Work, Industry & Canadian Society

Fourth Edition

Harvey J. Krahn
University of Alberta

Graham S. Lowe
University of Alberta

THOMSON

NELSON

Australia   Canada   Mexico   Singapore   Spain   United Kingdom   United States

THOMSON

NELSON

**Work, Industry, and Canadian Society,
Fourth Ed.,**

by Harvey J. Krahn and Graham S. Lowe

Editorial Director and Publisher:
Evelyn Veitch

Executive Editor:
Joanna Cotton

Marketing Manager:
Karen Howell

Managing Developmental Editor:
Christine Langone

Managing Production Editor:
Susan Calvert

Production Coordinator:
Hedy Sellers

Copy Editor/Proofreader:
Gilda Mekler

Creative Director:
Angela Cluer

Interior and Cover Design:
Ken Phipps

Cover Image:
Paul Schulenberg/
Stock Illustration Source

Compositor:
W.G. Graphics

Indexer:
Andrew Little

Printer:
Transcontinental Printing Inc.

National Library of Canada Cataloguing in Publication Data

Krahn, Harvey
Work, industry, and Canadian society

4th ed.
Includes bibliographical references and index.
ISBN 0-17-616948-2

1. Work—Social aspects—Canada.
2. Industrial sociology—Canada.
I. Lowe, Graham S. II. Title.

HD6957.C3K72 2002   306.3'6'0971
C2001-904034-2

CONTENTS

CHAPTER 1 Capitalism, Industrialization, and Postindustrial Society 1

Contents

Contents

Contents

LIST OF TABLES AND FIGURES

PREFACE

This fourth edition of *Work, Industry, and Canadian Society* discusses new research findings, incorporates new theoretical perspectives, and provides a more international perspective on employment trends. However, the most significant change from the third edition is the updating of every table and figure, and most text discussions of data, using the most current information available. We have also incorporated several hundred new references (and deleted many old ones) to reflect the most up-to-date findings and debates in the research literature. We have not changed the basic structure of the text. Rather, we have modified each chapter, in some cases adding new sections and deleting old ones.

In the four years since we last revised the text, there have been major changes in the world of work. The dramatic drop in national unemployment rates, a booming end-of-century North American economy that began to sputter with the meltdown of the high-tech sector in 2001, the Asian financial crisis, employers' anticipation of baby-boomer retirements—these are some of the broad transformations in the work landscape since we prepared the last edition of this text. And even as this edition went to press, the terrorist attacks of September 11 and their economic and social ramifications introduced new and as yet incalculable factors. While the fast-changing and fluid nature of the national and international contexts of work is part of what makes this research area so interesting, this continual change also presents a large challenge to textbook authors. Students using this text should be encouraged to consider the patterns of change and continuity since the summer of 2001, when we prepared this fourth edition.

As with previous editions, we continue to work as equal partners on this textbook. Even if we might want to take individual credit for specific ideas, by now it is difficult to remember where an idea originated. We are very grateful to Wolfgang Lehmann who served as an excellent research assistant, hunting down new sources, assisting with the updating of information in the figures and tables, and compiling the references. We also thank Statistics Canada for making available the high quality data that we have mined extensively in all four editions of the text. In planning this edition, we received helpful advice from various colleagues across the country who have used the book in their teaching, among them Trevor Harrison, University of Alberta, Denis Laplante, Lambton College, John Metcalfe, Humber College, and Andrew Okolie, University of Toronto. Equally important, feedback from undergraduate students at the University of Alberta has led to other modifications. At Nelson, Joanna Cotton encouraged us to take on another revision and agreed to a deadline that fit our schedules, and Christine Langone managed the editorial process. We would also like to thank Gilda Mekler, our copy editor, for her many helpful editing suggestions, which improved the text. Any errors and omissions are, of course, our own responsibility.

Harvey J. Krahn and Graham S. Lowe
University of Alberta
Edmonton and Kelowna, August 2001

INTRODUCTION

Work is undeniably an essential human activity. It is the basis for the economic survival of individuals and society. Beyond this, an individual's work activity structures much of her or his time and, one hopes, provides a source of personal fulfillment. An occupation also shapes identity and, in the eyes of others, largely determines an individual's status or position in society. Stepping back to gain a wider perspective, one also sees that Canadian society and the quality of life we have come to enjoy are the historical products of the collective work efforts of millions of women and men. Thus, while the *sociology of work and industry* may at first glance seem as potentially boring as the part-time job you just quit at your local shopping mall, it is not difficult to justify the subject's social relevance.

When we wrote the third edition of this book we began by noting that the pace and scope of change in Canadian workplaces, the national labour market, and the global economy had increased in the 1990s. Four years later, we still stand by this conclusion. But despite some truly remarkable developments in the local, national, and global contexts, the overall pattern of change is still best called evolutionary rather than revolutionary. As we note in various places in the text, debates continue about the extent to which "postmodern" or post-Fordist work systems, jobs, or organizations have swept away older forms of work. But many of the hierarchical and conflict-prone features of the capitalist workplace and labour market remain, albeit in somewhat different forms.

At the same time, some of the prominent trends documented in the third edition have clearly shifted direction. For example, global economic integration continues, but the grass-roots opposition so evident in Seattle, Quebec City, and Milan in 2000 and 2001 has placed the actions of transnational corporations and national governments under greater scrutiny. New information and communication technologies continue to push the frontiers of work, but the recent shakedown in the high-tech sector raises a host of questions about the sustainability of the so-called "new economy" as well as the implications this may have for the livelihood of workers in this sector. In the third edition, prepared in 1997, we described the new, powerful national economies in East Asia; yet soon thereafter, they were shaken by a deep financial crisis. We also described how a North American continental free trade agreement had begun to leave its mark. The debates on continental integration continue and the political agenda is now broadened with discussions of a *Free Trade Area of the Americas* that will extend throughout Central and South America. Unemployment was a leading public policy issue four years ago, but by the end of the 1990s robust economic growth in many, but not all, parts of Canada had pushed down the national jobless rate. Yet corporate downsizing, a trend widely associated with the retrenchment of the 1990s, has continued, often due to mergers and acquisitions and, in the past year (2001), the troubles in the technology sector. In short, the problems of structural unemployment have not disappeared. While the trend towards more nonstandard employment continues, it does seem to have leveled off in some respects. However, in other ways described in the following chapters, employment is becoming still more fragmented and tenuous. Overall, labour market polarization continues and social inequality has increased.

In this fourth edition we examine these and other trends that continue to influence the work opportunities and experiences of Canadians. In particular, we are concerned with the consequences of different types of work arrangements for both the individual and society. As the book's title suggests, a sociological analysis of work must be grounded in its industrial context—hence, our emphasis on the underlying economic forces that have shaped and continue to shape work opportunities. But a comprehensive understanding of the world of work also requires us to consider other features of society. For example, there are basic connections between a person's paid work and her or his family responsibilities. Society-wide value systems influence the work expectations of employees, as well as the behaviour of employers. The state plays a pivotal role in determining the nature and rewards of work through its employment standards and labour legislation, various labour market programs, and the educational system. Consequently, our discussion of work, industry, and Canadian society frequently ranges well beyond the work site.

The sociology of work and industry is not a neatly defined area of scholarship. This is an advantage, in our view, because, more than is the case for most sociological specialties, we are forced to incorporate the insights of related disciplines. Classic sociological theory, political economy, organization and management studies, industrial relations, labour history, labour economics, macroeconomics, women's studies and feminist theory, stratification, race and ethnic relations, and social policy are some of the diverse literatures upon which we draw. Because of this scope, our coverage of the literature is far from exhaustive. Instead, we selectively examine theoretical discussions and research findings in an attempt to highlight key themes and debates in the sociology of work and industry.

A few brief definitions may be useful. First, *work* refers to activity that provides a socially valued product or service. In other words, through our work we transform raw materials as diverse as information, iron ore, and wheat into something that is needed or desired by all or part of society. The emphasis in this definition is on activity; action verbs such as *cook, hammer, clean, drive, type, teach, sculpt,* or *serve* are typically used to describe work. Obviously, such a definition is very broad, including both paid and unpaid work, activities ranging from the legal to the illegal, and from the highly esteemed to the undesirable and despised.

But, with a few exceptions, we have restricted our focus to paid work. This approach recognizes the centrality of the employment relationship in modern capitalist societies, both in terms of the production of wealth and the quality of life. Hence, we discuss housework and child care—the major forms of unpaid work in our society—only briefly. Similarly, volunteer work receives only a few comments, as does work in the expanding "informal economy," where goods and services may be exchanged without cash transactions, and work in the traditional hunting and gathering economies that still exist among some of Canada's Aboriginal peoples. By spending less time on these nonpaid forms of work we are not suggesting they are unimportant, but that they warrant careful study in their own right. But we do recognize that, throughout the life course, paid work is variously combined with school work, child rearing, care of dependent relatives, household work, and community volunteering. Therefore, at various points in the following chapters, we examine the interaction of paid employment with some of these other types of work.

The relationship between employer and employee forms the cornerstone of the sociological study of work. By centring our analysis on workplace relations and the organizational structures in which these are embedded, we are able to address many of the core themes of classical sociological theory, including *inequality* and the distribution of scarce resources, power and how it takes shape in authority relations, and the shaky balance between the ever-present potential for *conflict* and the need for *cooperation* and *consensus*. A basic problem in all societies involves the distribution of wealth, power, and prestige. Paid work is central to this dilemma of distribution. Put more concretely, who gets the well-paying, interesting, and high-status jobs? Who is most vulnerable to unemployment? How does cooperation among employees and between management and employees occur? To what extent are employees integrated into their work organizations? Are there inherent conflicts of interest between employers and employees?

Another key theoretical concern in research on the sociology of work and industry is the interplay between the actions of individuals and the constraints exerted on them by social structures. For us, the *agency–structure debate* translates into some very basic and practical questions: How limiting and restrictive are work organizations? How much can employee actions, individually or collectively, reshape these structures? It is easy to detect the themes of *stability* and *change* just beneath the surface of these questions. In addressing these obvious tensions between individual action and social structures, it is helpful to distinguish between *macro* (social structure) and *micro* (individual) *levels of analysis*. At the macro level, we focus on the changing global economy, labour markets, industries and occupations, bureaucracies, unions and professional associations, and a variety of institutions that *structure,* or establish, regular and predictable patterns of work activity in society. We must be careful, however, not to place too much emphasis on social structures, because in doing so we risk losing sight of the individuals who are engaged in performing the work and, sometime, reshaping these structures.

As a counterbalance to this macro view, a more individual-level micro perspective on work in Canadian society is needed. This we provide by asking questions such as: How do individuals experience their work situation? What are the ingredients of job satisfaction? Or, looking at the negative side, what causes job dissatisfaction, alienation, and work-related stress? What types of work values are held by Canadians? Do most individuals accept their work situation, or do they attempt to change it? If so, how? In short, a micro-level analysis investigates how people experience their jobs, how they adapt to working conditions that are often far from ideal, and how, in some instances, they attempt to improve these conditions within the confines of what is possible given existing work institutions.

To elaborate this point, while an individual's work options may be constrained by social structures, there is nothing inevitable about the daily work routines, employment relationships, and legislative frameworks found in capitalist societies. Thus, we will argue that work can be demeaning or rewarding, depending in large part on how it is organized and who has authority. Further, we will highlight some of the possibilities offered by more egalitarian and humanized forms of work. However, we stop well short of advocating a utopian vision of work. Instead, we approach the subject of work from a *reformist perspective,* arguing that even within the confines of postindustrial capitalism the quality of working life can be improved for many. We believe that through careful theoretical reasoning and rigorous empirical research, sociologists can further the development of enlightened public policy and help individuals create better workplaces for themselves.

It will quickly become clear that we are not presenting a strictly Marxist analysis of work. Similarly, we go beyond a simplistic Weberian approach that gives undue emphasis to employees' understandings of their work situations. And we certainly do not advocate a functionalist or Durkheimian model of the work world that allows the need for social integration and stability to take on a larger-than-life presence. To varying degrees we have been influenced by all of these theoretical orientations, although our starting point is, more than anything, that of a *conflict perspective* of the social world. Thus, a Marxist perspective has strongly influenced the book's emphases on inequality, power, conflict, and control. The Weberian approach sensitizes us to the centrality of individual actors, and their beliefs and behaviours, in sociological analysis. The Durkheimian tradition reminds us that social integration, consensus, and stability within work organizations are the motivation for much management theory and practice.

Throughout the text we also strive to provide a comprehensive overview of the sociology of work and industry from a Canadian perspective. At the same time, we have incorporated more comparative material than in previous editions, recognizing that our understanding of work in Canada is enriched by comparisons with other nations, especially in today's global economy. Thus, this fourth edition of *Work, Industry, and Canadian Society* retains the basic themes and guiding questions addressed in the three earlier editions. However, a considerable amount of new material has been added since we last revised the book in 1997, while a few sections have been eliminated. As much as possible, empirical trend data have been updated to the year 2000.

As with the previous editions, the book is written with university undergraduates in mind. But it could also be used profitably by graduate students seeking a general assessment of the literature from a Canadian perspective, and by non-students seeking a better understanding of contemporary work trends. We have provided an extensive guide to sources, including relevant websites, allowing readers to directly access the printed literature and electronic information they require to find answers to their own research questions.

Chapter 1 of this book begins with an overview of the industrialization process and the rise of capitalism in Europe. This short history lesson provides a backdrop against which we can compare the somewhat later Canadian industrialization experience and the even more recent process of industrialization in a number of Asian countries. This first chapter also introduces some aspects of the theoretical writings of Karl Marx, Adam Smith, Max Weber, and Émile Durkheim. These social philosophers developed their assessments of the problems and prospects of work in industrial capitalist societies from their observations of how Europe was transformed during the Industrial Revolution. But the global economy, the industrial structures of advanced capitalist societies, and the employment opportunities found within them have all changed dramatically over the course of the twentieth century. Thus, we also examine a number of more recent theoretical perspectives on work in postindustrial society. Both the classical and contemporary theories resurface throughout the text as we focus on more specific topics within the sociology of work and industry.

Chapter 2 offers a detailed overview of the major industrial, labour market, and labour force trends in Canada. We begin by examining changes in the composition of the labour force over the past few decades, and then focus on how the industrial and occupational distribution of employment has also changed. Labour force participation patterns and unemployment rates are then examined, along with the rise in nonstandard forms of work (temporary and part-time, for example).

Labour markets are central institutions in the contemporary work world, basically determining who gets the good jobs and who ends up in the less desirable ones. Chapter 3 examines how the Canadian labour market operates by comparing recent findings with the predictions of two competing theories, the human capital model and the labour market segmentation approach. This chapter also focuses directly on the problem of growing labour market polarization and increasing social inequality.

The growing labour force participation of women is clearly one of the most remarkable social changes of the twentieth century. The question of how gender affects labour market outcomes is woven into the discussions in Chapters 2 and 3. But, given the importance of gender issues in the workplace, Chapter 4 provides an in-depth analysis of women's employment. This chapter outlines the transformation of women's economic roles, emphasizing the ways in which gender has become a source of entrenched divisions both within the labour market and within work organizations. The current push for gender equality is also highlighted, with specific reference to employment equity and pay equity programs.

Chapter 5 shifts the focus to how work activities are typically organized and managed in large bureaucracies. Here we discuss organizational theories that attempt to explain the structure of large organizations, as well as the way change occurs within them. Equally important, we introduce the range of management theories that have been developed over the past decades. We examine these models of management with particular attention to whether they counter some of the problems of bureaucracy and attempt to humanize working conditions, and whether they offer workers more autonomy or managers more control.

Chapter 6 is, in some ways, a debate with the mainstream management approaches. Our starting point is the labour process perspective, a much more critical assessment of employer–employee relationships in capitalist society. We examine different methods managers have used to control and gain compliance from workers, and ask whether new computer-based technologies, as well as the new management approaches, really provide workers with more autonomy and a chance to enhance their skills. Then, looking for alternatives, we discuss current approaches to addressing health and safety concerns in the workplace since, to some extent, they require co-management by workers and management. Going further afield, we conclude by discussing different forms of industrial democracy as well as examples of worker ownership, arguing that these approaches to organizing and managing work do have something to offer.

Unions receive some comment in earlier chapters, but Chapter 7 is devoted to this subject. We discuss various theories about the origins and functions of unions and document the development of the organized labour movement in Canada. We also describe the legal framework that has emerged for regulating union–management relations. This chapter concludes by examining worker militancy, particularly strike patterns, and by asking whether unions represent a revolutionary or reformist collective response by workers to the greater power of employers.

We conclude, in Chapter 8, by examining the individual experience of work. After commenting on society-wide work values and how they vary across time and culture, we then discuss work orientations, asking what individual employees seek to obtain from their work. Are their work orientations (or preferences) perhaps shaped by the work opportunities available to them? Equally important, are we seeing the emergence of new work orientations in response to growing employment insecurity and income inequality? From here we go on to discuss a wide array of research findings on job satisfaction, alienation, and workplace stress. A major theme developed in this chapter is that negative work experiences can have serious and lasting effects on individuals.

Finally, in a short conclusion, we review the trends described and the main conclusions drawn in the previous chapters. We also raise some important questions about the future of work in Canada. Work humanization through new human resource management strategies, job redesign, industrial democracy, occupational health and safety initiatives, the information technology revolution, and the forces of industrial restructuring all hold out possibilities for creating better workplaces. But these trends could just as easily have negative effects on the quantity and quality of work. We do, however, have some control and room to manoeuvre. In our opinion, what Canada needs is more public debate among employers, unions, professional associations, governments, and other labour market stakeholders to determine how best to balance the interests of workers, who want both a decent standard of living and an improved quality of work life, with the economic growth, profits, and labour market flexibility sought by employers and government.

CAPITALISM, INDUSTRIALIZATION, AND POSTINDUSTRIAL SOCIETY

INTRODUCTION

Nellie McClung, a Western Canadian political activist who championed the right of women to vote, was also, like many other women in the early decades of the twentieth century, involved in the Women's Christian Temperance Union. The story is told of her visits to schools where she would try to convince children of the evils of alcohol. Her method involved bringing two glasses into the classroom, one filled with water and the other with whiskey. She would then take a worm from a box and, after dropping it in the water, pull it out to show the children that it was still alive and healthy. She would then drop the same worm into the whiskey, where it would quickly die. When asked what they had learned, children would usually comment that whiskey was not healthy, and could even kill you. However, after one such demonstration, Johnny, waving his hand excitedly from the back of the classroom, was asked what he had learned. "It looks to me," he said, "that if you drink whiskey, you won't get worms."[1]

This anecdote highlights an important principle of sociological analysis. The conclusions we draw about our immediate world, about the significance of particular social patterns, and about what we might like to see changed, are greatly influenced by our vantage point, by the comparisons we make, and by our assessment of what is desirable and good. This book examines the types of paid work done by Canadians today. Most work for wages or a salary in bureaucratic organizations. In two out of three two-adult households, both partners are employed outside the home. In a labour force of just under 16 million individuals, almost three in four workers are in the service sector. Compared to the past, fewer workers are full-time employees. More than one in four are working either in temporary or part-time jobs; more than one in six are self-employed. For every thirteen employed Canadians, one is unemployed.

These present labour market realities become more interesting when we realize that only a generation ago some of these trends had just begun to emerge. And going back a century, the differences in work patterns are huge. What social and economic forces led to the shifts from agriculture to manufacturing, then to services? Why are women still underrepresented in better-paying jobs? Why are many jobs in today's high-tech information economy so mindless? Why have two-earner households become the norm, and what are the social consequences?

To answer these and many related questions, we examine the complex process of industrialization by looking back in history and at other societies. This historical and comparative approach will help us to understand present patterns and trends, assess their significance for individuals and society, and respond to the future challenges they pose.

Industrialization refers to the technical aspects of the accumulation and processing of a society's resources. *Capitalism* is a term used to describe key aspects of the economic and social organization of the productive enterprise. An industrial society is one in which inanimate sources of energy such as coal or electricity fuel a production system that uses technology to process raw materials. But labelling a society "industrial" tells us little about the relationships among the individuals involved in the productive process. A capitalist system of production is one in which a relatively small number of individuals own and control the means for creating goods and services, while the majority have no direct ownership stake in the economy and are paid a wage to work for those who do.

Studying the rise of capitalism requires us to make sense of large, complex processes spanning generations and leaving no aspect of daily life unaffected. The theoretical writings of Adam Smith, Karl Marx, Émile Durkheim, and Max Weber help us to explain, not just describe, the causes and consequences of capitalist development. But as we will see, the sociological concepts of *power, control, inequality,* and *conflict* that these early social scientists used to analyze changes in their times continue to be central to today's debates about the nature of 21st-century postindustrial society. Therefore, in this chapter and later in the book, we address questions such as: Is the rise of a knowledge-based, high-tech economy creating more flexible ways of organizing economic activity that benefits both workers and employers? How are new information technologies transforming the content and organization of work? Are there more losers than winners as a result of the economic restructuring of the past two decades? Are well-educated knowledge workers becoming a new elite in society? Is economic globalization increasing the power of transnational corporations at the expense of national governments? And with the rapid economic development of East Asia, the collapse of the Soviet Union and the uneven transitions of Eastern European countries towards market-based economies, do we need to rethink long-accepted explanations of capitalist development?

THE ORIGINS OF INDUSTRIAL CAPITALISM

Capitalism and industrialization dramatically reshaped the structure of European society, economically, socially, and spatially. These changes occurred over centuries, with a different pace and pattern in each country. While the details of these changes differed internationally and regionally within countries, the result was profound change in how, where, for whom, and under what conditions individuals worked.

The emergence of capitalism in Europe consisted of two basic periods: *mercantile or commercial capitalism,* which began in the 1500s, and *industrial capitalism,* which evolved somewhat later.[2] In the mercantile period, merchants and royalty in Spain, Holland, England, and France accumulated huge fortunes by trading internationally in a variety of goods, including spices, precious stones and metals, sugar, cotton, and slaves. An elaborate trading network evolved, linking Africa, Asia, and the American colonies with Europe.

This global trade and the pillage of cultures (slaves from Africa, for example, and vast amounts of gold and silver from Central and South America) provided wealth that would subsequently fuel the growth of industrial capitalism in Europe (Beaud 1983).

These early signs of capitalist commercial activity emerged out of a *feudal society;* the *Industrial Revolution* had not yet begun. Most people still lived in the countryside. The class structure of these agrarian societies consisted of a relatively small aristocracy and merchant class, most of whom lived in the cities, a rural landowning class, and a large rural peasantry. Work typically involved peasants farming small plots of land they did not own. Landowners received rent, usually in the form of agricultural produce, little of which was sold for cash. Generations of peasant families lived and died on the same feudal estates.

Thus, feudal Europe was predominantly a *pre-market* economy in which the producer was also the consumer. It was also a *pre-capitalist* economy because wage labour was rare and a business class had not yet become dominant. Feudal lords accepted rent and expected services in the form of manual labour required for the upkeep of the estate. In return, they allowed historical tenancy relationships to continue and provided some protection, if necessary, for their tenants. Thus, feudalism was built upon a system of mutual rights and obligations, reinforced by tradition. One's social position was inherited. But this relatively stable society also stifled economic progress.[3]

Did the decay of feudalism lead to the rise of capitalism, or was it the other way around? Scholars are divided on this question. Some argue that factors internal to feudal society, such as growing rural populations, deterioration of land, and landlords demanding more rent, forced people off the land and into the cities where they could form an urban working class. Others counter that as mercantile capitalism developed in urban areas, and as the market economy slowly began to make an impact on rural life, cities began to attract landless serfs. This debate is difficult to resolve, since the two processes influenced each other (Hilton 1976; Aston and Philpin 1985). What is undisputed is that capitalism brought with it an entirely new social order.

Early Capitalism

Industrial capitalism began to emerge in the early 1700s. The production of goods by artisans, or by the home-based *putting out system* in which merchants distributed work to peasant households, led to larger workshops ("manufactories") that made metal, cloth, glass, and other finished goods (Beaud 1983). By the late 1700s, various inventions were revolutionizing production techniques. James Hargreaves's spinning jenny transformed work in textile industries. Growth in trade and transportation, the construction of railways, and military demand for improved weapons encouraged new techniques for processing iron and other metals. Inventors also were devising ways of harnessing water and steam, as exemplified in James Watts's steam engine.

These early inventions facilitated a new form of work organization: the *industrial mill.* A technical breakthrough that involved harnessing many machines to a single inanimate energy source, the mill also had immense social implications, consolidating many workers under one roof and the control of managers (Beaud 1983: 66–67; Burawoy 1984). A growing class of impoverished urban wage-labourers endured horrific working conditions in early industrial mills. Some workers resisted this trend, particularly artisans who previously had controlled their own labour. Episodes of destroying textile machinery occurred between 1811 and 1816 in a number of British communities. The unemployed craftsmen involved (called *Luddites*) were not unthinking opponents of technological innovations, but skilled workers frustrated by changes that were making their skills obsolete. These uprisings were quashed by the state; some participants were jailed or deported, others were hanged (Beaud 1983: 65; Grint 1991: 55).

The emergence of industrial capitalism also changed the *gender-based division of labour.* While women, men, and children had done different types of work in feudal times, much of it at home, they were often engaged in parallel work activities (Middleton 1988). The putting out system, particularly in the textile industries, brought many women into the paid labour force along with men, since they could work out of their home and still carry out domestic work and child care. Early textile factories also employed men, women, and children (Berg 1988). But as manufacturing developed and expanded, it became the preserve of men. While a gendered division of labour had long existed, it became more pronounced with the rise of industrial capitalism.[4]

The Great Transformation

In only a matter of decades, factory production dominated capitalist societies. The urban landscape also changed as manufacturing cities grew to accommodate the new wage-labour force. Mechanization and the movement to factory-based production proceeded even faster in the 1800s than it had in the previous century. Manufacturing surpassed agriculture in its annual output. Industrial production in Britain, for example, increased by 300 percent between 1820 and 1860. The portion of the labour force employed in agriculture in Britain, France, Germany, the United States, and other industrializing countries declined, while employment in manufacturing and services rose rapidly. By the end of the nineteenth century, industrial capitalism was clearly the dominant system of production in Western nations.

According to Karl Polanyi, the *great transformation* that swept Europe with the growth and integration of capital, commodity, and labour markets—the foundation of capitalism—left no aspect of social life untouched.[5] The struggle for democratic forms of government, the emergence of the modern nation-state, and the rapid growth of cities are all directly linked to these economic changes.

Along with new technologies, the replacement of human and animal sources of energy with inanimate sources and the emergence of an integrated market system for finance, commodities, and labour, this era also saw dramatic changes in how work was organized. In time, the relatively stable landlord–serf relationships of feudalism were replaced by wage-labour relationships between capitalists and labourers. Employers paid for a set amount of work, but also determined exactly how, and under what conditions, work would be done. Previously independent artisans lost out to the factory system. In the end, the result was a higher standard of living for most residents of the industrialized countries. But the interrelated processes of change that created a market economy also led to new problems of *controlling, coordinating, and managing* work—central themes in this book.

CANADA'S INDUSTRIALIZATION

The process of industrialization in Canada lagged behind that in Britain and the United States, and can be traced back to the mid-1800s.[6] As a British colony, Canada's role had been to provide raw materials, rather than to produce finished goods that would compete on world markets with those of the mother country. Canadian economic elites focused on traditional activities such as exporting *staple products* like timber and fur to sell on world markets, and developing transportation networks (particularly railways) that could link the resource-producing regions of the country with the port cities involved in export trade.

Work in Pre-Industrial Canada

The first half of the nineteenth century, then, was a pre-industrial economic era in Canada. Canada still had a pre-market economy, since most production and consumption took place in households. In fact, given the peculiarities of a colonial economy dependent on Britain, even land was not really a marketable commodity. By the mid-1830s, less than one-tenth of the vast tracts of land that had been given by the French, and later British, monarchy to favoured individuals and companies had been developed for agriculture.

At the same time, immigration from Europe was increasing. Shortages of land for small farmers, potato famines in Ireland, and dreadful working conditions in many British factories fuelled immigration to the New World. Large numbers of immigrants landed in Canada, only to find shortages of urban factory jobs and little available agricultural land. Thus, the majority of these immigrants sought employment in the United States, where factory jobs and land were more plentiful (Teeple 1972).

Some of the immigrants who stayed in Canada were employed in building the Welland and Rideau Canals—the first of many transportation megaprojects—in the first half of the nineteenth century. The influx of unskilled workers created a great demand for such seasonal jobs, which often involved fourteen to sixteen hours a day of very hard and poorly paid work. Consequently, poverty was widespread. In the winter of 1844, the *St. Catharine's Journal* reported that:

> the greatest distress imaginable has been, and still is, existing throughout the entire line of the Welland Canal, in consequence of the vast accumulation of unemployed labourers. There are, at this moment, many hundreds of men, women, and children,

apparently in the last stages of starvation, and instead ... of any relief for them ... in the spring ... more than one half of those who are now employed must be discharged.[7]

The Industrial Era

By the 1840s, Canada's economy was still largely agrarian, even though the two key ingredients for industrialization—an available labour force and a transportation infrastructure—were in place. Prior to Confederation in 1867, some of Canada's first factories were set up not in Ontario or Quebec, as we might expect, but in Nova Scotia. Shipbuilding, glass, and clothing enterprises were operating profitably in this region before the Maritime Provinces entered Confederation (Veltmeyer 1983: 103). After 1867, manufacturing became centralized in Ontario and Quebec, resulting in the *deindustrialization* of the Maritimes. A larger population base, easy access to U.S. markets, and railway links to both Eastern and Western Canada ensured that the regions around Montreal and Toronto would remain the industrial heartland of the country.

At the time of Confederation, half of the Canadian labour force was in agriculture. This changed rapidly with the advance of industrialization. By 1900, Canada ranked seventh in production output among the manufacturing countries of the world (Rinehart 2001; Laxer 1989). The large factories that had begun to appear decades earlier in the United States were now springing up in Toronto, Hamilton, Montreal, and other central Canadian cities. American firms built many of these factories to avoid Canadian tariffs on goods imported from the United States. This began a pattern of direct U.S. foreign investment in Canada that continues today.

These economic changes brought rapid urban growth and accompanying social problems. Worker exploitation was widespread, as labour laws and unions were still largely absent. Low pay, long hours, and unsafe and unhealthy conditions were typical. Workers lived in crowded and unsanitary housing. Health care and social services were largely nonexistent. In short, despite economic development in the decades following Confederation, poverty remained the norm for much of the working class in major manufacturing centres (Copp 1974; Piva 1979).

The Decline of Craft Work

Traditionally, *skilled craft workers* had the advantages of being able to determine their own working conditions, hire their own apprentices, and frequently set their pay. Some worked individually, while others arranged themselves into small groups in the manner of European craft guilds. But this craft control declined as Canada moved into the industrial era. Factory owners were conscious of the increased productivity in American factories obtained through new technology and "modern" systems of management. Dividing craft jobs into many simple tasks allowed work to be performed by less skilled and lower-paid employees. Mechanization further cut costs while increasing productivity.

As these systems entered Canada, the job autonomy of craft workers was reduced, resulting in considerable labour unrest. Between 1901 and 1914, for example, more than 400 strikes and lockouts occurred in the ten most industrialized cities of southern Ontario (Heron 1980; Heron and Palmer 1977). While these conflicts may look like working-class revolt, they are more accurately seen as a somewhat privileged group of workers resisting attempts to reduce their occupational power. While there were large numbers of skilled workers who experienced the "crisis of the craftsmen" (Heron 1980; also see Rinehart 2001), there were larger numbers of unskilled manual labourers whose only alternative to arduous factory work was seasonal labour in the resource or transportation industries, or unemployment.

There were, in fact, thousands of workers employed in the resource extraction industries throughout Canada, and many others worked on constructing the railways. In *The Bunkhouse Man,* Edmund Bradwin estimates that up to 200,000 men living in some 3,000 work camps were employed in railway construction, mining, and the lumber industry during the early twentieth century. These workers were from English Canada and Quebec, as well as from Europe and China. Employers considered immigrants to be good candidates for such manual work, as they were unlikely to oppose their bosses. This hiring strategy often did ward off collective action, although immigrants sometimes were the most radical members of the working class.[8]

The creation of a transcontinental railway led to a high demand for coal. Mines were opened on Vancouver Island and in the Alberta Rockies, with immigrants quickly taking the new jobs. Mine owners attempted to extract a lot of work for little pay, knowing they could rely on the military to control unruly workers. It has been estimated that in the early 1900s, every 1 million tons of coal produced in Alberta took the lives of 10 miners, while in British Columbia the rate was 23 dead for the same amount of coal.[9] These dangerous conditions led to strikes, union organization, and even political action. In 1909, Donald McNab, a miner and socialist, was elected to represent Lethbridge in the Alberta legislature. The same year, the Revolutionary Socialist Party of Canada elected several members to the British Columbia legislature (Marchak 1981: 106; Seager 1985). But, although the labour movement did take root in resource industries, it never had the revolutionary spark that some of its radical leaders envisioned.

RETHINKING INDUSTRIALIZATION

Our overview of European and Canadian industrialization had several goals. One was to highlight issues of power, conflict, and inequality in what is sometimes viewed as simply a period of rapid technological change and economic growth. An equally important goal was to draw attention to differences in patterns of industrialization.

But while countries differ in the timing, pace, and form of industrialization, there still appear to be some similar underlying dynamics and processes. Industrialized countries tend to be highly urbanized; production typically takes place on a big scale using complex technologies; workplaces tend to be organized bureaucratically; and white-collar workers make up most of the workforce. Citizens are reasonably well educated, and generally an individual's level of education and training is related to her or his occupation. Such similarities led American social scientists in the 1950s to claim

> The world is entering a new age—the age of total industrialism. Some countries are far along the road, many more are just beginning the journey. But everywhere, at a faster pace or a slower pace, the peoples of the world are on the march towards industrialism. (Kerr et al. 1973: 29)

This is the *logic of industrialism* thesis, a deterministic and linear argument about the immensity and inevitability of industrial technology. It contends that industrialism is such a powerful force that any country, whatever its characteristics at the outset, will eventually come to resemble other industrialized countries. Hence, this argument is also known as the *convergence thesis*. In current debates about globalization, the same argument has been restated as a thesis of economic, political and cultural convergence. Yet, as we will see in later chapters, comparisons of work patterns in various industrialized countries do not support this prediction. For example, there are pronounced cross-national variations in unemployment rates, innovative forms of work organization, unionization and industrial relations systems, and education and training. And as noted below, globalization also is not a standardized process, but rather is played out in quite different ways at the national, regional and community levels.

Our historical overview also shows that Canada's industrialization occurred later and was shaped by its colonial status; that immigration was a major factor in creating a workforce; and that resource industries played a central role. Other countries such as Sweden and Japan also industrialized later, but their experiences differed from Canada's. In recent decades, Central and South American nations such as Mexico and Brazil have undergone much more rapid industrialization. Again, the process differed. In particular, inequality has become even more pronounced in these countries (Chirot 1986: 251–55). By reflecting on the experiences of the recently industrialized nations of East Asia, and on the stirrings of capitalism in China and the former Soviet Union, we will come to appreciate even greater diversity in this process. Other than at the broadest level of analysis, there does not appear to be an inherent "logic of industrialism."

This becomes clear when we compare the nineteen countries in North and South America, Asia, and Europe presented in Table 1.1. Keep in mind that comparing nations at different phases and levels of development presents methodological challenges, mainly because perfectly comparable data are lacking. However, the World Bank has constructed basic comparative measures that perhaps are as precise as we can get, so we use these in Table 1.1. Canada provides a useful benchmark for interpreting the relative socioeconomic conditions in other countries. After noting which countries are included in Table 1.1, scan each column to get a sense of the huge differences in population, urbanization, per capita income, average annual economic growth rate, women as a proportion of the total labour force, and inequality (share of all income or consumption accounted for by the top and bottom *quintiles,* or equal groupings of 20 percent). Keep in mind that in many developing nations, significant economic activity still occurs in the informal sectors of the economy, which makes it difficult to capture in the official government statistics presented in Table 1.1 (Martin, 2000). Still, these basic social and economic development indicators raise a host of questions about the underlying historical, cultural, and political contexts in which countries industrialize. Also interesting are the consequences for work and workers of the current level and form of industrialization in a country. And what the table does not show, because it presents data for only one time point, is how inequality among nations changes over time. Does economic growth lead to a higher standard of living and lower inequality? These are big topics, so we will explore them from several angles at various places in this chapter and elsewhere in the book.

The East Asian Tigers

The *Four Tigers* of East Asia—Singapore, Hong Kong, Taiwan, and South Korea—are attracting much attention from scholars, businesses, and politicians around the world. In a few decades, these economies have become highly industrialized and have either surpassed (the first two) or are fast approaching (the last two) per capita incomes in the major western industrial nations. For example, it took Britain 58 years (1780 to 1838) and the U.S. 47 years (1839 to 1886) for per capita gross domestic product (the total output of the economy) to double; it took South Korea only 11 years (1966 to 1977) (*The Economist,* 16 October 1993: 80). In the same region, another set of *newly industrializing countries* (NICs)—Thailand, Indonesia, and Malaysia— are following just behind the Four Tigers. While the Four Tigers and the NICs exhibited impressive economic growth rates through most of the 1990s, a major financial crisis in 1997–98 shook the foundations of these economies (particularly South Korea, Malaysia, Indonesia, Thailand, and the Philippines), revealing the tenuous nature of their new-found prosperity. However, recovery has been strong (World Bank, 2001; International Labour Office, 1998: Chapter 1; Barro, 2001). And the hand-over in 1997 of Hong Kong to China raised uncertainties about the future of this former British

TABLE 1.1 *Social and Economic Indicators for Selected Countries, 1999*

	Population 1999 (millions)	Urban Population as % of Total (1999)	GNP per capita (PPP) 1999 Current International Dollars [a]	Average Annual Growth per capita 1998–99 [b]	% of Relevant Age Group Enrolled in Secondary Education (1997 [c])	Labour Force: % Female (1999)	% Share of Income or Consumption in Lowest 20% of Income Earners [d]	% Share of Income or Consumption in Highest 20% of Income Earners [d]
Canada	31	77	23,725	2.8	95	46	7.5	39.3
United States	273	77	30,600	3.1	96	46	5.2	46.4
Brazil	168	81	6,317	-3.2	66	35	2.5	63.8
Mexico	97	74	7,719	2.4	66	33	3.6	58.2
Chile	15	85	8,370	-2.6	85	33	3.5	61.0
India	998	28	2,149[e]	4.9	60	32	8.1	46.1
China	1,250	32	3,291	6.3	70	45	5.9	46.6
Indonesia	207	40	2,439	0.3	56	41	8.0	44.9
Thailand	62	21	5,599	4.1	58	46	6.4	48.4
South Korea	47	81	14,637	10.1	100	41	7.5	39.3
Singapore	3	100	27,024	3.6	76	39	–	–
Japan	127	79	24,041	0.8	100	41	10.6	35.7
Russian Federation	147	77	6,339	1.6	88	49	4.4	53.7
Ukraine	50	68	3,142	-0.4	–	49	8.6	41.2
United Kingdom	59	89	20,883	1.6	92	44	6.6	43.0
Germany	82	87	22,404	1.2	95	42	8.2	38.5
Sweden	9	83	20,824	3.8	100	48	9.6	34.5
France	59	75	21,897	2.0	99	45	7.2	40.2
Switzerland	7	68	27,486	1.2	84	40	6.9	40.3

Source: World Bank, *World Development Report 2000/2001: Attacking Poverty* (Oxford: Oxford University Press, 2001). See the report (also available on line at http://www.worldbank.org/poverty/wdrpoverty/report/index.html) for technical details. Reprinted with permission.

a Parity Purchasing Power. The PPP conversion factor is defined as the number of units of a country's currency required to buy the same amount of goods and services in the domestic market as one dollar would buy in the United States.

b GNP is calculated using the *World Bank Atlas* method. GNP measures the total domestic and foreign value-added claimed by residents. It comprises Gross Domestic Product plus the net factor from abroad, which is the income residents receive for factor services (labour and capital) less similar payments made to nonresidents who contribute to the domestic economy. GNP per capita is calculated using the resident population in the corresponding year.

c UNESCO enrollment estimates and projections as assessed in 1999.

d Data in these columns are for different years.

e The estimate for India is based on regression; others are extrapolated from the latest International Comparison Programme benchmark estimates.

Crown Colony, while giving the world's largest communist society an instant link to global capitalism through Hong Kong's dynamic financial sector.

The World Bank (1993: 277) considers rapid economic growth and greater reductions in income inequality than in other developing nations to be the signal features of the "East Asian miracle." But other factors are also important, such as rising output and productivity in agriculture at the same time that a manufacturing export sector was developing, steep declines in birth rates so that population growth was constrained, heavy investment in human resources through the expansion and improvement of educational systems, and a bureaucratic state run by a career civil service.

But this overstates the similarities among these nations; in fact, there are striking differences. For example, capitalism has taken distinctive forms in the Four Tigers.[10] A few giant diversified corporations (called *chaebol*) that have close ties to the state dominate the South Korean economy. Taiwan's dynamic export sector is sustained by a network of highly flexible small and medium-sized manufacturing firms with extensive *subcontracting systems* that often extend into the informal sector of the economy. In Hong Kong (and also Taiwan) the main organizing unit of business is the Chinese *family enterprise*. These firms give utmost priority to the long-term prosperity and reputation of the family—a very different concept than the rugged individualism of North American capitalism. Singapore is set apart by the prominent role of the state in setting the direction of industrialization, which has involved much greater reliance on direct investment by foreign multinational corporations. These variations in business systems account for diverse industrialization paths and approaches to work organization within firms. In Richard Whitley's (1992) view, these business systems are rooted in each nation's unique history, cultural values, political system, and traditional authority relations.

Signs of Capitalism in China and the Former Soviet Union

We've all seen media reports of rich "peasants" in China buying German luxury cars, and of the garishly lavish lifestyles of Russia's new entrepreneurs. Does this mean that capitalism has taken hold in the two pillars of the communist world? Social scientists have asked this question, attempting to understand the complex transitions these societies are undergoing. Recent research has looked beyond "markets" in a narrow economic sense, attempting to present a more comprehensive explanation of what influences the economic behaviour of individuals in these societies. The emergence of market structures and the ways in which individuals pursue opportunities within these structures are influenced by factors such as the society's customs, culture, and norms, as well as by existing social networks, the organization of work, and state policies (Nee and Matthews 1996: 403).

China became the leading recipient of foreign direct investment by the capitalist world's multinational corporations in the 1980s, a trend that continues.[11] As the world's most populous nation, with 1.25 billion inhabitants, China is seen by these corporations as a huge market to conquer. Its workers also are being integrated into the global economy; "Made in China" now appears on a growing number of consumer items that Canadians buy. Between 1980 and 1995, China experienced an unprecedented annual economic growth rate of just under 10 percent (compared with slightly more than an average of 2 percent in all the major Western industrial economies) (*The Economist*, 9 March 1996: 5). As Table 1.1 shows, China's rate of growth has declined only slightly in the wake of the Asian financial crisis – it still continues to outpace Canada, the U.S., and most other industrialized countries.

Is communist China being overtaken by capitalist free enterprise? The short answer is no, but there is a remarkable transformation occurring, mostly localized in a few coastal industrial regions. Market reforms in China began in the mid-1970s. But the Chinese version of an entrepreneurial spirit is deeply rooted, and can be seen in the rich and powerful dynasties established by mainland Chinese families who migrated throughout Asia around a century ago (*The Economist*, 9 March 1996: 10). Chinese-style capitalism, influenced of course by the Western version, built Hong Kong, Singapore, and Taiwan. Now that Hong Kong has been reunited with China, it will be interesting to observe how China responds both politically and economically to the free market ways of this former British colony.

Unlike the former Soviet Union, where privatization is now widespread, state ownership of property remains dominant in mainland China. Furthermore, the bureaucratic systems of state-run work units and the Communist Party remain important influences on income levels and access to housing for many workers (Adamchak, Chen and Li, 1999). But the rules have changed: farming has shifted from collective farms to households, giving farmers full return on anything they produce over a set quota. And while state-owned enterprises are still very prominent, at the local level hybrid corporations straddling the state sector and the private sector are permitted. The Communist Party and state institutions continue to strongly influence individuals' occupational rewards, and therefore patterns of social inequality (Zhou, 2000). Market mechanisms do not simply take over; rather, they are adapted within the context of powerful state institutions and policies (Cao and Nee, 2000). So even in Guangzhou, a booming industrial centre, less than one-third of the jobs are in the market or private sector. As Nee and Matthews (1996: 417) conclude, "the Chinese approach did not conform to textbook economics ... Chinese reformers emphasized piecemeal incremental change, not by design, but by trial and error ... " The looming question now is whether and when these economic reforms will precipitate political reforms and increased human rights.

The fall of the Berlin Wall in 1989 marked the collapse of the once powerful Soviet Union. Robert Brym observes that a "strange hybrid of organized crime, communism and capitalism grew with enormous speed in the post-Soviet era" (Brym 1996: 396). Private enterprise, or market liberalization, was introduced in the mid-1980s, but competitive capitalism as we know it failed to emerge. The reason, in Brym's view, is that the old Communist Party elite, along with organized criminal gangs that had prospered in the corruption of the Soviet economy, were well placed to take advantage of any new opportunities. The result is a predatory variety of capitalism that enriches a small elite while breeding corruption and making life worse for ordinary Russians. Thus, despite the emergence of a private sector and state policies aimed at economic reform, and contrary to *market transition theory* – which has been developed to explain recent social and economic change in China and the former Soviet Union – Russia has not really experienced increased entrepreneurial activity, greater labour market returns to education, or reductions in inequality (Gerber and Hout, 1998).

A broadly similar pattern is typical of other Eastern bloc nations. Former Communist Party elites, who still control state resources and have good business networks, continue to benefit in the post-Soviet era, while living standards for the majority have declined (Rónas-Tas 1994; Szelényi and Kostello 1996). Unlike earlier transitions to capitalism in western Europe and North America, what is occurring in the former Soviet bloc does not involve the rise of a new economic elite or the creation of a working class—both of which existed in different forms under communism. Thus, Polanyi's "great transformation" from feudalism to a market economy in nineteenth-century Europe represented a unique experience of social and economic change. Subsequent transformations to market-based capitalism have taken some unexpected twists and turns.

THEORETICAL PERSPECTIVES

Now that we have some historical and comparative background on industrialization and capitalism, we can examine major explanations of the causes and consequences of these changes. The following sections present a range of classical and contemporary theories of social and economic change. After acquainting ourselves with these theories and their analytic concepts, we can apply their insights throughout the book when considering specific work issues.

Karl Marx on Worker Exploitation and Class Conflict

Karl Marx spent a lifetime critically examining the phenomenon of industrial capitalism. His assessment of this new type of society was presented within a very broad theoretical framework. He called the overall system of economic activity within a society a *mode of production*, and he identified its major components as the *means of production* (the technology, capital investments, and raw materials) and the *social relations of production* (the relationships between the major social groups or classes involved in production).

Marx focused on the manner in which the ruling class controlled and exploited the working class. His close colleague, Friedrich Engels, documented this exploitation in his 1845 book, *The Condition of the Working Class in England*. Engels (1971: 63) described one of London's many slum districts, noting that other industrial cities were much the same:

> St. Giles is in the midst of the most populous part of the town, surrounded by broad, splendid avenues in which the gay world of London idles about....The houses are occupied from cellar to garret, filthy within and without, and their appearance is such that no human being could possibly wish to live in them. But this is nothing in comparison with the dwellings in the narrow courts

and alleys between the streets, entered by covered passages between the houses, in which the filth and tottering ruin surpass all description .... Heaps of garbage and ashes lie in all directions, and the foul liquids emptied before the doors gather in stinking pools. Here live the poorest of the poor, the worst paid workers with thieves and the victims of prostitution indiscriminately huddled together.

It was from such first-hand observations of industrializing Europe that Marx developed his critique of capitalism.

Class conflict was central to Marx's theory of social change. He argued that previous modes of production had collapsed and been replaced because of conflicts among class groups within them. Feudalism was supplanted by capitalism as a result of the growing power of the merchant class, the decline of the traditional alliance of landowners and aristocracy, and the deteriorating relationship between landowners and peasants. Marx identified two major classes in capitalism: the capitalist class, or *bourgeoisie,* which owned the means of production, and the working class, or *proletariat,* which exchanged its labour for wages. A third class—the *petite bourgeoisie*—comprising independent producers and small business owners, would eventually disappear, according to Marx, as it was incorporated into one of the two major classes. Marx argued that capitalism would eventually be replaced by a socialist mode of production. The catalyst would be revolutionary class conflict, in which the oppressed working class would destroy the institutions of capitalism and replace them with a *socialist society* based on collective ownership of the means of production.

Marx sparked ongoing debate regarding the nature of work and of class conflict in capitalist societies (Zeitlin 1968; Coser 1971). Ever since, social, political, and economic analysts have attempted to reinterpret his predictions of a future worker-run socialist society. No capitalist society has experienced the revolutionary upheavals Marx foresaw. And the collapse of the Soviet communist system in Eastern Europe ended speculation that communism would evolve into true socialism. In fact, Marx probably would have been an outspoken critic of the Soviet communist system, given its extreme inequalities in power distribution and harsh treatment of workers. He would also have condemned the inequalities in today's capitalist Russia.

Marx's critique of capitalism has also shaped research in the sociology of work and industry, as analysts attempt to refine or refute his ideas. First, Marx emphasized how the capitalist profit motive is usually in conflict with workers' desires for better wages, working conditions, and standards of living. Second, Marx argued that the worker–owner relationship led to workers losing control over how they did their work and, hence, to the dehumanization of work. Third, Marx predicted that the working class would eventually organize to more actively oppose the ruling capitalist class. In short, Marx wrote about inequality, power, control, and conflict. His enduring legacy for sociology was this more general *conflict perspective.* He recognized that the relations of production in industrial capitalist society typically are exploitative, with owners (and their representatives) having more power, status, and wealth than those who are hired to do the work. Almost all of the debates about better ways of organizing workplaces and managing employees, the need for unions and labour legislation, and the future of work in our society stem from this basic inequality.

Adam Smith: Competition, Not Conflict

Adam Smith wrote *The Wealth of Nations* in 1776, during the early Industrial Revolution in England, extolling the wealth-producing benefits of capitalism. Thus, he is often portrayed as the economic theorist whose ideas outlasted those of Marx who, writing some time later, predicted the eventual downfall of capitalism. Even today, Adam Smith's ideas are frequently used to call for less government intervention in the economy, the argument being that "the unseen hand of the market" is best left alone.

It is important to note, however, that Adam Smith did not condone the exploitation of workers. He recognized that working conditions in the industrializing British economy were far from satisfactory, and actually argued that higher wages would increase the productivity of workers and the economy as a whole (Weiss 1976; Saul 1995: 150). But Smith was very clear about what he saw as a key underlying principle of capitalism. *Competition among individuals and enterprises,* each trying to improve their own position, led to growth and the creation of wealth. As he put it: "It is not from the benevolence of the butcher, the brewer, or the baker, that we expect our dinner, but from their regard to their own self-interest" (Smith 1976 [1776]: Book 2, Chapter 2: 14).

Thus, for Adam Smith, the "profit motive" was the driving force of capitalism. Individuals and firms in aggressive competition with each other produced the "wealth of nations." Where Marx (some decades later) saw conflict, exploitation, and growing inequality, Adam Smith saw competition leading to greater wealth.

These different perspectives continue to underpin arguments for, on the one hand, restructuring employment relationships to reduce inequality and, on the other, eliminating barriers to competition that are perceived to be holding back the creation of wealth. These counter-positions highlight a central contradiction of capitalist economies. Many people like to believe that the "marketplace" is best left unchecked if greater wealth is to be produced. At the same time, it is clear that social inequality increases without labour legislation, employment insurance, and other programs that smooth the rough edges of capitalism. The question, then, is, What kind of society do we want?

Diverse Perspectives on the Division of Labour

Human societies have always been characterized by a basic *division of labour*—essentially, how tasks are organized and distributed among workers. In primitive societies, work roles were assigned mainly according to age and gender. But with economic development these roles became more specialized, and the arrival of industrial capitalism further intensified this process. Once a certain scale of production was reached, it was much more efficient to break complex jobs into their component tasks.

Pre-industrial skilled craft workers are often idealized. C. Wright Mills, for example, emphasized the personal satisfactions derived from being involved in all aspects of the creation of some product, being free to make decisions about how the work should be done and to develop one's skills and abilities (Mills 1956: 220). Obviously not all pre-industrial workers were fortunate enough to be craft workers, but it is clear that such opportunities were reduced with the growth of industrial capitalism. Part of the change was due to the loss of control over work that accompanied the spread of wage-labour. Equally significant was the division of work processes into simpler and smaller tasks, each done by an individual worker.

In *The Wealth of Nations*, Adam Smith identified the division of labour as a key to capitalism's success. Using the example of a pin factory, he described how productivity could be greatly increased by assigning workers to specific tasks such as stretching wire, cutting it, and sharpening it. Whereas individual workers might produce 20 pins a day each by doing all of the operations themselves, with a well-defined division of labour, 10 people could make 48,000 pins a day. The greater productivity, Smith reasoned, came from the increased dexterity a worker could master in repeating a single task over and over again, the time saved in not having to change tasks and shift tools, and the added savings obtained from designing machines that workers could use to repeat the single task (Smith 1976; Braverman 1974: 76). The real advantage of this form of work organization would only be realized when factories made large quantities of a product—precisely the goal of industrial capitalism.

In 1832, Charles Babbage translated Smith's principles into practical cost-cutting advice for entrepreneurs. By subdividing tasks, he argued, less skill was required of any individual worker. Consequently, employers could pay less for this labour. Workers with fewer skills simply cannot demand as high a reward for their work (Braverman 1974: 79–83). The early history of industrialization is full of examples of this basic economic principle at work. The advent of factories with detailed divisions of labour invariably replaced skilled craft workers with unskilled factory workers who were paid less—just the sort of outcome that Marx criticized.

Returning to Mills's description of the craft ideal, we can easily see some of the problems. A central feature of *craft work* was the degree to which one individual was involved in all aspects of the creation of some product. The resulting sense of pride and self-fulfillment was an early casualty of industrialization. Furthermore, the minute subdividing of tasks in an efficient mass-production factory or administrative system inevitably led to repetitious, boring work. Little wonder, then, that many craft workers actively resisted factory-based production.

Marx's discussions of work in capitalist society focused on the negative consequences of an excessive division of labour. For him, capitalism itself was the source of the problem. The division of labour was simply a means to create greater profits from the labour of the working class. The development of huge *assembly-line factories* in the early twentieth century epitomized this trend. Henry Ford, the inventor of the assembly line, took considerable pride in recounting how his Model T factory had 7,882 specific jobs. Ford calculated that about half the jobs required only "ordinary men," 949 required "strong, able-bodied men," while the rest could be done by women, older children, or men who were physically disabled, he reasoned. These observations do not reflect a concern for disabled workers, but instead highlight the extreme fragmentation of the labour process, to the point that even the simplest repetitions became a job.[12]

Émile Durkheim, an early 20th-century French sociologist, provided the alternative, conservative assessment of capitalist employment relations, particularly the division of labour. He noted that industrial societies contained diverse populations in terms of race, ethnicity, religion, occupation, and education—not to mention differences in beliefs and values. Durkheim pointed to evidence in European industrialization of group differences creating conflict over how scarce resources should be distributed, over rights and privileges, and over which beliefs and values set the standard. Durkheim saw the division of labour as a source of *social cohesion* that reduced this potential for conflict.[13] He reasoned that individuals and groups engaged in different tasks in a complex division of labour would recognize their mutual interdependence. In turn, this would generate tolerance and social harmony.

Durkheim believed that individuals in modern society are forced to rely on each other because of the different occupational positions they fill. In simple terms, lawyers need plumbers to fix their sinks while plumbers need teachers to educate their children. By the same logic, capitalists and their employees are interdependent. Without cooperation between the two groups, the economy would grind to a halt. We will see in later chapters how Durkheim's positive assessment of the division of labour shaped management theories that assume shared interests in the workplace. While Marx has influenced conflict perspectives on work in modern society, the conservative assumptions of Durkheim's general model are the backbone of the *consensus approach*.

Max Weber on Bureaucratic Organizations

Max Weber, a German sociologist also writing in the early twentieth century, addressed yet another major change accompanying capitalist industrialization—*bureaucracy*. Weber noted that Western societies were becoming more rational, a trend most visible in the bureaucratic organization of work. Informal relationships among small groups of workers, and between workers and employers, increasingly were being replaced by more formal, impersonal work relations in large bureaucracies. Rules and regulations were now determining workers' behaviour. While Weber was concerned about the resulting loss of personal work relationships, he believed that this was far outweighed by greater organizational efficiency. For Weber, bureaucracy and capitalism went hand in hand. Industrial capitalism was a system of rationally organized economic activities; bureaucracies provided the most appropriate organizational framework for such activities.

What defined Weber's "ideal-type" bureaucracy was a precise division of labour within a hierarchy of authority (Weber 1946: 196–98). Each job had its own duties and responsibilities, and each was part of a chain of command in which orders could be passed down, and rewards and punishments used to ensure that the orders were followed. But the power of the employer could not extend beyond the bureaucracy. The contract linking employer and employee was binding only within the work relationship. Also necessary for efficiency were extensive written records of decisions made and transactions completed.

Recruitment into and promotion within the bureaucratic work organization were based on competence, performance skills, and certifications such as educational credentials. Individual employees could make careers within the organization as they moved as far up the hierarchy as their skills and initiative would carry them. Employment contracts assured workers a position so long as they were needed and competently performed the functions of the office. In short, rationality, impersonality, and formal contractual relationships defined the bureaucratic work organization.

Yet bureaucracies were not unique to 19th-century capitalism. A somewhat similar form of centralized government had existed in ancient China, and European societies had been organizing their armies in this manner for centuries. What was unique, however, was the extent to which workplaces became bureaucratized under capitalism. At the beginning of the 20th century, increased competition and the development of big, complex industrial systems demanded even more rationalized production techniques and worker control systems. Large bureaucratic work organizations would become the norm throughout the industrial capitalist world. But bureaucracy also became the norm during the 20th century in industrialized communist countries of the former Soviet bloc. So, while closely intertwined, bureaucracy and capitalism are, in fact, separate phenomena.

The Managerial Revolution

Large corporations had begun to dominate the Canadian economy by the early 20th century. Formerly, most manufacturing enterprises had been owned and controlled by individuals or families. Then came the joint-stock companies in which hundreds, sometimes thousands, of investors shared ownership and profits. Such a diverse group of owners obviously could not directly control the giant corporation in which they had invested. Consequently, a class of managers who could run the enterprise became essential (Berle and Means 1968).

As this pattern spread, observers began to question the Marxist model of industrial capitalism that portrayed the relations of production as a simple two-class system: capitalists who owned and controlled the means of production versus workers who had little choice but to exchange their labour for a wage. An alternative model became popular. The *managerial revolution* theory predicted a new era of reduced conflict and greater harmony in the workplace (Burnham 1941). The theory held that *managers*, who were salaried workers and not owners, would look beyond profits when making decisions; the good of both the company and the workers would be equally important. Since ownership of the firm was now diffused among many individuals, power and control of the enterprise had essentially shifted to a new class of professional managers.

Several decades of debate and research later, it is generally agreed that this perspective on industrial relations in capitalist society exaggerated the degree of change (Zeitlin 1974; Hill 1981: 71–76; Scott 1988). First, family ownership patterns may be less common, but they certainly have not disappeared. In Canada, the prominence of names like Molson, McCain, and Bronfman demonstrate the continuing role of powerful families in the corporate sector. Furthermore, while ownership of corporations involves more individuals, many corporations are still controlled by small groups of minority shareholders. Individuals who serve as directors of major corporations are linked in a tight network of overlapping relationships, with many sitting on the boards of several major corporations simultaneously. Another postwar trend has been the corporate ownership of shares. Concentration of ownership increased as a few large holding companies replaced individual shareholders. Thus, the belief that the relatively small and very powerful capitalist class described by Marx has virtually disappeared is not supported by current evidence.[14]

Advocates of the managerial revolution theory also must demonstrate that, compared with earlier capitalists, the new breed of managers is less influenced by the bottom line of profit. But research continues to show that senior managers and corporate executives think and act in much the same way as capitalist owners. They share similar worldviews, often come from the same social backgrounds as owners, and hold large blocks of shares in the corporation, where they frequently serve as directors as well. In brief, the optimistic predictions of an era of industrial harmony brought on by new patterns of corporate ownership and management are largely unfounded.

POSTINDUSTRIALISM AND GLOBALIZATION

Postindustrial Society

Continuing social and economic change has led some social scientists to argue that we have moved out of the industrial era into a *postindustrial society*. Daniel Bell, writing in the early 1970s, was among the first to note these transformations in the U.S. occupational structure.[15] The Industrial Revolution had seen jobs in the manufacturing and processing sectors replace agricultural jobs. After World War II, jobs in the service sector had become much more prominent. The number of factory workers was decreasing, while employment in the areas of education, health, social welfare, entertainment, government, trade, finance, and a variety of other business sectors was rising. White-collar workers were beginning to outnumber blue-collar workers.

Bell argued that postindustrial societies would engage most workers in the production and dissemination of knowledge, rather than in goods production as in industrial capitalism. While industrialization had brought increased productivity and living standards, postindustrial society would usher in an era of reduced concentration of power (Bell 1973: 358–67). Power would no longer merely reside in the ownership of property, but also in access to knowledge and in the ability to think and to solve problems. *Knowledge workers*— technicians, professionals, and scientists—would become a large and important class. Their presence would begin to reduce the polarization of classes that had typified the arrival of the industrial age. In contrast to the managerial revolution thesis, which envisioned a new dominant class of managers, Bell proposed that knowledge workers would become the elite of the postindustrial age.

Not long after Bell published his ideas about postindustrial society, John Naisbitt popularized them in *Megatrends*. By including occupational groups as diverse as secretaries, data entry clerks, lawyers, librarians, and scientists in his category of "information workers," Naisbitt observed that a majority of the workforce in the United States was employed in the information sector. He argued that knowledge, unlike property, cannot be possessed by a small elite. Since a majority of the population is involved in creating, processing, and distributing information, society must be moving into a new, more democratic era. "The new source of power is not money in the hands of a few but information in the hands of many," he concluded (Naisbitt 1982: 7). What's interesting is that decades after Bell and Naisbitt, the same arguments are being made in discussions of the digital, knowledge-based economy of the early 21st century.

While continuing to focus on knowledge workers in his book *The Work of Nations*, Robert Reich disputes the arguments of Bell and Naisbitt about declining inequality. Reich distinguishes *symbolic analysts* (engineers, scientists, consultants, and so on) from the many individuals performing *routine production work* (most manufacturing employees, along with data entry clerks and many other lower-level white-collar workers) and from those providing *in-person services* (retail sales clerks, workers in the food services, and security guards, for example). Reich recognizes that inequality has increased in American society in the past decades. He argues that the symbolic analysts whose skills are in great demand have become wealthier, while other American workers have become poorer (Reich 1991: 174–76).

Why the optimism in the early theories of postindustrial society? These explanations of social and economic change were developed in the decades following World War II, a time of significant economic growth in North America.[16] White-collar occupational opportunities were increasing, educational institutions were expanding, and the overall standard of living was rising. Hence the optimistic tone of the social theories being developed. Yet, as we discuss at various points in the book, other commentators paint a negative picture of the rise of service industries and an expanding white-collar workforce. These critical perspectives point to job deskilling, reduced economic security, the dehumanizing impact of computers, and widening labour market polarization—trends that seem more pronounced since the early 1980s.

Today, these themes are being revisited in debates about the so-called *new economy*, which essentially refers to industries based on new information and communication technology, especially the Internet. As Don Tapscott (1996: 43) argues, what distinguished the old industrial economy from the new "digital economy" is that the latter is "built on silicon, computers, and networks" and its main inputs and outputs are information. Thus the new economy is also a knowledge-based economy. Taking stock of these trends, sociologist Manuel Castells (1996, 1998) concludes that a new technical-economic paradigm, or model, has emerged—a networked society. As old boundaries imposed by time and space have broken down, opportunities to organize our collective and individual lives in more flexible ways emerge—with profound implications for society. The big unanswered question, of course, is who the winners and losers will be. There are growing concerns about a "digital divide," based on social groups or communities that are included in or excluded from the technology and knowledge of the new economy. However, more research is required to assess the many ways that access to and use of information technology can affect working conditions and work rewards (Hughes and Lowe, 2000).

Industrial Restructuring

Technological change is accelerating at a time when the international economy is in upheaval. The deep recessions of the early 1980s and early 1990s, fierce international competition, multinational free-trade arrangements, and the spectacular growth of Asian economies have had a major impact on Canada. In fact, it is becoming more difficult to think in terms of discrete national economies. In the words of Robert Reich (1991: 6), "[m]oney, technology, information, and goods are flowing across national borders with unprecedented rapidity and ease." This *globalization* of economic activity continues to bring about fundamental readjustments in the Canadian economy and labour market, including plant shutdowns, job loss through downsizing, corporate reorganization and mergers, and the relocation or expansion of company operations outside Canada.[17]

But are these trends new ? Writing in the early twentieth century, economist Joseph Schumpeter considered *industrial restructuring* a basic feature of capitalism. According to Schumpeter, this process of "creative destruction" involved breaking down old ways of running industry and building up more competitive, efficient, and high-technology alternatives.[18] North American industry clearly is engaged in this process today. But while necessary for the economy as a whole, industrial restructuring can also diminish the quality and quantity of work for individuals. Job losses may be part of the process for some, while others may find themselves with much less job security.

Industrial restructuring involves interrelated social, economic, and technological trends. Crucial is the shift from manufacturing to services. Canada's service industries have rapidly grown in recent decades, compared with declining employment in agriculture, resource, and manufacturing industries. Indeed, both Canada and the United States have experienced *deindustrialization.* This concept refers to declining employment due to factory closures or relocation, typically in once-prominent manufacturing industries: steel, automotives, textiles, clothing, chemicals, and plastics. Once mainstays of the Canadian and U.S. economies, these industries are now sometimes referred to as "sunset industries," because they have failed to adapt quickly to shifting consumer demands. Factories have been sold off, shut down, or relocated to areas such as Mexico, China, or other developing nations where labour is cheap and employment rights and environmental standards are lax. As Bluestone and Harrison (1982: 9) observe, "left behind are shuttered factories, displaced workers, and a newly emerging group of ghost towns."

Canada has been more vulnerable than the United States to deindustrialization. By the early 1990s dozens of large multinationals, encouraged by the Canada–U.S. free trade agreement, had announced or implemented plant closures in central Canada, seeking cheaper labour and fewer regulations. For example, after purchasing the Bauer hockey equipment company, Nike announced in 1997 that it was closing the Ontario factory.[19] But Canadian-owned firms have also been making similar moves. As Canadian corporate giants like Bombardier and Nortel have become global competitors, they have shifted more of their operations, and therefore job opportunities, out of the country.

Globalization

The term *globalization* has become part of everyday language, but what does it really mean, and can evidence document such a trend? The basic idea is not new; in Canada's colonial past, the masters of the British Empire no doubt envisioned their reach as global. Yet searching for a definition of globalization, one is struck by the great many meanings it conveys. Advocates of globalization echo earlier themes in this chapter: the "logic of industrialism" view that predicts the inevitable spread of capitalist markets and national convergence, and the postindustrial vision of economic progress through technology and information. As Gordon Laxer (1995: 287–88) explains, globalization typically refers to four interrelated changes:

> Economic changes include the internationalization of production, the harmonization of tastes and standards and the greatly increased mobility of capital and of transnational corporations. Ideological changes emphasize investment and trade liberalization, deregulation and private enterprise. New information and communications technologies that shrink the globe signal a shift from goods to services. Finally, cultural changes involve trends toward a universal world culture and the erosion of the nation-state.

Corporations, and often governments, promote globalization as a means by which expanding "free markets" will generate economic growth and elevate living standards. Signs of an increasingly global economy are visible in multinational trade agreements, financial markets, and economic treaties. Examples include NAFTA, the European Union, and the Association of South East Asian Nations; international regulatory frameworks such as the World Trade Organization (WTO); and the integration of financial markets through information technology. Critics—and there are many—detect more sinister aspects of globalization. For example, the protesters at the Summit of the Americas in Quebec City in April 2001 (where government leaders from Canada, the United States, and Central and South America discussed creating a Free Trade Area of the Americas by 2005) raised concerns that such treaties threaten national cultures, workers' rights, the environment – and ultimately, democracy.

Even champions of globalization recognize these basic challenges. For example, as Thomas Friedman (2000: 42) writes in his book on globalization, *The Lexus and the Olive Tree:*

> Any society that wants to thrive economically today must constantly be trying to build a better Lexus and driving it out into the world. But no one should have any illusions that merely participating in this global economy will make a society healthy. If that participation comes at the price of a country's identity, if individuals feel their olive tree roots crushed, or washed out, by this global system, those olive tree roots will rebel.

Community-based opposition is only one of the reasons why a globally-integrated economic system remains largely an ideal. In a truly global economy, corporations would operate in a completely transnational way, not rooted in a specific national economy. But research suggests that there are few such corporations (Hirst and Thompson 1995). While McDonald's, IBM, and General Motors may do business in many countries, operating vast networks of subcontractors and suppliers, they remain U.S.-based. The United States, Japan, and Europe still account for most of the world's trade, largely through corporations located in these countries. While multinational corporations account for 25 percent of the world's production, they employ only 3 percent of the world's labour force (Giles 1996: 6). Even so, computers, software, clothes, shoes, cars and a vast range of other goods are produced by global business networks that span several continents (Rinehart, 2001: Chapter 6). Some observers argue that large corporations' sustained power will depend on creating and controlling these networks or "business alliances" (Harrison 1997). However, Anthony Giles (1996: 6) cautions, "Beyond the obvious technological, economic and logistical hurdles, there are a host of cultural, legal, political and linguistic factors which complicate the development of genuine globally integrated production systems."

It is much easier to imagine production systems spanning several continents than it is to envision a largely global labour force. Despite expanding international markets for some goods and services, labour is still a local resource. According to Hirst and Thompson (1995: 420), "Apart from a 'club-class' of internationally mobile, highly skilled professionals, and the desperate, poor migrants and refugees who will suffer almost any hardship to leave intolerable conditions, the bulk of the world's populations now cannot easily move." In fact, Canada plays an important role in this regard, being one of the few nations to accept relatively large numbers of immigrants annually.

Although labour might not be part of a global market, globalization may still have an impact on labour practices, notably through the public's growing concern about the labour practices of nationally based firms operating in developing countries (one could say the same about environmental practices). Global media coverage has helped to raise North Americans' awareness. Recently, multinational corporations like Nike have been the targets of public campaigns because of their labour practices in Asian countries (Heinzl 1997). Reflecting these concerns, a 1997 survey of 98 of Canada's largest corporations by the Montreal-based International Centre for Human Rights and Democratic Development found that while 42 percent of the responding firms agreed that international business has a role to play in promoting human rights and sustainable development, only 14 percent had a code of labour standards that protects basic human rights—freedom of association, nondiscrimination, and elimination of child labour and forced labour.[20]

Canada and Free Trade

The 1989 Free Trade Agreement (FTA) with the United States and the 1994 North American Free Trade Agreement (NAFTA), which included Mexico, committed Canada to a policy of more open, less regulated markets. As a NAFTA proponent commented: "Free trade is Darwinian. In the absence of tariff protection, the inefficient expect to be weeded out if incapable of competing" (Dana 1992: 7). He was referring to inefficient industries and firms, but individuals, families, and communities end up being the real victims. While claims of massive job losses directly from the FTA and the NAFTA have not been borne out, the permanent factory closures and job losses that occurred in central Canada in the early 1990s have partly been linked to free trade. Nevertheless, strong economic growth and job creation in Canada and, in particular the U.S., at the end of the decade have offset these losses. Significant industrial restructuring was already taking place, but the FTA probably accelerated the process, allowing the individuals and communities negatively affected less time to respond. Between the first quarter of 1990 and the second quarter of 1991, Canada lost 273,000 manufacturing jobs, a decline of 13 percent in the industry as a whole. As the Economic Council of Canada (1992a: 4) concluded, "Many of the jobs that were lost will not return." These issues are presumably being monitored, since NAFTA includes both an accord on labour and a commission for labour cooperation, which is mandated to track labour market trends in the three NAFTA countries and to address complaints about workers' rights, collective bargaining, and labour standards.[21]

To put NAFTA in perspective, the three participating countries had a combined labour force of 183 million workers in 1995: 72 percent in the U.S., 20 percent in Mexico, and 8 percent in Canada (Secretariat of the Commission for Labor Cooperation 1996: 8). Mexico's labour force has been growing at a considerably faster rate than have the labour forces of its two northern neighbours, but since 1990 manufacturing employment in that country has actually declined (Arsen 1996: 46). The migration of jobs from Canada or the U.S. to Mexico was a major concern of NAFTA opponents. There is little doubt that the *maquiladora* factories along Mexico's northern border have been booming. In January 1995, for example, there were 300 new maquilas started by Canadian and Japanese investors and 6,000 new workers hired (Kopinak 1996: 197). Were these "new" jobs, or jobs relocated from high-wage Canada or Japan? From available evidence, it seems that fewer jobs than expected have migrated south.[22] And much of the new foreign investment in Mexico is from firms based in Japan, East Asia, and Europe seeking a base from which to supply the North American consumer market.

Jobs may be migrating south, but only in some manufacturing industries, and if these employers are in search of low wages, they would likely relocate to China, not Mexico. Actually, there is as much concern that competitive pressures from NAFTA in some manufacturing industries, such as auto and auto parts manufacturing, have accelerated the trend toward *nonstandard or contingent* work (part-time, temporary, contract) in the U.S. and Canada (Roberts, Hyatt, and Dorman 1996). Others would argue that the group most negatively affected by NAFTA is Mexican workers. Drawing our attention to Mexico's industrial and social development, one commentator notes: "Of the many arguments against NAFTA the most cogent was the case made by many Mexican opposition activists: that it would artificially prop up a decadent political monopoly, delaying democratic reform and ultimately making it harder for Mexico to modernize" (Orme 1996: xxv).

It is not difficult to find supporting evidence for this view. Mexico's industrialization in the 1980s led to increased social and economic inequalities. The workers in the border maquiladora factories numbered about half a million prior to NAFTA. While their dollar-an-hour pay, lack of rights, and working conditions may be deplorable by Canadian standards, they were part of an emerging middle class in Mexico, able to "cross-border" shop in the U.S. But few workers were spared the ravaging effects of the devaluation of the Mexican peso in late 1994, which saw per capita income instantly plummet from $4000 to $2600 U.S. (Orme 1996: xi). Maquiladora workers, already advantaged by Mexican standards, had the most militant response to this devaluation, and, through illegal strikes, did gain better pay and benefits (Kopinak 1996: 199). Furthermore, NAFTA debates tended to overlook the circumstances of the majority of Mexicans—the rural poor. The Zapatista uprising in the rural state of Chiapas briefly drew the world's attention to those who would not benefit from NAFTA.

THE ROLE OF THE STATE IN TODAY'S ECONOMY

Clearly, the information technology revolution, industrial and labour market restructuring, and economic globalization are proceeding in a political context dominated by *laissez-faire* beliefs that advocate free markets with little or no government interference.[23] In a sense, this political environment is also a key determinant of Canadians' future employment prospects. These three large trends have the potential to either improve employment opportunities for Canadians or lead to further labour market disruptions. It is difficult to predict just what their ultimate impact might be, but it is important to consider how these forces could be shaped to our collective advantage. Public policy in other industrial countries in Europe and Asia has been more proactive in attempting to influence the course of technological, labour market, and economic change.

The FTA and NAFTA were negotiated by governments, and have been hotly contested political issues in all three countries affected. These trade agreements underscore the evolving role of the state (or government) in the economy and the labour market. The history of industrial capitalism is replete with instances of different forms of state intervention. For example, in the early industrial revolution, the French government forced unemployed workers into factories in an attempt to give manufacturing a boost. We noted above that in the early nineteenth century the British government dealt harshly with the Luddite protests against new technologies. And the Canadian government adopted its National Policy in 1879 to promote a transcontinental railway and settlement of the West.

In fact, as Canada industrialized, the government heavily subsidized the construction of railways in order to promote economic development. It also actively encouraged immigration to increase skilled labour for factory-based production and unskilled labour for railway construction. At times, it provided military assistance to employers combating trade unionists, and introduced laws discriminating against Chinese and other nonwhite workers. But the Canadian government also passed legislation that provided greater rights, unemployment insurance, pensions, and compensation for workplace injuries. While some might argue that these initiatives were designed mainly to ensure industrial harmony and to create an environment conducive to business, it is nonetheless true that these labour market interventions benefited workers.

A consensus, or compromise, was reached between employers and workers (mainly organized labour) in the prosperous post–World-War-II period. Acting on *Keynesian economic principles* that advocated an active economic role for the state, the Canadian government attempted to promote economic development, regulate the labour market, keep unemployment down, and assist disadvantaged groups—in short, develop a "welfare state." While the Canadian state was never as actively involved in the economy and the labour market as some European governments, it nevertheless saw itself playing an important role.[24]

But industrial restructuring in the 1980s was accompanied (some would say facilitated) by new conservative political doctrines based on free-market economics (Marchak 1981; Saul 1995; Kapstein 1996). Ronald Reagan in the U.S., Margaret Thatcher in Britain, and Brian Mulroney in Canada argued that economies would become more productive and competitive with less state regulation and intervention. Public policy was guided by the assumption that free markets can best determine who benefits and who loses from economic restructuring. The ideas of Adam Smith were used to justify the inevitable increases in inequality. High unemployment came to be viewed as normal. In some jurisdictions, labour rights were diluted, social programs of the welfare state came to be seen as a hindrance to balanced budgets and economic competitiveness, and government-run services were privatized – changes that directly or indirectly affected employment relationships.[25] As John Ralston Saul (1995) argues, these free-market ideologies erode democratic freedoms, threatening to bring about what he calls "the great leap backward." Similarly, with the rapidly developing economies of East Asia, governments routinely use economic imperatives to restrict individual and collective rights.

Thus, in today's economic climate of globalization and restructuring, proponents of free-market economics seem to have more influence. But as we noted when discussing the ideas of Adam Smith, an unchecked marketplace generally leads to greater inequality. So, when answering the question "what kind of society do we want?" it will be important to determine the role of the state in achieving the desired society. Looking back, we can see that differing government policies have interacted with economic globalization to produce different effects at the local level. Looking forward, there is no fixed trajectory for globalization. Political choices by citizens and their governments undoubtedly will continue to shape the process in diverse ways (Cameron and Stein 2000). Canadians are concerned about labour market inequalities, employment, workers' rights, and employers' responsibilities to communities. The extent to which governments are held accountable for these issues will determine the impact of global economic forces on our daily economic lives.

CONCLUSION

From feudalism to NAFTA and globalization – we have covered a lot of territory in this chapter. We began with an historical overview of the origins and development of industrial capitalism, then discussed various theories that explain and evaluate the causes and consequences of this complex process. As economies and societies continually evolve and the nature of work is transformed, new social theories have been constructed accordingly.

We have highlighted important social and economic changes initially unleashed by the Industrial Revolution in Europe. As feudalism gave way to capitalism, markets grew in importance. A new class structure evolved and a predominantly rural society became urban. Factory-based wage labour became the norm, while craft work declined. Larger workplaces demanded new organizational forms and, in time, bureaucracies evolved to fill this need. And while industrial innovations led to substantial increases in productivity, it was some time before the standard of living of the working class began to reflect this increase. These far-reaching social and economic changes were the focus of early sociologists like Marx, Durkheim, and Weber, and economists like Adam Smith. Having had a brief look at the changing worlds that these social theorists were observing, we are now better equipped to understand their concerns and conclusions.

Our overview of the industrialization experience in Canada and several other countries takes us into the present. Much larger workplaces, new technologies, a more complex division of labour, growth in white-collar occupations, and a new class of managers were among the changes observed as industrial capitalism matured in twentieth-century Canada. Once again, these changes generated a variety of new social theories dealing with technology, social inequality, skill, knowledge workers, increasing convergence, and labour–management cooperation. But the optimistic predictions of reduced inequality and conflict in a postindustrial era are not well supported by the data. Instead, as we will see in the next chapter, employment trends suggest a growing gap between more and less advantaged workers.

We have also highlighted a number of global economic and technological forces now reshaping employment patterns. Like other advanced capitalist societies, Canada has become a service-dominated economy. The information technology revolution is having a major impact on both the quantity and quality of work in the Canadian labour market, as are processes of industrial and labour market restructuring. The eventual outcomes of these trends are still unclear. We will also have to confront the limits to growth, as environmental sustainability becomes a more pressing global problem (World Commission on Environment and Development 1987). We may see a general improvement in the standard of living and the quality of working life, or the benefits may go primarily to those who already have better jobs, thus contributing to increased polarization in the labour market and in society as a whole. In subsequent chapters, we will return frequently to this basic question about increasing or declining inequalities.

NOTES

1. We thank Pat Armstrong for this story.

2. Beaud's (1983) history of capitalism is a major source for our brief discussion; also see Grint (1991: 48–83) on pre-industrial and early industrial work patterns.

3. Over the centuries, however, technological innovations did lead to important changes in work patterns. See, for example, White's (1962) detailed historical analysis of the impact of draught horses and the wheeled plough on agriculture, and of the effects of the invention of the stirrup on the practice of warfare.

4. Grint (1991: 69–73). Cohen (1988: 24) concludes that industrialization in Canada did not lead to a sharper gender-based division of labour since, as was not the case in England, such segmentation already existed prior to industrialization.

5. Polanyi (1957). See Boyer and Drache (1996: 8–12) for an application of Polanyi's ideas to the current era.

6. This discussion is drawn from a variety of sources, many cited individually below. For a useful overview of this period in Canadian history, see Ryerson (1968), Laxer (1989), Kealey (1995: Part One), Palmer (1992), and the Canadian labour studies journal, *Labour/Le Travail.*

7. Bleasdale (1981: 13); see Wylie (1983) on the building of the Rideau Canal.

8. Bradwin (1972); see Avery (1995) and Creese (1988–89) on strikes and radical behaviour among immigrant workers.

9. Mine accidents that took the lives of many miners at one time are mainly responsible for these high averages. For example, 189 miners died in a mine explosion in Hillcrest, Alberta, in 1914. A memorial to these miners and background on the disaster can be found at http://members.tripod.com/~coalminersmemorial/hillcrestminedisaster.html. See McCormack (1978: 9) on British Columbia, and Caragata (1979: 16–21) on Alberta coal miners during this era.

10. See World Bank (2001), Holzer (2000), Whitley (1992), Shieh (1992), and Hsiung (1996) for accounts of economic development in the region. The argument about the critical role of a 'Weberian' form of government bureaucracy is presented by Evans and Rauch (1999).

11. More than $40 billion U.S. in direct foreign investment was made in China during each of 1998 and 1999 (www.asiacentre.net).

12. Toffler (1980: 50) provides the quote from Henry Ford.

13. Durkheim (1960) did allow that a "forced" division of labour, where individuals have no choice over how they participate in the productive system, would not lead to increased social solidarity. But he argued that this and other abnormal forms of the division of labour would disappear as industrial capitalism matured further.

14. See Antoniou and Rowley (1986) on family ownership patterns; Dhingra (1983) on concentration of ownership; and Carroll et al. (1982) on crosscutting directorship ties.

15. Bell (1973); current and more critical perspectives on postindustrial society are reviewed by Kumar (1995), Clement and Myles (1994), and Nelson (1995).

16. The managerial revolution perspective (Burnham, 1941; Berle and Means, 1968) was developed earlier, during an era when corporate concentration in North America was proceeding rapidly and when concerns about the excessive power of the corporate elite were being publicly debated (Reich, 1991: 38).

17. See Lowe (2000: Chapter 4) for a discussion of industrial restructuring and the rise of the 'new economy' in Canada. Also see Boyer and Drache (1996) and Barnet and Cavanagh (1994: Part Three) for critical perspectives on restructuring, globalization, and work.

18. Schumpeter's views are discussed in Bluestone and Harrison (1982: 9).

19. Drache and Gertler (1991: 12-13). See Heinzl (1997) on Nike's closure of the Bauer factory. Also see Mahon's (1984) analysis of restructuring in the Canadian textile industry.

20. International Centre for Human Rights and Democratic Development, 1997. The organization's web site (http://www.ichrdd.ca) has a number of reports on globalization and labour rights. On human rights at work, and the goal of promoting 'decent work' for all, see the International Labour Organization (ILO, 1999) [http://www.ilo.org/public/english/]. Also see Adams and Hallock (2001) on the anti-sweatshop movement and its impact on corporate codes of conduct.

21. Commission on Labor Cooperation (2000). For current information, see the North American Institute's web site (http://www.northamericaninstitute.org) and the Commission on Labor Cooperation (http://www.naalc.org). The latter monitors the North American Agreement on Labor Cooperation. The NAALC's study of adjustments in the North American garment industry under NAFTA focuses on the importance of labour standards [www.naalc.org/english/publications/garment_sum.htm/]. See Adams and Singh (1997) and Gunderson (1998) for an assessment of the impact of NAFTA on labour policies and worker rights. Vosko (1998) contrasts the different regulatory responses under NAFTA and the European Community to the spread of temporary employment.

22. Orme (1996: 13); Arsen, Wilson, and Zoninsein (1996); for different perspectives on NAFTA, see Bognanno and Ready (1993).

23. See Saul (1995) for a critique of this ideology.

24. See Olsen's (1999) comparative review of recent changes to Sweden's welfare state.

25. See Bamber and Lansbury (1998) for a comparative analysis of how employment relations and labour-management relations have changed recently in 10 industrialized nations.

CANADIAN EMPLOYMENT PATTERNS AND TRENDS

INTRODUCTION

Pick up a copy of any Canadian daily newspaper and flip through it, looking for feature stories on work-related topics. You'll likely come across articles based on labour force statistics collected by Statistics Canada, or by some other public or private sector data collection agency. Most common are the unemployment rates, updated monthly. But the news media also carry stories on a wide range of other employment themes, including income patterns, industry and occupational changes, gender differences in employment opportunities, part-time work and self-employment, strikes, and workplace health and safety.

Many of these labour force statistics are examined in this chapter. Becoming more statistically literate is an important goal: in a society in which the media constantly bombard us with the latest figures on one social trend or another, it is helpful to have some understanding of the definition and source of these numbers, and even more important, to be able to interpret them critically. Hence, we will discuss these trends with reference to some of the broad theories of social and economic change discussed in Chapter 1. At the same time, this statistical overview will provide us with the background needed to evaluate, in Chapter 3, competing theories of how labour markets operate.

We begin by outlining key demographic factors shaping the workforce. We then go on to discuss labour force participation trends and Canada's occupational and industrial structures, emphasizing the rise of the service economy. Canada's unemployment trends and the growth in nonstandard jobs in this country are other focuses of this chapter. We conclude with an analysis of where current labour market trends may be taking us, raising important issues about the future of work.

DATA SOURCES

A major data source is the Canadian census, a survey of the entire population of the country conducted by Statistics Canada. The most recent national census was completed in 2001, so the results are not available for this edition of the book. The huge effort and cost involved in collecting information about 31 million Canadians means that only a limited number of questions can be asked about each household and the individuals within it. Furthermore, because a census takes place every five years, results are seldom up to date. Despite this, a census provides the most complete picture of the Canadian labour market at specific points in time, and allows us to accurately plot historical changes.

A second useful source is the monthly *Labour Force Survey*, also conducted by Statistics Canada. Unlike the census, which attempts to cover a range of topics, this random sample survey is designed to collect only work-related information and so provides much more detail. Because the survey is done every month, information is always updated. In order to get precise estimates of the labour market activities of Canadians aged 15 and older, a large sample is needed. Approximately 52,000 households (most providing information on more than one individual) are included in the sample.[1] Households remain part of the sample for six months before being replaced.

The *Labour Force Survey* provides, for example, monthly estimates of unemployment and labour force participation rates and descriptions of industries and occupations experiencing job growth or decline.[2] Frequently, more detailed surveys, designed to study specific work-related topics, are "piggy-backed" onto the *Labour Force Survey*. Examples of such topics include student summer employment, involuntary part-time work, and job search behaviour. Many of the statistics cited in this chapter are obtained from this useful source.[3]

THE DEMOGRAPHIC CONTEXT OF LABOUR MARKET CHANGE

Whether our focus is on the labour market today or 10 to 20 years in the future, there is no denying that *demographic shifts* (population changes) under way in Canadian society set some basic parameters. Of all the employment trends we will consider in this chapter, those related to the demographic composition of the labour force are perhaps the only ones we can confidently project into the future. So while economists debate whether the unemployment rate may rise or decline next year, demographers (who specialize in studying the structure and dynamics of population) can quite accurately predict birth rates, life expectancy, population growth, age distributions of the population, and related trends. Three of these trends deserve particular attention: aging, cultural diversity, and educational attainment.

Workforce Aging

While we might dispute David Foot's claim in his best-selling book, *Boom, Bust and Echo*, that "[d]emographics explain about two-thirds of everything," we do agree that Canada's demographic trends influence many economic and social changes.[4] Foremost among these demographic factors is *population aging*, which has significant implications for job opportunities, pensions, work values, and organizational structures. The *baby boom generation*, born between 1946 and 1964, is the largest generation in Canadian history. In the words of historian Doug Owram (1996: xiv), "Economics, politics, education, and family life would all have been considerably different without the vast demographic upsurge of births after the Second World War." As baby boomers move through the life course, they are leaving few institutions unchanged—from a revolution in popular music in the 1960s to the rapid expansion of post-secondary institutions in the 1970s to the burgeoning mutual fund industry of the 1990s. Coupled with smaller birth cohorts following in their wake, due to sharply declining birth rates, the aging of the baby boom has fundamentally altered the demographic shape and social structure of Canada.

This huge and slowly aging bulge in the workforce has affected the career opportunities of many Canadian workers. The baby boom generation entered the workforce when the economy was still expanding, and many obtained good jobs. Some of the smaller generations that followed them into the labour force have been less fortunate, since higher unemployment and global economic uncertainties have frequently led to lay-offs, not hiring. Yet many baby boomers found their careers beginning to *plateau* in the 1990s. Because most work organizations are pyramids, career success has been defined in terms of climbing a ladder that has room for fewer and fewer people on each higher rung. But with more older workers, the competition for the few top jobs has intensified. For younger workers experiencing difficulty finding satisfactory entry-level jobs, this may not seem a serious problem. But, for long-term employees who have learned to view personal success as upward movement, career blockages can be very unsettling (Foot and Venne 1990). Generally, work organizations have not adapted to changing demographic pressures, maintaining pyramidal structures and recruitment policies that are no longer appropriate and focusing on downsizing for the past decade (Foot and Stoffman 1998: Chapter 4).

Figure 2.1 documents the workforce aging process by profiling the *age distribution* of labour force participants in 1975 and 2000. Note the decline in the relative proportion of teenagers (15 to 19 years) and young adults (20 to 24 years) over the 25-year period. Compare this with the increased size of the 35-to-44 and 45-to-54-year-old cohorts over this time. What is also interesting is the decline in the proportion of 55- to 64-year-olds in the workforce since 1975. This marks the trend toward "early" retirement, in part due to older workers being affected by labour market restructuring and organizational downsizing in the 1980s and 1990s.

In 1921, only 5% of Canadians were 65 years of age and older. Over the next 50 years, this figure grew slowly to 8%. Then the aging of the Canadian population began to accelerate, and by 2000 almost 13% of Canadians were senior citizens. Statistics Canada predicts that, by 2041, seniors will account for 23% of the total population.[5] The relative size of the working-age popula-

FIGURE 2.1 *Age Distribution of the Labour Force by Gender, Canada, 1975 and 2000*

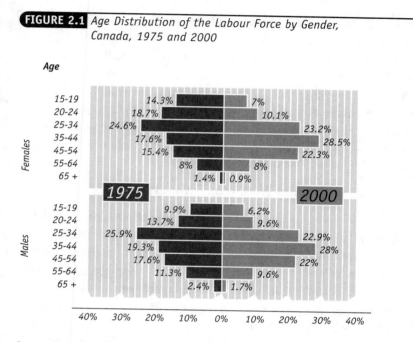

Source: Statistics Canada 2001. *Labour Force Historical Review.* Cat. no. 71F004XCB.

tion that funds government old-age security programs through payroll contributions will shrink considerably during this period. The earliest baby boomers are now in their mid-50s, and many have begun to think seriously about their retirement options. Hence, pensions have become a prominent public concern. Will the Canada/Quebec Pension Plan (C/QPP), one of Canada's main *social safety nets*, be able to support all the retiring baby boomers, or will today's youth have to pay more to cover the added costs? Or, as an alternative solution, will Canadians have to wait until they are a few years older than 65 to begin collecting a government pension? Will employer-sponsored pension plans make up the difference? Probably not. In 1998, for example, 88 percent of Canadian labour force participants paid into the C/QPP and, therefore, will receive small government pensions. However, only 39 percent made Registered Retirement Savings Plan (RRSP) contributions, and fewer (only 32%) participated in employer-sponsored registered pension plans (RPPs).[6]

It would seem reasonable to expect that workforce aging would open up opportunities for younger workers, who are far outnumbered by middle-aged baby boomers (Easterlin 1980). This has not been the case yet, mainly because employers have been restructuring and sometimes downsizing their organizations, rather than hiring to fill the vacancies left by retirees. But consider the relatively small size of the 15- to 19-year-old and 20- to 24-year-old cohorts in today's labour force (Figure 2.1). In another ten years, when the first wave of baby boomers have entered retirement, there is a distinct possibility of labour shortages. Even so, we need to recognize that the generation in between continues to have difficulty finding satisfactory jobs.

Greater Workforce Diversity

Immigration is an important determinant of Canada's population mosaic. For centuries, Canada has been a country of immigrants. In the post–World-War-II era, Canadian governments have attempted to tailor immigration policy to labour market trends, partly in anticipation of labour shortages in key areas. Immigration levels have been kept low when unemployment was high, but have been allowed to rise when economic expansion required extra workers. In fact, there have been times (around 1910, for example, when the Western provinces were being settled) when immigration levels were considerably higher than they are today. But, along with economic factors, immigration policies have also been influenced by demographic trends. For almost three decades now, birth rates have been below replacement level, so low that our population would have declined unless supplemented by immigration. ·

Between 1991 and 1996, the immigrant population in Canada increased more than three times as quickly as the native-born population (growth rates of 14.5% and 4.0%, respectively). Thus, by 1996, 17.4 percent of all Canadians were immigrants, up from around 15 to 16 percent between 1951 and 1991. This increase in the immigrant population reflects federal government quotas that are currently set around 200,000 immigrants per year (less than one percent of the total population). Despite concerns by some that immigrants are taking jobs away from native-born Canadians, research shows that this is rarely the case. Immigrants frequently create their own jobs, or are willing to take jobs that others do not wish to have, and are carefully selected to match shortages of workers in specific occupational categories. Given the impending shortage of labour force participants a few decades ahead, maintenance of current levels of immigration is a necessary policy decision.[7]

· Until quite recently, the majority of immigrants to Canada were from European countries; most were white. For example, in 1981, two-thirds of all immigrants living in Canada (including those who had been here for many decades) were born in Europe. By 1996, immigrants from Europe were a minority (47%). The source countries have changed dramatically in the past few decades, leading to much greater cultural diversity in society and in workplaces. In fact, 57% of all immigrants who arrived between 1991 and 1996 came from Asia. Why? Canadian immigration policies no longer favour European immigrants but, more importantly, the demand to immigrate to Canada has declined in Europe, while it has increased dramatically elsewhere. Consequently, more immigrants are members of visible minority groups with distinctive cultural backgrounds.

According to the 1996 Census, 11.2 percent of Canadians (3.2 million people) identified themselves as a member of a *visible minority* group (excluding Aboriginal Canadians), up from 9.4% only five years earlier. In Toronto and Vancouver, visible minorities made up almost one-third of the city population. Chinese Canadians made up the largest visible minority group in Canada in 1996 (3% of all Canadians), followed by South Asians (2.4%) and Blacks (2.0%). Given current immigration patterns, the proportion of visible minorities in Canada is expected to increase to around 20 percent by 2016. Moreover, 2.8 percent of the nation's population is of Aboriginal origin. This figure will also increase in the decades ahead, given the much younger age profile of Aboriginal Canadians (about 10 years younger than the total Canadian population, according to the 1996 census). Immigrants are also younger, on average, so both Aboriginal Canadians and immigrants will make up a growing share of the workforce as older Canadians retire.[8] As discussed in later chapters, these demographic trends have prompted governments and employers to develop employment equity policies to facilitate greater workplace cultural diversity and reduce the potential for labour market discrimination.

A Better-Educated Workforce

On the whole, Canadians are becoming increasingly well educated, a trend that has also fundamentally changed the character of the labour force. Figure 2.2 shows the dramatic change in *educational attainment* of the labour force between

1975 and 2000. In 1975, 66 percent of females and 68 percent of males in the labour force had only a high school education or less. Very few (only 7% and 10%, respectively) had a university degree. In the 25 years since, large numbers of both men and women obtained post-secondary credentials. Almost one in five Canadian labour force participants had a university degree in 2000.

This rising educational attainment has been the backdrop for a debate on the role of education in a rapidly changing and increasingly global and technological economic environment. In fact, many analysts argue that a well-educated workforce is a nation's key resource in today's global marketplace. Business and government have argued that additional education and training, and an overhaul of the education system that makes it more job-relevant, will help Canada become more competitive internationally.[9] The latest variant of this perspective is found in the concepts of *lifelong learning* and *learning organizations*.[10] Essentially, these refer to continuous education, both formal and informal, in educational institutions and at work and home, throughout one's adult life. Educators, parents, and students have responded by raising concerns that closer links between education and the economy might mean too much business influence over what is taught at all levels of the educational system (Davis 2000, Turk 2000).

FIGURE 2.2 *Educational Attainment of the Labour Force by Gender, Canada, 1975 and 2000*

Source: Statistics Canada 2001. *Labour Force Historical Review.* Cat. no. 71F004XCB.

By international standards, Canadians are very well educated in terms of post-secondary credentials and enrollment levels.[11] But there is more to developing a nation's human resources than the acquisition of formal education. No doubt there are educational reforms that could lead to the graduation of more skilled, flexible, and enterprising labour force participants. Basic literacy and numeracy, along with other essential skills, are lacking in small pockets of the workforce.[12] But work-related training is not only the responsibility of the education system. Canada has a mediocre record of employer-sponsored workplace training. A recent national survey revealed that only about one-quarter of full-time employees participate in employer-supported training (Human Resources Development Canada 1997). Compared to the United States and western European countries, Canada's training record is average, at best (Kapsalis, 1998). Generally, it is the well-educated worker already in a good job who receives training, further accentuating labour market inequalities (see Chapter 3).[13]

The assumption underlying the "education and training" solution to economic growth is that our workforce is not sufficiently educated and trained, yet the above discussion suggests there is more to the problem. For one thing, while unemployment is higher among the less educated, a considerable number of Canada's unemployed are well educated. In addition, many Canadian workers are in jobs that require little education or training. In 1994 almost one in four (23%) of employed Canadians (aged 15 to 64) reported that they were overqualified for their job.[14] This *underemployment* highlights the need to go beyond the supply side of the education-job equation to examine how job content and skill requirements could be upgraded—in short, how the demand for educated labour could be improved. Clearly, there are deeper problems in the structure of our economy as well, and concerted efforts by government, the private sector, organized labour, and professional associations are needed to address them. As two American sociologists concluded about the United States: "The problem is a shortage of good jobs to a greater extent than it is inadequate training and development."[15]

LABOUR FORCE PARTICIPATION TRENDS

Now that we have a better demographic understanding of the workforce, we can examine key labour market and employment trends that define where, how, and for whom Canadians work. *Labour force participation* (LFP) is the main indicator of a population's economic activity, at least from the perspective of paid employment. Whether relying on census or monthly Labour Force Survey data, calculations of labour force size or participation rates are based on the number of individuals 15 years of age or older who are working for pay (including self-employed individuals working on their own or employing others) and those who are looking for work. Hence, the *unemployed* (those out of work but who have actively looked for work in the past four weeks) are counted as part of the labour force. However, individuals performing unpaid household and child care work in their home are not included in official labour force calculations, even though their labour makes essential economic and social contributions.

Using this official LFP definition to look at work patterns at the beginning of the last century, only 53 percent of Canadians (15 years of age and older) were participating in the labour force in 1901. The rate increased to over 57 percent by 1911 but did not go much higher until the 1970s (Figure 2.3). By 1981 almost two-thirds (65%) of the eligible population was in a paid job or

FIGURE 2.3 *Labour Force Participation Rates by Gender, Canada, 1946—2000*

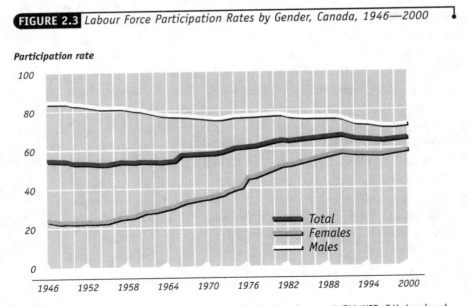

Source: Statistics Canada 2001. *Labour Force Historical Review.* Cat. no. 71F004XCB; F.H. Leach, ed., Statistics Canada 1983. *Historical Statistics of Canada,* 2nd ed. Series D205-222.

seeking one. Participation rates peaked in 1989 at 67 percent, and then fell a bit during the recession of the early 1990s. They have hovered between 65 and 66 percent since then. The 2000 LFP rate was 65.9 percent, representing a total of 15,999,000 labour force participants.

Gender Differences in Labour Force Participation

Breaking down the LFP rate by gender, we find striking differences. In 1901 only 16 percent of women aged 15 or older were in the paid labour force. However, this rate increased with each ten-year census. After World War II, the size of these increases was substantial (Figure 2.3). Between 1960 and 1975, female LFP jumped from 28 to 41 percent, and the following decade saw it rise to 55 percent. The landmark year was 1980, the first in which a majority of Canadian women were part of the labour force (which, as officially defined, leaves out unpaid family and household work).

The female LFP rate rose to almost 59 percent in 1990 and 1991, then dropped slightly for a number of years before rising again, to 59.5 percent in 2000. Thus, over the course of the last century, female labour force participation in Canada almost quadrupled, from 16 percent to 60 percent. As we will see in Chapter 4, the impact of this long-term trend on workplaces, families, and society as a whole has been immense. During the 1960s and 1970s, much of the growth in female LFP was due to larger numbers of women returning to paid employment after their children were in school or had left home. In contrast, most of the female employment growth in the 1980s and 1990s occurred among mothers with children at home. By way of example, a recent analysis of national data revealed that 86% of employed women who gave birth were back at work within a year, and 93% had returned to paid employment within two years (Marshall 1999a: 20).

While female participation rates have been climbing, male rates declined over most of the last century, although not as steeply. Between 1901 and 1931, the male LFP rate remained close to 90 percent, dropping in the decades before and after World War II to percentages in the mid-80s. In the 1970s and 1980s, the male rates fluctuated between 76 and 78 percent. More recently, the male LFP rate dropped quickly from 77 percent in 1989 to just over 72 percent in 1996, staying at this level until 2000. The economic recovery in the last half of the 1990s led to a small increase in female LFP but had no effect on male participation rates.

Thus, the long-term growth in total LFP rates in Canada has been the product of substantial increases for women and somewhat less dramatic declines for men. The latter change reflects two trends: men are living longer (with more men living past the conventional retirement age, the proportion of all men out of the labour force is increasing) and more men are retiring early (that is, before the accepted retirement age of 65). The causes of growing female labour force participation, which are more complex, are discussed in Chapter 4. A similar convergence of female and male rates has occurred in other industrialized countries (the United States, Britain, Germany, France, Italy, and Japan, for example) but, over the past few decades, Canada has experienced the largest jump in female labour force participation.

It is important to note that these labour force participation rates are annual averages. Given the seasonal nature of some types of work in Canada (jobs in agriculture, fishing and forestry, and construction and tourism, for example), higher levels of labour force participation are typically recorded in the spring, summer, and autumn months. Furthermore, taking a full twelve-month period, we observe higher proportions of Canadians reporting labour force participation at some point during the year. Thus, annual averages do not reveal the extent to which Canadians move in and out of different labour market statuses. A 1993 analysis of labour market activity showed that 27 percent of individuals who were in the labour force at some point that year experienced a change of status, either entering or exiting the labour force, becoming unemployed, or finding a job. Even though *job stability* (average length of time in a job) has increased somewhat since the early 1990s, the Canadian labour market still reflects a considerable amount of individual mobility.[16]

In addition, there are a number of groups that continue to have much lower than average rates of labour force activity. Many Aboriginal Canadians are economically marginalized, facing huge barriers to paid employment. For example, the 1996 census revealed that employment rates of Registered Indians living on reservations were 60% lower than that of the overall Canadian population. Another analysis of 1991 census data demonstrated that, among adult wage-earners in Northern Canada, only 33% of Aboriginals worked full-time for the full-year, compared to 58% of non-Aboriginals. The result, as one might expect, is that Aboriginal Canadians have much lower incomes, on average, and are much more likely to be living below the poverty line.[17] Similarly, research shows that disabled Canadians are much less likely to be in the paid labour force. In 1995, the LFP rate for disabled Canadians was only 43 percent.[18]

Labour Force Participation among Youth

With the exception of a small decline coinciding with the recession of the early 1980s, the labour force participation of Canadian youth (aged 15 to 24, females and males combined) rose more or less steadily from an annual average of 64 percent in 1976 to 71 percent in 1989. Figure 2.4 shows that the youth LFP rate then declined rapidly in the 1990s, dropping to 62 percent by 1996. Since then, it has risen again, to 64 percent. Over this period of time, the female and male youth LFP rates converged considerably, although male rates were still higher (66%) than female rates (63%) in 2000.

FIGURE 2.4 *Youth Labour Force Participation Rates by Gender, Canada, 1976-2000*

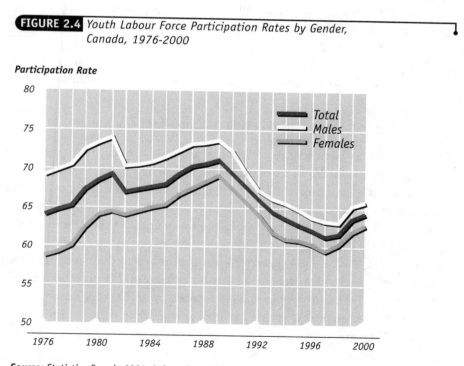

Source: Statistics Canada 2001. *Labour Force Historical Review.* Cat. no. 71F004XCB.

Over the past two or three decades, teenage (age 15 to 19) LFP rates have always been considerably lower than LFP rates for young adults (age 20 to 24), since a larger proportion of the latter group have left the education system. In 2000, female and male rates for teenagers were identical (52%) but, among young adults, male LFP rates (80%) were considerably higher than female rates (74%) (Sunter, 2001).

Why did youth LFP rates decline in the 1990s? The recession that lasted till mid-decade sharply reduced the number of "good" entry-level jobs for youth. In fact, during this period youth wages declined more than for any other age group in the labour force. In turn, a larger proportion of youth decided to continue their education to improve their employment prospects. For example, between 1989 and 1998, the percentage of Canadian youth (age 15 to 24) who were in school and not working rose from 29 to 40 percent. Furthermore, the size of the 20-to-24-year-old cohort declined, compared to the 15-to-19-year-old cohort. Since young adults have historically had higher LFP rates than teenagers, the overall youth LFP rate declined.[19] And, after dropping so dramatically, why did youth LFP rates increase slightly towards the end of the 1990s? A stronger economy, reflected in lower unemployment rates, is part of the answer. In addition, rapidly rising post-secondary tuition costs may have led some Canadian youth to choose work over school.

Labour Force Participation among Older Canadians

Over the past few decades labour force participation among older men has declined markedly. In 1976, more than three in four (77%) 55- to 64-year-old men were in the labour force. By 1997, the LFP rate for male members of this age cohort was only 61 percent. As we would expect, the oldest members of this cohort are most likely to be leaving the labour force. The 2000 LFP rate for men age 55 to 59 was 73 percent, much higher than the 46 percent rate for 60- to 64-year-old males. With somewhat better benefits provided to the elderly by government, compared with a generation or two earlier, and with a larger number of older men who have employer-sponsored pensions as well as other personal savings (RRSPs, for example), income security among older men has increased. Consequently, a greater percentage are opting to retire before age 65.[20]

However, there are other reasons for early labour market exit by men. Among all retired men, the 1994 General Social Survey found that health was the most frequent reason given for retirement (25 percent), followed by personal choice (24 percent). One in ten had been forced into retirement by unemployment (Statistics Canada 1995b). Looking just at retired men ages 55 to 64, in 1993 only 48 percent of this group had the support of employer pension plans. Thus, for many men in this age group, retirement still means subsisting on a very low income (Gower 1995). So it is not surprising to see a trend to re-employment after retirement. In 1994, for example, 16 percent of men who had ever retired had re-entered employment; one-quarter cited financial reasons for doing so, while about 20 percent wanted to occupy their free time, and a similar percentage cited personal choice (Monette 1996). Hence, in 2000, 16 percent of 65- to 69-year-old men were still in the labour force (Sunter, 2001). These recent trends challenge the traditional three-stage model of the work life—education, employment, then retirement. Instead, researchers are now using a *life-course perspective* that views individuals' roles as more fluid, and examines the choices and constraints underlying transitions across roles.[21]

Despite the small trend towards re-employment among "retired" men, the fact remains that older men who lose their jobs have more difficulty finding work, since many employers are reluctant to hire and retrain older workers. In addition, older men are more likely to be employed in industries where employment is declining (manufacturing and the resource-based industries, for example). Hence, the chances of being rehired by a former employer are lower than average (Tindale 1991). The small trend towards increased employment among men over age 65 actually reflects an increase in part-time work and self-employment (Walsh, 1999). But, as a rule, most unemployed older men decide to retire. Some are offered early retirement packages by employers attempting to downsize their workforce, while others decide that "retired" would be an easier label to live with than "unemployed." Thus, while a shortage of jobs may have pushed some men over the age of 55 out of the labour force, an adequate pension encouraged others to retire voluntarily.

A similar shift toward earlier retirement has not been observed for older women. In fact, LFP rates have been increasing among older cohorts of Canadian women. The LFP rate for women age 54 to 59 was 53 percent in 2000, up from 45 percent in 1989. For women age 60 to 64, the LFP rate increased from 23 to 27 percent over this decade (Sunter, 2001: 31). Rather than seeking to leave the labour force early, more older women appear to be re-entering (Marshall 2000), typically for financial reasons. Women earn less on average than men and receive fewer benefits, including government and employer pensions (see Chapter 4). Hence, compared with men of the same age, fewer older employed women have the financial resources needed to retire. Furthermore, the growing trend toward wives becoming the sole wage earner in families is most evident in families with husbands aged 55 or older (Crompton and Geran 1995: 28). In some of these families, women may have continued to work after their husbands became unemployed or retired.

Unpaid Work

As stated in the introduction to this book, our emphasis is on paid work since this is the primary type of work for the majority of adults in an industrialized capitalist economy. Nevertheless, if we define work as activity that provides a product or service used or valued by others in society, it is obvious that paid work constitutes only a portion of all work done in Canada. The largest and most serious omission is *unpaid household and child/elder care work*. The 1996 national census, the first to include questions about unpaid work, revealed that nine out of ten Canadians had done at least some unpaid household or caring work in the week prior to the census. Virtually all of these individuals had completed some housework or home maintenance, while 38 percent reported unpaid child care and 17 percent reported unpaid elder care. As we might expect, women, particularly mothers of young children, do much more unpaid work. But, as we have noted earlier in this chapter, many of these young mothers are also members of the paid labour force. Labour market analysts have estimated that, if given a dollar value, unpaid work would add $235 billion, or another one-third, to Canada's gross domestic product (GDP).[22]

Also omitted from labour force participation rates and employment statistics are those Aboriginal Canadians (and a few non-Aboriginals), typically resident in the northern parts of the country, who continue to participate in traditional hunting and gathering work. Such groups form only a very small part of Canada's population. Nevertheless, their *subsistence work* clearly provides useful and valued goods and services for their families and communities.

In addition, *volunteer work* is overlooked if we rely only on official labour force statistics. A national survey of Canadian adults revealed that, in 1987, about 5.3 million unpaid workers (27% of the population age 15 and older) contributed their time and energy to volunteer activities in the previous 12 months. In 2000, a replication of this survey revealed the same percentage (27%) of Canadians volunteering. Most of these jobs involved only a few hours per week. The 6.5 million volunteers reported an average of 162 hours of unpaid work in the previous year, down from 191 hours per year in 1987. Nevertheless, more than 1 billion hours of volunteer work were reported by the 2000 survey participants. Based on the earlier (1987) survey, analysts estimated that, if paid at minimum-wage levels, this volunteer work would have cost more than $75 million each week.[23]

Volunteer workers are found in a wide variety of clubs and associations, as well as in religious and political organizations. However, a very large number work in the publicly funded service industries, assisting in the provision of health, social, recreational, educational, environmental, and other types of services. In recent years, as government departments at all levels have attempted to cut costs and reduce payrolls, volunteers have also been replacing paid employees. This trend will no doubt continue, so volunteer work is likely to become an even larger part of the total amount of unpaid work performed by Canadians.

Official labour force participation statistics also omit some Canadians working in the *hidden economy,* or, as it is sometimes called, the underground or irregular economy. Such work includes illegal activities like selling drugs, prostitution, and gambling, as well as legal work done for cash or in exchange for other services. Mechanics working out of their backyard garages and not reporting this income and farmers assisting their neighbours in return for similar help at another time would be examples of this non-criminal group, some of whom would be represented in labour force surveys through their regular jobs. Others, if surveyed, might report themselves unemployed or out of the labour force in order to avoid detection by tax authorities.

There is little research on work in the hidden economy, since there is no direct way of systematically studying behaviour that people do not wish to have publicly documented. But the research available suggests that participation in the hidden economy is relatively common. During the mid-1980s, an assessment of concealed employment (legal but unreported work) in Western industrialized countries concluded that up to 1 in 5 adults might be involved at some point in a given year, although, for most of these individuals, this would reflect relatively few hours of work. Canadian researchers estimate that about 15 percent or more of total economic activity in Canada was not being reported to tax authorities in the mid-1990s.[24] The introduction of the Goods and Services Tax (GST) several years earlier may have prompted more independent self-employed workers to begin asking for "under-the-table" payment.

In short, official statistics clearly underestimate the number of working Canadians and the value of their work. Various types of informal work (household and child/elder care work, volunteer work, work in subsistence economies, and work in the hidden economy) are overlooked. This reflects how society values individuals' unpaid activities. Indeed, there is growing discomfort with conventional approaches to measuring economic activity. As articulated by three American economists, "the GDP [the nation's economic output] ignores the contribution of the social realm—that is, the economic role of households and communities. This is where much of the nation's most important work gets done, from caring for children and older people to volunteer work in its many forms. It is the nation's social glue."[25] Furthermore, it appears that informal work may be increasing. However, we could not even begin to provide an adequate overview of both paid employment and the various types of informal work in one volume. Consequently, with some exceptions, the rest of this book focuses on paid employment (including self-employment in the formal economy), which continues to represent the largest share of work performed by Canadians.

INDUSTRIAL CHANGES: THE EMERGENCE OF THE SERVICE ECONOMY

The work done by labour force participants can be categorized in several ways. We begin below by discussing industrial shifts and then examine occupational changes in the following section. *Industry* classifications direct our attention to the major type of economic activity occurring within the workplace. In the broadest sense, we can distinguish the *primary sector*, including agriculture, mining, forestry, and other resource extraction industries, from the *secondary sector* (manufacturing and construction), where goods are produced from the raw materials supplied by the primary sector, and the *tertiary sector*, where services rather than products are provided. A *service*, simply defined, is the exchange of a commodity that has no tangible form. These general industrial categories can be further subdivided into more specific industries. The service sector, for example, includes among others the finance, education, retail trade, government (public administration), and health service industries.

Service-Sector Growth

In 1891, the primary industries accounted for 49 percent of the Canadian labour force, the secondary sector for 20 percent, and the service sector for the remaining 31 percent (Matthews 1985: 36). In the following half-century, the primary sector lost its dominance, while the manufacturing industries expanded. At the same time, the service industries were also increasing in size. By 1951 almost half (47 percent) of all employed Canadians were working in the service industries, while the secondary sector accounted for almost one-third (31 percent) of employment (Picot 1987: 11). The relative size of the primary and secondary sectors have been declining steadily ever since. By 2000, 74 percent of employed Canadians held service sector jobs, 21 percent were working in the secondary sector, and only 5 percent were employed in the primary industries (Bowlby 2000). Agriculture, a dominant industry a century earlier, now accounts for less than 3 percent of all employment in Canada. In contrast, the portion of workers in the service sector has more than doubled over this time. This sector has also come to represent a much larger share of the total value of goods and services produced in the Canadian economy.[26]

These statistics clearly demonstrate that we are now living in a service-dominated economy. A similar transition from a pre-industrial to an industrial to a service economy occurred in other capitalist countries such as the United States, the United Kingdom, Japan, Sweden, and Germany. But manufacturing never played as great a role in Canada's development as in that of other countries. Consequently, while three out of four workers are now employed in the service sector in both Canada and the United States, the service industries still account for a somewhat smaller share of the employed labour force in these other countries (Akyeampong and Winters 1993: 36).

The rise of the service sector can be attributed to a combination of factors. Productivity gains due to new technologies and organizational forms in manufacturing, but also in the resource industries, have meant that fewer people could produce much more. In primary industries, the growing size and declining number of farms in Canada is perhaps the best indicator. Toward the end of the nineteenth and into the early twentieth century, factory mechanization greatly enhanced workers' productivity, despite a reduction in hours worked. In the last few decades, automated production systems (robotics and information technology) have once again accelerated this trend. Thus, the expansion of production in the primary and secondary sectors has been accompanied by a relative decline in the need for employees.

Industrial expansion and productivity gains over the years have also led to higher incomes and increased amounts of leisure time. These factors, in turn, have fueled the demand for a wider range of services, particularly in the last few decades when the recreation, accommodation, and food service industries have been growing rapidly. In addition, the expansion of the role of the state as a provider of educational and social services and a funder of health services contributed significantly to the growth of the service sector. In the 1990s, governments' vigorous pursuit of deficit reduction resulted in reduced program funding, organizational downsizing, and the privatization of work previously done by civil servants, thus slowing the trend towards public sector employment. However, both provincial and federal government departments have increased their hiring in the early years of the 21st century, in part because of the large number of baby boomer employees approaching retirement.

Employment Diversity within the Service Sector

The wide range of specific industries within the broad service sector can be usefully categorized into six broad groups: distributive services (transportation, communication, and wholesale trade); business services (finance, insurance, real estate, and other services to business); the education, health, and welfare sector; public administration; retail trade; and other consumer services. Distributive services differ from the others by being the final link in the process whereby raw materials are extracted, transformed, and then delivered to the ultimate consumer. Business services also provide support to the primary and secondary industries (the goods-producing sector), but in a less tangible way. Like public administration, the education, health, and welfare sector contains primarily noncommercial services provided by the state, while retail trade and other consumer services (for example, food and beverage, accommodation, and the tourism industries) are commercial services aimed directly at consumers.[27]

It is useful to further combine the six service categories into an *upper tier* (distributive, business, education, health and welfare, and public administration) and a *lower tier* (retail trade and other consumer services) since, as we will demonstrate later, many more good jobs are located in the former. Table 2.1 uses these concepts to profile the industrial distribution of Canada's employed (other tables in this chapter also include only employed members of the labour force). In 2000, just over one-quarter (26%) of employed Canadians were working in the goods-producing sector while, as already noted, 74 percent were employed in the service industries. Just over half (51%) of the employed were located in the upper-tier services, while not quite one-quarter (23%) had jobs in the lower-tier service industries.[28]

We have already observed that similar proportions of workers are employed in the service and goods-producing sectors in Canada and the United States. A more detailed comparison reveals only one major difference – the retail trade sector is considerably larger in the USA (about 17% of total employment, compared to 12% in Canada). However, we find a very different industrial distribution in Mexico, the other major North American economy. Here, 25 percent of the employed labour force is located in the primary industries, compared to only 5 percent in Canada and 3 percent in the United States. Similar proportions are employed in manufacturing in all three countries, but the business services sector is only about one-third as large (in relative terms) in Mexico as in Canada and the United States.[29]

Gender and Age Differences in Service-Sector Employment

Table 2.1 also reveals distinct gender differences in industrial locations. In 2000, almost 37 percent of employed Canadian men were working in the goods-producing sector, compared with only 13 percent of employed women. Women were more likely to be employed in the lower-tier services (27.5% compared with 19.1% of men). Within the upper-tier services, women were much more heavily concentrated in the education, health, and welfare industries than were men. Men were considerably more likely to be employed in the distributive services (transportation, communication, and wholesale trade).

Age plays an important part in further stratifying the employed labour force across these industrial categories. Younger workers (age 15 to 24) are much less likely to be employed in the upper-tier services. Instead, many

TABLE 2.1 *Industry by Gender, Employed Population, Canada, 2000*

	Total	Female	Male
Industry	%	%	%
Goods-producing sector (total)	26.0	13.2	36.7
Agriculture	2.5	1.6	3.2
Natural-resource-based	2.7	1.0	4.1
Manufacturing	15.3	9.3	20.4
Construction	5.5	1.3	9.0
Service sector (total)	74.0	86.8	63.3
Upper-tier services (total)	51.0	59.3	44.2
Distributive services	8.9	5.1	12.3
Business services	15.8	17.2	14.7
Education/health/welfare	21.2	31.8	12.2
Public administration	5.1	5.2	5.0
Lower-tier services (total)	23.0	27.5	19.1
Retail trade	11.9	13.9	10.1
Other consumer services	11.1	13.6	9.0
Total percent	100.0	100.0	100.0
Total (in 000s)	14,910	6,861	8,049

Source: Statistics Canada 2001. *Labour Force Historical Review 2000.* Cat. no. 71F004XCB.

young workers, particularly women, hold jobs in the lower-tier retail trade and consumer service industries.[30] Many of these young workers are students in part-time jobs. Thus, the expansion of the lower-tier service industries (for instance, shopping malls, fast food restaurants, and tourism) since the 1970s has relied heavily on the recruitment of student workers, creating a distinct student worker segment of the labour force. However, older female workers are also much more likely than older male workers to be employed in the retail trade and other consumer service industries.

OCCUPATIONAL CHANGES

While the industrial classification system is based on what is being produced, we also can categorize workers according to their *occupation*. Occupational distinctions are determined by the kind of work that an individual typically performs, the actual tasks that she or he completes. Thus, secretaries, managers, office cleaners, and accountants (occupational titles) work in mining companies, automobile factories, and government bureaucracies—that is, in the primary, secondary, and tertiary (or service) sectors of the economy. Other occupations are typically found only within specific industrial sectors. For example, teachers, nurses, and retail clerks are occupational groups largely unique to the service sector. So the two classification systems parallel each other to an extent but also overlap considerably.

For many years, Statistics Canada used the Standard Occupational Classification (SOC) system to categorize occupations. But a basic limitation of the SOC system was that it did not adequately capture the skill content of jobs. From our earlier discussions of education and training, it is clear that developing human resources—the skills of the workforce—has become a public policy priority. Consequently, in the 1990s, Human Resources Development Canada (HRDC) teamed up with Statistics Canada to develop a new occupational typology, the National Occupational Classification (NOC).

Table 2.2 displays the structure of the NOC with selected examples of occupations in each category. Essentially, the NOC identifies two dimensions of *skill*, providing information on skill level and generic skill type for each of the 25,000 detailed occupations in the Canadian labour market. Four basic skill levels are used, plus a separate level for management occupations, and each is directly related to the education and training required. For example, occupations in skill level A are mainly the professions and require a university education; occupations in skill level D require no formal education and only short demonstrations or some on-the-job training. The nine skill types indicate the kinds of tasks performed. Note that the highest skill groups are concentrated mainly in what we earlier referred to as "upper-tier services," while skill-level-D occupations are in lower-tier services and goods production.

Blue-Collar and White-Collar Occupations

Many but not all of the people employed in the primary and secondary industries would be classified as blue-collar workers, while most of those working in the service industries would be identified as white-collar workers. The term *blue-collar* has traditionally been used to distinguish occupations (for example, farmer, miner, truck driver, construction worker, and factory worker) with potentially dirty working conditions from *white-collar* (including clerical, sales, managerial, and professional) occupations. The explanation, of course, is that for the former jobs wearing a white collar would be inappropriate, since

TABLE 2.2 Classifying Occupations by Skill Type and Level—The National Occupational Classification*

Skill Level	Occupational Skill Type								
	Business, finance & administration	Natural & applied science	Health	Social sciences, education, government services, religion	Arts, culture, recreation, sport	Sales and service	Trades, transportation & equipment operators	Primary industries	Occupations unique to processing, manufacturing & utilities
Management	Senior managers, legislators, managers								
Skill Level A	auditors, accountants, human resource professionals, investment professionals	engineers, architects, systems analysts, computer programmers, physical and life science professionals	physicians, dentists, chiropractors, pharmacists, registered nurses, therapy professionals	judges, lawyers, professors, teachers, psychologists, social workers, clergy, probation officers, policy and program officers, researchers and consultants	librarians, writers, translators, public relations professionals, creative and performing artists				

(continued)

TABLE 2.2 Classifying Occupations by Skill Type and Level—The National Occupational Classification* (cont.)

Skill Level B	clerical supervisors, administrative occupations, secretaries	technical occupations in physical and life sciences, engineering, architecture, electronics	medical and health care technologists and technicians	paralegals; social service, religious and education occupations not classified above	technical occupations in libraries, museums, galleries; photographers, graphic artists, technical occupations in motion pictures, broadcasting, performing arts; announcers, athletes and coaches	sales and service supervisors, technical sales specialists, insurance and real estate sales, chefs and butchers, police officers and firefighters	supervisors, machinists, electrical trades and telecommunications occupations, plumbers, carpenters, other construction trades, mechanics, train crew, tailors, jewellers	supervisors, underground miners, logging machine operators, fishing vessel operators, fishermen/women; contractors, operators and supervisors in agriculture	supervisors, central control and processing operators

(continued)

TABLE 2.2 Classifying Occupations by Skill Type and Level—The National Occupational Classification* (cont.)

Skill Level C	clerical occupations, office equipment operators, library clerks, mail and message distribution occupations	assisting occupations in health services	retail sales clerks, travel and accommodation occupations, tour and recreational guides, food and beverage service occupations, childcare and home support workers	motor vehicle and transit drivers, heavy equipment operators, installers, repairers and servicers	logging and forestry workers, mine service workers, oil and gas drilling operators, agriculture workers, fishing and trapping workers	machine operators and related workers, assemblers
Skill Level D			cashiers, food counter attendants, security guards, cleaners	trades helpers, labourers	labourers	labourers

* This table gives examples of occupational groups (based on 3-digit Standard Occupation Classification). For a complete list see *Job Futures 1996. Volume One: Occupational Outlooks*, (Ottawa: Minister of Supply and Services Canada, 1996), xv - xviii, 455 - 57.

Source: Employment and Immigration Canada, *National Occupational Classification*. Ottawa: Canada Communications Group, 1993. Reproduced with the permission of the Minister of Public Works and Government Services Canada, 1997.

it would not stay clean. Thus, in the past, white-collar occupations tended to be viewed as having higher status. However, with the expansion of the service industries, including the lower-tier services where poorly paid, part-time jobs are quite common, the white-collar occupational category has come to include the majority of the labour force, including many people in less desirable jobs.

As primary sector industries became less important over the course of this century, we saw a huge decline in the size of some occupational groups and a proportional increase in others. A few examples can make the point. The 1911 census reported that 34 percent of the labour force was in agricultural occupations, compared with only 4 percent in clerical occupations, and a similarly small proportion in professional occupations. By 1951, agricultural occupations had declined to 16 percent of the labour force, compared with 11 percent in clerical occupations and 7 percent in professions (O'Neill 1991: 10). The 1996 census revealed less than 5 percent of the labour force in occupations unique to primary industry, 9 percent in management, 19 percent in business, finance, and administrative occupations, and almost 20 percent in natural science, social science, government, and other white collar occupations.[31] Thus, over the course of the past century, white-collar jobs have come to dominate the Canadian labour market.

Gender and Occupational Location

Many of the new white-collar positions have been filled by women, while the remaining blue-collar jobs in the primary and secondary sectors are still typically held by men. In fact, given the heavy concentration of women in clerical, sales, and service occupations, the term *pink collar* has been used to describe these occupational categories.

Using a revised version of the SOC to obtain comparability with earlier data, Table 2.3 presents a gender breakdown of Canadian occupational distributions for 1987 and 2000.[32] Note that the total employed labour force increased from 12.3 million to 14.9 million workers over this time. Hence, even though some occupational categories may have declined a bit in relative (percentage) size, they might still have increased in absolute size between 1987 and 2000. Considering first the total distributions (female and male combined), it is apparent that over the past 13 years, managerial and professional administrative occupations have become somewhat more common (an increase from 11 percent to 13 percent of all employed). At the same time, the other administrative and clerical category (office jobs without major planning and supervisory roles) decreased marginally, from 17 to 16 percent of all employed. The remaining white-collar occupational categories (both professional, and sales and service) also changed only to a limited degree, if at all. However, in the blue-collar occupations, we see relative declines in trades and transportation occupations (from 16% to 14% of all employment), in primary occupations (from 5% to 4%) and in manufacturing occupations (from 9% to 8%). The decline in blue-collar occupations is a result of the massive restructuring in the goods-producing sector outlined in Chapter 1, while the smaller decline in clerical occupations reflects a complex set of related changes, from advancing information technology to downsizing to the upgrading of some of these jobs to administrative categories.

Chapter 4 focuses on the unequal employment experiences and rewards of women and men, so we will comment only briefly at this point on the gender differences in Table 2.3. The 2000 data show a more even distribution of men than women across the occupational structure. Women are more heavily concentrated than men in "pink collar" occupations, with 24 percent employed in administrative and clerical occupations, 10 percent in retail trade, and 23 percent in other sales and service occupations, totalling 57 percent. In contrast, only 25 percent of men are employed in these three occupational groups. Women are also relatively overrepresented in health, social science, education and government occupations.

However, it is important to note the changes over time in the gender composition of the occupational structure. In 1987, only 8 percent of employed women were in managerial or professional administrative occupations. Thirteen years later, 10 percent of women were working in these higher-status white-collar occupations. Table 2.3 also shows a small increase over time in the proportion of women in other professional positions, and a corresponding decline in the percentage of women in clerical jobs.

To conclude, there have been some shifts in the gender composition of the occupational structure, although female–male differences have not disappeared. But we must remember that these are broad occupational categories. Health occupations, for example, include doctors, nurses, orderlies, nursing assistants, and other support workers. Women are still more likely to be in the

TABLE 2.3 *Occupation by Gender, Employed Population, Canada, 1987 and 2000*

	1987			2000		
	Female	*Male*	*Total*	*Female*	*Male*	*Total*
	%	*%*	*%*	*%*	*%*	*%*
Management occupations	6	12	9	7	11	10
Business, finance & administration						
Professionals	2	2	2	3	3	3
Administrative & clerical	30	8	17	24	6	16
Natural & applied science	2	7	5	3	10	6
Health occupations	9	2	5	9	2	5
Social science, education & government	7	5	6	9	5	7
Culture, recreation & sport	3	2	2	3	2	3
Sales & services						
Retail sales	10	3	6	10	3	6
Other sales & services	21	16	18	23	16	18
Trades, transportation & related	2	27	16	2	25	14
Occupations unique to primary industries	2	7	5	2	6	4
Occupations unique to manufacturing	6	10	9	5	11	8
Total percent	100	100	100	100	100	100
Total (in 000s)	5,299	7,021	12,320	6,861	8,049	14,910

Source: Statistics Canada 2001. *Labour Force Historical Review 2000.* Cat. no. 71F004XCB.

lower-status occupations within these broad categories, and are still typically supervised by men (Clement and Myles 1994). Hence, it is necessary to look in more detail at the specific occupations within which women and men typically are employed, as we do in Chapter 4.

SELF-EMPLOYMENT TRENDS

As in other industrialized capitalist economies, self-employment has dropped sharply over the past century. In 1946, for example, 33 percent of employed Canadians were self-employed. By 1981 this figure had fallen to 10 percent (Riddell 1985: 9). This shift toward paid labour can be explained to a considerable extent by changes in the agricultural sector. Early in this century, about three-quarters of those employed in agriculture were owner–managers, and most of the rest were unpaid family workers. But over the past sixty years, the number of farms in Canada has suffered a huge decline, from a high of 733,000 in 1941 to only 277,000 in 1996. At the same time, the remaining farms have been getting larger, and the proportion of paid workers in agriculture has been slowly increasing. By 1991, the 448,000 Canadians employed in agriculture consisted of paid workers (32 percent), unpaid family workers (9 percent), and self-employed individuals (59 percent). Thus, while wage labour has become more common in agriculture, a major decline in the number of family farms has also meant fewer self-employed individuals and unpaid family workers.[33]

Over the decades, self-employment in the secondary and service sectors also declined slowly. However, a reversal of this trend appeared about 20 years ago. Thus, in 2000, 16.2 percent of all employed Canadians (including those in agriculture) were self-employed, up from 10 percent in 1981 (but down slightly from 17 percent in 1999).[34] A similar increase was observed in most other industrialized capitalist economies, including the United States, during the 1980s, but the trend has continued longer in Canada. Thus, while self-employment in Canada continued to rise in the 1990s, the self-employment rate in the U.S. remained around 10 percent. In Canada, a decade ago the number of *self-employed employers* (who hire others to work for them) and *own-account self-employed* (without employees) were roughly similar, but the latter group has now become larger. More than half of the growth in Canadian self-employment in the 1980s involved employers setting up new businesses. In contrast, in the 1990s, 90 percent of the growth involved the own-account self-employed. But while slightly more than one in ten Canadian workers are now own-account self-employed, this figure is still very low compared to many less industrialized countries. For example, in 1995, 26 percent of the employed in Mexico were in this category.[35]

Self-employment increases with age. In 1997, for example, less than 10 percent of employed Canadians under 25 years of age were self-employed, compared to about 20 percent of those aged 35 to 54 and 30 percent of 55-to-64-year-olds (Manser and Picot 1999: 40). And self-employment is still more prevalent among men than among women. Thus, in 2000, 12.4 percent of employed women were self-employed, along with 19.5 percent of employed men. But the female self-employment rate has been rising steadily since the 1980s, and the rate of increase has been higher for women than for men. By 1997, women made up almost 40 percent of all own-account self-employed in Canada, and almost one-quarter of all employers (Hughes 1999: 14). Some of the women who have moved into self-employment over the past few decades may have done so to obtain the flexibility needed to deal with the "double day," that is, to balance paid employment and unpaid work responsibilities (Arai 2000).

The recessions in Canada at the beginning of the 1980s and the 1990s may have contributed indirectly to the rise of self-employment, particularly own-account self-employment. However, the direct relationship between economic downturns and growth in self-employment is weak at best (Arai 1997; Manser and Picot 1999: 43). Thus, while many employers in both the private and public sectors reduced the size of their labour force during these recessions, leading to higher rates of unemployment, it was not necessarily those who lost their jobs who then set up their own businesses. The majority of the self-employed typically come directly from the ranks of wage-earners. Furthermore, managerial, professional, and technical workers are more likely to become self-employed than are clerical and manual workers (the groups most affected by unemployment). The self-employed are more highly educated than the rest of the labour force, suggesting that at least some of the growth in self-employment may have been a response by more advantaged workers to perceived job insecurity.

The self-employed are dispersed across a wide range of industries and occupations, with considerable variation in income and other rewards. For example, in 1997, 16 percent of Canadians working in professional and technical occupations were self-employed, along with 31 percent of those working in sales occupations, and 60 percent of those working in primary occupations. Well over half of those employed in agriculture were self-employed, as were 37% of Canadians working in construction and almost 20 percent of those employed in the retail trade industry (Manser and Picot 1999: 40). Given this wide dispersal of the self-employed across occupations, and throughout the goods-producing and upper- and lower-tier services, it is not surprising that the income distribution of Canada's self-employed is bimodal. In 1996, almost half of the self-employed earned less than $20,000, compared to only 26% of paid workers. At the same time, 4 percent of the self-employed were among Canada's highest earners, reporting incomes in excess of $100,000, compared to only 1% of paid workers (Crompton and Vickers 2000: 13).

THE CANADIAN LABOUR MARKET: REGIONAL VARIATIONS

So far, we have treated Canada as a single economic entity, putting aside important regional differences. Anyone who has driven across Canada will have a strong sense of its regional diversity. The fishing boats and lumber mills of the West Coast are left behind as one begins to head east towards the Prairies, replaced by oil wells and grain elevators. The flat landscape disappears a few hours after leaving Winnipeg, and one is faced by the rocks, forests, and water of the Canadian Shield. The smokestacks of Sudbury and other mining communities are reminders of the natural resource base of that region, but they eventually give way to the old grey barns of Ontario, symbols of an agricultural economy older than the one observed several days earlier. But this is unlikely to be the only memory of the trip through Ontario and into Quebec. The huge Highway 401 pushing its way past miles of warehouses and suburban factories will also leave a strong impression as it takes one through the industrial heartland of the country. Then, repeating the pattern observed in the West (but in reverse, without the mountains, and on a smaller scale), the farming economies of Quebec and the Atlantic provinces begin to merge with a forest-based economy. Eventually, one returns to a region where fisheries are once again important. In short, regional diversity means economic diversity.

This description obviously overgeneralizes. There are high technology firms in the Fraser Valley, large factories in Calgary, and oil wells off the East Coast. And in the northern parts of Canada, energy development and mining compete uneasily with traditional Aboriginal hunting, fishing, and trapping. Still, it is essential to take into account the regional distribution of industries when considering work opportunities available to Canadians. Some regions are much more economically advantaged than others, as we point out below in our discussion of unemployment trends. Labour force participation rates also vary significantly across provinces. For example, in 2000, Alberta's labour force participation rate of 72 percent was much higher than the 56 percent rate in Newfoundland.

A brief comparison of industrial patterns of employment in 2000 highlights these regional variations (Table 2.4). For example, 9.2 percent of the employed labour force in Manitoba and Saskatchewan and 4.4 percent in Alberta had jobs in agriculture, compared with less than 2 percent in the other regions. Larger-than-average concentrations of workers in the resource-

TABLE 2.4 *Industry by Region, Employed Population, Canada, 2000*

Industry	Total %	Atlantic Provinces %	Quebec %	Ontario %	Manitoba/ Saskatchewan %	Alberta %	British Columbia %
Goods-producing sector							
Agriculture	2.5	1.8	1.8	1.7	9.2	4.4	1.5
Natural resource-based	2.7	5.4	2.0	1.4	3.2	6.0	3.4
Manufacturing	15.3	10.5	18.3	18.7	9.6	8.8	10.5
Construction	5.5	5.8	4.1	5.5	5.1	8.1	5.8
Service sector							
Upper-tier services							
Distributive services	8.9	8.8	8.8	8.3	9.9	10.2	9.3
Business services	15.8	11.7	14.4	18.0	11.8	15.2	16.8
Education/health/welfare	21.2	23.6	21.6	20.3	22.7	19.6	22.4
Public administration	5.1	6.8	6.0	4.7	5.8	3.9	4.7
Lower-tier services							
Retail trade	11.9	13.9	12.2	11.3	11.4	11.8	12.1
Other consumer services	11.1	11.7	10.8	10.1	11.3	12.0	13.5
Total percent	100.0	100.0	100.0	100.0	100.0	100.0	100.0
Total (in 000s)	14,910	1,023	3,438	5,877	1,039	1,588	1,949

Source: Statistics Canada 2001. *Labour Force Historical Review 2000.* Cat. no. 71F004XCB.

based industries reflect the presence of the fishing industry on the East Coast and in British Columbia, forest-based industries in the Atlantic provinces, Alberta, and British Columbia, and the oil and gas industry in Alberta. Meanwhile, 18 to 19 percent of workers in Quebec and Ontario had jobs in manufacturing, compared with only 10 percent or fewer in the other regions. It is also interesting to note that Alberta and Ontario, the two provinces taking the lead in scaling down government over the past decade, have the lowest employment in publicly-funded industries (education/health/welfare and public administration).

Canada is not unique in having some regions in which primary industries are most important, and others in which manufacturing is concentrated. But its economic history is marked by a reliance on exports of raw materials such as furs, fish, timber, wheat, coal, natural gas, and oil. This was Canada's colonial role in the British Empire, but even as an independent industrialized nation it has continued to provide natural resources to the global economy.

The *staple theory of economic growth*, developed by Harold Innis and others, documents the economic, political, and social consequences of this dependence on the export of unprocessed staple products. The theory argues that overcommitment to extraction and export of a single or few resources makes a nation or region vulnerable in world markets. The relative absence of manufacturing industries means that large portions of the workforce remain employed in lower-skill primary and tertiary sector jobs. In addition, a weak manufacturing sector does not encourage significant quantities of research and development and does not generate spin-off industrial activity. These factors create a "staples trap" in which there are few economic development alternatives (Watkins 1991).

Indicative of Canada's natural resource base is the number of single-industry communities scattered across the country. These towns and cities, often situated in relatively isolated areas, exist only because the extraction of some natural resource requires a resident labour force. While some of these communities have attempted to diversify their economies, few have been successful. Instead, their economic activity remains dominated by the primary resource extraction industry (oil in Fort McMurray, Alberta, for example, or nickel in Sudbury, Ontario). If the market for the staple declines or the resource is depleted, the economic base of the community will crumble. Mine shutdowns in Uranium City, Saskatchewan, Schefferville, Quebec, and Elliot Lake, Ontario in the 1980s are examples, as are the population declines in the 1990s in Labrador City, Newfoundland and Kirkland Lake, Ontario.[36] By contrast, a stronger world market for oil has made it economically feasible to invest in oil-sands production, creating another economic boom in Fort McMurray and other northern Alberta communities.

Over the decades, the prospects of better jobs and higher incomes have led many thousands of people to "go down the road" to the industrial cities of central Canada. But many have also been attracted to the resource towns of the hinterland for the same reasons. Such communities have historically provided work for unemployed or underemployed migrants from other regions of the country. However, the life cycle of resource towns, as they move through fairly predictable stages of development, is one in which work opportunities for residents and migrants do not remain constant. Moreover, since mining, forestry, the railway, and other blue-collar industries traditionally have been male occupational preserves, women have had trouble finding satisfactory employment. Many single-industry towns are located in areas with sizable Aboriginal populations, yet these groups seldom benefit from the employment opportunities generated by the towns.

UNEMPLOYMENT TRENDS

Counting the Unemployed

Labour Force Survey estimates indicate that, during 2000, there were 15,999,000 Canadians aged 15 and older in the labour force, with 14,910,000 of them employed (including self-employed). The unemployed, numbering 1,089,000, made up the difference. To put this in perspective, the number of unemployed people in 2000 was larger than the total population (children included) of Nova Scotia and Prince Edward Island combined. The official *unemployment rate* is calculated by dividing the number of individuals out of work and actively looking for work (the unemployed) by the total number of labour force participants (including the unemployed). Thus, in 2000, the national unemployment rate was 6.8 percent, down from 7.6 percent a year earlier and a considerably higher jobless rate (between 9 and 11 percent) in the earlier part of the 1990s.

Such calculations reveal the percentage of labour force participants who are unemployed at a particular point in time (an annual average provides the average of twelve monthly estimates). But over the course of a year, many people find jobs while many others quit or lose them. Consequently, if we were to count the number of people who had been unemployed at some point during a year, this alternative unemployment rate would be higher. For example, in 1997 when the annual average unemployment rate was high (9.1%), over the course of the entire year, 17 percent of individuals and 28 percent of all families had experienced unemployment (Sussman 2000: 11).

The official definition of unemployment, whether we calculate rates for a single point in time or over the full year, identifies a state of being without paid work (including self-employment). It excludes students who do not wish to work while studying, individuals performing unpaid work in the home, the disabled who are not seeking work, and the retired, all of whom are considered to be outside the labour force. It also excludes potential labour force participants who, believing there is no work available in their community or region, have not actively sought employment in the previous four weeks. In the wake of the 1981–82 recession, the Labour Force Survey estimated the size of the *discouraged workers* group at 197,000 (March 1983). The number of discouraged workers declined as the economy recovered, and did not rise as high again during the recession that began in 1990, peaking at 99,000 in March 1992. This lower number of discouraged workers reflects other basic labour market changes already discussed: declining youth labour force participation, rising educational enrollments, and earlier retirement. In other words, rather than waiting for new jobs to materialize, a larger proportion of jobless Canadians may have stayed in or returned to school, or retired early, during the 1992-93 recession. In 2000, when the unemployment rate was relatively low (6.8%), the Labour Force Survey identified only 48,000 discouraged workers.[37]

Canadian Unemployment Rates over Time

Canadian unemployment rates reached their highest point this century (around 20 percent) during the Depression of the 1930s (Brown 1987). But these hard times were quickly replaced by labour shortages during World War II and in the immediate postwar years. The average national unemployment rate was only 2 percent during the 1940s. Since the end of World War II, unemployment has slowly climbed higher, responding to successive business cycles of recession and expansion. Unemployment rates peaked at over 11 percent during recessions at the beginning of the 1980s (11.9 percent in 1983) and the 1990s (11.4 percent in 1993).

By 2000, the national jobless rate had again declined to below 7 percent, although there was little indication that the rate would fall any further. Still, over the past half-century, we see a long-term upward trend (Figure 2.5). The ten-year average unemployment rate was 4 percent in the 1950s, 5 percent in the 1960s, 6.7 percent in the 1970s, and 9.5 percent in the 1980s.[38] The ten-year average for the 1990s remained at the same level. Thus, some analysts argue that without a more proactive job creation strategy on the part of government, and more private, sector investments that generate demand for human capital, Canada's unemployment is unlikely to drop to the levels of the economically buoyant 1960s.

As unemployment rates have slowly climbed over the past decades, the duration of unemployment has also increased. In 1976, the average spell of

FIGURE 2.5 *Unemployment Rate by Age and Gender, Canada, 1946—2000*

Percent unemployed

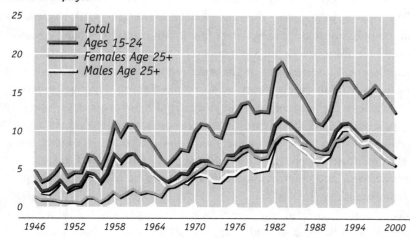

Source: Rachel Bernier, "The Labour Force Survey: 50 years old!". *The Labour Force,* November 1995. Statistics Canada, Cat. no. 71-001; Statistics Canada 2001. *Labour Force Historical Review.* Cat. no. 71F004XCB.

unemployment was only about 14 weeks. This rose to 18 weeks by 1989, and then to 26 weeks in 1994. In 1998, as the rate of unemployment had started to decline, the average duration of unemployment was still over 20 weeks. More than one in five (22%) unemployed Canadians had unsuccessfully tried to find work for 6 months or longer, and 10 percent of the unemployed had been seeking work for a full year or longer (Sharpe 1999: 21). Older workers laid off during the recessions of the early 1980s and 1990s were most likely to experience prolonged periods of unemployment.

Regional Variations in Unemployment

National rates of unemployment conceal considerable variation across regions of the country. In 2000, Newfoundland's unemployment rate averaged 16.7 percent, compared with 10.0 percent in New Brunswick, 8.4 percent in Quebec, 5.7 percent in Ontario, and 5.0 percent in Alberta. The Atlantic provinces, particularly Newfoundland, have had higher-than-average rates of unemployment for decades, while the manufacturing provinces of Ontario and Quebec have typically had lower rates. Alberta, with its oil-based economy, has recorded particularly low unemployment rates when high international oil prices have fueled the provincial economy. But with this exception, the regions most dependent on a few natural resources have typically experienced the most severe unemployment.

Unemployment also tends to be concentrated within specific occupational groups and industrial sectors. Seasonal work like fishing, logging, and construction carries a high risk of unemployment, and helps account for some of the higher levels of unemployment in the natural-resource-dependent regions of the country. Manufacturing jobs are also prone to unemployment, since economic downturns often lead to layoffs and plant shutdowns. On the other hand, professional and technical occupations tend to be somewhat more protected from unemployment.

Aboriginal peoples continue to experience exceptionally high rates of unemployment. When combined with lower than average rates of labour force participation, it is clear that this group faces serious disadvantages in the labour market. For example, a 1998 census of Alberta's eight Métis settlements revealed unemployment rates of 43 percent among 15–24-year-old residents, 32 percent among those age 25 to 44, and 26 percent among 45–64-year-olds. At the time, the provincial unemployment rate was only 5.4 percent.[39] These levels of unemployment are probably low compared with Aboriginal Canadians living on reservations in northern Manitoba, Saskatchewan, and Alberta, as well as in the Territories. The isolated Native communities in these regions offer few employment opportunities. In addition, low levels of education, limited work experience other than in short-term, low-skill jobs, minimal access to information about jobs and employers, and discrimination in hiring have all contributed to high rates of Aboriginal unemployment both on and off reserves.

Gender and Unemployment

A comparison of female and male unemployment rates in the post-war years reveals some interesting shifts in relative position (see Figure 2.5). Looking at adult workers (25 years and older), during the 1950s and early 1960s, male unemployment rates were generally about twice as high as those for females. The two rates converged in the mid-1960s, and by the 1970s, female rates were typically about 2 percent higher than male rates. This trend continued until the recession of the early 1980s when, for a second time, the two rates came together. For the rest of that decade, female rates of joblessness were again higher than male rates, but the difference was always less than 1 percent. During the 1990–92 recession and its aftermath, men were slightly more likely to be unemployed, but several years later there was a third convergence. In 2000, for adult (25 years and older) labour force participants, the female and male unemployment rates were 5.7 and 5.6 percent, respectively.

We would need a much more detailed analysis than is possible here to explain these shifts in female and male unemployment rates. Nevertheless, a large part of the explanation would focus on women's locations in the labour market. Female labour force participation was much lower in the 1950s and 1960s, and women were employed in a limited number of traditionally female occupations. Unemployment then, as now, was considerably higher in the blue-collar occupations, in which few women were found. Since that time, women have been making their way into a broader range of service-sector jobs alongside men. But many women continue to be employed in lower-level, less secure positions. Thus, during the past few decades, women have been somewhat more vulnerable to unemployment. However, the recessions at the beginning of the 1980s and 1990s led to widespread layoffs in blue-collar industries (manufacturing, for example). Since men continue to be overrepresented in these industries, their unemployment rate rose rapidly and passed the female rate when the economy weakened.

Youth Unemployment

Young Canadians (age 15 to 24), particularly those with the least education (high-school dropouts, for example) have experienced high rates of unemployment for several decades (Lowe and Krahn 1999). Youth unemployment fluctuated between 9 and 14 percent in the 1970s (Figure 2.5). The 1981–82 recession pushed the rate to about 20 percent, but it had dropped to around 11 percent by 1989. The recession that began in 1990 reversed this decline; rates in the 18-percent range were reached in 1993 and 1994. By 2000, as the economy strengthened and the total unemployment rate dropped to 6.8 percent, the youth unemployment rate also declined, to 12.6 percent. Thus, even though youth unemployment is affected by the same economic forces that determine the risk of joblessness for adults, young workers have fared much worse for several decades – the youth unemployment rate has not been below 10 percent since 1975. And even though young people typically have shorter spells of unemployment, because more of their previous employment has been part-time and part-year, they are less eligible for Employment Insurance (Betcherman and Leckie 1997).

A closer look at Figure 2.5 suggests that the gap between the youth and adult unemployment rates was largest in the early 1980s. Why? The shifting age distribution of the population provides a partial explanation. Canada experienced an exceptionally large baby boom during the 1950s and 1960s. The last of the children born in that era of high birth rates were making their way into the labour force during the early 1980s, just as a severe recession was reducing employment opportunities. Subsequent cohorts of school leavers became smaller. By way of example, in 1982, youth (age 15 to 24) made up 24 percent of the total Canadian population, compared to only 14 percent in 2000. Thus, since the early 1980s, when youth unemployment rates peaked, smaller cohorts of youth have meant less competition for jobs typically held by young workers (Foot and Li 1986; Gunderson et al. 2000).

Throughout the past several decades, teenage (age 15 to 19) unemployment rates have been higher than jobless rates among young adults (age 20 to 24). Compared with teenagers, young adults are typically better educated and have more work experience. In 2000, for example, the unemployment rate for 15-to-19-year-olds was 16.3 percent, compared with 10.2 percent for 20- to 24-year-olds. While female and male adult (age 25 and older) unemployment rates have again converged (see Figure 2.5), we still see a gender difference in joblessness among youth. For teenagers, the female unemployment rate in 2000 was 15.1 percent, compared to 17.5 percent for males. Among young adults, the female unemployment rate (8.7%) was also lower than the male rate (11.5%). These differences reflect, in part, the higher proportion of young males who seek employment in blue-collar industries where unemployment rates remain higher than in service industries (where a larger proportion of young women look for work).

Causes of Unemployment

We have already hinted at some of the causes of rising unemployment over the past several decades. Obviously, there is a demographic factor to consider. The sizable increase in the birth rate in the years following World War II led to rapid growth in the labour force several decades later. In addition, the increased proportion of women entering the labour force generated greater demand for jobs. But people working for pay are also people with money to spend, and the growth in labour force participation itself led to substantial job creation. Thus, econometric analyses conclude that these demographic shifts have had very little impact on the overall increase in unemployment in the past two decades (Gera 1991: 3).

Another basic type of explanation focuses on the characteristics of the jobless themselves. Such arguments are typically supported by anecdotal evidence and little else. One version suggests that many of the unemployed could be working if only they would accept the less attractive jobs that are available. But in many communities, the number of jobless far exceeds the total number of available jobs (Marsh et al. 1990). Furthermore, many of the jobs that may be available (and perhaps are even hard to fill) are part-time positions in the lower-tier services with pay rates so low that it would be impossible to support oneself, let alone a family. For many of the unemployed, accepting such work would be economically irrational, since it would force them to try to survive on very little income and discontinue actively searching for a better job.

A different version of the "blame the unemployed" explanation argues that they have insufficient skills and so are unable to compete for the jobs available in the new knowledge-based economy. However, recent studies have concluded that there is little evidence of a "skills gap" in Canada that might explain high rates of unemployment (Osberg and Lin 2000; Gingras and Roy 2000). In fact, as we argued at the beginning of this chapter, there is at least as much evidence of widespread underemployment in Canada as there is evidence of a skills shortage (Krahn and Lowe 1999a; Livingstone 1999). Yet another version of this type of explanation of high unemployment is the presumed laziness of the unemployed, in combination with the generosity of the government (Swanson 2001). But it is hard to believe that more than a few Canadians would prefer the low level of government social assistance to a higher and more secure earned income. Furthermore, stricter eligibility requirements were introduced in 1996 when the old Unemployment Insurance program was replaced by the Employment Insurance program. Thus, by the late 1990s only 36 percent of unemployed individuals received EI support, down from 74 percent in 1989 (Jackson, Robinson, Baldwin and Wiggins 2000: 153). Research on Canadians' work values (reviewed in Chapter 8) shows that few would choose the economic hardship and the stigma of unemployment over a regular job. Thus, as Betcherman (2000) concludes, we cannot blame our long-term high rates of unemployment on Employment Insurance policies, labour laws, or tax policies.

Economists often distinguish between *cyclical unemployment*, which rises during recessions and then declines as the economy recovers, and *frictional unemployment*. The latter results from the ongoing movement of workers in and out of jobs as they seek to match their skills and interests with the jobs offered by employers. Some unemployment, therefore, is normal, even in the strongest economy, since a perfect match between jobs and workers is never possible. However, research suggests that periods of cyclical unemployment over the past few decades have had the permanent effect on the Canadian labour market of increasing the "natural rate of unemployment" to such a degree that it is now unlikely to go back down. Thus, economists recognize that Canada has developed a serious problem of *structural unemployment*. More deep-rooted and permanent than cyclical or frictional unemployment, this problem requires new approaches to economic policy.[40]

Some of the emerging industrial and employment trends discussed in the previous chapter have contributed to the high and persistent level of unemployment in Canada. With industrial restructuring, many corporations have shifted their activities to countries and regions where labour costs are lower, and where government legislation regarding labour relations, worker safety, and environmental protection is less developed. Automation and information technologies are replacing workers in some industries. In both the private and public sectors, many employers have responded to financial problems by downsizing, cutting full-time jobs, and relying increasingly on temporary workers (a trend discussed later in this chapter). In addition, parts of Canada's staple-based economy have been hit hard by recent global economic shifts. Some of our basic resource industries (wheat and lumber, for example) have lately encountered unstable world markets. Others, such as the East and West Coast fishing industries, are suffering because of declining resource stocks.

As noted in Chapter 1, the impact of government policies on unemployment trends is equally important and must also be scrutinized. High unemployment in previous decades has been linked to the federal government's pursuit of low inflation via high interest rates (Fortin 1996). With a market-oriented approach to economic development that included entry into a continental free trade agreement, the federal government may have also made it easier for large corporations to close Canadian factories and lay off workers.

International Comparisons

In 1998, Canada's unemployment rate of 8.3 percent seemed high, when compared to Norway (3.2%), Japan (4.1%), the Netherlands (4.2%), the United States (4.5%), and Sweden (6.5%). However, jobless rates were much higher in Germany (11.2%), Belgium (11.7%), France (11.8%), Italy (12.2%), and Spain (18.8%) (Betcherman 2000: S132).[41]

Given that these countries are struggling with economic problems similar to those of Canada, why do some have high unemployment while others have nearly full employment? In terms of labour market policies, Canada lies between the *laissez-faire*, or free-market approach, of the U.S. and the more interventionist European approach. In countries like Norway, Sweden, and Japan, employers, organized labour, and governments frequently work together toward a common goal of full employment. Labour market programs are typically proactive. For example, in Sweden, 90 percent of government funds spent on labour market programs goes toward training, job creation, and assistance for workers moving to new jobs. The same approach has historically meant low unemployment in Germany, but re-unification in the 1990s led to rapidly increasing jobless rates as the communist economy of East Germany was merged with the capitalist economy of West Germany. In Canada, a collective effort has been missing, as has a well-developed industrial strategy that might counter some of the global economic forces negatively affecting our economy. The government has relied on the private sector to create jobs and to train and retrain workers, even though it has not had a particularly good record in this regard.[42]

Of most interest, perhaps, are comparisons of Canada's unemployment trends with those in other North American countries. Between 1984 and 1995, Mexico's jobless rate stayed below 6 percent, lower than the U.S. rate (between 6% and 8%), and considerably lower than Canada's rate (between 10% and 12%). By 1995, Canada's unemployment rate was just under 10 percent, while the Mexican rate had risen to meet the U.S. rate at around 6 percent.[43] The lower unemployment rates in Mexico are, in large part, a function of the much larger informal economy and own-account self-employment sector in Mexico. Individuals seeking work are more likely to find jobs, albeit low-paying and insecure jobs, in the informal sector, or to support themselves with small-scale entrepreneurial activities (Martin 2000).

The difference in unemployment levels between the United States and Canada has a different source. Looking back over time, we find that unemployment rates were very similar in the two countries in the 1950s, 1960s, and 1970s. However, beginning in 1981, Canada's jobless rate began to outstrip the U.S. rate, and the gap widened further in the 1990s. To some extent, the growing gap can be attributed to the more severe recessions in Canada in the early 1980s and 1990s, and the stronger U.S. economy in the 1990s. However, there is also evidence that Canada's unemployed remain in the labour market searching for work longer than their American counterparts (Riddell and Sharpe 1998). As a result, larger numbers of the jobless in the United States are not officially counted as unemployed. In addition, the United States is a society that imprisons many more of its citizens. In 1993, 13 percent of young males (25 percent of young black males) were either in prison or on parole or probation. While jobless, many of these young men would not be counted as unemployed.[44]

Canada has typically relied on the marketplace to reduce unemployment, while instituting Employment Insurance and social assistance programs to help deal with the social problems created by persistently high levels of unemployment. The present public policy challenge is how to create more employment opportunities for unemployed job seekers. While some other countries have devised more effective approaches to dealing with unemployment, we cannot simply import solutions. Canada has a unique economic history and industrial structure, a complicated political system where federal and provincial responsibilities are separate (and frequently disputed), and its own unique business and labour institutions. In short, we will have to fashion our own solutions. Nevertheless, the examples provided by other countries demonstrate that long-term high levels of unemployment need not be seen as inevitable, and that employers, the government, and organized labour will all have to be active participants in any attempts to solve our structural unemployment problem.

HOURS OF WORK AND ALTERNATIVE WORK ARRANGEMENTS

In 1870, the standard number of hours in a work week (the number beyond which overtime would typically be paid to full-time workers) in the Canadian manufacturing sector was 64. This was subsequently reduced because of trade union pressures and the introduction of new manufacturing technologies that could produce more goods in a shorter time. By 1901, 59 hours per week was standard in manufacturing. Twenty years later, 50 hours per week was typical, but this average changed little until after World War II. Between 1946 and 1949, the manufacturing standard dropped quickly from 49 hours per week to 44 hours. It then fell to 40 hours by 1957, fluctuated slightly around this point for the next two decades, and dropped to 39 hours per week by 1976. Since then we have seen a small further decline. In 2000, the average time worked per week for the total employed labour force was 36.7 hours. Thus, on average, Canadians spend considerably less time at work than they did a century ago, but recent changes have been minimal.

A closer look at the decline of about two hours of work per week over the past two decades reveals a very important change in Canadian work patterns. Specifically, we have witnessed a distinct polarization in hours worked – more people have been working long hours and more people have been working part-time.[45] In 2000, only 59 percent of the Canadian employed actually worked between 35 and 40 hours per week in their main job, down from 61 percent in 1993 and 71 percent in 1976 (Sunter and Morisette 1994). One in four (25%) worked less than 35 hours and 16 percent worked more than 40 hours per week. Thus, while the average number of hours worked has declined slightly, the much bigger story is the increase in both the proportion of part-time workers (less than 30 hours per week) and the proportion of Canadians working long hours.

We will return to the topic of part-time work in a moment. Meanwhile, a few observations about long working hours are necessary. For some workers, particularly self-employed professionals, longer hours may provide higher incomes. For others, the added work may simply be an attempt to avoid a decline in standard of living as real incomes have stagnated. But longer hours also cut into leisure and family time, and they have been shown to have detrimental effects on health (Shields 2000). Hence, it is not all that surprising that only one in four working Canadians would prefer more paid hours of work (Figure 2.6). In fact, many of these individuals were working part-time or were in temporary jobs (Akyeampong 1997: 50). Given the choice of more, less, or the same number of hours, 66 percent of working Canadians prefer the same number of hours, presumably with the same pay.

Shift work has long been common, but not always welcome, in some industries (e.g., health, consumer services), but there does seem to be some interest in alternative work schedules. *Teleworking* (working at home or in a remote site, often using computer technology), *flextime* (choosing the time to start and stop work), and *job sharing* have been receiving more attention in the

FIGURE 2.6 *Employees' Work Arrangements and Preferences, Canada, 1995**

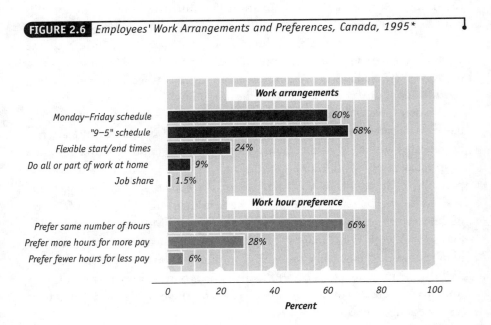

*Paid workers not enrolled full-time in school, excluding self-employed, aged 15 to 69. Work arrangement percentages do not add to 100% due to overlapping categories.

Source: Ernest B. Akyeampong 1997. "Work Arrangements: 1995 overview." *Perspectives on Labour and Income.* 9(1) (Spring 1997): 48–52. Katherine Marshall, "Job sharing." *Perspectives on Labour and Income* 9(2) (Summer 1997): 6–10.

past decade. These work options can help parents balance child care with their jobs. But they also have drawbacks, given that such arrangements often provide fewer benefits and can deprive workers of satisfying interactions with co-workers.[46]

But how common are flexible work arrangements in Canada? According to the national *Survey of Work Arrangements*, in 1995, most workers had Monday to Friday and "9 to 5" schedules (Figure 2.6). Just under one-quarter had flexible start and end times, only 9 percent worked at home all or part of the time, and fewer than 2 percent were in a job-sharing arrangement. Historical comparisons are not available, but it seems that widespread flexibility in work arrangements is still a long way off in most workplaces.

Although most employed Canadians do not appear to want to work less (presumably because of the loss of income), *shorter work weeks* do offer a potential solution to Canada's unemployment problem (Hayden 1999). Advocates claim that reducing full-time jobs a few hours a week could generate thousands of new jobs. A 1994 federal government advisory group, which included labour and industry representatives, recommended ways to redistribute work hours.[47] One Canadian organization, the Work-Well Network, is actively promoting a 30-hour work week. Speaking on behalf of the Network, Bruce O'Hara (1993: 3) concludes that "working harder is the problem, not the solution" to Canada's economic difficulties.

Shorter work weeks have recently been negotiated in several western European countries, in part to reduce unemployment by sharing work among a larger number of workers. For example, in the mid-1990s, German autoworkers negotiated a new deal with Volkswagen in order to preserve jobs, achieving a reduced work week with little pay loss. Perhaps the most significant, and contentious, move in the direction of a shorter hours is the French government's recent law introducing a 35-hour work week for all firms employing more than 20 workers in order to lower unemployment and create a more flexible labour market. Longer vacations also help spread work within a society – as well as contributing to the quality of life. Unlike a number of European countries where vacations of four weeks or longer are required by law, many Canadian workers continue to have only two weeks per year of paid vacation (in addition to statutory holidays). For the majority of Canadian employees, vacation entitlements might rise to three or four weeks per year only after many years in the job (Kumar et al. 1991: 388–89).

NONSTANDARD WORK ARRANGEMENTS

Varieties of Nonstandard Work

Most employed Canadians still have a full-time, year-round, permanent, paid job. However, alternatives to this standard type of employment arrangement are increasing slowly, not just in Canada, but in all industrialized societies.[48] Part-time work is the most common type of *nonstandard work*, but the number of multiple-job holders has also been increasing slowly. The own-account self-employed category has been growing, as we have already noted. And there are also indications that temporary (contract or "contingent") work has become more widespread. These four types of nonstandard work combined (not counting overlaps) accounted for 28 percent of all employed working-age (15 to 64 years) Canadians in 1989, rising to one-third by 1998 (Krahn 1995; Gunderson and Riddell 2000: 22).

Nonstandard work may be mandated by employers or initiated by individual workers. Many employers, in both the private and public sectors, have responded to the economic difficulties of the past decades by replacing full-time with part-time workers (and sometimes part-year workers), and by eliminating permanent positions. The latter have sometimes been replaced with temporary (limited-term contract) positions or workers hired from a temporary help agency (a form of sub-contracting). These employment strategies allow employers greater flexibility in responding to uneven demands for goods and services, and they clearly reduce labour costs (probably a more important factor, in many cases). This "flexible firm" model is discussed in Chapter 5. At the same time, a slowly-increasing number of labour market participants have chosen to set up their own business (the own-account self-employed) or to take on a second job.

Some workers choose alternative forms of employment (part-time work or self-employment, for example) because of personal preference. But for many others, such choices are a response to a difficult labour market. Workers may create their own jobs because few paid jobs are available; accept temporary or part-time work only when permanent, full-time jobs are scarce; or take on a second job because their first job pays poorly. Since nonstandard jobs typically pay less, provide fewer benefits, are less likely to be covered by labour legislation, and have less employment security (Grenon and Chun 1997; Kalleberg et al. 2000), an increase in nonstandard employment also means an increase in the precariousness of employment (and income) for many Canadian workers. Furthermore, evidence is beginning to appear that a job history of nonstandard work carries a long-term cost – controlling for other factors, previous part-time work has a negative effect on current wages (Ferber and Waldfogel 1998).

We have already commented on the small increase in *own-account self-employment* in the past decades. Just over 10 percent of employed working-age Canadians are in this category, which includes farmers, doctors, lawyers, and business consultants, as well as the small entrepreneurs we typically associate with self-employment. Multiple job holding increased from 2 percent in 1977 to over 5 percent in the late 1990s.[49] People take on a second job for a variety of reasons, including topping up an inadequate income, paying off debts, and saving for the future. Economic hard times undoubtedly have contributed to the growth in multiple job holding. However, since the majority are supplementing a full-time job, and since about one-third have a professional or managerial first job, we should be cautious about assuming that all Canadians with more than one job are in a precarious financial or employment situation. The same applies to the own-account self-employed.

Nonstandard jobs are much more common in some sectors of the economy. In terms of industry variations, agriculture has the highest rate of nonstandard work, 65 percent in 1994 (Krahn 1995). A large proportion of these nonstandard workers are the own-account self-employed. Construction also has a high rate of nonstandard work (45%), reflecting extensive self-employment and temporary contract work. But it is the lower-tier service industries—retail and other consumer services—that are the main source of nonstandard employment, given their relative size in the economy. Thus, in 1994, 42 and 47 percent, respectively, of Canadians working in these sectors were in nonstandard jobs. There is also considerable nonstandard work in the upper-tier services, particularly in the education/health/welfare sector (39%) where part-time and temporary work has become very common.

A worker's demographic characteristics also influence her or his likelihood of being employed in a nonstandard job. In 1994, for example, 40 percent of employed women were in nonstandard jobs, compared to 27 percent of men. Young workers were most likely to be in such positions (64% of females aged 15 to 24, and 52% of men in this age cohort). Older workers (55 to 64 years) also have somewhat higher rates of nonstandard employment (41% for women and 30% for men).

Part-Time Work

Half a century ago, in 1953, less than 4 percent of employed Canadians held part-time jobs. But during the 1960s and 1970s, *part-time work* became more common and today it is the most prevalent type of nonstandard work. Until quite recently, *full-time work* was defined by Statistics Canada as working 30 or more hours per week in total. But the rise in multiple job holding forced a rethinking of this definition, since some people holding several part-time jobs (totalling more than 30 hours) were being counted as full-time workers. Since 1996, part-time workers have been defined as those who work less than 30 hours per week in their main job.

Figure 2.7 displays part-time rates for the past several decades, calculated using the new definition. Back in 1976, the national part-time rate for all employed Canadians (aged 15 and older) was 13 percent. The recession in the early 1980s pushed the part-time rate much higher, to 17 percent by 1983. The recession at the beginning of the 1990s led to another increase in part-time employment rates, to 19 percent in 1992. The part-time rate remained at this level until 1999 when it dropped slightly. Thus, by 2000, a total of 2.7 million Canadians, 18 percent of all employed, were working part-time. As a group, they averaged 16.9 hours of work per week, up from the 15.5 hours per week worked by the (much smaller) cohort of part-time workers in 1976 (Pold 2001: 38).

Part-time rates for adult women and men (age 25 and older) are also plotted in Figure 2.7. It is apparent that few employed men age 25 and older are working part-time, although the rate for this group has climbed from 2 percent to 6 percent over the past 24 years. As for adult women, their much higher part-time rates have fluctuated between 23 and 26 percent throughout this period. In 2000, a full 69 percent of all part-time workers (aged 15 and older) were women. The most prominent trend observed in Figure 2.7 is the increase in part-time employment among youth (age 15 to 24). In 1976, the youth part-time employment rate was 21 percent. By 1983, the rate had soared to 31 percent, and it reached 41 percent by 1991. The youth part-time rate continued to rise, to 46 percent by 1995, before dropping marginally to 44 percent by 2000. Thus, at the beginning of the 21st century, almost half of the

FIGURE 2.7 *Part-time Employment by Age and Gender, Canada, 1976-2000*

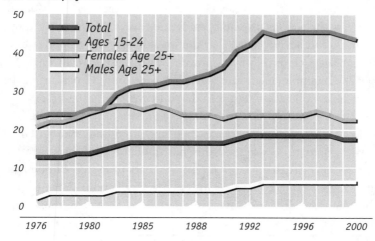

Part-time employment rate

Legend:
- Total
- Ages 15-24
- Females Age 25+
- Males Age 25+

Source: Statistics Canada 2001. *Labour Force Historical Review.* Cat. no. 71F004XCB.

employed 15-to-24-year-olds in Canada, just over one million in total, were working part-time. While Figure 2.7 does not break down the youth part-time rate by gender, we should note that the male rate was 37 percent in 2000, compared to a part-time rate of 51 percent for 15-to-24-year-old women.

Some people choose part-time work because it allows them to balance work and family responsibilities, to continue their education while still holding a job, or simply to have more leisure time. Others, *involuntary part-time workers*, are forced to accept part-time jobs because they cannot find one that is full-time. The monthly Labour Force Survey asks part-time workers why they are working part-time, providing the following possible answers: cannot find a full-time job (involuntary); going to school; personal/family responsibilities; do not want a full-time job (no specific reason provided); and other reasons. Figure 2.8 displays the reasons given by Canadian part-time workers in 1975 and in 2000.

In 1975, 37 percent of less than one million part-time workers stated that they did not want a full-time job. In 2000, this reason was given by a smaller proportion (25%) of a much larger cohort of part-time workers. However, in

2000, 25 percent of the 2.7 million part-timers in Canada were involuntary part-time workers, compared with only 11 percent several decades earlier. This long-term increase in involuntary part-time work reminds us that there is more to the rise in part-time rates than simply changing worker preferences. Much of the increase reflects the actions of employers seeking ways to cut labour costs. That said, we must still acknowledge that the involuntary part-time rate does decline somewhat when the economy improves (Marshall 2001a). In 1995, for example, when the unemployment rate was still 9.4 percent, 31 percent of the 2.5 million part-time workers could not find a full-time job.

Figure 2.8 reveals that almost one-third (30%) of part-time workers choose this type of work arrangement because they are attending school. For a majority of young part-time workers, this nonstandard work arrangement may fit quite well with their educational pursuits. Part-time jobs can be held while attending high school, college, or university. The Labour Force Survey also shows that many adult women working part-time, especially those with

FIGURE 2.8 *Reasons for Part-Time Work, Canada, 1975 and 2000*

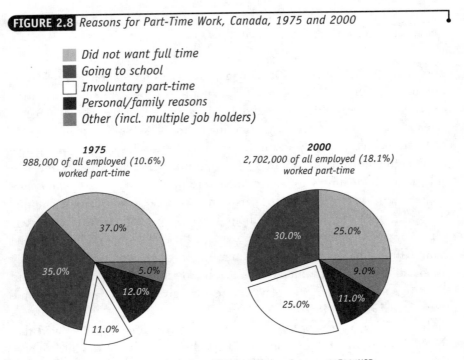

Did not want full time
Going to school
Involuntary part-time
Personal/family reasons
Other (incl. multiple job holders)

1975
*988,000 of all employed (10.6%)
worked part-time*

37.0%
35.0%
5.0%
12.0%
11.0%

2000
*2,702,000 of all employed (18.1%)
worked part-time*

30.0%
25.0%
9.0%
25.0%
11.0%

Source: Statistics Canada 2001. *Labour Force Historical Review.* Cat. no. 71F004XCB.

children, are likely to cite personal or family reasons, or simply state that they do not want full-time work. But had these women been asked whether they would still prefer a part-time job if they had access to adequate and affordable child care, it is likely that at least some would have expressed interest in full-time employment. In other words, traditional assumptions about female child care roles, together with a shortage of affordable, quality child care may create an underestimate of the real level of involuntary part-time employment among adult women (Duffy and Pupo 1992).

Part-time rates vary considerably across industries and occupations. In 2000, the part-time rate in the goods-producing sector was still very low (only 6%). Thus, most of the part-time jobs are in the service industries, in both the lower- and upper-tier services. For example, the part-time rate in the retail trade industry in 2000 was 32 percent, not that much higher than the rate (26%) in the health care industry. However, many of the part-time jobs in the upper-tier services (nurses and teachers, for example) are better paid than the part-time jobs (often held by students) in the retail trade and other consumer services. As for occupational differences, only 6 percent of managers were working part-time in 2000, compared to 18 percent of clerical workers, 39 percent of child care and home care workers, and 46 percent of retail sales clerks. As we will see in the next chapter, there is a strong correlation between occupational status, income, and the prevalence of nonstandard work arrangements, including part-time work.

As in Canada, part-time employment rates have been rising in most other western industrialized countries. Canada's current part-time rate is not unusual. For example, in 1998, about one in four workers were holding part-time jobs in Japan, the United Kingdom, Australia, and Mexico, along with about 30 percent in the Netherlands. In contrast, Sweden, the United States, Germany, and Italy reported part-time rates lower than Canada's 19 percent rate in 1998.[50]

Temporary Employment and Part-Year Work

Some forms of temporary employment, like seasonal employment in the tourism or construction industries, have been part of the Canadian labour market for many decades (Marshall 1999b; Vosko 2000). However, both private and public sector employers have begun to hire more employees on a limited-term (perhaps six months or a year) contract basis, rather than offering permanent positions, as was the custom a decade or two ago. In addition, temporary help agencies have been hiring more workers to be sent out on assignment to employers seeking to fill a temporary employment need. But, in terms of detailed statistical trends, we know considerably less about the growth in *temporary employment*, since Statistics Canada only began monitoring this phenomenon on a regular basis a few years ago. Defining temporary jobs as those with a specific end date, the 2000 *Labour Force Survey* revealed 13 percent of Canadians in such positions, up from 11 percent in 1997. About one-quarter (23%) of all temporary workers were in seasonal jobs, slightly more (27%) were in casual jobs (very short-term, with no specific contract), while most of the rest (47%) held positions with a specific, contracted term.[51]

Adult (age 25 and older) women and men were about equally likely to be in a temporary job (10% and 8%, respectively). Once again, as with part-time employment, it is young workers who are heavily overrepresented in temporary jobs. In 2000, a full 30 percent of 15-to-24-year-old employed Canadians were in a job with a specific end date. Young student workers are more likely to be employed in the lower-tier consumer services, where low-paying temporary jobs are more common. Also, in the upper-tier services (the education and health and welfare industries, for example), it is much easier to offer a new (young) employee a contract position than to move someone already in a permanent position to a contractually-limited job. Quite often, contract employees work alongside permanent employees, performing similar tasks and for comparable pay, but without the guarantee of continued employment beyond six months or a year. While some people, often those with highly marketable skills, find such arrangements quite satisfactory, others are frustrated and worried by their employment and income insecurity.

FUTURE TRENDS

The 20th century recorded profound changes in how, where, and for whom Canadians work. The late 19th and early 20th centuries were times of rapid industrialization and workplace rationalization. The years that followed saw further growth in white-collar occupations, expansion of the service sector, and a decline in self-employment. By the 1960s, the Canadian work world had been largely transformed. But, as our examination of more recent trends has shown, the Canadian labour market was once again going through a significant restructuring at the end of the 20th century.

The service sector has expanded enormously, producing both good and bad jobs, with many more of the latter in the lower-tier service industries. Meanwhile, manufacturing industries have continued to contribute less to employment growth in Canada. We have seen a substantial increase in part-time employment, while other forms of nonstandard work (temporary or contract work, for example) have also become more prevalent. Unemployment rates declined towards the end of the 1990s but are still high enough to cause concern, and could very well rise again in the next several years. Compared to the mid-1990s, when the general public was highly concerned about unemployment, anxiety about employment and income security has abated somewhat. Nevertheless, some groups in the labour market (young workers, for example) have not really experienced the same economic recovery.

What lies ahead? By simply posing this question, we enter the debates and controversies surrounding the future of work. There is a burgeoning literature on the future of work, offering a bewildering range of contradictory scenarios. Students of the sociology of work and industry should be encouraged to critically appraise these writings for themselves. From our perspective, the evidence presented in this chapter does not support the extreme positions taken by many futurists. The trends we have documented suggest neither a "workerless world" as technology displaces humans (Rifkin 1995) nor a "de-jobbed world" in which work is repackaged into a variety of more flexible and rewarding entrepreneurial forms for a majority of Canadians (Bridges 1994).[52]

We can be fairly certain that several of the trends we have documented will continue. Demographic factors are a given, especially workforce aging and the increasing diversity of the labour force. In addition, we can expect a bit more expansion in the service sector's share of total employment. Nonstandard work is still slowly increasing. The big unknown is unemployment: will jobless rates stay around 7 percent, as they were in 2000, or will they once again rise? Is an unemployment rate of, say, 5 percent even a remote possibility? How would public policy have to mesh with employers' strategies to create adequate numbers of well-paying and satisfying jobs? (Lowe 2000; Lowe and Schellenberg 2001)

Examining Canadian work trends most likely to affect the future, Gordon Betcherman and Graham Lowe (1997) identify a cluster of interacting forces creating considerable economic anxiety for Canadians. Foremost among these are persistently high levels of unemployment and underemployment, especially among young people; the uncertainties created by spreading nonstandard work; and the creation of a more polarized labour market, resulting in the economic marginalization of poorly educated or unskilled individuals. By throwing more of the risks associated with economic change onto individuals and families, and by widening the gulf between haves and have-nots, these trends are eroding our sense of social cohesion.

Some of these trends—higher levels of structural unemployment, declining employment in manufacturing, and increasing nonstandard employment—are linked to global economic restructuring. An unstable world market for some of Canada's staple products has reduced the prospects of regions most dependent on primary industries. Increased international competition has prompted some Canadian-based firms to rationalize their operations, shut down or relocate, replace workers with automation, or resort to low-cost nonstandard employment. Canada's economy, then, is not insulated from global economic forces. The Canadian government's laissez-faire labour market policies have, in some ways, made working Canadians more vulnerable to the negative effects of these economic changes.

NOTES

1. Excluded are residents of Nunavut and the Northwest Territories, people living on Indian reservations, full-time members of the armed forces, prison inmates, and others living in institutions such as hospitals or nursing homes. For additional information about this and other Statistics Canada data sources, check out the Statistics Canada website: www.statcan.ca

2. See Statistics Canada (1995a) for an overview of changes made to the content of the *Labour Force Survey* in the mid-1990s to reflect changing patterns of work in Canada.

3. Unless otherwise noted, the 2000 data presented in this chapter are from annual averages compiled by Statistics Canada (2001) from the monthly *Labour Force Surveys*. These historical labour force data are now available on CD-ROM, updated annually, for easier analysis. Other data sources are individually identified.

4. Foot and Stoffman (1998: 8). These authors provide a fascinating account of how demographic trends, particularly the baby boom, influence all aspects of society. However, in our opinion, they underestimate the effects of the profound economic, political, ideological, and organizational changes that have also occurred in the past several decades. For additional discussion of demography and the labour market, see Sunter (2001).

5. Lindsay (1999: 24). This article is one of many on the topic of aging and retirement in Statistics Canada's quarterly publication *Canadian Social Trends*.

6. Anderson (2000). This article is one of many useful discussions of Canadians' participation in private and public pension plans in Statistics Canada's quarterly publication *Perspectives on Labour and Income*. See, for example, Akyeampong (1999b) and Morissette and Drolet (2001). The *Monthly Labor Review* provides similar articles on retirement and pension trends in the U.S. See, for example, Purcell (2000) and Dohm (2000).

7. Immigration statistics in this section are from national census data (*The Daily*, Statistics Canada, November 4, 1997. Cat. No. 11-001E). See Boyd and Vickers (2000) on Canadian immigration trends and policies over the past century, and Iacovetta et al. (1996) for a comparison of the contributions to labour force growth of immigration in Canada and Australia.

8. Visible minority and Aboriginal statistics are based on census data presented by Statistics Canada, *The Daily* (13 January 1998) and Chard and Renaud (1999). Dai and George (1996:29) provide the 2016 projection. See Fullerton (1997) for similar trends in visible minority population growth in the United States, where the Black, Hispanic, and Asian populations are growing most rapidly.

9. See Reich (1991), Drucker (1993), OECD et al. (1998), and Laroche et al. (1999) on the importance of education in today's global economy. The Economic Council of Canada (1992a) and the Ontario Ministry of Education and Training (1996) are two examples of many calls for educational reform. In its discussion of Canada's potential role in the "knowledge economy," the Expert Panel on Skills (2000) presents a broader, more balanced set of observations and recommendations.

10. On learning organizations, see the discussion in Chapter 5; also see Lowe (2000). For a broader perspective on lifelong learning that emphasizes informal learning, see Livingstone (1999).

11. Zhao et al. (2000: 33). Also see Clark (2000), who provides a long-term overview of the growth of the formal education system in Canada, and Riddell and Sweetman (2000) who detail current educational participation and attainment trends.

12. Gilbert and Frank (1998). Also see Statistics Canada and HRDC (1996), OECD et al. (1998), and Krahn and Lowe (1999a) on workplace literacy concerns.

13. On workplace training, also see Betcherman et al. (1998), Statistics Canada and HRDC (1998; Chapter 3), Hum and Simpson (1999a) and Lowe (2000).

14. Kelly et al. (1997). For additional discussions of underemployment, see; Livingstone (1999); Krahn and Lowe (1999a); Lowe (2000); Frenette (2001).

15. Bellin and Miller (1990: 187). Also see Green and Ashton (1992), Noble (1994), Krahn (1997), Krahn and Lowe (1999a), Gingras and Roy (2000), and Smith (2001) on the debate over presumed skill shortages and their effects on competitiveness.

16. See Statistics Canada, *The Daily* (26 June 1996) on movement in the labour market, and Heisz and Coté (1998) on changes in job stability.

17. Armstrong (1999) profiles socioeconomic conditions in First Nations communities with 1996 census data, while Grenon (1997) uses the 1991 census to calculate Aboriginal earnings in the North. For 1996 census data on Aboriginal incomes, see Statistics Canada, *The Daily* (12 May 1998) as well as Maxim et al. (2000). Drost (1996) presents a general overview of the labour market activity and economic conditions of Aboriginal Canadians.

18. Federal, Provincial and Territorial Ministers Responsible for Social Services (2000:32). Also see Hum and Simpson (1996). Hale et al.(1998) and Kruse (1988) provide information on labour market activity of the disabled in the United States.

19. See Morissette (1997), Sunter and Bowlby (1998), Marquardt (1998), Clark (1999a), Sunter (2001), and Labour Market Ministers (2000) on labour market difficulties faced by Canadian youth in the 1990s, Picot (1998) on declining youth wages, and Bowlby (2000) on school-to-work transition trends, including information on the number of youth attending school and not working.

20. For LFP rates among the elderly, see Sunter (2001:31) and Statistics Canada (1998a). Akyeampong (1999b) and Morissette and Drolet (2001) discuss participation in pension plans. Also see Centre for Studies of Aging (1996) and Lindsay (1999) for more general discussions of aging in Canada, Purcell (2000) for similar comments on the U.S. experience, and Gendell (1998) on retirement trends in Germany, Japan, Sweden, and the United States.

21. Myles and Street (1995) use a life-course perspective to discuss pension reform. See Krüger and Baldus (1999) for an interesting German study of work, gender, and the life course.

22. See Statistics Canada, *The Daily* (17 March 1998) for 1996 census information on unpaid work. Frederick (1995: 7) uses time-use survey data to conclude that Canadians spend as much time on unpaid work as on paid work, while Jackson (1996: 29) places a dollar value on unpaid work.

23. See Hall et al. (2001) on the 2000 national survey and Hall et al. (1998) for discussion of a similar survey completed in 1997. Jones (1999, 2000) uses the 1997 data base to provide detailed analyses of the volunteering activity of seniors and youth, respectively, while Reed and Selbee (2001) demonstrate that a very small minority of Canadians do the majority of volunteer work in Canada. Pold and Wong (1990) present the estimate of the dollar value of volunteering work based on the 1987 survey. For a more theoretical analysis of volunteer work, based on trends in the United States, see Wilson (2000).

24. Methods of studying work in the irregular economy include unofficial surveys (assuming one can gain the confidence of respondents), examination of law enforcement records (in an attempt to estimate amounts of illegal economic activity), and assessments of the amount of cash in circulation in an economy (compared with taxation reports of the total amount of reported income). See Mirus et al. (1994) and MacKinnon (1999) for estimates of the size of the irregular economy in Canada. Felt and Sinclair (1992) present an interesting study of legal unpaid work in rural Newfoundland.

25. Cobb, Halstead, and Rowe (1995: 76). See Brown and Stanford (2000) and Osberg and Sharpe (1998) on quality of life indicators that can supplement standard economic measures (e.g., GDP) of societal progress.

26. Crompton and Vickers (2000) provide a century-long overview of labour force trends in Canada.

27. See Krahn (1992: 17–18) for further discussion of this classification system, which is quite similar to the industry typology developed by the Economic Council of Canada (1990) in its studies of the service sector. The Economic Council distinguished *dynamic services* (distributive and business services) from *nonmarket services* (education, health and welfare, public administration) and *traditional services* (retail trade and personal services).

28. Statistics Canada, *The Daily* (17 March, 1998) presents census data on shifts in employment by industry between 1991 and 1996. Note that comparisons of the percentages in Table 2.1 to similar industry distributions in previous editions of this textbook are inappropriate, because of changes to Statistics Canada's industry classification system in 1999.

29. See Statistics Canada (1998b) for Canada – U.S. comparisons, and Commission for Labor Cooperation (1997) for labour market profiles for Canada, the United States, and Mexico.

30. Betcherman and Leckie (1997). Also see Marquardt (1998).

31. Statistics Canada, *The Daily* (17 March, 1998). As some occupations (e.g., agricultural occupations) have declined in relative size, Statistics Canada has begun to combine them with others (e.g., occupations unique to primary industry). Alternatively, as some categories have grown, they have been subdivided and renamed in Statistics Canada data presentations.

32. Starting in 1999, Statistics Canada began to use a revised Standard Occupational Classification System (SOC91), rather than the SOC80, for presentations of Labour Force Survey and census data. The biggest impact of the change was on the management category, with some occupations formerly coded in this category now being placed in other categories. Statistics Canada has only revised its databases back to 1987, so Table 2.3 begins with that year.

33. Statistics Canada, *The Daily* (4 June 1992; 26 April, 1999); also see Winson (1996). Ilg (1995) documents the same trend in the United States.

34. Bowlby (2001: 14) observes that 2000 was the first year since 1986 that Canadian self-employment dropped. However, it is probably too soon to know whether this small decline indicates a longer-term trend.

35. Gunderson and Riddell (2000: 25) place 12 percent of employed Canadians in the own-account self-employed category in 1998. Manser and Picot (1999) compare self-employment in the United States and Canada. Also see Crompton and Vickers (2000:13) for Canadian data on self-employment. The Commission for Labor Cooperation (1997: 46) provides comparisons between Canada, Mexico, and the United States.

36. See Lucas (1971), Clemenson (1992), and Angus and Griffin (1996) on single-industry communities, Statistics Canada, *The Daily* (28 April 1992; 15 April 1997) for Census data on population decline in resource-dependent communities, Palmer and Sinclair (1997) on the collapse of the Newfoundland fishing industry, and Finnie (1999) on patterns of inter-provincial migration in Canada.

37. Akyeampong (1992) discusses the number of discouraged workers during the recessions in the 1980s and 1990s; See *Perspectives on Labour and Income* (Spring, 2001, p. 64) for the 2000 estimate of discouraged workers.

38. For discussions of unemployment trends and policy responses, see MacLean and Osberg (1996), Betcherman and Lowe (1997), Battle and Torjman (1999), and a *Canadian Public Policy* special supplement (July 2000) on "Structural Aspects of Unemployment in Canada."

39. Krahn et al. (1998); see also Statistics Canada (1994a), Drost (1996), Grenon (1997), de Silva (1999), and Armstrong (1999) on the labour market position of Aboriginal Canadians.

40. See Osberg (1996), Betcherman and Lowe (1997), Battle and Torjman (1999), and the July 2000 special issue of *Canadian Public Policy*.

41. See Sorrentino (1995) and Gitter and Scheuer (1998) on difficulties in comparing unemployment rates cross-nationally.

42. For discussions of the role of government in job creation, see Drache and Gertler (1991: 19–22), Tobin (1996), Battle and Torjman (1999), Roy and Wong (2000), and Riddell and St-Hilaire (2000).

43. See Commission for Labor Cooperation (1997: 67-78) for a discussion of unemployment trends in Canada, the United States, and Mexico.

44. Riddell and Sharpe (1998) provide a useful overview of research and debate about the Canada-U.S. unemployment rate gap. Their article introduces a special issue of *Canadian Public Policy* (July 1998 Supplement) devoted to this topic. Sherman and Judkins (1995:53) comment on the impact of high rates of imprisonment on unemployment figures.

45. Hall (1999) discusses the polarization of hours worked in Canada. See Rones et al. (1997) for American trends.

46. See Hamblin (1995), Nadwodny ((1996), and Mirchandani (1999) on the benefits and costs of teleworking, Akyeampong (1993) on flextime work arrangements, and Marshall (1997) and Huberman and Lanoie (2000) on job sharing.

47. Human Resources Development Canada (1994); also see Yalnizyan et al. (1994).

48. For discussions of nonstandard or "contingent" work, see Clinton (1997), Booth (1997), Kalleberg et al. (2000), Carré et al. 2000; and Lowe and Schellenberg (2001).

49. Sussman (1998) reports a 5.2% rate of multiple job holding in 1997. Based on data from a smaller sample survey in 1994, Krahn (1995) provided an estimate of 7 percent. Both sources, however, show a systematic increase in "moonlighting." For discussions of U.S. trends and implications, see Stinson (1997) and Kimmel and Powell (1999).

50. Marshall (2001a: 21). See Commission for Labor Cooperation (1997: 47-51) for a discussion of nonstandard work in Canada, the United States, and Mexico, and Felstead et al. (1999) for a comparison of nonstandard work trends in Canada and the United Kingdom.

51. Lowe and Schellenberg (2001: 12) suggest that, because some individuals working for temporary help agencies report themselves to be in permanent jobs, *Labour Force Survey* estimates of temporary employment may be too low. See Vosko (2000) for an analysis of temporary work in its historical context, and Henson (1996) for a personal account of temporary employment. Marshall (1999b) analyzes trends in seasonal employment, and Grenon and Chun (1997) compare the quality of permanent and temporary jobs.

52. See Betcherman and Lowe (1997) and Lowe (2000) for counter-arguments.

3

LABOUR MARKETS AND JOBS: OPPORTUNITIES AND INEQUALITY

INTRODUCTION

Why do high school teachers earn more than retail sales clerks, or engineers more than construction workers? Presumably, these income differences are a result of teachers and engineers investing in extra years of education that, in turn, lead to more skilled and responsible jobs. So why do dentists make more money than child care workers? While dentists spent more years training for their profession, caring for and teaching young children is also a very complex and responsible task. Why are the children of middle-class parents much more likely to go to university, compared with the children of less affluent Canadians? Why are women, the disabled, Aboriginal Canadians, and members of visible minority groups overrepresented in less rewarding jobs?

Such questions about variations in educational outcomes, career patterns, job security, and other job rewards are central to the sociological study of labour markets. We can define a *labour market* as the arena in which employers seek to purchase labour from potential employees who themselves are seeking jobs suitable to their education, experience, and preferences. In the labour market, workers exchange their skills, knowledge, and loyalty in return for pay, status, career opportunities, and other job rewards.

A number of other institutions and organizations support or interact with the operation of the labour market. Among their other functions, schools and families prepare individuals for entry (or re-entry) into the labour market. Government legislation affects how labour markets operate—minimum wage laws and legislation governing the activities of trade unions are examples. Government agencies may also assist the unemployed with financial support or job-training programs. Unions and professional associations are active in the labour market, looking after the interests of their members by bargaining for additional job rewards and, sometimes, by limiting access to better jobs. Organizations representing employers also try to influence labour market operations, lobbying governments to change laws regarding unions or encouraging schools to include more employment-related subject matter in their teaching.

Labour economists and sociologists study many of these institutions and how they influence labour market operations.[1] Of particular interest to sociologists are the distributive aspects of the labour market. Specifically, does the labour market provide opportunities for hard-working individuals to improve their social position and quality of life, or does it reinforce patterns of inequality in society? Perhaps it does both.

The previous chapter discussed Canada's changing industrial and occupational structures, its patterns of unemployment, and the growth in nonstandard jobs. It indicated that some jobs are much more rewarding than others and that some people are at much greater risk of unemployment. This chapter continues this discussion. It begins by reviewing some of the criteria by which individuals evaluate the desirability of jobs. We then ask several basic questions: Who has the good jobs? How did they get them? And how do they manage to keep them? Our attempt to answer these questions is built around a comparison of two alternative approaches to explaining labour market outcomes in societies like ours, the human capital model and the labour market segmentation perspective.

According to *human capital theory*, jobs requiring more effort, training, and skill typically receive greater rewards. This theory assumes that labour market participants compete openly for the best jobs, and that the most qualified people end up in the jobs requiring their particular skills. The outcome should be an efficient and productive economy and a fair allocation of job rewards. But in reviewing research on differences in job rewards, educational and occupational choice, status attainment, and labour market segmentation, we observe that the labour market does not always operate in this manner. In fact, there is evidence that the open competition assumptions of human capital theory need to be seriously challenged, and that a segmented labour market often allows the perpetuation of social inequalities.

Thus, the study of labour markets is not only about who gets better or worse jobs; it also addresses broader questions about social stratification and class structure.[2] Consequently, this chapter also discusses class inequalities within Canadian society and the growing polarization of living standards and life chances.

GOOD JOBS AND BAD JOBS

We have already begun to assess the quality of different jobs in our discussion of nonstandard employment relationships. Compared with being unemployed, a part-time or temporary job may be preferable. For most labour force participants, though, a full-time, full-year, permanent job would be much more desirable because of the income security it provides. Thus, recognizing that some Canadians do prefer nonstandard jobs for educational, personal, or family reasons, and allowing that some nonstandard jobs (business consultants working on a contractual basis, for example) might pay very well, we would still classify only a minority of nonstandard jobs as "good jobs."[3]

Clearly, the criteria for deciding whether a particular job is good or bad are not universal. Individuals compare the rewards a job provides against their own needs and ambitions and against the personal costs of working in such a job. Since most workers are concerned about maintaining or improving their standard of living and quality of life, material or *extrinsic job rewards* are very important. How much does it pay? What kinds of benefits come with the job? Is it dangerous? Is it full-time and permanent?

In the following section, we examine variations in pay and other employment benefits in the Canadian labour market. We also present data on work-related injuries and deaths, our rationale being that a job with few risks to personal health and safety is, in a very crucial sense, a better job. We then comment on the types of jobs that require workers to use computers. Recognizing that not all jobs involving computer use are highly rewarding, a subject we will return to in later chapters, we reason that in today's economy, computer use provides workers with technology skills that could enhance their future employment prospects. Finally, we discuss occupational status (the prestige ranking of a particular job), even though it is not really an extrinsic job reward in the same sense as pay and benefits. However, occupational status is also not as subjectively (individually) determined as are the more *intrinsic job rewards* (the chance to be creative, to work independently, to develop friendships in a job, and so on) discussed in Chapter 8. While power relationships within Canadian workplaces are obviously also central to discussions of good jobs and bad jobs, we will introduce them briefly in this chapter and then provide a fuller discussion in Chapter 6.

Income Differences

Statistics Canada uses the Census to collect income information, along with a number of other annual surveys including the *Labour Force Survey*. We draw on several of these data sources to highlight some of the most important factors influencing income differences in the Canadian labour market.

Considering only *paid employees* (that is, excluding the self-employed), incomes in the service industries are about 20 percent less than in the goods-producing industries (Grenon 1996). For example, in 2000, the annual average weekly wage (excluding overtime) was $892 in the natural resource-based industries and $699 in manufacturing. In contrast, the average weekly wage was only $459 in trade (wholesale and retail combined) and even less ($295) in accommodation and food services, both areas with substantial part-time employment. But the large and growing service sector contains both lower-tier and upper-tier services, with many better-paying jobs in the latter. Hence, in 2000, we also observed high average weekly wages in professional, technical, and scientific services ($806), educational services ($732), and public administration ($788). In short, there is more variation in employees' incomes within the service sector than within the goods-producing sector.

Comparing incomes of several major occupational groups, we find that (employed) managers reported average weekly wages of $999 in 2000, while

Canadians in natural and applied science occupations earned an average of $911 per week. Individuals in health occupations, a broad category that includes both well-paid doctors and poorly paid orderlies and nursing assistants, reported an average weekly wage of $627 in 2000. But these earnings were still much higher than the weekly wages of Canadians in sales and service occupations ($376). While the *Labour Force Survey* cannot provide reliable income estimates for detailed occupational categories, we can use 1996 Census information for this purpose. So, by way of example, we find that Canadian dentists earned an average of $102,433 in 1995, while lawyers reported average earnings of $81,617. Cashiers earned only a fraction of this ($17,613), as did service station attendants ($16,203) and nannies ($12,713).[4]

Higher earnings in some goods-producing and upper-tier services, and in managerial and professional occupations, can be traced, in part, to the presence of unions and professional associations that have bargained for higher incomes and full-time jobs. It is also apparent that workers with specific professional skills (for example, teachers, doctors, and engineers) and more formal education are generally paid much more than those with less training. Thus, some of the industrial and occupational differences in earnings are due to supply and demand factors in a labour market that rewards educational investments. Also important are differences in the bargaining power of the various groups participating in the labour market, a subject to which we return in Chapters 6 and 7.

These occupational earning patterns hide large gender differences. Thus, according to the 1996 Census, among people working full-time and full-year, women's earnings were 71 percent of men's. More specifically, female dentists earned an average of $71,587 in 1995, two-thirds of the earnings of their male counterparts ($109,187). Among senior managers, men earned an average of $104,715 compared to $71,270 for women. Female university professors reported 1995 earnings of $55,909, about 77 percent of the earnings of male professors ($72,532). Among the lower-paid occupations, we find male bartenders reporting annual 1995 earnings of $18,899, considerably higher than the earnings of female bartenders ($14,940). Similar gender differences are observed in all occupational groupings but, as these specific examples demonstrate, the *female-male earnings ratio* does vary considerably.

These examples from the 1996 Census compare women and men in full-time, full-year jobs. However, even among full-time workers, men average more hours per week (43.8 hours in 1997) than do women in full-time jobs (39.5 hours). This apparently small difference can still add to about five or six weeks of extra paid work per year. When this difference in the annual volume of paid work is adjusted in the calculation of an average *hourly wage*, *Labour Force Survey* data for full-time, full-year employees reveal women earning about 81 percent of what men earned in 2000.[5] The female-male earnings ratio is higher among younger and better-educated workers (Galarneau and Earl 1999).

The *gender wage gap* has been decreasing for several decades as women's earnings have been rising slowly while the earnings of men, on average, have stalled. One likely reason for rising female incomes is that more women have invested in higher education and, as a result, have gained access to better-paying jobs. This explanation does have some merit, since the proportion of female labour force participants with university degrees has certainly risen. However, if this were the complete explanation, we might even expect female incomes to be higher than male incomes, since the proportion of female labour force participants with university degrees is now higher than the proportion for men (see Chapter 2). Hence, in Chapter 4 we examine in more detail other features of the labour market (for example, hiring and promotion practices, and the presence or absence of unions) and its related institutions (for example, the influence of families and schools on educational, occupational, and career choices) to obtain a more complete explanation of the remaining gender differences in income.

By restricting our discussion to broad occupational categories, we also overlook the extreme ends of the *income distribution* in the Canadian labour market. At the top of the earnings hierarchy, chief executive officers (CEOs) of Canada's largest firms typically earn huge incomes (based on salaries, performance bonuses, and options to purchase stocks in their company at below-market value). In 2000, the CEOs of the top 60 companies listed on the Toronto Stock Exchange received a median compensation package of $3.7 million (only four of the 60 earned less than $1 million). The fact that the average compensation was much higher ($6.1 million) indicates that a few CEOs were exceptionally well paid. John Roth of Nortel Networks led the pack, with $70.8 million. Coming in second was Jacques Bougie, the outgoing CEO of Alcan Aluminum, with a $32.8 million compensation package.

Dominic D'Allesandro, CEO of Manulife, was a distant third, receiving only $17.8 million in 2000 (Silcoff 2001). It would take the average Canadian employee, with annual earnings of about $32,000 in 2000, about 550 years to accumulate as much money as D'Allesandro and over 2200 years to earn what Roth received in one year.

At the other end of the wealth scale are numerous workers with very low incomes. Legislated minimum wages in Canada have always been very low, and in the past several decades they have not kept up with inflation. Thus, in 2000, if a worker earning a minimum wage worked 40 hours a week for 52 weeks in the year, she or he would earn $11,440 annually in Newfoundland (the province with the lowest minimum wage), $12,272 in Alberta and New Brunswick, $14,248 in Ontario, $14,560 in Quebec, and $16,640 in British Columbia (the highest minimum wage in Canada).[6] However, virtually no minimum wage workers would be employed year round for 40 hours a week, so these estimates of annual income are too high for this group of workers.

Many, but not all, of these lowest-paid workers are students working in the lower-tier services (retail trade and consumer services), frequently part-time. Some older, full-time workers also have minimum wage jobs, but many more are hired at pay rates only a few dollars above the minimum wage. As a second income in a household, such salesclerk, waitress, cashier, and service station attendant jobs might help pay some bills. However, if this were the only income, the household, especially if it contained children, would likely be living well below the official *low income cutoff,* more commonly called the *poverty line.*[7]

Hourly wage rates in blue-collar occupations, such as construction or manufacturing, are typically at least twice as high as the minimum wage. Yet even with a $13-per-hour wage, and working full time and year round, these earnings would still make it extremely difficult to raise a family in most major Canadian urban centres. Furthermore, many of these blue-collar jobs are seasonal and are subject to frequent layoffs. Consequently, when we look closely at the characteristics of Canadian families living below the poverty line, we find that low wages, insufficient work (part-time or part-year), and periodic unemployment are usually the problem (Crompton 1995; Laroche 1998). Some of the working poor lack education or marketable skills, but many simply cannot find well-paid and secure employment.

Other Employment Benefits

Additional *employment benefits* – a form of indirect pay and increased security – are an important dimension of the quality of jobs, representing almost one-third of employers' total labour costs. Benefits required by law (employer contributions for Employment Insurance, Canada/Quebec Pension Plan, and Workers' Compensation) make up only about one-sixth of the cost of all employee benefits provided in Canada. A much larger portion of the indirect income provided through employment benefits comes from paid vacation and statutory holidays and from employer contributions to private pension and employee health and dental plans.[8]

In 1995, 51 percent of paid employees in Canada had an employer-sponsored pension plan. Slightly more were the beneficiaries of a health plan (59%), a dental plan (55%), and paid sick leave (57%). A much smaller proportion (21 percent in 1994) received formal work-related training paid for by their employer.[9] Such training can lead to promotions, higher income, and an improved ability to compete for other jobs. Five years later in 2000, when the economy was considerably stronger, a national survey showed that the proportion of Canadian workers receiving these benefits had not really changed (Figure 3.1). This more recent survey also asked about paid maternity/parental leave, a benefit reported by 46% of Canadian workers.

Further analysis of the 2000 survey data revealed that 30 percent of Canadian workers had none of these five benefits in their job, in contrast with 29 percent who received all five benefits.[10] In other words, the distribution of additional benefits is highly polarized. As shown in Figure 3.1, full-time employees are more than twice as likely as part-time workers to receive each of these benefits, and permanent employees about twice as likely as temporary workers. The self-employed, particularly the own-account self-employed, typically do not receive such benefits since it is expensive (and sometimes quite complicated) to "purchase" health and dental plans for oneself. These types of benefits are also more frequently provided in larger firms (where pay is also typically higher) and in unionized workplaces. Similarly, better-educated workers, those employed in larger firms, and those in full-time positions are more likely to receive employer-sponsored work-related training.[11] It is apparent, then, that pay differences within the Canadian labour market are accentuated by the uneven distribution of fringe benefits.

FIGURE 3.1 *Job Benefits by Labour Market Status, Canada, 2000*

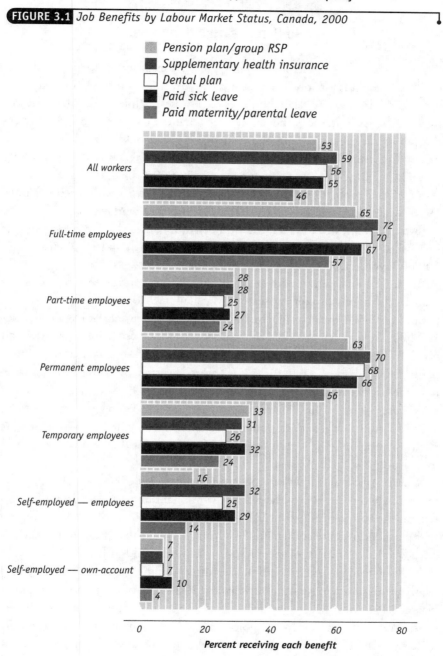

Pension plan/group RSP
Supplementary health insurance
Dental plan
Paid sick leave
Paid maternity/parental leave

Percent receiving each benefit

Source: Canadian Policy Research Network, *CPRN/Ekos Changing Employment Relationships Survey* (Lowe and Schellenberg 2000).

Risks to Personal Health and Safety

We can extend this discussion of job quality by examining the personal risks of different kinds of jobs. For example, every year hundreds of Canadian workers die from work-related injuries or illnesses. While work-related deaths may receive less attention, the fact remains that the chances of being killed on the job are still greater than those of being killed on the road by a drunk driver. On average, three work-related fatalities are recorded every working day. Thus, in the past 25 years more than 20,000 Canadians have died as a result of their job. Over that period, *industrial fatality rates* declined until 1996, when the rate was 5.14 deaths per 100,000 workers (a total of 703 industrial fatalities). However, the number of fatalities then rose (833 deaths in 1997 and 798 in 1998), bringing the 1998 rate back up to 5.57 deaths per 100,000 workers.[12]

Industrial fatality rates are generally much lower in the service industries than in the goods-producing sector (Marshall 1996). For example, over the period 1988-93, the manufacturing sector saw an average of 8 deaths per 100,000 workers per year. The construction and transportation industries had much higher fatality rates, with about two dozen work-related deaths per year per 100,000 workers. But these rates were dwarfed by those found in the resource-extraction industries: between 1988 and 1993, the annual fatality rates were 63 (per 100,000 workers) in mining, 82 in logging and forestry, and 113 in fishing and trapping. The 26 miners killed in Nova Scotia's Westray mine on May 9, 1992 are a tragic example of the high risks involved in working in Canada's resource industries.

Certain occupations within these industries carry extremely high risks. The most dangerous are those involving cutting, handling, and loading of materials in the mining industry (281 deaths per 100,000 workers) and working with insulation in the construction industry (246 deaths). However, since relatively small numbers of people work in these and other high-risk jobs (including fishing and trapping), the three leading causes of work-related death are exposure to harmful substances (20 percent of all industrial fatalities between 1988 and 1993), accidents involving transportation vehicles (19 percent), and being struck by an object. Since the high-risk jobs are typically filled by men, 96 percent of the workers who died because of work-related reasons between 1988 and 1993 were men.[13]

The incidence of work-related injury and illness rose in Canada during the 1970s and 1980s, but then began to decline in the early 1990s. It continued to decline even though the rate of industrial fatalities rose again in the late 1990s. In 1994, Workers' Compensation Boards and Commissions across the country compensated 430,756 individuals for work-related injuries and illness resulting in time loss and permanent disability. By 1998, this number had dropped to 375,360. Even so, the compensation costs for these injuries totalled $4.65 billion in 1998. As with work-related fatalities, rates of *time-loss work injuries* are much higher in the goods-producing industries, particularly in forestry, manufacturing, and construction (Figure 3.2). However, the distributive services (transportation and wholesale trade) also have high injury

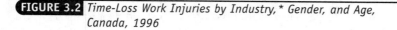

FIGURE 3.2 *Time-Loss Work Injuries by Industry,* Gender, and Age, Canada, 1996*

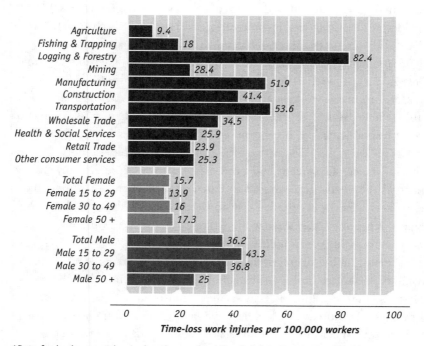

Time-loss work injuries per 100,000 workers

*Data for business services, education, and public administration not provided by source.

Source: Health Canada and Statistics Canada 1999, *Statistical Report on the Health of Canadians,* Table 6.1.

rates. Time-loss work injury rates for men are more than twice as high as for women, while young men (age 15 to 29) have particularly high rates (43.3 injuries per 1000 workers in 1996). The explanation for these gender and age differences is found in the different industrial sectors in which women and men tend to be employed.[14] Young men are most likely to be working in the most dangerous occupations in the goods-producing sector and in the distributive services.

Not all work-related injuries and illnesses get reported and compensated, and the effects of some do not become apparent for many years. Hence, it is useful to also look at research on *workplace stressors* that might be harming workers' health. In a 1994/95 national survey, for example, about 40 percent of Canadian workers aged 15 to 64 indicated that their job was very physically demanding. About 20 percent experienced high job strain as a result of hectic jobs and little opportunity to control the pace and content of these jobs, and almost as many were stressed by feelings of job insecurity. These stressors were more widespread among low income earners. They were also associated with negative health outcomes. For example, the more physically demanding the job, the higher the rate of self-reported work injuries. And the higher the job strain, the more frequent the reports of poor physical and mental health.[15]

In addition, many workers are exposed to *workplace hazards* that can be harmful to their health. A 1991 national study revealed that 34 percent of employed respondents had been exposed to dust or fibres in the air at their job site in the previous 12 months. One in four (26 percent) reported exposure to loud noise, 22 percent had been exposed to poor quality air, and 18 percent said they had been exposed to dangerous chemicals or fumes. Blue-collar workers were much more likely to be exposed to dust or fibres, loud noise, and dangerous chemicals, while white-collar workers were more likely to report poor quality air in their work environment.[16]

There are a number of important conclusions to be drawn from this brief discussion of workplace health and safety in Canada. First, it is clear that work-related stress, injuries, illnesses, and fatalities constitute an extremely serious social problem. Hundreds of Canadians die in work-related injuries each year, and hundreds of thousands are injured or become ill. But even though work time lost to injuries and illnesses continues to far exceed the time lost due to strikes and work stoppages in Canada (15.4 million days versus 2.5 million days in 1998, for example), the latter is much more often perceived to be a problem.

Second, workplace health and safety problems constitute a huge cost for employers. In addition to the direct costs of compensation ($4.65 billion in 1998, as noted above), there are indirect costs resulting from production losses, damage to equipment, lower efficiency, decreased employee morale, and lost supervisory time. Although such indirect costs are notoriously hard to calculate precisely, estimates of total costs are typically about twice as high as the direct costs of compensation.[17] In other words, the current annual costs of workplace health and safety problems are probably approaching $10 billion annually. Third, industrial and occupational differences in injuries and fatalities demonstrate that the risks of injury, illness, and death are an additional important dimension of overall job quality. Some of the best-paid groups within the labour market experience many fewer risks to their personal health and safety. Workers with lower incomes and fewer benefits also tend to be at greater risk of ill health and injury because of their job.

Computer Use in the Workplace

The impacts of new *information technologies* (IT) on employment opportunities and on the quality of work are still hotly debated topics in the sociology of work. Proponents of the new technologies point to long-term increases in employment as new types of jobs appear, and to increased skill requirements in jobs employing computers and automated technologies. Critics remind us that new technologies have frequently led to job loss for many workers as employers have used the technology to cut labour costs. They also draw attention to examples of jobs that have been *deskilled* as automated systems have replaced some of the previously required manual and cognitive skills of workers. We will return to this larger debate in Chapter 6, while focusing here on which workers actually use computers in their jobs. With respect to characteristics of good jobs and bad jobs, we reason that computer use on the job provides workers with technology skills that might enhance their future employment prospects (Oderkirk 1996; Marshall 2001b).

The 2000 *General Social Survey* revealed that 57 percent of employed Canadians used a computer (personal computer, mainframe, or word processor), the most common form of information technology, in their main job (Marshall 2001b). This figure had risen substantially, from 35 percent in 1989 and 48 percent in 1994. However, computer use was far from equally distributed across the labour force. While 86 percent of workers in professional occupations used computers in their job, along with 78 percent of managers, 84 percent of clerical workers, and 71 percent of technical workers, Canadians working in sales and service occupations and in blue-collar jobs, were much less likely to work with computers (Figure 3.3). The higher the education of Canadian workers, the more likely they were to use a computer in their daily work. Young workers and the oldest members of the employed labour force, groups somewhat less likely to be in good jobs, are also underrepresented among computer users at work.

These patterns of computer use parallel the distribution of other work rewards in the Canadian labour market. Workers with better pay, more benefits, more access to training, and safer jobs are, on average, also more likely to be using computers, thus acquiring skills that might be transferable to other employment situations. These survey results correlate with other research

FIGURE 3.3 *Computer Use in the Workplace by Occupation, Gender, Age, and Education, Canada, 2000*

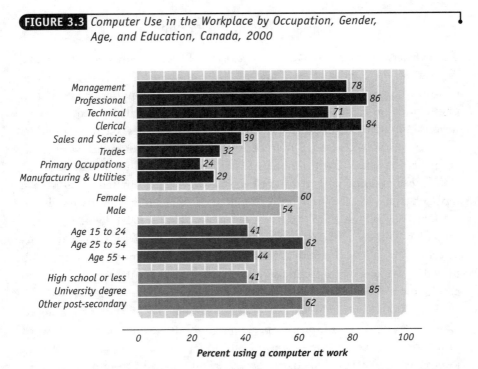

Source: Katherine Marshall. "Working with computers," *Perspectives on Labour and Income* (Summer, 2001): 11.

showing that more affluent households are more likely to own personal computers (Dickinson and Sciadas 1999). However, there are two important exceptions. First, clerical workers (most of whom are women) are typically not as well paid as are managers and professionals, but they report high levels of computer use. Second, manufacturing, construction, and primary sector workers, a largely male group that has been reasonably well paid, exhibit low workplace computer use. Thus, to understand how computer use and skills fit into the good jobs–bad jobs equation, we also need to look at how this new technology is actually used and at the gendered patterns of employment in the labour market (Hughes and Lowe 2000).

Occupational Status

We seldom find doctors, lawyers, scientists, or professors blushing when they are asked, "What do you do?" But for clerks, janitors, parking lot attendants, and many others, the same question might elicit an apologetic "I'm just a...." In short, there is consensus in our society about which jobs have higher status. While less important than income and benefits (which directly determine one's standard of living) and job security (which ensures continuity of that standard), *occupational status* is something we must also consider when comparing different jobs. To a great extent, our self-image and the respect of others is determined by our occupation.

Not surprisingly, there is a strong relationship between occupational status and income. It may seem that both higher pay and higher status are a direct result of the greater skill and responsibility required by certain jobs. Generally, higher status jobs do require more education, cognitive ability, and skill (Hunter and Manley 1986). It is also possible that some occupations have come to be seen as more prestigious because, over time, incomes in this line of work have risen. Higher incomes, in turn, might be the result of skill increases, but they may also reflect the ability of a powerful occupational group to limit entry into its field. It is also quite clear that some occupations have traditionally had higher social status because they were viewed as men's work rather than women's work, a topic we examine in the next chapter.

The links among income, education, and occupational status have led to widespread use of *socioeconomic status* (SES) scales in sociological research. In Canada, the most frequently used SES measures are the *Blishen scores*. Bernard

Blishen began with the results of a mid-1960s national study that asked respondents to rank the "social standing" of almost two hundred detailed occupational titles. He calculated the statistical relationships between these prestige rankings and the average education and income (from Census data) of men employed in these occupations, and then estimated SES scores for almost five hundred occupational titles. An updated version of this SES scale, based on 1981 Census data for both men and women, began to address one of the major criticisms of the original scale—it was biased toward traditionally "male" jobs.[18] This version of the Blishen scale ranges from low status scores, such as 17.8 for newspaper carriers and 21.5 for service station attendants, to high evaluations for professionals such as nuclear engineers (75.4), university teachers (75.9), and physicians (101.3).

A useful alternative occupational classification system consists of a sixteen-category typology developed by Peter Pineo and others from the occupational codes used in the 1971 Census and subsequently updated from 1981 Census information. This ranking focuses more on the work tasks done by different occupational groups, the skill and knowledge levels required, and the nature of the employment relationships. Self-employed professionals (doctors and lawyers, for example) are at the top of the list. Further down, we find categories such as semiprofessionals, technicians, middle management, skilled clerical, semiskilled manual workers, and so on. Compared to the Blishen scores, which remain numbers with no meaning in themselves, the advantage of the Pineo scale is that the title assigned to a rank (for example, semiskilled clerical, sales, and services) actually tells us something about the occupations included.[19] Both the Blishen and the Pineo scales have become somewhat dated, however, as new occupations (in the IT field, for example) have emerged and the relative status of other occupations changes.

CANADA'S CLASS STRUCTURE

The question of who has better and worse jobs in the Canadian labour market is really a question about social inequality. Therefore, answering the question requires us to examine the class structure of our society. The term *social class* is used in a variety of ways by social scientists. Some treat it as equivalent to socioeconomic status, discussed above, referring to an individual's position in a fluid social hierarchy determined by occupation, education, or income.

However, social class can have a much more precise meaning. It refers, at one level, to a particular position within a stratified social structure and, on another level, to the power relationships among groups directly engaged in the production process. These "relations of ruling"[20] have an impact on individuals' life chances (their living standard and the opportunities to improve it), and, sometimes, on the way they perceive the social world around them and react to it.

Marx on Social Class

Class relationships were central to the social and economic theories of Karl Marx. In his analysis of capitalism, Marx focused primarily on the relationship between the class of *capitalists*, who owned the means of production, and the *proletariat*. The latter class owned no production-related property, and so had little choice but to exchange labour in return for a wage. Marx also discussed the middle class of small business owners (the *petite bourgeoisie*) and predicted that, in time, it would largely disappear; small businesses would be swallowed up by bigger competitors, and self-employment in agriculture would gradually be replaced by wage labour. The result would be an even more polarized society. Conflict between an increasingly impoverished class of workers and the capitalist class would eventually lead to the emergence of a new type of egalitarian society.

As documented in Chapter 2, historically Canada has moved in the direction of less self-employment, as have other industrialized capitalist societies. However, we have also observed an increase in self-employment in the past decade. In addition, expansion of the service industries, a growing number of skilled (and well-paid) workers in white-collar occupations, and the emergence of distinctly different patterns of employment for women and men force us to rethink Marx's model of social class relationships. What, then, are the characteristics of Canada's class structure?

Postindustrial Class Structure of Canadian Society

Marx's original classification system cannot accurately map the complexities of social class in Canadian society today. For example, while an individual whose store has three employees is classified as an employer, her or his responsibilities, power, and job rewards are hardly comparable to the president of a corporation employing thousands of workers, wielding a great deal of power, and taking home a pay package of several million dollars a year. Similarly, while both a senior manager in a large corporation and a sales clerk in a retail store may be paid workers, their work experiences and rewards are very different. A variety of attempts have been made to incorporate such important distinctions into theories of social class.

A widely used approach was developed by Eric Olin Wright (Wright et al. 1982). In his classification of labour force participants, Wright took into account ownership, the employment of others, the supervision of others, and control over one's own work. He distinguished between large employers and small employers, two groups that have legal ownership and also employ others, and the *petite bourgeoisie*, who own their businesses (or farms) but do not have others working for them (the own-account self-employed). Large employers (the group most closely resembling Marx's class of capitalists) are in a different category from small employers with only a handful of employees, since the latter would typically be directly involved in the production process (working alongside employees).

The large class of paid employees was separated by Wright into managers, who, while not owning the enterprise, would be involved in decision making, along with (or in the absence of) the legal owners; supervisors, who are not involved in planning and decision making but who nevertheless exercise authority over others; and workers, who have no ownership rights, decision-making power, or authority over others. One final class grouping, *semi-autonomous workers* (for instance, social workers, university professors, and other salaried professionals), are identified by the relatively greater control they retain over their own work.

Census and *Labour Force Survey* data do not contain information on planning, decision making, and the exercise of authority over others, so these sources cannot be used to profile the Canadian class structure. However, a 1982 national survey designed to examine such issues suggested the following class distribution: large employers (1 percent); small employers (3 percent); the own-account self-employed (12 percent); managers (14 percent); supervisors (11 percent); semi-autonomous workers (16 percent); and workers (43 percent). While a small sample size (less than 1800 respondents) means that these estimates are not precise,[21] the study does demonstrate that the large class of paid workers contains several distinct types. Within this category, some workers (in unionized blue-collar settings, for example) would be much better paid and receive more benefits compared to workers in less secure jobs in the lower-tier services.

Wallace Clement and John Myles use the same data to develop a more concise typology of class relationships. They identify four main classes based on whether an individual controls the means of production and/or commands the labour power of others. In brief, the *capitalist-executive class* contains self-employed owners with three or more employees, along with senior executives and managers who make strategic decisions about how an organization operates. The *new middle class* contains individuals who control and manage other employees, while the *old middle class* are the self-employed with two or fewer employees. The *working class*, the largest category, contains all other employed labour force participants. Thus, the capitalist-executive class controls both production and the employment of other workers. The working class does neither. According to this classification system, in 1982 the majority of employed Canadians (58 percent) were in the working class. About 6 percent were members of the capitalist-executive class, 25 percent were in the new middle class, and 11 percent were in the old middle class (Clement and Myles 1994: 17–18).

By focusing explicitly on power relationships and using a smaller number of categories, Clement and Myles downplay some of the "ownership" distinctions made by Wright, as well as his emphasis on semi-autonomous workers. They also go beyond Wright's class analysis by integrating gender differences in employment outcomes into their model of class relations in post-industrial society.[22] Whichever approach we use, these are still large groupings that disguise major differences in job rewards. Consequently, there is merit in continuing our discussion of labour market outcomes by examining other approaches to the subject.

Furthermore, the class-based approach does not directly address questions about how a society allocates better or worse jobs to individuals and groups, how individual workers might improve their employment situation, or how some groups of workers might manage to exclude others from access to better jobs. Such questions about *labour market processes* are central to the human capital and labour market segmentation perspectives discussed in the remainder of this chapter.

THE HUMAN CAPITAL MODEL OF LABOUR MARKET PROCESSES

We have argued that, on a variety of dimensions, some jobs are better than others, while recognizing that some jobs also require more skills and training. Ideally, jobs with specific requirements would be filled by individuals most suited for these positions. If being suited for a particular job meant that one must first obtain an advanced education, then it would seem only reasonable that, having done so, one would be rewarded with a better job. Stripped to its essentials, these are the basic premises of *human capital theory*, a major economic explanation of how the labour market operates.

This theoretical perspective assumes that a job's rewards are determined by its economic contribution to society. It also predicts that more dangerous and unhealthy jobs should be paid more, since workers would have to be compensated for these greater risks. The model assumes that labour market participants are all competing for jobs in a single, open labour market. Information about available jobs is widely circulated. All potential employees with the necessary qualifications have equal access to job openings. When it comes to choosing whom to hire, employers make rational decisions, based on an assessment of an individual's ability.

In order to "get ahead," it makes sense for job seekers to get more education and training. This means delayed entry into the labour market and forgoing immediate earnings. Yet this is not a permanent loss because by obtaining more education one is investing in *human capital*, which can later be "cashed in" for a better job. In short, the human capital model emphasizes the *supply side* of labour markets, and largely overlooks the behaviour and characteristics of employers and work organizations (the *demand side*). It also ignores questions about class structure and unequal power relationships within the labour market. The human capital perspective on labour markets is premised on a *consensus* view of society, in contrast to the assumptions of *conflict* underlying class-based and labour market segmentation approaches.[23]

The basic logic of human capital theory is compelling, given the evidence that better educated individuals generally are less likely to be unemployed and more likely to hold well-paying, high-status jobs. But it is also difficult to ignore the contrary evidence. As we have seen, the most dangerous and unhealthy jobs are not necessarily the best-paid jobs. There are also many examples of well-trained and highly motivated people working in poorly paid, low-skill jobs. For example, although most recent university graduates have managed to find reasonable jobs, compared to graduates a decade or two ago, a larger minority have had difficulty finding full-time, permanent work that matches their training.[24] The problem is clearly not one of insufficient education or effort.[25] Instead, much of this youth underemployment can be traced directly to organizational downsizing and large-scale cutbacks in the hiring of entry-level workers by employers in both the public and private sectors.

Similarly, many of the wealthiest members of our society are no more educated than the rest of us. However, many of them appear to have had a head start in the career race. A 1986 study of the CEOs of large U.S. companies provides a good example. It showed that almost two-thirds of these wealthy and powerful individuals came from upper-class or upper-middle-class families (Boone et al. 1988). In Canada, we continue to see the powerful influence of huge firms largely controlled by individuals who inherited their money (Yakabuski 2001). Thus, the social class of one's family can strongly influence later labour market outcomes.

Effort and competence do not always correlate neatly with labour market rewards. Indeed, a 1996 Canadian study by the consulting firm KPMG revealed that the CEOs of poorly performing large firms on the Toronto Stock Exchange actually received higher total compensation packages (an average of $682,000) than did the CEOs of the best-performing firms ($657,000). A similar study in 1999 showed that, in some recent years, up to a third of CEOs of companies that had lost money still received performance bonuses. In some cases, these bonuses involved hundreds of thousands of dollars, on top of already huge salaries, while company losses for the year were in the millions of dollars (Church 1996, 2001).

Thus, the relationships among initiative and effort, education and training, and risk, on the one hand, and occupational attainment and income on the other, are not nearly as consistent as the human capital model would suggest. In fact, research shows that some groups are systematically less likely than others to have benefited from their investments in human capital, and that reasonable returns on education and training are obtained only in certain industrial sectors or only from some types of employers. Furthermore, a great deal of evidence shows that some groups in society are more likely to have access to higher education. To understand who gets the good jobs, we must look beyond the labour market to families, schools, and other institutions that shape labour market outcomes.

Social Structure and Occupational Choice

The human capital model attempts to explain how people are sorted into different occupational positions by focusing on the characteristics of individual workers. People whose skills and abilities are more valued by society, and who have invested more in education and training, will be leading candidates for the better jobs, according to the model. Another assumption it makes is that individuals choose among work options, eventually settling in the occupational niche that best suits them. But to what extent do individuals actually have a choice from among the wide range of occupations? Does everyone start the "career race" from the same position, or are some groups disadvantaged at the outset? Does chance also play a role in matching individuals and jobs?

We probably all know a few people who accidentally ended up in their present job, with little planning, or who landed a great position by being in the right place at the right time. We probably also know people who, as children, decided they wanted to be a teacher or a doctor, and then carefully pursued the educational route to these goals. Such behaviour and outcomes are consistent with human capital predictions, although the theory does not ask why these individuals had such high occupational goals.

In fact, we can easily imagine how socioeconomic origins might influence career patterns. It would be hard to picture a member of the wealthy Bronfman or McCain families aspiring to be a bus driver. Similarly, many people who make their living as farmers would probably cite growing up on a farm as a major career influence, while growing up in a working-class family in a single-industry community would likely channel a youth into one of the local mills or mines. It is also clear that many women in today's labour force were constrained in their career choices by society's attitudes about appropriate gender roles. Until quite recently, it was typically assumed that women could work as teachers and nurses, for example, but not in traditionally male occupations (see Chapter 4). Thus, while aptitudes and investments in education do play an important role, it is also clear that for many working Canadians, family circumstances, social class background, and community of origin, along with personal attributes such as gender, race, and ethnicity, are important determinants of educational and occupational choices and outcomes.[26]

Equality of Educational Opportunity

One of the core values underlying our education system is that of *equality of opportunity*. This is the belief that gender, race, ethnicity, family background, region of residence, or other individual characteristics should not be an impediment to obtaining a good education and, through this, access to good jobs and a decent standard of living. As we have already noted, gender differences in levels of education are small (although, as Chapter 4 discusses, there are substantial gender differences in types of educational choices). But research continues to show large differences in educational attainment depending on one's family background.

Analysis of data collected in a 1994 national survey reveals that among Canadian adults age 26 and over, a total of 16 percent had acquired a university degree. But among those from families where one or both parents had a degree, 59 percent had completed university, compared to only 12 percent of those from families where neither parent had a degree. Thus, among previous generations of potential university students, being a member of a family with a tradition of university attendance increased the chances of completing university by almost five times.[27]

How do such patterns of *intergenerational transfer of advantage* develop? An important study from three decades ago began (in 1970) by surveying 9,000 Ontario students (grades 8 through 12), as well as some of their parents. The researchers found that middle- and upper-class parents had high expectations of their children and also served as role models for successful entry into the labour market. Furthermore, more advantaged children had higher assessments of their own ability. All of this translated into higher *educational aspirations* (Porter et al. 1982: 311–19). The original sample members were re-interviewed several years later and asked about their educational attainment. As expected, given their higher aspirations and the financial advantages provided by their parents, middle-class youth were much more likely to have completed high school and gone on to obtain a university education. Another Ontario study of the "class of 1973" replicated these findings and, with a series of follow-up studies over the next two decades, conclusively demonstrated that a more advantaged background leads to higher educational and occupational aspirations, greater educational attainment and, in time, higher status occupations and higher incomes (Anisef et al. 2000).

Since these Ontario studies were begun, the proportion of Canadian youth going on to postsecondary education has risen dramatically because of the opening of new postsecondary educational institutions, continued demand by employers for higher qualifications, and the introduction of new student finance systems.[28] Have social class differences in educational attainment been reduced? Research reveals that the efforts to improve access to higher education largely eliminated gender differences in educational attainment and reduced class differences somewhat (Wanner 1999). Even so, children from more affluent and better-educated families continue to be significantly over-represented among university students (Wotherspoon 1995; Broucker and Lavallée 1998). And, as a recent comparison of Canadian *school-work transition studies* from the 1970s, 1980s, and 1990s demonstrates, children from more advantaged families continue to have higher occupational aspirations (Andres et al. 1999).

Findings from other recent studies of this type clearly reinforce this conclusion. In 1985, we began a longitudinal study of high school graduates in three Canadian cities (Edmonton, Sudbury, and Toronto). As in the 1970s Ontario studies, we found much higher educational aspirations among young people from higher-SES families. For example, 64 percent of high-school graduates from families where at least one parent had a supervisory, managerial, or professional occupation planned to obtain a university degree, compared with only 38 percent of those from lower-SES families. Four years later in 1989, we observed that 43 percent of sample members from higher-SES families had attended university during at least three of the four intervening years, compared with only 21 percent of those from lower-SES families.

A more detailed analysis of the Edmonton sample, and of a similar 1989-93 study in Vancouver, revealed that respondents from families where at least one parent had a university degree were much more likely to graduate from university themselves. In Edmonton, the odds of acquiring a university degree were about three times higher for respondents from families with a university-attendance tradition, compared to those whose parents were not university-educated. In Vancouver, the difference was not as large. Even so, 48 percent of sample members with a university-educated parent obtained a degree within four years of leaving high school, compared to only 25 percent of those whose parents did not have a degree (Andres and Krahn 1999).[29]

Economic Advantage and Cultural Capital

The fact that children of university-educated parents are more likely to graduate from university themselves is not simply a function of their higher educational and occupational aspirations. More highly educated parents also have higher incomes, on average, and more money means access to more and better postsecondary education (Davies and Guppy 1997). The rapid expansion of Canada's post-secondary system several decades ago increased access to higher education, and the introduction of new student finance systems allowed more children of working-class parents to take advantage of the new universities, community colleges, and technical schools. However, some of these gains were lost in the second half of the 1990s when post-secondary tuition fees began to rise rapidly, as did student loan debts.[30]

So, parents' money continues to matter. But the process whereby advantaged backgrounds translate into educational success and better jobs begins long before students reach the end of their high school studies and begin to pay university and college tuition fees. Statistics Canada's *National Survey of Children and Youth* reveals the disturbing fact that children in Canada's poorest families are three times more likely than children of the wealthy to be in remedial education classes at school. In contrast, the most advantaged children are twice as likely to be in classes for "gifted" students (Mitchell 1997). A long list of studies has also demonstrated that, even though the high school dropout rate has been declining over the past few decades, teenagers from less affluent families are still much more likely to leave school without a diploma.[31]

Children in Canada's poorest families frequently go to school hungry. Parents with low incomes may have to work long hours to cover basic living costs, and will have less time and money to invest in their children's education. The schools in poorer neighbourhoods may also have fewer resources. These are among the more obvious explanations of the relationship between economic disadvantage and less successful educational outcomes. In his analysis of social stratification systems, Pierre Bourdieu introduces the concept of *cultural capital* to further explain why middle-class youth perform better in the education system. Schools encourage and reward the language, beliefs, behaviour, and competencies of the more powerful groups in society. Middle-class youth bring more of this cultural capital to school with them, and so have a distinct advantage. They are more likely to speak like their teachers, to be comfortable in a verbal and symbolic environment, to know something about the subjects being taught, to have additional skills (music training, for example), and to have access to learning resources in their home.[32]

A 1994 national survey of Canadian adults provides some examples of this process. Considering only those respondents with children aged 6 to 18, 78 percent of those with a university degree reported that their children read every day for pleasure, and 70 percent stated that their children had a specified daily time for reading. Among parents without a university degree, only 41 percent said that their children read daily, while 49 percent reported a specified daily time when their children read at home.[33]

Thus, schools are not neutral institutions. Instead, they are part of the process whereby structural inequalities and power differences within society are reproduced, within and across generations, because the culture of the more powerful classes is embedded within them. Obviously, not all middle-class youth do well in school, and not all children from less affluent families do poorly. But the probability of doing well in school, graduating from high school, successfully completing postsecondary studies, and choosing an educational path that leads to a higher-status, better-paying job is much greater for middle-class youth.

Differences by Gender and Region

Several decades ago, Canadian studies showed that young women had lower educational and occupational aspirations than young men. More recent studies of high school graduates show equivalent aspiration levels among young women and men (Andres et al. 1999), although female and male teenagers still report quite different types of specific career goals. As female labour force participation has increased and gender role attitudes have slowly changed, the proportion of young women going on to higher education has risen to match the male rates. However, young women are still more likely to enroll in traditional "female" areas of study such as education, nursing, and the arts and humanities. As the next chapter documents, gender differences in educational choice continue to shape labour market outcomes for women and men.

The Ontario studies from the 1970s also examined the effects of students' region of residence on educational and occupational aspirations. The researchers noted that rural youth were less likely to plan on higher education, and speculated that the more "limited horizons" of rural youth might be due to their underexposure to attitudes favouring higher education. In addition, the absence of local institutions of higher learning forces rural youth to leave their home communities to go to college or university, making the transition more difficult. Recent studies in Nova Scotia and British Columbia reinforce such conclusions about problems faced by rural youth.[34] Consequently, rural youth acquire less post-secondary education than young people in large urban centres, limiting their occupational choices and their future earning potential.

Occupational Mobility Research

The term *social mobility* generally describes how individuals or groups move from one position within a social hierarchy to another. For example, we might find that the status of an immigrant group has risen over several generations in Canada. Or we might document the misfortunes of previously well-off individuals (and their families) who, because of industrial restructuring, lost their jobs and became downwardly mobile.[35] Because social standing is to a great extent influenced by occupational position, most social mobility research has examined occupational mobility.

We can usefully distinguish between *intergenerational* and *intragenerational* mobility.[36] The former involves comparisons between an individual's occupational status and that of someone in a previous generation, most frequently his or her parent (or grandparent). The latter involves comparisons between an individual's present and previous occupations.

There is also an important difference between *structural mobility* and *circulatory (or exchange) mobility*. Chapters 1 and 2 documented massive changes in industrial capitalist societies over the past century: a huge decline in agriculture and a parallel expansion of the urban workforce, the rise of large bureaucracies, and extensive growth in the service industries. These changes precipitated enormous growth in white-collar occupations. Because of this occupational shift, we would expect to find much larger proportions of labour force participants in middle-level occupations today than a generation or two ago.

Using data from surveys asking respondents about their occupation and the occupations of their parents, researchers employ sophisticated statistical techniques to determine how much structural mobility has been occurring within a society. Such research addresses a potentially more interesting question: how much intergenerational mobility do we observe independent of the effects of changing occupational structures—in other words, how open is a given society to occupational mobility?

A basic democratic value is that the most talented people end up in the more responsible and rewarding jobs. If this were the case, we would observe a great deal of circulatory mobility across generations, rather than a closed society in which occupational positions are typically inherited. Theoretically, circulatory intergenerational mobility occurs when those with more talent, skill, training, and motivation are able to move into the higher occupational positions. Merit, not social origin, determines occupational position. But no society has ever realized the goal of becoming a true *meritocracy*, raising the question: To what degree are occupational position and social status inherited in a given society?

An equally interesting question is whether some societies are more open than others to occupational mobility. Early mobility studies examined intergenerational mobility across three basic occupational categories—agricultural, manual, and nonmanual work. In 1959, Seymour Martin Lipset and Reinhard Bendix compared the United States with a number of European countries. Many might have predicted that occupational inheritance would be more pronounced in European countries, with their entrenched class structures, and less significant in the United States, with its stronger democratic values. However, few important cross-national differences were observed.[37] Studies using more recent data (from the 1970s and 1980s) and a larger number of occupational categories suggest few differences between mobility patterns and trends in Canada and the United States. However, they do indicate that Canada may have a somewhat more open stratification system than Sweden, the United Kingdom, France, and the Netherlands.[38]

To examine shifts over time in Canadian mobility patterns, researchers have compared results from two national surveys on occupational mobility, the first completed in 1973 and the second in 1986. The Canadian occupational structure became somewhat more open for both women and men, but in different ways. The steep decline in agricultural employment since the middle of the twentieth century meant that many men moved out of the agricultural occupations held by their fathers. For women, the shift was away from the housework that had been the main female occupation for their mothers' generation. For both, expansion of educational opportunities, leading to higher status occupations, played an important role (Wanner 1993).

These Canadian mobility studies find only a limited amount of direct occupational inheritance across generations and conclude that the occupational stratification system became somewhat more open during the 1970s and 1980s. Yet those at or near the top of the occupational hierarchy are still more likely to pass their advantages on to their children: "Canada is still a stratified society characterized by a considerable amount of inheritance of privilege" (Wanner 1993: 175). However, the most recent mobility study was conducted in 1986. Since then, there have been profound changes in the Canadian labour market. As we have seen, young Canadians have been particularly disadvantaged. If another Canadian occupational mobility study were to be conducted, would we still find the trend toward a more open stratification system?[39]

Status Attainment Research

Social mobility and *status attainment* studies address similar questions, but the latter focus more explicitly on intragenerational mobility and on the role of education in determining occupational outcomes. The most recent national Canadian status attainment study was conducted in 1986.[40] The researchers used Blishen scores to index the status of respondents' current and first occupations, as well as those of their fathers. The study found that the most important determinant of an individual's current job is his or her first job, that is, the level at which the person enters the labour market. In turn, the status of that first job is heavily influenced by the amount of education obtained.

Taken alone, these findings lend support to the human capital model—greater investments in education allow one to enter the labour market at a higher level, and, consequently, to move up to even higher status positions. However, the intergenerational component of the status attainment model also yields clear evidence of status inheritance by way of education. Canadians with more education (and, hence, who have entered the labour market at higher levels and have advanced further) tend to come from families with well-educated parents in high-status occupations.

While these are not new insights, they do reinforce our earlier conclusions. First, education strongly influences occupational outcomes. Second, parents' occupational status is often transmitted to their children via differences in the amount of children's educational attainment. Status attainment studies do not explain how social origin affects labour market opportunities, but we have already mentioned some of the processes. Obviously, wealthier parents can afford more (and better) education for their children, and can provide the cultural capital needed to succeed in school. They can have a strong influence on aspirations. Being better situated in the labour market, they may also be able to provide more information about how to find good jobs or to put their children in touch with useful contacts.

The 1986 *General Social Survey* also revealed that, compared with men, women in the Canadian labour force had completed more years of schooling (12.9 years versus 12.3 years). This translated into a slightly higher-status first job, but the advantage ended there; men had experienced more upward mobility within their own career (intragenerational mobility). Canadian-born men had moved up 3.6 points on the Blishen occupational status scale, compared with 1.6 points for Canadian-born women. The comparable figures for foreign-born men and women were 1.9 and 0.2 points, respectively (Creese et al. 1991: Chapter 7).

Despite marginally higher levels of education, women are less able to "cash in" these credentials for jobs with career potential. This may partly be due to the different types of education completed by women and men. If women become nurses and men become engineers, for example, then perhaps the higher status (and pay) of men's jobs makes sense. But this line of reasoning simply raises other questions: Why do traditionally female jobs have lower status and less pay? Are the contributions made by individuals in these occupations really less valuable to society?

A large part of the female–male difference in career mobility is a function of the gender-segregated nature of the labour market; women are more likely to be employed in industries and occupations where promotion opportunities are limited. Some of the gender difference in mobility also can be traced to women's interrupted careers due to child-rearing responsibilities. The human capital model would predict that less career experience (as a result of interruptions) would mean less upward mobility. To fully understand the careers of women and men, we must also examine the societal values and institutions that put the biggest share of responsibility for child rearing on women (see Chapter 4).

The 1986 study also demonstrated that foreign-born Canadians had higher-status social origins, more education, and higher-status first jobs. The explanation is quite simple: Canadian immigration policies over the last few decades have favoured well-educated and higher-status applicants. But these more advantaged beginnings did not translate into more upward career mobility. Foreign-born Canadians, particularly women, experienced little upward movement in the course of their careers. Limited knowledge of the labour market, language difficulties, licensing requirements that keep some immigrants from practising in their area of training, and discrimination in hiring and promotion can create substantial career barriers (Krahn et al. 2000).

In summary, we have found some support for the human capital model by identifying the central role education plays in determining one's occupational status and income. However, this must be weighed against evidence of considerable status inheritance, frequently passed on through the better education obtained by children in more well-to-do families. The fact that access to good education is not all that equal suggests that, to some degree, the issue of who gets the good jobs is class-based rather than an outcome of merit-based labour market processes.

By further examining the status attainment process, we observed that the Canadian labour market is not equally open to all labour force participants. Some groups of workers—men and individuals born in Canada, for example— are better able to cash in their education and training for higher-status and higher-income jobs. So there may be more than one labour market in operation, a possibility not considered by the human capital model. And factors other than skill, training, and effort may determine access to preferred jobs.

LABOUR MARKET SEGMENTATION

Labour market segmentation researchers begin with the proposition that there is not a single, open labour market operating in our society. Instead, better and worse jobs tend to be found in different settings and are usually obtained in distinctly different ways. Certain types of labour force participants (women and visible minorities, for example) are concentrated in the poorer jobs.

Segmentation theories also highlight the slim chances of moving out of the *secondary labour market* into jobs in the *primary labour market*. This is a key proposition, since the human capital model does not deny that some jobs are better than others; it simply maintains that those individuals who have the most ability and initiative and who have made the largest investment in education and training will be more likely found in the highly skilled and rewarding jobs. However, the segmentation perspective emphasizes the barriers that limit access for many qualified individuals into the primary labour market, along with the ability of primary labour market participants to maintain their more advantaged position.[41]

There are actually several varieties of labour market segmentation research. All share these basic propositions, but they differ in their explanations of the origins of segmentation and in their breadth of analysis. The broader dual economy approach has evolved out of the work of Marxist scholars tracing the growth of dual economic sectors in industrial capitalist societies. The narrower approach has grown out of studies of labour market dynamics within private-sector firms and government bureaucracies (internal labour markets), and out of examinations of tactics used by various occupational and professional groups to restrict entry into their field of work (labour market shelters).

Dual Economies

The *dual economy* model assumes that an earlier era of *competitive capitalism* was succeeded in the twentieth century by an age of *monopoly capitalism*.[42] Thus, a few large and powerful firms came to dominate automobile manufacturing, the oil and mining industries, the transportation sector (airlines and railways), and the computer industry, for example. Similarly, the finance sector came to be controlled by a handful of large banks, investment firms, and insurance companies. These dominant firms exert considerable control over suppliers and markets and are also able to manipulate their political environment. Examples of the power of such firms include instances in which automobile manufacturers have been able to limit foreign imports, mining and oil companies have influenced government environmental policies, and a handful of giant computer companies have come to dominate the IT industry.

Although global economic restructuring during the last decade has led to more intense competition among some of these large *core sector* firms, they still operate in an economic environment very different from the *periphery sector*, where we find numerous smaller firms. Because they have less control over their environment and generally face more intense competition, such businesses have a much greater chance of failure. Many lower-tier service-sector firms (for example, small retail shops and restaurants) would be found here, as would some smaller firms in the upper-tier services (for example, small office supply firms in the business services) and in the goods-producing sector (for example, small manufacturing companies).

Such enterprises are typically less profitable since they cannot control their markets and suppliers, they have low capital investments, and they are often less technologically advanced and generally more labour-intensive. Compared with the core sector firms, these enterprises typically do not require the same level of skill, education, and commitment from employees. Indeed, replaceable unskilled or semiskilled employees are often ideal.

This segmentation model basically proposes that the core sector contains a primary labour market with better jobs, while the periphery sector contains secondary labour markets. Capital-intensive core enterprises, by definition, require fewer workers to equal or exceed the productivity of firms that are more labour-intensive, although they frequently require workers who are more highly trained and better educated than those hired in the periphery sector. The large and bureaucratic nature of these enterprises means that there are reasonably good opportunities for upward mobility. The workers in these types of enterprises tend to be well paid and to have good benefit packages, are more likely to receive training, and may have greater job security.[43] Some segmentation writers have also placed government employees in the primary labour market because of the above-average job rewards that they typically receive.

Why would core sector employers be willing to pay more than the going rates in the secondary labour market? Part of the answer lies in the collective strength of labour unions and professional associations, which have been far more active in the primary sector. Labour market segmentation theorists have also argued that it would be too costly for core sector firms not to pay well. These enterprises have sizable capital investments and, thus, wish to avoid costly shutdowns due to labour disputes. High labour turnover would lead to the expense of training many new employees. Hence, it is simply good business practice to offer job security (negotiated with a union, if necessary), provide generous wage and benefit packages, and attempt to improve working conditions. Besides, higher profit margins mean that these employers can afford to pay more.

In the peripheral sector, employers are much less likely to provide high wages, extensive benefits, and long-term job security. We may also find more unhealthy working environments in this sector. Here, smaller profit margins, more intense competition, difficulties in imposing increased labour costs on customers, and greater vulnerability to economic cycles keep wage levels down. In addition, labour turnover is less of a problem for periphery sector employers; lower skill requirements and little on-the-job training make workers easily replaceable. Consequently, low-paying jobs are common and labour turnover is high, making union organizing more difficult.[44] The term *job ghettos* has frequently been used to describe work in such labour markets. Job insecurity, higher chances of unemployment, and irregular career earning patterns are a fact of life in secondary labour markets.

An interesting example of work in a secondary labour market is provided by Ester Reiter (1991), who writes about the time she spent working in a Burger King restaurant in Toronto. The restaurant, like most other enterprises in the fast-food industry, relied heavily on student labour, since few other workers would be available to work at a job that was part-time, had irregular hours, paid very little, and offered virtually no additional benefits. However, some middle-aged women were also employed in this industry, since such work allowed them to arrange their hours of work around family responsibilities. In addition, the industry employed recent immigrants who could not find better jobs.

Reiter describes how, in her particular restaurant, shifts were shortened to three hours so that employees could be expected to work hard for the duration of the shift without taking a break. The company actively discouraged the unionization of its employees, believing that its ability to control workers and the speed of work would be handicapped (as would its ability to pay very low wages). The work was highly standardized; the food-preparation and cash-register technology, along with specific rules for almost all tasks, left workers with virtually no opportunity to make decisions of any kind. In short, employees were interchangeable and easily replaced, as they are in many such workplaces.

Internal Labour Markets

There are typically fewer chances for career mobility within firms in the periphery sector. A carwash attendant or a mechanic in a small automobile repair shop would have few promotion prospects simply because the workplace would not have a bureaucratic hierarchy with well-defined career ladders. But many employees of IBM, Shell Canada, the Royal Bank, and other large private-sector firms do have such mobility opportunities, as do university professors, government employees, and many health care workers. In contrast to the often dead-end jobs within secondary labour markets, most large corporations and public institutions have a well-developed internal training and promotion system, or what may be called an *internal labour market*. From the perspective of the work organization, such internal labour markets help retain skilled and valuable employees by providing career incentives and also transmit important skills and knowledge among employees. From the perspective of employees, internal labour markets mean additional job security and career opportunities (Stark 1988: 327).

Researchers who study internal labour markets have usually sidestepped larger questions about the changing nature of capitalism, concentrating instead on specific features of these self-contained labour markets. Focus has been on *ports of entry*, specifically, the limited number of entry-level jobs that are typically the only way into such an internal labour market; *mobility chains*, or career ladders, through which employees make their way during their career within the organization; and training systems and seniority rules, which govern movement through the ranks.[45] Essentially, these concepts elaborate Max Weber's theory of bureaucracy while also emphasizing the career advantages held by workers in such labour markets.

There is some obvious overlap between studies of internal labour markets and the broader dual economy perspective. Early segmentation researchers tended to assume that all core sector firms contain well-developed internal labour markets open to all employees. However, there are important exceptions. For example, many major corporations have long career ladders, but these are open to only some of their employees. Clerical workers (usually women) are often restricted from moving into higher ranks (Diprete and Soule 1988; Hachen 1988). Some large corporations, like Burger King, consist of many small workplaces that have all the characteristics of a secondary labour market. In addition, corporation and government downsizing, and increased use of temporary and other nonstandard workers (Vosko 2000) means that the number of advantaged workers in internal labour markets has declined.

Labour Market Shelters: Unions and Professions

Most internal labour markets have been put in place by employers. In contrast, unions and professional associations have tried to improve job and income security for their members by setting up *labour market shelters*, sometimes within specific work organizations but more often spanning a large number of similar types of workplaces (Ashton 1986; see Chapter 7). Some occupational groups have restricted access to certain types of work since government legislation requires that such tasks be completed only by certified trades (for example, electricians). Public safety is the rationale for this legislation, but it also serves to protect the jobs and (relatively high) incomes of members of these often unionized trades.

Industrial unions, such as the Canadian Auto Workers, bargain collectively with employers to determine the seniority rules, promotion procedures, and pay rates within manufacturing establishments (see Chapter 7). Such contracts shelter these industrial workers from the risk of job loss or pay cuts for a specified period of time. Negotiated staffing restrictions also restrict nonmembers from access to the better jobs by giving laid-off members priority if new jobs open up.

Professional associations using tactics different from those of unions also serve as labour market shelters for their members. *Professions* have been distinguished from occupations in a variety of ways, but certain key features appear in most definitions. Professionals such as doctors, lawyers, engineers, and psychologists work with specialized knowledge acquired through extensive formal education in professional schools. They enjoy a high level of work autonomy and are frequently self-regulating, policing themselves through their own professional associations. Professionals also exercise considerable power over their clients and other lower-status occupational groups, and typically emphasize the altruistic nature of their work.

For example, doctors spend many years training in medical schools where they acquire knowledge specific to their profession. They go on to determine their own working conditions in virtually all health care institutions. In fact, in the past decades, many doctors have increased their work autonomy by setting up professional corporations. Through their own professional associations, doctors can censure colleagues who have acted unprofessionally in the course of their work. Doctors have a great deal of power over their patients and those in assisting occupations, such as nurses and medical laboratory technicians. Finally, members of this profession emphasize their code of ethics, by which they are committed to preserving human life above all other objectives.

In short, professions are far more powerful than occupations.[46] Randall Collins (1990) uses the term *market closure* to describe the ability of professionals to shape the labour market to their advantage, rather than simply responding to it, as do most occupational groups. Like the craft guilds of an earlier era, or higher castes in India's caste-stratified society, professional groups in contemporary Western society can restrict others from doing their type of work by controlling entry into their profession. Professional associations have close relationships with their (typically university-based) professional schools and can strongly influence both course content and entrance quotas. Many professional groups have actively lobbied for and obtained legislation that both requires practitioners of their profession to be officially licensed and prohibits anyone else from performing certain tasks. Over time, however, some occupational groups have gained more autonomy and power, while others may have experienced a process of deprofessionalization.[47]

Barriers to Primary Labour Market Entry

Returning to our original focus on structural barriers to labour market movement, we can now see how internal labour markets and labour market shelters not only provide more work rewards to some groups of labour market participants but also contribute to their ability to maintain labour market closure. Generally, there are only a limited number of positions within the primary labour market, and entry is often restricted to those with the proper credentials—a degree, union membership, or professional certification. Often, superior credentials (an MBA from a prestigious university, for example) will further improve one's chances of getting into the system and moving up through it. And, as we argued earlier, a higher-SES background typically gives one a significant head start.[48]

Specific credentials are not needed for all jobs in the primary labour market, but information about vacancies is not always widely distributed. In some cases, it may be passed only through small and informal networks. Since a large portion of all jobs are obtained through personal referrals, it is clear that access to information is extremely important. Without contacts within the primary labour market, qualified applicants might never be aware of job openings.

Barriers to mobility out of the secondary labour market may also be more subtle. For some individuals, a history of employment in marginal jobs may itself act as a barrier. In some regions of Canada, the prevalence of seasonal work means that many people are forced into an annual cycle where income is obtained from part-year jobs, employment insurance, and welfare assistance. A work record showing frequent layoffs or job changes may simply be reflecting the nature of the local labour market. But it could also be interpreted as an indication of unstable work habits. Similarly, a long sequence of temporary jobs, a common experience for many well-educated and highly motivated young Canadians, could nevertheless handicap them because employers might assume the problem originates with the job applicant rather than the labour market.[49]

Geography itself can limit one's work opportunities. A highly motivated and skilled worker living in Newfoundland, where the cod fishery has been decimated (Palmer and Sinclair 1997), or in Uranium City after the mine was closed, is clearly at a disadvantage compared with residents of large cities in Ontario or Alberta where unemployment rates have historically been much lower. Our discussion in Chapter 2 of employment opportunities in single-industry communities made the same point. There are simply fewer good jobs available outside of the wealthier regions of Canada.

In addition, residents of the hinterland regions are less likely to have obtained the credentials necessary for participation in primary labour markets. Dianne Looker's study of rural Nova Scotia youth leaving high school and entering the labour market highlights some of these geographic disadvantages. Compared with urban youth in Halifax and Hamilton, rural youth had less work experience, fewer course options while in school, and less knowledge about the labour market. They were also more likely to evaluate local labour market opportunities negatively, and were much more likely to conclude that they would have to leave their communities to find reasonable jobs.[50]

Some years ago, a research team in Atlantic Canada spent considerable time examining that region's employment opportunities. They argued that the high level of poverty and unemployment in the region cannot simply be explained with reference to inadequate education, training, or effort on the part of local residents. A "casualty" model of poverty, which would hold that most of the poor are incapable of working, or of working in good jobs, does not fit the facts. Rather, an explanation that focuses on the nature of the local labour market is much more useful. In short, many Atlantic Canadians have spent their working lives in a *marginal work world* where low pay, few benefits, limited career opportunities, and little job security are a way of life.[51]

Historical Patterns of Racial and Ethnic Discrimination

Employer *discrimination* in hiring and promotion can also block movement into better jobs, thus contributing to the overrepresentation of specific disadvantaged groups in secondary labour markets. Before we discuss the forms such discrimination might now take, it is instructive to look back in Canadian history at some examples of officially sanctioned racial and ethnic discrimination.

After Canada was colonized, members of various Aboriginal nations frequently participated in the pre-industrial labour market, acting as guides, fighting for the French against the English (and vice versa), and providing the furs sought by the trading companies for their European markets.[52] But as central Canada began to industrialize, and later as the West was opened for settlement, the traditional economies of the Aboriginal nations in these regions were largely destroyed. Usually the presence of Aboriginal groups was seen as an impediment to economic development. The most common solution was to place them on reservations, out of the way.

Nevertheless, some Aboriginal workers were employed in the resource industries (forestry, mining, and commercial fishing and canning, for example), in railway construction, and in agriculture, particularly in Western Canada. Not all of this paid employment was completely voluntary. For example, in the 1950s and 1960s, by cutting off social assistance benefits, the provincial and federal governments forced many Aboriginal workers to migrate to southern Alberta to work in the sugar beet industry (Laliberte and Satzewich 1999). But the decline in demand for large numbers of unskilled and semiskilled workers in Canada's resource and transportation industries also meant declining wage-labour opportunities for Aboriginals. Even when jobs were available for Native workers, racist attitudes and labour market discrimination were rampant (Knight 1978). This should not be surprising in a society that clearly viewed members of First Nations as second-class citizens, not even allowing them to vote until 1960.

As Canada industrialized in the late 19th century, manufacturing enterprises began to take root in Quebec and Ontario. However, patterns of ethnic stratification based on English ownership of key industries meant that French-Canadian workers were typically underrepresented in the higher-status, better-paying positions. For example, in 1938 in the Quebec industrial town of "Cantonville," French Canadians provided most of the factory labour while English-speaking outsiders filled the management and technical positions (Hughes 1943: 46). French-Canadian men frequently also worked as labourers in the natural resource sector and in railway construction where discrimination on the part of English-Canadian employers and supervisors was common.

During the 1880s, many Chinese men were recruited to work on railway construction in Western Canada and in the resource-based industries. They were generally paid about one-half to two-thirds of what others received for the same job and encountered a great deal of hostility from the white population (Anderson 1991: 35). Labour unions lobbied for legislation restricting Chinese workers from entering specific (better paid) trades. Chinese workers were forced into marginal jobs in a racially split British Columbia labour market. In addition, the British Columbia government passed legislation that severely restricted the civil rights of Chinese residents of the province. For its part, the federal government required Chinese immigrants to pay a head tax on entering Canada, while other immigrants did not, and, later, passed the Chinese Immigration Act which, for several decades, virtually stopped all Chinese immigrants from entering the country (Li 1982; Anderson 1991).

Perhaps the discrimination faced by Chinese workers was the result of white workers' fears that they would lose their jobs to nonwhites who were willing to work for lower wages. However, studies of this era suggest that racist attitudes—fears about the impact of too many Asian immigrants on a white, Anglophone society—were frequently the underlying source of publicly expressed concerns about job loss and wage cuts. White workers seldom tried to bring Chinese workers into their unions (a tactic that would have reduced employers' ability to pay lower wages to nonwhites), even though the latter frequently showed interest in collectively opposing the actions of employers.[53]

Peter Li (1982) has described how, in the first half of the 20th century (1910 to 1947), Chinese Canadians living in the Prairie provinces encountered similar forms of racial discrimination. Barred from entry into many trades and professions, Chinese workers were mostly restricted to employment in *ethnic business enclaves*, where, by supporting one another and working extremely hard, they could make a living. Chinese restaurants and laundries, for example, provided employment for many members of the Prairie Chinese community.

Similar experiences of racial discrimination were encountered by Black Canadians, many of whom were former American slaves who had settled in the area west of Toronto to the Detroit River. During the mid-19th century, white residents frequently lobbied to have Blacks sent back to their former owners in the United States (Pentland 1981: 1–6). By the 1860s, officially sanctioned discrimination against Blacks had largely disappeared, but labour market discrimination continued. For example, many Blacks worked for railway companies but were restricted to a limited number of lower-paying jobs, such as sleeping-car porter. White workers were found in the better-paying, less menial jobs such as sleeping-car conductor or dining-car steward. The system was supported by societal values that took for granted that Blacks should work in menial jobs. It wasn't until 1964 that the arrangements (embedded in the contracts between railway companies and their unions) that legitimized this *racially split labour market* were completely abolished (Calliste 1987).

Disadvantaged Groups in Today's Labour Market

Today, labour laws and human rights legislation make it more difficult for employers to discriminate against specific types of labour market participants. In fact, a series of recent studies have demonstrated that French-English differences in educational attainment and income have disappeared.[54] Nevertheless, some groups are still severely disadvantaged in the labour market. Some of this inequality of employment opportunity results from unequal access to higher education and specialized training. Some of it is a product of regional differences in employment opportunities. But there is also evidence of continued patterns of discrimination in hiring and promotion in the Canadian labour market, although it is typically not as blatant and institutionalized as in the past.

By 1996, visible minorities (excluding Aboriginal Canadians) made up 11 percent of the adult (age 15 and older) Canadian population (a total of 3.2 million people). Seventy percent of these Canadians were immigrants (born outside of Canada). Compared to the rest of the adult population, nonwhites are more likely to have a university degree and more likely to be in the labour force, in part because of their somewhat younger age profile. Despite this, they are also somewhat more likely to be unemployed (Latin American, South Asian, and Black Canadians are more likely to be unemployed, while Chinese and Japanese Canadians have lower-than-average unemployment rates). As for occupational differences, visible minority males are overrepresented in both lower- and higher-status occupations, while nonwhite women are heavily overrepresented in lower-paying, low-skill jobs. Overall, visible minority Canadians report significantly lower incomes than the population as a whole, and this difference is growing. (Kazemipur and Halli 2001).[55]

Since Canadian immigration policies favour better-educated immigrants, the higher education and higher-status occupations (at least for some men) are not surprising. Nevertheless, it is also apparent that large proportions of visible minority women, along with many men, are employed in the secondary labour market. Language difficulties, few personal contacts within the primary labour market, and professional licensing regulations that often keep well-educated immigrants from practising their professions are part of the explanation. For example, a 1999 study of recent refugees who had settled in Alberta showed that, even though 39 percent had held management and professional positions in their home country, only 11 percent had found similar employment in Canada (Krahn et al. 2000). For many of the former professionals interviewed in this study, the problem lay in Canadian employers and educational institutions being unwilling to recognize their foreign credentials.

In addition, prejudiced attitudes on the part of employers continue to keep some members of visible minority groups from improving their employment prospects. A 1984 study in Toronto compared the experiences of Black and White subjects, with equivalent qualifications, in applying for the same job. Blacks obtained fewer interviews and job offers, and were frequently told that the advertised position was filled, even though, in some cases, a White member of the research team was offered the same job only minutes later. In another part of the same study, subjects with names and accents identifying them as members of nonwhite or immigrant groups telephoned for job interviews. Out of a total of 237 advertised positions, South Asian subjects were told that the job was no longer available 44 percent of the time, while 36 percent of Black West Indians and 31 percent of White immigrant subjects were told this. But only 13 percent of white nonimmigrant subjects got this response (Henry and Ginzberg 1985).

A 1989 replication of this study revealed no discrimination against Blacks in the in-person portion of the study. However, the telephone survey showed that employers still favoured job applicants who had no accents (Economic Council of Canada 1991: 30). Thus, there is some evidence that prejudiced attitudes against hiring visible minorities may be decreasing, at least in Toronto where the proportion of visible minorities is the highest in the country. Or employers may have become more cautious about discriminating in a face-to-face situation. While a more recent replication of this particular study has not been completed, a series of focus groups with visible minority workers conducted in Toronto, Montreal, Halifax, Winnipeg, and Vancouver in 2000 revealed many instances of perceived employment-related discrimination. Thus, there is evidence that racial discrimination continues to handicap visible minorities seeking to improve their employment situation.[56]

While some members of visible minority groups (usually men with higher educational credentials) do find professional, technical, and managerial jobs in the primary labour market, many others are concentrated in a limited number of marginal occupations in the secondary labour market—taxi drivers, janitors, domestic workers, parking lot attendants, security guards, and workers in ethnic restaurants are obvious examples. Because of the high proportion of workers from specific ethnic groups in some of these occupations (airport taxi services in some Canadian cities, for example), we might call them *ethnic business enclaves.*

A somewhat different picture emerges of the underlying causes of Aboriginal Canadians' severely disadvantaged labour market position. Aboriginal labour market participation rates have been low for decades. In turn, unemployment and poverty rates in their communities have been extremely high. Aboriginal Canadians living in larger urban centres also have a much more precarious labour market status. When employed, either in their own communities or elsewhere, they have been heavily overrepresented in the secondary labour market. The 1996 Census revealed that fewer Aboriginals (aged 15 and older) than non-Aboriginal Canadians reported employment income (57% versus 66%). Among those who did, their average 1995 income was 34 percent below the national average.[57] Why?

On average, Aboriginal Canadians are not as well educated as other Canadians (Statistics Canada 1994; Davies and Guppy 1998). Access to good schooling has been a serious problem for generations, as has racism and discrimination within the education system (Pauls 1996). But lack of education does not fully explain their marginal labour market position. Many live in isolated communities where employment opportunities are severely limited. Large industrial megaprojects in Northern Canada (mines, mills, dams, and so on) have typically offered only limited employment to residents of local Aboriginal communities while, at the same time, these projects have often damaged traditional hunting, trapping, and fishing economies and have undermined traditional culture (Waldram 1987; Stabler and Howe 1990; Niezen 1993).

Aboriginal Canadians who seek employment in larger urban settings consequently bring with them a patchy employment record, which can seriously restrict entry into the primary labour market. They may also often encounter prejudice among employers which, along with a lack of contacts and limited job-search resources (such as transportation), further handicap them in their search for satisfactory employment. Thus, an explanation for the disadvantaged labour market position of Aboriginal Canadians must examine the many other factors that contribute to the segmenting of the Canadian labour market.

Disabled Canadians are another group characterized by low labour force participation and high unemployment rates, fewer hours of work, and lower incomes. As with the Aboriginal population, disabled people who do manage to obtain employment are frequently found working in low-skill, poorly paid jobs in the secondary labour market.[58] A study from the early 1990s estimated the number of working-age disabled Canadians at 1.8 million, and concluded that about 80 percent were either unemployed or underemployed (McKay 1991). While some of these individuals were incapable of paid employment of any kind, many could have been making much more useful contributions in the workplace.

Huge barriers keep disabled people from obtaining satisfactory employment. Many employers, and even some of those involved in assisting the disabled, assume that all those with visual, hearing, cognitive, and movement handicaps are equally impaired, though many of these individuals could cope well in a variety of jobs, with limited assistance. Some employers are uncomfortable with or fearful of disabled people. While a significant number of employers say they would hire disabled workers, few actually do so. In addition, many disabled people also face serious transportation problems and are held back by buildings designed without their special needs in mind.[59] While there has been a little progress in improving their labour market position in recent years, disabled people continue to be overrepresented in the secondary labour market. In fact, many find work only in special institutional settings where pay rates are low and career opportunities are nonexistent.

Women have faced prejudice and discrimination in the Canadian labour market for decades. Employment and human rights legislation have eliminated much of the systemic discrimination against women in recent decades, but more subtle forms of discriminatory hiring and promotion behaviour remain. For example, male employers or managers may sometimes decide that a female applicant, no matter how qualified, does not have the personality supposedly needed for a particular high-level position, or the career commitment that the corporation thinks it requires. We will address such labour force difficulties and their effects in more detail in the next chapter.

This discussion of discrimination has focused so far on the experiences of visible minorities, Aboriginal Canadians, disabled people, and women, the four groups of labour force participants designated for special attention in the federal government's efforts to promote *employment equity*. But other groups that can also encounter discrimination are not necessarily protected by legislation.

Age discrimination occurs when older workers, laid off in a plant shutdown and applying for another core sector job, are rejected in favour of younger applicants because of the belief that older workers are harder to retrain and will have difficulty adapting to new technologies. On the other hand, youth attempting to find their first permanent job also face age discrimination. Finding employment in the part-time student labour market within the lower-tier services is generally much less difficult than getting an interview for a full-time career position in a major corporation or a government department, even if one has the necessary educational qualifications. "Lack of experience" is a term heard all too frequently by unsuccessful young job applicants.

Discrimination on the basis of sexual orientation may be prohibited by human rights legislation, but this does not ensure that all employers act accordingly. For example, in 1991 in Alberta, a postsecondary educational institution (with funding from a specific religious denomination) fired a gay instructor, arguing that his sexual orientation was not acceptable among the supporters of the school. The provincial courts rejected his claim that this discriminatory behaviour on the part of the school was unacceptable, but ultimately the Supreme Court of Canada ruled in his favour.[60] Even so, gay and lesbian Canadians continue to face a less than welcoming climate in many workplaces (Mitchell 1999), while same-sex couples continue to struggle to obtain the benefits received by opposite-sex couples (Carter 1998). These examples, and the range of other research reviewed above, demonstrate that employer discrimination continues to be one of the factors accounting for persistent patterns of labour market segmentation in Canada.

NEW PATTERNS OF LABOUR MARKET SEGMENTATION

In a sweeping historical analysis of labour market segmentation trends in the United States, David Gordon and his colleagues separate the last two centuries into three major epochs (Gordon et al. 1982). During the period of *initial proletarianization* from about 1820 to 1890, a large, relatively homogeneous industrial working class was emerging. While modern forms of capitalist management were still in their infancy, craft workers were beginning to lose control over the labour process. However, this trend did not develop fully until the era of *homogenization of labour,* from the end of the 19th century until the start of World War II. This period saw extensive mechanization and deskilling of labour, the growth of large workplaces, and the rise of a new managerial class within American capitalism. The period following World War II to the early 1980s (when these authors wrote their book) was one of *segmentation of labour,* in which distinct primary and secondary labour markets emerged.

Canada began to industrialize later and has always remained more of a resource-based economy. Thus, the same three stages do not precisely describe our economic history, although there are some similarities (see Chapter 1). However, the emphasis on change in this historical overview encourages us to ask: Have further changes in labour market segmentation been occurring as the 1990s have given way to the 21st century? The answer is yes. There is considerable evidence of fundamental realignments in the industrial and occupational structures, and in the nature of employment relationships, not only in Canada, but also in the United States and other Western industrialized countries.

Labour Market Polarization

The goods-producing industries have declined significantly since the 1980s. Factory closures due to increased overseas competition and the movement of manufacturing bases to low-wage countries have led to what Barry Bluestone and Bennett Harrison (1982) called the "deindustrialization of America." The widespread introduction of computer technology has allowed many industries to maintain production levels with fewer employees (Sherman and Judkins 1995; Menzies 1996). A similar situation has developed in Canada's resource industries, where unstable world markets, in combination with technological innovations that reduce the need for labour, have led employers to substantially reduce their workforces.[61] During the 1990s, *downsizing* and hiring cutbacks were the norm in many large corporations in the business and distributive service industries. Similar trends emerged in the public sector as governments (both federal and provincial) cut deficits by laying off employees and privatizing some of the services they had previously provided directly to the public.[62]

Although a shrinking workforce has been observed in both the goods-producing and service sectors, there has still been employment growth over the past two decades. Most of it has been in the service industries. While new high-skill, well-paying jobs have been created, leading some observers to proclaim the emergence of a "knowledge economy" (Reich 1991; Drucker 1993; Lowe, 2000), there has also been a significant increase in the proportion of jobs in the secondary labour market. Many of the new jobs created have been part-time or temporary, paying less and offering fewer benefits and career opportunities than the full-time, permanent jobs that have disappeared. In addition, workers in some industries experienced substantial wage rollbacks that have still not been recovered, even with stronger economic growth in the past few years. In other work settings, traditional employment relationships have been altered when workers retired—temporary positions and contract work have replaced the previously permanent positions. Thus, nonstandard jobs with less security have been increasing (Krahn 1995; Vosko 200; Lowe and Schellenberg 2001).

The industrial realignment and the growth in nonstandard work, along with a decade or more of high levels of unemployment, have led to *labour market polarization*. Compared to the 1970s and 1980s, the 1990s saw more Canadians unemployed, and relatively fewer people employed in the well-paying, full-time, permanent jobs that used to be taken for granted. Put another way, the primary labour market shrank during the 1990s, leaving fewer workers with access to its good jobs, as defined by income, benefits, and job security. The economic recovery at the end of the last century and the beginning of the 21st century slowed, but did not reverse, this trend.

Within the broadly defined secondary labour market, two relatively distinct new segments appear to have emerged. The first is a *student labour market*, consisting mainly of part-time jobs, most of them in the lower-tier consumer services and retail trade industries (Marquardt 1998; Lowe and Krahn 1999). Many young Canadians participate voluntarily in this labour market, using their part-time jobs to earn discretionary income or to pay for their education. But this part-time workforce also contains non-students, women who cannot work full-time because of their family responsibilities, and others who simply cannot find a full-time job (see Chapter 2). The new *temporary/contract labour market* exists in both the upper- and lower-tier service industries (Lowe and Schellenberg 2001). As employers in both the private and public sectors have come to rely more heavily on temporary workers for both low- and high-skill jobs, a larger proportion of well-educated young adults are finding themselves spending a number of years in contract work before they are able to obtain more secure employment.

Rising Income Inequality

One of the results of labour market polarization has been an increase in individual-level income inequality in Canada. While real earnings (taking inflation into account) rose systematically in Canada in the three or four decades following World War II, this trend stopped in the 1980s. For many workers, real incomes have declined since then. A smaller proportion have seen their real incomes increasing. Compared to women's incomes, inequality in men's incomes has been more pronounced (Picot, 1998).[63]

Even more significant has been the growing income differences across age groups. Despite their high levels of education, on average, the real earnings of young Canadians have been dropping over the past two decades. For example, between 1981 and 1993, the real annual earnings of 17- to 24- year-old males dropped by 33 percent, while the earnings of women in this age cohort declined by 23 percent (Betcherman and Leckie, 1995: 5). However, since a larger proportion of workers in this age cohort are in the student labour market, it would be more appropriate to examine changes in earnings for young adults (age 25 to 34), most of whom have left the formal education system. Table 3.1 compares weekly earnings between 1981 and 1995 for women and men in this age cohort with their counterparts age 45 to 54 (older workers are omitted to eliminate the effects of some members of this cohort beginning to work less as they approach retirement).

In 1981, average weekly earnings for men age 25 to 34 were $738 (translated into 1995 equivalents). By 1995, weekly earnings for this group had declined by 14 percent, to $633. Older men were earning the same amount in 1981 and 1995. Table 3.1 shows that women were earning less than men, on average, in both 1981 and 1995. However, as we have already noted in this chapter, the female-male earnings ratio increased over that time. But the increase was not felt by younger women, whose incomes remained essentially the same over this 15-year period. Instead, older women saw their weekly earnings increase by 22 percent between 1981 and 1995. It is apparent that corporate and public sector layoffs and hiring freezes, and the increase in non-standard jobs, particularly temporary employment, have seriously disadvantaged younger workers, particularly young men.[64]

At the household level, however, there is less evidence of an increase in earnings inequality. While the strong growth in real family incomes that characterized Canadian society in the 1950s, 1960s, and 1970s had stopped by the 1980s, the rising proportion of employed women and dual-earner families since then has meant that family income inequality has not really increased over the past several decades (Rashid 1999). But we have seen a significant change in the composition of low-income households. In the 1970s, the elderly made up a sizable portion of Canada's poor. Since then, improvements in income security for senior citizens have reduced poverty among the elderly

TABLE 3.1 *Weekly Earnings by Gender and Age, Canada, 1981–1995*

| | Weekly Earnings (in 1995 $) | | | |
	1981	1988	1995	% Change (1981–95)
Female				
Age 25-34	474	467	479	1.1
Age 45-54	439	490	536	22.1
Male				
Age 25-34	738	684	633	-14.2
Age 45-54	870	888	877	0.8

Source: C. Kapsalis, R. Morissette, and G. Picot, *The Returns to Education, and the Increasing Wage Gap between Younger and Older Workers* (Ottawa: Statistics Canada, Analytic Studies Branch, Research Paper no. 131, 1999), page 10, Table 1.

(Myles 2000). However, the combined labour market trends noted above point to an increase in problems of poverty among working-age Canadians. The *working poor* have become a larger group in the Canadian labour market. Younger households, particularly female-headed single-parent households, have been particularly disadvantaged (Rashid, 1999).

Some observers have used the term *declining middle class* to describe these trends toward greater inequality. Others have commented on the emergence of an *underclass* of citizens, individuals largely marginalized from the labour market. But neither concept has been precisely defined. Some writers use the term "declining middle class" to refer to a declining proportion of well-paying blue-collar and mid-level white-collar jobs. Others emphasize growing income inequality without necessarily distinguishing between individual and family income.[65] Similarly, when proposing that an underclass has emerged, some users of the concept are referring to a growing number of long-term unemployed. Others include people unable to work and dependent on declining levels of social assistance in the category, while still others reserve the term to describe the homeless and absolutely destitute.[66]

Because of this conceptual confusion and the need for more research to test some of the assumptions underlying these concepts, we prefer to use the broader term labour market polarization to refer to the interrelated trends we have described—industrial and occupational realignment, rising levels of non-standard work, and growing individual income inequality. Nevertheless, we strongly emphasize that social inequality has increased as a result of these polarizing trends. Greater inequality means fewer labour market opportunities and reduced life chances for more Canadians.

POLICY RESPONSES TO LABOUR MARKET BARRIERS AND GROWING INEQUALITY

What might be done to create better jobs and to counter the trend toward greater labour market polarization? Responses based on a human capital perspective would primarily emphasize access to education as the most important public policy goal. In fact, this has been a central concern of Canadian governments throughout the second half of the twentieth century, particularly during the 1960s and 1970s when a wide array of new postsecondary educational institutions were opened and student loan systems were introduced.

These policy efforts did have an effect, as we have noted earlier. The average educational attainment of the Canadian population has risen dramatically, and some of the systemic barriers to equal access to education were reduced. Even so, research continues to show that not all groups in Canadian society have equal educational opportunities. Consequently, continued policy responses targeting this goal are needed. In fact, with rising postsecondary tuition costs occurring as a result of government reductions in funding for postsecondary education, we may well see a reversal of the slow trend toward greater equality of educational opportunity that characterized the latter decades of the 20th century.

During the 1980s and 1990s, government education policies shifted from building schools to encouraging young Canadians to stay in school and promoting skill upgrading among older labour force participants, particularly the unemployed. At the same time, more emphasis was placed on policies promoting formal training and skill upgrading in the workplace.[67] Reducing labour market inequalities gave way to concerns about Canada's competitive position in the global economy. Unemployed youth, older workers affected by industrial restructuring, and the marginal labour market position of other groups came to be seen not so much as social problems of inequality, but as economic problems. Unless we invested even more heavily in and took more advantage of current stocks of human capital, it was argued, Canada would fall behind in the global economy.[68] At the same time, greater investments in education and training should help disadvantaged groups (the unemployed, for example, and residents of economically depressed regions) to improve their labour market position.

Clearly, greater investments in education and training are important. Indeed, some groups of Canadian labour force participants continue to be educationally disadvantaged. Some could clearly benefit from improvements in their literacy skills. The Canadian record on workplace training is not very good. Thus, with global competitiveness as the goal, greater investments in human capital are part of the longer-term solution (Hum and Simpson 1999a; Lowe 2000). But we also need to look at other structural factors including inflation-fighting interest rate policies that slowed economic growth and kept unemployment high in the 1980s and early 1990s, the currently popular and misguided (in our opinion) belief that governments have no role to play in stimulating the economy when unemployment is high,[69] a limited emphasis on research and development by Canadian firms, and trade agreements that have been more beneficial to some sectors (and regions) than others.

If reducing labour market inequalities is our goal, human capital investments are only part of the solution. We know that additional education and training would assist some Canadians in improving their labour market position. But we are also aware that about one in four working Canadians consider themselves to be overqualified for their jobs, including many with university degrees. Research on literacy requirements in the workplace document large proportions of workers who are seldom required to use their literacy skills in their jobs.[70] Thus, *underemployment* is a serious problem in the Canadian workplace. While unemployment is lower among the better educated, many of Canada's unemployed have good educational qualifications. Simply put, even with a decline in unemployment rates towards the end of the 1990s, there are not enough good jobs. Or, as John Myles recently concluded in a critique of "market based" solutions to social inequality in Canada, "[t]he ultimate Achilles heel of the job training strategy is the assumption that the problem is mainly on the supply side."[71]

While the human capital explanation of labour market processes focuses our attention on education as the key policy variable, the labour market segmentation perspective encourages us to identify the barriers that keep large numbers of qualified individuals out of better jobs. Obviously, a shortage of good jobs is part of the problem. Beyond that, we will also continue to need strong legislation that discourages discrimination against disadvantaged groups in the Canadian labour market. Equity programs that help disadvantaged groups to catch up with mainstream labour market participants are also part of a policy package that could help reduce labour market inequality. Improved school-to-work transition programs are needed to assist young people in their search for rewarding jobs and careers, given that young Canadians have been particularly hurt by labour market polarization trends.[72] Finally, we believe that unions have a larger role to play in the Canadian labour market. If more Canadian workers were covered by union contracts, some of the inequality within the labour market could be reduced. If unions were involved on a more equal basis in decisions about national, regional, and firm-level industrial strategies, we might also move further toward the goal of global competitiveness. We will return to many of these topics in the following chapters.

CONCLUSION

After profiling good jobs and bad jobs in terms of income, benefits, risks to personal health, and other extrinsic work rewards, we began our analysis of these patterns by discussing the class structure of Canadian society and the power relationships that underlie it. In order to answer questions about who gets the better jobs, we shifted our attention to the human capital and segmentation explanations of labour market processes. While the human capital model highlights the central role of education in determining occupational outcomes, it fails to adequately account for the many examples of qualified and highly motivated individuals working in unrewarding jobs, and ignores intergenerational transfers of advantage. In contrast, the segmentation approach recognizes inequalities in labour market outcomes and provides a better account of how such power differences are created and maintained. In turn, studies of status attainment demonstrate both the importance of educational attainment and the extent to which status and power can be inherited (frequently through unequal access to higher education).

While not directly applying the concepts of class analysis, we address the issues examined in class analyses in our descriptions of structured patterns of labour market inequality, intergenerational transfers of advantage, labour market polarization, and the intersecting effects of gender, race, and ethnicity.

Questions about who gets the good jobs and why are essentially questions about social inequality and the power relationships that underlie it. In the following chapters on gender, management strategies, conflict in the workplace, and industrial relations we will revisit this central theme.

NOTES

1. See Van den Berg and Smucker (1997) on the neoclassical economic approach and more sociological analyses of labour markets.

2. See Clement and Myles (1994), Westergaard (1995), Breen and Rottman (1995), Ashton (1986), and Spilerman (2000) on labour markets, social inequality, and class analysis.

3. Lowe and Schellenberg (2001) discuss the importance of employment relationships for evaluating the quality of jobs.

4. *Labour Force Survey* estimates of weekly wages for 2000, by industry and occupation, are presented in the Spring 2001 issue of *Perspectives on Labour and Income* (p. 81). Census data on 1995 earnings (for full-time, full-year workers) are reported by Statistics Canada, *The Daily* (12 May 1998).

5. *Perspectives on Labour and Income* (Spring 2001: 81). This method of calculating the female-male earnings ratio differs from the method used by Statistics Canada until the late 1990s: it uses a different data source (the *Labour Force Survey* rather than the *Survey of Consumer Finances*); adjusts for average hours worked; is based on hourly pay rather than annual earnings; excludes overtime pay; and excludes the self-employed. Galarneau and Earl (1999) provide a useful comparison of the two approaches. The previous method of calculating the female-male earnings ratio (for full-time, full-year workers) produced a 1997 estimate of 73%, up from 58% in 1967 (Statistics Canada 1999: 12). This method is used in Chapter 4 because it allows us to track changes in the earnings ratio over time.

6. See the Canadian Council on Social Development (www.ccsd.ca) for minimum wage rates.

7. Statistics Canada's "low income cutoff" (LICO) is the measure most often used to measure poverty in Canada (see Statistics Canada, 2000a: Chapter 8; National Council of Welfare, 2000). A family (of a given size) is considered to be in the low-income category if, compared to the average Canadian family of that size, it spends at least 20 percent more of its total income on food, clothing, and shelter. LICOs are calculated separately for communities of different sizes since the cost of living is higher in larger communities.

8. Kumar et al. (1991: 373) provide Canadian data (covering 1953–1989) on employee benefit costs by type of benefit. See Lettau and Buchmueller (1999) on benefit costs in the U.S.

9. Akyeampong (1997) profiles the distribution of benefits using data from Statistics Canada's 1995 *Survey of Work Arrangements*. Grenon and Chun (1997: 26) compare benefits received by permanent and temporary workers. For data on training benefits from the 1994 *Survey of Adult Education and Training in Canada*, see Human Resources Development Canada (1997).

10. Additional analysis also shows that a small minority of workers without a dental or health plan can take advantage of their spouse's family plan (Lowe and Schellenberg 2000: 16).

11. See Akyeampong (1997: 52) and Human Resources Development Canada (1997: 1–2) on the advantages of employment in larger firms; for U.S. data, see Kalleberg and Van Buren (1996).

12. Marshall (1996) provides data from 1976 to 1993. See Human Resources Development Canada (2000c: 10) for additional data from 1994 to 1998.

13. Industry and occupation comparisons are from Marshall (1996).

14. Human Resources Development Canada (2000a: 10) provide 1998 data. Rates for 1996 are from Health Canada and Statistics Canada (1999: Table 61). See Conway and Svenson (1998) on a similar decline in occupational injury and illness rates in the United States, which they attribute to legislative reforms brought on by increased compensation payments to injured workers.

15. Stress-at-work results from the 1994/95 *Population Health Survey* are discussed by Statistics Canada (2000b); also see Wilkins and Beaudet (1998).

16. Grayson (1994) discusses self-reported work hazards using data from the 1991 *General Social Survey.*

17. See Human Resources Development Canada (2000b) for an assessment of the costs of occupational injuries and fatalities.

18. Pineo and Porter (1967) conducted the original study of occupational prestige; Blishen et al. (1987) provide the most recent version of the Blishen SES scale; see Fox and Suschnigg (1989) on gender bias in SES scales.

19. Even so, the Pineo (1984) ranking system is highly correlated with the Blishen scores (Hunter and Manley, 1986: 64). While not as up to date (in terms of newly-emerging occupations) as the 1993 National Occupational Classification (NOC) discussed in Chapter 2, the Pineo rankings are more finely differentiated in terms of skill (the NOC contains only four skill levels), and also distinguish the self-employed from paid workers. See Ollivier (2000) for an interesting discussion of how people situated higher in the stratification system place more emphasis on occupational status.

20. Clement and Myles (1994); also see Grabb (1997) and Forcese (1997) on differing theoretical and empirical conceptions of social class.

21. Black and Myles (1986: 162); see Clement (1990) for comparisons with results from similar surveys in Sweden, Norway, Finland, and the United States.

22. In their study of Hamilton, Ontario, Livingstone and Mangan (1996: 61) provide another example of a social class typology influenced by Wright's theorizing. See Wright (1997) for his more recent theorizing about social class and social mobility, including the intersection of gender and class.

23. Becker (1975: first published in 1964) is generally credited for developing human capital theory, although its basic premises originate in neoclassical economics. As we describe it here, the model is closely linked to the functionalist theory of stratification (Davis and Moore, 1945). See Laroche et al. (1999) and a 1997 issue of *Policy Options* (volume 18, no. 6) on the concept and measurement of human capital.

24. See Morissette (1997), Sunter and Bowlby (1998), Marquardt (1998), Picot (1998), Clark (1999a), Sunter (2000), Lowe (2000), and Labour Market Ministers (2000) on problems of underemployment among Canadian youth.

25. See Zhao et al. (2000: 33), Clark (2000), and Riddell and Sweetman (2000) on high levels of investment by Canadians in postsecondary education. Krahn and Lowe (1995) and Human Resources Development Canada (1997: 1) report that young labour force participants are the most likely to invest in additional job-related education and training.

26. Looker and Thiessen (1999) describe how young women and men from different class backgrounds evaluate their parents' occupations, as well as housework.

27. Unpublished analysis (by the authors) of data from the 1994 Canadian component of the International Adult Literacy Survey (Statistics Canada and Human Resources Development Canada 1996). See de Broucker and Lavallée (1998a) for a similar analysis of the same data set.

28. Clark (2000) presents a long-term overview of the growth of the formal education system in Canada. Riddell and Sweetman (2000) provide data on current educational participation and attainment trends.

29. See Krahn and Lowe (1999b), Hartnagel and Krahn (1995), and Lowe and Krahn (1995, 2000) for additional results from the Edmonton study. Similar research demonstrating how family background influences educational aspirations and outcomes has been conducted in Nova Scotia (Looker 1994, 1997; Looker and Dwyer 1998; Looker and Thiessen 1999), Newfoundland (Sharpe and White 1993), and British Columbia (Andres 1993; Andres and Krahn 1999; Andres and Looker 2001).

30. In 1995, Canadian universities received 24 percent of their total revenues from student fees, up from 13 percent in 1980 (Little 1997: 2). Since 1995, university tuition fees have continued to rise. See Finnie and Garneau (1996) and Clark (1996b) on rising student debt.

31. See Corak (1998) for a collection of empirical studies examining the impact of family background on physical and mental health, educational attainment, and income. Gilbert et al. (1993) and Tanner et al. (1995) review Canadian research on high school dropouts. Alexander et al. (1998) and Duncan et al. (1998) present similar information for the United States.

32. Bourdieu (1986); also see Looker (1994, 1997) on the impacts of cultural capital on educational outcomes.

33. Unpublished analysis (by the authors) of data from the 1994 International Adult Literacy Survey. De Broucker and Lavallée (1998a) present similar findings from an analysis of the same data set.

34. See Porter et al. (1982: 67) and Anisef et al. (2000: 143) on rural-urban differences in the 1970s Ontario studies. Looker (1993), Looker and Dwyer (1998) and Andres and Looker (2001) present more recent findings from Nova Scotia and British Columbia. Furlong et al. (1996) develop similar ideas in their study of how neighbourhood contexts affect occupational aspirations of Scottish youth.

35. See Swift (1995) on the downward mobility experiences of Canadian families in the 1990s. Newman (1989), and Dudley (1994) tell similar U.S. stories about restructuring in the 1980s and 1990s.

36. Wanner (1993) provides a useful discussion of social mobility definitions and the important stratification questions addressed by social mobility research. See Birdsall and Graham (2000) for recent contributions to this research tradition. Harrington and Boardman (1997) study people who have done exceptionally well in American society, despite their disadvantaged family background.

37. Lipset and Bendix (1959: 12). More recently, Kerckhoff et al. (1985) have again concluded that there are few differences between the United States and Britain in occupational mobility opportunities.

38. Wanner (1993) and Sawhill (2000) report results from recent comparative studies of mobility patterns; see Wanner and Hayes (1996) on similarities and differences in the mobility patterns of men in Canada and Australia; and Breen and Rottman (1995; Chapter 5) on social mobility patterns in Britain.

39. While Statistics Canada's 1994 *General Social Survey* could be used to answer questions about social mobility with more recent data, such analyses have not yet been published. Wanner (1999) uses data from all three studies to show that the effects of gender and language (French/English) on educational attainment have largely disappeared, while social class effects remain relatively strong. He also uses the data to describe how the value of a first university degree (in terms of the status of the first full-time job obtained following graduation) has declined over time (Wanner 2000).

40. Most status attainment studies are modelled on Blau and Duncan's (1967) original study of American men. Creese et al. (1991; Chapter 7) present status attainment results from the 1986 *General Social Survey* conducted by Statistics Canada. See Hauser et al. (2000) for recent U.S. status attainment analyses.

41. See Blaug (1985), Ashton (1986; Chapter 3), and Rubery (1988) on segmentation theory; Kalleberg (1988) and Stark (1988) comment on cross-national differences in segmentation.

42. Edwards (1979), Hodson and Kaufman (1982), and Gordon et al. (1982) are examples of this perspective on labour market segmentation.

43. See Akyeampong (1997: 52), Human Resources Development Canada (1997: 3), and Lowe and Schellenberg (2001) for Canadian data, and Kalleberg and Van Buren (1996) for U.S. data.

44. Gordon et al. (1982) argue that the emergence of dual economies and segmented labour markets in the United States divided the working class and reduced class conflict. Essentially, some workers were "bought off" at the expense of others.

45. See Althauser (1989) and Smith (1997) for overviews of research in this area. Examples of specific studies of internal labour markets include Bernard and Smith (1991), Ospina (1996), Walsh (1997), and Barnett et al. (2000).

46. See Freidson (1986), Abbott (1988), Macdonald and Ritzer (1988), Leicht and Fennell (1997) and Rossides (1998) on the sociology of professions.

47. Cant and Sharma (1995) discuss the "professionalization" of practitioners of nontraditional medicine, Wallace (1995a, 1995b) writes about variations in professional commitment among lawyers, and Randle (1996) analyzes the "deprofessionalization" of scientists.

48. Useem and Karabel (1986) discuss the advantages of an upper-class background and a degree from the "right" school; Davies and Guppy (1997) show the connection between SES and entry into prestigious universities; Boone et al. (1988) demonstrate the link between higher-status social origins and entry into senior management positions.

49. See Burchell and Rubery (1990) and Ferber and Waldfogel (1998) on the liabilities of irregular work histories.

50. See Looker (1993), Looker and Dwyer (1998) and Andres and Looker (2001) on the school-to-work transition experiences of rural and urban youth in Nova Scotia and British Columbia

51. See Clairmont et al. (1983) and Apostle et al. (1985) on the Marginal Work World research project. Apostle and Barrett (1992), Osberg et al. (1995), and Palmer and Sinclair (1997) present more recent research conducted in the same region.

52. See Jenness (1977: 250–51) and Patterson (1972); Pentland (1981: 1–3) reports that some Aboriginals were also kept as slaves in Quebec, but this practice had largely disappeared by the early 1800s.

53. Baureiss (1987); Creese (1988–1989); Muszynski (1996); Anderson (1991).

54. Shapiro and Stelcner (1997); Lian and Matthews (1998); Hum and Simpson (1999b); Wanner (1999).

55. Statistics Canada, *The Daily* (13 January 1998; 12 May, 1998) provides 1996 Census data on visible minorities in Canada. See (Kelly 1995) for 1991 Census data.

56. Kunz et al. (2000). See, also, Satzewich and Li (1987); Shadd (1987); Reitz (1988); James (1990); das Gupta (1996), Satzewich (1998), and Krahn et al. (2000). Peterson et al. (2000) and Baldi and McBrier (1997) show that, in the U.S., visible minorities are less likely to be hired and, once hired, less likely to be promoted.

57. Statistics Canada, *The Daily* (12 May 1998). For additional information on the labour market problems faced by Aboriginal Canadians, see Statistics Canada (1994a), Drost (1996), Grenon (1997), de Silva (1999), Armstrong (1999), and Maxim et al. (2000).

58. See Shain (1995), Hum and Simpson (1996), and Federal, Provincial and Territorial Ministers Responsible for Social Services (2000: 32) on the labour market status of disabled Canadians. Hale et al. (1998) and Kruse (1998) provide U.S. data on the employment situation of disabled people.

59. Rioux (1985) and McKay (1991) discuss employment barriers faced by disabled people; see Wilgosh and Skaret (1987) on employers' attitudes toward hiring disabled people

60. "Court protects gays" (*Globe and Mail,* 3 April 1998: A1).

61. Clement's (1981) study of technological change at INCO documented the beginning of this trend; see Osberg et al. (1995) and Bob Russell (1999) for more recent examples.

62. Gera (1991), Dudley (1994), Swift (1995), Osberg et al. (1995), Sherman and Judkins (1995), Menzies (1996), Hughes et al. (1996), Sharpe (1999), Gunderson and Riddell (2000).

63. See Myles (1996), Picot (1998), and Rashid (1999) on inequality trends in Canada. Ryscavage (1995) and Bernstein and Mishel (1997) discuss similar trends in the United

States, Wolfson and Murphy (1998) compare Canada to the U.S., and Westergaard (1995) and Sherman and Judkins (1995) present British data.

64. On the declining labour market position of young workers, see Betcherman and Leckie (1995, 1997), Sunter (1997), Picot (1998), Morissette (1997), Sunter and Bowlby (1998), Marquardt (1998), Clark (1999a), Sunter (2000), and Labour Market Ministers (2000).

65. See Picot (1998) and Wolfson and Murphy (1998) on definitions of income inequality and polarization

66. In some media accounts, the term "underclass" is used to describe poor families who, *presumably* having become dependent on social assistance, have passed such values of "welfare dependency" along to their children. For discussions of the term "underclass" and/or criticisms of the notion of "welfare dependence," see Edin (1991), Morris and Irwin (1992), Payne and Payne (1994), Breen and Rottman (1995: 91–93), Westergaard (1995: Chapter 8), Wilson (1997), Leonard (1998), Schwartz (1999), Schecter and Paquet (1999), and Buckingham (1999).

67. Gilbert et al. (1993), Betcherman (1993), Tanner et al. (1995), Human Resources Development Canada (1997),Betcherman et al. (1998), Statistics Canada and HRDC (1998; Chapter 3), Hum and Simpson (1999a).

68. Reich (1991), Laroche et al. (1999), Expert Panel on Skills (2000), Lowe (2000).

69. See Osberg and Fortin (1996) for discussions of the role of government in stimulating the economy and the impact of inflation-fighting policies on unemployment in Canada. Battle and Torjman (1999) and Riddell and St-Hilaire (2000) present useful collections of essays discussing the role of public policy in today's labour market. Bluestone and Harrison (2000) argue for the active role of government in maintaining economic growth and reducing inequality in the United States.

70. See Kelly et al. (1997), Livingstone (1999), Lowe (2000), and Frenette (2001) on self-reported underemployment in Canada; on literacy underutilization, see Krahn (1997) and Krahn and Lowe (1997a).

71. Myles (1996: 18); see Leadbeater and Suschnigg (1997) on the inadequacy of a "training solution" for communities where the economic base that provided employment has disappeared.

72. See Pauly et al. (1995) and Stern et al. (1995) on high-school-based programs, and Gitter and Scheuer (1997) and Lehmann (2000) on youth apprenticeship programs.

WOMEN'S EMPLOYMENT

INTRODUCTION

The last three decades have brought wide-ranging change to the economic roles of women. In 1970, 38 percent of all adult women in Canada worked outside the home for pay. By 2000, this figure had jumped to 59.5 percent.[1] Traditional barriers to female employment have slowly been eroding. Feminism challenged the conventional wisdom about women's capabilities. Rising education levels and job opportunities made more women career-minded, and the economic necessity of being self-supporting or contributing to the family income left some women little choice but to find a paying job.

This chapter examines these transformations in women's employment patterns. We will review the dramatic increases in female labour force participation rates during this century, showing how the labour market has become segmented into men's and women's jobs. We will also discuss two seemingly contradictory trends: on the one hand, significant gains in women's employment opportunities and rewards, and on the other, the persistence of major work-related gender inequities. A central theme is that women's work has been undervalued and poorly rewarded throughout history. Consequently, gender remains a key determinant of inequality in our society. The chapter ends optimistically, however, by reviewing two significant policy initiatives—employment equity and pay equity—that have started to redress this long-standing problem.

To better grasp the causes and consequences of gender inequity in the work world, we shall address the following questions: What forces have either pushed or pulled women out of the home and into paid employment in recent decades? Why are women concentrated in a limited range of jobs at the bottom of the occupational ladder? How did these jobs come to be labelled female, and, conversely, how have the most challenging and rewarding jobs come to be defined as male? What barriers still prevent equality of opportunity and rewards for women in the labour market? And finally, but perhaps most importantly, how can greater equality for women be achieved in the workplace?

A word of clarification before we proceed. To avoid confusion, we should define how we use the terms *sex* and *gender*. Basically, sex is the biological distinction between men and women; gender is socially constructed in the sense that it refers to how a particular society defines masculine and feminine roles. Thus, one can observe the sex segregation of occupations. But to explain this it is necessary to look at how jobs are *gendered,* that is, how they take on societal images of appropriate male or female behaviour. We tend to prefer the term gender, given that male–female differences in employment are almost solely a product of socially created gender roles and ideologies.

WOMEN'S ECONOMIC ROLE IN HISTORICAL CONTEXT

Although history has for the most part been written from the perspective of men, even a quick glance back to the past reveals that women have always performed a vital, if somewhat unacknowledged, economic role. Native women, for example, were indispensable to the fur trade, the major industry during much of Canada's colonial period (Van Kirk 1980). White male traders relied on Native women to act as interpreters, prepare food, clean pelts for market, and teach them wilderness survival skills. Little wonder that fur traders sought out Native women as wives. When an agrarian economy began to develop in Upper Canada (Ontario) during the 19th century, the family was the basic production unit, in which women played a key role. Men worked the fields, while women looked after all domestic work associated with child rearing, tending the livestock and garden, making clothes, and preparing food.[2] Similarly, in the west in the early 1900s, women contributed significantly to agricultural development by working on their family farms and by making the farm home "a haven of safety and healthfulness."[3]

Industrialization and Women's Work

In Chapter 1, we noted that one consequence of the rise of large-scale factory production was a growing separation between men's and women's work. Men were drawn into the industrial wage-labour market; women were increasingly confined to the domestic sphere of the household. Marjorie Cohen's feminist analysis of economic development in 19th-century Ontario reveals that, prior to wide-scale industrialization, an integration of family and household existed within the emerging market economy (Cohen 1988). Traditional theories of industrialization, Cohen points out, tend to ignore the contribution of households to the economy. Ontario's early economy was primarily based on two staple exports, wheat and timber, which were subject to unstable international markets. Consequently, women's household labour had to fulfill two functions: generate family income by producing agricultural goods to sell in the local consumer market, and perform the domestic chores necessary for the family's survival. Cohen's research underlines the importance of examining how the public and private spheres of market and household have been intertwined in diverse ways during all phases of economic development, with women always performing pivotal roles, albeit quite different from those performed by men.

The absence of a wage-labour market and the necessity of contributing to the household economy meant that few women were employed outside the home prior to the rise of industrial capitalism. Even in late 19th-century Canada, only a fraction of women were engaged in paid employment. In 1891, for example, 11.4 percent of girls and women over the age of 10 were employed, accounting for 12.6 percent of the entire labour force (Lowe 1987: 47). But as factories sprang up in the late-19th century, they began to redefine women's economic role. Employers in some light industries, such as textiles, recruited women as cheap unskilled or semiskilled labourers who, according to prevailing stereotypes, would be less likely to unionize and more tolerant of boring tasks.

By focusing only on paid employment, we risk ignoring the work activities of the vast majority of women during this era. The *unpaid domestic labour* of women—raising the future generation of workers and feeding, clothing, and caring for the present generation of workers—was an essential function within capitalism. Out of these competing pressures on women emerged a gendered division of labour that persists today. As we document below, this now takes the form of the *double day* (or, in equally graphic terms, the *second shift*), whereby most married women spend their days in paying jobs, yet still assume most of the responsibilities of child care and domestic chores when they get home.

Early 20th-century attitudes about women's economic roles distinguished between single and married women. Expanding manufacturing and service industries had an almost insatiable demand for both blue- and white-collar workers. The employment of young, single women prior to marriage came to be tolerated in domestic, clerical, sales, and some factory jobs. Once married, women were expected to retreat into the matrimonial home. Of course, some wished to remain in the labour force and still others were forced to stay through economic necessity. In these cases, married women laboured at the margins of the economy in domestic and other menial jobs that usually had been abandoned by single women.[4]

Industrialization accentuated age and gender divisions in the economy. Examining the work patterns of working-class women in Montreal, Canada's first large industrial city, Bettina Bradbury documents how age and sex determined who was drawn into wage-labour. Women made up about 35 percent of the city's industrial workforce during the 1870s. In certain industries, such as domestic work and the sewing and dressmaking trades, 4 out of 5 workers were women, and the vast majority of them were single. Given the scarcity of wage-labour for wives because of strong sanctions against their employment, such women could make a greater contribution to the family economy by being *household managers*. In this role, wives stretched the wages of male family members and single daughters as far as possible, occasionally supplementing this by taking in boarders or turning to neighbours or charities for help (Bradbury 1993).

The Family Wage Ideology

Powerful social values justified this division of labour. Especially influential in perpetuating women's subordinate role as unpaid family workers was the ideology of the *family wage*. As working-class men began organizing unions to achieve better wages and working conditions, one of the labour movement's demands was that wages should be high enough to allow a male breadwinner to support a wife and children. The labour movement's successes in this regard had the effect of drastically reducing women's presence, and the cheap labour they provided, in the workplace (a policy that was typical of unions until a serious male labour shortage arose in World War I). Middle-class reformers also lobbied for restrictions on female industrial employment due to its presumed harmful personal and social effects. In response, employers limited their hiring mainly to single women, further reinforcing this ideology. Despite its sexist tone, the family wage ideology may have benefited those women who were dependent on a husband by raising the standard of living in working-class families. The price, of course, was the restriction of women's labour market opportunities to areas in which they would not compete directly with men—hence the endurance of the term "male breadwinner."[5]

However, the family wage ideology tells only part of the story of women's lives during early industrialization. Joy Parr's case studies of two Ontario industrial towns, Paris and Hanover, between 1880 and 1950, caution us against thinking in binary oppositions—masculine/feminine, market/nonmarket, public/private, waged/nonwaged (Parr 1990: 8). Parr shows how the specific combinations of community context, gender roles, household forms, and industrial development patterns interacted to fashion different gender ideologies. Her study shows the variations in outcome within the broad contours of gendered work patterns.

On the surface, both Paris and Hanover appeared to be small, thriving manufacturing communities. Parr probes beneath the surface, documenting how the knit-goods industry based in Paris relied on a largely female workforce, while in Hanover's large furniture factory the workers were almost exclusively male. Consequently, different gender identities based on women's employment patterns arose to maintain each town's labour force. In turn, these were reinforced by attitudes and behaviour in households and the community. Certainly Paris was the exception at the time in Ontario. Nonetheless, its flow of daily life during the 80 years covered by Parr's study forces us to reconsider a model of industrialization based on one dominant mode of production in which males are the breadwinners.

This brief historical sketch has identified a number of prominent themes. First, although their widespread participation in the paid labour force is a recent development, women have always made essential economic contributions. Second, women's entry into paid employment occurred in ways that reproduced their subordinate position in society relative to that of men, although the specific forms this took varied across time and place. Third, the changing interconnections among households, families, and the wage-labour market are crucial to understanding women's roles in the continuing evolution of 21st-century capitalism.

FEMALE LABOUR FORCE PARTICIPATION PATTERNS

Few changes in Canadian society since World War II have had as far-reaching consequences as evolving female employment patterns. Virtually all industrial nations have experienced rising *female labour force participation rates* since the end of World War II. This trend has been especially rapid in Canada. Figure 4.1 provides a comparison of labour force participation rates among adult women (aged 15 and older) for ten major industrial nations between 1975 and 1998. Note that rising female employment is a general cross-national trend. Canada and the Unites States experienced larger increases than all but the Netherlands. The tremendous expansion of white-collar service-sector jobs, coupled with rising educational levels and a declining birth rate, drew millions of Canadian women into employment at an accelerated rate. By 1998, Canada's female labour force participation rate surpassed all the advanced industrial nations except the United States and Sweden. The latter is an interesting case, given that it experienced the least change of all ten countries over the 1975-98 period, largely because women's employment outside the home has been actively encouraged by state policies for decades.

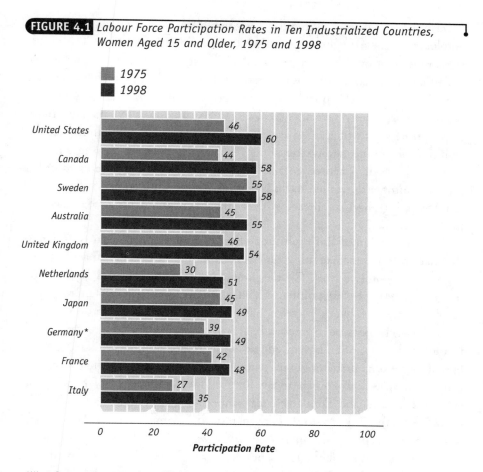

FIGURE 4.1 *Labour Force Participation Rates in Ten Industrialized Countries, Women Aged 15 and Older, 1975 and 1998*

- 1975
- 1998

Country	1975	1998
United States	46	60
Canada	44	58
Sweden	55	58
Australia	45	55
United Kingdom	46	54
Netherlands	30	51
Japan	45	49
Germany*	39	49
France	42	48
Italy	27	35

Participation Rate

*West Germany in 1975; the unified East and West Germany in 1998.

Source: U.S. Department of Labor, Bureau of Labor Statistics 2000. Comparative Civilian Labor Force Statistics, Ten Countries 1959-1999.

Influences on Women's Employment

What social and economic factors account for this remarkable increase in Canada's female labour force participation? Clearly there was no single cause. The huge post-war baby boom generation was completing its education and flooding into an expanding job market by the late 1960s. Young women were becoming much better educated, which raised their occupational aspirations and made them more competitive with men in the job market. Traditional stereotypes of women's work no longer fit reality. The massive expansion of white-collar service-sector jobs boosted the demand for female labour, and the growth of feminism contributed to more liberal social values regarding women's work roles. As we have seen, service-sector growth also fuelled a trend to part-time jobs, which often are convenient for women with family responsibilities. Shrinking family size allowed married women to pursue employment more readily. Moreover, rising separation and divorce rates forced a growing number of women to find their own source of income. And in many families, the reality (or threat) of declining living standards made a second income essential.

The interaction of this multitude of supply and demand factors underlay the sharp rise in female employment.[6] Interpreting the overall impact of these changes on women's lives, Charles Jones, Lorna Marsden, and Lorne Tepperman (1990: 58–59) point out that as more women have entered paid employment, their work patterns have not come to mirror those of men. Rather, largely because women are heavily concentrated in the secondary labour market and often have to juggle family responsibilities with a job, their lives have become increasingly individualized. Compared with their mothers' generation, younger women today have adopted new ways of combining work, education, and family. Hence, since the 1950s, there is now much greater variety, fluidity, and idiosyncrasy in women's roles. For Jones, Marsden, and Tepperman, the *individualization process* is defined by these elements: (1) variety, through greater opportunities for employment and education; (2) fluidity, in terms of increased movement among these roles and domestic/household roles; and (3) idiosyncrasy, in the sense that it is now exceedingly difficult to predict whether, when, and where a woman will be working for pay.

These observations raise further questions about how women actually make choices and trade-offs between paid employment, marriage and child rearing. Some researchers examine women's *life-course patterns*, looking for sources of greater discontinuity – departure from a more standardized sequencing and timing of education, work and family events – than experienced by men (Krüger and Baldus 1999). Other studies have looked at the effect of career choices and occupational conditions on motherhood decisions.

As Gillian Ranson concluded, after interviewing a sample of Alberta university graduates: "Women who make non-traditional career choices may enjoy many of the benefits of increased pay and promotion prospects – but at the price of prolonged postponement of pregnancy, and/or much more of a struggle to combine paid work and children" (Ranson 1998:531). As we see below, such research findings challenge employers to ensure that career expectations and working conditions enable women (and men) to meet their personal goals.

There is no question that many factors have a bearing on the likelihood of a woman participating in the labour force. Figure 4.2 identifies important variations in 2000 participation rates by region, age, marital status, family circumstances, and educational level. Provincially, women in Alberta have the highest participation rate (65 percent), followed by those in Ontario (61 percent). Newfoundland and New Brunswick have the lowest (51 and 56 percent, respectively). Certainly local and regional job opportunities have a direct bearing on female participation rates, as do regional differences in age structure and educational attainment. For example, Alberta has a relatively strong service sector and a young and well-educated workforce—hence its high rate of labour force participation for both women and men. In contrast, Newfoundland has limited employment opportunities for women (and men) due to chronic economic underdevelopment and the decline of the fisheries. Consequently, much work occurs outside the sphere of paid employment in a thriving informal economy and through self-provisioning (Sinclair and Felt 1992).

Personal characteristics also influence work patterns. Among youth (aged 15-24) single women are less likely than their married (or cohabiting) counterparts to work for pay—because more of them are full-time students. But what's changed in the past several decades is a convergence of participation rates for married and single women over age 25. Indeed, 83 percent of women between the ages of 25 and 44 are in the labour force. By comparison, just under half of women aged 45 or older are in the labour force. Women with higher levels of educational attainment are more active in the labour force—79 percent of women with university degrees compared with 63 percent who have a high school diploma. Family situation also matters. However, because a high proportion of mothers with children under the age of 15 are relatively young and well educated, their labour force participation rates are above average. For example, 68 percent of mothers with preschool children participate in the labour force.

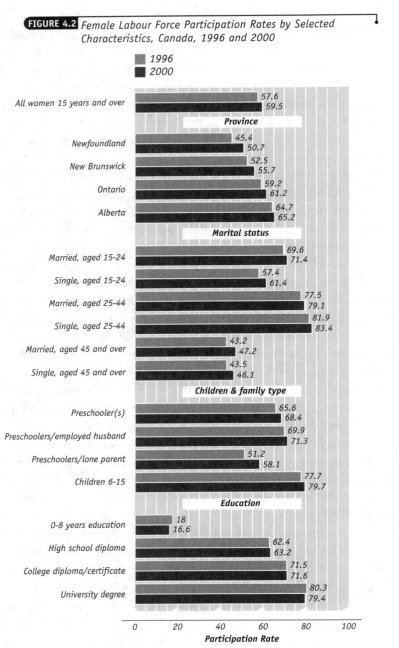

FIGURE 4.2 *Female Labour Force Participation Rates by Selected Characteristics, Canada, 1996 and 2000*

■ 1996
■ 2000

All women 15 years and over — 57.6 / 59.5

Province
Newfoundland — 45.4 / 50.7
New Brunswick — 52.5 / 55.7
Ontario — 59.2 / 61.2
Alberta — 64.7 / 65.2

Marital status
Married, aged 15-24 — 69.6 / 71.4
Single, aged 15-24 — 57.4 / 61.4
Married, aged 25-44 — 77.5 / 79.1
Single, aged 25-44 — 81.9 / 83.4
Married, aged 45 and over — 43.2 / 47.2
Single, aged 45 and over — 43.5 / 46.1

Children & family type
Preschooler(s) — 65.6 / 68.4
Preschoolers/employed husband — 69.9 / 71.3
Preschoolers/lone parent — 51.2 / 58.1
Children 6-15 — 77.7 / 79.7

Education
0-8 years education — 18 / 16.6
High school diploma — 62.4 / 63.2
College diploma/certificate — 71.5 / 71.6
University degree — 80.3 / 79.4

0   20   40   60   80   100
Participation Rate

Source: Statistics Canada 2001. *Labour Force Historical Review 2000,* Cat. no. 71F004XCB.

Financial necessity is a major factor, often the most important one, in many women's decisions to seek employment. Generally, wives in low-income families or women who are lone parents may be compelled to work to meet, or help meet, basic expenses. In fact, the most common dual-earner family combination in Canada is a blue-collar husband and a wife in a clerical, sales, or service job (Chawla 1992: 24). The participation rate for single mothers with preschool children at home was 58 percent in 2000, while the rate for mothers of preschoolers who had an employed husband (or partner) was 71 percent. For many single mothers, finding or keeping a job may be difficult, given such factors as lower educational attainment and difficulties arranging adequate and affordable child care. Low-paid, unstable work is a major reason for the high incidence of poverty in this group.[7] In 1997, 56 percent of female-headed families lived below Statistics Canada's low income cut-off (the unofficial poverty line), compared with only 12 percent of two-parent families with children (Statistics Canada 2000a: 151). Growing concern about child poverty in Canada is clearly linked to the difficulties lone-parent females face in the labour market (Canadian Council on Social Development 2001). In contrast, better-educated, urban, middle-class women who are married and whose spouse or partner is a professional or a manager have greater opportunities and the luxury of choice with regard to employment (Lowe and Krahn 1985: 4). Among families with the highest incomes in Canada, it is very likely that the female partner is a high-earning manager or professional.[8]

Women's organizations, such as the National Action Committee on the Status of Women, and social policy experts point to these patterns to support their calls for better child-care facilities, higher minimum wages, and less punitive welfare programs. Such reforms would remove some of the barriers that economically disadvantaged mothers of young children now face in the labour market.

WORK AND FAMILY

Traditional gender roles and values have defined women's work as household tasks and child rearing. This enduring male–female division of labour underlies much of the gender inequality we see today. For example, domestic responsibilities continue to limit women's availability for paid work, keeping many married women financially dependent on their husbands. Feminists argue that women's subordination results from the combination of two systems of domination: capitalism and patriarchy. Capitalism incorporated earlier patriarchal social arrangements. Broadly speaking, *patriarchy* refers to male domination over women, but more specifically it describes forms of family organization in which fathers and husbands hold total power.[9] Remnants of patriarchy still reinforce stereotypes of women as cheap, expendable labour. Furthermore, women's traditional family roles of wife and mother often restrict their employment opportunities and, for those who are employed, create a *double day* of paid and unpaid work.

Changing Family Forms

Women in the 1950s saw the home as their major priority. They sometimes were employed before having children, stayed home to raise them, and then returned to the labour force in middle age after the children had grown up.[10] Because most wives in the 1950s and 1960s responded to the demands of child rearing by leaving the labour force, employers assumed that women must have a weaker attachment to paid work than men. A 1952 national study found that the major reason married women under the age of 40 left their employment was for child-raising responsibilities (Boyd 1985). Similar family constraints on employment for women still exist. However, between 1981 and 1991, there was a pervasive national trend for mothers with children at home to seek paid jobs, with this group accounting for most of the increase in female participation (Logan and Belliveau 1995: 25). As a result, many more women are facing the stresses and conflicts of juggling paid work with family roles.

Today, however, far fewer women leave the labour force, and those who do leave for a shorter time. Consequently, the dual-earner family is now the norm in Canada. Since the 1960s, the traditional family in which the husband was the sole earner has been eclipsed by dual-earner families, which make up 61 percent of all husband–wife families.[11] At the same time, the number of lone-parent families is on the rise. According to the 1996 Canadian Census, 22 percent of families with children present are headed by lone parents, more than 83 percent of whom are women. The number of mother-led families with children nearly doubled between 1971 and 1996 (Statistics Canada, 2000d: 32, 43).

The Domestic Division of Labour

While there are some indications of greater equality in the gender division of household chores, changes in this area of domestic life have not kept pace with the rising employment rate of married women. Evidence gleaned from *time budget studies*, which ask people to record in detail how they spend their time, leads to the conclusion that many employed wives often work what Arlie Hochschild calls a "second shift" in the home.[12] After putting in seven or eight hours on the job, some wives return home to cook, clean, shop, and look after children—the domestic chores their mothers and grandmothers did as full-time housewives. This echoes the findings of a 1971 study by Martin Meissner and his colleagues, which found that taking a job outside the home meant a decrease of 13.5 hours per week in leisure time for a sample of British Columbia wives. Yet their husbands experienced no loss of leisure time because they had not shared the housework to begin with.[13] The researchers concluded that time pressures and added workloads create a "double burden" for many employed wives.

Recent investigations show some change, but women still continue to shoulder this double burden. Statistics Canada's 1998 *General Social Survey* (GSS) documented that employed women devoted an average of 4.4 hours daily to total unpaid work, compared with 2.7 hours for men. Most of this difference reflects the fact that women, on average, devote twice as much time to domestic work and primary child care (Figure 4.3). An earlier GSS found that in dual-earner families in which both spouses had full-time jobs, more than half of the wives had sole responsibility for housework (meal preparation and cleanup, cleaning, and laundry); these tasks were shared equally in just 1 in 10 such families.[14] Yet there are considerable variations in the domestic division of labour. In addition to age and education—younger and university-educated women tend to have less traditional roles—recent Canadian studies have identified single parenthood, continuing gender role stereotypes, power relations shaping the household division of labour, and wives' earnings relative to their husbands' as influencing time spent on household tasks and how these are divided.[15].

Population aging also has implications for women in that they often provide care to elderly and dependent parents and relatives. *Elder care* is becoming a concern amid predictions of a "care-giving crunch," as fewer women are available to meet such demands because of the constraints of jobs, which would not have been the case a generation ago (McKinnon and Odynak 1991: 31). Actually, elder care has become quite common, as the 1991 *Alberta Survey* documented: 41 percent of full-time employed women in the province and 35 percent of full-time employed men reported they provided assistance to an elderly relative.[16] The heaviest burden falls to the "sandwich generation": adults who combine child care with caring for their elderly parents. In 1996, 15 percent of women in the 25 to 54 age group (the majority of whom are in the labour market) provided both kinds of care, compared with 9 percent of men in the same age group (Statistics Canada 2000d: 114)

Wives' household work varies, depending on their social class position and their husbands' occupation. Working-class wives have a higher probability of facing the combined stresses of poverty and menial employment. Women married to managerial and professional men may be expected to comply with the traditions of a two-person career. It has been commonly assumed in large corporations that male managers climbing the career ladder will have the

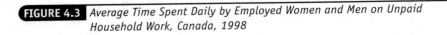

FIGURE 4.3 *Average Time Spent Daily by Employed Women and Men on Unpaid Household Work, Canada, 1998*

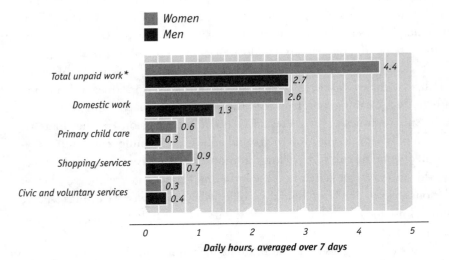

Daily hours, averaged over 7 days

*Includes primary child care, meal preparation, meal clean-up, cleaning and laundry, and shopping and services performed by employed individuals with spouses.

Source: Statistics Canada 1999. *Overview of the Time Use of Canadians in 1998,* Cat. no. 12F0080XIE.

unpaid services of a wife. Success in the corporate world demands unwavering dedication to one's career, often resulting in very low family involvement. Wives are expected to put on dinner parties, accompany their husbands to company social functions, make travel arrangements, and plan household moves. They are what Rosabeth Moss Kanter (1977: Chapter 5) calls "unpaid servants of the corporation." These antiquated vestiges of male corporate culture are eroding as more women pursue their own careers. However, women attempting to establish themselves in management still face disadvantages, given lingering expectations about two-person careers. Unfortunately, their husbands are seldom willing to take on extra child care and housework.

Balancing Work and Family

"Work has changed. Women have changed," writes Arlie Hochschild. "But most workplaces have remained inflexible in the face of the family demands of their workers and at home, most men have yet to really adapt to the changes in women. This strain between the change in women and the absence of change in much else leads me to speak of a 'stalled revolution'" (Hochschild 1989: 12). Perhaps the most pervasive consequence of this stalled revolution is the rise of *job–family conflict* – or what could be called more broadly work-life conflict. When the Conference Board of Canada surveyed 11,000 employees across Canada in 1989, it discovered that two-thirds had some difficulty balancing work and family (MacBride-King 1990; Stone 1994). A follow-up study, ten years later, discovered that stress due to difficulties balancing work and family responsibilities had increased. In 1999, 17 percent of survey respondents experienced "a lot" of stress trying to balance work and family, compared with 9 percent reported in the 1989 survey (MacBride-King and Bachmann 1999).

Juggling the demands of job and family also can affect quality of life. As Figure 4.4 documents, 21 percent of women and 16 percent of men between the ages of 15 and 64 responding to the 1998 *General Social Survey* (GSS) reported feeling severely "time-crunched"– a substantial increase in overall stress since 1992. The most highly-stressed age group are 25-to-34-year-olds, who are most likely to be juggling jobs and family responsibilities. Taking a closer look at these GSS findings, we find little difference in time-crunch stress between men and women ages 25 to 44 who are single, with no children and

FIGURE 4.4 *Time-Crunch Stress* by Gender and Age, Canada, 1992 and 1998*

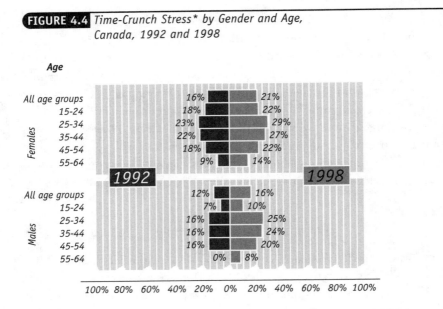

Age

Females
- All age groups: 16% / 21%
- 15-24: 18% / 22%
- 25-34: 23% / 29%
- 35-44: 22% / 27%
- 45-54: 18% / 22%
- 55-64: 9% / 14%

1992   *1998*

Males
- All age groups: 12% / 16%
- 15-24: 7% / 10%
- 25-34: 16% / 25%
- 35-44: 16% / 24%
- 45-54: 16% / 20%
- 55-64: 0% / 8%

100% 80% 60% 40% 20% 0% 20% 40% 60% 80% 100%

*Respondents were asked to answer "yes" or "no" to a series of ten questions on their perception of time. Those who agreed with seven or more were considered to have high levels of time stress.

Source: Statistics Canada. "Time Stressed Population." Adapted from *The Daily,* November 9, 1999. Cat. no. 11-301E.

working full-time. In sharp contrast, married female parents of the same age who work full-time have a much greater rate of stress – again, most likely a result of the combination of job and family demands (Statistics Canada, *The Daily,* 9 November 1999). This is not to suggest, though, that child care and family responsibilities are strictly women's concerns. In fact, men increasingly are expressing more interest in family-friendly policies, and some are contributing to the changing configuration of work, gender, and family by redefining their roles.[17] Male gender roles are changing slowly; for example, there were "stay-at-home-dads" in 6 percent of all families with a parent at home in 1997, up from 1 percent in 1976 (Marshall 1998: 11). It will be important for future research to monitor male attitudes and behaviour on work-family balance issues.

The pressures created by work-family imbalance have costs for employers, too (Glass and Estes 1997). For example, a survey of employees in medium-sized and large organizations in Saskatchewan found that a combination of heavy workloads and a lack of workplace supports for balancing work and family contributed to absenteeism, intent to quit, lack of commitment to the organization, and job dissatisfaction (Duxbury and Higgins 1998). Absenteeism caused by competing job and family demands is a significant source of lost productivity for employers. Indeed, Statistics Canada documents that while male rates of absenteeism have risen only slightly since the late 1970s, female rates rose steadily, mainly due to family or personal obligations as growing numbers of mothers with preschool children sought employment (Akyeampong 1995). In 1998, employed women lost an average of 9.2 days, compared to 6.9 for men, due to illness, disability, personal or family responsibilities (Akyeampong 1999a: 31).

While some employers have moved to create family-friendly work environments, firms in the most dynamic sectors of the economy face a range of pressures that make work-life balance difficult. A study of knowledge workers in the seven largest Ottawa-area high-tech workplaces found that work cultures in these firms were defined by heavy workloads and long hours. This culture is not sustainable, however. It may suit younger, single workers who have no dependent care responsibilities, but lack of attention to work-life balance issues will cause increasingly serious problems—notably high quitting rates, especially among key female knowledge workers—as the high-tech workforce moves into its 30s, marries and starts raising children (Duxbury, Dyke and Lam 2000).

The Conference Board asked employees what type of employer support would help them to better integrate their job, family, and personal life. Common responses included child-care support, flexible work hours and schedules, improved personal and family-related leave, and a more understanding approach by management to employees' nonwork needs. Slowly, in part due to studies such as these, heightened awareness of the economic and individual costs of job-family conflict is challenging employers to reconsider some long-standing policies. Yet on-site child-care facilities are rare; many managers seem rigidly locked into a nine-to-five day and five-day-week schedule; and paid maternity or paternity leave (in addition to the period covered by EI) or elder care support are provided by only a minority of employers.[18] Of all these needs, perhaps the issue of child care requires the most urgent attention. According to the 1988 *National Child Care Survey*, arranging child care that is affordable, of high quality, and convenient presents an ongoing problem for many parents – although preferences for different forms of child care vary widely among working parents (Crompton 1991; Beaujot 1997). The growth of licensed child care spaces in the 1990s has by no means filled the need. In 1996, there were about 300,000 supervised day care spaces nationally for preschoolers, clearly insufficient to meet the requirements of the 900,000 dual-earner or employed lone-parent families that had at least one preschool child (Statistics Canada 2000d: 101). Many children of working parents are looked after informally by sitters, neighbours, nannies, or relatives. So far, Quebec is the only jurisdiction in Canada to make a concerted effort to address these issues, having introduced in 1997 a comprehensive program of universal subsidized day care, early childhood education, support for parental leaves, and improved family allowances. This no doubt explains why half of the 338 work-related child-care centres in Canada are located in Quebec.[19]

All in all, what we have just documented surely amounts to a "stalled revolution." Over a decade ago, the Conference Board predicted that more employers would respond to these needs as the drain on productivity became more visible and employee pressure for such policies mounted (Paris 1989). Unfortunately for many working parents, there are few tangible signs of this happening. And for some employees who do have flexible work arrangements, recent research suggests that these may not meet expectations in terms of reducing the stresses of balancing job and family. After examining a variety of alternative work arrangements, Janet Fast and Judith Frederick (1996) concluded that self-employment, flex-place (working some hours at home), and shift work had no effect on workers' perceived time stress. Both women and men in part-time jobs are less time-stressed than full-timers, although far more women than men choose part-time work for family-related reasons. Flextime (employees choosing when their work day starts and stops) helps to reduce time pressures, but it is less available to women than to men. Compressed work weeks (fewer days per week with longer hours each day) seem to increase women's level of time stress, likely because they interfere with family routines. Job sharing, which now is available to only 8 percent of part-time workers, was not examined in this study, but it may have the potential to contribute to reduced time pressure and better integration of work and family (Marshall 1997).

However, the barriers to achieving work-family balance are numerous and complex. Arlie Hochschild's research suggests that even in organizations that provide family-friendly policies and programs, employees may experience difficulties finding enough time for their families. One of the largest barriers is the fact that society places great value, and confers rewards, on people who are successful in their careers. The result, especially among professionals and managers, is that employees spend more, not less, time at work. As Hochschild (1997: 198-99) suggests: "...in a cultural contest between work and home, working parents are voting with their feet, and the workplace is winning."

GENDER SEGREGATION IN THE LABOUR MARKET

At the heart of gender inequality in the work world is the structuring of the labour market into male and female segments. *Occupational gender segregation* refers to the concentration of men and women in different occupations. A potent combination of gender-role socialization, education, and labour market mechanisms continue to channel women into a limited number of occupations in which mainly other females are employed.

Female Job Ghettos

Female *job ghettos* typically offer little economic security and little opportunity for advancement; furthermore, the work is often unpleasant, boring, and sometimes physically taxing. Women in job ghettos lack ready access to the more challenging and lucrative occupations dominated by men. These male segments of the labour market operate as *shelters*, conferring advantages on workers within them through entrance restrictions.[20] The concepts of ghettos and shelters emphasize the unequal rewards and opportunities built into the job market on the basis of a worker's sex. It is especially important to recognize that job opportunities determine an individual's living standard, future prospects, and overall quality of life—in Max Weber's words, her or his *life chances.*

Simply put, women in Canada are more likely to be poor than men. Poverty among employed women has grown at five times the rate of growth among men since the early 1970s. The root causes of this can be traced to a combination of gender-based labour market segmentation and domestic and child-care responsibilities. Gunderson et al. explain the broader context of these realities:

> ... working poverty has not decreased and appears to be on the increase, highlighting the fact that something is fundamentally

amiss in the labour market. The fruits of economic growth are not being shared evenly. The evidence of this is striking. Regional disparities in employment opportunities in Canada are glaring. The labour market is volatile with international competition, technological change, and deindustrialization leading to layoffs and plant closures, creating hardship and leaving many people out of work. The quality of the jobs now being created is in question, as part-time and low-wage service sector jobs have proliferated. These are the jobs that tend to be open to women, and they are the jobs that produce working poverty. (Gunderson, Muszynski, and Keck 1990: 220)

One of the fundamental mechanisms underlying segmentation is the *gender labelling* of jobs. Employers do not always make hiring decisions on strictly rational grounds, despite what economics textbooks would have us believe. If all hiring decisions were totally rational, women would have been recruited much earlier in the industrialization process and in far greater numbers, given their cost advantage as cheap labour. As already mentioned, men typically opposed the employment of women in their occupations for fear of having their wages undercut. Furthermore, traditional values narrowly defined female roles as child rearing and homemaking. Women, therefore, were relegated to the less rewarding jobs that men did not want. Because these occupations came to be labelled "female," future employers would likely only seek women for them, and, regardless of the skills demanded by the job, pay and status would remain low.

Dominant social values about femininity and masculinity have long been used to define job requirements. For instance, by the late 19th century, teaching, social work, nursing, and domestic work were socially acceptable for women. Society could justify this on the ideological grounds that these occupations—caring for the sick, the old, and the unfortunate, transmitting culture to children, and performing domestic chores—demanded essentially female traits. Exclusive male rights to the better jobs and higher incomes thus went unchallenged, and the role of women as homemaker and wife was preserved. Once a job was labelled male or female, it was difficult for workers of the opposite sex to gain entry (Lowe 1987).

Trends in Labour Market Gender Segregation

In Chapter 2, we outlined gender differences in the occupational distribution of the labour force. Figure 4.5 explores this further, summarizing employment distribution and concentration in 1996. The left-hand set of bars in Figure 4.5 identify the percentage of employees in each occupation who are women. Clerical/administrative jobs and nursing and other health-related occupations (excluding physicians) have the highest concentrations of women, who make up 75 and 87 percent, respectively, of all employees. Teaching, social sciences, and sales/service occupations (for example, jobs in restaurants, bars, hotels, tourism, hairdressing, and child-care facilities, and domestics and building cleaners) are around 60 percent female. All these could be labelled job ghettos

FIGURE 4.5 *Employment Concentration and Occupational Distribution of Women, Canada, 1999*

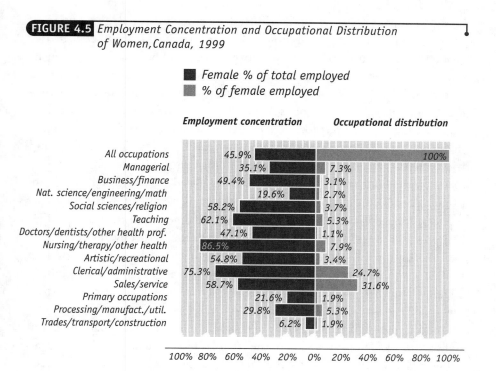

■ *Female % of total employed*
■ *% of female employed*

	Employment concentration	Occupational distribution
All occupations	45.9%	100%
Managerial	35.1%	7.3%
Business/finance	49.4%	3.1%
Nat. science/engineering/math	19.6%	2.7%
Social sciences/religion	58.2%	3.7%
Teaching	62.1%	5.3%
Doctors/dentists/other health prof.	47.1%	1.1%
Nursing/therapy/other health	86.5%	7.9%
Artistic/recreational	54.8%	3.4%
Clerical/administrative	75.3%	24.7%
Sales/service	58.7%	31.6%
Primary occupations	21.6%	1.9%
Processing/manufact./util.	29.8%	5.3%
Trades/transport/construction	6.2%	1.9%

100% 80% 60% 40% 20% 0% 20% 40% 60% 80% 100%

Source: Statistics Canada. *Women in Canada 2000. A gender-based statistical report,* p. 128. Cat. no. 89-503-XPC.

in the sense that the majority of employees are women, although the pay and security provided in some (particularly nursing and teaching) are relatively good. By contrast, women form a small minority of workers in natural sciences, engineering and mathematics occupations, primary occupations (e.g., forestry, mining, fishing, farming), and in trades, transportation, and construction.

The right-hand series of bars in the figure show the distribution of the female labour force across all occupations. Clerical and administrative jobs employed one in four women workers in 1999. And service and sales jobs accounted for just under one in three female jobs. Taken together, these two occupational categories account for over half of the female labour force. This attests to women's continuing overrepresentation in lower-status occupations.

For a more complete understanding of where men and women are located in the labour market, we need to investigate the industrial distribution of employment. You will recall from Chapter 2 that Canada's service-based economy is generating polarization between good and bad jobs. How then are men and women distributed within the upper and lower tiers of the service sector? Referring back to Table 2.1 will help to answer this question. Two-thirds of men work in the goods sector. Potentially this has negative implications for the male labour force, given the massive restructuring occurring in manufacturing. Women's jobs are far more likely to be found in service industries. Overall, 87 percent of employed women in 2000 were in the service sector, with about one-third employed in its lower tier (retail trade and consumer services). In comparison, 19 percent of men worked in the lower-tier services. Interestingly, a higher proportion of women than men also worked in upper-tier services (59 percent and 44 percent, respectively). The main explanation for this is the concentration of women in the education/health/welfare sector. But in overall terms, our discussion of service sector jobs in Chapter 2 suggests that relatively more women than men are in nonstandard, low-quality jobs.

Indeed, there is a growing body of research on the gendered nature of nonstandard work. The very notion of the "standard job" can be considered a masculine norm of employment—the husband as family breadwinner, working full time and in a more or less permanent job with the same employer. These standard job assumptions underlay the post-war employment contract, which has changed dramatically with the spread of a range of nonstandard employment relationships (Vosko 2000). A major reason women seek self-employment is to gain the independence and flexibility they feel they need to balance work with their family and personal life. But there are costs, including considerably lower wages than their counterparts who are employees and lack of benefits and career supports, such as access to training or business networks (Hughes 1999; Arai 2000). Linked to gender, there also is a racial dimension to non-standard work (Zeytinoglu and Muteshi 2000). Visible minority women, often recent immigrants, have historically been employed in some of the most economically marginal forms of work, in family-run businesses, domestic labour, or the garment industry. Perhaps the most feminized form of nonstandard work is temporary employment. As Leah Vosko (2000) argues, the expanding temporary help industry is based on traditional stereotypes of "women's work," even though the flexible and impermanent employment relationships it offers are seen as a hallmark of the "new economy."

How much has gender-based job segregation diminished over the course of this century? Table 4.1 shows that in 1901, 71 percent of all employed women were concentrated in five occupations. Within this small number of socially acceptable women's jobs, that of domestic servant employed the greatest portion of working women at 36 percent. Next in importance were seamstressing and school teaching, each employing roughly 13 percent of the female labour force. These three occupations fit our description of a job ghetto, given that three-quarters or more of all workers in the job were female. In the early twentieth century, outright exclusion was the prominent form of gender-based labour market segregation, with professions such as law and medicine barring women, while others, such as dentistry, allowed women to enter but under conditions that ensured their marginalization (Adams 1998).

This was not the case, however, for the two other main female occupations. Clerical work at the turn of the century was still a man's job, although by the 1940s the gender balance had shifted toward women. Interestingly, clerical work was one of the few traditionally male jobs to undergo this *feminization* process. Behind this change was the rapid expansion of office work accompanied by a more fragmented and routinized division of labour. As a result, a layer of new positions emerged at the bottom of office hierarchies, opening office doors to women (Lowe 1987). Finally, the fact that farmers and stock raisers appear as one of the five prominent female occupations may seem peculiar. Considering that Canada was an agricultural economy in 1901, it is

TABLE 4.1 *The Five Leading Female Occupations in Canada, 1901, 1951, 1986 and 1996*

Occupation	Number of Employed Women	Percent of Total Female Employment in Occupation	Females as Percent of Employment in Occupation
1901			
1. Domestic servants	84,984	35.7	87
2. Seamstresses	32,145	13.5	100
3. School teachers	30,870	13.0	78
4. Office clerks	12,569	5.3	78
5. Farmers and stockraisers	8,495	3.6	2
All five occupations		71.1	
1951*			
1. Stenographers and typists	133,485	11.5	96.4
2. Office clerks	118,025	10.1	42.7
3. Sales clerks	95,443	8.2	55.1
4. Hotel, café and private household workers n.e.s.+	88,775	7.6	89.1
5. School teachers	74,319	6.4	72.5
All five occupations		43.8	
1996			
1. Retail salespersons	339,025	5.0	61.2
2. Secretaries	311,835	4.6	98.3
3. Cashiers	235,585	3.5	85.9
4. Registered nurses	220,625	3.2	94.8
5. Accounting clerks	219,895	3.2	83.0
All five occupations		19.5	

+n.e.s.: Not elsewhere specified. Excludes a few persons seeking work who have never been employed.
*1951 Census does not include the Yukon or the NWT.

Source: Canada, Dominion Bureau of Statistics, *Occupational Trends in Canada, 1891-1931* (Ottawa, 1939), Table B; Statistics Canada, *Women in Canada: A Statistical Report*, 2nd ed. (Ottawa: Statistics Canada, Cat. no. 89-503E, 1990), 82; Canada, 1951 *Census, Volume 4, Labour Force—Occupations and Industries*, Table No. 4; Canada, 1986 *Census, The Nation, Population and Dwelling Characteristics: Occupation* (Statistics Canada, Cat. no. 93-112), Table No. 1; Canada, *1991 Census, Industry and Occupation: Industry and Class of Worker* (Statistics Canada, Cat. no. 93-327), Table No. 1; "Ten most frequent jobs for women, Canada, 1996," adapted from Statistics Canada, *The Daily* (17 March 1998: 6), Cat. no. 11-001E.

understandable that women would form a small part of the paid agricultural workforce.

The twentieth-century march of industrialization saw a decline of some female jobs, such as domestic work and seamstressing, and the rise of new employment opportunities in booming service industries. By 1951, the two leading female occupations were in the clerical area. Along with sales clerks, hotel, café, and domestic workers, and teachers, they made up 44 percent of the female workforce just after World War II.

As we have seen, female job ghettos still exist. Office and sales jobs have topped the list since World War II. However, women are now entering a broader range of occupations and professions. For example, according to the 1996 Census, the five main female-dominated job titles accounted for only 20 percent of the entire female labour force. This is a positive sign of occupational diversification; but how far have women moved into nontraditional (in other words, male-dominated) occupations? Karen Hughes's analysis of the 484 detailed occupations in the 1971 Census discovered that 86 percent of women worked in traditionally female occupations.[21] Over the next 15 years, the proportion of women in these traditional occupations declined to 79 percent, then changed little between 1986 and 1991. This raises questions about the degree to which women can move out of gender-typed occupations over their working lives – the idea that "female" jobs are a way station through which some women pass on their way to better jobs that are not gender-typed (Chan 2000).

Yet, at the same time, women were making gains in what can be called *nontraditional jobs*, those in which men have predominated. By 1991, women had achieved equal representation with men in optometry and financial management, and nearly equal representation in sales management and government administration (Hughes 1995).

Additional insights can be gleaned about the shifts taking place in female employment by focusing on professional occupations. Because professions are organized around specific bodies of knowledge and expertise, usually acquired through a university degree, women's access to these jobs should improve as their level of education rises. The proportion of all university degrees granted to women has been rising steadily. Women's share of undergraduate enrollment jumped from 43 to 53 percent between 1972–73 and 1992–93, and continued to rise through the 1990s (see Figure 4.6). There were also large increases at the master's and doctoral levels. All major program areas saw rising female enrollments. Math, science, and engineering fields are the only disciplines in which women do not make up more than half of all students; in fact, women are significantly underrepresented in these areas.

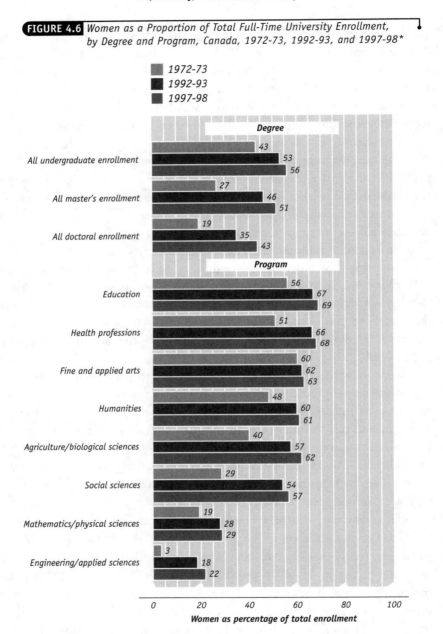

FIGURE 4.6 *Women as a Proportion of Total Full-Time University Enrollment, by Degree and Program, Canada, 1972-73, 1992-93, and 1997-98**

1972-73
1992-93
1997-98

Degree

All undergraduate enrollment — 43, 53, 56

All master's enrollment — 27, 46, 51

All doctoral enrollment — 19, 35, 43

Program

Education — 56, 67, 69

Health professions — 51, 66, 68

Fine and applied arts — 60, 62, 63

Humanities — 48, 60, 61

Agriculture/biological sciences — 40, 57, 62

Social sciences — 29, 54, 57

Mathematics/physical sciences — 19, 28, 29

Engineering/applied sciences — 3, 18, 22

0 20 40 60 80 100
Women as percentage of total enrollment

*Includes udergraduate and graduate students, except those in graduate certificate and diploma programs.

Source: Adapted from Statistics Canada, *Women in Canada 2000: A Gender-Based Statistical Report*, p. 94. Cat. no. 89-503-XPE.

Consistent with the direct connection between educational and occupational attainment discussed in Chapter 3, women accounted for two-thirds of the growth in professional occupations between 1981 and 1986 (Marshall 1989). Especially strong gains were made in male-dominated professions —a trend that continued through the 1990s. Pharmacy is an interesting case, having become 50 percent female by 1986. Research examining Ontario pharmacists sheds light on this feminization process. Despite gender parity, pharmacy remains segregated horizontally and vertically. Women pharmacists are more likely to work in chain stores or hospitals than in independent pharmacies, they are more likely to be employees than owners or franchisees, and their earnings are significantly lower (Tanner et al. 1999). However, women are more satisfied with their current job and careers than are men. Men, on the other hand, have shown no signs of retreating from pharmacy as more women entered.

Still, many traditional male professions present hurdles to female entry. Furthermore, there has been considerably less movement of men into female-dominated occupations. For instance, since 1987 women's share of nursing and other health-related professions (excluding medicine and dentistry) has remained steady at around 87 percent.[22] Thus, to the extent that occupational gender segregation is breaking down, it is due to women moving into male-dominated areas, not vice versa. And finally, despite the changes outlined above, women still have considerably fewer occupational and career avenues open to them.

Gender Stratification within Occupations

Thus far, we have traced broad historical patterns of *horizontal* occupational gender segregation. Now we will examine a related obstacle women face, *vertical* segregation. This refers to how a gendered division of tasks, statuses, and responsibilities exists within specific occupations. As a rule, men tend to be in positions of greater authority in organizations and, consequently, usually receive better job rewards than women. Consider the teaching profession. Even though women made up 69 percent of all school teachers and counsellors in 1996, they occupied only 38 percent of school administrative positions. Approximately 53 percent of the women in teaching are in elementary school classrooms, while men are concentrated in the higher-status, better-paying jobs in universities, colleges, high schools, and educational administrations (Statistics Canada 1996b: Table 713).

The situation is much the same in other professions. Women have made significant inroads recently, particularly in law and medicine, although there is a tendency for them to opt for lower-status specialties such as family law or general medical practice.[23] This reinforces assumptions often made by the male establishment in these professions about female colleagues being best suited to tasks calling upon their "natural instincts" as wives and mothers.

In their probing investigation of the changes in legal careers in Canada, John Hagan and Fiona Kay portray a gender-stratified profession in which work environments are not family-friendly. Large numbers of women entered law in the 1970s and 1980s, when the profession was expanding and reorganizing into larger firms. According to Hagan and Kay (1995: 182):

> ... women were recruited into the profession during a period when they were needed to fill entry- and intermediate-level positions and were perceived to be compliant employees .... It is possible that ... many partners in law firms were encouraged by the belief that as in the teaching profession of an earlier era, women would assume entry-level positions in the profession, work diligently for a number of years, and then abandon their early years of invested work to bear children and raise families, leaving partnership positions to men assumed to be more committed to their occupational careers.

These assumptions were largely borne out in research findings. The changing professional climate of the 1980s restricted opportunities for both men and women to attain partnerships—a financial and management stake in the firm that results in much higher earnings. However, women lost out even more than men, mainly because of the conflicts and compromises engendered by the interplay of professional demands and expectations with family roles. Still, women who continue to practise law full-time after having children have high work commitment and high job satisfaction, despite lower earnings than men. Other researchers (Robson and Wallace 2001) have examined the persistence of lower female earnings in law, despite similar human capital investments by both sexes, concluding that while there is no direct pay discrimination, women are disadvantaged by factors such as experience, work hours, and job autonomy that affect earnings. A number of trends deserve monitoring. The job market for lawyers has improved considerably since Hagan and Kay's study and women continue to enter the profession. To what extent have the experiences of the earlier generation of female lawyers led to a better adaptation of careers and work practices to women's desire to strike a balance in their lives – without economic penalty?

During the 1970s, women began making major breakthroughs in the male domains of business and finance professions and medicine and dentistry. These trends continue, for in 1999 women made up close to half of the workers in these occupations (Figure 4.5). They have also made gains in other high-status occupations, and in 1999 made up 35 percent of managers. How does this compare with other advanced industrial countries? The general category of managerial work in the United States and Australia was over 40 percent female by the early 1990s, well ahead of Japan (9 percent), Germany (19 percent), and Mexico (20 percent).[24] This selective comparison suggests that labour market and cultural barriers to women may be more resistant to change in some countries than in others.

However, a detailed analysis of the managerial category reveals that women are clustered in the least responsible and lowest-paying jobs. By reviewing detailed occupational titles contained in the 1996 Census, we learn that women accounted for 8 percent and 17 percent, respectively, of senior managers in key goods-producing industries and in business and distributive service industries (see Table 4.2). Looking more closely at the latter sector, a study of women in Canada's investment industry (investment dealers) found that gender stereotyping, exclusion from informal networks and role models, and a lack of family-friendly policies were major barriers to women advancing into senior management positions (Women in Capital Markets, 2001). Moreover, few women have entered management positions in natural sciences and engineering or in the mining and oil sector—all economic activities dominated by men. Conversely, women managers are concentrated in predominantly female enclaves within organizations, such as office administration, personnel, and sales. In conclusion, despite women having entered management in sizable numbers in North America and Europe, real power and decision-making authority continue to be exercised by male corporate executives and directors (Clement and Myles 1994).

TABLE 4.2 *Average Employment Income of Full-time, Full-year Workers in the 16 Highest-Paying Occupations, Canada, 1995*

	Income, Men	Income, Women	F-M Earnings ratio	Total number employed	Number of women employed	Women as % of total
Judges	$128,791	$117,707	91%	1,765	405	23%
Specialist Physicians	$137,019	$86,086	63%	12,560	3,220	26%
General Practitioners and family physicians	$116,750	$81,512	70%	21,670	5,615	26%
Dentists	$109,187	$71,587	66%	8,530	1,535	18%
Senior managers - goods production, utilities, transportation & construction	$102,971	$58,463	57%	35,510	2,880	8%
Senior managers - financial, communications and other business services	$104,715	$71,270	68%	23,055	3,860	17%
Lawyers and notaries	$89,353	$60,930	68%	44,385	12,080	27%
Senior managers - trade, broadcasting and other services	$84,237	$48,651	58%	28,655	4,060	14%
Primary production managers	$78,421	$48,479	62%	7,075	405	6%
Securities agents, investment dealers and traders	$90,391	$47,323	52%	14,520	4,880	34%
Petroleum engineers	$73,657	$56,506	77%	2,765	180	7%
Chiropractors	$71,032	$56,764	80%	2,370	370	16%
Engineering, science and architecture managers	$69,792	$53,138	76%	17,835	1,665	9%
University professors	$72,532	$55,909	77%	31,395	8,190	26%
Senior managers - health, education, social & community organizations	$78,012	$56,190	72%	8,025	3,615	45%
Air pilots	$68,219	$43,991	64%	7,490	195	3%

Source: Statistics Canada, "Number and average earnings of full year, full time workers in the 25 highest and 25 lowest paying occupations, by sex, Canada 1995", adapted from *The Daily*, Cat. no. 11–001E, May 12, 1998.

Women still encounter a *glass ceiling*—subtle barriers to advancement that persist despite formal policies designed to eliminate them. Looking at the 333 employers covered by the federal Employment Equity Act (discussed in more detail below), in 1998 women made up 44 percent of the 586,199 employees. Yet close to two-thirds of these women worked in three occupational groups: clerical personnel; administrative and senior clerical personnel; and supervisors of clerical, sales and service personnel. However, in 1997 and 1998 women's concentration in these jobs decreased somewhat, partly due to their increasing share of managerial and professional occupations. However, women's representation in management ranks was inversely related to the authority and rewards of these positions. Even though employers covered by the Act have been recruiting more women into upper-level management, in 1998 they held about one in five of these senior positions. By way of comparison, in 1989 women made up only 6 percent of upper-level managers in this group of employers.[25] Yet, it has been exceedingly difficult for women to gain entry into the executive suites of major corporations. Despite some recent appointments of women to the top corporate jobs, such as president, chief executive officer (CEO), executive vice-president or chief operating officer, in 1999 women occupied only 3.4 percent of these positions, compared with 5.1 percent in the U.S. (Hughes, 2000: v).

In sum, although the evidence of wider employment horizons for women bodes well for the future, progress toward full gender equality in the workplace is halting and uneven. As Figure 4.5 illustrates, achieving this goal would see women represented in each occupation proportional to their overall share of the labour force, which is now at 46 percent. This immediately raises the question (which we address shortly) of how best to reach this objective. But would women want full access to all male jobs, given that a good number are dirty, dangerous, physically exhausting, insecure, low-paying, or at risk of being restructured out of existence? The implication, of course, is that unless all jobs at the bottom of the occupational hierarchy are upgraded in terms of pay and working conditions, gender equality as defined above would only be a partial advance for women.

THE WAGE GAP

One of the most obvious consequences of labour market segmentation is the *gender wage gap* (or female–male earnings ratio, as we labelled it in Chapter 3). Figure 4.7 shows that women who work full-time for the entire year earned an average of 73 percent of what similarly employed men earned in 1997. This is an accurate way to compare male–female earnings differences, because part-time or part-year workers, who have lower earnings and are disproportionately female, are not included. Despite women entering some of the higher-paying managerial and professional jobs during the 1980s, the

FIGURE 4.7 *Average Earnings in Constant (1997) Dollars for Full-time/Full-year Workers,* by Gender, Canada, 1969—1997*

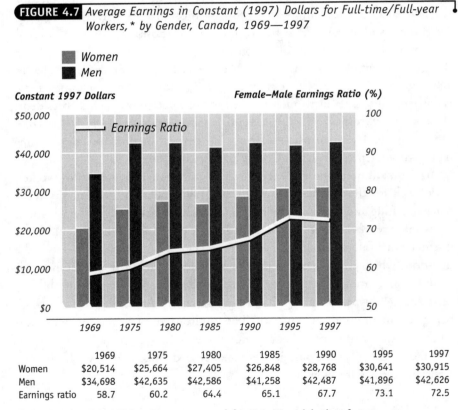

	1969	1975	1980	1985	1990	1995	1997
Women	$20,514	$25,664	$27,405	$26,848	$28,768	$30,641	$30,915
Men	$34,698	$42,635	$42,586	$41,258	$42,487	$41,896	$42,626
Earnings ratio	58.7	60.2	64.4	65.1	67.7	73.1	72.5

*A person who worked 30 hours or more per week for 49 to 52 week in the reference year.

Source: Adapted from Statistics Canada, *Women in Canada 2000: A Gender-Based Statistical Report*, p. 155. Cat. no. 89-503-XPE.

wage gap has narrowed by less than 9 percentage points since 1980 and seems to have plateaued at 73 percent in the mid-1990s. This partly reflects the way in which employment growth trends often counteract each other. During the 1970s, the number of women in the twenty highest-paying occupations swelled more than fourfold, compared with a twofold increase for men (Boulet and Lavallée 1984: 19). But this trend was offset by an expansion of female employment at the lower end of the pay scale. While not used in our calculation of the wage gap, the big rise in the number of part-time jobs is important because it has reduced the earning potential of many women. This distinction between full- and part-time earnings reflects the growing employment disparities among women and between the sexes in the service economy.

Gender-Based Inequality of Earnings

Trends in earnings between 1969 and 1997 deserve brief comment. Figure 4.7 displays *real earnings*, which means that the effects of inflation have been eliminated by adjusting earnings for all years to 1997 dollars. This provides the startling realization that male real earnings did not increase between 1975 and 1997, while women's earnings have nudged upward. Quite different labour market and organizational processes underlie these divergent earnings profiles. While women were being recruited into intermediate-level professions and junior and middle-level management, males were losing ground as traditionally well-paying (often unionized) manual occupations became less common and downsizing pushed older professionals and managers (mostly men) into early retirement. Within the labour market as a whole, some of men's loss was women's gain. A rising proportion of employed women, with incomes somewhat higher than the incomes of women a generation earlier, have kept family incomes from dropping as far as they otherwise might have. Without the wife's income, many husband–wife families now in the middle or working class would likely join the ranks of the poor.

Wages are a basic indicator of overall job quality. Recall from Chapter 3 that high wages also are part of a larger package of extrinsic and intrinsic job rewards. Stated simply, in addition to paying relatively well, "good jobs" usually offer other advantages: a range of benefits, job security, advancement opportunities, and interesting and challenging work. Turning to Figure 4.8, we find that female employees and self-employed individuals are less likely than men to receive benefits such as supplementary health insurance and a dental plan. Furthermore, 40 percent of female workers in 1994 were in non-standard jobs, compared with 27 percent of men (Krahn 1995: 40). Men are also more likely to receive promotions. Jobs occupied by men tend to offer more decision-making authority, have higher skill requirements, and be less repetitive (Krahn 1992: 96). In short, the gender wage gap is part of a broadly based discrepancy between the quality of jobs performed by men and women.

Women's lower earnings also mean reduced living standards. In other words, women in Canada are more likely than men to be poor. Some 54 percent of lone-parent mothers with children under age 18 lived in poverty in 1998, compared with only 10 percent of two-parent families with children. Along with female lone-parents, women over the age of 65 are among the groups in Canadian society most vulnerable to poverty. In 1998, 39 percent of all elderly unattached women lived in poverty, mainly due to inadequate pensions. On the positive side, improvements in income support programs for the elderly have helped to reduce this number from 69 percent in 1980.[26]

Shifting our focus from the bottom to the top of the income distribution, male and female earnings in the 16 highest-paying occupations are displayed in Table 4.2. First observe that the female–male earnings gap is somewhat greater in this top range of jobs than in other occupations. Specifically, the ratio is lower than 73 percent (see Figure 4.7) in eleven of these jobs. The gap is narrowest for judges (91 percent), and widest among investment dealers and stockbrokers (52 percent). Thus, in the most well-paying occupations, as elsewhere, women have a greater chance of receiving a lower salary. Still, women who do succeed in entering Canada's top-paying occupations can expect to earn considerably more than $31,000, which is the average female income (for full-time, full-year workers) in all occupations. But we also need to note that, with one exception (senior managers in health, education, social and community services) all of the highest-paid occupations are male-dominated. In fact, if we examine the list of Canada's 50 best-paid CEOs in 1995, we find that none were women.[27]

When interpreting such data, we must keep in mind that because of the quite recent entry of women into managerial and professional jobs, gender differences in age and experience will account for part of the earnings gap—but by no means all of it. This is underscored when we examine earnings of recent university graduates. Studies comparing men and women who have identical university education, who are similar in age, and who have comparable work experience have found that a wage gap existed (albeit a small one) immediately after graduation.[28]

Accounting for Women's Lower Earnings

Two forms of discrimination affect female earnings. The first is *wage discrimination*, whereby an employer pays a woman less than a man for performing the same job. The second stems from the gender-segregated structure of the

FIGURE 4.8 *Job Benefits Received by Employees and Self-Employed, by Gender, Canada, 2000*

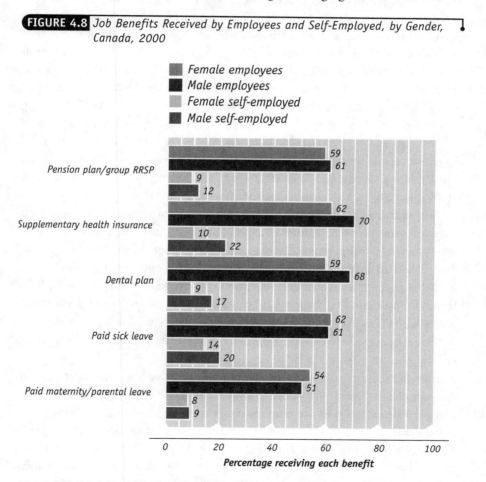

Source: Canadian Policy Research Networks,CPRN/Ekos, *Changing Employment Relationships Survey,* microdata file (n = 2500).

labour market documented earlier. Occupational gender segregation results in lower female wages by channelling women into low-paying job ghettos which, in turn, provide few opportunities for mobility into more rewarding jobs.

To what extent does each form of discrimination contribute to the overall wage gap? To answer this question, one must look at an employee's education, training, and work experience, as well as at the occupation, industry, and geographic location of employment. These factors may influence a worker's productivity and thus his or her earnings. Research by Morley Gunderson, a labour economist, shows that when these productivity factors are taken into account (or are statistically controlled), the earnings ratio in Ontario increases from around 60 percent to between 75 and 85 percent.[29] Differences in work experience, combined with the segmented structure of the labour market, emerge as the main determinants of gender differences in earnings. Applying this analysis to men and women employed in the same jobs within a single establishment, the wage gap narrows even further, as the earnings ratio rises to between 90 and 95 percent. In short, there is little direct pay discrimination by employers, at least in Ontario; rather, it is the division of the labour market into male and female jobs that creates pay inequality.

Human capital theory emphasizes that education is the great equalizer in the job market. Ideally, people with identical educational credentials should have the same amount of human capital and, therefore, be equally competitive in their earning power. But as Chapter 3 emphasized, human capital theory fails to explain why some individuals with equivalent education are much better paid. Nonetheless, education does matter. Ever since World War II, obtaining a good education has been a route to upward mobility for many young Canadians, particularly males from working-class families.

Does the same hold true for women? There is little doubt that women have become better educated. Between 1975–1976 and 1988–1989, women's enrollments made up 73 percent of the increase in university enrollments in undergraduate degree programs (Labour Canada 1990: 69–70). Women also entered a wider range of programs during this period and more of them went on to graduate studies. Dramatic gains were made in male-dominated professional faculties, notably law and medicine. By 1993, women received 51 percent of law degrees and 44 percent of degrees in medicine, representing huge increases from 9 percent and 13 percent, respectively, in 1971 (Statistics Canada 1996a: Table 36). However, women continue to be concentrated in education faculties: in 1997-98, 14 percent of all females enrolled in university were pursuing education degrees (Statistics Canada 2000d: 94).

Professional training for science- and technology-based careers remains heavily male-dominated. For example, in 1997-98, 21.5 percent of the students in Canadian engineering and applied science university programs were women, up slightly from 18 percent in 1992-93 (Statistics Canada 2000d: 94). The challenge of attracting more women into engineering was the focus of a study jointly sponsored by the federal government and the engineering profession. In its 1992 report, the Canadian Committee on Women in Engineering highlighted the complex social and cultural barriers that have obstructed women's way into engineering:

> The cultural influences that channel girls and young women away from non-traditional roles start with parents and other caregivers in pre-school years. Once in school, many girls and young women continue to be discouraged from pursuing interests in mathematics and science and from considering careers in engineering by teachers and guidance counsellors who are not sensitive to gender stereotyping. Because there are so few female science and mathematics teachers and even fewer women engineers to act as role models, young women are not likely to meet and interact with them. These influences are compounded by the perception that engineering is a male profession, that high grades are needed to succeed in engineering studies, and that engineers only build bridges and roads.[30]

Given that more women than ever before are graduating from university, a question worth considering is, have they been able to find the types of jobs for which they have been educated? Overall, a university education is a good predictor of higher occupational attainment for both women and men. However, this generalization requires careful qualification to account for the combined impact of gendered enrollment patterns, mentioned above, and occupational gender segregation. And, as also documented above, a well-educated woman cannot expect to earn as much as a comparably educated man. In short, human capital theory alone fails to explain the employment realities of Canadian female university graduates.

THEORETICAL PERSPECTIVES
ON WORK-RELATED GENDER INEQUALITY

Our key question is, how has occupational gender segregation become so deeply entrenched? Once we can answer this, we will be better able to inform public policy discussions about strategies for achieving equality in the workplace. However, a comprehensive theoretical model capable of adequately explaining the origins, development, and perpetuation of work-related gender inequities has yet to be formulated. Feminist analysis has provided a necessary antidote to the long-standing male bias in much of the sociological research on work. Feldberg and Glenn characterized research in the 1970s in terms of *job* and *gender models* of the workplace. Studies of male workers focused on working conditions and organizational factors (the job model); explanations of women's employment discussed their personal characteristics and family roles (the gender model).[31] Since then, feminist analysts of women's work have probed the intersections of the private and public spheres of domestic work and paid employment, seeking a unified framework For example, women's involvement in various nonstandard forms of work bring the public and private domains into much closer contact, both in time and space. Professionals doing some of their work from home, immigrant women involved in industrial homework, and women who co-own home-based small business with their husbands all struggle, often without success, to maintain home and work as distinct parts of their lives.[32]

Human Capital and Labour Market Segmentation Models

Nonetheless, most theories remain narrowly focused, dealing selectively with gender-role socialization, the family division of labour, the operations of the labour market, employee attitudes and behaviour in organizations, and so on. But the problem of occupational gender segregation is multifaceted, resulting from "the interaction of a well-entrenched and complex set of institutions that perpetuate the inferior position of women in the labour market, since all pressures within society, be they familial, legal, economic, cultural, or historical, tend to reinforce and support occupational segregation" (Reagan and Blaxall 1976: 2).

The two main competing theories of how labour markets operate are *human capital theory* and *labour market segmentation* (or *dual labour market*) *theory* (see Chapter 3). We have already criticized the human capital model for its inability to explain the persistence of gender segregation.[33] While the human capital model is concerned with factors influencing the characteristics of workers—the supply side of the labour market—the segmentation model examines how job requirements within organizations create a demand for particular kinds of workers. Labour market segmentation theory distinguishes between secondary and primary labour markets. Secondary labour markets are located in marginal, often uncompetitive industries that must struggle constantly to keep wages and operating costs down. In contrast, corporations and state bureaucracies in the primary sector can afford to provide employees with relatively high wages, decent benefits, job security, and pleasant working conditions. Furthermore, internal labour markets are found almost exclusively within the primary sector. Employers thus obtain a stable, committed workforce by providing employees with opportunities to develop careers within the organization.

For the segmentation model to accurately explain why men and women hold different kinds of jobs, women would have to be concentrated in the secondary segment of the labour market. This is partly true, since, it will be remembered, relatively more women than men are employed in lower-tier service industries, which form a large part of the secondary sector. However, critics point out that many women are also employed in job ghettos as typists, cleaners, or food servers within the primary sector. In short, an overly general segmentation perspective does not adequately account for gender differences in employment within the same industry or establishment, or inequalities among women. Moreover, the model cannot explain how gender segregation developed in the first place.[34]

Additional factors need to be considered in order to explain why gender is a major source of inequality in the labour market. Some researchers, for instance, link women's labour market position to their traditional roles within the family. Women's family roles have centred on activities such as raising children and caring for dependents; cooking, cleaning, and other services essential to enabling family members to hold down jobs; and contributing a secondary income to the family budget—roughly in that order. Many employed wives experience a conflict when forced to choose between their job and their family. According to this view, women's loyalty usually goes to the latter, and employers consequently often view these women as lacking commitment to their work. Barriers to interesting and better-paying jobs consequently persist (Garnsey et.al. 1985).

Gender Role Socialization

But how are employers' stereotypes of women, women's expectations and restricted employment opportunities, and women's family roles linked to their employment patterns within the workplace? Are such patterns best explained with reference to women's early socialization, including awareness of family roles and feminine qualities, or as a response to their employment conditions? Clearly, both processes may be involved.

The socialization of girls and boys into traditional gender roles creates cultural norms and expectations that they will carry into the workplace as adults. For example, a survey conducted in the early 1980s of children aged 6 to 14 in Ontario, Quebec, and Saskatchewan documented the effects of *gender-role socialization*. While the girls recognized the expanding occupational horizons of women, at a personal level they still held very traditional aspirations. As the researchers conclude: "Many seem to be saying 'Yes, women can become doctors, but I expect to be a nurse'" (Labour Canada 1986: 55). Further discussions with these girls revealed that when they imagined themselves as adults, most saw women who were mothers with small children, supported by a husband.

Have these attitudes changed? Our survey of 1996 Albertan grade 12 students shows that while gender role attitudes are becoming more egalitarian among youth—the vast majority of female and male respondents agree that a woman should have the same job opportunities as a man—more traditional work preferences continue to influence career choices. Nurse, social worker, and teacher were the popular career choices for females, compared with computer programmer/analyst, engineer, and auto mechanic for males.[35] As Jane Gaskell's research illuminates, the choices young working-class women make while they are in school, and upon leaving it, prepare them for domestic labour and employment in female job ghettos. Gaskell (1992: 134–35) explains that the young women whom she studied

> ... end up recreating the world they are not happy with. They see what men are like; they see what jobs pay and how one gets trained for them; they see the lack of child-care options. Within the world

as they experience and know it, they do their best. The young men take their gender privilege equally for granted. The result is the reproduction of gender divisions, not because they are desired, but because these young people don't believe the world can be otherwise.

Gender Inequality and the Organization of Work

Also indispensable to an understanding of female work behaviour is how socialization patterns are strengthened and reproduced within the workplace. Rosabeth Moss Kanter's research suggests that the main sources of gender inequality must be located within work organizations. Kanter's (1977: 67) core argument is that "the job makes the person." She elaborates:

> Findings about typical behaviour of women in organizations that have been used to reflect either biologically based psychological attributes or characteristics developed through a long socialization to the female sex role turn out to reflect very reasonable and very universal responses to current organizational situations (Kanter 1977: 67).

In Kanter's view, then, men and women employed in similar jobs in an organization will react in similar ways to their job conditions. (We return to this subject in Chapter 8.) A good example is Donald Roy's (1959–60) study of male machine operators. These men escaped the drudgery and isolation of their work—"kept from 'going nuts,'" in Roy's words—by engaging in idle chatter, playing games, and fooling around. Female key punch operators, file clerks, or assembly-line workers may seek similar relative satisfactions to cope with the numbing tedium of their work. In either case, management can use the coping behaviour as evidence that these workers are incapable of performing more demanding jobs. This creates a double bind for employees: the most effective ways of personally coping in jobs at the bottom of the organization are also indications to management that workers in these jobs deserve to be kept there.[36]

Kanter does not ignore possible gender differences in socialization or non-work roles. Rather, she underlines the pervasive influence of an individual's job content and organizational position on her or his attitudes and behaviour. This perspective is similar to what Pat and Hugh Armstrong (1994: Chapter 6) call the *materialist* explanation of the gendered division of labour. These researchers document the strong connection between women's self-perceptions and the kinds of work they do. The historical fact that men and women have performed different tasks in the home and in the labour force creates gender differences in work orientations. For example, women may be aware of their subordinate economic role, but they either rationalize it as an outcome of their domestic responsibilities, or else feel powerless to change it.

Gender is a potent controlling device within organizations. Male managers draw on social stereotypes of women as more oriented toward pleasing others, and therefore compliant, to devise paternalistic methods of supervision. Another dominant perception employers have is that women put their domestic responsibilities first, therefore devoting less effort and commitment to their employment. The assumption that women choose to allocate more effort to their domestic than to their employment roles is central to human capital theory's account of why women receive lower wages than men and have limited career opportunities. However, this myth was exploded by Denise and William Bielby (1988), who document that women do not allocate less physical and mental energy to work than men. In fact, women are more efficient workers, given that the majority put greater effort into their work than men with similar attributes. This finding leads the researchers to suggest that women, therefore, should be preferred by employers.

Kanter advances the analysis of gender divisions in organizations by showing how management is a social process that relies heavily on trust and conformity.[37] To reduce uncertainty in decision making—the essence of managerial activity—a premium is placed on recruiting individuals who are predictable. The best way to achieve this is to recruit only those people who have social characteristics identical to the existing group of managers. This social cloning reproduces male dominance in management and, moreover, creates an enormous barrier to women.

In sharp contrast, the role of the secretary is built on a combination of female stereotypes. Kanter uses the term *office wife* to describe the subordinate, paternalistic, and almost feudal relationship secretaries usually have with their male employers. The job becomes a trap through the dependency of managers on their secretaries and the personal loyalties that result. Many competent secretaries are not promoted because their good performance makes them indispensable to the boss. Unlike other positions in modern bureaucracies, there are no safeguards in place that would curb or restrict the exercise of managerial authority and the expectation that personal services, like fetching coffee, are part of the job. Because secretaries are often stuck in this role, their behavioural responses, such as self-effacement or timidity, may undermine advancement prospects.

Men who have more opportunities take advantage of them, developing behaviours, values, and work attitudes that help them do so. Once young male management trainees are identified as "fast trackers," the resulting halo effect creates the impression that they do not make mistakes and gives them the momentum to move up. Conversely, women in dead-end jobs quite rationally decide to give up, losing both work commitment and motivation. This signals to supervisors that they do not deserve promotions or raises.

Women who succeed in entering management face the problem of *tokenism*. Kanter argues that a goldfish bowl phenomenon, resulting from being an identifiable minority, leads women or members of visible minorities to work harder to prove themselves. In turn, this confirms the dominant group's impression that these individuals are different and, therefore, do not belong. Furthermore, tokens lack the support systems so essential for surviving in the middle and upper ranks of organizations. But the problem is not sex or race, per se; rather, it is one of being part of a group underrepresented in a particular environment. Other empirical research into tokenism concludes that it is limited to women in traditionally male occupations and, further, that by focusing on the imbalance in numbers as the causes of the problem, it deflects attention away from the more complex mechanisms of discrimination (Yoder 1991). However, Kanter's more general point still holds: the *structure of opportunities* in an organization—basically, who has access to which positions, resources, and rewards—tends to create self-fulfilling prophecies that only serve to reinforce the subordinate status of women.

Recent research pursues these issues raised by Kanter in several directions. New evidence suggests that *ascription* – allocating opportunities or positions, such as in hiring and promotion decisions, on the basis of ascribed characteristics such as a person's sex – operates through an organization's personnel practices. Ascription can be reduced or eliminated if formalized procedures replace informal networks to identify candidates for management jobs (Reskin and McBrier 2000). Other research uses gender as an explicit analytic category. For example, while acknowledging that women's work experiences are shaped by organizational structure and power, Rosemary Pringle's (1989: 162) study of secretaries adds the dimension of sexuality:

> Far from being marginal to the workplace, sexuality is everywhere. It is alluded to in dress and self-presentation, in jokes and gossip, looks and flirtations, secret affairs and dalliances, in fantasy, and in the range of coercive behaviours that we now call sexual harassment. Rather than being exceptional in its sexualization, the boss–secretary relation should be seen as an important nodal point for the organization of sexuality and pleasure.

By focusing on sexuality, researchers are able to advance our understanding of how employment relations and work structures contribute to defining gender, both for men and for women. This new area of *gender studies* challenges us to rethink how masculinity, femininity, and heterosexuality are socially constructed categories reinforced by existing work institutions.[38]

On a larger scale, *sexual harassment* is the most draconian use of male power over women in the workplace. According to the 1993 national *Violence Against Women Survey*, 23 percent of Canadian women aged 18 and over had experienced some form of workplace sexual harassment, the most common being inappropriate comments about their bodies or sex lives. Other Canadian surveys suggest that the incidence is much higher, since there is likely underreporting of "poisoned environment" harassment – the display of a demeaning attitude toward women or unwanted sexual attention.[39] The secretaries Pringle interviewed confirmed that sexual harassment is quite pervasive and can drive women to quit jobs. Such harassment, or the fear of it, also deters women from entering nontraditional occupations, all the while reinforcing their subordinate status to men (Pringle 1989: 164). From the perspective of workplace health and safety, other researchers consider sexual harassment to be one form of the rising trend of aggression and violence in the workplace (DiGiacomo 1999).

ACHIEVING WORKPLACE EQUALITY

We have catalogued the inequities women face in terms of work opportunities and rewards. Some of the evidence leads to optimism that the stumbling blocks to equal labour–market opportunities and rewards are slowly being pushed aside. But the agenda of equality in employment can be achieved more effectively and sooner through bold public policy initiatives. This chapter will conclude by assessing two major policy thrusts: employment equity and pay equity. Unions too can play a decisive role in women's quest for greater workplace equality; their role will be examined in Chapter 7.

Employment Equity

The 1984 Royal Commission on Equality of Employment, also called the Abella Commission, defined *employment equity* as a strategy to eliminate the effects of discrimination and to fully open the competition for job opportunities to those who have been excluded historically. Four groups in Canadian society were identified as having been disadvantaged in terms of employment: visible minorities, persons with disabilities, Aboriginal peoples, and women. It is important to recognize that women do not constitute a homogeneous group. Indeed, we can speak of women who are also Aboriginal, or disabled, or members of a visible racial or ethnic minority as facing a double disadvantage. Focusing on women, the Abella Commission asserted that:

> … equality in employment means first a revised approach to the role women play in the workforce. It means taking them seriously as workers and not assuming that their primary interests lie away from the workplace. At the same time, it means acknowledging the changing role of women in the care of the family by helping them and their male partners to function effectively both as labour force participants and as parents. And it means providing the education and training to permit women the chance to compete for the widest possible range of job options. In practice this means the active recruitment of women into the fullest range of employment opportunities, equal pay for work of equal value, fair consideration for promotions into more responsible positions, participation in

corporate policy decision-making through corporate task forces and committees, accessible child care of adequate quality, paid parental leaves for either parent, and pensions and benefits (Canada 1984: 4).

The Abella Commission articulated the growing belief that all individuals, regardless of their personal characteristics, should be treated fairly in recruitment, hiring, promotions, training, dismissals, and any other employment decisions. The commission provided the rationale for the federal 1986 Employment Equity Act by arguing that *systemic discrimination* creates employment barriers that can only be dismantled through strong legislation. Systemic discrimination is the unintentional consequence of employment practices and policies that have a differential effect on specific groups. This form of discrimination is built into the system of employment, rather than being the conscious intent of individuals to discriminate. For example, minimum height and weight requirements (using Caucasian males as the norm) for entry into police or fire departments have the effect of excluding women and members of certain visible minorities, even though this was not the intent.

The 1986 Employment Equity Act covers federal government employees, 370 federally regulated employers and Crown corporations, and employers that have 100 or more employees and bid on government contracts worth more than $200,000. The thrust of the act is twofold. First, it requires these employers to identify and remove employment practices that act as artificial employment barriers to the four *designated groups* (women, visible minorities, Aboriginal peoples, and disabled people). Second, it establishes targets and timetables for achieving a more representative workforce that will reflect the proportion of qualified and eligible individuals from designated groups in the appropriate labour pool (not in the entire population). As the preamble to the act spells out, the ultimate goal is "to achieve equality in the work place so that no person shall be denied employment opportunities or benefits for reasons unrelated to ability" (Canada 1985).

Employment equity policy also recognizes a need for positive measures that will rectify historic imbalances in staff composition (for example, special training programs for Aboriginal peoples) and the reasonable accommodation of differences (such as changing the RCMP's dress code to permit Sikhs to wear turbans and Aboriginal officers to have braids) to make workplaces more accessible and hospitable for a greater diversity of individuals. In this way, organizations are able to become more representative of the increasingly varied composition of Canadian society.

The Employment Equity Act requires employers to file annual reports showing their progress in recruiting and promoting members of the four designated groups. Generally, these reports demonstrate the slow pace of change. However, recent research does provide a measure of success, suggesting that increased access for designated groups to professional, supervisory, and upper management positions has contributed to reducing the wage gap between these groups and white males.[40] Yet there is wide-ranging criticism of employment equity, to which the Special Committee of the House of Commons that reviewed the act responded by recommending stricter monitoring and enforcement; broadening the act to include more workplaces; greater employer commitment to the equity goals, timetables, and plans; and the establishment of a comprehensive national employment equity strategy.[41] Overcoming male resistance to gender equality in organizations and backlash against what some men view as the threat of feminism in action will require these measures and more.[42]

Stronger legislation may indeed speed progress toward equality. But business motives may be a more powerful influence: a growing number of employers realize that, despite current high levels of unemployment, they will face labour shortages early in the 21st century. Employers are being confronted by the reality that women and members of the other three designated groups will make up a large majority of new labour force entrants in coming years.

Employment equity seems least effective at eradicating racial discrimination, based on the growing number of racial discrimination cases coming before human rights tribunals (Jain and Al-Waqfi 2000). In the current language of employers, "diversity" is becoming a major human resource management challenge, which means making workplaces welcoming for everyone, regardless of their gender or race or their disability status.

At the forefront of this approach is the Bank of Montreal's 1991 Task Force on the Advancement of Women in the Bank (Bank of Montreal 1991). The task force examined how to correct the following imbalance: three-quarters of the bank's 28,000 employees were women, yet only 9 percent of executives and 13 percent of senior managers were women. The president of the bank committed the institution to the goal of gender equality in the following statement:

I am convinced ... that establishing equality for our workforce is not just the right thing to do but the smart thing to do. It makes the best of business sense, especially in a world where balance has become a priority. The full participation of women in our enterprise is the giant step that will allow us to take the lead in that world. It will make us more creative and more competitive ... The glass ceiling is now officially smashed (Bank of Montreal 1991).

The task force exposed five dominant myths that had served to justify why women did not make it into senior management ranks: "They're too young or too old"; "they have babies and quit"; "they just need more education"; "they don't have the right stuff" (that is, they show weaker job performance); and "they'll catch up soon." By developing a thorough statistical profile of women and men in the bank, the task force demolished these misconceptions. A survey tapped employees' suggestions regarding how to promote women and help all staff balance multiple commitments to their job, family, community, and education. Employees' main suggestions included training in people development skills, internal posting of management vacancies, cross-training between departments, flexible work hours, child-care assistance, and time off to care for sick dependents. To bring about the necessary organizational change, the bank made managers accountable for meeting equity objectives. Starting in 1993, all managers set annual hiring, retention, and advancement goals for women, visible minorities, Aboriginal people, and people with disabilities. To ensure accountability, individual managers' performance appraisals evaluate their success in meeting these goals, as well as their general contributions to workplace equality (Bank of Montreal 1993).

Pay Equity

A related policy initiative is *pay equity*. Pay equity, or *comparable worth* as it is called in the United States, focuses specifically on the most glaring indicator of gender inequality in the labour market: the wage gap. Pay equity is a proactive policy, requiring employers to assess the extent of pay discrimination and then to adjust wages so that women are fairly compensated. Frequently a topic of heated public debate, pay equity recognizes that occupational gender segregation underlies the wage gap. It attempts to provide a gender-neutral methodology for comparing predominantly female jobs with predominantly male jobs that are in different occupational classifications under the same employer. For example, a secretarial job (female) would be compared with the job of maintenance technician (male) in the same organization. A standardized evaluation system assigns points to these jobs on the basis of their skill level, effort, responsibility, and working conditions.

Underpinning the process is the recognition that women's work is valuable but has been under-rewarded in the past. The objective is to pay employees on the basis of their contribution to the employer. This will establish *equal pay for work of equal value,* a more far-reaching concept than *equal pay for the same work,* which only compares women and men in the same (or "substantially similar") jobs. However, developing and applying a truly gender-neutral system for evaluating jobs has proved exceedingly difficult because it challenges long-standing assumptions about the nature of skill (Steinberg 1990).

Pay equity legislation mainly covers the public sector, although laws in Ontario and Quebec apply to parts of the private sector as well.[43] Pay equity policies are explicit in their intent. As the British Columbia Public Sector Employers' Council (1995: 1-2) states in the introduction to its pay equity policy: "Pay equity programs address the undervaluation of work traditionally or historically done by women. Employment equity initiatives are required to address other aspects of the wage gap including attitudinal barriers and occupational segregation." Opponents claim that the economy cannot afford the resulting wage increases, that some businesses may be driven into bankruptcy, or that it interferes with the operation of the labour market. But for millions of employed women, comparable worth may provide long overdue recognition of their economic contributions to society.

Pay equity legislation has gone some distance toward creating fairer, gender-neutral compensation schemes. One example of the successful implementation of pay equity is found in the Manitoba provincial government. Five thousand women employees received wage adjustments averaging 15 percent at a cost of 3.3 percent of the provincial civil service payroll.[44] Ontario pay equity legislation was heralded as the most comprehensive in North America. Yet loopholes, exclusions, and cumbersome procedures have muted its impact. For instance, casual workers and private-sector firms with fewer than 10 employees are exempted, as are women who are unable to find a suitable male job to use for comparison within their place of employment.[45] Under the scrutiny of feminist analysis, the technical issues and problems of pay equity become the barriers to eliminating the gender wage gap and redefining the value of women's economic worth. So while comparable worth policies cannot eliminate the female–male wage gap, they have contributed to narrowing it. Furthermore, by increasing earnings at the bottom of the female earnings distribution, they have benefited more than just middle-class women.[46]

Another policy instrument for achieving gender equality in employment is section 15 of the Canadian Charter of Rights and Freedoms. This section of the Charter became law in April 1985. It established for the first time in our history a constitutional entitlement to full equality for women in law, as well as in the effects of law. This latter point is a crucial one, for regardless of the wording or intent of a law, if in practice it results in discrimination against women, the courts can rule it to be unconstitutional. This legal process may gradually come to have an influence on gender inequality in the workplace.

CONCLUSION

We are beginning to rectify some of the most glaring problems women confront in the work world. The employment equity and pay equity programs now operating in Canada are reform oriented, aiming to modify existing employment institutions, values, processes, and social relationships. But how effective will workplace reforms be in altering women's traditional nonwork roles—especially within the family—and the supporting socialization processes and ideologies? The limitations of such reforms prompt some feminists, for example, to call for an eradication of the patriarchal relations underpinning the exploitation of women. Clearly any successful strategy must recognize that employment inequities are firmly embedded in the very structure and values of our society. So while we look for ways of reducing the impacts of patriarchy in our families, schools, and other institutions, we also need to continue to focus directly on the organizational barriers that stand in the way of gender equality in the workplace.

NOTES

1. The female labour force participation rate is the number of women in the paid labour force (employed, or unemployed and actively looking for work) divided by the female

population 15 (14 prior to 1975) years of age and older. This calculation undervalues women's economic contribution because it overlooks unpaid household work.

2. See Cohen (1988). Useful sources for women's history in Canada are Strong-Boag and Fellman (1997), and the labour studies journal *Labour/Le Travail.*

3. Danysk (1995: 150) examines the gendered construction of work roles in western Canadian agriculture. The quotation is from a 1923 prairie farm publication. Rollings-Magnusson (2000) presents further useful information on the vital contribution of women to the development of the West.

4. For historical background on the transformation of women's work inside and outside the home during the rise of industrial capitalism, see Cohen (1988), Bradley (1989), Armstrong and Armstrong (1994: Chapters 2–3).

5. On the family wage, see Humphries (1977), Land (1980), and Bradbury (1993: 80, and also Chapters 3 and 5). For a related discussion of how the norm of the "male breadwinner" has recently changed in working-class steelworker families in Hamilton, see Livingstone and Luxton (1996).

6. These factors are discussed in Armstrong and Armstrong (1994: Chapter 6) and Jones, Marsden, and Tepperman (1990: Chapter 12). A comprehensive source for trends related to female employment is Statistics Canada (2000d).

7. On lone mothers in the workforce, see Crompton (1994). See Schellenberg and Ross (1997) for a detailed analysis of the working poor in Canada.

8. Rashid's (1994: 48) analysis of the top percentile of all families shows that wives in these families had incomes four times greater that the average for all wives, and that without this income 57 percent of these families would not reach the top income percentile. Statistics Canada's National Longitudinal Survey of Children and Youth revealed that, in 1994, 1 in 6 children under the age of 12 lived in lone-mother families, and that these children face far more disadvantages than those in two-parent families (*Canadian Social Trends* 1997: 7–9).

9. For differing perspectives on patriarchy, compare Johnson (1996), Walby (1990), Hartmann (1976), and Lerner (1986).

10. This post–World-War-II pattern is described in Ostry (1968). Also see Canada Department of Labour (1958).

11. Statistics Canada, 2000d: (144). On dual-earner families, see Oderkirk et al. (1994); Chawla (1992).

12. Hochschild (1989). See Harvey et al. (1991) for a Canadian time-budget study using the General Social Survey.

13. Meissner et al. (1975). For studies of the household division of labour, see Luxton (1980) and Pupo (1997).

14. Marshall (1993: 12). Data are from the 1990 General Social Survey (GSS). As a note of caution, there is some bias in how the GSS measures housework, because it is based on the perceptions of only one respondent per household (either male or female).

15. See, for example, Davies and Carrier (1999); McFarlane, Beaujot and Haddad (2000); Looker and Thiessen (1999).

16. McKinnon and Odynak (1991: 12). See Frederick and Fast (1999) for recent national trends.

17. On the changing role of fatherhood and how some men are trying to integrate work and family, see Gerson (1993) and Coltrane (1996). Organizations implementing work-family policies often promote them as not just a women's program, but one of benefit to male employees too.

18. For a review of work and family policies in Canada, see Skrypnek and Fast (1996). For a detailed analysis of the U.S. situation, see Spain and Bianchi (1996).

19. A work-related child care centre is one that is sponsored and supported by an employer, group of employers, union or employee group. Most are on the worksite. See Barbeau (2001). For an analysis of family-related policies and programs provided in six provinces, including Quebec, and by the federal government, see Jenson and Thompson (1999).

20. See Feuchtwang (1982: 251) for a definition of *job ghetto*. Freedman (1976) discusses the concepts of labour market segments and shelters (see Chapter 3, above, on these concepts).

21. Hughes (1990; 1995). Traditional occupations are those in which women constitute a greater proportion of employment than they do in the labour force as a whole.

22. Statistics Canada, (2000d: 128). On the nursing profession, see Sedivy-Glasgow (1992) and Armstrong, Choiniere, and Day (1993).

23. On women in medicine in Canada, see Gorham (1994). Also see Hagan and Kay (1995) for a detailed study of gender issues in Canadian lawyers' careers.

24. International Labour Office (1995: Table 3C). This category includes managers, legislative officials, and government administrators. German data are for 1991.

25. Data are from annual employment equity reports filed by the employers. Human Resources Development Canada (1999); Employment and Immigration Canada (1990: 33).

26. Statistics Canada (1996b: 32-33). See National Council of Welfare (2000) on poverty lines in Canada [www.ncwcnbes.net].

27. *Report on Business Magazine* (July 2001: 123–24); the total 1995 compensation packages of these 50 men ranged from $6.58 million to $70.7 million.

28. Using the *National Graduate Survey,* Davies et al. (1996) found a rise in the female–male earnings ratio between 1978 and 1988 from 84 to 91 percent (or stated differently, a closing of the wage gap).

29. The literature on the wage gap is reviewed by Gunderson (1994). For a more sociological analysis, see Coverman (1988). Research that examines productivity-related factors as determinants of the earnings gap can only account for a portion of the difference, however, suggesting that these factors themselves may be influenced by discrimination, or that factors outside the labour market are important (Drolet 2001).

30. Canadian Committee on Women in Engineering (1992: 1). On the male culture of engineering see Hacker (1989) and McIlwee and Robinson (1992: Chapter 6).

31. See Feldberg and Glenn (1979). Also see Acker (1988) and Calás and Smircich (1996) for critical discussions of the male biases in the sociological study of work and organizations.

32. On feminist approaches to understanding gender and work see Tancred (1995), Armstrong and Armstrong (1994), and Reskin and Padavic (1994). For studies of teleworkers, industrial home work, and women in family micro-businesses see Mirchandani (1999), Leach (1998) and Baines and Wheelock (1998), respectively.

33. On human capital explanations of sex differences in occupations and earnings, see Blau and Ferber (1986: Chapter 7).

34. For critical discussions of occupational gender segregation, see Siltanen (1994), Phillips and Phillips (1993: Chapter 4), and Armstrong and Armstrong (1990: Chapter 1). Hagan and Kay (1994) critically utilize human capital theory and a more general version of labour market segmentation theory in their study of gender inequalities in the legal profession. Developments in the measurement of occupational gender segregation and the underlying factors are discussed in Rubery and Fagan (1995) and Blackburn, Jarman, and Siltanen (1993).

35. Unpublished data from the 1996 *Alberta High School Graduate Survey*. Virtually all females (97 percent) and 85 percent of males agreed or strongly agreed with the statement "a woman should have the same job opportunities as a man." Career choices and other study findings are presented in Lowe, Krahn, and Bowlby (1997) [www.learning.gov.ab.ca/learning/96graduatesurvey/].

36. For an interesting discussion of the significance of workplace conversations about household work, see Hessing (1991).

37. For a summary of related research, see Powell (1993).

38. The growing area of *men's studies* examines the social construction of masculinity in work and unemployment (Morgan, 1997); on sexuality and power in organizational life, see Hearn, Sheppard, Tancred-Sheriff, and Burrell (1989). Coming at sexuality and work from another angle, Ross (2000) documents the history of erotic workers—strippers—in North America.

39. See Johnson (1994: 11) for the 1993 survey, conducted by Statistics Canada. A survey reported by Crocker and Kalemba (1999) found, in contrast, that 56 percent of working women surveyed had experienced workplace sexual harassment in the year prior to the survey. See Welsh (1997) and Sev'er (1999) for discussions of research evidence, theoretical interpretations, and measurement issues on this topic.

40. Leck, St. Onge, and Lalancette (1995). The study examined 1989–1993 changes in full-time earnings in all organizations covered by the Employment Equity Act.

41. Canada (1992). For a critical analysis of the act, see Lum (1995). For an overview of development of employment equity in Canada see Westmoreland-Traoré (1999).

42. Resistance to equity policies by males and managers (often the same) and the organizational barriers to the elimination of discrimination are analyzed by Cockburn (1991) and Collinson, Knights, and Collinson (1990). See Jo-Ann Wallace (1995) for an analysis of resistance to employment equity policy at the University of Alberta, and Creese (1999) for how gender, ethnicity, disability, and union politics combined to shape debates about employment equity at BC Hydro.

43. Pay equity laws, policies, or collective agreements negotiated with unions are in place in most provinces and federal jurisdictions, except the Northwest Territories and Alberta.

44. Weiner and Gunderson (1990: Chapter 10) outline the methodology of pay equity and its application across Canada. For a comparative perspective see Gunderson (1994).

45. Neale (1992). Under the former New Democratic government, Ontario extended pay equity into the private sector, but one evaluation of its impact suggests that pay equity awards have been small and that there are considerable difficulties administering and gaining compliance with the act (McDonald and Thornton 1998).

46. For critiques of pay equity and how it has been implemented, see Fudge and McDermott (1991) and Quaid (1993). Forrest (2000) discusses the large federal government pay equity settlement with female members of the Public Service Alliance of Canada in 1999. Simulations of the U.S. economy show that the wage gap would close 8 to 20 percent if comparable worth were nationally applied (Gunderson 1994: 111). Figart and Lapidus (1996) provide a positive evaluation, showing that such policies would generally contribute to reducing earnings inequality between the sexes and among women. However, other researchers suggest that the closing of the wage gap (at least in the United States) is in large part due to the increasing stagnation of white male earnings (Bernhardt, Morris, and Handcock, 1995).

5

THE ORGANIZATION AND MANAGEMENT OF WORK

INTRODUCTION

We live in an organizational society. Attending school, buying weekly groceries, negotiating a student loan, volunteering at our community foodbank, searching the Internet, or watching our favourite TV program all bring us into contact with formal organizations. Even more important, at least from our sociological perspective, are the organizations in which people work. In this chapter, we examine the organization and management of work, sampling selectively from an enormous and diverse literature on organizational analysis and management theory and practice. We consider different perceptions of work organizations. While a manager or executive may assess a particular work organization in terms of efficiency or profitability, other employees may use totally different criteria. Given these variations in the objective features and subjective experiences of work organizations, a number of interrelated questions can be asked.

First, what are the major factors that determine the structure—that is, the patterned regularities of work organizations? Second, looking specifically at process, how are organizations transformed over time? To what degree is organizational change a response to a changing external environment or to internal forces? Third, how much do the actions and beliefs of managers, employees, and other groups such as clients and customers influence the form, goals, and internal dynamics of an organization? Finally, our discussion raises a further question: how will the new organizational forms that emerged in the late 20th century continue to transform working life in the future?

Managers have played a key role in constructing modern organizations, mainly because they make critical decisions about goals, structure, personnel, and technology. We will therefore examine the various schools of management that have emerged over the past century. This chapter's focus on mainstream organization and management literature is reflected in the prominence given to the themes of *consensus* and *integration*. Then, in Chapter 6, we present a more critical perspective on organizations and management, focusing on the themes of power, control, resistance, and conflict. While some of the basic problems of organizing and managing work in a capitalist economy will be introduced here, a more systematic critique appears in the next chapter.

WHAT'S WRONG WITH BUREAUCRACY?

As we saw in Chapter 1, a major step along the road to industrialization was the division of craftwork into simpler components. Less skilled labourers could then perform each of these narrow tasks more cheaply. But once all the parts of a craftworker's job had been simplified and reassigned, coordinating and integrating these tasks became a problem. This helps to account for the role of managers, who, since the late 19th century, have become central actors in most work organizations. Questions about how best to integrate and coordinate the activities of large numbers of workers within a single enterprise gave rise to early theories of management.

Weber, Bureaucracy, and Capitalism

The organizational structure adopted by 19th-century businesses was the bureaucratic hierarchy. As we have already seen, Max Weber considered *bureaucracy* to be the organizational form best able to efficiently coordinate and integrate the multitude of specialized tasks conducted in a big factory or office. Without bureaucracy, he predicted, "capitalist production could not continue."[1] Although he described the general features of bureaucracy, Weber did not provide a practical guide for managers on how it should be organized. Nevertheless, his description has become the model for a highly mechanistic type of organization. Gareth Morgan defines bureaucratic organizations as those "that emphasize precision, speed, clarity, reliability, and efficiency achieved through the creation of a fixed division of tasks, hierarchical supervision, and detailed rules and regulations."[2]

No doubt bureaucracies were an improvement over the tradition-bound "seat of the pants" methods used in running most 19th-century businesses. Their predictability greatly increased the productivity of industrial capitalism. Furthermore, a bureaucracy is a system of authority. Its hierarchical structure, formal lines of authority, and impartial rules and regulations are designed to elicit cooperation and obedience from employees. One advantage of a hierarchy with an elaborate division of labour was that employers could gain employee commitment by offering the prospect of career advancement. This is the internal labour market described in Chapter 3. Given that a bureaucracy's specialized division of labour meets Adam Smith's conditions for increasing industrial productivity, noted in Chapter 1, it would seem that bureaucratic work organizations are ideal.

The Ills of Bureaucracy

All things considered, most sociologists would agree that bureaucracies have serious flaws. Organizational researchers have amassed considerable evidence showing that bureaucracies are often overly complex and, therefore, difficult to manage, resistant to change, and unable to cope with uncertainties. Working conditions in bureaucracies are frequently unsatisfying, as we will show in Chapter 8 (Daft 1995; Perrow 1986). A paradox of bureaucracy is that, far from achieving machine-like efficiency, it often unintentionally creates inefficiency, a problem Weber largely failed to see. Furthermore, sociologists have documented a dark side of organizations, where things can go seriously wrong (Vaughn 1999). Examples of such mistakes, misconduct, or disasters are plentiful, and would include the Bre-X stock fraud, the town of Walkerton's water contamination, and the fatal Westray mine explosion.

A number of classic sociological studies challenge the notions of bureaucratic rationality and efficiency. For example, Robert Merton described how employees who slavishly obey the rules could undermine the efficiency of a bureaucracy (Merton 1952). The rules become ends in themselves, rather than the means of achieving organizational goals. Officials acquire a *bureaucratic personality*, compulsively following procedural manuals to the last detail. Similarly, Peter Blau's fieldwork in American government agencies revealed how workers behaved according to their own unofficial rules.[3] In doing so, they were directly responding to organizational pressure to attain certain goals, such as handling a quota of clients or cases in a given period. Blau identified the tension between the official rules of the bureaucracy and workers' counter-rules. By striving to make their jobs easier, employees often erode bureaucratic efficiency.

Another example is Alvin Gouldner's (1954) classic study of an American gypsum plant. He argues that organizational life cannot be made as fully predictable as the bureaucratic model would suggest. Events such as promotions, layoffs, or dismissals are unpredictable. Moreover, rules reducing uncertainty for management may be a major source of discontent among employees. In fact, Gouldner argues, often the bureaucratization process is implemented not for reasons of greater efficiency, but as a result of power struggles between workers and managers. In short, there is nothing inevitable about bureaucracy; rather, its many faces reflect the shaky balance of power between workers and managers within an organization.

The notion of bureaucratic efficiency rests, in part, on the assumption that employees will readily submit to *managerial authority*. In Weber's view, workers accept the legitimacy of the existing authority structure, abide by the rules, and obey their bosses because they believe the basis for such authority is impartial and fair. Underlying capitalist bureaucracies is a *rational–legal value system*. However, the assumption that there is general acceptance of goals is contradicted by the realities of employee–employer relations, which are punctuated by conflict and resistance (see Chapter 6). People in positions of power set organizational goals. These goals are, therefore, "rational" from management's perspective, but not necessarily from the perspective of workers. What is rational for them is what reflects their own interests, such as higher pay, a safer and more comfortable work environment, or more scope for making work-related decisions. These goals are often in conflict with those of management. Hence, conflicts over the distribution and use of decision-making power are normal.

Weber's model of bureaucracy neglects employee resistance to such authority. As we will also see below, resistance can be frequently detected in workers' informal group norms and codes of conduct that run counter to the official systems of production. Not surprisingly, a major concern of management has been to find ways of gaining worker cooperation. Managers have gone to great lengths to convince workers to accept organizational goals as their own personal goals, and to justify their decisions to those below them. The development of *management ideology* justifying superior rewards and the right to give orders is part of this process. Reinhard Bendix (1974: 13) explains: "All economic enterprises have in common a basic social relation between the employers who exercise authority and the workers who obey, and all ideologies of management have in common the effort to interpret the exercise of authority in favourable light."

Bureaucracy and Fordism

As an organizing principle, the bureaucratic hierarchy was integrated with technology to create the huge factories that formed the backbone of industrial capitalism. When Henry Ford introduced the moving assembly line in 1914, launching the era of mass-production manufacturing, he was building on the machine-like logic of bureaucratic organization. *Fordism*, based on assembly-line mass production, combined technology with bureaucracy to shape 20th-century work and economic growth.

Robert Reich (1991), in *The Work of Nations*, provides a trenchant critique of Fordism. Reich's treatise ranges over the sprawling terrain of the emerging global economy, which has shifted the locus of economic activity (as we documented in Chapter 1) from goods production to services. The key to prosperity used to be large volume production in giant factories by corporations that dominated world markets. In today's global marketplace the distinction between goods and services is blurred. Specialized expertise in finance, research and development, and marketing adds value to products and responds to constantly changing market needs. Furthermore, service and production networks tie together working units that are scattered across many countries.

Reich's portrayal of post–World-War-II corporate America is an indict-
ment of Fordism and bureaucracy. It is also a recipe for how not to organize
work in the new global economy:

> America's corporate bureaucracies were organized like military
> bureaucracies, for the efficient implementation of preconceived
> plans. It is perhaps no accident that the war veterans who manned
> the core American corporations of the 1950s accommodated so
> naturally to the militarylike hierarchies inside them. They were
> described in much the same terms as military hierarchies—fea-
> turing chains of command, spans of control, job classifications,
> divisions and division heads, and standard operating procedures to
> guide every decision. When in doubt go by the book. All jobs were
> defined in advance by pre-established routines and responsibilities.
> Organization charts graphically mapped out internal hierarchies,
> starting with a large box at the top containing the chief executive
> officer, and proceeding downward through levels of ever smaller
> and more abundant boxes. As in the military, great emphasis was
> placed upon the maintenance of control—upon a superior's ability
> to inspire loyalty, discipline, and unquestioning obedience, and
> upon a subordinate's capacity to be so inspired (Reich 1991: 51).

A crucial question, then, is whether alternatives to the Weberian model of
bureaucracy have emerged. In addition to Reich's argument, consider three
examples that reveal a shift away from bureaucracy. The first is the decline of
internal labour markets in the 1990s, as large organizations downsized and
increasingly relied on contingent workers who did not have access to internal
careers. Research on managerial careers suggests that today fewer managers are
likely to spend their entire career climbing the ladder of one organization than
in the 1950s or 1960s – the heyday of the "organization man" (Osterman
1999). The second example revisits the Weberian emphasis on rational and
impersonal norms of worker behaviour. Researchers have studied how some
customer service organizations cultivate employees' use of emotions and
informality. For example, Martin, Knopoff and Beckman (1998) described
how work relations in The Body Shop were defined by "bounded emotionality," encouraged by a corporate leader who emphasized the values of caring,

sharing and love. The third example is how work has become de-institution-alized—that is, has moved outside the structure of a single large organization. One response to rapidly changing markets and globalization is the rise of net-worked forms of business organization, including franchises, joint ventures, outsourcing agreements and strategic alliances (Podolny and Page 1998; Hendry 1999). These decentralized and flexible forms of business organization raise anew the old questions about how coordination and control are achieved.

In short, the triumph of Western industrial capitalism was founded on what is now recognized as an outmoded model of organization and management. This is a leading theme in the new management literature we review below. As Danny Miller (1990) suggests in *The Icarus Paradox*, the life cycle of North American corporations resembles the character Icarus from Greek mythology, who flew so high that the sun melted the wax on his wings and he fell to the sea and drowned. The moral: The very strengths of the traditional bureaucratic and Fordist organization have become the source of its downfall.

THEORETICAL PERSPECTIVES ON ORGANIZATIONS

Organizational theory offers a range of perspectives from which to analyze the structure, functions, and dynamics of organizations (Clegg et al. 1996; Pfeffer 1997; Morgan 1997). This section will touch on several major theoretical currents in this rich literature: contingency theory, organic models, sociotechnical systems, and strategic choice. Some of these ideas will resurface later in the chapter—for example, the sociotechnical model in our discussion of work redesign, and strategic choice in our discussion of managerial decision-making. A newly emerging theoretical interpretation of the changes reshaping organizational life comes from the application of postmodernist theories. As we will see, this critique of conventional organizational theory shares common elements with the much more practically oriented new management literature. We have already provided an overview of feminist perspectives on organizations in Chapter 4. We can expect that issues of gender, ethnicity, and race will receive increasing attention from researchers as workplaces continue to become more socially diverse (Reskin 2000). The Marxist-inspired radical critique of organizations, itself a distinct perspective, will form part of our exploration of conflict, control, and power in Chapter 6.

Structures, Systems, Strategies

The weaknesses and gaps in the Weberian model of bureaucracy have led to alternative theories of organizations. Weber's thesis that a bureaucratic structure is most appropriate for any type of capitalist economic activity has been largely replaced by *contingency theory*. It proposes that organizational structures and processes are contingent upon the immediate problems posed by their environment. There is no single best way to organize or to manage work. A basic question guiding organizational research today is, What structures and strategies does a particular organization require to survive?[4]

The many possible answers to this question are typically based on an organic model, which views organizations as social systems adapting to internal and external changes. This conventional view of organizations as adapting social systems is grounded in the general sociological theory of *structural functionalism*. Hence, there is an emphasis on goal attainment, functions, structural adaptations, and a value consensus among organizational members. Conventional organization theory has been criticized for being too concerned with structure, per se, and, as a result, losing sight of the larger socioeconomic, political, and historical context of which organizations are a part. Other weaknesses include ignoring the attitudes and behaviours of employees (the informal side of organizations discussed later in this chapter), and glossing over the realities of workplace power and conflict (see Chapter 6).[5] Nonetheless, some useful insights about organizations can be found in this empirical literature.

For example, in the 1950s, Burns and Stalker studied synthetic fibre, electronics, and engineering industries, proposing a continuum of organizational forms from the *mechanistic* (or highly bureaucratic) to the *organic*. More open and flexible organizational structures and management styles were required, they concluded, in industries with rapidly-changing technologies and market conditions (Burns and Stalker 1961). Joan Woodward's studies revealed a direct relationship between production technology, on the one hand, and structural forms and management styles on the other. She concluded that bureaucracy and tight management controls are more appropriate in industries with mass production technology. When the workflow is varied, and production processes are nonroutine and complex—as in craft or continuous process technologies—more flexible, organic structures function best (Woodward 1980).

Woodward's research attests to the importance of technology as a key variable in organizational analysis. The concept of a *sociotechnical system*, introduced by researchers at London's Tavistock Institute of Human Relations, takes this idea one step further. In their study of the mechanization of British coal mining, Trist and Bamforth documented how social relations in teams of miners were dependent on the technology used.[6] When the traditional hand method of mining was replaced by mechanical conveyer belts, thus destroying the technical basis for the work teams, the negative social–psychological consequences for workers hampered the operations of the new system. Consequently, the notion of optimizing the fit between social and technical aspects of production has become an important principle in work design. The information technology revolution, discussed below and in other chapters, underscores these and other concerns about the impact of technological change on work organization, the quality of work life, workers' skills, and organizational performance (Liker et al. 1999; Burris 1998).

There is a tendency in the literature on workplace structures to *reify* organizations, that is, to discuss them as if they had a life of their own, independent of the actions and decisions of their members. We should remember that organization theory is largely about decision making. Given the constraints of technology, markets, government regulations, labour negotiations, and so on, what are the most appropriate choices for managers to make? This issue is taken up by the *strategic choice perspective* on organizations.[7] In contrast to contingency theory's emphasis on environmental and other constraints imposed on decision making, the concept of strategic choice draws our attention to the ways in which dominant groups (coalitions) actually choose among various strategies for structuring an organization, manipulating its environment, and establishing work standards. To fully comprehend the nature of work organizations, we must examine the guiding theories, actual practices, and supporting ideologies of management.

Despite the persistence of these established approaches, organizational theory is evolving. As Chapter 4 documented, feminist researchers have effectively challenged the one-sided male perspective traditionally found in organizational literature, illuminating how workers' experiences, opportunities, and rewards in workplaces are shaped by gender.[8] The latest attempt to recast it comes from *postmodernism*. This emergent perspective on organizations touches on the major trends reshaping the workplace, thereby contributing to the debate about the nature of post-industrial society. According to this critique, organization theory was the product of *modernity*—the age of the bureaucracy and the assembly line (Clegg 1990; Cooper and Burrell 1988; McKinlay and Starkey 1998). The driving force was rationality and an increasing division of labour, and everything that flowed from these principles. *Postmodernity* (to risk simplifying an elaborate theory) in organizational life is marked by less differentiation and more unpredictability (Lash 1990). Stewart Clegg argues that a postmodernist view of organizations is more consistent with the assumptions of contemporary North American management writers, reviewed below, or Japanese-style management. He explains the basic distinction between modernist and postmodernist organizations this way:

> Where modernist organization was rigid, postmodern organization is flexible. Where modernist consumption was premised on mass forms, postmodernist consumption is premised on niches. Where modernist organization was premised on technological determinism, postmodernist organization is premised on technological choices made possible through "de-dedicated" microelectronic equipment. Where modernist organization and jobs were highly differentiated, demarcated and de-skilled, postmodernist organization and jobs are highly de-differentiated, de-demarcated and multi-skilled (Clegg 1990: 181).

Change and Innovation

There is a huge management literature on strategic planning in organizations. While reminiscent of strategic choice theory, mentioned above, strategic planning has a more practical thrust, helping managers achieve specific goals. Still, it raises sociological questions about how managers (individually or as a group) are able to influence an organization's performance and shape its future. Certainly the new management literature assumes that conscious decisions and strong leadership form the basis of survival strategies. But as Henry Mintzberg (1994) argues, managers have not learned from the failures of strategic planning. The problem with strategic planning, according to Mintzberg, has been its formalization of the planning process, which stifles strategic thinking about creative alternatives and visions for the future of the organization. This is yet another example of how bureaucratic procedures can inhibit innovative behaviour in organizations.

A basic definition of strategy is "a plan for interacting with the competitive environment to achieve organizational goals" (Daft 1995: 45–49). This is vague, so to add some precision, Mintzberg and his colleagues (Mintzberg et al. 1998) identify ten distinct schools of strategy, each with its own definition of strategy formation in organizations, how this happens, and who the key actors are.

For example, one perspective views strategy formation as an emergent process, in which organizations learn from their strengths, continuously adapting them to the future. This describes many high-tech firms that are scrambling to make order out of a chaotic environment and therefore cannot have a fixed master-plan (Brown and Eisenhardt 1998). Another school focuses on power. From this perspective, sociologists David Knights and Glenn Morgan (1990) argue that the core issue is whether organizations really act according to strategic plans, or whether these plans are post hoc explanations by social scientists trying to make sense of organizational changes and power structures. Strategy, they suggest, is primarily a mechanism of power. To understand it, we must uncover how corporate strategies are rooted in power relations and serve to reproduce existing organizational hierarchies and inequities, but nonetheless are subject to ongoing negotiations with interest groups inside the organization. While it is difficult to know whether a particular strategy actually makes a difference, it could have the implicit effect of making managers and employees more goal-oriented and self-disciplined (Knights and Morgan 1990). More broadly, an organization's strategy provides a description of how it deals with internal and external change.

Understanding Organizational Change

The difficulties of strategic planning reflect the larger challenges of organizational change. How do organizations change? Observing that organizational turmoil became the norm in the 1980s, Bob Hinings and Royston Greenwood (1988) argue that it is essential to recognize and manage change. Their research on local governments in Britain focuses on "strategic organizational design change," which is change that signals a fundamental shift in the orientation of the organization. Their study emphasizes that change and stability are two sides of the same coin. Theoretically, Hinings and Greenwood introduce the concept of a *design archetype* to describe an organization's structure, management system, and supporting beliefs and values. They also suggest that organizations can be classified according to *tracks*. The metaphor of a track captures the extent of change occurring, specifying whether an organization remains within one design archetype over time or moves between archetypes.

Hining's and Greenwood's theory is intended to account for both successful and unsuccessful attempts at organizational change. Because the late 20th century saw an increase in organizational decline, this process has become the subject of considerable research. Distinguishing between decline, on the one hand, and cutbacks and retrenchment on the other, William Weitzel and Ellen Jonsson (1989: 94) suggest that the root cause of decline is the failure of organizations "to anticipate, recognize, avoid, neutralize, or adapt to external or internal pressures that threaten the organization's long-term survival." Whether it is avoiding decline or pursuing growth and innovation, these issues reflect two strong themes in contemporary organizational and management literature: how change can be "managed," and the conditions under which change leads to innovation in products and services (Hage 1999; Tushman and Anderson 1996). One basic research finding is that change is disruptive for organizations. The challenge this presents for firms in volatile sectors, such as high tech, is that new organizational models designed to adapt to rapidly evolving markets create employee turnover because of how they alter employment relationships. This in turn can undermine future firm performance (Baron and Hannon 2001).

Technology has, historically, precipitated huge changes in the organization of work, as we saw in Chapter 1. To more fully understand technological change, it is useful to view it as a process of managerial decision making. This helps to demystify technology by showing how it too reflects organizational and human constraints and choices. John Child (1985) identifies four goals that managers have when they introduce new technology: reducing costs and boosting efficiency; increasing flexibility; improving quality; and achieving greater control over operations. These goals, which often overlap, are "evolving" and the end results may not be predictable. From this perspective, the same computer hardware or software will, for example, have a varying impact on workers depending on how managers pursue these goals.

However, this view credits managers with too much conscious planning and control. Various case studies underscore major organizational and human constraints on management's ability to plan and implement technological change. The complexity of new technology invariably requires attendant organizational change and job redesign—a tough challenge. Moreover, the full potential of automation cannot be realized without recognition of the human dimension. Only by involving workers in planning and implementing new technology, and giving them the responsibility to operate it, can a smooth transition be attained. For instance, often workers' detailed knowledge of old systems is indispensable to making new technology function (Hayes and Jaikumar 1988; Forester 1989; Wood 1989a). Shoshana Zuboff's (1988: 389) conclusion, drawn from her study of several high-tech firms, aptly expresses the contingent and often unpredictable quality of technological change:

> Even where control or deskilling has been the intent of managerial choices with respect to new information technology, managers themselves are also captive to a wide range of impulses and pressures. Only rarely is there a grand design concocted by an elite group ruthlessly grinding its way toward the fulfillment of some special and secret plan. Instead, there is a concentration of forces and consequences, which in turn develop their own momentum.

THE ROLE OF MANAGERS

We have alluded to the key role managers have in organizing and regulating work, but exactly what do managers do? We know that within any hierarchical organization authority resides at the top. This gives rise to one of the most vexing problems confronting management: how to obtain employee compliance and prevent opposition to authority. In this respect, the workplace is a microcosm of the larger society. Maintaining orderly and harmonious social relations among people who are not equals has always been a problem for those in power. Another pressing concern involves motivating workers to achieve the quantity and quality of output considered necessary by management. Employers do not have complete control over the amount of effort

expended by employees. Hence, conflict often erupts over different perceptions of the right amount of effort given a specific wage and work situation.

Management Ideology and Practice

Managers became a prominent new social group in the early twentieth century. *Cost accounting* techniques for calculating how much each factor of production, including labour, contributes to profits was one way capitalists
initially tackled the problems of running increasingly large and complex
enterprises. Appointing trained managers, often factory engineers, was an
equally important social innovation. As business historian Alfred D. Chandler
Jr. suggests, the visible hand of the corporate manager replaced the "invisible
hand" of market forces (Chandler 1977). Corporate boards of directors, representing the shareholders, delegated to managers the authority to operate the
business profitably. Recall from Chapter 1 that this growing power of managers and the separation of corporate ownership from daily control functions
has been labelled the *managerial revolution*. In striving to meet their broad
mandate, managers undoubtedly have transformed the organization and control of work.

In considering the evolving role of managers, it is important to distinguish
among *ideology, theory,* and *practice*.[9] Management ideologies, we noted earlier, are used to justify existing authority relations in organizations. Joseph
Smucker's research shows how Canadian managerial ideologies have undergone several shifts since 1900. The self-perception of managers moved away
from that of autonomous achieving individuals to one of organizational team
workers, while managers' image of workers was transformed from recalcitrants
to associates (Smucker 1980: 163). The economic and workplace transformations of the 1990s created, at least in some Canadian industries, yet another
new image of the ideal worker: someone who is educated, a life-long learner,
flexible and skilled in technology use (Adams and McQuillan 2000). A suc-
cession of theories influenced by these views has attempted to specify how to
manage. But these theories are merely prescriptions for action.

Henry Mintzberg's distinction between "folklore" and fact is a useful way
of deciphering what managers actually do. The words that supposedly guide
managers are, he argues, often little more than vague goals: "If you ask managers what they do they will most likely tell you that they plan, organize, coor-

dinate, and control. Then watch what they do. Don't be surprised if you can't relate what you see to those four words" (Mintzberg 1989: 9). This under-scores the importance of looking closely at how management theories are actually applied and at the results – especially at a time when there are so many management fads. Indeed, management researchers are now seeking to understand the factors shaping the discourse of these new management approaches, such at Total Quality Management (discussed in detail below). Often, the discourse leads to overly optimistic assessments of their impact and a gap between rhetoric and practice (Zbaracki 1999; Pollitt 1995). The resulting contradictions can undermine the credibility of corporate leaders in the eyes of employees.

Another sociological interpretation of managers views their activities as directed at defining and pursuing common problems, goals, and solutions, interpreting their actions as responses to situational constraints (Reed 1989; Godard 1994: Chapter 6). This view helps to demystify management, showing how a group possessing formal authority still faces the limits that institutions place on human agency. Seeing management as a socially-constructed practice avoids the trap of reifying organizations. This *social action perspective* on management also raises one of the thorniest problems in studying organizations: how to conceptualize individuals within organiza-tions. As Charles Perrow (1986: 66) puts it, "How can you talk about organi-zations without talking about individuals?" In response, it should be said that much of organization theory does just that.

Managers as Decision Makers and Leaders

This leads us into the area of *decision making*, a topic that has received much attention in writings on management. Perrow shows how one of the classic statements about the role of managers, Chester Barnard's 1938 book, *The Functions of the Executive*, falls into the trap of presenting a "nonpersonal" model of organizations (Barnard 1938). For Barnard, even the decisions made by executives are not personal choices (that is, individually determined) because they are embedded in a coordinated system. The logic and rationality often attributed to managers, for him, are actually imposed in a disciplined way by the organizational environment. Barnard's tremendously influential contribution to subsequent thinking about organizations (especially organic theories) is basically flawed, argues Perrow, because it "glorifies the organization and minimizes the person" (Perrow 1986). Organizational policies take on a moral tone, and are assumed to be functional for everyone involved, from executives to workers and customers.

Research on decision making examines the role of the manager and whether she or he, as an individual, can make a difference in the organization (Hickson 1987). What seems to matter more than the individual manager's role, however, is the process by which decisions are made, especially how other organizational actors are involved in this process (Rodrigues and Hickson 1995). Media reports of larger-than-life corporate empire builders and "white knight" turnaround artists suggest that successful business leaders are a rare breed. This image of managers as decisive visionaries – what leadership expert Warren Bennis (1999) terms the myth of the triumphant individual – is challenged by researchers who argue that leaders' roles are constrained by the specific context of their organizations and their wider environment. In fact, there are many accounts of management that debate whether leadership skills that can truly change organizations can be taught or are innate characteristics (Micklethwait and Wooldridge 1996: Chapter 8; Yammarino et al. 2001). From a sociological perspective, the underlying issue is how leadership practices are embedded in workplace relationships, group dynamics and the overall authority structure of an organization – all of which shift our focus beyond the CEO as an individual.

A related question, subject to ongoing controversy, is the relationship between leadership and an organization's performance. Empirical studies show that corporate executives do affect their firm's performance, but that this effect is overshadowed by other factors (for instance, industrial sector, markets, technology, and size) that differentiate firms (Thomas 1988). This is closely linked in the literature to the issue of executive compensation, which critics argue has reached a level that is both excessive and inequitable (Nichols and Subramaniam 2001). One study found a positive relationship between the level of CEO compensation and innovation (patents and research and development activity) in high-tech firms, but not in other industries (Balkin et al. 2000). Another study suggests that some CEOs gain legitimacy by introducing the latest management technique – such as quality programs, teams, or employee empowerment – resulting in an increase in their pay but not necessarily in the firm's economic performance (Staw and Epstein 2000).

Let's step back from this individualistic focus on executives as business leaders. Meeting any organizational goal depends largely on how people in the organization are managed. Specifically, an overriding management objective is to create motivated and cooperative employees, so this is a key criterion for assessing a manager's effectiveness, as well as organizational success. On this latter point virtually all theories of management agree. But as we now will show, various management theories have advocated different methods for achieving organizational goals. During the past century, several distinct schools of management appeared. The two most influential were scientific management and the human relations approach.

SCIENTIFIC MANAGEMENT

Charlie Chaplin's classic movie *Modern Times* humorously depicts the impact of scientific management on working conditions. The comedian plays a harried factory worker whose job has been analyzed and redesigned by stopwatch-wielding efficiency experts. Every few seconds, Chaplin tightens a nut as another identical piece of equipment zips past him on the assembly line. Chaplin is little more than an automaton whose actions are programmed by the production system. Once out on the street, he continues repeating the motions on anything that fits his two wrenches.

Taylorism

Scientific management began in the United States as a set of production methods, tools, and organizational systems designed to increase the efficiency of factory production. The term itself was coined in 1911. But this new approach to factory management and organization, popularized by an engineer named Frederick W. Taylor, had been developed by the end of the previous century. Taylor and other "efficiency experts" extolled the virtues of scientific management, and the method soon spread across North America and, to a lesser extent, Britain and Europe. Taylor's theories were at the cutting edge of what Bryan Palmer refers to as the broad "thrust for efficiency" that contributed to the rise of twentieth-century industrial capitalism.[10] These early management consultants advocated workplace reorganization, job redesign, and tighter administrative and employee controls, all in the name of efficiency and profits.

Taylor laid out the following steps for rationalizing the labour process: (1) shift the decision-making responsibility for doing a job from workers to management; (2) use scientific methods to determine the most efficient way of executing a job and redesign it accordingly; (3) provide a detailed description of how to perform each step in a job; (4) select the best worker to perform the job; (5) train workers to execute the job efficiently; and (6) closely monitor workers' performance (Morgan 1997: 22–26; Littler 1982: 51–52). Taylor believed his management techniques benefited all parties involved. Yet their overriding effect was to give management tighter control over workers' activities by making all major work decisions. Critics such as Harry Braverman (1974) view Taylorism as the cornerstone of all 20th-century management. As we will elaborate in Chapter 6, according to the *labour process perspective*, Taylorism degraded labour, minutely fragmenting tasks, reducing skill requirements, and eliminating workers' input about how their jobs should be done. While many have contested Braverman's claim about the pervasive influence of Taylorism, there can be little doubt that the basic principles of scientific management continue to influence the amount of control and discretion workers can exercise when performing their jobs.

Taylor was convinced that worker *soldiering*, or deliberate laziness, was the scourge of industry. He believed that workers consciously restricted production by keeping bosses ignorant of how fast a job could be done. In Taylor's rather alarmist language, "there could be no greater crime against humanity than this restriction of output."[11] His solution was to determine "scientifically" the one best way of performing a job through *time-and-motion studies* of each step. A base rate of pay was then tied to a production quota. If workers exceeded the quota, they received a pay bonus. Lazy workers unable to achieve the quota would be forced to quit because their base rate fell below a minimum level. Essentially, scientific management was founded on the assumption that workers were motivated by economic gain alone. Taylor preached that the scientific basis of a "fair day's wage" and the productivity gains through more efficient work methods would bring about a new era of industrial cooperation and harmony.

Taylor's view of human nature was coloured by his preoccupation with technical efficiency. In his mind, the ideal worker was more like a machine than a human being. Taylor was a leading ideologue for early 20th-century management, articulating its deep concerns about the "labour problem." Industrial cooperation would only replace class conflict, he predicted, once a complete mental revolution had taken hold of both management and labour. As Taylor stated in *Industrial Canada* (April 1913: 1224–25), a prominent Canadian business magazine just before World War I:

> The new outlook that comes to both sides under scientific management is that both sides very soon realize that if they stop pulling apart and both push together as hard as possible in the same direction, they can make that surplus [i.e., profits] so large that there is no occasion for any quarrel over its division. Labour gets an immense increase in wages, and still leaves a large share for capital.

Scientific management failed to provide a successful formula for labour–management cooperation. Taylor's package of managerial reforms was seldom adopted completely. Yet various aspects of scientific management were quickly introduced into Canadian factories and, by the 1920s, were used to overhaul large corporate and government offices.[12] Still, Taylor's rhetoric of scientific objectivity was little more than an ideological justification for greater management control over labour (Kelly 1982: Chapter 2). The most famous example of Taylor's system does not stand up to scrutiny. Careful analysis of Taylor's original documentation shows inaccuracies in his published claims about efficiency gains at the Bethlehem Iron Company, where in 1899 he redesigned the work methods and equipment for shovelling pig iron (heavy chunks of metal (Wrege and Hodgetts 2000). But this has not stopped scientific management's approach to job design and work organization—including job descriptions, planned work flows, detailed unit accounting, and time-and-motion studies—from becoming standard features of contemporary management.

The Legacy of Scientific Management

Indeed, these basic features of scientific management can still be found today in many organizations. For instance, in the service sector, Burger King attempts to maximize food sales and minimize labour costs by emphasizing SOS—

"speed of service" (Reiter 1991: 85). Complying with this motto requires highly standardized work procedures and strict management controls in all Burger King outlets. Time-and-motion studies dictate how long it takes to prepare the fries, burgers, and drinks, exactly how workers should do these tasks, and where they should be positioned depending on the design of the kitchen. Taylorism also is very much alive in manufacturing. One recent case study of an appliance factory in Wales documented the persistence of time-study, piece rate payment, and efficiency gains through reduced operator discretion, despite efforts by senior management to change these practices (Jones 2000).

History provides many examples of workers resisting scientific management. Skilled industrial workers besieged by managerial rationalizations in the early 20th century responded by striking (Heron and Palmer 1977; Kealey 1986). Auto workers were one occupational group that experienced a barrage of scientific management, along with extensive technological change. Chapter 8 will comment further on how Fordism combined scientific management techniques with mass-production, assembly-line technology to create some of the most alienating and stressful working conditions in modern industrial society.[13]

In many ways, Taylorism represented the practical application of bureaucratic principles to a manufacturing setting. Henry Ford's moving assembly line used technology to develop the logic inherent in scientific management and bureaucracy. The resulting increased monotony and speed of production sparked a huge increase in employee turnover. Only by doubling wages was Ford able to induce workers to accept the new production methods. Worker opposition to Fordism is never far from the surface. When General Motors opened a Vega plant in the early 1970s at Lordstown, Ohio, the relentless pace of the line, coupled with more restrictive management, led to massive labour unrest and sabotage (Aronowitz 1973: Chapter 2). As described in Chapter 6, lean production, the latest Japanese-inspired management system in North American auto factories, has retained elements of Fordism.

In short, major human costs often accompany increased efficiency, productivity, and profits. Other schools of management have attempted to counteract the harshness that resulted from Taylorism and Fordism by developing more humane working conditions. As one organizational researcher aptly concludes, scientific management principles "make superb sense for organizing production when robots rather than human beings are the main productive force, when organizations can truly become machines" (Morgan 1997: 26).

THE HUMAN RELATIONS MOVEMENT

Bureaucracy, scientific management, and mass-production technologies transformed work in the twentieth century. Many jobs became routinized and monotonous, stripped of opportunities for workers to use their minds or develop their skills and abilities. Employee dissatisfaction, often in the form of high turnover and absenteeism rates or industrial unrest, threatened to undermine the machine-like efficiency of the new industrial system. Taylor, Henry Ford, and a host of "efficiency experts" sought to redesign production systems so that control would be firmly in the hands of management. Technical efficiency was paramount.

Toward Normative Control: Workers as Human Beings

However, gaining the cooperation of workers within an increasingly bureaucratized, mechanized, and regimented labour process remained difficult. Some employers responded with programs, broadly known as *corporate welfare* or *industrial betterment*, which emphasized the need to treat workers as human beings. Popular in leading North American firms by the 1920s, corporate welfare programs tried to reduce the alienating effects of bureaucracy and worker dissatisfaction with routinized tasks. The goal was a loyal and productive work force; the means were healthier work settings and improved job benefits. Recreation facilities, cafeterias, cleaner and more pleasant work environments, coherent personnel policies, medical care, and pensions are major examples of corporate welfare efforts.

Taylor and other efficiency experts were quick to dismiss these schemes as a waste of money. Yet many firms committed to scientific management also used corporate welfare measures to gain greater cooperation from staff (Craven 1980: 100–105; Jacoby 1985). More than anything, the corporate welfare movement showed that the principles of bureaucracy and scientific management failed to address the key ingredient in modern industry—human beings. Not until the *human relations school of management* began to systematically examine some of the same concerns in the 1930s did the scientific management model face a serious challenge.

Control within organizations depends upon rank-and-file employees complying with management directives. Such *compliance* can be achieved in three different ways: coercive management techniques that rely on penalties and harsh discipline; utilitarian methods by which employees are motivated by economic self-interest; and normative approaches that assume that workers equate their own interests with organizational goals, thus becoming motivated to work hard (Etzioni 1975). Scientific management combined coercive and utilitarian methods, with mixed results at best. The normative approach, which cultivates a community of interests throughout the organization, is thought to be more effective. Workers are more likely to personally identify with management goals, pursuing them as their own. In short, a normative approach to employee relations sharply contrasts with scientific management in its assumptions regarding human nature and motivation.

A complementary perspective on these issues is the concept of *trust*. Trust means having positive expectations about another person's or group's conduct in a relationship, or put differently, believing that they are concerned about your best interests (Lewicki et al. 1998; Lowe and Schellenberg 2001; Sitkin et al. 1998). Some organizational researchers argue that a precondition for worker compliance and commitment is a relationship of mutual trust between employees and managers (Heisig and Littek 1995). Workplace and labour market restructuring often heighten insecurity and uncertainty, increasing the likelihood that employees will *distrust* their employer.

Theoretically, then, the big happy corporate family of the human relations school replaced the carrot of incentive wages and the stick of harsh discipline. In practice, however, scientific management and human relations often operate side by side. And beneath the changing workplace structures is a layer of fragile social relationships that influence individuals' work experiences and organizational success.

The Hawthorne Studies

The human relations school of management originated in the *Hawthorne Studies*, a program of research conducted by Harvard Business School researchers between 1927 and 1932 at Western Electric's Hawthorne Works on the outskirts of Chicago.[14] Western Electric management was initially concerned with the effects of fatigue and monotony on production levels. These were central concerns of industrial psychologists at the time. Various studies examining the effect of rest pauses, hours of work, and lighting levels on productivity led researchers to unexpected findings.

In the Relay Assembly Test Room study, workers were placed in two separate rooms. Researchers then recorded production while varying light intensity for one group but not the other. To their surprise, productivity in both groups increased, regardless of lighting level. Only when light intensity was reduced to that of bright moonlight did productivity decline. Several variations on this study came up with the same puzzling findings. Searching for possible explanations, the researchers speculated that a fundamental change had occurred in the workplace. Involving workers in the study had the unintended effect of raising their morale. They now felt that management cared about them as individuals. Productivity, concluded the researchers, increased as a result. This is the famous *Hawthorne effect*.[15] A basic axiom of human relations management had been discovered: the humane treatment of employees and the creation of an *esprit de corps* improves their motivation to cooperate and be productive.

In a subsequent phase of the research, interviews with employees revealed that work groups were governed by informal behavioural codes. This early attempt at employee counselling also tried to detect grievances and potential trouble spots in the factory (Wilensky and Wilensky 1951). The Bank Wiring Observation Room study further probed work-group behaviour. For seven months, 14 employees were observed as they wired telephone switching banks. Researchers documented how *informal group norms* replaced formal directives from management. The work team set its own production quotas, making sure that no member worked too quickly or too slowly. Infractions of the group's rules, such as reporting violations of company policy to management, were punished. Generally, strong pressures to conform to the group norms prevailed (Homans 1950: Chapter 3). This exposed the hidden side of the workplace, where workers consciously engage in practices to oppose or subvert established authority.

After the Hawthorne studies, worker needs and motivation became key management concerns. And the workplace came to be viewed as a social system rather than a purely technical system.

Cooperation and Conflict in Human Relations Theory

Human relations management theory emphasizes how workers' attitudes, values, emotions, psychological needs, and interpersonal relationships shape their work behaviour. This approach to management seeks the best match between the worker, given her or his personal background and psychological makeup, and the job. Careful recruitment and effective training of employees, as well as good supervision and communications, are therefore essential.

The human relations perspective also assumes that people naturally want to cooperate. This is an explicit rejection of the utilitarian assumption of scientific management. Yet Elton Mayo and other human relations theorists claimed that workers are unaware of their cooperative instincts, acting instead on the basis of irrational sentiments or beliefs. For Mayo, the survival of society depended on cooperation, so he advocated a new industrial order run by an administrative elite. The leadership of this elite would encourage the development of work environments that would bring out the cooperative instincts and productive potential of employees (Mayo 1945).

Mayo and other human relations advocates consider workers unable to act in their own best interests. Less authoritarian leadership, careful selection and training of personnel, an emphasis on human needs and job satisfaction— these are the central contributions of the human relations approach. Yet lurking behind these management tactics is a contradictory view of the workplace (Burawoy 1979: 7). On the one hand, human relations theory assumes that industrial harmony is normal and healthy and, conversely, that conflict is destructive. The possibility of conflicting interests between management and workers is denied, leaving no place for unions or other collective expressions of workers' interests. On the other hand, human relations theory argues that workers must be closely regulated by management in the greater interests of cooperation and harmony. These inconsistencies have led some critics to label human relations theory as an elaborate justification for management's manipulation of workers (Rinehart 2001).

Many strands of management thinking make up the human relations tradition. One durable strand, which draws on psychologist Abraham Maslow's concept of a hierarchy of human needs, was developed by Douglas McGregor in the 1950s and 1960s. McGregor saw in bureaucracy and Taylorism a mechanistic approach to managing and motivating people that stifles human potential by relying mainly on economic incentives. He called this Theory X, and contrasted it with Theory Y, which views a manager's main task as creating an environment that aligns workers' personal needs for growth, development, and participation with an organization's goals. McGregor reminded managers that Theory X and Y are not strategies, but sets of assumptions about human nature. While an influential idea, the humanistic Theory Y did little to influence day-to-day management practice when it was published 40 years ago. Today, McGregor's ideas are once again very much in vogue, as shown in our review below of current approaches to human resource management.[16] Most human resource (or personnel) managers sincerely want to treat workers as human beings. Yet the power structures of most large organizations, reinforced by their dominant cultures, still pose major barriers to putting these ideas into practice. In this sense, McGregor's thinking remains futuristic.

ORGANIZATIONAL CULTURE

Our overview of the Hawthorne studies documents how workers construct their own culture in the workplace, replacing official rules and norms with their own. Consequently, the potential for management–worker conflict is increased, since the official goals of management and the unofficial, more personal goals of workers and work groups are not the same. This issue is taken up further in Chapter 6. Yet informal workplace relations and organizational culture also provide another management tool for increasing employee conformity and integration. This apparent paradox between workplace social relations and culture as means for employee resistance on the one hand, and as the basis for a value consensus on the other, is rooted in the two divergent theoretical traditions we first identified in Chapter 1. The former, which derives from Marx's view of society, emphasizes the dynamics of conflict. The latter draws on the work of French sociologist Émile Durkheim and his concerns about achieving social stability (Ray 1986; Ouchi 1981: Chapter 6).

The Informal Side of Organizations

By focusing only on the formal structure of organizations and the role of managers, we overlook vital features of life in work organizations. Less visible but equally important in the daily operations of an organization is its *informal* side, where employees reinterpret, resist, or adapt to work structures and management directives (Blau and Scott 1963). Thus, to get a complete picture of a work organization, we must examine it from the vantage point of employees' informal practices and social relations. The glossy organizational charts found in corporate annual reports present management's image of how things ought to operate. Employees further down the hierarchy often see things differently, and act according.

In the seven decades since the Hawthorne studies, the *informal work group* has been under the microscope of social scientists. Some of this research has highlighted the dynamics of conflict and power within work organizations. Despite management's efforts to regiment work procedures, employees often respond in ways that do not fit these plans. Total control of people by bureaucratic structures, management discipline, and technology is difficult to imagine. Furthermore, there is an underlying tension between the cooperation necessary for any organization to function and the internal competition among individuals and groups over the distribution of power, rewards, and other scarce resources.

Donald Roy's (1952) participant observer study of a Chicago machine shop graphically portrays work-group dynamics and counter-systems of production. During the 1940s, Roy worked as a machinist in a shop that ran on a *piecework payment system*. Productivity was regulated by management through bonus payments for output that was above established quotas. Machine operators constantly battled over the base wage with time-study personnel trained in scientific management. The machinists invented ingenious shortcuts to maximize their wages while minimizing effort. This required conspiracies with other groups who supplied tools, maintained the machines, or delivered raw materials, all of which violated company rules.

The workers' informal system of production involved what in shop-floor jargon was called "goldbricking" on "stinker jobs." That is, on difficult jobs for which they could not possibly earn a bonus, workers relaxed and enjoyed some free time. On easy jobs, however, they could "make out" by exceeding the quota to receive a bonus. Any production beyond an unofficial quota was stored up in a "kitty" to be used to boost output figures on a slow day. Management rarely challenged the workers' system because production usually fluctuated within an acceptable range. Ironically, the workers had designed a more predictable and efficient production process.[17]

Managers, too, participate in the manipulation of informal work practices, as Roy observed in the machine shop. While able to exercise some authority over rank-and-file workers, many middle- and lower-level managers and supervisors feel constrained in their roles. Consequently, they may not entirely follow the directives of top executives. A revealing study of how managers sometimes operate is Melville Dalton's *Men Who Manage*.[18] Dalton illustrates how managers bend rules and short-circuit bureaucracy in order to achieve their objectives. Especially fascinating is his analysis of how official and unofficial rewards often complement each other, giving management a wider repertoire of means to achieve a particular goal.

On paper, the organizations Dalton studied were formal bureaucracies. In practice, unofficial systems guided actions. Obtaining a promotion depended less on merit than it did on social characteristics such as, for example, being a member of the Masonic Order or the local yacht club. Employees at all organizational levels regularly engaged in what, to the outside observer, was dishonest activity. The company's resources were dispensed as personal rewards in order to keep the bureaucracy running, to acknowledge someone's special services to the firm, or to solidify social relationships in order to get a job done. Workers borrowed tools and equipment; managers had home improvements done at company expense. According to Dalton, this sort of "freewheeling" frequently occurs just beneath the thin veneer of bureaucracy.

Organizational Culture

Based on insights like these about informal group relations, the concept of *organizational culture* has become a prominent theme in literature on management and organizations (Trice and Beyer 1993; Frost et al. 1991). Social-anthropological methods are useful in studying organizational culture. Viewed from the perspective of their members, organizations become mini-societies. The shared beliefs, customs, rituals, languages, and myths serve as "social glue," binding together the diverse elements of the organization. *Culture*, then, refers to a system of shared meanings about how organizational life ought to be conducted. It can express how things really get done at an informal level. The culture metaphor, used broadly, shifts our attention from the structure of an organization toward the processes by which employees actually carry out and collectively interpret work activities (Morgan 1997: Chapter 5; Ranson et al. 1980).

Shaping the *dominant culture* of an organization—that is, encouraging employees to identify strongly with the goals of the corporation—has become a management preoccupation (Pettigrew 1979). Viewed from this perspective, the norms and values of employee work groups become *countercultures* challenging the dominant organizational values. Corporations with strong internal cultures, as evident in Sears' customer service commitment or the Body Shop's culture of social responsibility, send a clear signal to all employees, as well as to customers. A strong corporate culture can create a self-selection process, whereby individuals are attracted to a firm because of its values and those who are already there either buy in or leave. Senior managers in the private and public sectors devote much energy to "branding" their organization by marketing their core values, partly in an effort to attract the kind of employees they want. More theoretically, attempts to develop strong organizational cultures are a means of achieving what Amitai Etzioni calls normative control. Critics argue that this management approach is used to enforce conformity and prevent dissent. This may not serve the overall goals of the organization if it stifles the kind of healthy debate that generates solutions to problems (Ray 1986).

Managing Consensus through Culture

Contributing to the boom in organizational culture studies in the 1980s was the belief among North American managers that strong collective values explained the growing success of Japanese firms. William Ouchi's (1981) research suggested that successful North American corporations that emulated this Japanese approach had developed clan-like internal cultures that made the firm's values the main guides for what employees think and do. Encouraged by such studies, many employers attempted to create a strong corporate culture, a dominant system of beliefs and behaviour to which, ideally, all members of the organization would be committed. These values were reinforced by mythology that revered the founders of the organization and legendary past leaders, and by rituals such as annual awards dinners at which employees' achievements were recognized.

The popular management literature often features organizations that have apparently transformed their culture. For example, some years ago, the Campbell Soup Company in Canada introduced a "New Age" form of culture into the organization, based on the concept of "breakthrough management," which encourages people to plan from a future perspective, and spread by "power coaches." While the Campbell Soup president admitted that some people "wonder what we've been smoking," the new thinking fostered by breakthrough management seems to have delivered real results in the form of costs savings and higher profits (*The Globe and Mail*, 4 August 1992: B18). Scholars also examine, with greater skepticism, attempts at cultural transformation. An example is Saturn Corporation's attempt to create illusions of empowerment among customers and employees through its advertising campaigns for the cars it produces. Postmodernist researchers focus on Saturn's use of "storytelling" as a mechanism for creating a symbolic community that appeals to the needs of consumers and workers for a sense of connectedness (Mills et al. 2001).

This is only one example of how researchers provide a critical lens through which to assess the claims about managers shaping a dominant organizational culture. Much of the management research on culture focuses on the functions of culture – how it contributes to an organization's goals. Other researchers, often sociologists or anthropologists, examine the meaning of the organization to participants, and how a diversity of understandings and values coexist or at times are in conflict (Rowlinson and Procter, 1999; Harris and Ogbonna 1999). Postmodernist researchers, in particular, have criticized the unitary, dominant model of organizational culture by highlighting the wide range of symbols and stories that have relevance for different groups in an organization. This is an important insight, given the great diversity of social, cultural and demographic backgrounds that individuals bring into organizations (Chemers et al. 1995). Feminist researchers argue that gender is constructed in workplaces through the use of language and other symbols, a process shaped by the interaction of workforce characteristics, the nature of the industry, and the larger cultural context—none of which managers can really control (Poggio 2000).

Do Organizations Have Different Cultures?

An organization's culture reflects many other characteristics, including the larger social and historical context. Research casts doubt on the view that an employer can "manage" culture. Using employee attitude data collected from IBM employees in 64 countries, Geert Hofstede and his colleagues investigated national variations in organizational culture (Hofstede et al. 1990; Hofstede 1984). In particular, the researchers asked whether measurable cultural differences among organizations are a function of the distinctive features of these organizations, or are shaped by the larger environment in which the organization is situated.

Hofstede's (1984: 252) international study of IBM employees found that national cultures directly influence individuals' behaviour in work organizations, the values they hold, organizational design, and even the theories used to explain organization. Follow-up studies frequently confirm that employee values are not the product of their organization, but are far more likely to vary by nationality, age, or education. Rather than values being at the core of organizational culture, the researchers found shared perceptions of daily practices (what needs to be done and how to do it) to be central (Hofstede et al. 1990: 311). The practical implications of this research are twofold. First, employee values are more likely to enter the organization through the hiring process than through on-the-job socialization that attempts to inculcate the dominant culture. Second, the effectiveness of popular management techniques, organizational design, and work humanization efforts will vary according to national context.

Canadian research by David Zussman and Jak Jabes (1989) comparing senior federal government managers with comparable levels of managers in the private sector also challenges the conception of a dominant culture of shared values. This study documented distinct differences between public and private sector managers in terms of personal and corporate values and leadership styles. Equally pronounced was what they termed "the vertical solitude" between levels of management within the public sector. This suggests morale and leadership problems among federal public service managers, although we hasten to add that all managers did share a commitment to doing a good job serving the Canadian public. What is more, interorganizational cultural differences may be less pronounced than the differences in values and orientations among groups within a specific organization.

In fact, most organizations have a variety of cultures—dominant and alternative—depending on the degree to which particular groups within them share similar work experiences. This cultural fragmentation can result in organizations saying one thing in their philosophy or mission statement, while their day-to-day operations reflect something quite different. In fact, an organization's culture can be a barrier to greater employee involvement, the very goal that managers seek when refashioning culture (Chelte et al. 1989). As well, work groups can develop cultural practices that are essential for performing effectively but that may be undermined by senior management because of their distance from the group. For instance, an anthropologist who studied Xerox copier machine repair technicians discovered that these workers had devised an elaborate oral culture, based on the circulation of stories that contained vital information about how to fix these idiosyncratic machines. However, this oral culture was invisible to senior managers, who planned the technicians' work on the erroneous assumption that corporate standards of design excellence ensured predictable machine operations (Orr 1996). In sum, research from a variety of perspectives clearly shows that the idea of a unitary corporate culture, fashioned by management to gain employee commitment to goals they had no say in setting, greatly oversimplifies the nature of organizational life.

IN SEARCH OF A NEW MANAGERIAL PARADIGM

Even a cursory glance at recent management literature leaves the impression that corporate North America is in constant upheaval. In many respects, the large bureaucracies that have come to dominate the economic landscape are like dinosaurs: cumbersome, slow to respond and adapt, and, according to some critics, a dying breed. The turbulent economic times in which we now live have prompted even the most vocal champions of bureaucracy to search for better ways to manage organizations. Managers, consultants, and some business school academics have created a new growth industry, producing a steady stream of popular management books. These seek a new *paradigm* that would be capable of inspiring managers to meet the huge challenges of what many observers perceive to be an increasingly chaotic, global, knowledge-based, technology-intensive economy.[19]

Tom Peters and Bob Waterman Jr. set the tone in their enormously influential 1982 book, *In Search of Excellence*, in which they documented how rigid, inflexible organizations are less able to survive, let alone grow and profit, in today's rapidly changing economy (Peters and Waterman 1982). Despite the fact that many of Peters and Waterman's "excellent" firms later experienced problems (*Business Week*, 5 November 1984), the writers fuelled debates about the need to rethink old ways of organizing and managing derived from the legacies of Weber, Taylor, and Ford. In this respect, much of the *new management literature* corresponds with the sociological critique of bureaucracy.[20] It also enunciates some additional themes at the core of organizational studies: how change occurs, the role of managers, issues of power, and the possibilities for gaining cooperation and forging a consensus among all organizational participants. A brief overview of several major contributions to the new management literature will elaborate these themes.

The Critique from Within

Revolution is a widely used metaphor in this new management literature, as is seen in Joseph H. Boyett and Henry P. Conn's *Workplace 2000: The Revolution Reshaping American Business* (Boyett and Conn 1991). This book begins with a case study of the kind of revolution the authors argue is necessary. Picture a plant employing 130 people, where, in a six-year period, output rises 80 percent, absenteeism drops to 2 percent, and turnover drops to 1 percent. There are no time clocks, no supervisors, no job classifications, and no definite work assignments. Everyone is salaried and productivity reaches that of plants employing a third more staff. The ingredients of this apparently remarkable turnaround are captured by Boyett and Conn in their use of terms such as work teams, participative management, employee empowerment, flatter and leaner organization structures, flexibility, creativity, innovation, pay-for-knowledge, continuous learning, quality, service, and doing more with less. This is the language of the new management.

Tom Peters has become one of the best known of the new management gurus. In his book, *Thriving on Chaos: A Handbook for a Management Revolution,* he recants some of the tenets put forward in *In Search of Excellence,* arguing that there is no such thing as an excellent company because a firm can always be run better and rapid change requires constant adaptation (Peters 1987). His model of what he calls a "winner" is based on five sets of characteristics: an obsession with responsiveness to customers; constant innovation in all areas; the full participation and empowerment of all people connected with the organization; leadership that loves change and promotes an inspiring vision; and non-bureaucratic control by simple support systems.

Peters (1987) clearly articulates the necessity of, as he puts it, turning the organization "upside-down and sideways." He has an abundance of anecdotes from the corporate trenches, such as an anti-bureaucratic inversion of a cherished status symbol, whereby one reformed corporation jokes about still having an "executive dining room"—the Chinese restaurant or the deli across the street from its headquarters (Peters 1987). Finally, Peters's obsession with embracing change sets a new goal for managers: create internal stability in an organization so that it can be constantly adapting to an ever-changing external environment. Peters drives this message home in an article in the *California Management Review* with the appropriate title, "Get innovative or get dead" (Peters 1990; 1991). Echoing similar themes is Henry Mintzberg (1989: 2), who defines organizations simply as "collective action in pursuit of a common mission, a fancy way of saying that a bunch of people have come together under an identifiable label ('General Motors,' 'Joe's Body Shop') to produce some product or service."

Mintzberg's (1989: Chapter 11) work on innovative organizations introduces the concept of *adhocracy*. Adhocracy is a hallmark of the innovative organization, one that has a fluid and decentralized operating structure. This contrasts with the inflexibility of what Mintzberg calls the "machine organization," or traditional bureaucracy, and even with the "entrepreneurial organization," which is too performance-oriented. The work of an adhocracy is performed by multidisciplinary teams. Hierarchical top–down control, rigid lines of authority, and narrow job functions are replaced by a *matrix structure*. This injects elasticity, allowing experts to move between functional units for specialized administrative tasks and multidisciplinary project teams. Mintzberg points to Canada's National Film Board as a good example of an operating adhocracy, with its artists, technical experts, and administrators forming and reforming teams to create the documentaries and animated films for which the agency is famous. Mintzberg's view of fluid, flexible, innovative organizations is shared among management thinkers, and it raises larger questions about how organizations change. Peter F. Drucker (1993: 59), the dean of management gurus, argues that in a knowledge- and technology-based economy, successful organizations must be able to continuously change and renew themselves. Essentially, these writers are elaborating the concept of the "learning organization."

But continuous change is not easy. Rosabeth Moss Kanter evokes the image of elephants learning how to kick up their heels in her book *When Giants Learn to Dance* (Kanter 1989). In it, she advocates a "post-entrepreneurial revolution." She observes that change has become the new management orthodoxy and wonders if the resulting managerial innovations designed to harness change will infiltrate the old elephantine corporations most in need of reinvigorating. The crux of the problem is that bureaucracy is a hindrance to a cooperative, creative, and flexible workplace. Kanter cautions, however, that the "cowboy management style" typical of many young successful firms—"lean and mean," glamorizing individualism, highly competitive—is not the solution.

Eastman Kodak and Apple Computer exemplify the old elephantine corporation and the new entrepreneurial cowboy, respectively. "Too-bureaucratic Kodak had begun to stagnate," Kanter explains, adding that it "had become burdened with a cumbersome organization that encouraged bureaucratic turf-consciousness and stifled innovation. Too-entrepreneurial Apple, mired in the problems of transition from the founder and the chaotic start-up mode, was caught in internal rivalries that wasted resources, and had not yet harnessed the achievement drives of individuals to shared purposes" (Kanter 1989: 52). These two contrasting firms launched themselves on similar new management strategies. They reorganized according to their strengths, established closer relationships with suppliers and customers, emphasized cooperation and the generation of new ideas, cut out management layers, and developed self-managing employee teams. The result, in Kanter's (1989) words, was "a triumph of process over structure."

In a later book, *World Class*, Kanter examines successful "cosmopolitan" firms that rely on ever-changing global business networks. Viewing corporate life from this perspective of globalization (see Chapter 1), a more negative picture of management initiatives emerges. The problem, she points out, is that "as cosmopolitan businesses extend their market scope, tap new and better supply sources, and link up with global chains, they inevitably loosen local ties and relationships" (Kanter 1995: 145). This results in increased temporary work, outsourcing, and growing workloads and longer hours for core staff, with no guarantee of future security. Kanter advocates human resource policies that create new forms of security within the context of rapid change. She gives examples of global firms that have introduced a "new social contract" based on the concept of employability—ensuring that employees receive the kind of ongoing training, learning opportunities, and career counselling that will keep them employable (Kanter 1995: 156–63).

This brief sampling of some of the most influential management writers gives the flavour of the issues still being raised in this now-vast literature. To expand this discussion, we will consider three prominent themes – quality, downsizing, and learning – that have come to characterize the challenges and contradictory pressures that employees and managers face in putting "new paradigms" into practice.

The Quality Mission

Putting quality and customers first are two axioms of the new management. To this end, some organizations have embraced the *total quality management* or TQM (sometimes called *total quality improvement)* model. Skeptics may view TQM as just a catchy label applied to a particular combination of cus-tomer-service initiatives, often with the help of computers (Micklethwait and Wooldridge 1996: 26; Abrahamson and Fairchild 1999). However, TQM champions claim that the model reduces costs and increases productivity, cus-tomer satisfaction, quality of working life, and firm competitiveness.

TQM was North American management's response to the competitive edge Japanese firms had gained in the 1980s through an obsession with product quality. However, its roots lie in the U.S. government's efforts to set quality standards for suppliers to the Defense Department during World War II and the pioneering work of American statistician W. E. Demming on quality control systems, which Japanese firms readily adopted (Clarke and Clegg 1998: 257; Aguayo 1990). TQM advocates, first and foremost, a customer-based emphasis on quality. "Customers" can be external consumers or citizens in the case of public sector organizations, or other units or indi-viduals within the organization ('internal customers'). TQM's emphasis on continuous improvement focuses on involving employees in identifying and quickly resolving problems, or anticipating future problems. Like other man-agement schools, there is no unifying model of TQM. Some perspectives on TQM converge with the ideas on organizational learning reviewed below, sug-gesting that quality goals require much more learning and creativity among employees (Eskildsen et al. 1999; Argyris 1999). In addition to quality control systems, typical elements of TQM include performance measures, improved communications and feedback systems, problem-solving work teams, employee involvement, and a culture of trust and cooperation (Clarke and Clegg 1998: 254-65).

Based on this description, TQM could have major implications for employees. But as with other new management trends, it is difficult to sort out real change from the rhetoric of TQM. Again, much of the so-called evidence consists of nothing more than anecdotes. Overall, it does seem that if a quality improvement strategy is part of a comprehensive set of high performance work practices (discussed below), then there is a higher likelihood that there will be tangible movements towards less bureaucracy, greater customer responsiveness, organizational flexibility, and employee participation. Yet more research is needed to unravel the links between quality improvement, on one hand, and specific organizational change initiatives, on the other. For example, many retail and consumer service organizations, such as Marriott hotels and Wal-Mart, call employees "associates" and "empower" them to take initiatives to satisfy customers. Two of the winners of a national U.S. quality award, Xerox Corporation and Milliken & Company (a textile manufacturer), have made heavy investments in employee training and use teams extensively. However, these and related examples are not based on a systematic analysis of how specific changes actually contribute to measurable improvements in quality.

Other criticisms abound. For example, in the public sector, TQM has been widely applied in health care. Patients are treated as "customers" and quality committees rethink processes and procedures in order to improve the quality of patient care and to cut costs. In an era of health care spending cuts, often the end result has been more stressful working conditions for nurses and other health care workers (Armstrong et al. 1994). A case study of the introduction of a major TQM initiative at the University of Alberta Hospital, in Edmonton, found that much of it turned out to be counterproductive because it was linked in employees' minds with downsizing, which was happening at the same time. Increased workloads, reduced competence resulting from multi-skilling, and the overall impact of doing more with less created "role ambiguity, conflicts and demoralization" – with potentially negative impacts on health care costs and quality (Lam and Reshef 1999: 741).

Some analysts argue that the "quality movement" has stimulated thinking about how to change workplaces so that employees become the key factor in improved organizational performance (Pfeffer 1994: Chapter 9). Among those firms using some form of TQM, relatively few have had very positive results. As one major international evaluation of quality management practices concluded, Canadian managers "have learned the jargon, read the books and attended the seminars, but have failed to bring the theory to the shop floor."[21] There is frequently resistance to TQM changes at various levels of the organization, largely because it may be perceived as disrupting the existing power structure. Middle managers balk at the idea of empowering employees, knowing that it is their power that will be redistributed downward. Employees and unions may resist bringing the logic of the marketplace inside an organization – such as treating university students as "consumers" and measuring their "satisfaction'" through course evaluations. Furthermore, employees no doubt have trouble with such vague goals as "continuous improvement," which suggests that their best efforts today may not be good enough tomorrow.

The Downside of Downsizing

Despite the people focus of human resource management in the last decade, the most common management strategy has been *downsizing*. Job cuts, accompanied by organizational restructuring, occurred in close to half of Canadian firms with 100 or more employees between 1991 and 1996, and one-third expected more downsizing to come. Smaller firms, with fewer than 50 employees, were far less likely to downsize, which is not surprising considering that small businesses created the majority of new jobs in the 1990s.[22] A 1993 national survey of more than 700 firms in the resource, manufacturing, and business services sectors found that the most common management strategy (reported by over 60 percent) was "cost cutting" through reduced labour and operating costs (Betcherman et al. 1994: 20–21). In the United States, the 100 largest firms in the *Fortune 500* list have downsized an average of 15 times over the past 15 years, eliminating 2.5 million workers from their payrolls (McKay 1996: 56). These figures do not include the public sector, where deep budget cuts in the 1990s aimed at reducing government deficits resulted in more significant staff cuts than in the private sector (Lowe 2001). Downsizing has continued in the 21st century, more often as a result of mergers, acquisition, and large-scale reorganization than of cost cutting *per se*.

Downsizing has been likened to corporate anorexia. Organizations that may have started out reasonably healthy become lean and mean, but sometimes also dysfunctional. Underlying organizational problems are not addressed. There is now considerable evidence that downsizing has inflicted damage not only on individual employees and communities, but also on the downsized organization. The 1990s witnessed public reactions against the downsizing trend, fuelled by widespread feelings of job insecurity (Betcherman and Lowe 1997). *The New York Times'* (1996: 21) report on "The Downsizing of America" observed that the tally of jobs eliminated in the 1990s "...has the eerie feel of battlefield casualty counts. And like waves of strung-out veterans, the psychically frazzled downsized workers are infecting their families, friends, and communities with their grief, fear, and anger." Many of these laid-off workers end up downwardly mobile, unable to find comparable jobs.

A growing body of research by academics and management consultants documents three areas—economic, organizational, and human—in which downsizing can create more problems for organizations than it solves.[23] Economically, the short-term cost savings associated with downsizing often do not translate into improved profits. Expenses may actually increase over time as managers realize they need to rehire workers or contract out work that otherwise would not get done. Organizationally, downsizing is often a quick fix that is not part of a comprehensive change strategy. When organizations shrink rapidly, structures, processes, values, and goals must also change. Downsizing may be incompatible with other organizational change initiatives, such as TQM. And researchers on organizational learning suggest that wide-scale staff cuts weaken the social networks that are vital for the organization's capacity to learn and share knowledge (Fisher and White 2000).

The human costs are also extensive and often not anticipated. Medical researchers have tracked individuals who have been downsized, documenting damage to their health (Kivimäki et al. 2000). The term *survivor syndrome* has been coined to describe the negative psychological effects of downsizing on employees who remain behind, although this is only one possible response (Mishra and Spreitzer 1998). Workers experience elevated levels of stress, and generally become demoralized and dissatisfied. Motivation, loyalty, and productivity can suffer as employees avoid taking risks in their jobs and become absorbed in protecting their own interests. This is exacerbated by increased workloads (and sometimes wage cuts) as the organization tries to "do more with less." People get reassigned to new duties without adequate training; layers of management may be eliminated without authority being delegated downward; departing employees may take with them "organizational memory"; long-term planning of any kind becomes very difficult; and customer service and quality can also suffer. So it is not surprising that a national survey of Canadian employees conducted in 2000 found that those who experienced downsizing and restructuring in the year prior to the survey had much lower levels of trust in and commitment to their employer, and reported poor communication and less influence on decision making, compared with employees who had not undergone such changes (Lowe and Schellenberg 2001). Building trust relationships and employee commitment is one of the most difficult challenges an employer faces in the wake of downsizing.

In short, downsizing has had serious unintended consequences, and, in this respect, provides lessons in how not to go about changing organizations. Ironically, downsizing became trendy at the same time as organizational researchers and human resource management experts were preaching the importance of managing employees in ways that empowered them and increased their skills. Recently, the importance of loyalty has been rediscovered, and firms now are being told that a high-loyalty strategy aimed at building committed and long-term staff—the opposite of downsizing, contracting out, or using temporary workers—is directly related to customer loyalty (Reichheld 1996: Chapter 4). Not only is this a longer-term view, but it also treats employees as more than another line in the budget.

Some organizations have reduced staff numbers more humanely. Nova Corporation of Calgary, for example, established the Employment, Transition and Continuity Program to achieve a 10 percent staff reduction. The objective, according to the vice-president of human resources, is "to ensure that those who leave feel good about how they were treated and that those who stay feel energized and ready to move Nova forward."[24] Whether it truly is possible to feel good about being laid off is questionable. However, the program underscores the importance of the process by which downsizing is carried out so that morale is not destroyed (Mishra and Spreitzer 1998; Lam and Reshef 1999). And in practical terms, it does provide employees whose jobs are affected with more options and support, including alternative work arrangements (job sharing, reduced work week, seasonal employment), financial support for education or working in nonprofit community organizations, small business start-up advice and grants, skills upgrading, leaves of absence, and help with relocation costs. While exacting a smaller toll on individual employees, staff reductions achieved by employees volunteering to leave under conditions such as those just outlined create new problems for the organization. This is especially true if the most experienced and productive employees are among those who leave, because it depletes the firm's knowledge assets and reduces its learning capacity (Fisher and White 2000). This highlights one of the dilemmas of balancing the fair treatment of employees against what is in the overall best interests of the organization.

Learning Organizations or Organizational Learning?

The concept of a *learning organization* has become popular recently. Employers increasingly are turning their attention to gaining a competitive advantage through effective use and development of employees' knowledge and skills. Not only is this the stated objective of most human resource managers, it is also echoed widely by governments across the industrialized world, which are giving high priority to lifelong learning as the means to continuous skill development (OECD 1996). It is widely assumed that better-trained workers will make an organization more adaptable, innovative, and flexible. So too, entire organizations must learn by continuously incorporating new knowledge, using it to improve their performance, and enabling individual workers to actively engage in learning.

A leading advocate of the learning organization is Peter Senge.[25] He proposes that employees and organizations follow five "learning disciplines": expanding your personal abilities and enabling others to do so; breaking out of old ways of thinking; developing a shared vision of the future; team learning; and holistic or systems thinking. These abstract principles describe a process, not a set of concrete changes. Senge claims that there is no "top 10" list of learning organizations, only individuals, work groups, and teams in various organizations engaged in "mastery and self determination" through learning. Such workers are better able to "embrace change." Senge and other champions of organizational learning present a humanistic image of self-development and self-learning in organizations, quite the opposite to the mechanistic model of organizations created by Taylor or described by Weber.

However, discussions of organizational learning lack clear definitions that could guide implementation strategies (Gherardi 1999; Popper and Lipschitz 2000). A stock definition of a learning organization is one that is "skilled at creating, acquiring, and transferring knowledge, and at modifying its behaviour to reflect new knowledge and insights" (Garvin 1993: 80). What remains ambiguous here is the relationship between individuals' learning activities in workplaces and organizations as learning systems. Too often, organizational learning initiatives become technical exercises in "knowledge management" using computer-based information systems (Easterby-Smith et al. 1999). Senge would argue that transforming an organization's culture is the best way of removing the barriers to learning that are rooted in traditional work practices and organizational structures. Learning must become a valued and rewarded process that employees have the autonomy to pursue. According to this view, a learning organization has a *learning culture* that empowers employees to take initiatives to solve problems and learn.[26]

Some firms appear to have moved toward developing a learning culture. At Harley Davidson Motorcycles, "intellectual curiosity" is now a core value, "Harley University" offers extensive training programs, and the president promotes learning at every opportunity (Gephart et al. 1996: 39). But experts on workplace skill development would argue that Harley Davidson simply has made greater investments in training, communicating this as a new value commitment. Training-intensive organizations, where skills are increased by regular on-site programs or through support for off-site courses, only go part way to ensuring that individuals engage in learning as they do their job and are able to apply and share that learning throughout the organization (Betcherman et al. 1998). By this standard, Canadian firms have a long way to go. Recall from Chapter 2 that, compared to other countries, Canadian employers underinvest in job-related training (Statistics Canada and Human Resources Development Canada 2001).

Thus, it would appear that for the majority of Canadian employers, creating a learning organization remains an ideal. Achieving this goal will require a more rigorous model of a learning organization that is informed by research (rather than consultants' anecdotes), a clearer understanding of the barriers to learning faced by individual employees, and the conditions that can enable knowledge generation and transfer throughout the organization (Argote 1999).

Revolution or Evolution?

Marx theorized that capitalism contained the seeds of its own demise. But, instead of workers revolting to replace capitalism with a worker-run socialist system, the "revolution" has taken an altogether different course. To the extent that the new management commentators such as Peters, Kanter, Mintzberg, Senge, and a host of other academics and business consultants are correct, we may be witnessing a management-inspired revolution, driven by an instinct for survival. Or, is it more accurate to call it the latest stage in the evolution of organizational forms and managerial strategies?

Regardless, we can detect a shift away from a mechanistic, bureaucratic model of work organizations and toward a model that strives to better manage its human resources. This greater "people emphasis" indeed may be the most significant feature of the new direction in management, although it is in constant tension with the pressure to downsize and cut labour costs. This people orientation has shown some positive results for both management and employees in the private as well as the public sector.

To conclude, this brief review of the new management literature raises four pressing issues that researchers and practitioners must consider. The first concerns the nature of change in organizations, as well as the barriers that must be overcome for them to succeed. The changes heralded above as "revolutionary" suggest a shift from traditional approaches to organizing and managing work. Many managers may be talking about these changes, but, in practice, they are limited. Indeed, "management fads" and their diffusion have become a focus of academic research. Studies show that recent fads are launched by "management-knowledge entrepreneurs," have a short life cycle, and are difficult for senior managers to successfully implement (Carson et al. 2000; Abrahamson and Fairchild 1999). Second, the basic assumptions and prescriptions being advocated fall short of a new paradigm. Many of the ideas are recycled from various streams of earlier thinking, some of which are reviewed below. So it would be helpful to have more careful assessments of the intellectual origins and innovative contributions of "new" management approaches. Third, it should be clear by now that most new models for managing and organizing work focus on large organizations, mainly in the private sector. This rather exclusive approach leaves out small and medium-sized businesses and the self-employed, which combined account for far more employment than do large corporations (see Chapter 2). It also tends to overlook the unique operating environments of public-sector and nonprofit organizations.

A fourth issue concerns the likely impact of these changes on employees at all levels of the organization. The research on management fads, just noted, raises the distinct possibility that the effect of new management techniques on employees is most likely neutral or negative. Probing this further, can the rhetoric of participative management, team work, and employee empowerment now in vogue be taken at face value? Or is it a more sophisticated managerial control strategy aimed at getting workers to make even greater commitments and sacrifices to the organization and to "do more with less"? These questions are taken up in Chapter 6, where we discuss critical perspectives on work. For now, we will demonstrate that the idea that people matter in work organizations is firmly rooted in earlier attempts to reform and humanize work.

WORK HUMANIZATION, JOB REDESIGN, AND THE HIGH-PERFORMANCE WORKPLACE

So far, we have documented the problems of bureaucratic hierarchies, assembly-line technology and a fragmented division of labour, and organizational downsizing. The costs to workers, management, and society take the form of job dissatisfaction, stress and anxiety, poor morale, low productivity, and failure to meet the challenges of today's changing economic environment. Central to the new management approaches just reviewed are team work, greater employee participation in decision making, and skill development. But these are hardly new ideas. To help locate them historically, we will take a brief journey through the various theories and some of the actual applications of more democratic forms of work organizations and innovative job designs.

Human relations theory strongly influenced work reform schemes such as job enlargement, job enrichment, participative management, sociotechnical planning, quality circles, and various quality-of-working-life programs. A common ideological thread unites these approaches. Employees should be treated humanely and provided with good working conditions. Even so, beyond a few concessions in the realm of decision making, most of the authority remains with management. However, some reforms in Canada and elsewhere, particularly in Sweden and Norway, have come closer to achieving the dual goals of significantly redistributing power and enhancing the quality of working life. In some instances, the reforms described below may also improve productivity, resulting in mutual gains for employees and employers (Kochan and Osterman 1994).

Swedish Work Reforms

The potential of work humanization has been most fully realized in Sweden, which pioneered work reforms. Decades of social democratic government, a strong labour movement, and legislation giving individuals the right to meaningful jobs provide fertile grounds for the humanistic work reforms that have taken place in Sweden. The widely publicized Volvo Kalmar plant, which opened in the early 1970s, is based on a *sociotechnical work design.* The assembly line was replaced by battery-powered robot carriers, which automatically move car bodies to different work teams, each of which is responsible for a phase of assembly. Productivity and quality improved, but a major limitation of the Kalmar plant's sociotechnical design was that a computer (not teams) controlled the movement of the carriers and short task cycles. Despite Kalmar's team approach and elimination of the conventional assembly line, most jobs provide little scope for personal development or for the use of skills and initiative. Workers still complain that their jobs are boring. Volvo's short-lived Uddevalla factory, which opened in 1989 and shut in 1993 due to a market downturn, resolved some of these problems by pushing sociotechnical design much further. Small work teams were able to build entire cars at ergonomically designed stationary work locations. By comparison with other Volvo facilities, this plant achieved high levels of quality, productivity, and worker satisfaction.

Another solution to the alienating monotony of assembly-line work can be found in Saab's main auto plant at Trollhattan. The body assembly shop faced problems typical in mass production: high turnover and absenteeism, low quality, widespread dissatisfaction, and a numbingly fast work pace. Reforms initiated in the early 1970s sought to improve the work environment, make jobs intrinsically more satisfying, and boost productivity. As at Volvo, the local union played an active role.

Some remarkable changes resulted. The assembly line was eliminated. Autonomous teams of workers, or *matrix groups*, devote about 45 minutes at a time to completing an integrated cycle of tasks. Robots took over arduous, repetitive welding jobs. Groups of 12 workers control the entire production process in the welding area. This involves programming the computers and maintaining the robots, ensuring quality control, performing related administrative work, and cleaning up their workspace. Buffer zones allow teams to build up an inventory of completed bodies, giving them greater flexibility over how they use their time. Skill development, new learning opportunities, and a broader approach to job design provide the teams with what Saab calls "control and ownership" of their contribution to the production process. Far from being victims of work degradation and deskilling through robotics, these Saab employees have reaped the benefits of upgraded job content and decision-making autonomy.[27]

North American Quality of Working Life Programs

Quality of working life (*QWL*) became a buzzword among managers, public policy makers, academics, and consultants during the 1970s. QWL is an umbrella term covering many different strategies for humanizing work, improving employee–employer cooperation, redesigning jobs, and giving employees greater participation in management. The underlying goal has been to improve employee satisfaction, motivation, and commitment. The expected payoffs are higher productivity, better quality products, and bigger profits. Its proponents have argued that employers and employees alike will benefit.[28] These basic ideas of QWL have been appropriated by the new management literature reviewed earlier, especially notions of employee participation. Often missing, however, is the original QWL goal of improving the quality of the work environment as a worthy goal in its own right.

QWL has diverse intellectual roots. Its core ideas came from Swedish studies on work reform, the Tavistock Institute's sociotechnical systems approach to job design, Norwegian E. Thorsrud's experiments on self-managing groups, Frederick Herzberg's theory that work is satisfying only if it meets employees' psychological growth needs, and McGregor's "Theory Y," outlined above.[29] In addition, QWL themes are congruent with an emphasis on worker participation in decision making as a means of creating cooperative work relations. *Human resource management*, an influential revision of human relations theory, assumes that employee satisfaction and morale are nurtured in a climate of participative management (Miles 1965). Theoretically, QWL claims to combine both humanistic and economic objectives: challenging, involving, and rewarding work experiences for employees and, for the employer, more productive utilization of the firm's human resources. Yet the lofty rhetoric of QWL advocates often fails to translate into successful applications (see Chapter 6).

A quick overview of some of the major QWL techniques would be useful. *Job enlargement* is meant to expand a job horizontally, adding related tasks to put more variety into the work done by an individual worker. *Job enrichment* goes further by combining operations before and after a task to create a more complex and unified job. For example, in the case of a machine operator in a clothing factory, job enrichment might mean that the operator would now be responsible for obtaining necessary materials, doing the administrative paperwork associated with different production runs, and maintaining the machines. This might not be an enormous change, but it would lead to a somewhat more varied, demanding, and responsible job. *Job rotation* has workers moving through a series of work stations, usually at levels of skill and responsibility similar to their original task. This tactic is frequently used to inject variety into highly repetitive, monotonous jobs. When job rotation is combined with more fundamental redesign strategies (especially the use of work teams), an employee can develop a considerable range of new skills.

An *autonomous work team* consists of roughly a dozen employees who are delegated collective authority to decide on work methods, scheduling, inventory, and quality control. They might also perform what previously would have been supervisory tasks, such as administration, discipline, and even hiring. *Quality circles (QCs),* with a narrower mandate of having workers monitor and correct defects in products or services, are perhaps the best-known application of the team concept. But quality circles often fall short of redistributing authority to rank-and-file workers. By the late 1980s, the "team concept" had become quite common in some industries and Canadian auto production plants were embracing quality or "employee involvement" schemes (Robertson and Wareham 1987). And throughout the 1990s, both researchers and managers in many industries became increasingly interested in various forms of employee participation or "involvement" (Heller et al. 1998; Bélanger 2000).

Attempts at work reform have generated heated debate between advocates, usually managers and QWL consultants, and critics, who are often trade unionists. As revealed later in the chapter and in Chapter 6, when we discuss "lean production" in the auto industry, team-based production and employee participation do not necessarily humanize working conditions (Wells 1986a; Milkman 1997). In fact, the smorgasbord of QWL programs, or what now is referred to as *workplace innovation*, introduced by Canadian employers has resulted in both successes and failures (Betcherman et al. 1990; Lowe 2000, 2001). On the negative side, QWL initiatives have resulted in declining work performance, heightened union–management tensions, employee dissatisfaction, and a breakdown in communications. Positive effects can include higher employee satisfaction and commitment, better earnings, improved labour relations, and even productivity gains. The context into which changes are introduced, the level of management commitment to fundamental reform, and the process by which this happens all strongly influence outcomes.

Shell's Sarnia Chemical Plant

The flagship of the North American QWL movement is Shell's chemical plant in Sarnia, Ontario (Rankin 1990; Davis and Sullivan 1980). Here we can see the importance of context and process. What makes the plant unique is that union and management actively collaborated in the sociotechnical planning and design of the new plant. Furthermore, compared with existing facilities, brand-new plants, or "greenfield sites," offer greater scope for innovative work arrangements. Shell's goal was a "post-bureaucratic organization," suitable for the continuous-process technology used in the petrochemical industry, that would facilitate employee control, learning, and participation.

Six teams of twenty workers run the plant around the clock, 365 days a year. Along with two coordinators, a single team operates the entire plant during a shift, and is even responsible for hiring new team members when vacancies occur. Teams are supported by technical, engineering, and managerial personnel, along with a group of maintenance workers, who also teach team members craft skills. The organizational structure is flat, having only three authority levels from top to bottom. Team members have no job titles and rotate tasks. Pay is based on knowledge and skills obtained through job training. It takes about six years of training for an operator to reach the maximum pay level.

This design empowers workers and allows them to apply and develop their skills. Continuous-process technology may lend itself more readily to this approach because of the huge capital investment per worker and the enormous losses to the firm should the system malfunction. Thus, management has a strong economic incentive to obtain a high level of employee commitment. By tapping the talents of its employees, Shell created a safer and more productive operation. According to the director of the union, the Shell plant eliminated authoritarian bureaucracy and provided members with opportunities to improve the quality of their work life (Reimer 1979: 5). This sociotechnical design seems to have achieved its objectives: a high level of production efficiency, smoothly functioning teams, and mutually beneficial collaboration between union and management (Halpern 1984: 58–59).

On the whole, autonomous work teams appear to have the greatest potential for significantly reallocating decision-making power, as well as for creating more interesting, challenging, socially integrated, and skilled work. Why, then, has the Canadian labour movement often been a vocal critic of QWL? The drawback for unions is that management frequently has used QWL to circumvent collective agreements, rationalize work processes, and co-opt workers into solving problems of quality and productivity. QWL has often been used to undermine union bargaining power and frequently spearheads labour relations schemes intended to keep firms union-free. As discussed in Chapter 7, from labour's perspective, gains in the quality of work life are therefore best achieved through collective bargaining. For example, the Canadian Auto Workers (CAW) adopted a policy on work reorganization that supports the involvement and empowerment of workers, provided there is a true partnership and union objectives are not undermined. Rarely does this happen, though.

The Shell experience appears to be atypical. In the Shell chemical plant, the union's involvement came only after guarantees that it would be a full partner in the QWL process, and that its ability to represent the interests of employees would not be undermined. It is noteworthy that members of the same union at an adjacent, older refinery wanted nothing at all to do with

QWL. But the story of innovation at Shell's Sarnia plant is now history, because a change in management ushered in more traditional work organization and management systems. It is not unusual for work redesign initiatives to be abandoned when top management changes, especially if the new managers are mainly concerned about costs.

The High-Performance Workplace

Earlier we posed this question: Is a new management paradigm emerging? A tentative answer is yes, and perhaps it is most visible in a human resource management approach called the *high-performance workplace (HPW)*. Despite the downsizing and rationalizations, a small but growing number of organizations have combined various elements discussed above. A high performance workplace is defined by employee involvement in decision making, team organization and flexible work design, extensive training and learning opportunities, open information sharing and communication, financial incentives for improved performance, support for family responsibilities, and a work environment that improves health and reduces stress. Given these defining characteristics, the working conditions and rewards in such organizations typically are very good, and employers reap the benefits of a productive and loyal workforce.[30]

The Human Resource Management Project at Queen's University conducted an extensive analysis of human resource practices in Canadian private sector workplaces in the early 1990s. It concluded that while an HPW may cost an employer more initially, improved economic performance and worker productivity occurs over time when compared with traditionally run firms. The study also showed that there is no single model of an HPW, just as we noted in discussions of various approaches to work teams. One typical approach to HPW emphasizes QWL-style employee participation and enhanced job quality; another focuses more on providing employee incentives through improved performance-based compensation. But extensive application of all the HPW elements is found in only a minority of workplaces in Canada; at most, an estimated 30 percent of firms in wood products, metal fabricating, electrical and electronic products, and business services reported varying degrees of an HPW in 1993 (Betcherman 1995: 116). Firms with the most complete applications tend to be large, technologically advanced, and with national and international operations in complex markets.

In some respects, the HPW is an updated version of QWL in an internal labour market system (see Chapter 3), but with much greater emphasis on employee participation and human resource development. As such, the HPW approach may contribute to further polarization of the labour market by creating a core of advantaged employees. Yet for this core of employees who have access to good working conditions, high performance appears to mean just that—lots of dedicated hard work and continual upgrading of skills. However, less clear is to what extent, and how, HPW systems actually increase organizational performance (Wood 1999). On balance, the overall weight of the evidence would point to some productivity gains when "bundles" of HPW practices are introduced, especially if these changes increase employee involvement and skill levels (Black and Lynch 2000, Appelbaum et al. 2000; Bélanger 2000). This is an important question for future research, along with the conditions that encourage the diffusion of HPW practices (Osterman 2000; Whitfield and Poole 1997).

JAPANESE INFLUENCES ON MANAGEMENT AND ORGANIZATIONS

Canadians can learn from Swedish experiences of industrial democracy and work humanization, but the Japanese approach to work has captured most of the attention recently. The global success of Japanese corporations has led many people to conclude that their management systems, industrial organization, and technology are superior. Many studies have examined Japanese industry to cast light on what is distinctive about the Japanese approach, why it is so successful, and to what extent it can work in North America. Sociologically, the important issue is whether the Japanese industrial system can be explained by theories of social and economic organization, facilitating its adoption elsewhere, or whether Japanese industry's distinctiveness owes more to its culture and history, in which case application outside Japan would be difficult (Lincoln and McBride 1987).

The Japanese Employment System

The four basic elements of the Japanese approach, which typically are found only in the major corporations, include: (1) highly evolved internal labour markets (discussed in Chapter 3), with features such as lifetime employment (*nenko*), seniority-based wages and promotions, and extensive training; (2) a division of labour built around work groups rather than specific positions, a feature that is the basis for the well-known quality circles; (3) a consensual, participative style of decision making involving all organizational levels *(ringi);* and (4) high levels of employee commitment and loyalty. A closer analysis of these aspects of Japanese firms leads to some interesting conclusions. The differences between North American and Japanese firms and management styles are probably overstated. Moreover, the Japanese system of employment owes more to principles of industrial organization than to any uniqueness in Japan's history or culture (Lincoln 1990; Hamilton and Biggart 1988). Even so, Japan seems to be at the cutting edge of the new approaches to management and work organization discussed throughout this chapter.

To elaborate briefly, the core of the Japanese work organization is the *internal labour market.* As James R. Lincoln and Kerry McBride (1987) observe, Japanese employers strive to maintain a well-functioning internal labour market and to obtain a high level of employee commitment to the firm over the long term. Teams share responsibility and accountability. When this is coupled with the consensus-building networking process used to make decisions, it is easy to see how individual workers are well integrated in their workplace. But how bottom-up is Japanese corporate decision making? Actually, it is a hybrid system, combining centralized authority in the hands of executives who bear final responsibility for decisions with consultations that ensure everyone has some input. *Ringi* refers to lower- or middle-level managers making petitions that circulate and slowly build consensus, thereby gaining a high probability of adoption.

On the shop floor, participation commonly takes the form of *quality circles* (*QCs*). Made famous by Toyota, QCs are now common in Japanese industry (Cole 1979). Some, such as those at Toyota, are essential to maintaining and improving high levels of quality. Yet, as Lincoln and McBride (1987: 300) observe, others "may be little more than collective suggestion-making exercises, imposed by management, for which workers receive little training." While the contribution of QCs to Japan's industrial success remains a moot point, sociologist Stephen Wood offers an insightful analysis of how they represent a potentially useful approach to worker participation (Wood 1989a).

Wood (1989a) notes that the issue of workers' *tacit skills*, or intuitive expertise about how to do their job, figures prominently in debates about the introduction of new technology, deskilling, and management control (also see Chapter 6). For example, without the aid of workers' informal expertise, the bugs in many new automated systems simply would not be overcome. What is especially innovative about Japanese organization, then, is how it harnesses the tacit skills and latent talents of workers. Wood dismisses arguments that this may be just another power grab by management, or Japanese-style Taylorism. Instead, he argues, Japanese industry has shown that production systems can always be improved and that industrial engineers and other technical experts do not have the final word on these matters. QCs and other forms of participation enlarge workers' overall knowledge of the business and sharpen their analytical and diagnostic skills.

The Japanese Approach in North America

How far have these Japanese management and organizational innovations infiltrated North America? Quality, teams, and participative management are the new management buzzwords. Some organizational design concepts, particularly Toyota's *just-in-time (JIT)* system of parts delivery, have been more readily adapted for use outside Japan than have other aspects of Japanese management or work organization. JIT reduces inventory overhead costs, forges a stronger alliance between a firm and its suppliers, and makes it easier to change production specifications, but does not require major changes in job design. However, JIT assumes a smoothly operating transportation system. In the wake of the September 2001 terrorist attacks in the U.S., a number of manufacturing firms, including auto plants in Canada, had to shut down some days because they quickly ran out of parts when the border closed and trucks were held up. So there may be a return to the old practice of stockpiling inventory, a practice that JIT advocates viewed as inefficient.

QCs have also become popular among North American firms facing Japanese and other foreign competitors. However, they do not go as far as delegating authority to autonomous work teams. QCs seem to place responsibility for monitoring quality and troubleshooting problems on production workers without a parallel expansion of their authority or increased rewards.[31] As Lincoln and McBride (1987: 301) conclude, QCs are often seen by North American workers as just one more chore imposed on them by management.

The obvious place to look for the successful adaptation of Japanese employment techniques is in *Japanese transplants* (local plants owned and operated by Japanese firms) or in their joint ventures with North American firms. Even here we find very mixed results. At one end of the continuum is the NUMMI plant in California, a unionized joint venture between Toyota and General Motors. Using methods imported by Toyota, employees work in teams and contribute ideas, but the daily management style is distinctly American (Kanter 1989: 274). However, the norm in transplants or joint ventures may be much closer to the other end of the continuum. As Ruth Milkman's investigation of employment conditions in Japanese transplants in California found, these firms closely resembled American firms employing nonunion labour. Few had introduced QCs, and many local managers were unfamiliar with the principles of Japanese work organization or management approaches (Milkman 1991). These firms' employment strategies mainly emphasized cost reduction, leading them to take full advantage of low-wage immigrant labour.

By the early 1990s, Canada had 530 Japanese-owned plants. The most prominent are the Ontario plants of Honda, Toyota, and CAMI (a Suzuki–GM joint venture). The Japanese managers at these three plants have had to develop a hybrid system, modifying aspects of the Japanese approach in a way that is acceptable to Canadian workers (Walmsley 1992). For example, one key to Japanese management's success is "fastidious housekeeping," which emphasizes cleanliness, reduced clutter, and keeping things orderly, as well as consistency in maintaining these goals and mutual respect. Canadian workers at Honda replaced this with their own version of good housekeeping, but dropped the principles of mutual respect and consistency. The major success story among Japanese transplants is Toyota's Cambridge, Ontario, plant, whose Corollas have won the coveted J. D. Power and Associates award for the highest quality car in North America (based on surveys of car owners). From the Toyota workers' point of view, benefits include job flexibility, free uniforms, consensus decision making, team work, good pay, and job security. However, there are drawbacks, including regular overtime, open offices for managers, no replacement workers for absent team members, health problems, close scrutiny of absenteeism and lateness, and only selective implementation of employee suggestions. Despite attempts by the CAW to organize this Toyota facility, it remains non-union.

Probably the peak performance of the Japanese model described above occurred in the 1970s. Even then it faced criticism, such as the stifling of individual creativity through *nenko* and groupism; discrimination against nonpermanent employees, particularly women; labour market rigidities that made the horizontal movement of workers among firms difficult; and long hours of work often at an intense pace (Kamata 1983). Japanese industry faced a barrage of new challenges in the 1980s and 1990s, including a prolonged recession, that altered its employment system (Whittaker 1990). The pressures of new technologies, globalization, the shift to services, a strong yen that drove up the cost of Japanese exports, and a recession have precipitated major changes. Additional stimuli for change included an aging workforce, the different attitudes of young workers, and the growing number of women workers. Firms have struggled to cut jobs without resorting to North American-style downsizing, but this trend also has begun. The pure seniority principle has given way to other means of rewarding and motivating workers. And the mobility of workers during their careers and across firms is increasing. It will be interesting to see if this restructuring signals a growing convergence of Japanese and North American approaches to organizing and managing work.

Flexible Specialization

Standardized mass production techniques have been the hallmark of industrial capitalism for over half a century. The extensive division of labour and elaborate assembly-line technologies in large factories generated huge volumes of goods. But hefty investments in mechanical technology alongside the small amounts spent on training and skill development also meant that the North American manufacturing sector (automobile companies, for example) would be slow to respond to aggressive competition from outside the country. Consequently, according to some observers, assembly-line mass production of standardized goods is becoming much less economically viable, while *flexible specialization* in production is the way of the future. Attention again turns to Japan, where many firms have moved into more flexible, computerized production systems that can be quickly adapted to produce new product lines.

Flexible production systems, which use computers at each stage (from designing a product to selling it), link all aspects of production into a coordinated system. Much smaller product runs are possible than with assembly-line systems, and because sales trends and consumer tastes are closely monitored, changes in design or product lines can readily be made. Microelectronic production technology, including advanced programmable robots, is also much more versatile than mass production methods in its ability to produce a wide range of goods, including electronic equipment, automobiles, furniture, clothing and shoes, and engineering products. Computers also reduce stock control costs ("zero inventory") and improve product quality ("zero defects"). In addition to Japan, some firms in Germany, Scandinavia, and northern Italy have implemented this new system. Describing the success of northern Italian consumer goods firms, Piore and Sabel (1984: 17) write:

> Flexible specialization is a strategy of permanent innovation: accommodation to ceaseless change, rather than an effort to control it. This strategy is based on flexible (multi-use) equipment; skilled workers; and the creation, through politics, of an industrial community that restricts the forms of competition to those favouring innovation.

This model of flexible specialization in manufacturing firms is based on the use of advanced microelectronic technology, highly skilled and versatile workers, and a political environment that favours innovative firms but does not protect ailing industries. The emphasis on skilled workers is particularly interesting, given that some labour process critics (reviewed in Chapter 6) take the opposing view, namely that job deskilling results from computerization. Flexible specialization, at least for Piore and Sabel, signals a return to the craft forms of production that were eclipsed with the rise of mass production. These writers also suggest that we may see a greater convergence of interests between workers and management because highly skilled workers are indispensable in such production settings. In addition, because smaller firms will be as or even more competitive in this new manufacturing environment, the global dominance of giant multinational corporations may be reduced.

The evidence of an increase in flexible, computerized manufacturing systems in Japan and other countries is indisputable, but it remains unclear whether the full range of manufacturing industries, in all industrialized countries, can and will move in this direction (Wood 1989b; Neis 1991; Macdonald 1991). There is, to date, only scattered evidence of improvements in working conditions in specialized flexible production settings. As for predictions of a shifting balance of power between workers and management, and between small firms and huge multinationals, these appear to be more in the realm of hope than of reality. As Stephen Wood notes in a detailed assessment of the flexible specialization model, this part of the theory is really "an intellectual manifesto," a description of the type of workplace that Piore and Sabel believe would be preferable (Wood 1989b: 13). In a way, Piore's and Sabel's optimistic predictions are reminiscent of the postindustrial society theorists, such as Daniel Bell, who were convinced that general skill levels would increase while inequality declined.

Piore and Sabel also overlook the potential for job loss that the adoption of new technologies entails. Nor do they recognize the possibility of its leading to a two-tiered employment system in which a small group of highly skilled workers, primarily male, would be the main beneficiaries of the new production system, while the majority continue to perform routine, unskilled, or semiskilled work. Furthermore, as Jenson (1989) argues, Piore and Sabel fail to recognize the role of gender in the labour market – a serious oversight.

The Flexible Firm

While evidence of a significant shift toward flexible specialization production is limited, there are clear indications that many employers, in both the manufacturing and service sectors, have begun to reorganize their workforces to gain greater flexibility and to reduce payroll costs. Frequently, these employer initiatives have involved greater reliance on part-time or part-year workers, as well as on temporary or contract employees. Thus, the economic uncertainties experienced by employers in the past decade have also meant an increase in *nonstandard jobs*. Although some workers prefer part-time or other nonstandard jobs, as noted in earlier chapters, these positions still pay less and typically offer little job security. Consequently, an increase in nonstandard employment also means greater employment insecurity and, potentially, more workplace inequality.

Some observers of these trends suggest that a new type of employment system is needed, with a core of full-time workers and a periphery of low-cost nonstandard workers whose numbers and functions vary with business conditions. John Atkinson labels this the *flexible firm*. The employment practices of such firms are thought to give them a competitive advantage in an environment of quickly changing markets and technologies. This adaptability could be achieved three ways: *functional flexibility* (training workers to perform a variety of different tasks, thus making them more interchangeable); *numerical flexibility* (being able to quickly alter the size of the workforce, or the number of hours worked, through hiring of part-time, temporary, subcontracted, and other types of nonstandard workers); and *pay flexibility* (the ability to reduce pay and benefit costs by using alternative wage rates for nonstandard workers and by avoiding traditional collective agreements).[32] Thus, Atkinson's model describes an alternative work organization that is more flexible than a traditional bureaucracy, and that also has lower payroll costs. What more could an employer want?

A number of researchers have examined the employment practices of contemporary private- and public-sector work organizations to see how well they fit Atkinson's model. The research results show that, despite growing reliance on nonstandard workers, many organizations have not initiated other forms of employment flexibility. Among those that have, however, it is not all that clear that they have done so for the long-term strategic reasons Atkinson identified (Booth 1997). Many public-sector organizations have relied on nonstandard workers as one way to cut costs. Furthermore, cross-national differences in the extent to which firms resemble Atkinson's model suggest additional political and cultural factors that must be taken into account.[33]

As with the flexible specialization model of production, we will have to wait and see whether flexible firms become the dominant type of work organization in industrial capitalist societies, or whether traditional bureaucratic organizations remain the norm. Both of these theoretical perspectives describe work organizations that, it is argued, will be more successful in a highly competitive, rapidly changing economic world. However, each has the potential to increase workplace and labour market inequalities and contribute to the intensification and destabilization of work (Smith 1997). As Samuel Rosenberg (1989: 8) cautions: "Behind flexibility—a word with extremely positive connotations—lies the more serious question of the relative balance of power between different groups in society." Competitiveness and productivity are clearly important goals, but so too are employment security and the quality of working life.

Lean Production

Let us return one last time to the question, Is a new management paradigm emerging? Earlier, we documented that the high-performance workplace model had the potential to be a new paradigm. The HPW approach drew on various strands of thinking—from work teams and QWL to issues of healthy work environments and family-friendly workplaces. In general terms, the HPW can be interpreted as the latest reincarnation of the human relations tradition: a humanistic view of workers resulting in a strong emphasis on good human resource management practices. But there is yet another alternate management paradigm emerging in Canada—*lean production (LP)*.[34] Three features of lean production distinguish it from HPW. First, it is modelled directly on the Japanese approach to production described above and is well established in Japanese transplants. Second, it is most fully developed in manufacturing, particularly in the North American auto industry. Third, it revolves around an integration of advanced production technology with team organization, based on a detailed analysis of the work process reminiscent of Taylorism. In this respect, LP exemplifies what is called *re-engineering*, or the radical redesign of a firm's entire business process to achieve maximum output and quality with the least labour by tightly integrating technology and tasks (Hammer and Champy 1993: 65–66).

A number of elements define LP: continuous improvement (*kaizen*), continuous innovation, flexible production, work teams, zero downtime, zero defects, just-in-time inventories and production, and employment security (Drache 1994). Lean production is presented by its advocates as a major improvement over mass production and bureaucratic organization. In other words, it has been held up as the production system for a *post-Fordist* work organization. GM's new Saturn plant in Tennessee and the GM–Toyota NUMMI factory in California are often portrayed as models of lean production. Like the Shell Sarnia plant, both are unionized, but only Saturn was a greenfield site.

At Saturn, workers and the United Auto Workers union played an active role in all phases of designing the plant (Appelbaum and Batt 1994: Chapter 8). A sociotechnical approach was adopted, integrating technology and the social organization of production. Work teams of 6 to 15 members are self-managed, with responsibility for deciding important issues like work flow and quality. Teams also manage human resources, including hiring, absenteeism policies, and replacement of absent workers. Like the high performance workplaces described earlier, but unlike traditional North American auto plants, workers at Saturn are paid 80 percent of the industry wage in an annual salary (as opposed to hourly), but they can receive up to an additional 40 percent if production and customer satisfaction goals are met or exceeded. A unique feature is the partnership approach to strategic planning, operating, and problem-solving decisions, whereby managers are "partnered" with elected union representatives. This approach has generated considerable mutual respect, and productivity and quality also seem to have benefited.

NUMMI differs from Saturn in that it was an old GM factory plagued with labour and production problems. When it reopened as a GM–Toyota joint venture, a new approach to work organization and human resource management was applied (Pfeffer 1994: Chapter 3). The NUMMI system included extensive employee training, job security, teams of multiskilled workers, reduced status distinctions, an elaborate suggestion system, and extensive sharing of what used to be exclusively management's information. Compared with the old GM factory, this new work system resulted in impressive reductions in absenteeism and grievances, and significantly improved quality and productivity. In fact, NUMMI produced high-quality products in less time than other GM plants and was almost as productive as a comparable Toyota plant in Japan. An employee survey showed 90 percent satisfied or very satisfied with work at NUMMI.

Thus, the NUMMI experience shows us that the work environment and industrial relations climate can affect the economic performance of a firm. Both the Saturn and the NUMMI cases demonstrate the potential for lean production to positively alter the worker–management relationship. But, as we will see in Chapter 6, the lean production approach to work organization redesign has also been harshly criticized. As with previous new management models that arrived with great promise, implementation often falls short of the mark.

CONCLUSION

We have covered a vast terrain of research and theory in this chapter. We have seen that there are many effective ways to structure and to manage an organization. Yet there is a continuity, a set of unifying themes underlying the various theories and models that attempt to explain what happens inside work organizations. Let us reiterate these dominant themes.

Viewed as structures, most work organizations in capitalist societies (1) have been put together according to the principles of bureaucracy; (2) have a specialized and coordinated division of labour; and (3) have been run by professional managers. Technologies, the nature of markets, the type of product or service being produced or provided, management's strategic preferences, and constraints in the social and political environment are among the factors influencing the specific features of an organization's structure. But we must also look beyond these structural aspects of organizations. The actions and reactions of ordinary employees must all be taken into account if we are to understand the dynamics of work organizations.

Human actors create organizations. Even huge bureaucracies consist essentially of social relationships among individuals and groups. Especially fascinating is how these employees, from the night janitor to the president, compete to varying degrees for control of scarce organizational resources such as rewards, opportunities, power, influence, and status. To draw a fixed battle-line between management on one side and subordinate employees on the other would be to caricature the often subtle and complex give-and-take processes at work. This important point will be further explored in Chapter 6. Certainly, worker–management conflict is central to organizational studies. Sometimes conflict erupts, but, typically, truces, negotiations, and tradeoffs create a workable level of stability and cooperation. In sum, the dynamics of conflict and consensus, rooted in unequal power relations, are integral parts of work organizations. But these relationships can assume a myriad of different forms.

Looking ahead, there are signs of a growing emphasis on the human assets of organizations. We can detect a subtle shift in the human resource management literature, from the view that an organization's human resource functions merely support its larger goals, to *strategic human resource management,* which emphasizes how human resource activities drive the overall strategy of the organization (Mabey, Salaman and Storey 1998). Why?

First, the North American economy entered the new century relatively healthy and with unemployment at levels low enough that some industries faced serious labour shortages. Second, the impending retirement of large numbers of baby-boomers led some analysts to predict intense competition for talent and labour shortages that could undermine Canada's national competitive advantage (Conference Board of Canada 2000). For a growing number of employers, a top priority is finding effective ways to recruit and retain employees (Lowe 2001). Third, governments, employers and individuals recognize that skills and knowledge are the key resources in the global economy of the future. This emerging economy is increasingly knowledge-based, so employers are seeking ways to develop what ar now referred to as *intellectual assets* – the skills, competence and commitment of workers (Ulrich 1998). As more jobs become knowledge-intensive, a wide range of experts argue that knowledge workers must be treated as assets, not costs, and inspired by managers to learn and be creative (Drucker 1999; Mintzberg 1999; O'Reilly III and Pfeffer 2000).

But despite these reasons for developing a stronger people focus in organizations, evidence from a new national survey of workplaces by Statistics Canada (the 1999 *Workplace and Employee Survey*) suggests that most employers in this country still place insufficient value on these assets. For example, only 36 percent of Canadian employers state that they view employee skill development as a crucial or very important part of their overall business strategy (Statistics Canada 2001).

To conclude, the challenges of workplace reform that we have addressed in this chapter are very much alive. How they are addressed by employees, managers and unions will shape the workplace of the future. To what extent can work be reorganized and tasks redesigned in order to achieve a better balance between the goals of making work satisfying, socially useful, and rewarding on the one hand, and of achieving economic efficiency and profitability on the other? Is this an impossibility? Are bureaucratic, managerial hierarchies essential for the smooth functioning of capitalism? Can the excesses of Taylorism and Fordism be eradicated? As we have seen, there are some alternative forms of work organization that might be capable of democratizing and humanizing work. The approaches called for in the new management literature—a top-down revolution, TQM, QWL, and Japanese-style employment systems—all contain potential for meaningful change. How far they go in creating nonbureaucratic, democratic, and fulfilling work environments will likely form the script for the drama of workplace change and conflict in coming decades.

NOTES

1. Weber (1964: 338); also see Weber's essay on bureaucracy (1946: Chapter 6).

2. Morgan (1997: 15–17). This book gives an excellent overview of the multiple images, or metaphors, of organizations found in the literature, as does Bolman and Deal (1997). Also see Jones (1996: Chapter 2) on theories of bureaucracy.

3. Blau (1963); also see Crozier (1964), whose case studies of French bureaucracies show workers regularly circumventing formal rules.

4. Daft (1995: 25); also see Morgan (1997), Pfeffer (1997), and Clegg et al. (1996) for overviews of the field of organizational studies.

5. See Burrell and Morgan (1979: 154–60) for a discussion of the influence of functionalism on organization theory. Donaldson (1989, 1996) offers a clear overview and defence of this conventional brand of organization theory. For a critical debate of Donaldson's views, see *Organization Studies* (1988).

6. Trist and Bamforth (1951). The work of Trist and the Tavistock Institute is summarized in Pugh et al. (1985: 84–91). Also see Rankin (1990: Chapter 1).

7. The key source for strategic choice theory is Child (1972). Also see Chandler (1962) for a historical discussion of the importance of managerial strategies in shaping modern business enterprises in the United States.

8. Billing (1994); Calás and Smircich (1996). The journal *Gender, Work and Organization* is a good resource on this topic.

9. See Kelly (1982: Chapter 2) for an analysis of Taylorism using this typology. Jacoby (1999) examines the historical roots of modern human resource management practices as found in the early 20th century management ideology of welfare capitalism.

10. Palmer (1975). Also see Haber (1964), Bendix (1974), Merkle (1980), Nelson (1980), and Littler (1982).

11. *Industrial Canada* (March 1913: 1106)also see Taylor (1919).

12. The application of scientific management in Canada is discussed in Lowe (1984; 1987: Chapter 2), Palmer (1979: 216–22), and Craven (1980: 90–110).

13. Classic studies of auto assembly-line workers include Walker and Guest (1952), Beynon (1984), Linhart (1981), and Meyer (1981). Hamper (1986) and de Santis (1998) offer more personal accounts of this type of work.

14. The research was originally described in Whitehead (1936) and Roethlisberger and Dickson (1939). The original interpretation of the study's findings have been rigorously debated; see, for example, Carey (1967), Franke and Kaul (1978), Sonnenfeld (1985), Jones (1990), and Gillespie (1991).

15. The Hawthorne effect also refers to the problem of reactivity in research methodology. The fact that people are aware of being part of a study may itself confound the results.

16. See McGregor (1960) on "the human side of enterprise." Heil et al. (2000) revisit McGregor's ideas, arguing they are more relevant now than ever.

17. Another study by Roy (1959–1960) showed how work groups also cushion the drudgery of low-skill, monotonous jobs by engaging in games and "goofing off."

18. Dalton (1959). Another insightful investigation of workplace "fiddling," or cheating, is Mars (1982).

19. Kuhn (1970) described scientific revolutions in terms of the shift from old to new paradigms. A paradigm is a set of assumptions, principles, and guides to action. For useful overviews of shifting paradigms of management knowledge, see Clarke and Clegg (1998). Pfeffer (1997) describes the debates generated by the different theoretical paradigms of organizations.

20. Wood (1989c) reviews nine books representative of what he calls "new wave management." Micklethwait and Wooldridge (1996) offer a scathing critique of management gurus and their ideas. Carson et al. (2000) review 16 management fads over the past five decades.

21. Enchin (1992: B1); also see *The Globe and Mail* (25 April 1992: B4). A survey by the Arthur D. Little consulting firm of 500 U.S. firms found only one-third reporting that total quality programs significantly improved their competitiveness. A study of 100 firms in the United Kingdom came up with similar findings.

22. *Report on Business* (April 1996: 16). Based on a poll of 880 business owners and senior executives across Canada conducted for *Report on Business* by Dunn & Bradstreet Canada, 20 percent of small businesses had downsized and 10 percent expected to do so.

23. On the negative impact of downsizing, see Cascio (1993), Hitt et al. (1994), Freeman and Cameron (1993), and Murray Axmith and Associates (1997).

24. *The Globe and Mail* (21 March 1995: B12); *Nova Now* [monthly employee publication] (July–August 1995).

25. Senge (1990); Senge et al. (1994). For a critical assessment of Senge, see Micklethwait and Wooldridge (1996: Chapter 6). Mintzberg et al. (1998: Chapter 7) offer a useful overview of strategy formation as a learning process within organizations.

26. See Shien (1992: Chapter 18) on "learning cultures" and Yanow (2000) and Lipshitz (2000) on organizational learning.

27. On Volvo Kalmar, see Jonsson (1980) and Aguren et al. (1985). Rinehart (2001: 195-96) describes the Uddevalla plant. On Saab's work reorganization, see Logue (1981) and Helling (1985). These accounts of the Volvo and Saab factories are also based on Graham Lowe's personal observations and discussions with union officials, management, and shop-floor workers during visits to both plants in late 1985. The two case studies are meant to highlight different applications of sociotechnical principles; the situation in each factory could be quite different now. For a critical view, see Van Houten (1990).

28. See, for example, Levine (1995). See Rinehart (2001: Chapter 7) for a critical assessment.

29. Emery and Thorsrud (1969); Thorsrud (1975); Herzberg (1966, 1968); Cherns (1976); Gardell (1977, 1982); Gardell and Gustavsen (1980). On the development of QWL in Canada, see Rankin (1990), Long (1989), and Jain (1990).

30. See Betcherman et al. (1994); Appelbaum and Batt (1994); Osterman (1994, 2000); Black and Lynch (2000); Appelbaum et al. (2000); OECD (1999, Chapter 4).

31. See Knights et al. (1985). On quality circles, see Bradley and Hill (1983) and Rinehart's (1984) Canadian case study. Hampson (1999) suggests that key features of Toyota's production system are not transplanted.

32. Atkinson (1984, 1985); also see Pinfield and Atkinson (1988) for a Canadian perspective on flexible firms, and Lowe (2001) for these practices in governments.

33. See Rubery (1988), Pollert (1988), and Martha Macdonald (1991) for discussions of the utility of the flexible firm model. Walby (1989) comments on the absence of gender in this theoretical perspective, while Lane (1988, 1989) provides examples of cross-national variations in employer practices.

34. On lean production in manufacturing, particularly in the auto sector, see Womack et al. (1990), Rinehart et al. (1997); Kochan et al. (1997); Green and Yanarella (1996), Appelbaum and Batt (1994: Chapter 8). Nilsson (1996) examines lean production in a white-collar setting. Benders and van Bijsterveld (2000) review its reception in Germany.

6

CONFLICT AND CONTROL
IN THE WORKPLACE

INTRODUCTION

Throughout the past century, employers sought new ways of managing workers in order to increase efficiency and productivity and to reduce workers' resistance to authority. Scientific management, with its emphasis on complete managerial control and an extreme division of labour, gave way to the softer human relations approach, which tried to motivate workers by making them feel that they were an integral part of the larger work organization.

By the 1970s, management consultants were advocating changes to organizational structures and job design. Japanese-style management strategies, quality of work life programs, and total quality management models, for example, tried to reduce the negative effects of bureaucracy, increase job skills, and enhance worker decision making. Downsizing, organizational restructuring, and new technologies have been the favoured approaches to increasing productivity in the past two decades. Even so, the lean production and high-performance workplace models claim to empower workers, enhance their skills, and involve them as partners in the production of goods and services.

If we were to draw a conclusion about consensus, cooperation, skill development, and fairness in today's workplace from the management literature in Chapter 5, it might be that new approaches to management have solved most of the problems of conflict and worker exploitation observed in the past. But this would ignore a great deal of contradictory evidence.

First, we continue to hear about massive layoffs as employers rely on downsizing and restructuring to improve company performance and/or deal with declines in market demand for their goods and services. For example, in August 2001, Air Canada announced that it would lay off another 4,000 employees in the coming year, on top of the 3,500 it had let go the year before. At the same time, Nortel, another Canadian corporate giant, was beginning the process of laying off 10,000 employees worldwide, bringing to 30,000 the total number of jobs cut in one year. These two downsizing decisions reflected reductions in the total Air Canada and Nortel workforces of about 16 percent and 32 percent, respectively.[1] Along with downsizing, replacement of full-time permanent workers with part-time and temporary employees continues to be the competitive strategy for many Canadian private and public sector work organizations (Vosko 2000; Lowe and Schellenberg 2001).

Second, despite the rhetoric about the need for better human resource utilization and worker empowerment in order for Canadian firms to be globally competitive, management practices in this regard have been slow to change. Recent studies of large Canadian workplaces continue to show that many still rely on Taylorist management approaches, and that most make, at best, limited investments in employee training. Responses to employees' desires for more autonomy and responsibility and their needs for more family-friendly workplace benefits and policies continue to be the exception rather than the rule (Betcherman et al. 1994; Livingstone 1999; Lowe 2000).

Third, in response to such employer practices, we regularly see workers resisting and opposing management policies, in all sectors of the economy. In 1992, for example, 99 percent of the employees in the Ingersoll, Ontario, CAMI plant, a state-of-the-art lean production factory, voted to strike. Their union president stated that "if the company's rhetoric of fairness, worker input and commitment to a non-confrontational relationship with our union had been meaningful, this company would have never forced this strike." In 1997, Vancouver employees of the Starbucks coffee chain approached the Canadian Auto Workers for help in organizing a union. As an employee explained, "The whole idea of being called 'partners' by the company backfired. They used it to brainwash us, and some of us took it seriously. We thought that in order to be a partner, we needed to have a say in what was taking place. And that wasn't happening" (*Globe & Mail,* 4 July, 1997, p. B1). Two years later, technical workers at the Canadian Broadcasting Corporation (CBC) went on strike for two months. One of the CBC employees walking the picket line described the dissatisfaction of his colleagues. "You look at the faces of the people here, they're frustrated. There are a lot of talented people out here and [striking] isn't what they want to do for a living." And in 2001, when B.C. nurses and other health care professionals were forced by the provincial government to accept a wage settlement, hundreds went out on wildcat strikes and thousands threatened to resign, an act that would have left the provincial health care system in absolute disarray. Commenting on the government's heavy-handed action, one of the union leaders observed that "[t]he workers are very angry. Nurses are feeling very disrespectful today."[2]

These examples demonstrate the need to counterbalance the discussion in Chapter 5 of management approaches by returning to the themes of power and control, conflict and resistance. These themes are central to an adequate understanding of workplace dynamics. It is also helpful to characterize the management theories and strategies introduced in the previous chapter as sharing a *consensus* perspective. In contrast, this chapter's critical analyses of worker–management relationships have been influenced by the *conflict* perspective in sociological analysis.

It is appropriate, then, to begin by reviewing Karl Marx's critique of work in capitalist society, since his arguments shaped the conflict perspective. We then outline the *labour process perspective*, an attempt to update Marx's ideas to explain contemporary worker–management relationships. This alternative approach begins with the assumption that conflict is to be expected in work settings, where the interests of owners and managers are in opposition to those of workers. It focuses directly on attempts by management to control workers, and on how workers resist such efforts, trying to gain more control over their own labour. While the labour process approach has itself been criticized on various grounds, it does provide a much more critical assessment of quality of work life, lean production, and other contemporary management strategies, as well as the introduction of new information technologies in the workplace.

This chapter is really a debate with the assumptions and conclusions of the mainstream management and organizational literature reviewed in Chapter 5. But we also go further by asking whether workplace health and safety might be one area in which workers and management have come closer to reaching a consensus. We conclude with a discussion of industrial democracy and worker ownership. Both of these approaches to organizing workplaces help workers to gain more control over the conditions of their work. In Chapter 7, we continue the discussion by examining the origins, functions, and future of trade unions, another vehicle through which workers have attempted to look after their interests.

MARX ON EMPLOYMENT RELATIONSHIPS WITHIN CAPITALISM

As we have observed in Chapters 1 and 3, class conflict was central to Marx's perspective on social change. Looking back, he argued that feudalism had been transformed into a new mode of production—capitalism, characterized by wage-labour relations of production—because of conflict between different class groupings. Looking forward, he predicted that capitalism would eventually give way to socialism because of the inherently conflictual and exploitative relationships between owners and workers.

Central to Marx's view of social change was a specific economic theory of the capitalist labour market. Beginning with the premise that the value of a product was a direct function of the labour needed to produce it, Marx proposed that, in a capitalist economy, wage labourers produced more than the amount needed to pay their wages. *Surplus value* was being created. Consequently, the relationship between capitalist and worker was exploitative in that the workers who produced the profit were not receiving it.

Unlike feudalism, which greatly restricted the mobility of serfs, workers under capitalism were free. They could always quit and search for another job. However, by purchasing labour, capitalists gained control over the labour process itself. Factory organization and mechanization further increased employer control. Thus, the craftsmen forced into the industrial mills of Marx's time were, according to one commentator, "subjected to inflexible regulations, and driven like gear-wheels by the pitiless movement of a mechanism without a soul. Entering a mill was like entering a barracks or prison."[3]

These relationships of production led, according to Marx, to feelings of *alienation* among workers in a capitalist economy. Lacking control over the process and products of their labour, and deprived of the surplus value (profit) they were creating, workers felt separated (or alienated) from their work. We will discuss alienation in greater depth in Chapter 8, along with other subjective reactions to work. For now, it is sufficient to note that Marx believed that the working class would eventually rise up in revolt against this alienation and exploitation.

But things have changed since Marx's time. The harsh, dangerous, and exploitative working conditions of early industrialization have been largely eliminated in first-world countries. The combination of labour legislation, unions and professional associations, and more sophisticated employers has led to higher incomes and standards of living, safer working conditions, and more responsibility and autonomy for workers, at least in relative terms.

However, earlier chapters have documented the growing number of working poor in Canada, a polarization of work rewards, the rise in involuntary nonstandard employment, and continued high levels of structural unemployment. Unions continue to resist management attempts to reduce wages while most nonunionized workers have little choice but to accept what they are offered. Hundreds of workers are still killed on the job each year, and thousands suffer workplace injuries. Despite the calls for new management approaches to empower workers, some employers continue to act as if control over work belongs to them. As the president of McDonald's Restaurants of Canada explained a few years ago:

> A McDonald's outlet is a machine that produces, with the help of unskilled machine attendants, a highly polished product. Through painstaking attention to total design and facilities planning, everything is built integrally into the technology of the system. The only choice open to the attendant is to operate it exactly as the designers intended.[4]

Marx's descriptions of working conditions in early capitalist society may no longer be applicable, but the core themes in his writings can still help us to gain a better understanding of work in today's economy. These themes— power relationships in the workplace, attempts by owners and managers to control the labour process, resistance to these attempts by workers, and conflict between class groups—are central to the labour process perspective on worker–management relationships.

THE LABOUR PROCESS PERSPECTIVE

Harry Braverman on the "Degradation of Work"

In his influential and provocative book, *Labor and Monopoly Capital*, Harry Braverman (1974) argued that twentieth-century capitalism was considerably different from the mode of production examined by Karl Marx. A relatively small number of huge, powerful corporations controlled the national and international economies; the role of the state in the production process had expanded; new technologies had evolved; workplace bureaucracies had become larger; and the labour process itself had become increasingly standardized.

Analyzing the transformation of office work in large bureaucracies, Braverman argued that clerical work had once included fairly high-status and responsible jobs. Turn-of-the-century male clerks and bookkeepers had been able to exercise considerable control over their work, and had been responsible for a wide variety of tasks. But this was no longer the case. What the feminization of the occupation masked was how the extensive division of labour in offices had narrowed the scope of the work done by one clerk. Office work had been standardized and mechanized. Clerks essentially processed an endless stream of paper on a white-collar assembly line, their routine tasks devoid of much mental activity. In short, clerical work had been degraded and deskilled.

Braverman attributed these changes to management strategies designed to improve efficiency and gain more control over the office labour process. Thus, office workers experienced the same degradation of work that skilled craft workers had experienced in the 19th century when factory-based production was expanding. Many of the management principles introduced to the factory were now also in use in private sector and government white-collar bureaucracies.

For Braverman, Taylorist tendencies lay at the heart of all modern management approaches since they all fragmented and routinized work. As he saw it, these negative trends were also beginning to affect the working conditions of technicians, professionals, and middle-level managers. In other words, both lower- and higher-status white-collar workers were becoming part of the same working class. Management strategies to control workers' every movement, introduce more advanced forms of technology, and refine the division of labour were leading to the deskilling and degradation of work, setting the scene for future class conflict.

Braverman's Contribution to the Sociology of Work

Braverman's analysis of changing employment relationships in 20th-century capitalism has been widely influential, giving rise to scores of illuminating studies with a labour process perspective. His book encouraged sociologists to look much more closely at the skills used in different jobs, and at the ways in which the labour of employees was controlled by managers. But it has also been severely criticized by researchers sympathetic to its general critical approach.[5]

First, critics point out that Braverman assumed, but did not demonstrate, that all clerical workers in an earlier era were highly skilled and had considerable responsibility in their position. Braverman also overgeneralized from scattered evidence in North America to assert that deskilling was a universal pattern present in all occupations within all industrial capitalist societies. Important cultural differences in the labour process were consequently ignored, as were situations in which automation, work reorganization, and employee relations policies actually provided more autonomy and responsibility to workers. Furthermore, while focusing on declining skills in some occupations, Braverman overlooked the new skills that were required in industrial and postindustrial economies. For example, the management of large numbers of employees involved in different tasks required the development of a wider range of leadership skills, office work in service industries required sophisticated "people skills," and efficient use of new manufacturing and information technologies required the ability to operate computers.[6]

Second, Braverman ignored the gendered nature of workplace skills, as have many other researchers (see Chapter 4). Technical skills, frequently more central to "male" jobs, have been valued more highly than people skills, which figure more prominently in jobs typically held by women.[7] Where Braverman observed the feminization of clerical work, he may have underrated the skill requirements of this rapidly expanding occupational group. Along with his failure to consider the independent effects of gender on workplace relationships, he also overlooked how race and ethnicity have played a major part in determining access to better jobs in North American labour markets (see Chapter 3).

Third, Braverman implied that workers passively accepted management assaults on their job skills and autonomy. Seldom in *Labor and Monopoly Capital* does one find mention of workers resisting management, even though, as we saw in Chapter 5, power struggles have always been part of the informal side of bureaucracy. Furthermore, workers have organized in unions for well over a century to collectively oppose their employers (see Chapter 7). The main flaw in Braverman's theory of the degradation of work is its determinism, which suggests that the inner logic of 20th-century capitalism pushed capitalists to devise Taylorism, Fordism, human relations management approaches, and their many variants.

Why, then, has Braverman's thesis been so influential? The answer is that he challenged work researchers to ask new questions about changes in the labour process in contemporary capitalist societies. The ensuing debate has brought into sharper relief how, to what degree, and under what conditions jobs may have been degraded, deskilled, and subjected to various types of management control. As Vicki Smith notes in her commentary on Braverman's legacy, twenty years after the publication of his book, he brought the sociology of work and organizations back to issues of class and inequality, power and control, resistance and conflict. Even in his failings—overgeneralizing about deskilling, not taking account of gender, and overlooking worker resistance—he motivated other researchers to try to revise the basic labour process perspective (Smith 1994). The following sections on models of managerial control and the deskilling debate review some of this research.

Models of Managerial Control

The diversity of workplace control mechanisms documented by labour process researchers is not easily classified. This is to be expected, if we concede that there is not a single inherent control strategy within capitalism, and that workers have historically resisted efforts to control them, with varying degrees of success. What we find is a patchwork of control strategies that has emerged through the confrontations, compromises, and negotiations that regularly occur between managers and workers. As the editors of a book of Canadian labour process case studies observe, "Workers and their employers are simply too stubborn and too resourceful to conform to an overly tidy theory" (Heron and Storey 1986: 33).

Yet looking back over the past century of maturing capitalism, we do find signs of shifting preferences for control strategies among North American employers. Richard Edwards and his colleagues developed a theory of labour market segmentation around such changes in workplace control systems.[8] As discussed in Chapter 3, working conditions and work rewards vary significantly across labour markets in the primary and secondary sectors of the economy. But these radical economists took the idea of segmentation considerably further, asserting that methods of worker control also differ across labour markets.

They distinguished three basic types of managerial control. With *simple control*, most common in secondary labour markets, employers regulate the labour process with coercive or paternalistic methods, or, in larger organizations, through a hierarchy of authority. *Technical control* is achieved by machine pacing of work (an assembly line is the best example) and can, in part, replace the direct supervision of simple control methods. *Bureaucratic control* has evolved in large corporations in the core sector of the economy. Good salaries, generous benefits, and pleasant work settings are the inducements provided, usually to middle- and upper-level white-collar employees and some groups of skilled manual workers. The internal labour market, and the prospects of an interesting and rewarding career, are part of an employment package designed to win employees' commitment.

Edwards and his colleagues argued that the evolution of segmented labour markets, with their different control systems, resulted in a socially fragmented and politically weak working class. As they saw it, employers in the United States gained the upper hand over workers in the "contested terrain" of the workplace by developing new and more effective means of control. While impressive in its scope, this historical theory is still quite deterministic, suggesting that changes in the means of production and periodic economic crises forced capitalists to devise new methods for directing, monitoring, evaluating, and disciplining workers. Like Braverman, these economists portray workers as largely passive.

Other observers of the capitalist labour process have emphasized the agency of workers—how they resist, reshape, or participate in management control strategies. Andrew Friedman (1977: 82–85), for instance, describes a shifting *frontier of control*, which is influenced alternately by conflict and accommodation between employers and employees. At issue is who sets the pace of work, hours of work, and order of task execution, and what constitutes fair treatment and just rewards. Sometimes workers gain a say in these matters through union bargaining. Or management may initiate work reforms, giving workers what Friedman calls *responsible autonomy*, which is a way of obtaining cooperation by granting workers some scope for making task-related decisions. Some degree of responsible autonomy is found, for example, in the quality of working life (QWL) programs and other participative management schemes described in the previous chapter. The opposite strategy in Friedman's model is *direct control* (like the simple control described by Richard Edwards) which involves strict supervision with very little job autonomy for workers. These two types of control systems are best viewed as opposite ends of a continuum of employer–employee relationships and work decision-making arrangements, with many combinations in between.

Examples of both types of control are found in the Canadian mining industry. Wallace Clement's (1981: 204) study of the International Nickel Company described the introduction of sophisticated "people technology" at the modern Copper Cliff Nickel refinery. Inco's emphasis on a "one big happy family feeling," a flatter job hierarchy, and a new on-the-job training system looked progressive. However, these changes led to a breakdown of traditional job autonomy and the erosion of the bargaining power of the unionized refinery workers. This increased the level of direct control by management. In contrast, Inco's teams of underground miners possessed considerable responsible autonomy. These small, closely knit groups decided among themselves how and when to do each phase of the mining operation.

A more recent study of potash mining in Saskatchewan (Russell 1999: 193-4) revealed that managers in post-Fordist work settings were less likely to employ a "rough" style of management or, in Friedman's terms, traditional direct control. However, it was also apparent that management could not afford to act in this manner, since this might jeopardize the cooperation of workers who were expected to maintain high levels of productivity in a lean-production environment. Ultimately, the researcher concluded that, despite the rhetoric, workers had not really been empowered.

Shifting our attention to the service sector, a nightclub in a Western Canadian city provides an interesting example of the shifting frontier of control. Mike Sosteric (1996) describes the strong informal workplace culture that had emerged in the club and the considerable degree of job autonomy enjoyed by workers. As a result, they were loyal and committed, and customers received high-quality, personalized service. But new management saw some of the norms of the informal workplace culture as problematic, and tried to take charge by implementing what might be seen as a system of responsible autonomy. The workers were put off by the training seminars, disliked the new system of job enlargement, and found that elimination of supervisors made their work more difficult. Consequently, they actively resisted the changes. In turn, management adopted a direct and coercive control strategy that led, ultimately, to workers quitting and the quality of service in the nightclub deteriorating.

While Friedman describes responsible autonomy being offered to selected groups of workers in return for their cooperation, Michael Burawoy (1979; 1984) goes even further, suggesting that in many work settings employees choose to cooperate. Rather than asking why workers resist management initiatives, Burawoy reverses the question and asks why they typically work as hard as they do. His answer is that workers' consent is manufactured, largely through their own actions at the point of production. In his study of machine shop workers, he describes how an unspoken agreement with company goals emerged. Some employees, for example, adapted to management's control system by simply treating wage bonuses as a game they tried to win. Participation in the game of "making out," or earning wage bonuses, was essentially an individualistic response or adaptation to an otherwise boring job. As long as each worker had a fair chance of "winning" bonuses, management's rules went unchallenged. For these workers, coercion (or the *despotic organization of work*, in Burawoy's terms) was unnecessary since, by accepting the rules of the workplace, they basically motivated themselves.

Burawoy also describes the *hegemonic organization of work* in a manner similar to Richard Edwards's bureaucratic control. In large corporations and government departments, employees often see their own futures linked with the success of the organization. Hence, management's values are dominant, or hegemonic. The presence of internal labour markets and responsible autonomy helps to maintain management control. Individual workers are subtly encouraged to adopt the company's or department's value system, and good job conditions foster long-term commitment to the organization. A recent study of how the Klein government in Alberta restructured the department responsible for museums and cultural heritage sites in the 1990s is a good example (Oakes et al. 1998). By requiring all government departments to develop standardized business plans, an apparently neutral strategy from which everyone would benefit, senior management shifted the department's emphasis from public education and cultural preservation to the logic of business while, at the same time, gaining greater control over professionals employed in the department as they adopted the language and values of business planning.[9]

The rapid growth of computer-based information technologies appears to be giving rise to yet another type of management control system. *Electronic control* may simply be a replacement for technical control since, like assembly lines, computers can be used to determine the speed of work and reduce job autonomy in some industries. Joel Novek has described, for example, how the individual decision-making opportunities of Thunder Bay grain terminal operators were reduced when computers were installed in the control room (Novek 1988). But electronic control can be much more direct and intrusive when supervisors monitor workers' telephone calls and electronic mail or send warning messages to workers who are not meeting a performance standard. Or it may be somewhat more subtle, although equally controlling, when workplace performance norms (the number of sales made by co-workers, for example) are collected electronically and used to push for higher performance from individuals.[10]

Different types of control may be more effective in some industries or with some occupational groups. We have seen examples where control strategies lost their effectiveness as work contexts changed. There may even be cultural differences in control strategies successfully employed by managers. For example, efforts to introduce Japanese forms of management to North American workplaces have frequently been met with considerable resistance by workers. Unaccustomed to paternalistic managers and peer criticism, and perhaps unwilling to give up some of their individuality, North American workers have been reluctant to participate actively in attempts to develop a consensus-based corporate culture.[11]

Having reviewed some of the research on managerial control strategies, we can now see the variety of ways in which managers might try to control the labour process. Direct, technical, bureaucratic, hegemonic, and electronic control, along with responsible autonomy, are all possibilities, alone or in some combination. The balance of power and control in any given workplace can range from strictly coercive, with management holding all the cards, to situations where workers have considerable responsibility for regulating their own work, essentially controlling themselves. As John Jermier (1998: 241) wrote when introducing a recent collection of studies on the subject, regimes of control range from those "anchored in the iron fist of power [to] those that rely on the velvet glove." Nevertheless, workers continue to find ways to resist many management control efforts. In Friedman's words, the labour process remains a shifting frontier of control and conflict.

The Skill Debate

Questions about changes in the skill level of workers' jobs are central to both our evaluation of Braverman's thesis (as well as the contrasting theories of postindustrial society) and to current public policy discussions about the link between investments in human resources and Canada's economic competitiveness. Are the forces of globalization, technological change, industrial and labour market restructuring, and new management techniques requiring more or less skill from today's workers?

For Braverman, the application of Taylorist-style management was systematically deskilling both blue-collar and white-collar work in capitalist society. In contrast, Daniel Bell and other postindustrial society theorists argued that a new economy relying heavily on highly skilled "knowledge workers" was taking shape (see Chapter 1). More recently, other writers have put forward a similar *enskilling* argument about the growing number of multiskilled workers required with "flexible specialization," "lean production," and other postindustrial forms of production (see Chapter 5). And public policy debates about competitiveness have been characterized by warnings that more investments in education and training are needed to increase the skill levels of Canadian workers.

Before we can address the skill debate, we need some agreement on definitions. What exactly is skill and how can we measure it accurately?[12] A first basic question is whether skills reside in workers or whether they are characteristics of jobs. In other words, is deskilling something that happens to individual workers or to the jobs they occupy? The answer to both questions is "yes," since jobs can be redesigned to increase and decrease skill content, and workers can lose skills if they do not have the opportunity to use them regularly.

Second, are skills such as the ability to use advanced computer software, drive a semi-trailer, or teach children to read completely objective job requirements that can be reliably measured and ranked in terms of their importance and complexity? Or are skills to some extent socially constructed, reflecting the social status, power, and traditions of a particular occupation? Feminist researchers have shown, for example, how the social construction of skill has placed more value on traditionally male skills and devalued those possessed by women.[13] A useful concept in this regard is *tacit skill*, a term describing the informal knowledge workers have gained through experience or from co-workers about how to do their job. Tacit skills obviously are not part of formal job descriptions and, thus, often go unrewarded.

These observations highlight the importance of thinking about skill in a multidimensional way. The research literature contains a variety of detailed skill classifications, and personnel experts who conduct formal job evaluations have their own lists. But there is considerable consensus that, in general terms, work-related skills have two components: *substantive complexity* (the level and scope of intellectually, interpersonally, and manually challenging tasks performed in a job), and *decision-making autonomy* (the opportunity for individual workers to decide how, when, and at what speed to complete a task).

There are also important research design and measurement issues to be addressed in the skill debate. While case studies of specific workplaces or occupations can illuminate deskilling or enskilling processes, they seldom have the breadth to test Braverman's sweeping conclusion about deskilling within capitalism. Hence, larger-scale studies (both in terms of occupational coverage and the time period examined) are needed. Can we assume that jobs typically held by well-educated people are, in fact, highly skilled? Alternatively, do formal job requirements really indicate the skill levels of the work tasks performed? The answer to both questions is "not necessarily." Recall, for example, that rising levels of educational attainment among Canadians, in the absence of enough jobs requiring the skills acquired through education and training, can lead to significant problems of underemployment (Chapter 2).

Wallace Clement and John Myles (1994: 72) summarize the skill debate by asking if we are faced by "a postindustrial Nirvana of knowledge where everyone will be a brain surgeon, artist, or philosopher (Bell) or, alternatively, a postindustrial Hades where we shall be doomed to labour mindlessly in the service of capital (Braverman)." Some case studies of skill change in specific occupations and work settings have supported the deskilling hypothesis, while others have not. But with larger-scale studies using multiple measures to examine skill shifts over several decades in the complete occupational structure, a more definitive conclusion has emerged. On average, the long-term trend in North America and western Europe has been in the direction of increased skill requirements in the workplace. Although Daniel Bell's overly optimistic predictions of an emerging knowledge society have not been fulfilled, "the net result of the shift to services has been to increase the requirements for people to think on the job."[14]

This conclusion, however, comes with several important caveats. First, Myles and Clement comment on the "net result," acknowledging that deskilling has occurred in some work settings. Second, we also need to recognize that an overall increase in skill requirements need not be accompanied by other improvements in the quality of work life. For example, TQM, lean production, and other recent management innovations may require workers to learn additional skills, but in downsized organizations workers also have to work harder and faster, under more stressful conditions (Russell 1999). In fact, some of the critical assessments of these management strategies (summarized below) distinguish between *multitasking* (simply adding more tasks to a worker's job description) and *multiskilling* (adding to the skill repertoire of workers), arguing that the former merely makes employees work harder, not smarter.[15]

Furthermore, the studies leading to the conclusion of increased skill requirements over time did not include data from the 1990s. Until the 1980s, growth in higher-skill jobs, most in the upper-tier services and the goods-producing industries, outstripped the expansion of less-skilled positions, many in the lower-tier services. But we have continued to see substantial industrial restructuring and organizational downsizing, and widespread introduction of automated technologies, the sum of which might have slowed or stopped the enskilling trend. This might account for Michael Smith's (2001: 17) conclusion that "recent technological change has not distinctly raised average skill levels" in Canada.

Finally, while providing overall support for the enskilling hypothesis, research also demonstrates an increasing polarization between skilled workers and those with less skill.[16] Some case studies, for example, have shown substantial skill increases for specific groups of workers within an organization, because of automation or new information technologies, while the jobs of other workers have been deskilled.[17] Observing the more general society-wide trend toward skill polarization, Robert Reich (1991) worries about the social implications of growing inequality between "symbolic analysts" and "routine production workers." Clement and Myles (1994: 76) discuss the skill polarization issue in terms of social class, noting that almost all executives and a majority of the new middle class are in skilled jobs, compared to less than a quarter of the working class. Thus, the polarization of skills may be accenting the already pronounced class differences in income, status, and power in the Canadian labour market.

TECHNOLOGY AND THE LABOUR PROCESS

Technology is a central concept in the sociology of work. It figures prominently in theories and debates about industrialization and postindustrial society. Most of the management approaches developed over the past century relied on new technologies, at least to some extent, to improve efficiency and increase productivity. In turn, labour process researchers have focused on how employers have used technology to deskill work and increase control over employees. The following sections examine the effects of new technologies from a critical perspective.

Technology and Social Inequality

Classical theorists like Adam Smith and Karl Marx and more contemporary observers of postindustrial society such as Daniel Bell have all emphasized technology's role in social and economic change. Gerhard Lenski, a sociologist analyzing North American industrial society in the 1960s, placed technology at the centre of his theory explaining differences in the level of social inequality. Since critical perspectives on technology focus on inequality in power, skill, income, and job security, it would be useful to begin our discussion with an overview of Lenski's (1966) theory of power and privilege.

Lenski proposed that a society's technological base largely determines the degree of inequality or the structure of the stratification system within it. In simple hunting and gathering societies, he argued, the few resources of the society were distributed primarily on the basis of need. But, as societies became more complex, privilege, or the control of the society's surplus resources, came to be based on power. Ruling elites received a much larger share. In agrarian societies, a governing system had evolved that gave the privileged class control of the political system and access to even more of the society's wealth. However, the arrival of the industrial era reversed this "age old evolutionary trend toward ever-increasing inequality" (Lenski 1966: 308).

Lenski's explanation hinged on the complex nature of industrial technology. Owners of the means of production could no longer have direct control over production. In the interests of efficiency, they had to delegate some authority to subordinates. This led to the growth of a middle level of educated managerial and technical workers who expected greater compensation for their training. Education broadened the horizons of this class of workers, introducing them to ideas of democracy, as well as making them more capable of using the political system to press their demands for a greater share of the profits they produced.

In short, Lenski's theory proposed a causal link between complex industrial technology, rising levels of education, and workers' insistence on sharing in the growing wealth of an industrial society. But why would employers give in to this demand? Lenski believed that the industrial elite needed educated workers; the productive system could not operate without them. Equally important, the much greater productivity of industrial societies meant that the "elite can make economic concessions in relative terms without necessarily suffering any loss in absolute terms" (Lenski 1966: 314). Because so much more wealth was being produced, everyone could have a larger share.

Lenski accurately described the social and economic changes accompanying industrialization. Twentieth-century capitalism had provided a higher standard of living for the working class. Compared to the era observed by Marx, workers were not as exploited and powerless. Social inequality was slowly declining in the decades of economic expansion and full employment immediately following World War II. However, it is virtually impossible to prove that industrial technology was the underlying cause. A better explanation might focus on changing social relations of production. Within capitalism's shifting frontier of control and conflict, workers had gained relatively more collective power—through unions, for example—and the state had legislated rules governing the labour market and provided a social safety net that reduced the level of poverty.

But as we have argued, we are again seeing evidence of growing inequality in North American society. Industrial restructuring, organizational downsizing, the growth of nonstandard jobs, and a reduction in the social safety net are all part of the explanation. But going back to Lenski's starting premise that a society's technological base determines the degree of inequality, is it possible that computer-based technologies have also contributed to the slow increase in social inequality?

The Information Technology Revolution

The new technologies of the industrial age increased productivity largely by reducing the amount of physical labour required in the goods-producing industries. In contrast, today's computer-based information and automated production technologies are reshaping both the physical and mental requirements of work, in both the goods-producing and service sectors. Factory robots, globally-linked office computer networks, e-commerce in the retail sector, automated materials-handling systems in transportation, computer-assisted design in engineering firms, computer-assisted diagnostics in health care, and modems and fax machines in workers' homes are all part of a rapidly changing technological context for work at the beginning of the 21st century.[18] It would not be an exaggeration to describe the changes occurring as an information technology (IT) revolution. The change has been extensive and rapid. At the beginning of the 1980s, only a small minority of Canadian workers used computers, in any form, in their jobs. By 1985, a survey of Canadian employers indicated that about 16 percent of their workers were using computers (McMullen 1996). This figure had more than doubled (to 35%) by 1989, had tripled (to 48%) by 1994, and then rose again to 57 percent by 2000 (Marshall 2001b).

We will not even attempt to catalogue the proliferation of new computer-based information and production technologies and how they are being used. However, several general observations about the trends would be useful. As already noted, the new technologies are reshaping work in all sectors of the economy. Computer-based technologies are now linked throughout entire production and service-delivery processes, within workplaces, across multi-site work organizations, and globally. And computer technologies are becoming remarkably sophisticated in their abilities to approximate human thinking. Despite claims about "artificial intelligence," human beings and machines will remain different "species." Yet, it is clear that computer designers are creating machines capable of extremely complex decision-making processes.

How have these new technologies affected employment patterns and the labour process? Technological innovations have contributed to increased productivity. But have these technologies also led to improvements in job quality? Have the skills of workers been enhanced, and have they been able to use the technologies to gain greater control over their work? Have the new technologies eliminated some of the unhealthy and boring jobs of the previous industrial era? Equally important, have the new technologies created more jobs than they have replaced?

Skill Requirements of New Technologies

Having addressed some of these questions in our earlier discussion of the labour process perspective, we will now focus on the role of new technologies in reshaping jobs and workplaces, with particular emphasis on *robotics* (automated production technologies) and *information technologies (IT)*.

Automation's potential to eliminate dirty, dangerous, and boring factory jobs has been partly realized through robotics.[19] Robots are ideal for work in cramped spaces, in extreme temperatures, or in otherwise hazardous situations, and they have been used to eliminate dangerous jobs in many factories (welding and painting automobiles is an example). It is possible to organize production around robots in a way that offers workers considerable opportunity for skill improvement and job autonomy. The Saab factory described in Chapter 5 is an example.

Frequently, though, the new jobs involved in operating or maintaining robots have not been organized in this manner. Factory robots are seldom programmed by those running them. In some situations, operators do little more than position the material, and the robot does the rest. The retooling of a U.S. automobile plant provides an example (Milkman and Pullman 1991). Until the mid-1980s, the GM factory in Linden, New Jersey, produced luxury-sized cars using traditional assembly-line technology. Around 1985, the factory was retooled in order to start producing smaller cars. Over 200 robots were added to the production system, along with more than 100 automated guided vehicles (AGVs), which moved the cars in production through the system. In addition, management introduced some organizational innovations including just-in-time delivery, quality control circles, and special training programs for workers. However, the basic hierarchy separating production workers on the line from skilled trades workers (electricians, machinists, and carpenters) remained unchanged.

The automated system required 25 percent fewer production workers to do less skilled jobs. This deskilling of production jobs could be traced to the replacement of welders by robots as well as the reorganization of several production processes. Previously, a group of workers with a broad range of skills relieved others, one at a time, from their various positions on the line. With the new technology, everyone took breaks at the same time, so the multiskilled relief workers were no longer needed. Under the old system, production workers frequently repaired defective component parts. With the just-in-time delivery system, defective parts were returned to the suppliers. And even though production workers used computers in the new assembly system, few new skills were needed. By contrast, a reduced number of skilled trades workers found themselves doing a larger variety of tasks that required more skills. Compared with the traditional assembly-line technology, the installation and maintenance of the robots and AGVs were challenging jobs with a great deal of variety.[20]

Computer numerical control (CNC) machines, used to make metal parts and tools, have also, in some cases, led to an erosion of workers' knowledge requirements and responsibilities. These machines have been used to replace tool and die makers, who traditionally were among the most skilled manufacturing workers, with cheaper semiskilled CNC operators. As one skilled Canadian machinist described the impact of CNCs on his job:

> "You don't even need a man to monitor [the CNC], the machines will monitor themselves. They've got all these electronic scans that tell when the tool edge is wearing, what horsepower the machine is using. They've got all these tool change systems, so they even can

change tools whenever they want, so you don't even need a man there."[21]

As for white-collar employees, case studies reveal that the impact of IT has been positive more often than negative.[22] The extent of the improvements in work quality depend on organizational characteristics such as size, industry, and occupation, the specific type of technology, and managerial decisions about how to reorganize work. Thus, some of the dreary filing and typing chores of office work have disappeared, and opportunities to acquire word processing, graphics, data base management and Internet skills have provided more challenging, varied, and interesting jobs for some clerical staff.

But the full potential of IT for enhancing the quality of work has not always been realized. On the basis of her case studies, Shoshana Zuboff (1988: 57) concludes that IT "creates pressure for a profound *reskilling.*" Yet old-style management control and bureaucracy often prevent workers from learning how to effectively interact with the computers. Fearing loss of power, many middle managers in the firms she studied were reluctant to give workers the training and responsibility they needed to make the leap to *informated* (as opposed to simply *automated)* work.

As these case studies indicate, IT has had mixed effects on the skill levels of workers. Even so, nationwide surveys suggest that skill upgrading has been more common than downgrading, at least from the perspective of workers (Lowe 1997). However, opportunities to learn a wide range of new skills are usually limited. A 1995 survey of Canadian firms revealed that *know-how skills* (simply knowing how to use a new technology) were more likely to be enhanced than *problem-solving* and individual *decision-making* skills (autonomy). Workers in professional and managerial positions were more likely to have experienced skill upgrading (McMullen 1996: vii). There is also some evidence that the introduction of IT may lead to the loss of informal expertise (tacit skills) that is difficult to build into computer systems (Fearfull 1992: 441).

Furthermore, the spread of new computer-based technologies has led to greater polarization of skills within the labour force (Burris 1998). Case studies and Statistics Canada's *General Social Survey* show that workers who already are highly skilled (professionals, managers, and technicians) are more likely to have the opportunity to work with IT and to receive the necessary training (Lowe 1997; Marshall 2001b). Kathryn McMullen's 1995 survey of Canadian firms reveals that professional positions accounted for 56 percent of new jobs created by IT, while 60 percent of the jobs eliminated were in intermediate-level positions. However, employers appeared to be doing little to upgrade the skills of workers made redundant by IT so that they could move into the new, more skilled jobs (McMullen 1996: viii). As Thomas Idle and Arthur Cordell conclude, "We are beginning to see the creation of a workforce with a bi-modal set of skills. Highly trained people design and implement the technology, and unskilled workers carry out the remaining jobs" (1994: 69).

New Technologies and Control of Workers

Henry Ford's assembly line gave managers a powerful means of controlling the pace of work. As one observer of a Ford plant commented:

> Every employee seemed to be restricted to a well-defined jerk, twist, spasm or quiver resulting in a flivver. I looked constantly for the wire or belt concealed about their bodies which kept them in motion with such clock-like precision.[23]

Such technical control within a rigid bureaucratic setting (Fordism) gave North American industrial workers little autonomy. But as new information technologies became more common, so too did predictions that they would erode organizational power structures. With computers, workers would gain more control over their own labour and there would be less need for direct supervision by managers. John Naisbitt (1982: 282) was one of the early enthusiasts:

> The computer will smash the pyramid; we created the hierarchical, pyramidal, managerial system because we needed it to keep track of people and things people did; with the computer to keep track, we can restructure our institutions horizontally.

However, McMullen's 1995 survey of Canadian firms presents a much more cautious assessment. On the basis of employers' responses about the effects of new computer-based technologies, the know-how skills of employees were improved more than their problem-solving and decision-making skills (McMullen 1996: vii). In other words, the new technologies had not provided workers with that much more control over their own work. Furthermore, critics of IT have presented case-study evidence to show that computers and other new technologies can also be used by management to expand control over workers. The most obvious example is electronic control, defined earlier. Specifically, IT has been used in a range of different settings to monitor workers' productivity and to ensure that they are following rules.[24]

Nevertheless, it is difficult to draw an overall conclusion about the impact of the new technologies on workplace power structures. The case-study evidence presents a pessimistic picture, but it does not allow us to generalize about the labour market as a whole. In turn, while reaching a somewhat more positive conclusion, the 1995 survey of Canadian firms cannot really tell us what is happening at the point of production, based as it is on employers' responses to general questions about occupational change. Furthermore, new technologies are often introduced along with other managerial initiatives—TQM or lean production, for example—making it difficult to identify the specific causes of improvements or reductions in employee autonomy. The point to remember is that new technologies are almost always chosen and implemented by managers, not by the employees directly affected.

Job Creation or Job Loss?

Early in the 1800s in English milltowns, the Luddites, fearful about the loss of their jobs to new industrial technologies, rioted and smashed weaving machines. In Canada, at the end of that century, skilled workers in Ontario resisted efforts to mechanize their workplaces for the same reason. It is clear, though, that the eventual outcome of the move to factory-based production and, later, the introduction of assembly lines included economic growth, job creation, and a higher standard of living. In the last few decades, the rapid diffusion of new computer-based technologies has also led to economic growth. But will the new technologies create more jobs than they eliminate, and will the eventual outcome be a higher standard of living for more working Canadians?

The industrial revolution eventually produced many more jobs than it destroyed and, later, the service economy expanded to fill the void created by a shrinking manufacturing sector.* But the new technologies are replacing "mental" as well as "manual" forms of work. Some futurists like Jeremy Rifkin, therefore, have a very pessimistic view of the future. Describing the "end of work" as he sees it, Rifkin writes:

> Within less than a century, "mass" work in the market sector is likely to be phased out in virtually all of the industrialized nations of the world. A new generation of sophisticated information and communication technologies is being hurried into a wide variety of work situations. Intelligent machines are replacing human beings in countless tasks, forcing millions of blue and white collar workers into unemployment lines, or worse still, breadlines.[25]

Canada and other industrialized nations have been facing a serious problem of structural unemployment for some time now, although unemployment rates did drop somewhat as the 1990s gave way to the 21st century (see Chapter 2). New automated technologies have been introduced to reduce labour costs and have, no doubt, contributed to the structural unemployment problem. But so have corporate downsizing, the shrinking of the government sector, and global business systems that have moved some jobs overseas. The direct link between the introduction of new information technologies and job loss is not as clear. In some cases, the IT revolution has led to layoffs while, in others, new jobs have been created, although it is evident that workers made redundant by new technologies are seldom first in line for new jobs (McMullen 1996). Furthermore, the 1990s witnessed significant job growth in the service industries where IT has had the largest effect (Marshall 2001b), even though many of these were nonstandard jobs (see Chapter 2). Thus, there is insufficient evidence to support Rifkin's apocalyptic view of the future, and the targeting of new technologies as the primary cause of job loss (Smith 1999a).

Even so, it is unlikely that we will see sufficient computer-induced job growth in the next decades to counterbalance the effects of a decade of downsizing, automation, and globalization (Menzies 1996: 89–102). As Idle and Cordell conclude in their discussion of the automating of work, "these are not the best of times." High levels of unemployment, increased employment insecurity, and growing income inequality have made life more difficult for millions of Canadians. Reductions in government spending have meant a reduction in support for the unemployed and the working poor. As a society, we are faced with a serious challenge: how do we maintain sustainable economic growth, reduce social inequalities, and ensure social cohesion (Betcherman and Lowe 1997; Lowe and Schellenberg 2001)?

Part of the answer is recognizing, as Charley Richardson puts it, that "computers don't kill jobs, people do" (1996). Technology is a tool that humans have used to their advantage historically, to create jobs and to improve the quality of life. Technology has also been used to eliminate jobs, to destroy the natural environment, and to kill people. There is evidence that the new technologies being developed today can create jobs, increase skill levels, and provide workers with more control over their working environment. New technologies also have the potential to do the opposite, as our quick review of the research literature demonstrates. Hence, as a society, our challenge is to find ways to use technology to provide economic opportunities for as many citizens as possible.

Technological, Economic, or Social Determinism?

We began our critical assessment of technology with Lenski's theory proposing that a society's technological base determines the degree of social inequality. Writing in the 1960s, Lenski viewed industrial technology positively, arguing that it had led to reduced inequality. At the same time, Marshall McLuhan presented a far more pessimistic analysis of the impact of technology on social life. He concluded that human beings were at risk of becoming the servants of technology. His actual words were stronger; he suggested that if trends continued, we might simply become "the sex organs of the machine world ... enabling it to fecundate and to evolve ever new forms."[26]

We do not agree with either of these positions since they attribute too much independent power to technology. *Technological determinism*, the belief that the developmental pattern and effects of a given technology are universal and unalterable, removes the possibility of human agency, the potential for people to shape technology for the greater social good. Furthermore, this position ignores the strong evidence that new technologies have been used in very different ways, with different outcomes, in different work settings and societies.

We also reject *economic determinism*, the belief that the "market knows best" how to choose and implement new technologies. Such a perspective would argue that, despite current problems with job loss, deskilling, and loss of worker autonomy, new technologies will in time lead to more positive than negative outcomes. Behind the "free hand of the market" are real people, making decisions about how to implement the new technologies. These decisions typically have been made by managers guided by the profit motive, so only a small minority of citizens have participated in making these decisions.

Instead, we prefer a *social determinism* perspective, advocating education, wide-ranging discussion, and open decision-making about how technologies will be used, by whom, and for whose benefit. We believe that technology should be used to serve human needs, not merely the needs of a particular company or work organization. Consequently, workers need to be able to participate in decisions about the choice and implementation of new workplace technologies that affect them directly, and citizens need a voice in shaping broader technology strategies.

Because the quest for increased competitiveness through technology has frequently meant job loss or job downgrading for workers, labour movements in North America and Europe generally have opposed the introduction of new technology by management without any input from unions. But this does not mean that unions oppose technological change in principle. Instead, they have insisted that employees be consulted so that the negative effects can be minimized and opportunities for upgrading jobs and improving working conditions maximized. Unions also have argued that any productivity gains should be shared equitably. But while European unions have been successful in obtaining some of these goals, similar gains for organized labour have yet to be achieved in Canada (see Chapter 7).

Canada presently lacks strong legislation requiring prior consultation with employees on technological change. Legislation at the federal level and in four provinces merely requires up to 120 days' notification of technological changes, but notification does not mean consultation and joint decision making. Fewer than 40 percent of major collective agreements require the employer to notify or consult with the union prior to making technological changes, while fewer than 20 percent establish joint labour–management technological change committees.[27] Clearly, Canadian employers' strong sense of "management rights" extends to decisions regarding automation and technological change.

Involving unions and employees in the technological change process in Canada would constitute a major step toward balancing economic and social goals. Research indicates that in countries with strong labour movements, consultation on technological change is more often the norm. Negative effects such as deskilling and income polarization have been less pronounced, and workers have not been as opposed to technological change.[28] Because Sweden and Norway have powerful unions that take an active role in shaping social policy, legislation requires employers to consult with employees prior to automating. Workers have direct input regarding the reorganization of work around new technologies. Widespread layoffs due to technological change have generally been avoided, and, in cases of redundancy, employers have retrained or found other jobs for those affected. In the past few years, however, some of these policies have been weakened and others are being questioned (Smith et al. 1995: 713). It remains to be seen whether Sweden can maintain the system that has provided a model for North American trade unionists.

NEW MANAGEMENT APPROACHES: A CRITICAL PERSPECTIVE

Chapter 5 introduced some of the recent management approaches that have promised to flatten workplace hierarchies, provide workers with additional job autonomy, and enhance their skills. The labour process literature has identified many of the ways in which these promises have not been fulfilled, as documented earlier. Still, it would be useful to itemize some of the specific criticisms of several prominent management approaches. While the management literature itself has addressed problems and contradictions within these models (see Chapter 5), the labour process critique is far more penetrating.

Quality of Working Life (QWL)

The quality of work life (QWL) model of management grew out of several different traditions, including the British sociotechnical systems approach, early Swedish work reforms, and Herzberg's writings on job satisfaction. The emphasis in QWL programs was primarily on workers' immediate job tasks, with job enrichment, job enlargement, job rotation, and autonomous work teams being among the most common innovations. In some settings, management hierarchies were also reduced as work teams took on some of the basic management tasks. The QWL package was typically presented to workers as an effort on the part of management to improve the quality of work life, but obviously managers were hoping to improve productivity as well.

Some QWL initiatives resulted in model "high performance" workplaces, such as the Shell Sarnia refinery and GM's Saturn factory. Unions participated in the design of the program, workers received extensive training, and considerable autonomy and decision-making responsibility was given to self-directed work teams. But more often, critics charge, changes in workers' job tasks were minimal, they did not gain the opportunity to influence decisions on larger workplace changes (the introduction of new technology, for example), and management imposed the programs rather than involving the workers in the decision.[29] In some cases, QWL programs were introduced in a cynical attempt to counter the organizing efforts of unions—if management could provide these benefits, who needs a union?

Total Quality Management (TQM)

Like QWL approaches, total quality management (TQM) programs have been heralded as a "win–win" approach to labour–management relations: workers benefit through improved working conditions and productivity increases. TQM emphasizes customer satisfaction and continuous improvement in addition to job redesign. It also places more emphasis on the need to develop a strong organizational culture. By the 1980s, when TQM was becoming popular, concerns about global competitiveness were becoming more pronounced. Hence, the need for workers to buy into the goals of the program and the values of the corporate culture took on a larger significance. The message for workers was that winning—being part of an ever-improving and more productive company or government workplace—was important not only for the workers and management, but also for the economy. By the same logic, losing meant more than just being part of an unsuccessful work organization. In the new, competitive economy, it might also mean losing one's job.

But TQM efforts have seldom invited workers to participate in decisions about whether to introduce new technologies, or to restructure or downsize organizations. Instead, critics point out, workers have been invited to find ways to work harder, often in an atmosphere of anxiety about possible job loss. Promises of improved working conditions as a result of organizational and job redesign have, consequently, often meant only superficial changes. As in the case of QWL, some TQM initiatives were presented to workers as alternatives to unions. Systems put in place to monitor quality, and to encourage team work and product/service improvement, have also been effective ways to control workers (Sewell 1998). Ironically, many middle managers also find it stressful to constantly reorganize work processes. Thus, while TQM may have increased productivity in some settings (see Chapter 5), it has done so by requiring employees to work harder. All too often, working conditions have not improved and workers have not been empowered (Zbaracki 1998).[30]

Flexible Specialization

Flexible specialization joined the list of new management approaches with considerable fanfare. It promised revolutionary change in Fordist manufacturing systems (computer-coordinated, small-run, flexible production) and the return of craft forms of production (highly skilled, autonomous workers involved in all aspects of the production process). Consequently, bureaucracy should be reduced and workplace conflict should subside. In addition, the power of multinational corporations employing traditional production methods would decline. Essentially, flexible specialization was seen as the production system of a postindustrial economy characterized by less conflict and inequality.

Unlike QWL and TQM, flexible specialization has limited applicability as a management model outside of the manufacturing sector. In fact, it remains unclear just how applicable it is to the full range of manufacturing industries. More important for our discussion here, there is little evidence of working conditions improving and workplace conflict subsiding in firms of this type. Multinational corporations have certainly not become less powerful over the past decade.

Thus, one critique of the flexible specialization model is that it is more a blueprint for a desirable workplace than a description of an emerging trend. However, if it were to become a trend, this model proposes no solution to the social problem of workers made redundant by technological change. Instead, it offers a vision of a severely segmented labour market in which a small elite group of highly skilled workers are the main beneficiaries, while the majority continue to perform routine, unskilled, or semiskilled work.[31]

Lean Production

The *lean production* system of manufacturing also relies heavily on computer-based and automated technology, but without the commitment to the small-scale, highly flexible production processes of flexible specialization. Nevertheless, it goes beyond the rigid and standardized mass production of Fordism by encouraging a flexible approach to product redesign and with its emphasis on quality, continuous improvement in production methods (*kaizen*), and just-in-time delivery. Like QWL and TQM, lean production claims to rely on highly skilled and thinking workers, and promises a reduction in workplace conflicts through its teamwork model of decision making. With all of these features, it is little wonder that lean production has been portrayed by its advocates as the final solution to Taylorism and Fordism (Womack et al. 1990).

Nevertheless, many critics have been harsh in their assessments of lean production's impact on the labour process.[32] They point out that multitasking (one person doing more jobs) is not the same as multiskilling. Instead, it is one of the ways in which management has squeezed more work out of a smaller number of workers. The elimination of replacement workers has also had this effect, as has *kaizen*, the consensus-based approach to continuous improvement. By emphasizing how workers in a particular factory need to outperform their competition elsewhere, management essentially harnesses peer pressure to speed up production.

By way of example, James Rinehart describes a California automobile factory that, before lean production, managed to keep its workers busy for 45 out of every 60 seconds they were on the job. Lean production brought this up to 57 out of 60 seconds. But, as he puts it, "[t]o call kaizen a democratization of Taylorism is to demean the concept of democracy" (2001: 162). Other critics agree, noting that management continues to tightly control the topics discussed in kaizen sessions (Graham 1993: 148). Essentially, lean production has not led to significant skill enhancement or to worker empowerment. It has meant a faster pace of (still repetitive) work, higher stress for employees, and, in some cases, higher injury rates. As a consequence, lean production has also led to resistance by workers—the 1992 strike at the CAMI plant in Ingersoll is an example. Thus, as Rinehart (2001: 197) concludes, "lean production constitutes an evolution of rather than a transcendence of Fordism," and therefore can be called neo-Fordism.

High-Performance Workplaces

The *high-performance workplace* is one of the latest additions to the list of new management strategies. This model shares a number of features with other recent management approaches, including an emphasis on reducing bureaucratic hierarchies and rigid job descriptions, increasing workers' decision-making opportunities, and offering them more training to enhance their skills. But it goes further by advocating human resource management programs that are family friendly and emphasizing the importance of a healthy, non-stressful work environment. It also recommends that employers share profits from productivity increases with workers through variable-pay plans that link some compensation to performance (Betcherman et al. 1994: 96).

Like flexible specialization, the high-performance workplace is more a model of a desirable future than a description of current practice, since only a minority of Canadian organizations have moved in this direction (Betcherman et al. 1994: 58). For workers in a high-performance organization, the potential benefits (skill upgrading, decision-making opportunities, profit sharing, improved working conditions) are considerable. But there are also drawbacks, since one of the assumptions of the model is that employment security can no longer be guaranteed, and that profit sharing also means risk sharing (if the company loses money, so do the workers). In fact, a large-scale study of hundreds of U.S. companies in the 1990s showed that layoffs were more common in high-performance workplaces (Osterman 2000).

Critics influenced by a labour process perspective would be skeptical of the commitment asked of workers in return for these benefits, pointing to previous examples of companies using QWL, TQM, and other similar approaches to speed up work and sideline unions. Nevertheless, there are occasional examples of unions and management working together to build high performance organizations. Clarke and Haiven (1999) describe how, in Saskatchewan in the 1990s, the Communications, Energy and Paperworkers

Union (the same union involved in the Sarnia Shell plant described in Chapter 5) participated in redesigning the Saskatoon Chemicals work organization, including profit sharing and payment for skills. As in other successful union-management projects, what made the difference was a very strong union that was centrally involved in all aspects of the change process. In addition, both parties agreed to a process of *continuous bargaining*, in contrast to the traditional approach of seeking a collective agreement that would remain unchanged for several years.

There have been few attempts to introduce higher performance work practices in the lower-tier service industries. However, a study of a handful of large U.S. retail companies like Wal-Mart and Home Depot that have attempted such organizational changes concludes that workers have not really benefited (Bailey and Bernhard 1997). Wages did not rise appreciably, skill sets were not significantly enhanced, and only a few workers found new career opportunities. High performance work organizations, while not widespread, are more likely to be found in the upper-tier services and in some of the goods-producing industries. Thus, the advent of this form of work organization may signal greater labour market segmentation. The result might be a society in which a small privileged elite of high-skill, relatively autonomous workers are well rewarded, while the majority of workers face a much greater risk of low-skill, less-rewarding work with greater employment insecurity. This, of course, is not a critique of the high-performance workplace model so much as a recognition that, despite its promise, it does not offer a solution to the larger social problem of growing labour market inequality.

New Management Approaches: A New Labour Process?

The management literature reviewed in Chapter 5, while recognizing some of the flaws and inconsistencies in these approaches, uses labels like *participative management* and *employee empowerment* to describe recent innovations. More critical observers have described them as *neo-Fordist* or *post-Fordist*, suggesting that the changes have not been nearly as significant as their proponents claim. By offering some small concessions to workers, these approaches have maintained the basic production framework and power structure of industrial capitalist society. Some critics go even further, using the term *hyper-Taylorism* to describe how managerial control over the labour process has increased and how "management by stress" requires workers to push themselves and each other to make more profits for their employers (Russell 1997: 28).

But labels are not as important as real outcomes. What do we see when we look back at three decades of new management approaches in North America? Summing up our overview of these initiatives, all of them offer some potential for skill upgrading, increasing worker participation in decision making, and reducing bureaucracy. In some cases (Shell's Sarnia refinery, the Tennessee Saturn plant, and the Saskatoon Chemicals workplace, for example), the implementation of these approaches has gone a considerable way toward improving the quality of work life for employees. None of these management models, however, really provides permanent and effective avenues for workers to have ongoing input into larger organizational decisions, such as the introduction of new technologies or a decision to restructure the organization.

The two approaches that go the furthest to counter Taylorism and Fordism—flexible specialization and the high-performance workplace—have not been implemented often. Other approaches typically do not deliver nearly as much as they promise. Furthermore, when we examine them more critically, we frequently find that they have also been used to increase control over workers and to speed up work. In addition, the advent of the new management approaches has been accompanied by widespread organizational restructuring and downsizing. The outcome, for society as a whole, has been a polarization of the labour force in terms of skill, income, and job security, leading to greater social inequality.

As we concluded about the impacts of new technologies on the labour process, the problem does not lie in the technology but in how it is implemented, by whom, and for what purposes. Overall, new management strategies—we might call them *social technologies*—have almost always been introduced with productivity and profit as the main goals. Improvements in quality of work life and worker empowerment have been secondary motivations, while reductions in social inequality have seldom figured in the decision. And workers have rarely been involved in the decision to implement new social technologies, either directly or through their unions. With a few exceptions, when invited to participate, workers' input has been restricted to smaller decisions about changes in their immediate work tasks. Consequently, we should not be surprised that much of the promise of the new management approaches has not been realized.

A CRITICAL PERSPECTIVE ON WORKPLACE HEALTH AND SAFETY

Our profile of good jobs and bad jobs in Chapter 3 documented the high costs to workers, employers, and society of workplace health and safety risks. Every year, hundreds of Canadian workers are killed and thousands are injured on the job. Acknowledging that it is impossible to put a price tag on human suffering and death, the magnitude of the problem is nevertheless indicated by the $4.65 billion paid as compensation for work-related injuries and fatalities in Canada in 1998 (Human Resources Development Canada 2000a: 10). In addition, the future health of many workers is regularly placed at risk. Every year, a sizable minority of all Canadian workers are exposed to workplace health hazards, including air pollution, excessive noise, physically demanding repetitive work, and stress-inducing work environments (Grayson 1994; Bachmann 2000).

Workplace health and safety is highly relevant to our discussion of conflict, control, and resistance in the workplace. Historically, dangerous machinery, unsafe work sites, polluted air, and exposure to carcinogenic substances and other risks have taken their toll on the working class in terms of shorter life expectancies and higher illness and disease rates. Most of the progress made over the years in reducing workplace health and safety risks has been the result of workers fighting for improvements, often against the strong opposition of employers. Furthermore, workplace health and safety continues to be a contentious issue in union–management contract disputes and in the larger political arena. At the same time, the area of workplace health and safety provides one example where, at least to some extent, workers and their employers have managed to identify and work together toward common goals.

The Politics of Workplace Health and Safety

In the early years of Canada's industrialization, workers had little protection from what were often extremely unsafe working conditions. Work in the resource industries, in construction of canals and railways, and in factories was hazardous, and the risk of injury and death was high. As in other industrializing countries, an *administrative model of regulation* slowly developed, in which the government set standards for health and safety and tried to enforce them (Lewchuk et al. 1996: 225). Employers frequently opposed these efforts, arguing that their profits were threatened and that the state had no right to interfere in worker–employer relationships. In turn, unions fought for change and the public was mobilized behind some causes, including restrictions on the employment of women and children in factories. Thus, the Factory Acts of the 1880s led to improvements such as fencing around dangerous machines, ventilation standards for factories, and lunchrooms and lavatories in large workplaces. The employment of women and children was also curbed on the grounds of protecting their health.

Over the years, additional safety standards were introduced. In unionized workplaces and industries, *collective bargaining* also made a difference as unions negotiated for better working conditions and the elimination of specific health and safety hazards. By the second decade of the 20th century, provincial workers' compensation boards had put in place *no-fault compensation systems* that still exist today. Injured workers are provided with some money, the amount depending on the severity of their injury, and with partial compensation for lost wages, no matter whose fault the accident. In return, they give up their right to sue for compensation if the employer was at fault. The system is funded by contributions from employers, with the amount based, in part, on their safety record. Thus, there is a monetary incentive for employers to reduce workplace health and safety hazards and to encourage safe working practices among employees.

All of these approaches to dealing with health and safety issues—standard setting and enforcement by the state, collective bargaining between unions and employers, and the no-fault compensation system—offer little room for direct involvement on the part of workers who are most directly affected by unsafe and unhealthy working conditions. But the introduction of the *internal responsibility system (IRS)* has changed this. A guiding principle of this approach is that workers' personal experience and knowledge of work practices and hazards are an integral part of any solution to health and safety problems. In addition, workers should have the right to participate in the identification and elimination of workplace hazards. Furthermore, health and safety is also management's responsibility. Overall health and safety is a workplace issue—an internal responsibility—too important to be left to government alone. In the IRS system, employees are directly involved with management in monitoring and inspection and in education and health promotion in their workplaces.

Direct worker involvement in health protection and promotion in the workplace increased dramatically in Europe in the 1970s. This trend grew out of demands for greater industrial democracy (discussed later in this chapter), and government reviews of traditional and unsatisfactory approaches to occupational health and safety (Tucker 1992). In Canada, the first major initiative of this sort was the 1972 Saskatchewan Occupational Health Act. It broke new ground by broadly defining occupational health as "the promotion and maintenance of the highest degree of physical, mental, and social well-being of workers" (Clark 1982: 200), and by making joint health and safety committees (JHSCs) mandatory. Other provinces and the federal government (about 10 percent of Canadian workers are covered by federal labour legislation) followed, and today the internal responsibility system, built around JHSCs, is part of the legislated workplace health and safety system across the country.

JHSCs range in size from two to twelve members, half of whom must be non-managerial employees (either elected or appointed by a union if one exists), and are required in any workplace employing twenty or more. In most provinces, workplaces with at least five but fewer than twenty employees must also have at least one non-managerial safety representative. The committees keep records of injuries, participate in safety inspections, make recommendations to management about health and safety concerns, inform employees about their rights with respect to such concerns, and develop safety enhancement and educational programs (Gordon 1994: 542–43).

Along with giving JHSCs the *right to be involved* in health and safety issues, legislation also allows workers the *right to refuse unsafe work*, the definition being based on the individual employee's own assessment that a particular task presents a genuine risk. If subsequent inspections determine otherwise, the legislation protects workers from reprisals from employers. Workers also have the *right to be informed* about potentially hazardous materials with which they might be working.

The IRS system appears to be effective. Research has shown that the recommendations of JHSCs to management are usually heeded (Gordon 1994: 548). A recent Ontario study examined data on claims for lost time due to accidents between 1976 and 1989 and concluded that "where management and labour had some sympathy for the co-management of health and safety through joint committees, the new system significantly reduced lost-time accidents" (Lewchuk et al. 1996: 225). If an organization reluctantly introduced JHSCs, the system had little effect. The success of JHSCs in Canada has led to recommendations that the Canadian system be copied in the United States. The more traditional U.S. system, which still relies primarily on legislation and, where unions are present, on collective bargaining, is less effective (Gordon 1994).

The Labour Process and Workplace Health and Safety

Does the relative effectiveness of JHSCs and the IRS system indicate that workers and management are no longer in conflict over health and safety issues, that this is a win–win situation? We would argue that workers and management have moved further in this direction on health and safety than they have elsewhere. In part, this is due to the economic incentives built into the system for employers; a better safety record means lower costs of production. More important, legislation has reduced some of the power differences between management and workers and directly involved each in addressing health and safety issues.

Even so, workplace health and safety remains a contested terrain. Critics of the IRS system have pointed out that, in many JHSCs, non-management members continue to have much less influence, particularly in nonunionized workplaces. Some employers largely ignore the joint committees, despite legislation (Lewchuk et al. 1996: 228). Research has shown that workers are often unaware of their rights and lack the knowledge needed to address complex health hazards, and that scientific and medical experts give the appearance of impartiality to a system that continues to be dominated by employers for whom profits come first.[33] In some tragic cases like the Westray mine explosion in 1992 in Nova Scotia, the system failed completely (Comish 1993; McCormick 1998). Local miners had warned that the mine site was unstable, and the initial mining plan was rejected for safety reasons. But the mine still opened, and remained open even after repeated problems with methane gas, coal dust, and roof falls. Eventually, twenty-six miners died in an explosion.

Joel Novek's (1992) case study of restructuring within the Canadian meatpacking industry provides another example of how worker health and safety can be jeopardized for profits. Industry-wide consolidation of production in the

1980s led to a rising injury rate among workers. The problem could be traced directly to changes in the labour process, specifically mechanization and speedups. Workers suffered more muscle strains and knife lacerations, and the hazards associated with handling live animals in cold, damp, and noisy environments increased. Productivity also rose, but because of more accidents and worker burnout, the companies faced higher workers' compensation board levies and had difficulty maintaining production. Only at this point did one firm address the problem, approaching a union-run health clinic for assistance.

While Canadian unions have fought for safer workplaces for well over a century, they have sometimes found themselves balancing concerns about their members' health and well-being with equally strong concerns about potential job loss. Robert Storey and Wayne Lewchuk (2000) describe how, in the early 1980s, the United Automobile Workers of America tried to force Bendix Automotive in Windsor, Ontario to deal with the deadly problem of asbestos dust in its brake shoe factory. Having already closed one of its plants because of this problem, the company announced that it now planned to close the remaining factory. Some of the workers wanted their union to insist that the workplace be made safer, whatever the cost. Others, fearful that the company would close the factory and they would lose their jobs, wanted the union to back down. The factory was eventually closed anyway. While highlighting how little power the workers really had, compared to the company, Storey and Lewchuk also describe the limits of provincial health and safety legislation, which is incapable of stopping an employer from closing a workplace rather than dealing with its heath hazards.

Along with disputes over management's and worker's rights, the definitions and sources of work-related health problems also continue to be contested. For example, there is mounting evidence that job-related stress takes a toll on employees' health. Stress-induced health problems can range from headaches to chronic depression and heart disease. But stress is frequently rejected as a legitimate concern by workers' compensation boards who administer claims.[34] They tend to use a narrow definition of health and illness, focusing mainly on physical injuries and fatalities. Employers and compensation boards sometimes also attempt to place the blame for workers' health problems on their lifestyles or family situations rather than on their jobs. Such a "blaming the victim" ideology assumes that workers are careless, accident-prone, or susceptible to illness.

Rather than accepting a narrow definition of workplace health and safety issues, Bob Sass (1986) argues that we need to

> "stretch" the present legal concept of risk, which covers dust, chemicals, lighting, and other quantifiable and measurable aspects of the workplace to cover all work environment matters: how the work is organized, the design of the job, pace of work, monotony, scheduling, sexual harassment, job cycle, and similar work environment matters of concern to workers.

Sass wrote this almost two decades ago. Since then, he has gone even further to argue that the "weak rights" workers now have within the IRS system need to be extended. "Strong rights," as he sees it, go beyond co-management and would involve *"worker control* in the area of the work environment."[35] In such a democratized work environment, workers would not have to accept the constant tradeoff between health risks to themselves and the efficiency and profit demanded by employers. Sass sees unions as the only vehicle for such change since they are worker-controlled, even though most unions continue to work within the current IRS system and accept its basic premises and goals.

However, with some exceptions, it has not been unions that have been pushing for a broader and more inclusive definition of worker health and well-being. Instead, corporate health promotion, or "wellness programs," emerged in the 1980s as yet another human resource management policy that would help to motivate workers and raise productivity (Conrad 1987; Sloan 1987). The orientation of these wellness programs has typically been to change workers' lifestyles or health-related behaviours (exercising more and quitting smoking, for example). Some have gone further to promote family-friendly and less-stressful employment policies and practices. But they have not addressed job redesign, added to workers' rights, or increased workplace democracy.

Corporate wellness programs no doubt have good intentions, and probably benefit employees who participate in them. But they have no real impact on the unequal distribution of power within work organizations, which contributes greatly to health and safety problems. Furthermore, because such programs are typically only available in larger work organizations, many workers are unable to participate. Thus, while offering some assistance to some workers, corporate wellness programs do not improve working conditions for the working class as a whole.

Terrance Sullivan (2000) introduces a collection of essays about "injury and the new world of work" by observing that we find ourselves, once again, in a period of revolutionary change, with new information and communication technologies, new types of work organization, and new management approaches. He argues that the legislation and the internal responsibility system that was developed to address workplace health and safety problems in the last century may not be adequate for the workplaces of the 21st century, an argument echoed by O'Grady (2000). Not only can we expect to see new types of injuries, we also know more today about long-term effects of workplace hazards and stressors, and about the wider array of physical and mental disabilities that might be caused in the workplace. Thus, like Bob Sass (1986), Sullivan (2000) argues for a broader definition of workplace health and safety issues, and calls for a re-examination of the legislation and programs developed to address the problem.

INDUSTRIAL DEMOCRACY: RETHINKING WORKERS' RIGHTS

Our evaluation of new management models concluded that none really offered workers input into decisions beyond their own jobs. New technologies generally have been imposed by management and then, perhaps, workers have been given more freedom to use the technology. Decisions about downsizing and organizational restructuring are rarely negotiated, and unions rarely consulted about policies that replace permanent, full-time jobs with nonstandard jobs. The IRS system attempts to go further, acknowledging the need to involve workers in the co-management of health and safety risks. But it does not give workers and employers equal control over the work environment.

Within capitalism, ownership carries with it the ultimate right to control how work is organized and performed. We have seen some employers relinquishing some of these rights, allowing workers greater autonomy over their immediate work tasks in the belief that efficiency and productivity could be improved and conflict reduced. *Industrial democracy*, in contrast, attempts to involve workers in a much wider range of decisions within the organization.

Industrial democracy applies the principles of *representative democracy* found in the political arena to the workplace. Workers have a voice at the work-group level, as well as indirectly through elected representatives on corporate boards and other key policy-making bodies. A greater degree of open discussion and consensual decision making involving all employees is the goal of democratized work environments. The essence of workplace democracy, according to Donald Nightingale (1982: 49), is "that labour as a legitimate stakeholder in the enterprise has a moral right to play a role in the management of the enterprise."

Even so, industrial democracy in its various forms has not eliminated power differences within work organizations. Typically, owners reserve the right to make the most important decisions themselves, such as closing a factory, for example. Also, the shared decision-making structures of industrial democracy still tend to give owners and managers more influence. Furthermore, industrial democracy does not guarantee less bureaucracy, reduced income inequality, skill upgrading, or even more task-related autonomy for workers. Even if workers are involved extensively in decision making through elected representatives, the debates might not be around these issues. Job security, for example, or health and safety might be the major concern. Thus, in some settings, industrial democracy has led to job redesign and profit sharing. In others, the results may have been fewer layoffs or more consultation about technological change. Overall, however, industrial democracy has been implemented to a greater degree in European countries than in North America.

Industrial Democracy in North America

Attempts to involve workers in management, at least to some extent, actually have a long history in North America. Following World War I, *works councils* including elected workers and management representatives were set up in large workplaces in a number of industries in both Canada and the United States. The councils met to discuss health and safety, workers' grievances, efficiency, and sometimes even wages. In a number of settings, particularly the coal industry, the impetus for these initiatives was a series of long, bitter, and violent strikes.[36]

Mackenzie King, who later became prime minister, was a labour consultant to some of these companies at the time. He was a strong advocate of the principles of industrial democracy, believing that works councils and related initiatives would reduce industrial conflict and help usher in a new era of social harmony (King 1918). Critics argued that mechanisms to encourage more cooperation between workers and management continued to favour the latter, and that works councils were just a way to deter workers from joining unions. Clearly, in many companies this was the case. With the onset of the Depression at the end of the 1920s, interest in these earlier forms of industrial democracy waned, perhaps because unemployment reduced labour unrest.

Since then, calls have periodically been made for a revival of such worker–management decision-making systems. Not coincidentally, industrial democracy has attracted more interest during periods of labour unrest—immediately after World War II, for example, and again in the 1970s. During those strike-filled eras, employers and politicians looked to Germany and other European countries where industrial democracy had been implemented more widely. North American unions have generally opposed the idea, believing that works councils and other similar forms of industrial democracy undermine collective bargaining, the more traditional means by which workers have negotiated with management for improved working conditions (Guzda 1993: 67).

The spread of industrial democracy in North America has been slow. Most employers have been more interested in avoiding strikes than in really sharing power, and unions have not been supportive. One estimate from the mid-1980s suggested that about one-third of Fortune 500 corporations allowed some form of employee participation in decision making. But the scope of this worker involvement appeared to be limited to joint worker–management consultation committees, special project teams, and problem-solving groups reporting to a top executive. Another estimate from the early 1990s indicates that four out of five Fortune 500 companies have set up "worker involvement programs." This more general term probably includes a wide variety of QWL, TQM, lean production, and other management programs that may provide only limited opportunities for worker involvement in decision making beyond their immediate work tasks (Rothschild and Russell 1986; Guzda 1993: 67).

Although most North American industrial democracy initiatives have not had a significant impact on the power structure of work organizations, a few examples have gone further toward reaching Nightingale's goal. Shell's Sarnia chemical plant (see Chapter 5), for example, combines QWL principles of job redesign with a commitment to involving workers in decisions about all aspects of the operation. But even this organization has not gone as far as Semco, a fascinating Brazilian case study in worker participation (Semler 1993). The financially successful company with 300 employees (another 200 workers run "satellite" businesses that subcontract to Semco) allows workers to set their own production quotas, redesign products, develop marketing plans, and determine salary ranges. Every six months, workers evaluate their managers. For big decisions, such as buying another company or relocating a factory, every worker gets a vote. Workers also participate in profit sharing and decide how large the shares should be. Thus, Semco appears to have gone far beyond basic principles of industrial democracy to give workers rights and obligations normally reserved for owners.

Institutionalized Industrial Democracy in Germany

North American experiments in industrial democracy have usually been introduced by management, occasionally with some pressure from unions. In contrast, in Europe principles of industrial democracy have been institution-alized in a number of countries through government legislation. In Norway, Sweden, Austria, and Germany, for example, legislation gives workers the right to elect representatives to sit on works councils or corporate boards, the right to consultation regarding technological changes, and more grassroots control over health and safety matters.[37]

The German model of *co-determination* has a century-long history. In the 1890s, concerns about widespread labour–management conflict motivated Bismarck to bring in legislation giving works councils the right to advise management on workplace regulations. This legislation was broadened in the 1920s as the Weimar government sought ways to counter the threat of the Russian Revolution spreading into Germany. After World War II, concerned that labour strife would hold back the reconstruction of Germany's devastated economy, the British, American, and French administrators of occupied Germany extended the co-determination legislative framework. A number of additional changes were made in the 1970s and 1980s (Guzda 1993; Beaumont 1995: 101–08).

In its current form, German legislation makes works councils mandatory in any workplace with more than five employees. Elected representatives of the workforce (their number proportional to the size of the firm) share decision making with management representatives. The legislation stipulates that in larger work organizations where unions are present, a proportion of the elected members must be from the union. But nonunionized white-collar workers must also be represented. In larger companies, there are several layers of shared decision making. The most powerful management board, a small group of three or four individuals, has only one worker representative, selected from within the larger works council.

The co-determination legislation requires employers to advise and consult with works councils about plans to introduce new technologies, restructure work, reallocate workers to different tasks or locations, or lay off workers. Works councils can demand compensation for workers negatively affected by new technologies or organizational restructuring. Consequently, the North American strategy of downsizing has been much less common. Elected representatives are jointly involved with management in determining hours of work, pay procedures (bonus rates, for example), training systems, health and safety rules, and working conditions. However, collective bargaining between employers and unions about overall pay rates takes place outside the works councils on an industry-wide level. Consequently, the right to strike remains with the larger unions, not with the local works councils. The unions, however, have much less influence in the joint decision-making process at the local level.

‣ The German *dual representation system* of industrial democracy—industry-wide unions and local works councils—is viewed relatively positively by both employers and workers. There are some concerns that unions may be weakened by the dual system of representation (in the long term, this could jeopardize workers' employment security), but union members still constitute a majority of elected representatives on the works councils. Overall, joint decision making has meant better communication between workers and management, greater protection of workers' rights, improved working conditions, and a reduction in labour–management conflict. The latter was, of course, one of the original goals of the co-determination legislation, and this is also what has frequently impressed North American observers concerned about strikes and reduced productivity.

During the 1990s, the German economy began to lose some of its momentum, in part because of the costs of reuniting West and East Germany. Employers have begun to call for changes in the dual system of representation. In particular, there are pressures to reform the industry-wide collective bargaining system that has meant similar pay rates and conditions of employment in different-size firms and in different parts of the country. Employers argue that they need more flexibility to remain competitive. Whether changes will be made in Germany's labour legislation and whether the rights and working conditions of workers are protected remains to be seen (Beaumont 1995: 107-08).

Sweden: Industrial Democracy as a National Goal

In Germany, concerns about strikes and social unrest led to co-determination legislation. In Sweden, the motivation to implement industrial democracy was somewhat different. An exceptionally strong union movement and the governing Social Democratic Party worked together to improve employment conditions and give workers more rights. In fact, tripartite cooperation and consultation among large and centralized unions (representing 85 percent of the workforce), the employers' federation, and the state has been a hallmark of Swedish democracy. More than in most other countries, unions and employers have been viewed as social partners (see Chapter 7). Thus, in Sweden in the 1970s and 1980s, industrial democracy was elevated to a national goal within a much broader policy of commitment to reduced inequality and full employment.[38]

The full-employment policy has three key elements. A wage policy, based on the concept of equal pay for equal work, removes pay differentials among regions, industries, and firms by pushing low-wage firms to pay decent wages, and by allowing profitable enterprises to pay less than they would under conventional collective bargaining. The reasoning is that weaker enterprises will either become more efficient or go out of business. The relatively lower wages in expanding industries should stimulate economic growth. Active labour market interventions, including heavy investments in training, assist new labour force entrants, as well as workers displaced from declining industries, in finding work. Selective employment policies also attempt to create jobs in regions or industries affected by structural shifts in the economy.

As in Germany, Swedish law mandates employee representation on corporate boards of directors in all but the smallest firms. Elected members are involved in joint decision making with management in a wide range of areas, but cannot participate in discussions regarding negotiations with unions. But the 1977 Act on Employee Participation in Decision Making extends Swedish employees' rights beyond the rights of German workers. Specifically, in addition to the obligation to inform and consult with workers on major decisions (factory closures, transferring employees, introducing new technologies), Swedish employers must negotiate with unions prior to making such decisions. Unions must also be given complete access to information on the economic status of the firm, its personnel policies, and so forth. In 1984, Sweden went further by setting up Wage Earner Funds that redirected corporate taxes into share purchases on behalf of employees in manufacturing and related industries.

The 1978 Work Environment Act goes beyond the goal of industrial democracy—joint decision making throughout a work organization—to address problems of worker satisfaction and personal fulfillment, a subject we examine in more detail in Chapter 8. The act aims to achieve "working conditions where the individual can regard work as a meaningful and enriching part of existence." It is not enough for work to be free of physical and psychological hazards; it must also provide opportunities for satisfaction and personal growth, and for employees to assume greater responsibility. Thus, unlike QWL and other recent management models that view improved productivity and less conflict as desirable outcomes of worker satisfaction, this legislation makes worker satisfaction and individual growth a high priority.

During the 1970s and 1980s, Sweden's impressive economic performance, low unemployment, and reduction of wage inequalities were seen as strong evidence of the success of its model of society-wide industrial democracy. But the 1990s brought changes. Some of the active labour market policies encouraging worker mobility and maintaining full employment were eliminated, and unemployment was allowed to rise. Employers were seeking more flexibility in the allocation of labour in the production process. Lean production made its appearance in Swedish factories, some of the most progressive factories (in terms of workers' autonomy and skill enhancement) closed, and employers introduced new technologies to cut jobs.[39] But the framework legislation that supports the Swedish system of industrial democracy is still in place.

Globalization and Industrial Democracy

In 1993, the twelve nations in the European Community at the time formed a single trading and labour market. This required common rules governing labour–management relations. One of the proposed policies would require multinational companies operating in more than one member country to set up works councils. Among the objectives of such a policy would be the desire to reduce worker–management conflict since strikes in one country could seriously affect production in another. All but one of the twelve countries agreed to the policy, with Britain being the exception (Guzda 1993: 70). Even though this form of industrial democracy has proven its potential for reducing conflict and maintaining high production, the Conservative British government of the day opposed the policy, largely on ideological grounds that it undermined management rights.

Canada has entered into a somewhat similar trading agreement with the United States and Mexico. The North American Free Trade Agreement (NAFTA) has brought calls for the harmonization of labour legislation and labour market policies. Since there is no tradition of formally legislated industrial democracy in any of the three countries, it is unlikely that a policy promoting works councils or other such initiatives will be developed. Instead, the challenge may be to try to maintain Canada's current labour legislation which, to an extent, protects workers more than American or Mexican legislation (Block and Roberts 2000).

WORKERS TAKING OVER OWNERSHIP

A basic capitalist principle is that ownership carries with it the right to control how work is performed and how the organization is run. By offering some degree of co-management or co-determination, the various forms of industrial democracy have given workers some of the rights traditionally attached to ownership. But as Stephen Marglin (1976) provocatively asked, are bosses really necessary? Why don't workers run enterprises collectively, thereby dispensing altogether with authority relationships?

In this final section of the chapter, we ask three basic questions about the possibilities of worker ownership: How common is it? Does worker ownership provide more opportunity for control over the labour process? And how economically viable is worker ownership within a capitalist economy?

Employee Share Ownership Plans

In North America, *employee share ownership plans (ESOPs)* have been widely promoted as a way for workers to share in the profits of production and as a means of generating more consensus in the workplace. If workers are part-owners, the reasoning goes, they should be more likely to identify with the company, work harder, and cooperate with management. In the past decade, ESOPs have been part of the package offered to employees in many private-sector high performance workplaces.

In companies with ESOPs, shares in the company are purchased for employees and provided as part of a benefit package. Depending on the details of the plan, some categories of employees might receive more shares than others. In some ESOPs, employees can also make additional share purchases for themselves. Thus, employees receive some of the company profits, in the same way as would other shareholders. However, when shares available through the ESOP are provided as benefits in lieu of wages, employees will also lose when the company is losing money, since their shares then lose value.

A recent estimate (Brohawn 1997:1) indicates that there are more than 10,000 ESOPs in existence in the United States, in firms representing over 11 million employees (not all of these employees would necessarily take advantage of the stock option plan). In Canada, about two-thirds of the firms listed on the Toronto Stock Exchange have ESOPs. About half of these are available to all employees with the company paying at least some of the cost. Similar plans are in existence in a number of European countries, frequently as part of a legislated industrial democracy strategy. In Sweden, for example, the Wage Earner Funds have been used to make share purchases for employees in some industries since 1984. Because the principles of industrial democracy have not been widely promoted in Britain in recent years, ESOPs are less common. In the mid-1990s, less than 100 were in operation in Britain.[40]

In North America, ESOPs have been set up primarily to provide additional benefits to workers or to allow them to purchase shares, but not to promote joint decision-making. In workplaces where employees participate in an ESOP as well as some form of joint decision making, it is usually because some other managerial model (QWL, for example) has also been implemented. A British study of the recently privatized bus industry shows that firms with ESOPs are somewhat more likely to have workers on the board of directors, although there is no evidence that share ownership by employees led to this weak form of industrial democracy. The study also reveals that workers participating in ESOPs were no more likely to have control over their own work tasks, although management was concerned that workers might begin to demand more control. Unions representing the workers were more interested in using their seats on the board of directors to preserve jobs than to gain control over the labour process (Pendleton et al. 1996).

Employee Buyouts

Economic restructuring and factory closures over the past several decades have made worker ownership of a different kind a frequent news item in Canada. Workers have bought out their employers (or attempted to do so) in an effort to save their jobs when the company was about to close. In some cases, huge firms were bought out, while in others, much smaller enterprises were involved. *Employee buyouts* or attempted buyouts have occurred in both the service industries (the attempted buyout of Canadian Airlines in the late 1990s, for example) and the manufacturing sector. One of the most prominent examples of the latter was the purchase of Algoma Steel in Sault Ste. Marie in 1992. The company had been operating in the community since 1901 and employed about 5,000 workers at the beginning of the 1990s. If the company had folded, the community would have been devastated.[41]

Through their union (the United Steel Workers of America) and with the assistance of loan guarantees from the New Democratic provincial government, workers negotiated the purchase of a majority of shares in the company. Cost savings were obtained by a voluntary pay reduction and through a plan to eliminate 1,600 jobs through attrition. The company has been running successfully since the employee buyout, under the direction of a 13-person board of directors, four of whom are nominated by the union. When the workers bought the company, they also took the opportunity to reorganize the front-line management system, replacing a hierarchical system with a team-work approach. Thus, in this case, aspects of both an industrial democracy model and a participative management system were introduced. The employee buyout was economically successful and also led to greater control over the labour process by workers.[42]

When failing companies are rescued by their employees, the new management systems can take many different forms. However, more often than not, traditional management schemes are maintained. The Algoma Steel example is an exception in this respect. Typically, new worker-owners do not attempt to introduce industrial democracy or innovative participative management schemes. Instead, as shareholders they delegate authority back to a management team, although job security in return for wage concessions is usually negotiated at the same time. Thus, after the buyout has occurred and production resumes, the worker–management relationship would resemble that in a company with an employee share ownership plan (ESOP). But, there is still one critical difference. With majority ownership, workers retain the option to change the governance structure of the organization.

Research has shown that worker-owners typically report more job satisfaction and exhibit more commitment to the organization than workers in conventional companies. But it is unclear whether it is ownership per se that makes the difference. However, the research is clear on the viability of firms bought by their employees. Most companies bought by workers become successful once again. The chances of success are increased when all the participants, including the union if one is present, support the buyout plan. In addition, workers typically need expert advice to assist them in deciding how to restructure the organization since major changes (often in wage rates and staffing) are usually needed. Government support is also critical, particularly with respect to financing, since many lenders are reluctant to gamble on worker buyouts, despite their better-than-average track record.

Overall, the evidence is quite clear on the profitability and viability of worker-owned firms, whether they are employee buy-outs or producer co-operatives (see below). A recent meta-analysis of 43 published studies (Doucouliagos 1995) showed that profit-sharing, worker ownership, and other forms of formal participation in decision making (industrial democracy, in the language we have used) are associated with higher levels of productivity. The impact was strongest in worker-owned firms, compared to firms with ESOPs or some type of formalized industrial democracy.

Producer Cooperatives

Producer cooperatives have a long history in North America and Europe (Oakeshott 1978). The first examples appeared in Britain over a century ago as workers looked for alternatives to the exploitative excesses of early capitalism. However, the producer cooperative movement was overshadowed by another form of collective response by workers, the formation of trades unions (see Chapter 7). Nevertheless, the cooperative alternative continues. In Atlantic Canada, for example, records show that 221 worker cooperatives were founded between 1900 and 1987. Three-quarters came into existence after 1975. Recent estimates indicate that about 300 producer cooperatives are functioning in Canada, with a total of about 6,000 members.[43] About 60 percent of these organizations are in Quebec, in large part because the provincial government has put in place programs that provide financing for producer cooperatives. While producer cooperatives are not a widespread phenomenon, and those that exist are quite small, they nonetheless offer another alternative to conventional employer–employee relationships. Examples in Canada include everything from construction companies to day care centres, taxi firms to fish farms, as well as small manufacturing companies, consulting firms, restaurants, and forestry management firms.

Producer cooperatives must be distinguished from other collective enterprises, including consumer cooperatives (such as co-op food stores) or housing co-ops, in which a number of individuals or families jointly own and maintain a dwelling or housing complex. They are also different from marketing co-ops (the wheat pools set up by Western farmers are the best example) and financial services co-ops, such as credit unions. While sharing with these other organizations a general commitment to collective ownership and shared risk-taking, *producer cooperatives* are distinguished by their function as collective producers of goods or services.[44]

Distinguishing producer cooperatives from other types of worker-owned enterprises is not quite as easy. However, there are several characteristics that do stand out. First, to a much greater extent, producer cooperatives have typically been established because of a desire to collectively solve problems faced by their members. For example, discontent with low pay and erratic work schedules have led some truckers to leave the large companies they worked for and set up their own trucking cooperatives. On a much larger scale, some employee buyouts of a company have been instigated by imminent job loss and the possibility of a community's economic base disappearing. Thus, unlike most enterprises in a capitalist economy where profit-making is the first priority, producer cooperatives have a social purpose interwoven with the need to be successful in the marketplace. Second, central to the philosophy of producer cooperatives is a commitment to the democratic principle of "one person—one vote." This defining characteristic would eliminate companies with employee share ownership plans (ESOPs) and many examples of employee buyouts. Third, and related to the second point, producer cooperatives typically do not allow non-members to own shares. As a result, members cannot benefit financially from the success of the cooperative by selling shares. Instead, some arrangements are usually made to reimburse members for their own contributions when they leave the organization.

It has often been assumed that producer cooperatives, like employee buyouts, are typically a response to difficult economic times. In other words, workers decide to set up a cooperative, or take over a company and reshape it into a cooperative, because their jobs are at risk. However, analysis of the cooperative experience in Atlantic Canada over the course of this century indicates no relationship between economic cycles and the formation of producer cooperatives (Staber 1993). This suggests that the social goals of producer cooperatives' members may be as important as their economic goals.

Small producer cooperatives can survive in a capitalist economy. The study of Atlantic Canada showed an estimated median lifespan of 17 years for rural producer cooperatives and 25 years for those in urban settings (Staber 1993: 140). But producer cooperatives face many challenges. It is difficult to finance such enterprises, since banks are often skeptical of their ability to survive. This problem is also faced by other small businesses and by employees attempting to buy out their company. In situations where producer cooperatives are set up as a solution to high unemployment caused by economic downturns, the new worker-owned enterprises are at a disadvantage from the outset. And, as with any attempts to democratize workplaces, participants in producer cooperatives have to learn how to work collectively toward common goals, something that is not taught or encouraged in a competitive capitalist society.

Do producer cooperatives offer workers greater control over their work tasks and the organization as a whole? Some accounts suggest that many are organized much like other profit-oriented work organizations (Nightingale 1982: 227), but this conclusion may be the result of including as examples companies with ESOPs and employee buyouts that maintain traditional management approaches. Leslie Brown (1997) draws the opposite conclusion, arguing that producer cooperatives actually incorporate many of the democratizing and work-humanizing features of workplace reform promised, but not always delivered, by the many new management approaches of the past decades. She also concludes that producer cooperatives are a viable solution to problems of community economic development that have not been solved by attempts to encourage traditional forms of capitalist enterprise in underdeveloped regions of the country.[45]

The most successful producer cooperative is found in Mondragon, a city in the Basque region of Spain, where some 20,000 worker-owners run a wide range of firms, including heavy equipment manufacturers and consumer goods and services companies. Each worker has an economic stake in the enterprise where she or he works and, as a member of the firm's general assembly, establishes policies, approves financial plans, and elects members to a supervisory board, which, in turn, appoints managers. Mondragon co-ops have replaced the private ownership of industry in this region with a system of collective ownership and control. By all accounts, these co-ops have achieved high levels of growth, productivity, and employment creation, strong links with the community, harmonious labour relations, a satisfying and non-alienating work environment, and a close integration between workplace and community (Whyte and Whyte 1988; Macleod 1997).

Mondragon's success is linked, among other things, to the Basque region's decades-long struggle for greater autonomy from Spain, the destruction of the area's industrial base during the Spanish Civil War in the 1930s, and support from the local Catholic church and unions. This unique historical mix of political, cultural, and economic circumstances has sometimes been used as an argument that producer cooperatives could not be successful in other settings such as North America. Granted, it is never easy to transplant production systems from one cultural and political context to another. But, if we are willing to accept that Japanese lean production or German co-determination, for example, offer alternatives to the North American approach to organizing workplaces, we should not ignore the Mondragon-style producer cooperative alternative (Macleod 1997).

CONCLUSION

In this chapter, we have debated the assumptions and conclusions of the mainstream management literature outlined in Chapter 5. From a critical perspective influenced by the labour process research tradition, we focused on power relationships within the workplace, management attempts to control workers, and their efforts to regain control over their labour. We questioned whether new management models and new computer-based technologies really empower workers and allow them to enhance their skills. And we critically scrutinized the systems that have been put into place to improve workers' health and safety. We then shifted our focus to an examination of alternative ways of organizing work that might reduce conflict and provide workers with more control over the labour process and their work organizations.

Several general conclusions sum up this discussion. First, concentration of power in the hands of owners and managers continues to characterize workplaces within our society, and the desire to increase profits continues to overshadow any commitment to empowering workers. Managers continue to systematically control workers, although their methods have changed. Second, employees' expectations of reasonable wages and working conditions, and their desire for more control over the labour process, are frequently at odds with the goals of management. Consequently, conflict and resistance are often present in the workplace, manifested in many different ways.

Third, it is apparent that the new management models intended to empower workers and enhance their skills, while reducing conflict and improving productivity, have frequently not lived up to their potential. In fact, in some cases, the rhetoric of new management models has been used to gain additional control over workers. New technologies have the potential to raise workers' skill levels, humanize the workplace, and improve the quality of life for society as a whole. We have seen evidence of this but have also observed how information technology has been used to control workers and to eliminate jobs. Fourth, new technologies and management models are created and implemented by human beings. The social problems generated by these "hard" and "soft" technologies are a result of human choices. By the same reasoning, it is our responsibility to try to use these technologies to improve working conditions, empower workers, create jobs, and reduce social inequality.

Workplace health and safety continues to be a contested issue in the workplace. Even so, our assessment of the systems put in place to address health and safety concerns reveals some evidence of workers and management finding common ground. When we examine different approaches to creating industrial democracy and examples of worker ownership, we observe that these alternative methods of organizing work offer considerable potential for worker empowerment and conflict reduction. Hence, our last and most general conclusion is that there are alternatives to traditional employment relationships within capitalism that deserve serious consideration.

Despite our emphasis on the need to examine worker resistance when analyzing the labour process, resistance has been only one of many themes in this chapter. In fact, we have talked more about management control systems, the deskilling debate, the impact of new technologies, and alternative approaches to organizing the workplace. In the next chapter, we examine the primary collective vehicle for worker resistance in Canada over the past century, namely, the organized labour movement.

NOTES

1. Information on Air Canada and Nortel layoffs from the *Globe and Mail* (2 August, 2001, p. A1) and the *Edmonton Journal* (19 June, 2001, p. F1), respectively.

2. CAMI workers quoted by CAW–Canada Research Group on CAMI (1993: 55); Starbucks workers, CBC technicians, and B.C. nurses quoted in the *Globe and Mail* (4 July, 1997, p. B1), (15 April, 1999, p. B1), and (10 August, 2001, p. A6), respectively.

3. Paul Mantoux, quoted by Beaud (1983: 66).

4. George Cohon, president of McDonald's Restaurants of Canada, Ltd., quoted in *Report on Business* (October 1990: B8).

5. See Littler (1982), Tanner et al. (1992), Smith (1994), and Warhurst (1998) for useful critiques. Thompson and Smith (2000/1) make the interesting observation that, had Braverman not died two years after publishing his book, he might well have responded effectively to some of his critics. Also see Heron and Storey (1986), Wood (1989b), and Sturdy et al. (1992) for labour process case studies.

6. See Littler and Salaman (1982), Spenner (1983), Penn and Scattergood (1985), Attewell (1987), Form (1987), Diprete (1988), Gallie (1991), Lewis (1995), Burris (1998) Gallie et al. (1998), and Thompson and Smith (2000/1) for contributions to the deskilling debate. Canadian studies addressing this issue include Heron and Storey (1986), Lowe (1987, 1997), Myles (1988), Hunter (1988), Clement and Myles (1994: Chapter 4), Russell (1995, 1999), and Hughes and Lowe (2000).

7. See Jenson (1989), Horrell et al. (1990), Gaskell (1991), Wajcman (1991), Hughes (1996), and Clarke (2000) on the gendered nature of occupational skills.

8. Edwards (1979); also see Gordon et al. (1982). For critiques of their theory, see Penn (1982) and Nolan and Edwards (1984).

9. Wallace (1995a) uses the term "corporatist control" to describe the high level of organizational commitment among professionals.

10. See DeTienne (1993), Menzies (1996: 117-22), Frenkel et al. (1995), and Sewell (1998) on workplace electronic surveillance, and Haggerty and Ericson (2000) on the increase in surveillance in general in postmodern society.

11. Graham (1993, 1995); CAW–Canada Research Group on CAMI (1993: 30).

12. See Spenner (1983, 1990), Form (1987), Vallas (1990), Gallie (1991), Clement and Myles (1994: 74–75), Noble (1994), and Smith (2001) on the definition and measurement of skill.

13. Jenson (1989); Steinberg (1990); Gaskell (1991); Clarke (2000).

14. Clement and Myles (1994: 72); also see Spenner (1983), Myles (1988), Hunter (1988), Gallie et al. (1998), de Witte and Steijn (2000), and Burris (1998).

15. See Russell (1995, 1997, 1999), Menzies (1996), and Rinehart et al. (1997) for examples.

16. Myles (1988); Gallie (1991); Burris (1998); Hughes and Lowe (2000).

17. Milkman and Pullman (1991); Stewart and Garrahan (1995).

18. See Hughes (1989, 1996), Zuboff (1988), Block (1990), Idle and Cordell (1994), Rifkin (1995), Noble (1995), Menzies (1996), Maclarkey (1997), Burris (1998), and Hughes and Lowe (2000) on the impact of new technologies on work.

19. On robotics, see Robertson and Wareham (1987, 1989), Block (1990: 100–03), and Suplee (1997).

20. See Milkman (1997) for an excellent study of technological change, new management strategies, and downsizing and layoffs in the same factory.

21. Robertson and Wareham (1987: 28); also see Noble (1985, 1995) and Block (1990: 100–03).

22. See, for example, Hughes (1989, 1996), Zuboff (1988); Fearfull (1992), Menzies (1996), McMullen (1996), Lowe (1997), and Maclarkey (1997).

23. Ewan (1976: 11), quoted by Swift (1995: 30).

24. See Fearfull (1992), DeTienne (1993), Noble (1995), Frenkel et al. (1995), Menzies (1996: 117-22), and Sewell (1998).

25. Rifkin (1995: 3); for equally concerned but somewhat less pessimistic views, see Idle and Cordell (1994), Sherman and Judkins (1995), Noble (1995), Swift (1995), Menzies (1996), and Richardson (1996).

26. McLuhan (1964: 56), quoted by Menzies (1996: 44).

27. Giles and Jain (1989: 339); also see Kumar et al. (1991: 62–65).

28. Mahon (1987); several recent Canadian studies have also demonstrated how a strong union (Clarke and Haiven 1999) and a positive labour relations climate (Smith 1999b) can influence workers' willingness to accept change; see Smith et al. (1995, 1997) and Smucker et al. (1998) for comparisons of the industrial relations environment in Canada and Sweden. Yun (1995) proposes that low unemployment rates in Singapore have meant that workers have not been as concerned about technological change, while Smith

(1999b) argues that Canadian workers who believe that they can find another job, if laid off, are less likely to oppose workplace changes.

29. See Wells (1986), Robertson and Wareham (1987), and Rinehart (2001: Chapter 7) on QWL.

30. For additional critiques of TQM see Webb (1996), Sosteric (1996), Menzies (1996: 102–108), Redman et al. (1997), Fox and Sugiman (1999), McCabe (1999), and Knights and McCabe (2000). The last two studies in this list also provide examples of workers, individually and via their union, resisting management's attempts to gain greater control of the labour process. For a study that concludes that TQM benefits workers, see Rosenthal et al. (1997).

31. See Wood (1989a), Jenson (1989), Neis (1991), MacDonald (1991), and Fox and Sugiman (1999) for critiques of flexible specialization.

32. Graham (1993, 1995), Rinehart et al. (1997), Kochan et al. (1997), Russell (1999), Benders (2000), Rinehart (2001: 160-63); see Nilsson (1996) for a somewhat more positive assessment.

33. Walters and Haines (1988), Walters (1985); also see Sass (1995).

34. See Lowe and Northcott (1986: Chapter 1), Karasek and Theorell (1990), and Jex (1998) on job stress research. Kompier et al. (1994) note that Sweden, the United Kingdom, and the Netherlands recognize work-related stress in their health and safety legislation, while Germany and France do not.

35. Sass (1995: 123); elsewhere, Sass (1996) criticizes the organized labour movement for accepting the status quo in terms of legislation and policies regarding health and safety.

36. See Russell (1990: Chapter 3) and Rinehart (2001: 48–50) on early work councils in Canada. Also see Guzda (1993) on the U.S. situation.

37. Guzda (1993); Beaumont (1995: 101–08).

38. This discussion of Sweden draws on Erikson et al. (1986–1987), Alestalo and Kuhnle (1986–1987), Milner (1989), and Olsen (1991). Also see Smith et al. (1995, 1997) and Smucker et al. (1998), who compare the effects of different labour market policies in Canada and Sweden on workers' reactions to technological change.

39. Sandberg (1994); Smith et al. (1995, 1997); Smucker et al. (1998); Nilsson (1996).

40. See Pendleton et al. (1996: 212) for British estimates, and Gunderson et al. (1995: 418) for Canadian data. For a useful overview of ESOPs in the U.S. labour market, see Bruno (1998) and Logue and Yates (1999).

41. Most of this discussion of worker buyouts is based on Gunderson et al. (1995). For more information on the Algoma Steel example, see Nishman (1995).

42. At the time this edition was being completed (late 2001), Algoma Steel was again in financial difficulty because of low international steel prices. But the union was hopeful that a solution to the financing problem would be found, perhaps involving many early retirements as well as loan guarantees by government.

43. Staber (1993) provides the Atlantic Canada figures while Quarter (1992) presents the national count. Also see Co-operatives Secretariat (2000) for a similar estimate of the prevalence of producer cooperatives in Canada and a dozen case studies of successful organizations of this type.

44. This discussion of producer cooperatives is based on Nightingale (1982: 224–33), Quarter (1992: 27-32), Staber (1993), Cornforth (1995), Lindenfeld and Wynn (1997), and Brown (1997).

45. Brown (1997); also see Staber (1993) and Macleod (1997), who make similar arguments.

UNIONS, INDUSTRIAL RELATIONS, AND STRIKES

INTRODUCTION

We begin this chapter with three examples of the challenges facing Canada's unions. Each example highlights some of the key issues that likely will dominate labour–management relations in the coming years.[1]

- At midnight on March 25, 1997, more than 10,000 unionized workers at 73 Canada Safeway supermarkets in Alberta went on strike, rejecting the company's "final offer." The battle lines were drawn in what became a long and bitter dispute. The workers, represented by the United Food and Commercial Workers Union, had been attempting to negotiate a new contract with the California-based corporation for over a year. The issues at stake—a living wage, concessions, flexibility—resonated throughout workplaces in the 1990s, making this strike emblematic of broader trends in industrial relations. The Alberta public, not known for its pro-union views, widely supported the striking workers on the principle of fairness. The firm lost an estimated 70 percent of its customers for the duration of the strike. Still, the dispute dragged on for 11 weeks. Despite pressure from clergy and other community leaders, the government would not intervene. In the end, workers made very modest gains—part-timers were guaranteed 12 hours weekly—but the company got a two-tier wage structure with three-quarters of its workers in the lower tier.

- In Canada's restaurant industry we can detect signs that young employees are seeking union representation. More than anything, these workers want decent treatment and respect. Yet two failed attempts in the mid-1990s by McDonald's workers to unionize, one led by a 17-year-old high school student in Orangeville, Ontario, attest to the enormous barriers corporations can erect to union representation. In 1998, the Canadian Auto Workers' (CAW) breakthrough in gaining certification at the Squamish, BC, McDonald's was short-lived, with the workers later voting to decertify the union. Around the same time, the 20-something Starbucks workers at 12 Vancouver cafés also had turned to the CAW. They wanted management to make good on its rhetoric of calling employees "partners" by granting them more say. Starbucks, like other multi-location firms in the low-wage consumer-services sector, feared a domino effect. So it extended the wage terms of the union's first contract to non-union employees, removing a major motivation for other Starbucks workers to join. These events at McDonald's and Starbucks send clear messages to unions and potential recruits: exercising the right to collective bargaining in such workplaces is very difficult and, for unions, costly.

- Our third example is from the public sector. The ongoing troubles in health care across the country erupted into a series of job actions in 2001. These range from physicians closing their offices for several days, to nurses refusing overtime, to hospital support staff going on wildcat strikes. Sparking these protests are a decade of deteriorating working conditions and rising workloads due to cutbacks, declining real pay levels, and a lack of say in restructuring. One result is a serious shortage of nurses. In July 2001 this volatile mix erupted in Nova Scotia, where the province's 9,000 unionized health care workers were slapped with the most draconian anti-strike law in Canada, a law that set heavy fines and did not permit arbitration as a dispute resolution mechanism. In defiance, the workers threatened mass resignation. This would have crippled the province's health care system and speeded the exodus of workers to other parts of Canada or the United States. The government had little choice but to back down on its legislation and to send the dispute, which revolved largely around workloads and pay, to a form of binding arbitration. But the damage to employment relationships, especially trust and commitment, will take years to heal.

Viewed from a distance, these three examples raise questions that go to the very heart of contemporary *employee–employer relations*, a topic we raised in Chapter 6 and continue here. The Safeway, McDonald's, and Starbucks cases pit the free-market principles of capitalism against the rights of workers to collective bargaining, a decent wage, fair treatment and economic security. The nurses' dispute reveals the very same issues in the public sector. When is it justifiable for market pressures, or "the public good," to take precedence over the rights and interests of employees? What responsibilities do employers have to their employees? Is there an inherent conflict between workers' desires for good jobs and employers' goals of profits, flexibility, and competitiveness? Conversely, to what degree are interests between workers and employers shared? Are there circumstances under which labour and management can cooperate to their mutual benefit? What is the role of government in regulating the relations between labour and capital? Why do workers join a union in the first place? Finally, what improvements in wages and working conditions have unions achieved through collective bargaining?

These are the sorts of industrial relations issues that will be examined in this chapter. From a sociological perspective, we will focus on power, conflicts, and compromises over the distribution of resources in the workplace, as well as on employee collective action. These themes are highlighted in the study of unions, the major organizations representing the interests and aspirations of employees in capitalist societies. As we concluded in Chapter 6, much of the resistance to employers by North American workers has been channelled through their unions. We will, therefore, explore the nature and development of the labour movement in Canada, as well as how union–management relations are regulated through a complex legal framework. The causes and implications of industrial conflict are the subject of later sections in this chapter.

THEORETICAL PERSPECTIVES ON THE LABOUR MOVEMENT

We can begin to understand why unions developed in the first place by reviewing some of the early theories of the labour movement. No single issue stands out as the driving force of unionization. Rather, workers historically have rallied collectively to oppose the imposition of arbitrary management power, to protect their jobs and retain some semblance of control over the labour process, and to obtain improvements in rights, wages, and working conditions.

Why Do Workers Unionize?

In a classic work on British trade unionism, Sidney and Beatrice Webb (1894/1911) suggested that workers' pursuit of higher wages expressed a more basic desire to reduce employer domination. Collective action could improve working conditions and reduce the competition for jobs that drives wages down. Furthermore, the Webbs argued that it could curb an employer's authority by instituting common rules governing the employment relationship. Selig Perlman (1928) later stressed the role of unions in controlling jobs. After studying the International Typographical Union, the oldest union in America, Perlman concluded that workers develop an awareness that jobs are scarce and must, therefore, be protected through unionization. Michael Poole sheds additional light on the emergence of the labour movement in his discussion of the various goals it pursued.[2] Unions can thus be viewed five different ways: as moral institutions, fighting against the injustices and inequities of capitalist industrialization; as revolutionary organizations intent on overthrowing capitalism; as psychological or defensive reactions against the threat early capitalism posed to workers' jobs; as responses to economic realities, aimed at achieving better wages and working conditions; and as political organizations extending workers' rights further into the industrial arena.

Generally speaking, the harsh working conditions endured by industrial workers in the late 19th century sparked the first major surge of unionization. Yet the basic idea that workers are motivated to unionize by the desire to gain greater control over their jobs, as well as fair treatment and just rewards, remains a dominant theme in industrial relations. Mainstream industrial relations theory views the *system of job regulation* as the core of worker– management relations.[3] In other words, the rules and regulations that form the basis of collective agreements are assumed to inject stability into employment relations by tilting the balance of power slightly away from management and toward workers.

However, this perspective overplays the importance of predictable and harmonious industrial relations, and downplays the frequency of conflict. That is, by focusing on the system of rules, regulations, and institutions governing industrial relations, the mainstream perspective does not question the existing distribution of power between workers and management. It also presents an incomplete picture of industrial relations, due to a narrow focus on the formal aspects of the system, such as legislation and collective bargaining. An equally important informal side involves the daily interaction between workers and employers, as "the rules of the game" are constantly being negotiated. It is, therefore, helpful to acknowledge that work is a power relationship in which conflict is always a possibility. As Richard Hyman (1975: 26) explains, "in every workplace there exists an invisible frontier of control, reducing some of the formal powers of the employer: a frontier which is defined and redefined in a continuous process of pressure and counter-pressure, conflict and accommodation, overt and tacit struggle." Echoing themes from Chapter 6, Hyman proposes a more critical perspective on industrial relations, defining it as the process of control over work relations—a process that especially involves unions.

Conflict and Cooperation in Union–Management Relations

It is important to understand the role of conflict in union management relations. Collective agreements, negotiated and administered under provincial and federal labour laws, seek to avoid open conflict. Indeed, the main thrust of modern industrial relations practice is the avoidance of conflict. Thus, for the system to operate with some degree of fairness and equity for workers, who on the whole are in the weaker bargaining position, there must be the threat of conflict that could disrupt the employer's business. A stock criticism of the Canadian industrial relations scene concerns its adversarial nature. A federal government task force on labour relations, responding to these concerns, explained the underlying conflict in these words:

Paradoxical as it may appear, collective bargaining is designed to resolve conflict through conflict, or at least through the threat of conflict. It is an adversary system in which two basic issues must be resolved: how available revenue is to be divided, and how the clash between management's drive for productive efficiency and the workers' quest for job, income and psychic security are to be reconciled (Canada 1969: 1, 19).

We must also view industrial relations as a continuous process. New problems regularly confront the parties in collective bargaining. Solutions for one side may create difficulties for the other, as in cases of wage rollbacks. Or an agreement may be based on compromises that both sides have trouble living with (for example, when a third-party arbitrator imposes a solution). Part of the difficulty is that workers and management have different definitions of social justice and economic reality.[4] Safeway considered competition from Superstore adequate justification for pursuing further economic concessions from its Alberta workers. Safeway employees considered it grossly unfair that the corporation would not share some of its healthy profits with them and replace the wage reductions they had already taken to improve its competitive position.

As pointed out in Chapter 5, work organizations typically have a division of labour that requires collective interdependence. Management, therefore, must balance the need to control employees with the necessity of achieving a workable level of cooperation and commitment from them. Stephen Hill (1981) has explored this basic tension and concludes that workers and managers must cooperate to provide goods or services. Yet in doing so, Hill notes, each side also strives to maximize its own interests. Workers aim for higher wages, better working conditions, and more autonomy in their jobs. Employers pursue higher profits, lower costs, and increased productivity. The chronic tension between these opposing interests forces tradeoffs on both sides, and may also generate open conflict. Of course, we must recognize that not all union–management negotiations are *a zero-sum game*: that is, a situation in which one side can gain something only if the other gives up something. Indeed, on some issues, such as improved health and safety conditions (see Chapter 6), negotiations can produce a win–win situation in which both workers and management benefit.

Unions as "Managers of Discontent"

There is a general consensus among scholars that the industrial relations systems in modern capitalist societies "keep the lid on conflict." Having observed the oppressive conditions under which mid-19th-century factory workers toiled, Marx concluded that eventually their misery and poverty would ignite a revolution. But, as Stephen Hill (1981: Chapter 7) points out, even Marxists, committed to the belief that capitalism pits the workers and bosses against each other in constant struggle, acknowledge that collective bargaining integrates workers into the existing economic system. For many Marxists, unionism itself embodies a basic contradiction by striving to solve workers' problems within the confines of capitalism. This is why Lenin, father of the Russian Revolution, dismissed trade unions as capable only of reform, not revolution. But to lay all the blame on capitalism is to ignore the basic dilemma of the distribution of scarce resources, which all societies must face (Crouch 1982: 37–38).

In some respects, then, unions function as *managers of discontent*.[5] Unions in Canada and other advanced capitalist societies channel the frustrations and complaints of workers into a carefully regulated dispute-resolution system. Unions help their members to articulate specific work problems, needs, or dissatisfactions. Solutions are then sought through collective bargaining, or through grievance procedures. In Canada, for example, labour legislation prohibiting strikes during the term of a collective agreement puts pressure on union leaders to contain any actions by rank-and-file members that could disrupt the truce with management. This may seem ironic, since unions developed in response to the deprivations suffered by workers in the early stages of industrial capitalism. But unions today operate in ways that contribute to the maintenance of capitalism, seeking reforms that smooth its rough edges.

In order to channel the discontent of their members, unions must legitimately represent the views of the majority of members. This raises the issue of internal *union democracy*. Generally speaking, unions are democratic organizations whose constitutions allow members to elect leaders regularly. Theoretically, this should make leaders responsive and accountable to rank-and-file members, translating their wishes into tangible collective bargaining goals. But, despite this, there has long been a sociological debate about the pitfalls on the road to union democracy.

Robert Michels was the first to investigate the problems of union bureaucracy and democracy. His study of German trade unions and the Social Democratic Party prior to World War I concluded that leaders in working-class organizations always dominate members. Michels's famous *iron law of oligarchy* draws on technical, organizational, and psychological explanations. According to this theory, leaders develop expert knowledge, which gives them power; once in office, leaders can control the organization to maintain their power; and, finally, the masses tend to identify with leaders, and expect them to exercise power on their behalf. But in Canada and elsewhere, we have recently witnessed the emergence of strong rank-and-file movements challenging entrenched union leadership cliques and, in effect, opposing oligarchic rule. Most unions today espouse democratic principles, but some have been more successful in putting these into practice than others. In fact, union officials seem to be constantly trying to increase the participation of rank-and-file members in union activities. Images of corrupt and autocratic leaders, while headlined by the media and reinforced by the history of a few unions (such as the infamous Seafarers' International Union led by Hal Banks) are far from typical. Thus, what Michels discovered was not a universal trait of unions, but a potential problem faced by all large bureaucratic organizations.[6]

WHAT DO UNIONS DO?

How do unions set goals and devise strategies to attain them? Of great interest to sociologists is why unions, rather than espousing revolutionary or even reformist aims, have engaged in largely conservative and defensive actions. Typically, the daily activities of unions focus on two types of goals: control over work and the rewards of work (Crouch 1982: Chapter 4). It is not inconceivable that demands for control over the work process could, if they escalated, spark radical challenges to the capitalist system of business ownership. Yet, historically, such demands often involved skilled craft workers fighting to defend their relatively privileged position in the labour market against the onslaught of modern production methods. Their goal, in short, was to preserve the status quo.

There are frequently compromises between control over the labour process and economic rewards. Workers may be forced by their immediate economic needs to pursue the latter to the exclusion of the former. In addition, employers are sometimes willing to give up more of their profits rather than concede to workers' greater decision-making authority. The emphasis on material gain rather than job control, known as *business unionism*, has become a hallmark of the North American labour movement. In the last decade, we can detect a shift away from business unionism toward what can be called *social unionism*. Public-sector unions, along with some leading private-sector unions such as the Canadian Auto Workers, have taken on a much broader agenda of reform, entering public debates about issues such as globalization, international human rights, and health care reform.[7]

Public Opinion about Unions

How does the public view the activities of unions? Canadian public opinion has become less favourable toward the role of unions in our society. Gallup polls in the 1950s asked respondents if they thought unions were good or bad for the country: 12 to 20 percent said unions were bad, while 60 to 69 percent said they were good. However, polls during the 1980s found an increase in "bad" responses to between 30 and 42 percent. One explanation of this declining support for unions is that in the last several decades, Canadians have become less trusting of major institutions. For example, a 1996 national Angus Reid poll found considerable cynicism toward corporations, the federal government, and unions, which can be interpreted as part of the shift in social values in a postindustrial society.[8] Thus, views about labour unions are part of the public's overall assessment of the institutions affecting their lives.

Public attitudes toward unions are, however, usually more ambiguous than suggested by Gallup polls. For example, in a study of Winnipeg and Edmonton residents, we found that individuals held both positive and negative images of unions, depending on the specific issues at stake (Krahn and Lowe 1984; Lowe and Krahn 1989). Many respondents believed that unions contributed to inflation, while also recognizing that they had achieved material gains for members. At a general level, this study identified two different images of unionism: a *big labour image* that sees unions as too powerful believes that they inflict harm on society, and thinks, therefore, that they require greater government regulation; and a *business unionism* image that focuses on the positive gains in wages and working conditions unions have made through collective bargaining. Both images are reinforced by the media.

Researchers also have linked non-union employees' attitudes toward unions to their level of support for joining a union (Barling, Fullagar and Kelloway 1992). This perspective has direct relevance for unions' future success. According to a national survey conducted by Canadian Policy Research Networks in 2000, 25 percent of non-union employees in Canada said it was likely or very likely they would join a union if one existed in their workplace or profession (Kumar, Lowe and Schellenberg 2001). Younger workers and members of visible minorities (including Aboriginals) expressed higher than average interest in joining a union. Lack of trust in one's employer, not having a supportive and healthy work environment, as well as dissatisfaction with pay and job security also are associated with support for joining a union. The relatively strong support for union joining among young workers is corroborated in other studies (Lowe and Rastin 2000). This bodes well for the labour movement, although it appears that workplace socialization reduces pro-union attitudes as these young workers gain more experience.

The Economic Impact of Unions

Unions benefit their members financially. Research by Canadian economists suggests that, on average, unionized workers earn about 10 percent more than nonunion workers do, with the impact being greater for women than men. However, this *union wage premium* has declined since the 1970s. But unions negotiate for more than wages. Consequently, union members are more than twice as likely to have pension plans provided by their employer. And unionized workers receive more paid vacations and holidays, and are more likely to have dental and medical plans and better job security than are comparable nonunion workers. Unions also contribute to reducing overall wage inequality in a nation's labour market. This is largely because the union impact on wages is greatest for workers in the lower and middle ranges of the income, education, and skill distributions. In other words, without unions income inequality in Canada would most likely rise. Indeed, in the United States and Britain growing income inequality has been linked, in part, to declining union membership.[9]

Access to these economic advantages of union membership depends mainly on where you work. In this regard, workplace size and type of employment matter. Unionization is significantly higher in large workplaces. Recall from earlier chapters that large firms make up much of the "core" sector of the economy, providing better wages and benefits, and are more likely to introduce new technologies and innovative forms of work organization. They are in a better competitive position than are smaller firms to provide decent wages and working conditions. In terms of employment type, recall from Chapters 2 and 3 that nonstandard jobs are often referred to as "bad jobs" because of their inadequate wages, security, and benefits—outcomes related to a lack of union representation (Kalleberg et al. 2000). Barriers to unionization include restrictive legislation and, until very recently, lack of interest among unions. The lack of union representation for temporary, part-time, and self-employed workers—groups that have been increasingly marginalized in the labour market—has become a recent research focus (Carré et al. 2000: Section IV; Vosko 2000).

Does the conventional wisdom that unions further their members' interests at public expense have a basis in fact? The most thorough analysis of what trade unions actually do is a study by two Harvard economists, Richard Freeman and James Medoff (1984: 5–11), who make a useful distinction between the two "faces" of unionism. The *monopoly* face represents unions' power to raise members' wages at the expense of employers and other workers. The *collective voice* face shifts attention to how unions democratize authoritarian workplaces, giving workers a collective voice in dealing with management. Freeman and Medoff admit that unions do impose some social and economic costs, but think that these are far outweighed by their positive contributions. Unions significantly advance workers' economic and political rights and freedoms. And, to the chagrin of their opponents, unions also boost productivity. As these researchers explain, unions improve productivity through lower employee turnover, better management performance, reduced hiring and training costs, and greater labour–management communication and cooperation. But because of higher wage costs, productivity gains do not necessarily make unionized firms more profitable.

Even though they are examining American unions, Freeman's and Medoff's conclusions deserve careful attention. They show that, in addition to raising members' wages relative to those of nonmembers, unions alter nearly every other measurable aspect of the operation of workplaces, from turnover to productivity to profitability to the composition of pay packages. The behaviour of workers and firms and the outcomes of their interactions differ substantially between the organized and unorganized sectors. On balance, unionization appears to improve rather than to harm the social and economic system.[10]

THE DEVELOPMENT OF THE CANADIAN LABOUR MOVEMENT

The Canadian labour movement has long been a major force in the economic life of the nation. Its history is tied to the development of capitalism. But, as workers in the late 19th and early 20th centuries reacted to the inequities and deprivations of their employment by organizing unions, they also had to fight to gain the right to do so. The story of unions is a human drama in which groups of workers often struggled against strong-willed employers and a reluctant state to gain higher wages, better working conditions, and some control over their daily working lives.

Craft Unionism

Skilled craft workers were the first to unionize. The earliest union in Canada was organized by printers in York (now Toronto). Carpenters, bricklayers, masons, cabinetmakers, blacksmiths, shoemakers, tailors—these were the pioneers of the union movement before the days of modern industry. A strike by Toronto printers in 1872 resulted in the Trade Unions Act, which for the first time legalized union activity. Prior to that, unions had been considered a conspiracy against the normal operations of business. Other significant events that laid the foundations for trade unionism in Canada were the Nine-Hour Movement in the 1870s, involving working-class agitation for shorter working hours, and the creation of the Trades and Labour Congress (TLC) in 1883 as the first central labour body.[11]

Craft pride based on the special skills acquired through a long apprenticeship, solidarity with fellow artisans, and a close integration of work and communities were the hallmarks of these early *craft unions*. Craftsmen (there were no women among them) were the aristocrats of the working class. Printers, for example, reinforced their status by referring to their work as a "profession." Like other crafts, shoemakers drew on a long heritage to bolster craft pride. "From medieval craft lore, the shoemakers brought forth St. Crispin as a symbol of their historic rights and their importance to the community," reports historian Greg Kealey (1980: 292).

Craft unions were organized according to specialized craft skills, and served their members in several important ways. They were benevolent societies, providing members with a form of social insurance years before the rise of the welfare state. They also protected their members' position in the labour market by regulating access to the craft, thus monopolizing its unique skills. Today, this would be referred to as a "labour market shelter" (see Chapter 3). And, as small local enterprises of the 19th century gave way to the factories and large corporations of the 20th, unions provided craftsmen with a defence against the erosion of their way of life. Artisans opposed scientific management, the mechanization and reorganization of craft production in factories, and other attempts by employers to undermine the skills and responsibilities on which their craft traditions were based. Moreover, the tightly knit social relations of working-class artisan communities—reinforced by educational institutes, parades, picnics, and other neighbourhood events—bolstered these reactions to the march of modern industry.[12]

Craft unions dominated the young Canadian labour movement well into the 20th century. These *international unions* were American-based and affiliated with the conservative American Federation of Labour (AFL). The iron moulders' union was the first international union to set down permanent Canadian roots, in 1859. This was a time when the labour market for many skilled trades spanned both sides of the Canada–U.S. border. The internationals quickly came to control the Canadian labour scene. At the 1902 convention of the TLC, the AFL unions purged their Canadian-based rivals by successfully moving that no organization duplicating one already in the AFL could be a member of the TLC. They thus stole power from more radical Canadian labour leaders (Babcock 1974).

Industrial Unionism

The craft principle underlying the early AFL unions contrasts with *industrial unionism*, where all workers in an industry are represented by the same union, regardless of their occupational skills. The Knights of Labour, the earliest industrial union in Canada, organized its first local assembly in Hamilton in 1875. For a brief period in the 1880s, they challenged the dominance of the AFL craft unions. Driven by an idealistic radicalism, the Knights' immediate goal was to organize all workers into a single union, regardless of sex, skill level, craft, or industry of employment. They saw their efforts ultimately leading to the abolition of the capitalist wage system and the creation of a new society. Their membership peaked in 1887, with more than 200 local assemblies representing workers in 75 occupations. A combination of factors led to the Knights' demise: rapid membership growth that made it difficult to maintain an idealistic philosophy; regular defeats at the hands of employers; internal political rivalries; the union's growing hostility with the AFL unions; and a recognition among craft workers that uniting with unskilled workers in industrial unions would jeopardize their privileged position. The Knights survived longer in Canada than south of the border, although by the early years of the 20th century they had all but disappeared (Kealey 1981b).

Only a handful of industrial unions surfaced in the early 20th century. Several were part of the rising tide of labour radicalism that reached a crest with the 1919 Winnipeg General Strike. There was a distinctive regional flavour to these working-class protests, as most were rooted in Western Canada. The Western Federation of Miners, an international union but the archrival of the AFL, gained a foothold in British Columbia mines. The radical ideology of the Chicago-based Industrial Workers of the World (the "Wobblies") attracted unskilled immigrants employed in lumbering, mining, agriculture, and railways in the West prior to World War I. The Wobblies advocated a form of *syndicalism*, which held that international industrial unions and general strikes are the main vehicles for working-class emancipation.

Our discussion would be incomplete without mention of the One Big Union (OBU). This revolutionary industrial union received widespread support in the Western provinces, particularly among miners, loggers, and transportation workers, around the time of the Winnipeg General Strike. The OBU called for secession from the conservative AFL and its Canadian arm, the TLC. Its support for the Russian Revolution brought counterattacks from employers, governments, and craft unions, and caused the union's eventual defeat in the 1920s.

Not until the 1940s did industrial unionism become firmly established in Canada. The breakthrough was the United Auto Workers' (UAW) milestone victory in 1937 against General Motors in Oshawa, Ontario. The UAW sprang up under the banner of the left-leaning Congress of Industrial Organizations (CIO) in the 1930s to organize unskilled and semiskilled workers in mass-production industries. Many of the initial forays into the auto, electrical, rubber, and chemical factories of corporate North America were led by communist organizers. Craft union leaders opposed the CIO largely on political grounds, despite the fact that Canadian workers embraced the CIO form of industrial unionism (Abella 1974; Moulton 1974).

In 1956 Canadian craft and industrial unions buried their differences, uniting skilled and unskilled workers within a single central labour organization. This marked the merger of the craft-based TLC and the industrial unions of the Canadian Congress of Labour, resulting in the creation of the Canadian Labour Congress (CLC). A similar merger of the AFL and the CIO had occurred one year earlier in the United States. The CLC remains Canada's "house of labour." Its affiliated unions represent 69 percent of union members in the country (Human Resources Development Canada, Workplace Information Directorate 2000: 68).

The CLC promotes the economic, political, and organizational interests of affiliated unions by providing research, education, and organizational and collective bargaining services, as well as by eliminating jurisdictional conflicts and organizational duplication. It sometimes becomes embroiled in inter-union disputes over jurisdictions and complaints about unions *raiding* each other's members. Prominent examples of such rivalries include the Canadian Auto Workers' (CAW) recruitment of Newfoundland fishery workers who were represented by the United Food and Commercial Workers International Union, and the raid on the Canadian Union of Postal Workers by the International Brotherhood of Electrical Workers. The CLC also has strong ties to the New Democratic Party, having taken a leading role in founding the party in 1961. The CLC has become active on the national political stage, for example, by forming coalitions with other community-based groups to oppose free trade. This more broadly based political action increased with the election of Bob White, the high-profile former head of the CAW, as CLC president in 1992.

Quebec Labour

The history and present character of the labour movement in Quebec contribute to the distinctiveness of social and economic life in that province (Boivin and Déom 1995; Lipsig-Mummé 1987). Quebec labour's history is a fascinating topic in its own right, and deserves more than the brief treatment we can afford to give it here. Many of the issues central to Canada's ongoing constitutional debates are amplified in the arena of labour relations. For example, industrial relations have been shaped by a different legal framework in Quebec (its laws are derived from the Civil Code of France, rather than British-based common law). A more interventionist state role has created a higher degree of centralized bargaining than in other provinces, as well as resulting in some innovative legislation such as the 1977 anti-strikebreaking law. And nationalist politics have left an indelible mark on union policies and priorities. Indeed, the question of special representation for Quebec on the executive of the Canadian Labour Congress at the 1992 CLC convention raised the spectre of a split between the CLC and the Quebec Federation of Labour, which represents CLC affiliates in that province.

The development of unions in Quebec followed a different path from that of the rest of Canada. For example, in the early 20th century the Catholic Church organized unions that, unlike their counterparts elsewhere, emphasized the common interests of employers and employees. During the years that Premier Maurice Duplessis and the ultraconservative Union Nationale party held power (from 1936 to 1960), repressive state actions attempted to stifle union development. Worker militancy flared up in response, the most violent manifestations being the 1949 miners' strike at Asbestos and the 1957 Murdochville copper miners' strike. Some analysts view these strikes as major catalysts in Quebec's Quiet Revolution, which ushered in major social, economic, and political reforms in the 1960s.

During this period, the old Catholic unions cut their ties with the church, becoming one of the main central labour organizations in the province (the CNTU, or Confederation of National Trade Unions) and adopting an increasingly radical stance. Hence the Quebec Federation of Labour, made up of CLC-affiliated unions, differs from its counterparts in other provinces; it represents a minority of union members in the province and operates in a more independent manner. Another influential union organization is the Quebec Teachers' Federation. Thus, there is no unified Quebec labour movement, although these central organizations have banded together on occasion, the most notable example being the 1972 Common Front strike by some 200,000 public sector workers against government policies.

THE ROLE OF THE CANADIAN STATE IN INDUSTRIAL RELATIONS

Canada's contribution to the quest for industrial peace has been the development of a legislative and administrative framework that casts the state into the role of *impartial umpire*, mediating between labour and capital. The architect of this system was William Lyon Mackenzie King, the first federal minister of labour and later a Liberal prime minister. King's 1907 Industrial Disputes Investigation Act (IDIA) became the cornerstone of Canada's modern industrial relations policy. The act provided for compulsory *conciliation* (fact finding) in disputes during a "cooling off" period, a tripartite board of *arbitration*, and special treatment of public interest disputes involving public services. At first the act was applied to disputes in coal mines and railways. Its scope was extended during World War I, and, in the 1950s its principles were incorporated into provincial legislation. In some instances, the state used the powers of the act to legislate an end to strikes. There is little question that this sort of intervention has shaped the pattern of industrial conflict in Canada – some would argue in the interests of employers (Craven 1980; Huxley 1979).

State intervention in industrial conflict is not a 20th-century invention, however. Claire Pentland, for example, documents the role of the British army in suppressing unrest among colonial labourers building the Rideau Canal in 1827. He concludes: "Intervention by the Canadian state on behalf of employers in more recent years should not be regarded as novelties, but as fruits of what employers and officials learned about labour problems in the middle of the nineteenth century" (Pentland 1981: 196). Yet, it was the 1907 IDIA that marked the first major step toward the institutionalization of industrial conflict through the control of law.[13]

We can identify four major phases in the development of the legal framework for industrial relations in Canada (Riddell 1986). In the first, or pre-Confederation phase, common law prohibited collective bargaining. The second phase was entered with the 1872 Trade Unions Act, passed by the Conservative government of Sir John A. Macdonald. This neutralized the legal restrictions on unionism, but did not grant workers positive legal rights or protections that facilitated collective bargaining. The National War Labour Order, regulation P.C. 1003, launched the third, or modern, phase in 1944. Modelled on the 1935 U.S. National Labour Relations Act (Wagner Act), P.C. 1003 granted employees in the private sector collective bargaining rights, set down union certification procedures, spelled out a code of unfair labour practices, and established a labour relations board to administer the law. These measures paved the way for a postwar labour–management pact designed to maintain industrial peace. This truce was enshrined in federal legislation in 1948 and in subsequent provincial legislation.

Another milestone in the legal entrenchment of *collective bargaining rights* came out of a 1945 strike by the United Auto Workers at the Ford Motor Company in Windsor. The *Rand Formula*, named after Justice Ivan Rand of the Supreme Court, whose ruling was instrumental in settling the strike, provided for union security through a *union shop* and *union dues checkoff.* According to the Rand Formula, while no one should be required to join a union, because a union must act for the benefit of all employees in a workplace it is justifiable to automatically deduct union dues from the paycheques of all employees in a workplace regardless of whether or not they actually belong to the union.

The fourth phase involved the rise of public-sector unions. The movement toward full-fledged public-sector unionism began in Saskatchewan in 1944. The real push, however, started when Quebec public employees were granted collective bargaining rights in 1964. Another major breakthrough was the 1967 Public Service Staff Relations Act, which opened the door to unions in the federal civil service.

The intent of all these legislative changes was to establish industrial peace. It is obvious that one of their unintended effects was to spur the growth of unions. But the goal of conflict reduction should not be underestimated. The centrepiece of the 1907 IDIA was the regulation of work stoppages through compulsory postponement of strikes and lockouts, provisions for mediation or conciliation, the banning of strikes or lockouts during the term of a collective agreement, and alternative means of dispute resolution. The act also made strikes or lockouts illegal in key industries (transportation, communications, mines, and public utilities) until a board of inquiry had studied the problem and its conciliation report had been made public. These methods of *institutionalizing conflict* have been fine-tuned over the years. But work stoppages are still illegal during the term of a collective agreement (although they do occur) and the state has taken away the right to strike altogether from certain public employees who perform essential services.

Some analysts would argue that industrial relations entered a coercive phase during the 1980s. Leo Panitch and Donald Swartz view government imposition of wage controls, more restrictive trade union legislation, and the use of courts to end strikes as signals of the end of "free collective bargaining" as established by the industrial relations system set out in the 1948 federal legislation. Panitch and Swartz characterize this new era as *permanent exceptionalism*, reflecting how the suspension of labour's rights and more heavy-handed state intervention that were once the exception have become the rule.[14] As we shall see below, there is now considerable debate over whether Canadian industrial relations have entered troubled times.

UNION MEMBERSHIP TRENDS

Canadian Union Membership Growth and Stabilization

Figure 7.1 traces union membership growth in Canada since 1911. In 2000, there were more than 4 million union members, representing 32 percent of the nonagricultural paid workforce.[15] Considering that only 4.9 percent of all nonagricultural paid employees belonged to unions in 1911, this is an impressive record of expansion. This percentage measures *union density* and reflects the proportion of actual union members to potential members. The exclusion of agriculture, where most workers are self-employed and are, therefore, ineligible for union membership, allows more accurate comparisons with earlier historical periods (when agriculture was a much larger sector) and with other countries at different levels of industrialization. However, some employees in agriculture belong to unions. And unlike some countries, labour legislation in Canada usually prohibits managers and supervisors from joining.[16]

It is also important to note that collective representation and collective bargaining extend beyond union members. A slightly higher percentage of workers are covered by collective agreements since, in some cases, nonmembers in a unionized workplace are entitled to the wages and benefits negotiated by the union. In 1999, there were a quarter of a million Canadian workers in this situation. Among them were supervisory employees who are excluded because of their management role, new hires on probation, and individuals who because of their religious or other personal beliefs opt not to join. Furthermore,

FIGURE 7.1 *Union Membership in Canada, 1911—2000*

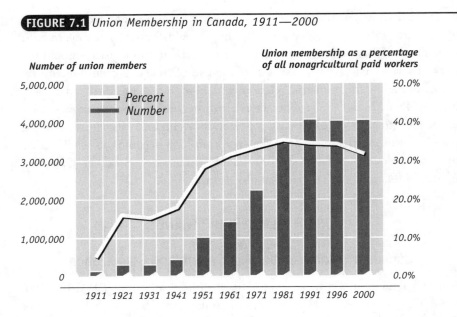

Source: For 1911-1981: Human Resources Development Canada, Workplace Information Directorate, *Directory of Labour Organizations in Canada* 1996. Ottawa: Canada Communication Group-Publishing; For 1991-2000: "Union membership in Canada - 2000," *Workplace Gazette* 3(3) 2000, p. 69 (http://labour.hrdc-drhc.gc.ca/milieudeltravail_workplace/gazette/articles//gaze_articles.cfm] Reproduced with permission of the Minister of Public Works and Government Services Canada.

Canadian labour law permits nonunion forms of collective representation, such as staff associations, which represent 5 percent of all employees. Finally, another 9 percent of employees belong to professional associations, and some of these set wages and working conditions for members.[17]

Scanning the chart, we can identify three major spurts in membership growth. The first two coincided with the two World Wars. This is not surprising because national mobilization for these wars resulted in economic growth, labour shortages, and the need for a high level of cooperation between employers and employees, all of which are key ingredients for successful union recruitment.

In the years during and immediately following World War II, Canada's contemporary industrial relations system took shape. Massive changes in the size, composition, legal rights, and goals of unions have occurred since the 1940s. The third growth spurt took place in the 1970s. The rise of *public-sector unions* in that decade, largely facilitated by supportive legislation, brought many civil servants, teachers, nurses, and other public employees into organized labour's fold.

In the three decades since 1971, union density has remained at about one-third of nonagricultural paid employment, hitting a peak of 37.2 percent in 1984. In part, the decline since that year occured because two recessions and industrial restructuring cut deeply into the traditional membership strength of unions in manufacturing and other blue-collar occupations. Similarly, budget cuts and downsizing in the public sector during the 1990s eroded membership ranks. Furthermore, employer pressures for concessions and the whittling away of collective bargaining rights by governments and the courts have contributed to a more hostile climate for labour relations. Despite these adversities, Canadian unions have held their own by adapting to these harsher realities, although membership numbers have levelled off in the 1990s – which, in an expanding labour force, results in a slight relative decline in union density.

The labour movement has undergone organizational changes as well. A notable trend is consolidation, resulting from mergers and membership growth since the 1960s. In 1968, there were 14 large unions (30,000 or more members), accounting for just under half of total union membership. By 2000, 32 unions had memberships of 30,000 or more, and these made up 75 percent of total union membership in the country.[18] There has also been an upswing in the number of small unions (under 1,000 members), but this has had a minor effect on the process of consolidation. One of the defining features of the Canadian labour movement is the large number of locals. In 2000, the 271 national and international unions comprised 15,674 *locals*, the basic self-governing unit of the labour movement and the legal entity for collective bargaining. Membership in locals ranges from just a few members to more than 45,000. In short, despite consolidations, Canadian labour remains fragmented and, consequently, collective bargaining is very decentralized. Unlike some European nations, where industry-wide national bargaining is the norm, the Canadian pattern of single-establishment, single-union bargaining results in thousands of collective agreements in effect at any one time.

A Comparative Perspective on Canadian Unions

A comparative perspective on Canada's unions provides insights about the nature of union–employer relations, and how these are institutionalized into national systems of industrial relations. Figure 7.2 provides two key measures for 12 countries: union membership density and the percentage change in density between 1985 and 1995. Keep in mind, though, that these comparisons are approximate because countries collect these data in somewhat different ways. As we noted above, density measures the extent of union membership in the non-agricultural workforce. Through their unions, these workers engage in *collective bargaining*, the decision-making process in which union and management negotiate wages, benefits, hours, and other employment conditions for a group of workers, resulting in a *collective agreement* (or contract) (OECD 1994: Chapter 5; Adams 1995).

In terms of union density, Canada is higher than many European countries, Australia and New Zealand, the United States and Japan, but lower than the Scandinavian countries (Norway, Sweden) and Austria. However, union density reveals only part of the strength of unions; collective bargaining coverage also must be considered. In Europe, it is more common than in Canada, the United States, or Japan for workers who are not union members to have terms and conditions of employment set by collective agreements. For example, in France, the Netherlands, and Germany, where relatively few wage and salary earners are union members, between 80 and 90 percent are covered by the provisions of collective agreements that these unions negotiate (International Labour Office 1997).

What accounts for these crossnational differences? In North America, key factors are management's traditional opposition to unions, labour laws that make the certification process for new bargaining units difficult, and a decentralized industrial relations system based in local workplaces. In Japan, where density and coverage are similar, collective bargaining also is decentralized and firm-based. But, unlike North America, in many European countries there is much greater coordination within each industrial sector. With the exception of Sweden, where the vast majority of workers eligible for union membership actually belong, countries with even moderate levels of union density can have extensive collective bargaining coverage because centrally negotiated contracts apply to most workers in a sector.

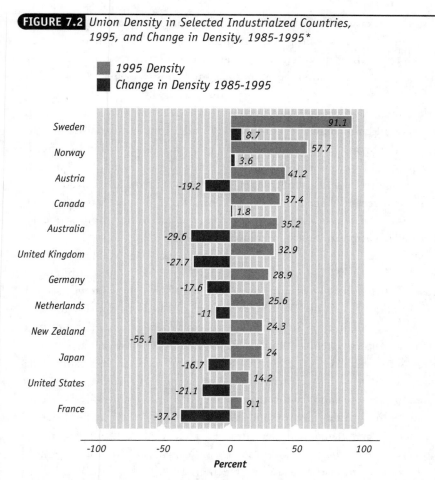

FIGURE 7.2 *Union Density in Selected Industrialzed Countries, 1995, and Change in Density, 1985-1995**

1995 Density
Change in Density 1985-1995

*Union density refers to the number of trade union members as a percentage of wage and salary earners. Methodological differences in how countries collected these data make comparison difficult. Canadian data are for 1993, Swedish for 1994.

Note: The Canadian data here are not comparable to those in Figure 7.1 because different definitions were used.

Source: International Labour Office 1997. *World Labour Report.* Genewa: ILO. [www.ilo.org/public/english/bureau/inf/pkits/wlr97.htm]

The European pattern is a result of highly coordinated and centralized collective bargaining systems, supported by law, in which national unions negotiate with large employers' federations. Pay and other basic working conditions are set nationally or by industrial sector, greatly reducing competition among individual workplaces on these issues (unlike Canada, where a firm may resist union pay demands because it would increase its wage costs relative to local competitors). So, in France, for example, despite a union density of only 9 percent, employer associations are legally required to regularly negotiate broad agreements with unions, the benefits of which are extended to virtually all employers and employees. In addition, industrial democracy systems at the firm level in some European countries (discussed in Chapter 6) give workers and unions a voice in a wide range of local issues, from technological change to work arrangements. European systems of collective bargaining have recently become more decentralized, in some cases bringing greater industrial democracy to workplaces and providing more scope for worker participation in management decisions.

We noted earlier that Canadian union density has been stable for the last several decades. Of 92 industrialized and developing countries, only 20 saw increases in the number of union members, with the largest growth seen in Asia (International Labour Office 1997). Declines in both density and coverage were more common in nations with employer-centred, decentralized industrial relations systems—notably the United States and Japan. Drops in coverage were less likely in countries with strong sectoral or national bargaining regulated by the state to balance employers' and employees' interests. Britain and New Zealand, two countries with previously centralized systems, stand out with declining density and coverage. In each case, market-oriented governments deregulated and decentralized industrial relations systems in attempts to weaken the power of unions – basically, a shift to a more Americanized model of industrial relations (Freeman 1995). There are also various signs in other European countries, Australia, and New Zealand of a shift in collective bargaining from national or sectoral levels down to firms, largely due to the introduction of more flexible forms of work organization, although the extent and implications of this decentralization process varies considerably (International Labour Office 1997). The field of *comparative industrial relations* examines these trends. A central question is the extent to which labour and employment relations are undergoing a basic transformation across advanced industrial nations, and whether this is in the direction of convergence or divergence at the national level (Bamber and Lansbury 1998; Godard 1997). Both these issues generate much debate among researchers.

The Decline of U.S. Unions

Canada's union density and coverage have surpassed those of Japan and the United States, the two other countries with employer-centred industrial relations. It is significant that Canadian union membership remained stable while other countries, especially the United States, saw a decline. Canadian unions appear to have weathered the economic storms of the 1970s and 1980s, although the future looks far less certain (Lowe 1998). U.S. unions, in contrast, are engaged in a struggle for survival. Membership has plunged from one-third of the workforce in the mid-1950s to 14 percent now. Observers attribute this decline to a number of factors, but in particular to fierce anti-union campaigns launched by private-sector employers, labour laws that permit these coercive tactics, and ineffective responses from unions to these changes. Also significant is the shift of employment away from the union strongholds of the north-eastern industrial regions to the Sun Belt states, where *right-to-work laws* undermine union security; under these laws, neither union membership nor payment of union dues may be required as a condition of employment.[19]

Some industrial relations scholars have concluded that the American industrial relations system, which grew out of the New Deal in the 1930s and institutionalized collective bargaining, was replaced in the 1970s and 1980s by a nonunion approach to industrial relations. The breakdown of the old union-based industrial relations system can be traced to three trends: (1) *concession bargaining* (that is, unions agreeing to rollbacks in wages, benefits, and collective rights); (2) management innovations such as teamwork and greater employee participation; and (3) explicitly nonunion human resource management strategies in the private sector, in part a response to American unions' greater positive impact on wages compared with other countries, giving employers a strong incentive to oppose them. Taking a more historical view, Goldfield links the decline of American unions to changing class relations. He argues that the failure to form a solid working-class base for the labour movement during its period of greatest membership strength, from the 1930s to the 1950s, seriously weakened it as a political force. Hence, U.S. labour lacked the strategies, leadership, and membership solidarity necessary to survive in a more hostile environment.[20]

Another perspective is offered by Seymour Martin Lipset, probably the best-known student of Canadian–American differences. Lipset's thesis is that a core difference between the two societies is the historically stronger commitment among Americans to individualistic values, and the greater sense of collective rights among Canadians. For Lipset (1990a), these value differences underpin the greater propensity of Canadians to belong to unions. However, his thesis is disputed by a number of Canadian scholars (Bowden 1989; Lipset 1990b).

Furthermore, as the debate about Canadian-American differences in the unravelling of the postwar employment contract heated up, Lipset teamed up with Noah Meltz, a Canadian industrial relations expert, to survey the attitudes and values of workers on both sides of the border (Lipset and Meltz 1997). They discovered a paradox. On one hand, American workers were slightly more approving of unions than Canadian workers and considerably more nonunion workers (47 percent and 33 percent, respectively) would vote for a union if they had the opportunity. Yet on the other hand, the actual level of union membership in the U.S., as we noted, is less than one-third that of Canada. Lipset and Meltz resolve the paradox by pointing to the difference between deep-rooted *values*, which underlie the institutions of labour relations, and more immediate *attitudes* towards unions, which reflect current labour market conditions and union strength. So in the case of America, unions are so weak today that workers believe they should be stronger, while in Canada, the greater power of unions ends up being a source of criticism among many. This debate is far from finished, however. Two American academics (Freeman and Rogers 1999: 36) have argued that if one looks beyond unions to any collective form of representation, in both countries there is a gap between workers' desire for more say in decisions that affect their work lives and actual opportunities for participation.

To recap, several distinctive features of Canadian unions, as well as their social and political environment, help to explain why they have not suffered the same fate as their American counterparts. Most important are the somewhat more militant character of Canadian unions, widespread public-sector collective bargaining that has been facilitated through legislation, and demands for greater local control of union affairs in Canada. The U.S. experience shows the decisive role of legislation and management opposition in encouraging or inhibiting free collective bargaining. However, some industrial relations scholars detect signs of union revival in the U.S., which may reverse the trends described above. The main evidence of revival in the late 1990s includes: increased public approval of unions (seen, for example, in the widespread support for striking UPS workers in 1997); new leadership in the AFL-CIO (the equivalent of the CLC) committed to vigorous organizing; increased success in union certification elections; and innovative strategies among local unions that have appealed to low-wage workers, women, and racial and ethnic minorities. Other analysts are pessimistic, arguing that unions in both Canada and the U.S. lack the resources, institutional frameworks, and supportive public policies required for the massive new organizing successes required to increase membership substantially.[21]

THE CURRENT STATE OF UNIONS IN CANADA

Membership Patterns

The likelihood of a Canadian worker being a member of a union, or joining one in the future, varies according to province of residence, industry, and occupation. Figure 7.3 shows that in 2000, 30 percent of employees (excluding the unemployed and self-employed) belonged to a union. Provincial differences in labour legislation, industrial mix, and economic performance influence union membership. Newfoundland has the highest rate of unionization, at 39 percent, because of the disproportionately large size of the unionized public sector in a historically weak economy and the strength of unions in the fishing industry. Quebec is next, for reasons that largely reflect the unique political context noted above. At the opposite end of the scale, Alberta's union density is only 21 percent. A critical perspective would suggest that Alberta's industrial relations have moved closer to the American model, given this province's more restrictive labour legislation, the decimation of construction industry unions in the early 1980s, and American-style nonunion human resource policies found in key industries such as oil and gas (Panitch and Swartz 1993; Noël and Gardner 1990; Reshef 1990). To view this from a broader perspective, labour laws are one aspect of labour standards that provide workers with a range of protections. According to a comparison of legislated labour standards in all U.S. states and Canadian provinces and territories, Alberta ranks close to the bottom (Block and Roberts 2000).

Figure 7.4 provides a detailed industrial breakdown of union membership for men and women. For decades, there was a large gender gap in unionization: men had higher rates of union membership than women. However,

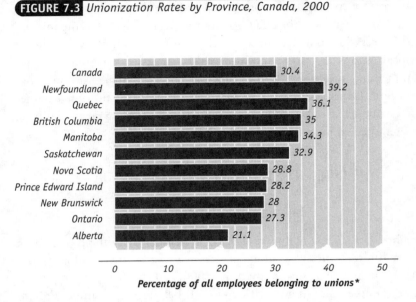

FIGURE 7.3 *Unionization Rates by Province, Canada, 2000*

Province	
Canada	30.4
Newfoundland	39.2
Quebec	36.1
British Columbia	35
Manitoba	34.3
Saskatchewan	32.9
Nova Scotia	28.8
Prince Edward Island	28.2
New Brunswick	28
Ontario	27.3
Alberta	21.1

Percentage of all employees belonging to unions*

*Unemployed and self-employed excluded.

Source: Statistics Canada, *Perspectives on Labour and Income*, Autumn 2000, p. 42. Cat. no. 75-00-1XPE.

Figure 7.4 shows that the gap has all but closed. Consider that the comparable figures in 1989 were 38 percent and 29 percent, respectively, for men and women (Statistics Canada 1992c: 48). In both education and public administration, women are more unionized than men, probably due to a combination of the overall high level of unionization and the fact that more males are managers, and, therefore, excluded from unions. Figure 7.4 underscores how industry of employment is more important than gender in explaining membership trends. For example, the five most highly unionized industries have small or reversed gaps between male and female membership. The low rates of union membership in service industries, such as finance, insurance, real estate and leasing, consumer services, and accommodation and food services, support this argument from the other side: the lack of opportunities to join a union, or difficulties in organizing one, affects men and women equally. Unions' lack of success in these industries does not bode well for the future of unions, given our discussion in Chapter 3 about the importance of these sectors in job growth.

FIGURE 7.4 *Unionization Rates by Industry and Gender, Canada, 2000*

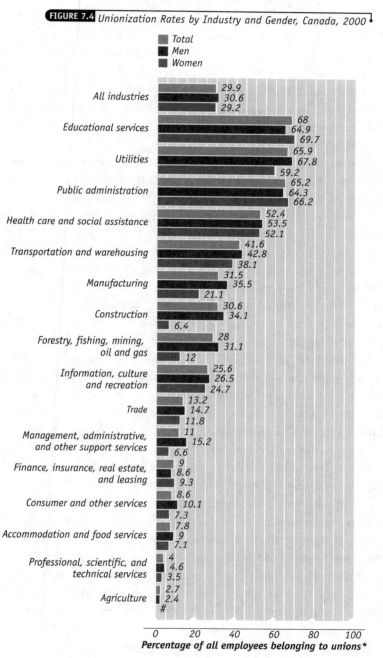

Legend:
- Total
- Men
- Women

All industries
29.9
30.6
29.2

Educational services
68
64.9
69.7

Utilities
65.9
67.8
59.2

Public administration
65.2
64.3
66.2

Health care and social assistance
52.4
53.5
52.1

Transportation and warehousing
41.6
42.8
38.1

Manufacturing
31.5
35.5
21.1

Construction
30.6
34.1
6.4

Forestry, fishing, mining, oil and gas
28
31.1
12

Information, culture and recreation
25.6
26.5
24.7

Trade
13.2
14.7
11.8

Management, administrative, and other support services
11
15.2
6.6

Finance, insurance, real estate, and leasing
9
8.6
9.3

Consumer and other services
8.6
10.1
7.3

Accommodation and food services
7.8
9
7.1

Professional, scientific, and technical services
4
4.6
3.5

Agriculture
2.7
2.4
#

Percentage of all employees belonging to unions*

0   20   40   60   80   100

*Unemployed and self-employed excluded. # Too few employees for reliable estimate.

Source: Statistics Canada, *Labour Force Survey* (special tabulation).

Union density is around the national average in manufacturing, construction and natural resources. However, here we find a large gender gap in membership levels, mainly due to the gender division of labour in these predominantly male, blue-collar areas of employment. Few women work in these industries. Those who do are located in office jobs, which unions have often ignored ; when unions have tried to organize these workers, they have encountered major hurdles.

Another way of examining union membership is by occupation. Figure 7.5 shows that individuals in wholesale, food and beverage, managerial, and retail occupations are least likely to be union members. In contrast, the most highly unionized jobs are in the public sector: nurses; teachers and professors; health care technical workers; protective service workers (e.g., police and fire); and health care support workers. Between 51 percent and 81 percent of workers in these occupations belong to unions. The unionization of these white-collar workers, many of whom are women, has given a whole new look to the labour movement. The traditional, blue-collar union strongholds in trades, manufacturing and processing, and transport equipment operations now have union densities ranging from 36 to 42 percent.

Other factors are also associated with union membership. In terms of sociodemographic characteristics, age and education are strong predictors.[22] In 2000, only 13 percent of young workers (aged 15 to 24 years) belonged to unions, compared with 31 percent of 25- to 44-year-olds, and 42 percent of those aged 45 to 54. This pattern of aging membership is the main reason why unions need to bolster their recruitment efforts (Lowe and Rastin 2000). Better-educated workers also have higher rates of union membership. For example, the unionization rate among workers with university degrees is 35 percent, compared with 24 percent among those with some high school.

However, while workers' personal characteristics help to predict union membership, employment characteristics are far more important in this regard. Workplace size is one of the strongest predictors of union membership: 54 percent of employees in workplaces with over 500 employees are unionized, compared with 12 percent of those in establishments with under 20 employees (Statistics Canada 2000c: 43). So too is one's employment status. Specifically, being a full-time, permanent worker improves your chances of being a union member, or, in other words, of having the opportunity to join. Unions represent

FIGURE 7.5 *Unionization Rates by Occupation, Canada 2000*

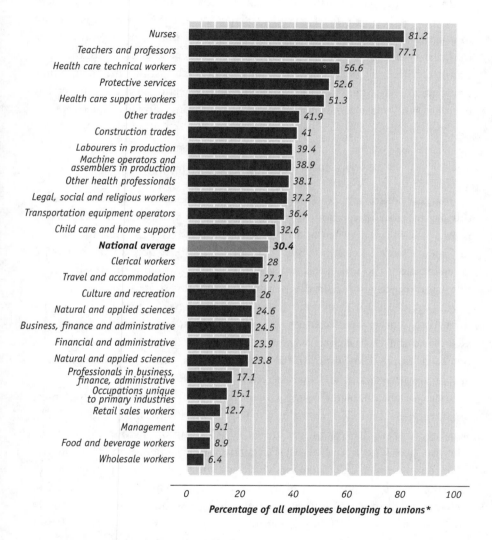

Occupation	Percentage
Nurses	81.2
Teachers and professors	77.1
Health care technical workers	56.6
Protective services	52.6
Health care support workers	51.3
Other trades	41.9
Construction trades	41
Labourers in production	39.4
Machine operators and assemblers in production	38.9
Other health professionals	38.1
Legal, social and religious workers	37.2
Transportation equipment operators	36.4
Child care and home support	32.6
National average	**30.4**
Clerical workers	28
Travel and accommodation	27.1
Culture and recreation	26
Natural and applied sciences	24.6
Business, finance and administrative	24.5
Financial and administrative	23.9
Natural and applied sciences	23.8
Professionals in business, finance, administrative	17.1
Occupations unique to primary industries	15.1
Retail sales workers	12.7
Management	9.1
Food and beverage workers	8.9
Wholesale workers	6.4

Percentage of all employees belonging to unions*

*Unemployed and self-employed excluded.

Source: Statistics Canada, *Perspectives on Labour and Income,* Autumn 2000, p. 43.
Cat. no. 75-001XPE.

22 percent of part-time and 24 percent of temporary workers, compared with 32 percent of full-time workers or permanent workers.

In short, the composition of the labour movement has been transformed since the 1960s. The typical unionist today is a white-collar worker employed in one of the service industries, quite likely in the public sector. Women have joined the ranks of organized labour faster than men, so chances are that new union recruits will be women. Labour's traditional bastion, the male-dominated manufacturing, construction, and resource sectors of the economy, has been shaken by the forces of industrial restructuring, downsizing, recession, and globalization.

The Rise of Public-Sector Unions

In marked contrast, membership grew in both relative and absolute terms during this time throughout the service sector. An example of this expansion is that of the Canadian Union of Public Employees (CUPE), the largest union in Canada since the early 1980s. The key to CUPE's success is membership diversification: the union has moved into new areas such as universities, airlines, and nursing homes in this period. Recently this strategy also seems to be paying dividends for some industrial unions. Witness, for instance, the Canadian Auto Workers' recruitment of workers in airlines, fisheries and food services. And the United Steel Workers have organized widely, in workplaces as diverse as hotels and hospitals, bakeries and banks, university campuses, and among security guards and taxi drivers.[23]

The present character of the labour movement is reflected in its largest organizations. Table 7.1 lists the ten largest unions in 1996 and in 2000, which, as a group, represent just under half of all union members in Canada. The top two, CUPE and NUPGE, represent government and other public-sector employees. CUPE members work in a wide spectrum of jobs in municipalities, electrical utilities, social services, child-care centres, schools, libraries, colleges and universities, hospitals, nursing homes, and many other public institutions. Typical of many government employee unions, CUPE evolved from a traditional and rather docile staff association. Established in the 1960s, it grew to 97,000 members by 1967. CUPE's fourfold growth in three decades made it the first union in the country to break the 400,000-membership mark. In 2000, it represented more than 13 percent of all union members in

TABLE 7.1 *Ten Largest Unions, Canada, 1996 and 2000*

	Membership (000s) in 1996	Membership (000s) in 2000	Change, 1996–2000 in Membership (000s)
Canadian Union of Public Employees	455.8	485.0	29.2
National Union of Public and General Employees	310.6	325.0	14.4
National Automobile, Aerospace, Transportation and General Workers Union of Canada (Canadian Auto Workers or CAW)	205.0	220.0	15.0
United Food and Commercial Workers International Union	185.0	210.4	25.4
United Steelworkers of America	170.0	190.0	20.0
Public Service Alliance of Canada	167.8	146.6	- 21.2
Communications, Energy and Paperworkers Union of Canada	165.2	144.3	- 20.9
International Brotherhood of Teamsters	95.0	100.2	5.2
la Fédération de la santé et des services sociaux(formerly la Fédération des affaires sociales)	97.0	96.8	- 0.2
Service Employees International Union	80.0	90.0	10.0
Total union membership	4,033.0	4,058	25.0
Membership of ten largest unions	1,931.4	2,008.3	76.9
Percentage of total membership in the ten largest unions	47.9%	49.5%	

Sources: Human Resources Development Canada, Labour Program, Workplace Information Directorate, *Directory of Labour Organizations in Canada 1996* (Ottawa: Canada Communications Groups – Publishing, 1996): xiv, xvii; "Union membership in Canada," *Workplace Gazette* 3 (3) 2000: 69-70. (http://labour.hrdc-drhc.gc.ca). Reproduced with the permission of the Minister of Public Works and Government Services Canada.

Canada. NUPGE is the umbrella organization for the various provincial government employee unions. Two other public-sector unions are among the top ten—one is based in Quebec, and the other, PSAC, represents federal government workers. The largest private-sector union is the CAW, which is Canadian-based. The largest U.S.-based union is the United Food and Commercial Workers, whose members were involved in the 1997 Alberta Safeway strike. Like the CAW, it has been actively organizing new members in service industries and has also grown by merging with smaller unions.[24]

A watershed in the Canadian labour movement was reached in 1967 when the federal government passed the Public Service Staff Relations Act. This opened the door to collective bargaining for federal civil servants. Provincial government employees were already moving in this direction, with the granting of collective bargaining rights to Quebec public employees in 1965. Unionism soon spread into municipal governments, hospitals, schools, prisons, social services, and other expanding public institutions. Consequently, the international unions representing mainly male craft and industrial workers have lost their once-dominant position in the Canadian labour movement. Thus, the large unions in Table 7.1 represent the wave of public-sector unionism that began in the late 1960s. They also signal a new brand of worker militancy. Nurses, teachers, librarians, social workers, clerks, university professors, and other white-collar employees have taken to the picket lines to pressure their employers (ultimately, the government) into improving wages and working conditions and maintaining the quality of public services.

"Canadianizing" Unions

The rise of public sector unions has also helped to *Canadianize* the labour movement. At the beginning of the 20th century, U.S.-based international unions represented about 95 percent of all unionized workers in Canada. By 1969, this proportion had dropped to 65 percent and, with the groundswell of nationalism since the 1970s, has continued to decline to 31.9 percent in 1990.[25] Not surprisingly, the recent upsurge in union growth is largely because of the efforts of national public-sector unions (such as CUPE, mentioned above). Equally important in explaining the Canadianization trend is the push for greater autonomy, or outright independence, within Canadian sections of international unions.

The vulnerability of Canada's branch-plant economy taught growing numbers of workers the need for greater local control of union activities. A strong argument in support of international unions is that they are labour's best defence against the global strategies of multinational corporations. Yet the internationals have not always been effective in dealing with the sorts of problems multinational corporations created for Canadian employees. For example, officials at the U.S. headquarters of these unions sometimes equated layoffs or plant closures in Canada—associated with multinational firms shifting production to their U.S. facilities—with more jobs for their much larger American memberships. The North American Free Trade Agreement and the rising tide of protectionism south of the border have compounded these problems.

Different bargaining agendas also tended to arise in the two countries, reflecting their distinctive industrial relations environments. Canadian auto workers, for instance, roundly rejected the concessions made to employers by the U.S. wing of their union. The issue of national autonomy came to a head in the 1984 strike against General Motors by the Canadian division of the United Auto Workers. These Canadian autoworkers found themselves pitted against not only GM, but also the UAW leadership in Detroit, who wanted Canadian workers to accept the concessions agreed to by their American counterparts. While autonomy was not the goal of the Canadian workers going into the strike, it became an inevitable result. Reflecting on the formation of the Canadian Auto Workers union in December 1984, Sam Gindin, research director with the CAW, offered this analysis:

> While the anti-concession objectives of the Canadian UAW was, of itself, a modest goal, it was another strong reminder that collective bargaining remains at the heart of unionism … The story of this fight against concessions obviously includes struggles beyond the Canadian autoworkers … But if the autoworkers, with their reputation for militancy, for being at the leading edge of collective bargaining developments, had fallen into line with their American parent, concessions would not only have been legitimated in Canada but an aura of fatalism would have enveloped them. The Canadian autoworkers were faced with either becoming the vehicle for spreading concessions into Canada or risking the uncertainty of establishing their own Canadian union. Their choice was critical to maintaining the vitality of the Canadian labour movement.[26]

Beyond having different bargaining priorities and strategies, some Canadian branches of international unions felt that their dues were flowing into the American headquarters with few services flowing back. These and other factors have prompted a growing number of separations. In addition to the Canadian Auto Workers Union, the Communications, Energy, and Paperworkers Union, the Communications and Electrical Workers, the Energy and Chemical Workers, and the Canadian Paperworkers Union were all created in this way.[27] Usually, good working relations are maintained, however, with their former U.S. parents. What will be interesting to watch in future is how unions create new forms of international cooperation – beyond Canada and the U.S. – to address the impact of economic globalization on workers.

WOMEN AND UNIONS

Why historically has the level of unionization been lower among female workers than among male workers? At one time, it was assumed that women would be less interested in unions because of their family responsibilities and presumed lower commitment to paid employment. Because of their domestic roles, the argument went, women's ties to the labour force were weak. Hence, work problems that might prompt unionization were of secondary concern. Old myths die hard, but close scrutiny of recent membership trends totally shatters this one. Women made up only 16.4 percent of all union members in 1962, yet by 2000, this figure had jumped to 48 percent. In fact, women have been joining unions at a much faster rate than men. Charlotte Yates's analysis of union organizing campaigns in Ontario during the 1980s and 1990s found that female-dominated workplaces were far more likely to vote in favour of union representation than were male-dominated workplaces. Clearly, women are not apathetic, passive, or indifferent to unions, if in fact they ever were. This is an important point that Yates believes unions have not adequately considered in their organizing campaigns.[28]

Indeed, women are often more pro-union than men because of their inferior positions in firms.[29] Kate Purcell rejects the "passive woman worker" argument on the grounds that industrial patterns of unionism are most decisive in who joins. Men and women alike join unions and engage in militant action according to the established patterns of their industries or occupations (Purcell 1979: 122–23). Miners and forestry workers are highly unionized, as we noted above, and have a history of militancy. But because these are non-traditional areas of women's employment, we would not expect to find many female unionists in these industries.

Thus, gender segregation in the labour market (discussed in Chapter 4) is the key factor in women's unionization patterns (Kumar and Cowan 1989). We have seen how, historically, women's employment has been restricted to a few predominantly female jobs. The oppressive and unrewarding character of this type of work, not the fact of being a woman, underlies the lower rate of female unionization. Such conditions in themselves can undermine collective action as a way of solving problems: workers, be they male or female, may be more likely to quit than to stay and fight for change.

What has been the role of male-dominated unions in keeping women out of certain jobs and, therefore, out of unions? There are numerous examples of craft and industrial unionists adopting policies that restricted female access to their jobs, mainly due to fears about having their wages undercut. In the early 20th century, craft unions lobbied with middle-class reformers to keep women out of the industrial labour force (allegedly to protect them). Such efforts discouraged union initiatives by women, thereby defining the union movement as a male institution. In Canada, for example, the failure of the 1907 strike by female Bell Telephone operators in Toronto was partly due to the lack of support their unionization campaign received from the International Brotherhood of Electrical Workers, an exclusively male craft union (Sangster 1978).

Consequently, for many women the option of joining a union has not existed. Only in the last 20 years, for example, were major organizing efforts launched in the largely female retail and financial industries. Massive counterattacks were mounted by management in banks and in retail stores. Despite a huge investment of organizing resources since the late 1970s, the CLC has achieved only limited success in unionizing banks. Breakthroughs during the 1980s in achieving union certification in big department stores, such as Eaton's, initially augured well for union expansion in the retail sector. Yet the 1987 *decertification* of unions by employees in five Ontario Eaton's stores was a major setback.[30] While some areas of the retail industry, such as grocery stores, have moderate levels of unionization, vast areas of the service sector still pose large hurdles, as witnessed in recent failed unionization attempts at Macdonald's and Wal-Mart.

Feminist scholars have cast new light on the collective struggles of women to achieve fairness and equality through unions. In predominantly female occupations, women have a long tradition of collective action. As professionals, female teachers have been organized for decades. While not based on trade union principles, the 1918 founding of the Ontario Federation of Women Teachers' Associations showed the growing commitment of women to organize for improved working conditions (Strong-Boag 1988: 69). Also, a history of union activism exists among women in the garment and textile industries, particularly in unions such as the International Ladies' Garment Workers (Gannagé 1986, 1995; Lipsig-Mummé 1987; Frager 1992). Women also have exerted pressure on the male-dominated unions to which they belong to have their concerns addressed. As Pamela Sugiman shows in her study of women's struggle for gender equality within the Canadian wing of the United Auto Workers during the 1960s, feminists active in the union used "gendered strategies of coping and resistance," drawing on women's combined experiences as auto workers, unionists, wives, and mothers. Yet while formally espousing this goal, male UAW members had difficulty getting beyond their patriarchal ideology (Sugiman 1992: 24).

This research underscores a prominent theme in women's growing influence in unions, namely the importance of coalitions with the organized women's movement outside the workplace. *Pay equity* has become a major new workplace objective, largely due to a broad alliance of feminists and some major unions. Indeed, the central thrust of pay equity is to challenge the gendered division of labour as enshrined in many union-negotiated job classifications. It also places equality squarely on the collective bargaining agenda, especially given that legislation in Ontario and elsewhere requires unions to negotiate pay equity with employers. Perhaps the most prominent example of how pay equity for women workers has become a rallying point for unions is the Public Service Alliance (PSAC) national strike of federal civil servants in 1991. However, it took until the end of the decade to reach a pay equity settlement with the government for these clerical and administrative workers. As Gillian Creese's (1999) case study of the white-collar workers' union at BC Hydro documents, public sector unions' quest for pay equity in the 1990s was made more difficult by the fact that it coincided with employers downsizing, restructuring and contracting out work. These organizational changes affected a wide range of workers, raising complex issues about standards of fairness in how workers are treated. Furthermore, even though the job hierarchy at BC Hydro did become more open to women and members of racial minorities, union traditions and culture continued to reflect the values and interests of white males.

In sum, women's demands for equality of opportunities and rewards in the workplace have already had a major impact on Canadian unions. The CLC elected its first female president, Shirley Carr, in 1986, and women are making up a growing share of elected union officers and paid staff, especially in public sector unions. The largest union in Canada, CUPE, elected Judy Darcy as its president in 1991. And a few unions, such as the Canadian Union of Postal Workers, have given top priority to concerns most often expressed by women (for example, paid maternity leave, sexual harassment, child care, and fair treatment of part-time workers) (Julie White 1990). Gradually, "women's issues"—which really are issues for all workers—have come to have higher stature in labour's collective bargaining and social action. Important bargaining items, at least for large unions, now include gender-neutral contract language and clauses dealing with discrimination, sexual harassment, family-related leave, child care, technological change, and rights for part-time workers (Kumar and Acri 1991; Briskin and McDermott 1993). Labour's success in achieving this bargaining agenda is obviously crucial to its future.

MANAGEMENT OPPOSITION TO UNIONS

Despite laws giving each employee the right to join a union and to participate in free collective bargaining, employer opposition to unionism has frequently been a major obstacle to putting these rights into practice. Workers who encounter strong management opposition to their union organizing activities may legitimately fear for their jobs, and this will have a chilling effect on the union campaign. Moreover, if an employer chooses not to recognize a union after it has been legally certified in the workplace, it is very difficult for members of that union to exercise their legal rights. Prior to the introduction of a legal framework for *union certification* and *collective bargaining* procedures during World War II, many industrial disputes occurred over the employer's refusal to recognize the workers' union. Surveying the historical record, Pentland observes: "It is sad but true that Canadian employers as a group and Canadian governments have never taken a forward step in industrial relations by intelligent choice, but have had to be battered into it."[31]

The New Human Resource Management

White-collar workers in the private sector remain the largest unorganized group in the labour force. Strenuous efforts by employers to remain union-free, with the help of the new human resource management practices already mentioned, and government inaction with regard to promoting private-sector union recognition, have created an inhospitable climate for unionism. There are several additional reasons for this climate (Bain 1978: 23). White-collar employees often have direct contact with management and, therefore, may identify more closely with the company ideology than do blue-collar workers. When management openly disapproves of unions, white-collar workers may be reluctant to join one. Workers join unions for the benefits, such as better working conditions, higher wages, job security, or access to a grievance procedure. Concrete proof that unions can "deliver the goods" is obviously lacking in industries that have never had high levels of unionization. The difficulty of overcoming these obstacles discourages unions from launching recruitment drives. Consequently, the option of joining a union has not been available to many private-sector white-collar workers.

Management usually prefers to deal with each employee individually. This creates a "David and Goliath" situation, pitting individual employees against the power of a corporation. However, the once virulent anti-unionism of Canadian business turned into grudging acceptance in the decades immediately following World War II (Smucker 1980: Chapter 7). Instead of fighting unions head on, managers now often criticize them as being unrepresentative organizations under misguided leadership. An underlying concern is what constitutes *management's rights*. There are still some employers today who zealously believe that the owners of a business should unilaterally define the employment relationship. In such cases, the right to manage takes absolute priority.

Some leading corporations have adopted a more subtle strategy. This is the *new human resource management*, which aims to maintain high-quality human resource policies and good working conditions, and encourages employee participation and commitment. Both lean production and high-performance workplace models, discussed in Chapter 5, have been adapted by some employers to maintain a union-free workplace. In some cases, a *company union* or employee association creates the appearance of democratic employee representation. The basic assumption, derived from the human relations management tradition, is that if management treats employees well and listens to their concerns, a union will be unnecessary. IBM is a good example of this approach in action. In Britain, the corporation's 13,000 employees were balloted at the request of the government's industrial relations board to find out if they desired union recognition. Only about 4 percent of the staff favoured unionization. This vote was not the result of corporate coercion or intimidation, as is becoming increasingly common in the United States (although not at IBM). Rather, it reflected the attention and resources that the company had devoted to employee relations. These human resource management policies produce a corporate culture based on strong employee loyalty and identification with management's goals (Keenoy 1985: 98–102). Some Canadian firms, most notably the Hamilton steel producer Dofasco, have developed their own unique brand of nonunion labour relations to obtain the cooperation of employees (Storey 1983).

Workplace reforms, particularly lean production and high-performance work systems, pose major dilemmas for unions. However, some of the most successful innovations of this kind suggest that union involvement is a prerequisite (Pradeep Kumar 1995: 148). The examples of Saturn, Shell, and NUMMI (see Chapter 5) make this point. But in most cases, unions have tended to respond with either passive acceptance of these initiatives or active rejection.[32] The CAW, after extensive experience with lean production, adopted a policy of very carefully assessing the benefits and costs of participation (CAW 1993: 12). Only if workers' interests can be advanced and the union as an organization strengthened will the CAW enter into such change programs with management. Crucial ingredients are worker education and openness on management's part to share information (Martin 1995: 118–21). Pradeep Kumar (1995: 148–49) explains why "workplace innovation" poses difficulties for unions as well as management:

> ... unions and management have different views of the goals of workplace innovations. Management goals are primarily efficiency-oriented. The general mission of HRM [human resource management] is to improve organizational effectiveness and achieve competitive advantage through a more efficient utilization and development of human resources ... Unions, on the other hand, are voluntary organizations of workers that serve as their

collective voice in order to improve their physical, economic, social, and political well-being. The underlying values of the unions are inherently pluralistic and collective. Union activities extend beyond the workplace to legislative and political action to effect economic and social change. Consequently, if the unions are to have an independent role in workplace change, the objective of HR innovations must be more than simply enhancing organizational effectiveness: it must include improving the lot of the individual worker and promoting societal well-being.

One of the most insightful studies of a union's experience with new systems for organizing and managing examines CAMI, a joint venture between General Motors and Suzuki (Rinehart, Huxley and Robertson 1977). The firm built a new factory in Ingersoll, Ontario and carefully recruited a relatively young workforce. The CAW represented the workers, making CAMI one of the few North American "transplants" to be unionized. The plant used *lean production*, a hybrid of Japanese and North American industrial organization and management systems. CAMI claimed its competitive advantage derived from its emphasis on four core values: *kaizen* (continuous improvement); team spirit; open communications; and worker empowerment. However, rather than representing a paradigm shift from old-style mass production to post-Fordism, CAMI basically just fine-tuned Fordism. Work under lean production was "arduous and intense" (204). The biggest problem was chronic understaffing, mainly due to CAMI management's intent to operate very lean from the start. "CAMI values" declined as worker discontent rose – the reality of conflict replaced the promise of "win-win." CAMI jobs were not challenging; most were low-skilled, repetitive and routinized, and had a high risk of injury. The logic of the system was a relentless push to reduce the labour component of each vehicle – hardly conditions that foster more humane work. Workers reacted to these conditions by going on strike for five weeks in 1992. As a result of the strike, the union gained more voice in setting production standards, in addition to higher wages. Not surprisingly, the researchers quote many workers who label CAMI "just another car factory." It is experiences like this that provide unions good reason to be skeptical and cautious when dealing with management strategies to reorganize work.

Unions in an Era of Continuous Restructuring

Crystal-ball gazing is not a very scholarly activity, but we should at least contemplate likely future scenarios in Canadian industrial relations. The collective bargaining agenda is being transformed. Declining productivity growth since the mid-1960s, recessions in the early 1980s and early 1990s, privatization and cuts in government spending, high taxes and shrinking real incomes, and the increasing use of legislation and courts to restrict labour's rights have forced unions to rethink their negotiating priorities. For organized labour, the challenge of the 1990s has been to protect members' jobs and incomes (Kumar, Murray and Schetagne 1998). Unions also face employer demands for wage and benefit concessions and greater flexibility in hiring practices. Concession bargaining began seriously in 1983, and, partly as a result, wage settlements have dropped sharply.

The 1985 strike by 3,000 Air Canada ticket agents brought together for the first time issues that have since become prominent. These included the use of part-time employees, technological change, the rights of women workers, and the effects of industry deregulation. Deregulation in 1984 forced airlines to reduce labour costs because of mounting competition. The union was concerned that management wanted to make ticket agents into part-time workers, because it intended to use machines to issue tickets and check in passengers. At stake were full-time incomes for female employees. The big issue raised by this dispute was the necessity of involving workers directly in the process of workplace change. In the 1990s, examples of concession bargaining include the restructuring of Canadian Airlines that depended, in part, on substantial employee wage rollbacks; pay cuts for public sector employees in the name of deficit reduction; and the hardball tactics used by Maple Leaf foods to improve their market position through lower wages.

In an era of industrial restructuring, downsizing, and public sector cutbacks, employers are increasingly using work reorganization, flexible employment systems, and contracting out ("privatization" in the public sector) to their advantage. There is little doubt that these are major collective bargaining challenges in the future. When 26,000 members of the Canadian Auto Workers union went on strike in October 1996 against General Motors Canada, the key issue was "outsourcing" of work (using other companies to make parts previously made by GM workers). The union gained some ground in its fight to restrict GM's ability to sell plants or to contract out "non-core" jobs (*The Globe and Mail* 23 October 1996: A1, A6). In the public sector, similar issues arose in November 1995 when 120 laundry workers at two Calgary hospitals staged an illegal strike, protesting the contracting out of their work to a private Edmonton company. They had previously taken a 28-percent wage cut that they thought would preserve their jobs. Other unionized hospital workers joined the picket line and there was considerable support from citizens fearful about the general deterioration of health services. Within a few days, the regional health authority and the provincial government had backed down on this particular privatization initiative, but the larger trend was unchecked.[33]

This realignment in collective bargaining in favour of management reflects underlying economic trends. Many factors are motivating employers to slash labour costs, boost employee productivity, intensify the work process, or even relocate jobs out of Canada. Included among these are globalization; pressures from NAFTA to bring Canadian employment standards into line with lower standards in the U.S., Mexico, or elsewhere; the acceleration of technological innovations; government deregulation of industry; the desire to obtain greater flexibility in staffing and production systems; and pressures to cut government deficits. Some analysts argue that, in response, organized labour must develop truly international strategies, given that large multinational corporations are leading the way in these respects. Not surprisingly, the impact of these trends on national and workplace industrial relations is a growing area of research (Robinson 1994; Bélanger, Edwards, and Haiven 1994; Pradeep Kumar 1995; Clarke and Haiven 1999).

THE NATURE OF COLLECTIVE ACTION

So far, we have assumed that union members' common interests and objectives make it likely that they will bargain collectively with their employer. But how do workers come to act collectively? We recognize the importance of work-group dynamics, informal norms, and social relations, topics already discussed in Chapter 5. But this is only a partial answer. A more complete understanding of collective action requires us to examine the underlying basis for unionization, which is the predominant form of collective worker action in industrial society. What makes this particularly interesting is that the very idea of collective action seems contrary to the individualistic norms of capitalist employment relations.

The Dilemmas of Collective Action

Drawing on the insights of informal group dynamics, sociologists portray unions as *social movements* that unite members so they can actively seek shared goals. But, as with bureaucracies, unions also require rules and sanctions to regulate the behaviour of members. As Allan Flanders (1970: 44) writes, "trade unions need organization for their power and movement for their vitality." Both qualities are essential for unions to achieve their social and economic objectives. At the individual level, this perspective focuses on why employees would organize themselves into unions to collectively pursue common goals. In addition, it incorporates an analysis of the economic and social conditions that encourage or inhibit unionism and, moreover, raises questions about the internal dynamics of unions.

It is helpful to consider two dilemmas that a worker must resolve if she or he is to seriously consider joining a union or, if already a member, becoming an activist. The first is the *free-rider problem*. Mancur Olson asserts that individuals will not naturally organize to further their collective interest. "The rational worker," explains Olson (1965: 88), "will not voluntarily contribute to a union providing a collective benefit since [s]he alone would not perceptibly strengthen the union, and since [s]he would get the benefits of any union achievements whether or not [s]he supported the union." Just like social movements concerned with environmental, peace, or feminist issues, unions provide *collective goods*. In other words, all potential members have access to the organization's achievements—a sustainable environment, a world with fewer weapons, employment equity programs, or a grievance procedure and negotiated regular wage increases—whether they have assisted in achieving these objectives or not (Crouch 1982: 51-67). This is one reason that unionization levels remain low in European countries such as France, the Netherlands, and Germany. Given that the centralized, state-regulated industrial relations systems in these countries guarantee many nonmembers the full benefits of union-negotiated wage agreements, the incentive to join is considerably reduced. In contrast, in the United States where such legislation is absent, "right to work" laws weaken unions by taking advantage of the "free rider" dilemma.

The second dilemma involves Albert Hirschman's (1970) *exit* and *voice* methods of expressing discontent. According to Hirschman, a dissatisfied employee can either leave her or his employer or stay and push for changes. The presence of a union increases the chances that the employee will pursue the latter strategy. But in nonunion workplaces, the poor employment conditions that could spark an organizing drive also increase the chances of an individual opting to quit. This is a major obstacle to unionization in low-wage job ghettos in the service industries today.

However, as we have already noted, many people do not have employment options. Unemployment may be high in their community, or their particular skills may not be in demand. Consequently, as we document in Chapter 8, such individuals adapt to their limited opportunities to find a better job, perhaps becoming increasingly apathetic and alienated from their work. But, while it is true that apathy and alienation stifle collective action, it would be wrong to assume that these conditions cannot be overcome. Instead, we should ask why some groups of employees mobilize while others do not.

The Mobilization Process

The process of mobilizing initial support for a union requires obtaining signed union cards from the majority of employees in the workplace. It also requires the financial assistance and organizational expertise of an established union. Once organized, a union faces the problem of rallying members in support of collective bargaining goals. Ultimately, this could involve strike action. According to Charles Tilly's (1979) research on the causes of social protest, what is essential here is a sense of shared identity with the group. Collective action in the workplace will be easier when the work group is an important part of each employee's life. Strong social ties inside and outside the workplace integrate employees into the group. Individual interests become synonymous with group interests, acting as a springboard to collective action. Good examples of groups possessing this *solidarity* are printers, miners, fishers, and members of other occupations in which the occupational culture encompasses all of a worker's life.[34] Levels of unionization and industrial militancy tend to be high under these conditions.

Assuming the existence of a cohesive group, what pushes its members into common action? The role of the group leader is obviously central. Especially important are *organic leaders* who, by virtue of being part of the group, are best able to tap its potential for collective action. This is because they understand the experiences of group members and can gain their trust better than an outsider could. In short, an effective leader will build up group solidarity, create an awareness of common interests, map out a realistic program of action, and seize opportunities to launch the plan.

But we are not suggesting that all union activity can be reduced to the characteristics of a particular group, its members, and its leaders. Also important is the environmental context, which might involve a supportive community, a hostile employer, or fair labour legislation—all factors that can either nurture or dampen union activity. Even if such conditions are favourable, employees ripe for unionization may still not act. Similarly, unionized workers facing a deadlock in negotiations with management over a new collective agreement may not strike. Often missing is one or more precipitating factors: an arbitrary change in work practices; the denial of a long-awaited salary increase; the dismissal of co-workers; or a pent-up sense of being treated unfairly by management. Such perceived injustices could serve as the catalysts for mobilization.

Research on the inner workings of two Canadian unions gives us glimpses of how some of these factors actually contribute to *militancy*. Julie White's (1990: 147) study of the Canadian Union of Postal Workers (CUPW) quotes a woman worker in a Saint John post office: "We're a militant union, and I really believe that Canada Post has made us that way." This view is typical of CUPW members, White argues. The union has developed a "culture of struggle," based on the belief that management does not have the interests of workers at heart and, further, that any past improvements have been extracted from management by militant action (Langford 1996). Against a background of unsuccessful attempts to resolve disputes through negotiation, mediation, and conciliation, this culture of struggle has been cultivated by an openly democratic structure based on rank-and-file involvement.

The importance of internal union dynamics was also a crucial factor in the militancy of Canadian autoworkers in the 1980s. Charlotte Yates attributes CAW's success at holding back on concessions demanded by North American auto firms to its greater membership solidarity, compared with the United Auto Workers union in the United States, which agreed to concessions. Some of the key features of union organization that contributed to CAW's militancy were members' influence over union decision making, including the rank-and-file's ability to mobilize opposition to the leadership if unpopular positions were being imposed, and effective communication channels linking all levels in the union (Yates 1990: 77).

In summary, a solid organizational base, strong leadership, union democracy that encourages rank-and-file participation, a shared understanding of who is responsible for employees' grievances, and support from other groups in the community are key ingredients for collective action. Equipped with this understanding, we can now turn our attention to the most common manifestation of collective action—strikes.

STRIKES

According to conventional wisdom, unions in this country are strike-happy, and our entire industrial relations system is far too adversarial. In this section, we will evaluate the popular complaint that Canadian workers are strike-prone. We will also probe beneath the surface of these conflicts, locating strikes within the context of the larger political arena. Are strikes a sign of worker militancy? Does industrial conflict have any connection with working-class politics? After all, many of the grievances fuelling strikes could be blamed on the economic system, but do workers make such connections? And what role do employers and governments, through legislation, play in industrial disputes?

What Are Strikes?

Strikes are high drama on the stage of industrial relations. The public views strikes as an inconvenience or even as a major social problem. Many politicians and business leaders argue that strikes harm the economy. The participants seldom want strikes, least of all the union members, who will never recoup the wages lost should the dispute drag on. But if conflict has been largely *institutionalized*, as described earlier, why do strikes occur at all? What motivates workers to strike, and what are the larger social and economic implications of their actions?

Let us begin with a widely accepted definition of a *strike* or *lockout*: "A temporary stoppage of work willfully effected by a group of workers, or by one or more employers, with a view to enforcing a demand" (Lacroix 1986:

172). Workers initiate strikes typically after a legally required strike vote, while lockouts (which account for relatively few work stoppages) are initiated by employers. In the 1990s, close to 90 percent of collective agreements in Canada's private sector were negotiated without a strike, although some did rely on third-party conciliation or mediation to reach this goal. The public sector is a different story. Some 70 percent of agreements are settled between the parties. However, strikes are actually less frequent than in the private sector, because governments can use legislation to prevent or terminate strikes – as they did in 22 percent of the collective agreements concluded with public-sector workers in the 1990s (Gunderson, Hyatt, and Ponak 2001: 327). The Nova Scotia nurses' strike, described at the start of the chapter, is an example of this kind of government action. Overall, strikes are infrequent events. Contrary to public opinion, settlement of union–management disputes without recourse to work stoppages is clearly the norm in Canada. There is evidently some truth to the argument that conflict has been institutionalized through the elaborate legal framework that regulates union–management relations.

Strikes are, nonetheless, central to the wage-labour relationship. If workers are selling their labour power to an employer in return for wages, their ultimate bargaining lever is to withdraw that labour. Even before the emergence of industrial capitalism in Canada, strikes erupted as workers protested against harsh treatment. For example, carpenters imported to build ships in colonial New France staged a slowdown to win living expenses above basic wages (Pentland 1981: 27). We have already mentioned that the struggling 19th-century labour movement mounted several landmark strikes, most notably the 1872 Toronto printers' strike and the Nine-Hour Movement agitation that happened around the same time.

But strikes are only one possible form of workplace conflict. Richard Hyman distinguishes between *unorganized* and *organized conflict* (1978: Chapter 3). The former is not a calculated group action, and typically involves workers responding to oppressive situations by individual absenteeism, quitting, or sabotage. The latter is a planned collective strategy, the aim of which is to change the source of the discontent. Recall that strikes in Canada are only legal after the collective agreement has expired and specific conditions, such as a strike vote, have been met. Unauthorized strikes during the term of an agreement, often spontaneous responses by rank-and-file workers to an immediate problem in the workplace, are known as *wildcat strikes*.[35] The Calgary laundry workers that we discussed earlier provide a recent example.

Not all strikes are over economic issues, nor do they exclusively involve working-class unionists. They can be political, as in the case of the Canadian Labour Congress's 1976 "national day of protest," when more than one million employees marched on the streets to register their opposition to the federal government's imposition of wage and price controls. The British Columbia Federation of Labour's concerted opposition in 1983 to new legislation that would seriously weaken unions is another example. So too are the 1996 "days of action" initiated by the Ontario Federation of Labour to protest the newly elected Conservative government's massive public-sector funding cuts. Industrial disputes also can involve work stoppages by high-status professionals. Examples include teachers, doctors, university professors, and airline pilots. Finally, strikes do not necessarily entail all members of the union leaving the worksite as a group. Under certain situations, *rotating strikes* across a number of worksites, *working-to-rule* (doing the minimum required or refusing overtime work, which has been used recently by health care workers), or staging work stoppages by "sitting down" on the job are variants of strike activity that can also communicate workers' demands to management.

Our emphasis on strike activity may leave the impression that workers are the disruptive factor in what otherwise would be harmonious labour relations. The key word here is *relations*, for there are two parties in every strike—three if the government intervenes, and possibly four if the public is directly affected. Seldom is the employment relationship a balanced one, however, since employers inevitably wield greater power. After all, management holds the final bargaining chip—the keys to the factory gate or office door, and, therefore, to the workers' jobs. Nonetheless, the public usually sees unions as the cause of strikes and labour unrest.

The United Auto Workers (1985: 153), now the CAW, attempted to set the record straight in their 1985 brief to the Royal Commission on the Economic Union and Development Prospects for Canada, saying, in part, "No matter how legitimate our demands are, it is the unions who have to initiate strike action. This reinforces the public bias of blaming workers for management–labour conflict." The brief debunks the myth that unions are too powerful and strike-happy by outlining the underlying causes of what, at the time, were three UAW disputes. These included the unwillingness of an employer to recognize a legitimately organized union local, employer attempts to force wage and benefit rollbacks, and concerns about plant closures. These are not isolated instances. Rather, they are typical of how employers are able to muscle unions into a tight economic corner from which strike action is often the only rational escape.

Canadian Strike Trends

On an annual basis, work stoppages rarely account for more than 0.5 percent of all working time in Canada (Table 7.2). This indicates that the seriousness of the strike "problem" often gets blown out of proportion. But, historically, we can identify eras when strikes were more common and widespread. There have been four particularly stormy periods of industrial conflict in Canada during the 20th century, gauged by the percentage of total working time lost due to strikes and lockouts.

A number of issues were at stake in early 20th-century strikes. Skilled artisans in the 19th century had been able to retain much of their craft status, pride, and economic security through their control of the production process. This privileged position was eroded by industrialization after 1900, as advancing technology and scientific management techniques undermined craft workers' autonomy. Thus, craft workers angrily resisted rationalization of their work, sparking many of the 421 strikes and lockouts that occurred between 1901 and 1914 in southwestern Ontario manufacturing cities (Heron and Palmer 1977).

Prior to union recognition and compulsory collective bargaining becoming encoded in law during World War II, many strikes were precipitated by an employer's refusal to recognize the existence of a union, much less bargain with it. The historic peak in labour militancy occurred at the end of World War I. Workers across the country were agitating against oppressive working conditions, low wages, and declining living standards due to soaring wartime inflation. Most of all, they wanted recognition of their unions. Western Canadian unions were far more militant and inclined toward radical politics than those in the rest of the country. Thus, in 1919 when Winnipeg building and metal trades employers refused to recognize and negotiate with unions over wage increases, the Winnipeg Trades and Labour Council called a *general strike*.

TABLE 7.2 *Work Stoppages Involving One or More Workers, Canada, 1976–2000**

Period	Number in existence during year	Total number of workers involved	Average number of workers per stoppage	Total person-days not worked	Average days lost per worker involved	Days lost as a percentage of estimated total working time
1976	1,040	1,586,221	1525	11,544,170	7.3	0.53
1977	806	217,647	270	3,320,050	15.3	0.15
1978	1,057	400,622	379	7,357,180	18.4	0.32
1979	1,049	462,386	441	7,819,350	16.9	0.33
1980	1,028	439,003	427	9,129,960	20.8	0.37
1981	1,050	341,852	326	8,850,560	25.9	0.35
1982	680	464,181	683	5,712,500	12.3	0.23
1983	645	329,472	511	4,440,900	13.5	0.18
1984	716	186,916	261	3,883,400	20.8	0.15
1985	829	162,333	196	3,125,560	19.3	0.12
1986	748	484,255	647	7,151,470	14.8	0.27
1987	668	581,882	871	3,810,170	6.5	0.14
1988	548	206,796	377	4,901,260	23.7	0.17
1989	627	444,747	709	3,701,360	8.3	0.13
1990	579	270,471	467	5,079,190	18.8	0.17
1991	463	253,334	547	2,516,090	9.9	0.09
1992	404	149,940	371	2,110,180	14.1	0.07
1993	381	101,784	267	1,516,640	14.9	0.05
1994	374	80,856	216	1,606,580	19.9	0.06
1995	328	149,159	455	1,582,321	10.6	0.05
1996	328	283,744	865	3,339,560	11.8	0.11
1997	284	257,664	907	3,610,206	14.0	0.12
1998	381	244,402	641	2,443,876	10.0	0.08
1999	413	158,612	384	2,445,770	15.4	0.08
2000**	228	92,623	406	783,370	8.5	0.05
1976-79 average	988	666,719	654	7,510,188	14.5	0.33
1980-89 average	754	364,144	501	5,470,714	16.6	0.21
1990-99 average	394	194,997	512	2,625,041	13.9	0.09

Notes:

* Work stoppages refers to strikes and lockouts

** 2000 data reflects January to June 2000 only.

Source: Human Resources Development Canada, Labour Program, Workplace Information Directorate, *Chronological Perspective on Work Stoppages in Canada 1990-2000* (http://travail.hrdc-drhc.gc.ca/doc/wid-dimt/ws-at/table.cfm). Reproduced with the permission of the Minister of Public Works and Government Services Canada.

A massive display of working-class solidarity erupted, bringing the local economy to a halt. Sympathy strikes spread to other cities across Canada, and even into the United States. The battle lines of open class warfare (one of the few instances of this in Canadian history) were drawn when, fearing a revolution, Winnipeg's upper class fought back with the help of the state. For several days, strikers squared off against police and employer-sponsored armed vigilantes. The confrontation ended in violence after the Royal Northwest Mounted Police, sent in by the federal government, charged a crowd of demonstrators. Strike leaders were arrested and jailed, while the workers' demands were still unmet (Bercuson 1974; Jamieson 1971; Kealey 1984).

Strike activity declined with rising unemployment during the Depression of the 1930s. As a rule, unions are less likely to strike in tough economic times. Conversely, when industry is booming and there is a relative shortage of labour, reflected in low unemployment rates, a strike becomes a more potent bargaining lever. The World War II era marked the rise of industrial unionism in manufacturing industries. Organizing drives accelerated as military production demands helped to restore the ailing economy. Again, union recognition was a dominant issue, driving workers in automobile factories, steel plants, and mines onto the picket line. As mentioned earlier in the chapter, the 1945 Ford strike led to the introduction of the Rand Formula to protect union security (Colling 1995). Subsequently, this became a standard feature of collective agreements, setting the tenor of labour relations by legitimizing unions while simultaneously ensuring orderly collective bargaining (Russell 1990).

Canada experienced a series of strikes in the mid-1960s. The fact that about one-third of these work stoppages involved wildcat strikes (mainly over wages) led the government to perceive a serious crisis in industrial relations. A task force, chaired by Professor H. D. Woods of McGill University, was set up to investigate the causes of industrial unrest and to recommend ways of achieving labour peace. Yet rampant inflation during the 1970s, and an increasingly militant mood among public sector workers, escalated labour–management confrontations.

The most recent strike wave reached its apex in 1976. The Trudeau government's imposition of wage and price controls in 1975 as part of its anti-inflation program made strikes over higher wages a futile exercise (Reid 1982). But in the 20 years since 1976, lost time due to work stoppages dropped to post–World War II lows. The recession-plagued 1980s and 1990s have dampened strike activity. Ironically, the fact that Canada's lost working time due to strikes and lockouts had dropped by the late 1980s was used by the federal government to attract foreign investors looking for a stable industrial relations environment (*The Globe and Mail* 4 April 1987: A3).

Table 7.2 profiles the labour relations patterns of the past two decades by reporting four characteristics of strike activity: *frequency* (number of strikes), *size* (number of workers involved), *duration* (days lost), and overall *volume* (days lost as percentage of total working time). For example, in 1999 (the last full year reported in Table 7.2) there were 413 work stoppages involving an average of 384 workers, with each striking worker on the picket line an average of 15.4 days. In comparison, 1980 witnessed more than three times the number of strikes, each involving fewer workers (an average of 427) but lasting considerably longer (20.8 days on average). A more systematic comparison over time can be found in the bottom three rows of Table 7.2. Here we provide averages for the last four years of the 1970s and the decades of the 1980s and 1990s. Note that all the trends are downward: the number of strikes, numbers of workers involved, average size, and time lost. Changing economic and industrial relations conditions in Canada have resulted in somewhat smaller and shorter strikes.

However, the greater number of public-sector workers who have faced legislated restrictions on strike action contributes to this trend. Most governments' deficit-cutting strategy during the 1990s involved imposing wage roll-backs through legislation, effectively suspending their employees' collective bargaining rights (Swimmer 2001). So the declining numbers in Table 7.2 do not necessarily signal the dawn of a new era of labour peace. Clearly the system of public-sector industrial relations needs reform. Taking stock of labour-management relations in the federal government, the Advisory Committee on Labour Management Relations (2001), led by John Fryer, recommended a new framework, based on collaborative problem-solving, that would be better able to address pressing human resource management issues. Extending the Committee's diagnosis across the public sector, what's needed is a fundamental shift to a less adversarial approach based on cooperation and mutual trust.

A Comparative Perspective on Strikes

How does Canada's strike record compare with that of other industrial nations? Recognizing the difficulties involved in making international comparisons of strike activity, due to differences in how strikes are defined and measured (Ross, Bamber and Whitehouse 1998), we can, nonetheless, get a rough idea of where Canada stands in this regard. Based on the annual averages of working days lost in nine industrialized countries between 1970 and 1992, Canada's rate was the second highest after Italy (Adams 1995: 512). But the earlier years in this period were historically high for Canada, inflating the overall average. Looking at the mid-1990s, Canada has significantly lower strike volume than Italy, France, or Australia, but considerably higher than other countries, in particular the United States and the Netherlands (International Labour Office 1997: 249-50). More importantly, the strike volume in highly industrialized countries has declined, in large part because of difficult economic times and high unemployment through much of the 1990s. Some experts suggest that while strikes are less frequent, when they do happen they are now more intense confrontations (Aligisakis 1997). However, other analysts argue that cross-national patterns in industrial disputes reveal considerable diversity, reflecting the unique institutional contexts in which employment relationships are shaped (Adams 1995; Ross, Bamber and Whitehouse 1998).

There are major institutional differences that account for international variations in strikes. For instance, in Italy, disputes, while short, are frequent and involve many workers. By contrast, the Swedish system of centralized bargaining, along with the country's powerful unions and their huge strike funds, mean that a work stoppage could quickly cripple the economy. This imposes considerable pressure to peacefully resolve potential disputes. In Japan, unions are closely integrated into corporations in what really amounts to a type of company unionism. Strikes are infrequent; workers voice their grievances by wearing black armbands or by making other symbolic gestures calculated to embarrass management. German union–management collective bargaining is centrally coordinated, but, at the individual workplace, employee-elected works councils frequently negotiate employment conditions (see Chapter 6). German laws require these participatory councils; they also make it very difficult to strike. Even though the strike rate in Canada is relatively low now, the fact that employees in this country have to confront employers when seeking collective bargaining has created a far more adversarial system (Adams 2000).

Thus, legislation governing the structure of collective bargaining is vitally important. The North American system of bargaining is highly decentralized and fragmented, involving thousands of separate negotiations between a local union and a single employer, each of which could result in a strike. Low-strike nations such as Austria, Germany, the Netherlands, and Sweden avoid these problems by having national or industry-wide agreements, and by legislating many of the quality-of-working-life issues that Canadian unions must negotiate with employers on a piecemeal basis. As Roy Adams (1995: 515) concludes, "As long as uncoordinated decentralized bargaining continues in North America, it is unlikely that the overall level of conflict will be reduced to the levels common in Northern Europe." In addition, as discussed in Chapter 6, laws in these countries give employees greater participation rights in enterprise-level decision making. This provides unions with more information about the firm's operations and opens up more communication channels with management, thereby encouraging more cooperation.

There are also major industrial and regional variations in strikes, which may be the result of how industries are organized. The least strike-prone Canadian industries are finance, trade, and services, which makes sense given their low unionization levels. Of the highly unionized industries, mining has historically been the most strife-ridden. Similarly, Newfoundland and British Columbia have significantly higher than average strike rates because of their high concentration of primary and other strike-prone industries.[36]

Explaining Strikes

One prominent but widely challenged interpretation of interindustry differences in strike behaviour is Kerr and Siegel's *isolation hypothesis*. These writers propose that isolated industries have higher strike rates than those where workers are integrated into the larger society. Isolated workers "... live in their own separate communities: the coal patch, the ship, the waterfront district, the logging camp, the textile town. These communities have their own codes, myths, heroes, and social standards."[37] Canada has always had large numbers of remote, resource-based, single-employer towns (see Chapter 2), where a combination of social isolation and a limited occupational hierarchy moulds workers into a cohesive group in opposition to management.

Research by Eric Batstone and his colleagues in a British auto plant adds to our understanding of strikes by highlighting the day-to-day processes that may culminate in a strike (Batstone et al. 1978). Strikes, argue these researchers, do not just happen. Rather, as a form of collective action, strikes require a high degree of *mobilization*. How production is organized, the type of technology used, and the formal institutions regulating union–management relations shape the context for this mobilization. But a crucial (yet largely ignored) ingredient of mobilization is how the social relations within the union allow certain individuals and groups to shape the course of events leading up to a strike. This mainly occurs through the identification of potential strike issues and through the use of rhetoric, by which the escalation of collective action is justified.

At the time of Batstone's study, most British strikes were unofficial stoppages initiated on the shop floor, not by top union leaders or by a democratic vote by all members. Laws more strictly regulate Canadian strikes, although recent British legislation has also moved in this direction. But the Batstone study offers some important insights about strikes in general. Typically workers are reluctant to strike, so there will not be much support for a strike until a vocabulary has developed that justifies such action. This involves the translation of specific grievances into the language of broad principles and rights. Furthermore, disputes over wages also typically involve *effort bargaining* (Gannagé 1995). That is, even if management refuses to grant wage increases, workers can informally shift their bargaining tactics to the other side of the "wage-effort equation" through slowdowns, refusal of overtime, and unauthorized work breaks. Finally, the study refutes the common view that the most powerful unions throw their weight around by striking. A basic contradiction of trade unionism, especially when examined in the workplace, is that "... the groups of workers most able to strike (in terms of bargaining awareness and collective strength) may rarely have to resort to strike action" (Gannagé 1995).

Case studies of strikes involving women workers add new insights to the dynamics of industrial disputes (Luxton and Corman 1991; Ferland 1989). Industrial conflicts in the past two decades were more likely than earlier disputes to occur in the public sector and to involve women, immigrants, and other workers new to collective bargaining. Jerry White's analysis of the 1981 illegal strike in Ontario hospitals highlights how the pressures of cutbacks and the resulting work reorganization in health care have the potential to push workers onto the picket line. White dismisses the "agitator" explanation of strikes, pointing out that, in this case, the union leadership generally did not support the strike. Rather, the strike was a grassroots protest by nonprofessional service workers such as orderlies, housekeepers, food handlers, registered nursing assistants, lab technicians, and maintenance workers. In the end, the strike won the workers slight wage improvements, but at a price: thousands of strikers were suspended, 34 were fired, and 3 union leaders were jailed.

Interestingly, the motivations to strike were different for men and women in this dispute. At issue was the transformation of the labour process associated with patient care due to massive cost-cutting. Male workers wanted compensation in the form of higher pay, reduced workload, and guaranteed benefits. Women, in contrast, were far more concerned with how cutbacks had led to deteriorating relationships with patients. As White (1990: 124–25) explains, for women:

> There was a complex of rewards, including formal *recognition* of the usefulness of the work, an *interaction* with other workers, and an intrinsic sense of a *job well done*. The hospital work provided this complex of rewards. Care-giving was a key aspect of this. Labour process changes broke this care-giving bond for many women workers. The desire to reestablish this bond was one consideration in the decision to strike.

◗ WORKER MILITANCY AND CLASS POLITICS

Social scientists often use strikes as a measure of worker *militancy*. Are strikes actually deeply rooted in class antagonisms, reflecting basic working-class discontent? Or do unionized workers act simply out of economic self-interest? General strikes have temporarily disrupted the economies of several advanced capitalist societies in recent years, and there is debate over how to interpret these events. Are they signs of heightened *class consciousness*, or are they merely pressure tactics to force changes in specific government or employer policies?

Economists have calculated that strikes have only a modest impact on the economy (Gunderson, Hyatt, and Ponak 2001: 345–47). As sociologists, we are equally interested in the broader implications of strikes for class consciousness and for working-class political action.

Comparative Perspectives on Working-Class Radicalism

Michael Mann's (1970) comparative study of industrial conflict addresses this question. Workers in France and Italy, he found, were more politically radical than those in Britain or the United States, who identified more closely with management. But the political potential of the French and Italian working classes was frequently limited by their failure to articulate an alternative social system and to chart a course toward it. Mann argues that strikes can be *explosions of consciousness*. But the working-class solidarity they generate rarely gathers momentum beyond the immediate event. For example, a test of the "explosion of consciousness" hypothesis among Hamilton, Ontario, postal workers who had participated in a strike found increased positive identification with fellow workers and the union, but little impact on class consciousness (Langford 1996). Ultimately, then, strikes by even politically radical workers are transformed into tactical manoeuvres to obtain concessions from employers.

Most workers, according to Mann, possess a *dual consciousness*. Instead of having a unified understanding of how their work dissatisfactions are organically linked to the operations of capitalism—real class consciousness in the Marxist sense—workers tend to compartmentalize their work experiences from the rest of their lives. They develop a "pragmatic acceptance" of the alienation and subordinate status they endure at work. Satisfactions in life are found in the basic pleasures of family, friends, and community, not in the quest for a new society.

Several other comparative studies have carried this discussion further, trying to identify which factors may transform varying degrees of working-class consciousness into collective action. This question gets at what perhaps is the weakest link in Marxist theories of class (Form 1983: 175). Duncan Gallie (1983) investigated the nature and determinants of worker attitudes to class inequality in France and Britain. At the time, these two countries had similar levels of socioeconomic development, but the French working class was radical, while its British counterpart was moderate. Indeed, Gallie (1983) points out that the May 1968 general strike in France was "arguably the most powerful strike movement unleashed in the history of capitalist society, shaking its very foundations." Why is it, asks Gallie, that British workers accept major social inequities as inevitable, while for the French they are a source of resentment and a catalyst for industrial militancy and political radicalism?

Gallie's evidence shows that workers in both France and Britain recognize class-based inequities in opportunity, wealth, and privilege. They differ, however, in their attitudes toward these inequities. For French workers, class position is an important part of personal identity. They identify with the larger working class, resent the system that puts them at the bottom, and believe that political action can improve their situation. British workers, in contrast, are more concerned about changing things in the workplace rather than in society as a whole.

Gallie's explanation of these differences hinges on the role of left-wing political parties in translating workplace experiences into a radical critique of society. French employers exercise greater unilateral power than do their British counterparts, and workplace industrial relations in France are not governed by mutually-agreed-upon rules. Thus, social inequality is more pronounced than in Britain. Furthermore, France has a revolutionary political tradition going back to the late 18th century. Hence, French workers' grievances with their employers are more intense and more readily carried outside the workplace, where they are moulded into a broad counter-ideology by exposure to trade unions and radical politics (especially the Communist Party).

Scott Lash (1990) provides another perspective on the determinants of worker militancy, with conclusions echoing those of Duncan Gallie. He compares the radical French with the conservative American working classes. Data collected at industrial sites in both countries show that differences in objective employment conditions cannot account for variations in militancy. Lash's alternative explanation focuses on how ideological and cultural factors shape militancy. Trade unions and political parties in a society or region are vehicles for socialization, transmitting to workers ideologies of natural rights in the workplace and in the political arena. Exposure to left-wing political parties determines *societal radicalism*. Socialization by trade unions, "industry's alternative rule-makers," is the most important cause of *industrial radicalism* (Lash 1984). Both kinds of radicalism aim to achieve the kinds of broader legal rights that would give power to individual workers. Militant workers do not, therefore, necessarily try to overthrow existing institutions; rather, they use them to their collective advantage.

Class and Politics in Canada

What about the Canadian situation? Gallie and Lash conclude that unions and political parties are the main vehicles for channelling general working-class discontent into collective action. Have Canadian unions, which are basically reformist in orientation, had the same role (Smucker 1980: Chapter 11)? The Canadian Labour Congress helped to found the New Democratic Party in 1961, and remains closely affiliated with it. However, if all union members voted for the NDP, it would have formed the federal government by now. And, despite the tough economic times that many workers have endured since the early 1980s, there are few signs that widespread discontent is on the rise. When New Democratic Party governments were elected in Ontario, British Columbia, and Saskatchewan in the 1990s, the victories actually involved little change from previous elections in the NDP's share of the popular vote. And the 1990-1995 Ontario NDP government's attempt to impose a "social contract"' on unionized public sector workers to reduce the government deficit backfired, creating what then Premier Bob Rae later called a "social contract tunnel of doom" that contributed to the NDP's electoral defeat (Rose 2001:73-74). Nor have two major recessions made the unorganized members of the working class more inclined to seek union representation. If anything, they have tended to blame their economic woes partly on unions (Palmer 1992: Chapter 7; Baer, Grabb, and Johnston 1991).

Despite theories suggesting that involvement in strikes may have a radicalizing effect on workers' political consciousness, our earlier discussion showed that this is seldom the case. Because strikes involve the organized and better-off members of the working class, resulting improvements in wages and working conditions may further divide the working class. Michael Smith (1978) claims that if strikes bring gains for the unionized workers involved, the more disadvantaged, unorganized workers may see this as proof of the unfairness of the system. Cynicism, political alienation, and antiunion feelings may result. So, even though strikes may briefly kindle the flames of class consciousness among strikers, their overall political impact within the Canadian working class appears small.

One of the few Canadian studies to probe these theoretical issues examined the ideologies of male manual workers in an aircraft repair plant where skill levels were high, and in a home insulation factory employing low-skilled labourers. No significant differences in political attitudes or class ideologies were found between the two groups (Tanner 1984; Keddie 1980). Furthermore, among those who were committed to left- or right-wing political beliefs, these beliefs were not related to other attitudes about work and society (Tanner and Cockerill 1986). The researchers concluded that a coherent and integrated set of political views was absent among the male blue-collar workers they studied. Worker consciousness regarding class and politics tended to be fragmented and often contradictory. For example, some of the same individuals who believed that corporate profits should be more equally distributed (a left-wing position) also agreed that trade unions are too powerful (a right-wing stance). But according to the researchers, this does not demonstrate an acceptance of the capitalist status quo or, alternatively, a rejection of socialism; rather, it suggests that workers' limited encounters with alternative ideologies lead them to question the system only on certain issues.

Other attitude surveys reinforce this assessment of class consciousness among Canadian workers. For instance, William Johnston and Michael Ornstein (1985) examined the political ideologies of employed men and women. They found class differences in support for social welfare programs and the redistribution of income, with the working class being the more egalitarian. But, despite being slightly to the left in political ideology, members of the working class were not more active in politics. "Left-wing political organizations and trade unions," conclude Johnston and Ornstein (1985), "have evidently failed to transform class differences in attitudes to social policy into coherent and durable perceptions of class structure and the political system." Even the economic crisis of the late 1970s and early 1980s, marked by high inflation and rising unemployment, did not further polarize class ideologies (Baer, Grabb, and Johnston 1991). However, a more recent Alberta study did reveal that individuals personally affected by the recession were somewhat more likely to be critical of the distribution of wealth in society (Krahn and Harrison 1992).

The Future of Worker Militancy

Despite the absence of a strong working-class radical ideology and, moreover, a decline in strike activity in Canada, there have been several examples of worker militancy that deserve careful scrutiny. Can we expect to see an upswing in industrial conflict in the future, coupled perhaps with a leftward shift in working-class politics? Some observers believe that future working-class mobilization could be provoked by employer and government demands for greater productivity, economic concessions, and more management rights.

A graphic illustration is the British Columbia Solidarity Movement, which sprang up in opposition to the Social Credit government's 1983 public-sector restraint program. Proposed legislation would have limited the scope of public sector bargaining, allowed the firing of employees at will, cut back on social services, ended rent controls, and abolished the B.C. Human Rights Commission. The launching of Operation Solidarity by the B.C. Federation of Labour was a delayed reaction, which followed the more militant responses by the grassroots Lower Mainland Budget Coalition.

Bryan Palmer's (1986) analysis of the B.C. Solidarity Movement raises some provocative questions. Class relations in Canada have begun to realign themselves, argues Palmer, and the 1983 events in British Columbia signal that class conflict may be on the rise. Palmer goes as far as calling the protest marches, public rallies, picket lines, and community-based resistance during the summer of 1983 "class warfare." These actions reflected mass opposition to the proposed legislation, rather than being merely the response of union leaders. In fact, the moderate leadership of Operation Solidarity rejected calls for a general strike that would have deepened the conflict. Negotiations between the government and mainstream union leaders eventually resulted in minor revisions to the legislation.

Not everyone would agree with Palmer's Marxist interpretation of the events in British Columbia. In hindsight, it may have been premature to draw conclusions about realignments in class relations on the basis of this case alone. It is interesting to speculate about other possible outcomes of this confrontation if organized labour had not become involved. What seems clear, though, is that government offensives against employee rights and social programs can provoke the labour movement into more broadly-based political action. Even though these reactions are often defensive, with unions scrambling to preserve past gains or members' jobs, public opinion can sometimes be rallied against unpopular government decisions, as in the case of the Calgary hospital laundry workers. Another example of widespread protests occurred in the mid-1990s when Ontario unions forged a broad coalition with community-based organizations to oppose policies proposed by the Harris Conservative government, which they saw as threatening social programs and undermining workers' rights. The political goal of this short-lived initiative was practical and immediate (and, we might add, unsuccessful): to pressure the Harris government into rethinking its agenda. The actions had no clear impact on class relations.

In general terms, however, the environment of labour relations became more restrictive after the recession of the early 1980s. Canadian employers increasingly resorted to lockouts. Several provincial governments introduced public-sector restraint legislation during this period, and the use of court injunctions and legislation to end strikes has escalated. Major private-sector strikes, such as the 1997 Alberta Safeway dispute, have been accompanied by the increased use of strikebreakers. On the other hand, there have been positive breakthroughs for labour, such as Quebec's anti-strikebreaking legislation. But these are exceptions, and some analysts believe that the new developments may undercut the established labour–management accord by placing severe restrictions on free collective bargaining, especially by public employees.[38]

These backward steps violate international labour conventions. In fact, the International Labour Organization (ILO) investigated two Alberta laws, one restricting the right of public servants to strike, and the other making unions liable to having up to six months' worth of union dues forfeited in the event of illegal walkouts. It also investigated Ontario's Inflation Restraint Act of 1982, which suspended public-sector collective bargaining rights for two years, and a 1983 Newfoundland law banning rotating public-sector strikes and preventing certain public employees from joining unions (*The Globe and Mail* 3 April 1985: A4). Organized labour took these cases to the Supreme Court of Canada, hoping that the new Charter of Rights and Freedoms would disallow these laws restricting workers' rights. But, in the spring of 1987, the Supreme Court ruled that the Charter guarantees neither the right to strike nor the right to bargain collectively. Clearly, this particular interpretation of the Charter's guarantee of *freedom of association* could, in time, reshape industrial relations in Canada (Kumar and Coates 1991: 17–19).

CONCLUSION

To return to the themes of conflict and cooperation introduced at the start of this chapter, do the new economic realities of the opening decade of the 21st century require that unions and management create new relationships? To answer this question, researchers have expanded the study of industrial relations far beyond just unions. Anthony Giles (2000) documents how, in response to the economic transformations of the last two decades of the 20th century, the focus of industrial relations research has expanded to encompass employment relations, management, and work organization issues. This interdisciplinary perspective has raised key questions about the future of unions that hinge on cooperative relationships and new forms of participatory work organization.

Today there are still many observers who believe that labour–management relations in Canada are too adversarial. In organized labour's experience, however, management wants workers to cooperate on its own terms. Cooperation is defined by management as a way of improving competitiveness and efficiency and lowering costs, rather than as a means of balancing workers' legitimate concerns with economic objectives. Unions do not dismiss the importance of productivity, competitiveness, or organizational flexibility. They simply want cooperation and consultation on these issues to be fully open and democratic. As documented elsewhere in the book (Chapters 5 and 6), there are models of a more equal partnership between labour and management. But this approach requires a fundamental shift away from adversarialism and toward full recognition of the rights of workers. This will require greater trust between workers and management. The end result could be significant benefits for labour, management, and society as a whole.

NOTES

1. The following examples are based on reports from the *Edmonton Journal* (Safeway dispute), *The Globe and Mail* (Safeway dispute, Starbucks campaign), Lorinc (1994) (McDonald's), the CAW website (www.caw.ca) (McDonalds, Starbucks), and Yahoo! News Canada (http://ca.news.yahoo.com) and *The Globe and Mail* (Nova Scotia nurses' dispute). A useful source for information on organizing drives, strikes and labour issues is the independent Canadian labour magazine, *Our Times* (www.ourtimes.web.ca).

2. Poole (1981: Chapter 1). This classification is based on Perlman (1958). Godard (1994: Chapter 7) provides a useful discussion of the role and function of unions as institutions.

3. Bain and Clegg (1974). The systems model of industrial relations was pioneered by John Dunlop (1971). For critical assessments, see Bamber and Lansbury (1998); Poole (1981: Chapter 2); Crouch (1982: Chapter 1); and Hyman (1975: Chapter 1). A systems approach is contrasted with a political economy approach to Canadian industrial relations by Taras, Ponak and Gunderson (2001).

4. See Poole (1981: Chapter 8) for a discussion of the importance of workers' values and perceptions (which are the basis of their actions) in the study of industrial relations. Keenoy (1985: 15–20) elaborates the point that workers and managers have different definitions of reality.

5. The phrase "managers of discontent" was coined by C.W. Mills (1948). An especially interesting discussion of the mobilization and management of discontent is provided by Batstone et al. (1978: Chapter 16).

6. Michels (1959); also see Crouch (1982: 163–74); Lipset, Trow, and Coleman (1956); and Freeman (1982). On the CSU and Hal Banks, see Kaplan (1987).

7. On the social unionism of the CAW, see Gindin (1995). Also see the issues and campaigns on the CAW website (www.caw.ca) and the Canadian Union of Public Employees' (CUPE) magazine, *Organize* (www.cupe.ca) for that union's perspective on broad social and political issues.

8. The data in this paragraph are from Riddell (1986: 5); Coates et al. (1989: 119); The Angus Reid Group (1996). On value shifts see Nevitte (1999).

9. Gunderson and Hyatt (2001: 392); Chaykowski and Slotsve (1999); Jackson, Robinson, Baldwin and Wiggins (2000: Chapter 4). On how unions reduce income inequality in 16 industrialized countries, see Gustafsson and Johansson (1999).

10. Freeman and Medoff (1984: 19); also see Gunderson and Hyatt (2001) on how unions affect compensation, productivity, and management practices in Canada.

11. Basic sources for historical accounts of the rise of the Canadian labour movement include Heron (1989), Morton (1989), Smucker (1980: Chapters 7 and 8), and Godard (1994: Chapter 4). The Canadian labour history journal, *Labour/Le Travail*, is an excellent source, as occasionally are *Relations Industrielles/Industrial Relations* and *Studies in Political Economy*.

12. On labour radicalism during the early 20th century, see Robin (1968), McCormack (1978), Bercuson (1974), and Frager (1992).

13. The institutionalization of conflict thesis was put forward by sociologists to explain the relative peacefulness of union–management relations in the immediate postwar period. Some U.S. academics went so far as to suggest that the decline in industrial disputes signalled a lessening of class distinctions and class conflict. See Crouch (1982: 106–9), Hill (1981: 124–27), and Ingham (1974).

14. Panitch and Swartz (1988). Also see Swimmer (2001); Fudge and Tucker (2000); Russell (1990); Kettler, Struthers, and Huxley (1990) Similar concerns about collective bargaining in the United States and the United Kingdom are discussed in Freeman (1995).

15. Note that the data in Figure 7.1 for 1981 and later are based on revised labour force estimates, to reflect changes to the *Labour Force Survey* in 1995 (see Chapter 2). This results

in higher estimates of nonagricultural paid employment, and, therefore, lower levels of union density than obtained using earlier labour force data series. The Labour Branch of HRDC website gives annual updates on union membership, industrial relations, and collective bargaining trends in its quarterly journal, *Workplace Gazette* [http://labour-drhc.gc.ca/millieudetravail_workplace/gazette/]. Also note that the data in Figures 7.3 to 7.5 use a slightly different method of reporting union membership, calculating it as a percentage of all employees, which is why the membership level for 2000 varies from that in Table 7.1.

16. See Murray (2001), OECD (1994: Chapter 5), and Chang and Sorrentino (1991) on measurement issues regarding union membership.

17. In 2000, collective bargaining coverage was 32.6 percent of all employees, or 2.2 percentage points higher than union density (Akyeampong 2000: 42). On nonunion forms of representation, see Taras (1997) and Lowe and Schellenberg (2001:25-29).

18. 2000 data in this paragraph are from the *Workplace Gazette* (2000).

19. For an assessment of right-to-work legislation from a Canadian perspective, see Ponak and Taras (1995); for a critical U.S. analysis, see AFL–CIO (1995).

20. See Goldfield (1987). On the breakdown of the old industrial relations system see Kochan, Katz, and McKersie (1986); Bamber and Lansbury (1998: 18 Chapter 1).

21. Those detecting signs of union renewal include Voss and Sherman (2000), Clawson and Clawson (1999), and Cornfield (1999). The pessimistic view is presented by Chaison and Rose (2001). Compare Yates (2000) and Martinello (2000) for different perspectives on union activity in Ontario after the election of Mike Harris's Progressive Conservatives in 1995.

22. Data in this paragraph are from Statistics Canada, "Unionization: an update," *Perspectives on Labour and Income* (Autumn 2000): 42-43. This publication provides detailed annual updates of union membership trends in Canada.

23. These unions have informative websites: Canadian Union of Public Employees (www.cupe.ca); Canadian Auto Workers (www.caw.ca), and District 6 of the United Steel Workers of America, the Canadian wing of the union (www.uswa.ca).

24. The websites for these unions are: NUPGE (www.nupge.ca), PSAC (www.psac.ca) and the UFCW Canada (www.ufcw.ca).

25. The website (http://labour.hrdc-drhc.gc.ca) of Human Resource Development Canada, Labour Program, Workplace Information Directorate has data on membership according to type of union. See Gindin (1989), Roberts (1990), and Chaison and Rose (1990) on the Canadianization trend.

26. Gindin (1989: 81–82); also see Gindin (1995). See Wells (1997) for an analysis of the CAW's shift away from principled militancy to, in some instances, more pragmatic cooperation with management. Yates (1998) examines the challenges posed by the growing diversity of the CAW's membership.

27. A history of the Energy and Chemical Workers Union and its drive for a Canadian approach is found in Roberts (1990). The Communications Workers, the Energy and Chemical Workers, and the Canadian Paperworkers Union later merged to form the Communications, Energy, and Paperworkers Union of Canada.

28. Yates (2000: 662-64). On women in unions in Canada, see Canadian Labour Congress (1997); Briskin and McDermott (1993); Creese (1999); Gannagé (1995); Julie White (1990); and Jerry White (1990).

29. Based on a major U.S. study of employee voting in union representation elections; see Farber and Saks (1980) and Antos et al. (1980). Once members, women are no less committed to their union than are men; see Wetzel et al. (1991).

30. Decertification refers to unionized workers voting to terminate their relationship with the union representing them. On the bank organizing drive, see Lowe (1981); Ponak and Moore (1981); and Beckett (1984). For an account of the unsuccessful 1948–1952 Eaton's organizing drive, see Sufrin (1982).

31. Pentland (1979: 19); also see Jamieson (1971: 51–52). See Bendix (1974) on U.S. employers' anti-union tactics.

32. Downie and Coates (1995: 177). For differing perspectives on this issue, see Rinehart, Huxley, and Robertson (1997); Clarke and Haiven (1999); Verma and Chaikowski (1999); Lowe (2000); Wells (1986); Appelbaum and Batt (1994); Nissen (1997); Payette (2000).

33. *The Globe and Mail* (23 November 1995: A13; 25 November 1995: A3). See Taylor (1995) for a discussion of organized labour's response to the Klein government's deficit reduction strategy.

34. Tilly's (1979: 64) example is Lipset, Trow, and Coleman's (1956) study of union democracy, which found that printers' union locals "have both distinct, compelling identities and extensive, absorbing interpersonal networks," and incorporate much of the members' lives. Clement's studies of miners (1981) and fishery workers (1986) provide Canadian examples. See Conley (1988) for a useful theoretical treatment of working-class action. Crouch's (1982) rational-choice model of trade unionism focuses even more directly on the attitudes and beliefs of individual employees, as well as on the larger contextual constraints on their actions.

35. Gouldner (1955) is the classic study of a wildcat strike. Jamieson (1971: Chapter 7) discusses the wildcat strikes that characterized the turbulent industrial relations climate in Canada during the 1960s. Also see Fisher (1982) and Zetka (1992) on wildcat strikes.

36. See Gunderson, Hyatt, and Ponak (1995) for a discussion of these trends. For historical perspectives on militancy and industrial conflict in mining, see Craven (1980: Chapter 8), Frank (1986), and Seager (1985).

37. Kerr and Siegel (1954: 191). For critiques, see Shorter and Tilly (1974: 287–305) and Stern (1976). Fisher (1982) finds empirical support in Canada for the Kerr and Siegel thesis.

38. Compare Panitch and Swartz (1993), Russell (1990) and Godard (1997).

8

THE MEANING AND EXPERIENCE OF WORK

INTRODUCTION

In previous chapters, we presented a structural analysis of work in Canada. Among other topics, we discussed labour markets, the occupational structure, work organizations, labour unions, and gender and other forms of stratification. Some of this material addressed individual reactions to work—workers' problems in balancing work and family responsibilities, and resistance and conflict in the workplace, for example. But in this final chapter, we get to the very core of the individual–job relationship by examining the meaning of work in our society and workers' subjective response to their employment situation.

The chapter begins with an overview of general work values. We ask: What does "work" mean in our society today, and how do our work values differ from those in preindustrial and early industrial societies? What can the experiences of the unemployed tell us about the meaning of work in contemporary society? Are there cultural differences in work values? Do we need a new set of values in a society where many citizens are having difficulty obtaining satisfactory employment?

We then become somewhat more specific in our analysis, asking about the types of work orientations (or preferences) held by individual Canadians. How are these work orientations shaped? Are we observing the emergence of alternative work orientations in response to long-term structural unemployment, the growth in nonstandard employment relationships, and demographic shifts in Canadian society?

The last section of the chapter focuses on job satisfaction. In general, how satisfied are Canadian workers with their employment situation? Is this changing? What factors influence job satisfaction and dissatisfaction? We then continue our discussion of individual responses to work by examining the related issues of alienation and job-related stress.

This micro-level analysis of individuals' responses to their work situation complements our macro analysis in the previous chapters. It encourages us to ask two basic types of questions. First, how does the structure of work influence individuals' experiences of work? Second, and related to the first question, what can individuals do to improve their work situation? More broadly, we are interested in the manner in which societal work values influence workplace structures, employer–employee relationships, and individual responses to work. Equally important is the question of how unequal power relationships in society might influence work values and workers' behaviours. Thus, this chapter brings together many of the book's themes by focusing on the core distinction in sociology between *individual agency* and *social structure*.

DEFINING WORK VALUES, WORK ORIENTATIONS, AND JOB SATISFACTION

Values, as sociologists use the term, are the benchmarks or standards by which members of a society assess their own and others' behaviour. We could talk about how personal attributes such as honesty and industriousness are valued in our society, about how we value the freedom of speech, or about the value placed on getting a good education. And we might ask how work is valued, or, in other words, what the meaning of work is in a particular society.

Having identified work values as societal standards, we can define *work orientations* more narrowly as the meaning attached to work by particular individuals within a society. Blackburn and Mann (1979: 141) define an orientation as "a central organizing principle which underlies people's attempts to make sense of their lives." Thus, studying work orientations involves determining what people consider important in their own lives. Does someone continue to work primarily for material reasons (a desire to become wealthy or because of economic necessity), because income from the job allows him or her to enjoy life away from work, or to get enjoyment and personal fulfillment from work? Even more specifically, what types of work and work arrangements do individuals prefer?

The distinction between work values and work orientations is not always clear, since it hinges on the extent to which the latter are broadly shared within a society. As we will argue below, several different sets of work values can coexist within a society, influencing the work orientations of individuals within that society. In fact, as our earlier discussion of managerial ideologies and practices showed, particular work values have often been promoted by employers to gain the cooperation of their workers.

An individual's work orientations are also shaped by specific experiences on the job. Indeed, a worker whose job or career is dissatisfying may begin to challenge dominant work values. Thus, over the long term, shifting work orientations on the part of many workers might also influence societal work values. *Job satisfaction* (or dissatisfaction), then, is the most individualized and subjective response of an individual to the extrinsic and intrinsic rewards offered by her or his job.

WORK VALUES ACROSS TIME AND SPACE

Historical Changes in the Meaning of Work

The meaning attached to work has changed dramatically over the centuries.[1] The ancient Greeks and Romans viewed most forms of work negatively, considering it brutalizing and uncivilized. In fact, the Greek word for "work," *ponos*, comes from the root word for "sorrow." According to Greek mythology, the gods had cursed the human race by giving them the need to work. Given these dominant work values, the ruling classes turned their attention to politics, warfare, the arts, and philosophy, leaving the physical work to slaves.

Early Hebrew religious values placed a different but no more positive emphasis on work. Hard work was seen as divine punishment for the "original sin" of the first humans who ate from the "tree of the knowledge of good and evil." According to the Old Testament, God banished Eve and Adam from the Garden of Eden, where all of creation was at their easy disposal, to a life of hard labour, telling them that "In the sweat of thy face shalt thou eat bread till thou return unto the ground."[2] This perspective on work remained part of the early Christian world view for many centuries.

A more positive view of work was promoted by Saint Thomas Aquinas in the 13th century. In ranking occupations according to their value to society, Aquinas rejected the notion that all work is a curse or a necessary evil. Instead, he argued that some forms of work were better than others. Priests were assigned the highest ranks, followed by those working in agriculture, and then craft workers. Because they produced food or products useful to society, these groups were ranked higher than merchants and shopkeepers. A comparison of this scheme to contemporary occupational status scales (see Chapter 3) reveals some interesting reversals. The status of those involved in commercial activity—bankers, corporate owners, and managers, for example—has increased, while farmers and craft workers have experienced substantial declines in occupational status.

During the 16th-century Protestant Reformation in Europe, Martin Luther's ideas marked a significant change in dominant work values. He argued that work was a central component of human life. Although he still viewed work for profit negatively, Luther went beyond the belief that hard work was an atonement for original sin. When he wrote, "There is just one best way to serve God—to do most perfectly the work of one's profession" (Burstein et al. 1975: 10), he was articulating the idea of a "calling," that is, industriousness and hard work within one's station in life, however lowly that might be, as the fulfillment of God's will. Whether or not peasants or the urban working class actually shared these values is difficult to determine. However, to the extent that the ruling classes could convince their subordinates that hard work was a moral obligation, power and privilege could be more easily maintained.

The Protestant Work Ethic

The Industrial Revolution transformed the social and economic landscape of Europe and also generated a new set of work values. In his famous book, *The Protestant Ethic and the Spirit of Capitalism,* Max Weber emphasized how the Calvinists, a Protestant group that had broken away from the mainstream churches, embraced hard work, rejected worldly pleasures, and extolled the virtues of frugality.[3] Weber was not attempting to prove that Calvinist beliefs were the cause of capitalism. Instead, he argued that religious doctrines that encouraged individuals to make and reinvest profits gave rise to work values conducive to the growth of capitalism.

Since then, other scholars have questioned whether these early Protestant entrepreneurs really acted solely on religious beliefs, and whether other groups not sharing these beliefs might have been equally successful (Dickson and McLachlan 1989). Nonetheless, Weber did draw our attention to the role of work values in capitalist societies. He also recognized that such an *ideology of work*, while justifying the profit-seeking behaviour of capitalists, might also help control their employees who, for religious reasons, would be motivated to work hard (Anthony 1977: 43).

Freedom and equality are additional secular values that fit into the belief system of capitalist democracies. A central assumption is that workers are participants in a labour market where they can freely choose their job. It must follow that some people are wealthier and more powerful than others because of hard work and prior investments in education. Hence, within this ideology of work, equality does not refer to the distribution of wealth and power, but to access to the same opportunities for upward mobility in a competitive labour market. But, as demonstrated in our discussion of labour market processes (Chapter 3), some workers are advantaged by birth, and some occupational groups are more protected in the labour market. Consequently, for many workers, the daily realities of the labour market often contradict the dominant set of work values.

Work as Self-Fulfillment: The Humanist Tradition

The importance of hard work and wealth accumulation are only one perspective on work in a capitalist society. The belief that work is virtuous in itself gave rise to another set of values in the 17th and 18th centuries. The *humanist tradition* grew out of Renaissance philosophies that distinguished humans from other species on the basis of our ability to consciously direct our labour. A view of human beings as creators easily led to the belief that work should be a fulfilling and liberating activity, and that it constituted the very essence of humanity. From this perspective, work was the means through which humans could fulfill their potential.

Karl Marx fashioned these ideas into a radical critique of capitalism and a formula for social revolution. He agreed that the essence of humanity was expressed through work, but argued that this potential was stifled by capitalist relations of production. Because they had little control over their labour and its products, workers were engaged in alienating work. For Marx, capitalist economic relations limited human independence and creativity. Only when capitalism was replaced by socialism, he argued, would work be truly liberating.

Marx's theory of alienation has had a major impact on the sociology of work, as we explain later in this chapter. Interestingly, a similar set of beliefs about the centrality of work to an individual's sense of personal well-being underlies a number of contemporary management approaches, which are decidedly non-Marxist in their assumptions (see Chapter 5). It is often argued, for example, that workers would be more satisfied if they were allowed to use more of their skills and abilities in their job. But these management perspectives do not see capitalism as the problem. Rather, they advocate better organizational systems and job designs within capitalism.

Humanistic beliefs about the essential importance of work have also been espoused by some contemporary theologians who address economic issues from a social justice perspective. For example, in response to rising levels of unemployment in Canada in the early 1990s, a group of Catholic bishops prepared a discussion paper on "the crisis of work." In their call for greater government involvement in the economy and more corporate responsibility for job creation, they argued that:

> It is through the human activity of work, that people are able to develop their sense of self-identity and self-worth, acquire an adequate income for their personal and family needs, and to participate in the building-up of one's community and society (Canadian Conference of Catholic Bishops (1991: 2).

Experiencing Unemployment:
Identifying the Meaning of Work in Its Absence

Many studies tell us that unemployment is extremely traumatic for jobless individuals and their families.[4] But the Catholic Bishops suggest that the unemployed are disadvantaged in ways that go beyond lost income, a lower standard of living, personal and family stress, and health problems. They take the humanist position that work gives meaning in our lives. Thus, by examining the experience of unemployment, the gaps left by the loss of a paid job, we can gain further insights about the personal and social functions of work.

Based on her research among the unemployed during the Depression of the 1930s, Marie Jahoda (1982) identified some of the *latent functions* of work, which people miss if they lose their jobs. While the *manifest function* of work is, primarily, maintaining or improving one's standard of living, the latent (less obvious) functions contribute to an individual's personal well-being. Work can provide experiences of creativity and mastery, and can foster a sense of purpose. It can be self-fulfilling, although, clearly, some jobs offer much less fulfillment than others. When hit by unemployment, an individual loses these personal rewards, as illustrated by the following comments by a nutritionist about her 14 months of unemployment:

> I feel like I'm wasting time. I feel like I'm not accomplishing anything. I don't really feel like I'm contributing to the marriage, to society, or anything like that.[5]

Work also provides regularly shared experiences and often enjoyable interactions with co-workers. When the job is gone, so are such personally satisfying routines. The unemployed individual quickly comes to miss these social rewards, and may also find that relationships away from work are no longer the same.[6] Such feelings are expressed in the following way by an unemployed teacher:

> The whole feeling that I had ... [was] that nobody really understood where I was, what I was going through, what I cared about, what was important to me. Because I was no longer talking about my job as a teacher, in fact I wasn't talking about my job as anything. I had a strong sense of not fitting in.

In addition, work structures time. Individuals who have lost their job frequently find that their days seem not only empty, but disorienting. A divorced mother of a four-year-old, living with her own mother to make ends meet, explains:

> If you went to work, at least you're coming home in the evening. When I'm home all day ... I get confused. My whole metabolism's gone crazy, because it's, like, I'm coming back from ... where I have been. Or I've gone and I'm still waiting to come home.

Being unemployed often requires that one seek financial assistance, sometimes from family members, but more often through government agencies. Dealing with the bureaucracy can be frustrating. Even more problematic, receiving social assistance carries a great deal of *stigma*. As a former factory worker, the mother of two small children, explains:

> When I went down there, I felt that I just stuck right out. I thought, "Oh, my God, people think I'm on welfare ... You used to think "It's those people who are on welfare," and now you discover you're one of those people.

The same value system that rewards individuals for their personal success also leads to what Jean Swanson (2001) calls "poor-bashing," the perpetuation in the media, in our legislation and social programs, and in our everyday discourse, of myths and stereotypes about the poor and the unemployed being lazy, unmotivated, and undeserving of assistance. This, in turn, can lead unemployed people to blame themselves for their own problems, even if they recognize the structural barriers they are facing. Swanson (2001: 10) quotes an unemployed former bank employee who exemplifies such contradictory feelings:

> I never chose to be poor. I'm ashamed of what I am now, but it's beyond my ability to change things. I'm still alive. I haven't committed suicide. I'm living with hope. Although I know with all my heart that it's not my fault, the system makes you feel guilty. Society makes you feel guilty.

These glimpses into the lives of unemployed Canadians reflect the value placed on work in our society as a potential source of self-fulfillment and social integration. At the same time, a set of more materialistic work values are highlighted through the stigma and self-blame that can result from joblessness, seen by some unemployed people as a mark of their own labour market failure. Thus, while career success and wealth accumulation are at the core of one of the value systems in capitalist society, the humanist perspective on work as a source of self-identity and personal satisfaction reflects an equally important alternative set of work values.

Cultural Variations in Work Values

Max Weber argued that the Protestant work ethic provided a set of work values that were conducive to the emergence of a new capitalist mode of production. Today, when we compare the economic performance of different countries in the global economy, we might be tempted to make a similar "cultural differences" argument. Do Japan and the Southeast Asian tiger economies owe some of their success to a different set of work values in these societies?

As Japan's economy outperformed the rest of the world in the 1980s, a common explanation was that Japanese workers simply had a much stronger work ethic. They willingly worked long hours, often went without holidays, and were more strongly committed to their employers than were Western workers.[7] Typically, explanations of this behaviour focused on cultural differences, suggesting that the Japanese have always exhibited strong patterns of conformity and social integration. In modern times, the corporation has assumed the once-central roles of the family and the community in the lives of Japanese workers. Hence, Japanese workers exhibit great loyalty to their employers and work extremely hard. From the vantage point of North America, the presumably stronger work ethic of Japanese employees appeared to be a key ingredient in the Japanese "economic miracle."

As the economies of Singapore, South Korea, Taiwan, and Hong Kong expanded rapidly, similar cultural explanations about different underlying work values have been proposed for their success. Like descriptions of the presumably more-motivated Japanese workers, this "Confucian work ethic" argument attributed the economic success of these economies to traditional habits of hard work, greater willingness to work toward a common social goal, and employees' ready compliance with authority.[8] Without such willing and motivated workers, it has been reasoned, these economies could not have grown as quickly.

Undoubtedly, there are cross-national differences in the way people respond to work in general, to new technologies, and to their employers' demands for compliance and/or new employment relationships. North American workers, for example, may be somewhat less accepting of Japanese-style management approaches that expect workers to show unwavering loyalty to company goals. Workers in Asian countries may think of their work organization in less individualistic and more family-like terms.[9] That said, it is overstating such differences to argue that a Confucian work ethic explains the rapid growth of the East Asian economies. If it does, why did the rapid growth not begin earlier? Why are there significant differences among the four "tigers" in the way firms are organized (see Chapter 1), in the extent to which democratic rights of workers are respected, and in the role of the state in economic development (Siu-Kai and Hsin-Chi 1988)?

Conceding that there are some cultural differences in work values (Super and Šverko 1995), we would argue that they are not central to explanations of national differences in economic development in today's global economy. Far more crucial are the production decisions of firms regarding technology, employment practices, and research and development, and the extent to which governments actively participate in economic development strategies. In fact, research suggests that the cause-and-effect relationship may frequently operate in the opposite direction—work values and, in turn, employee behaviour can be influenced by employment practices and labour market institutions.[10]

The Japanese labour market is highly segmented, even more so than in Canada. Only a minority of Japanese workers are employed in the huge, profitable, high-technology corporations so admired by Western observers. Most people work in smaller businesses that subcontract to make parts or provide services for the giant firms. The major advantages of this arrangement for the large corporations include the flexibility of being able to expand and contract their labour force without hiring permanent employees, and the reduction in inventory costs through the just-in-time delivery of components from the subcontracting businesses.

Along with higher wages, major Japanese firms offered their employees lifetime employment guarantees, a variety of fringe benefits, and opportunities for skill development and upward advancement within the corporation. However, this form of job security was eroded in the 1990s, as major Japanese corporations struggled to adapt to a weak economy. Even so, loyalty and commitment to the firm have long been part of Japanese corporate culture, with internal labour markets (see Chapter 3) playing a major role in maintaining the stability of the system (Hill 1988: 246–47). In fact, some critics have argued that company loyalty is built on fears of job loss, and that the economic benefits provided to workers in major firms simply make it easier for their employers to demand compliance and hard work.[11] By contrast, in small firms and family businesses, low pay, few benefits, and little job security mean workers have to work long hours to make a living. Thus, for both core- and periphery-sector Japanese employees, the willingness to work long and hard may have much more to do with organizational and economic factors than is often recognized.

Evidence supportive of this "internal labour market" explanation comes from a large comparative study that found Japanese workers more likely than U.S. workers to be employed in firms where benefits were extensive, where some employee participation in decision making was encouraged, and where mobility opportunities and job security were provided. However, given a similar organizational context, there were few differences in commitment to one's firm between the two countries. In short, in Japan economic and organizational factors have a significant influence on workplace behaviours and work values, just as they do in North America (Lincoln and Kalleberg 1985; 1990).

Yet global economic pressures are forcing even the largest Japanese corporations to alter their employment practices. High wages for all company employees are no longer the norm, and subcontracting of production tasks to peripheral firms has increased. New technologies have made more workers redundant and, perhaps most importantly, traditional patterns of lifelong employment have begun to disappear. As the Japanese labour force rapidly ages, it is frequently the older employees, with the most years of service, who find themselves without employment security (Kumazawa and Yamada 1989:

10; Whittaker 1990). This suggests a convergence in Japanese and North American management approaches and, perhaps, work ethics.

A Need for New (Nonpaid) Work Values?

Unemployment levels have risen in most of the Western industrialized economies over the past several decades. Nonstandard employment has increased significantly, placing more workers in jobs with limited hours and low pay. At the same time, other workers face a longer and more stressful work week. Given these significant changes, perhaps we need a different set of dominant work values. Specifically, if more citizens would come to recognize that there is a world outside the workplace and begin to value the benefits of nonpaid work and the pleasures of leisure activities, perhaps we would get back on track to a better society.

This is not a new idea. Two decades ago in his provocative book, *Farewell to the Working Class*, Andre Gorz (1982) argued that we need to recognize that higher levels of unemployment also mean more free time for individuals to participate in nonpaid work and leisure activities. Recognizing that people still need to work to make a living, he suggested that new technologies have reduced the time it takes to produce what is needed for a decent standard of living. Consequently, Gorz called for a new set of values that replaced hard work, labour market competition, and consumption of material goods with more emphasis on the personal fulfillment that comes from nonpaid work activities and leisure pursuits.

Similar ideas have been promoted in a number of recent books about the future of work in Western societies. Jamie Swift concludes his description of growing labour market inequality in Canada by noting that, along with many more poorer workers, we have another more advantaged group of workers, overworked and stressed from the long hours they put into their jobs. He reflects on "the lunacy of lives driven by the compulsions of work, speed, and consumption," and calls for more attention to "the good life" rather than "the goods life."[12] Like Gorz, Swift recommends a new set of work values that emphasize working less, consuming less, and seeking self-fulfillment not only in paid work but also in healthy leisure pursuits and in (nonpaid) caring for others around us. We need, he writes, a "radical rethinking of how we spend our time and what we find rewarding" (Swift 1995: 240).

Jeremy Rifkin develops similar ideas, arguing that the industrial transformations occurring today will be more traumatic for workers than were previous industrial revolutions. While manufacturing jobs replaced agricultural jobs and, in turn, service jobs replaced manufacturing jobs, new technologies and global production patterns essentially mean the "end of work" as we know it for many people (Rifkin 1995). Like Gorz and Swift, Rifkin advocates redefining work values, proposing that we involve more people in the voluntary sector of the economy. People without paid employment would find personal fulfillment in caring for others, improving the environment, and making a contribution to society in other ways.

Clearly, labour market polarization and growing social inequality are social problems that need to be addressed. Emphasizing the value of nonpaid work and reducing inequities in access to paid work are all part of a solution. So too are stressing the importance of caring for others and the environment and emphasizing that there is more to a good life than merely earning a high income and acquiring and consuming material goods. But writers like Gorz, Swift, and Rifkin fail to tell us how such a transformation of social values can be achieved. Nor do they explain how high levels of inequality between those with paid jobs and those without will be avoided.[13] In a society where women have traditionally been expected to do most of the "caring work" (see Chapter 4), would nonpaid voluntary work continue to be seen as "women's work"? There is also an intergenerational equity concern: since older workers are often more economically secure, is it fair to encourage young Canadians to change their values and reduce their career aspirations, arguing that they are the ones who will face the "end of work"?

While it is important to rethink dominant work values, an overemphasis on changing work values as *the* solution to labour market polarization can also divert our attention from the sources of growing inequality. Today's more precarious economy is not simply the product of natural market forces. Real people in positions of power make decisions to change technologies, to move factories, and to push workers to accept less income and fewer hours of work and less job security. Consequently, there is room for individuals, unions, and the government either to resist some of these trends or to reshape them (Noble 1995). In fact, we would argue that the work values of employers need to be reshaped as well, with commitments to profits at all costs being balanced with greater responsibility to employees and the larger community (Lowe 2000, Lowe and Schellenberg 2001).

Since many well-paid workers put in long hours while others have trouble making a living on part-time jobs, work redistribution must be part of the solution.[14] Alternative forms of work organizations such as worker-owned cooperatives can help reduce labour market inequalities and, in some settings, can also contribute to improvements in community life (Brown 1997). A greater emphasis on industrial democracy in its various forms (see Chapter 6) might reduce labour market polarization. And, as we have argued, there is still an important role to be played by government through labour legislation, income support, and retraining programs and industrial strategies that encourage job creation.

Critics might dismiss such efforts to reduce labour market inequalities as out of step with today's political and economic reality. In fact, evidence suggests that they are in line with the dominant social values of Canadians. A recent study concluded that concerns about people being self-reliant rather than relying on government and about the government being fiscally responsible were prominent among Canadians. But equally central to the *core social values* of Canadians were compassion and a feeling of collective responsibility for others, a concern about opportunities for future generations, and a belief that government had a role to play in reducing inequalities.[15] For example, in 1987, about 50 percent of Canadians agreed that government has a responsibility to see that everyone has a job and a decent standard of living. By 1993, the proportion agreeing had risen to 60 percent.

WORK ORIENTATIONS

Having discussed how societal work values have changed over time, might vary across cultures, and need to be re-examined in light of today's economic realities, we now shift our analysis to individuals' job expectations—the type of work orientations they bring to their jobs. Are most Canadians motivated by a desire to be successful and become wealthy? Do they merely work to earn money in order to purchase satisfaction elsewhere, or is their work a source of personal fulfillment? Do women and men have similar orientations to work? Are specific groups of labour force participants beginning to exhibit different types of work orientations, and if so, why?

Instrumental Work Orientations

Almost four decades ago, David Lockwood commented on some of the differences he observed in male British working-class "images of society." Lockwood was interested in the issue of *working-class consciousness* how British workers perceived social inequality. He identified three distinct world views originating in different community and workplace experiences. *Proletarian workers*, argued Lockwood, saw the world in much the way Marx had predicted: they perceived themselves to be in an "us against them" conflict with their employers. Lockwood (1966) concluded that this image of society was more pronounced in industries such as shipbuilding and mining where large differences between management and workers in terms of income, power, and opportunities for upward mobility had produced heightened class consciousness.

Deferential workers also recognized class differences, but accepted the status quo, believing that wealth and power inequities were justified. Provided they were treated decently, deferential workers were unlikely to engage in militant actions against employers. Lockwood located this world view in the traditional service industries and in family firms where paternalistic employment relationships foster acceptance of the existing stratification.

Both of these traditional orientations to work, Lockwood argued, were found primarily in declining industries. The third type, *instrumental work orientations*, were more typical of the attitudes of the contemporary (1960s) working class, whose members Lockwood labelled *privatized workers*. They viewed society as being separated into many levels on the basis of income and possessions. Rather than expressing antagonism or attachment to their employers, the dominant feeling of these workers was one of indifference. According to Lockwood, the "cash nexus" (the pay received), and not feelings of antagonism or deference, constituted the employment relationship for such workers. Work was simply a way to obtain a better standard of living, an "instrument" used to achieve other nonwork goals.

Lockwood and his colleagues went on to conduct a major study of the work orientations of a group of male auto workers in Luton, a manufacturing town north of London, England. These "affluent workers" had chosen to move to this new industrial town because the jobs available would provide them with the money and security needed to enjoy a middle-class standard of living. The fact that work in the Vauxhall automobile factory was not intrinsically rewarding did not seem to matter. In their book describing this study, the researchers essentially concluded that these workers exemplified the modern worker in western industrialized economies (Goldthorpe et al. 1969).

• But critics argue that contemporary workers appear to be instrumental only in comparison with an idealized proletarian worker of the past, and that the conclusions drawn from this study were overgeneralizations (MacKinnon 1981). Based on their study of the male labour market in another British city, Robert M. Blackburn and Michael Mann found that most workers reported a variety of work orientations. In addition, there was often little congruence between an individual's expressed work preferences and the characteristics of his job. Blackburn and Mann (1979: 155) explained this finding by arguing that the major flaw with an *orientations model* of labour market processes is that many people have few job choices, taking whatever work they can get, even if it is not what they would prefer. A further criticism is that only men were included in these studies, although the researchers assumed that the findings applied to all workers.

Individuals' work preferences can also be modified in the workplace. If a job offers few intrinsic rewards or little opportunity to develop a career, workers may adjust their values and priorities accordingly. This might explain why studies have shown instrumental work orientations to be more common among workers in monotonous, assembly-line jobs (MacKinnon 1981; Rinehart 1978). Richard Sennett and Jonathan Cobb (1972) examined this theme in their book, *The Hidden Injuries of Class*. Their discussions with American blue-collar workers revealed a tendency to downplay intrinsic work rewards, few of which were available to them, while emphasizing pay and job security. Workers interviewed by Sennett and Cobb also redefined the meaning of personal success, frequently talking about how hard they were working in order to provide their children with the chance to go to college.

Thus, we should not be surprised if some workers do have instrumental work orientations, given the strong emphasis on material success in our society, and current fears about job security. By way of example, in 1996, 35 percent of a national sample of employed Canadians agreed that "[m]y current job is a way to make money—it's not a career." In another study conducted several years earlier, almost 2,500 private sector and crown corporation employees across the country were asked to rank the relative personal importance of a number of job rewards. This 1991 survey showed that about one in four workers (23 percent) ranked pay higher than any other work reward.[16]

But most employed Canadians are not motivated primarily by instrumental work orientations. Instead, along with a desire for good pay, extensive benefits, and job security, workers also want intrinsically satisfying work. A national survey of 2,500 Canadian workers conducted in 2000 revealed, for example, that 85 percent or more felt that good pay, good benefits, job security, work that was interesting, work that provided a sense of accomplishment, and work that allowed the development of skills and abilities were "important" or "very important" to them personally. However, it is also noteworthy that the intrinsic work rewards (interesting work, accomplishment, and skill development) were rated as important by 95 percent or more of the sample members, compared to 85 to 90 percent for the extrinsic rewards (pay, benefits, security).[17]

Gender and Work Orientations

The early studies of work orientations that we reviewed focused only on men. When the work orientations of women were mentioned, it was often assumed that their interests were directed primarily toward the home, and less toward paid employment. The argument that *gender role socialization* might encourage women to place less value on intrinsic and extrinsic job rewards and more on social relationships in the family, the community, and on the job seemed plausible in the 1960s and early 1970s when many of these studies were completed.

However, there is another more compelling structural explanation. Women and men work in very different labour market locations, and women typically receive fewer job rewards. Hence, gender differences in work orientations might also be adaptations to their employment situation. Using the same logic as in our explanation of why unskilled blue-collar workers might have more instrumental work orientations—their low-level jobs discourage other types of work preferences—we could also argue that female work orientations, to the extent that they differ from those of men, are a function of workplace differences.[18]

In addition, the domestic and child-care responsibilities that many women continue to carry force some to readjust their work and career goals. As a part-time nurse explained:

"My career is important to me. I don't want to give that up. But my main concern is the children ... So I give about 100 percent to the children and maintain a career at the same time." (Duffy and Pupo 1992: 116)

Similarly, in her study of young university-educated women, Ranson (1998) observed that, particularly for those who had chosen nontraditional careers in science and engineering, the pressures of balancing family and job demands required a reassessment of either or both their parenthood and career aspirations. As one young women explained when asked about her parenthood plans:

Actually I've thought, would I work or would I stay home? ... I've spent a lot of time going to school. I've worked my way up. Like, do I want to give all that up? [Because] if you come back to the work force in five years you're not going to work where you left off. Then the other part of me thinks, well, you have to make that choice, it's one or the other. (Ranson 1998: 529)

Once again, these examples point to structural determinants—the gendered household division of labour and the frequent absence of family-friendly employment policies—rather than to female personality characteristics.

CHANGING ORIENTATIONS TO WORK?

In the 1960s, during a period of economic expansion and rising standards of living, the Affluent Worker research team concluded that a new set of work orientations—the instrumental sentiments of privatized workers—were emerging. Today, we are observing substantial industrial restructuring, along with a major shift in the nature of employment relationships. The characteristics of the labour force are changing as well (see Chapter 2). It is not surprising, then, to find observers of these changes concluding that work orientations may also be in flux. While we seldom have enough comparable data from different points in time to fully substantiate claims of changing work orientations, it would still be useful to examine some of these arguments.

Work or Leisure as a Central Life Interest?

Do most Canadians continue to see their jobs as central to their lives, or are we beginning to see a greater emphasis on leisure and satisfactions deriving from nonwork activities? The analysts of an Environics survey conducted in the late 1980s concluded that the latter was the case, quoting a young male Winnipeg technologist: "I like toys, and to pay for those toys I have to work. But if I could have four days of work and three days of leisure, I'd take it." The pollsters concluded that there is "a growing insistence on personal pleasure" (Maynard 1987: 114). At about the same time, in a book about "motivating and leading the new generation," Michael Maccoby (1988: 20) wrote that:

> Motivated to succeed in family life as well as in a career, and to balance work with play, they [the new generation] continually question how much of themselves to invest in the workplace. They want to know why they are working, as opposed to expressing themselves outside of the job.

This argument suggests that the types of (nonpaid) work values desired by Andre Gorz, Jamie Swift, and Jeremy Rifkin have already taken root in our society. It is interesting, however, to see such value systems being promoted as "new," given that industrial sociologists have been debating questions about *work as a central life interest* for many decades (Dubin et al. 1975). Thus, broad generalizations about the more diverse personal goals of today's workers may be based on an oversimplified one-dimensional view of the life interests of previous generations.

Nevertheless, American public opinion surveys indicate that, during the 1980s, the proportion of U.S. workers who said that their leisure time was more important than their work time increased until, by 1989, the leisure advocates were in the majority (Waldrop 1992). However, a more recent Ontario study introduced an important qualification. Three-quarters of the more than 1,500 employed subjects in the study stated that they would be interested in reduced time spent at work if they could maintain their income levels. The authors interpret this finding as indicating an increase in instrumental work orientations (Reid and Mannell 1994: 262). However, it might simply indicate a realistic assessment of today's more precarious employment climate and a sense of anxiety over possible permanent income loss if one decided to cut back on time spent at work.

In fact, the better-paid workers in the Ontario study were more likely to predict that their work time would decrease in the future. Similarly, as we observe the continued decline in retirement age in Canada (Sunter 2001: 36), we also observe that workers with better pension plans and more savings are more likely to be able to retire early.[19] Thus, individuals employed in the secondary labour market, where pay is lower and pensions are less common, may not have the luxury of thinking about leisure pursuits as alternatives to paid work.

The baby boom generation may also have helped to create the appearance of growing leisure interests among North American workers. As this very large cohort moves through middle age, many of its members are reaching their career peak in terms of both promotions and earning potential (Foot and Stoffman 1998). These employees may be finding that other personal and community interests are now as compelling as their jobs. The same aging process no doubt affected the life interests of previous generations of workers. But because the baby boom is such a large cohort, their mid-life responses would dominate public opinion surveys conducted today. Rather than societal values shifting, perhaps a larger proportion of today's workers are at that point in their life course when non-work interests begin to compete with work interests (Lorence and Mortimer 1985).

The Work Orientations of Youth

Socrates is reputed to have said that "[c]hildren today are tyrants. They contradict their parents, gobble their food and terrorize their teachers." If he had lived today, he might also have added that "they don't want to work hard" since such concerns about deficient work orientations have frequently been part of the public stereotype of youth. In the 1960s and 1970s, for example, the counterculture activities of some North American youth led to fears that the work ethic of this new generation was declining. Most members of that cohort are now settled into their careers, thus demonstrating that these fears were largely unfounded. It seems that each generation, when observing the generation following, sees lifestyle experimentation, forgets its own similar experiences, and concludes that values are slipping.

What are the concerns about the work orientations of today's youth? At first glance, debates about the possibly inadequate *employability skills* of young Canadians seem to have little to do with the subject of work orientations. The Conference Board of Canada, an organization representing large public- and private-sector employers, published an *Employability Skills Profile (ESP)* in 1993. In this pamphlet, the Conference Board (1993) listed a set of "critical skills required for the Canadian workplace" as identified by employers. Included in the list are *academic skills* (communication, thinking, ability to learn), *personal management skills* (positive attitudes and behaviours, responsibility, adaptability), and *teamwork skills* (the ability to work with others). The ESP has been influential, focusing debate on the types of skills that schools should be developing in students in order to prepare them for employment in the rapidly changing labour market. It has also at times fueled public criticisms of the educational system.

Clearly, all of the skills identified in the ESP are important, not only for young workers, but for all labour force participants, even though not all of these skills would be equally necessary in all jobs. However, more careful scrutiny of the public education system suggests that, with respect to teaching academic skills, Canadian schools are performing quite well.[20] Furthermore, research indicates that when hiring young people for entry-level positions, many employers focus mainly on motivation, perceived work ethic, and the personality of the applicant—in other words, on work orientations rather than on skills. Young job seekers are told that "proper attitude earns a job."[21]

Are today's youth less willing to "work hard" and to make a commitment to an employer? Unfortunately, there is little reliable data documenting shifts in the "soft" employability skills of youth. But a majority of high school students work part-time at some point while completing school, suggesting that there is a strong desire to work, even if only for the money. Continued high rates of participation in post-secondary education (see Chapter 2) indicate that youth are willing to work hard to obtain the credentials needed for better jobs. And studies of youth continue to show high levels of general work commitment. For example, in 1985 we conducted a survey of approximately 1,000 Edmonton Grade 12 students about their work and education plans and experiences. In 1996, we repeated the study. Only 9 percent of the first cohort agreed that "I'd rather collect welfare than work at a job I don't like," compared to 7 percent of the 1996 cohort. Similarly, only one in eight respondents in both surveys agreed that "I would not mind being unemployed for a while." (Lowe and Krahn 2000). Such facts leave us skeptical about the supposed "work attitude" problem of today's youth.

The employment difficulties faced by Canadian youth are real, as we have demonstrated in Chapters 2 and 3. Continuing high levels of structural unemployment, corporate and public sector downsizing, and an increase in nonstandard jobs have made it much more difficult for young people to cash in their educational investments for good jobs. It may also have led to a prolonged entry into adult roles, such as living on one's own, marriage, and parenthood.[22] Recognizing these trends, in 1993, Douglas Coupland wrote a fictional account of the experiences of today's youth moving between jobs and relationships. *Generation X: Tales for an Accelerated Culture* was a bestseller. Its portrayal of the post–baby-boom generation as cynical and alienated, with few career goals and largely instrumental work orientations, became part of popular culture.

The Generation X view of changing work orientations differs from public concerns about employability skills. It focuses on somewhat older, more educated youth rather than on recent high school graduates, and diagnoses "the problem" more specifically, pointing to a devaluing of careers and intrinsic work rewards, rather than simply a reluctance to work hard. It points to structural changes in the labour market—a lack of satisfactory employment opportunities—as the source of the problem, rather than to schools and their presumed failure to socialize appropriate work attitudes in youth.

Is there evidence of the emergence of Generation X work orientations? The answer appears to be no. A majority of young Canadians continue to invest in higher education, despite rising tuition fees, hoping to get good jobs. Many continue to pursue additional work-related training after obtaining formal qualifications (Lowe and Krahn 1995). Surveys of youth fail to reveal a decline in commitment to work or a reduced interest in intrinsic work rewards. For example, in 1985 we surveyed graduates of the five largest faculties at the University of Alberta, asking them about their work goals and career ambitions. In 1996, we repeated the study, asking identical questions of graduates from the same faculties. In response to a question about "how important would the following be to you when looking for a full-time job after leaving school?" 92 percent of the class of 1985 agreed that "work that is interesting" would be important to them, compared to 96 percent of the class of

1996. Similarly, over 90 percent of both cohorts agreed that "work that gives a feeling of accomplishment" would be important to them. For both questions, the proportion who answered "very important" increased over time (Rollings-Magnusson et al. 1999). Other findings from these studies lead to the same conclusion: young Canadians continue to aspire to good jobs and satisfying careers.

The 1996 survey also showed 74 percent of the university graduates agreeing that "it will be harder for people in my generation to live as comfortably as previous generations," a sentiment echoed by 65 percent of Alberta Grade 12 students (Rollings-Magnusson et al. 1999). Thus, while the basic work orientations of youth may not have changed, and while their work ethic has not declined, there is considerably more anxiety about future employment prospects. A generation ago, an expanding economy allowed a larger proportion of youth to launch satisfying careers. Today, labour market restructuring has made career entry more difficult for Canadian youth and heightened their employment anxiety.

At the same time, reduced loyalty and commitment by many employers to their workers, as reflected in greater reliance on part-time and temporary workers, may also translate into less commitment and loyalty to the work organization by employees, both young and old (Lowe and Schellenberg 2001; Gallie et al. 1998: 306). For example, a national survey conducted by Canadian Policy Research Networks in 2000 showed 50 percent of the 2,100 paid employees in the sample (the self-employed were excluded in this analysis) agreeing that "I feel very little loyalty to this organization." Another 23 percent agreed strongly with this statement.[23] However, rather than indicating a decline in the work ethic, this points to a possible change in the relationship between workers and their employers. It also indicates a problem that employers, not schools, need to address. How do you motivate workers without offering them some degree of employment security and satisfaction in return? As nonstandard work becomes more common, employers will be forced to face this issue more directly.[24]

Welfare Dependency and an Emerging Underclass?

The poor also have been the frequent target of public concern about a "declining work ethic," since it is often easier to blame them for their plight than to try to understand the structural conditions that create poverty (Wright 1993; Swanson 2001). During the 1970s, growing awareness of extensive poverty, particularly among Black Americans, prompted fears that fewer people were willing to work. By way of example, in 1972, U.S. President Richard Nixon stated that American society was threatened by the "new welfare ethic that could cause the American character to weaken."[25]

￼However, in both Canada and the United States, national surveys conducted in the 1970s failed to reveal a declining work ethic. Very few Canadian respondents agreed that they would rather collect unemployment insurance than hold a job. Most stated that, given the choice, they would prefer working to not having a job, and that work was a central aspect of their lives. Paradoxically, these same respondents doubted the work commitment of other Canadians. Four out of five agreed that "[t]here is an atmosphere of welfare for anybody who wants it in this country."[26] People seemed to be saying that they personally wanted to work, but that social institutions made it easy for others to avoid working.

Has anything changed over the past several decades? A national survey of Canadian workers conducted in 2000 led to the conclusion that the work ethic remains strong (Lowe and Schellenberg 2001: 40).[27] But negative public opinion about social assistance programs and the work orientations of recipients also remains relatively unchanged. National surveys conducted in 1994 showed 68 percent of Canadians agreeing that "the existence of our social programs makes it too easy for people to give up looking for work." A smaller majority (55 percent) agreed that "if people just took more responsibility for themselves and their families we wouldn't need all of these social programs." Sixty-three percent supported lower unemployment insurance benefits for frequent users of the UI system, presumably because they felt they were less deserving (Peters 1995: 115–16).

What has changed, however, are the social assistance programs themselves. During the 1990s, the Unemployment Insurance program (now called Employment Insurance) was altered, making it more difficult for seasonal workers to obtain benefits. In several provinces, social assistance benefits have been cut back for "able-bodied" recipients, and *workfare* programs that require recipients to work in public projects have been introduced.[28] Thus, in the past decade, long-standing beliefs that many of the poor are reluctant to work, perhaps because the *social safety net* is too comfortable, have had a significant influence on public policy.

In fact, with the number of long-term unemployed increasing in many Western industrialized countries, and with income inequality rising, some observers have begun to label the most marginalized members of society as an *underclass*, even though the term has been used very imprecisely (see Chapter 3). Some discussions of this new underclass are sympathetic, arguing that this level of social inequality is unacceptable. Other commentators treat the trend toward greater inequality as largely inevitable, worrying instead about welfare dependency. The argument, simply put, is that prolonged receipt of social assistance and unemployment insurance benefits leads to changed attitudes: both the stigma of receiving assistance and the desire to seek paid employment decline. Even more troubling, such accounts suggest, these welfare dependency orientations can be passed on to the children of the poor (Buckingham 1999).

Is there any basis to such fears about a declining work ethic within the poorest members of society, or are we simply seeing ideological justifications for reducing social assistance benefits to the poor and unemployed? The best test would be to determine whether the presumed weak work ethic of the poor translates into little effort to seek paid work or other sources of income. Research that has taken this approach invariably leads to the same conclusion —a weak work ethic and a lack of effort are seldom the problem. Much more often, the problem is one of not enough good jobs and inadequate social and labour market policies (Schwartz 1999; Jaynes 2000).

In fact, the majority of Canada's poor are not welfare-dependent but "working poor," seeking to maintain their standard of living on jobs with low pay and short hours. While long-term unemployment has increased in Canada, there is actually a great deal of movement in and out of poverty as individuals lose jobs, move from social assistance to a low-paying job, become divorced, or enter retirement without an adequate pension.[29] In regions or cities where unemployment is high, a great deal of productive work continues to take place in the informal economy, including subsistence work performed by street people and the homeless.[30] Such widespread initiative is hardly evidence of a failing work ethic.

Furthermore, when offered jobs that pay only a few dollars more than the minimum wage, welfare recipients have demonstrated a great willingness to work (Social Research and Demonstration Corporation 1996). As for the argument that welfare dependency attitudes are passed from one generation to the next, research shows little of this happening (Duncan et al. 1988). Thus, while we are concerned about rising social inequality, we are not convinced by accounts of welfare dependency and a declining work ethic among the poor and unemployed.

JOB SATISFACTION AND DISSATISFACTION

We began this chapter with an overview of societal work values and then examined the work orientations or preferences of individuals. Now we will focus on job satisfaction and dissatisfaction, the subjective reactions of individual workers to the particular set of rewards, intrinsic or extrinsic, provided by their job (Blackburn and Mann 1979: 167).

What do Canadians find most and least satisfying about their jobs? Are most of them satisfied? Do people's work orientations influence what they find satisfying in a job? Can job satisfaction or dissatisfaction affect workers off the job? Some researchers assume that productivity is a function of job satisfaction. Their goal has been to discover how to organize work and manage employees in a way that leads to increased satisfaction, productivity, and profits. Others, adopting the humanistic view that work is an essential part of being human, view satisfying and self-fulfilling work for as many people as possible as a desirable societal goal in itself.

The Prevalence of Job Satisfaction

The standard measure of job satisfaction in survey research is some variation of "All in all, how satisfied are you with your job?" In response, a very large majority of workers typically report some degree of satisfaction. Just how large that majority is depends on the response categories offered to survey participants. If they cannot choose a neutral mid-point, a larger proportion indicate that they are satisfied. For example, a 1998 Angus Reid – Royal Bank survey of 1,200 employed Canadians revealed that 42 percent were "very satisfied" while 46 percent indicated that they were "somewhat satisfied" with their job (the other two response options were "somewhat dissatisfied" and "very dissatisfied."[31] But when provided with a neutral mid-point on a job satisfaction scale, a significant minority choose this response. Using such a five-point scale, a Canadian Policy Research Networks (CPRN) national survey in 2000 found that 71 percent of Canadian workers were satisfied with their job (28% were very satisfied), 20 percent were neither satisfied or dissatisfied, while only 9 expressed dissatisfaction (Figure 8.1).

These results, and many similar findings over the past few decades (Firebaugh and Harley 1995), imply that job dissatisfaction is not a serious problem. However, there are several reasons why we could question such a

FIGURE 8.1 *Job Satisfaction* by Selected Demographic and Labour Market Characteristics, Canada, 2000*

*Survey respondents could answer "very satisfied," "satisfied," "neither," "dissatisfied," and "very dissatisfied." The last two categories have been combined in this chart.

Source: CPRN-Ekos 2000. *Changing Employment Relationships Survey.*

conclusion. James Rinehart points out that workers' behaviours—strikes, absenteeism, and quitting—all indicate more dissatisfaction with working conditions than do attitude surveys. Rinehart (1978: 7) proposes that answers to general questions about job satisfaction are "pragmatic judgements of one's position vis-à-vis the narrow range of available jobs." Most workers look at their limited alternatives and conclude, from this frame of reference, that they are relatively satisfied with their work.

Essentially, responses to general job satisfaction questions may be similar to replies to the question, "How are you today?" Most of us would say "fine," whether or not this were the case. Hence, more probing questions may be needed to uncover specific feelings of job dissatisfaction. We should also recognize that in a society with highly individualistic work values, people may be unwilling to express dissatisfaction with their jobs because it could reflect negatively on their own ability and efforts.

This is why more refined measures of job satisfaction are useful. We have already noted that, according to the 2000 CPRN survey, three out of four (73%) of paid employees in Canada agree that they feel little loyalty to their work organization. An earlier (1987) Environics survey asked Canadian workers whether they would choose the same occupation if they had another chance to choose. Almost half (46 percent) said that they would stay in their occupation, 42 percent said they would change occupations, and the rest were uncertain. A 1996 Angus Reid poll showed 32 percent of employed Canadians agreeing that they "would take a comparable job at another company if it were offered."[32] Thus, *behavioural intention* measures typically reveal somewhat more widespread job dissatisfaction. As Sandy Stewart and Bob Blackburn (1975: 503) put it, "satisfaction is expressed within a framework of what is possible, liking is expressed within a framework of what is desirable."

Age and Job Satisfaction

A consistent finding in job satisfaction research is that older workers generally report somewhat more satisfaction (Firebaugh and Harley 1995). Figure 8.1 displays this pattern clearly, with the proportion answering "very satisfied" increasing from 22 percent for the youngest respondents in this 2000 study to 38 percent for the oldest survey participants. Typical of the research on differences in job satisfaction, explanations for this age-related pattern take two basic forms. Some are individualistic, focusing on motivations and work orientations, while others are more structural, pointing to characteristics of the job and the workplace (Ospina 1996: 181).

Perhaps older workers have reduced their expectations, becoming more accepting of relatively unrewarding work. This is an *aging* effect. Alternatively, a *cohort* explanation emphasizes lower expectations (and consequently higher satisfaction) on the part of a generation of older workers, assuming that older workers grew up in an era when simply having a secure job was all one desired and when little self-fulfillment at work was expected. Third, a *life-cycle* effect argues that older workers are more likely to have family and community interests that might compensate for dissatisfying work. A fourth explanation emphasizes the nature of the work performed (a *job effect*), suggesting that older people have been promoted into more rewarding and satisfying jobs, or have changed jobs until they found one they liked. A final explanation points to *self-selection*, arguing that less satisfied workers will drop out of the labour force as they get older, leaving behind the more satisfied workers.

Which is the best explanation? No clear answer emerges from the many studies on this topic although, with today's high unemployment rates, fewer workers will have the luxury of changing jobs until they find one they like or of quitting work because of job dissatisfaction. Regardless, we know that older workers are more likely to report satisfaction with their work, and that this is due mainly to the better jobs they have obtained over time and to their cumulative social experiences and adaptations in the workplace and society.[33]

While the data we have displayed in Figure 8.1 do not reveal the pattern (perhaps because the very youngest workers – those under 18 – were not surveyed), several other recent studies have suggested that the relationship between age and job satisfaction is U-shaped (Clark et al. 1996: 75; Birdi et al. 1995). Specifically, satisfaction is moderately high among the youngest workers, lower in the next cohort, and then higher again in each successive cohort. The explanation is that the youngest workers are usually reasonably satisfied with their entry-level jobs, perhaps because many are still attending school. But if they remain in the student labour market after completing their formal education, the mismatch between low-level jobs and higher aspirations begins to have an effect. Hence, job satisfaction is lower among workers in their late twenties and early thirties. With time, however, the combination of better jobs and declining expectations again leads to higher levels of job satisfaction. This argument points to both individualistic and structural determinants of job satisfaction. It also raises an interesting question for future research. Because today's youth seem to be facing many more barriers to entry into good jobs, will we continue to observe the overall strong positive relationship between age and job satisfaction in the future?

Gender and Job Satisfaction

Given that women are more likely to work part-time in the secondary labour market, are they less satisfied with their jobs? The research evidence offers a clear answer: despite large differences in work rewards, there is typically little difference between men and women in self-reported job satisfaction (Northcott and Lowe 1987; de Vaus and McAllister 1991). Figure 8.1 tells the same story. Again, as with age differences in job satisfaction, an explanation of this non-difference brings us back to the subject of work orientations. Some researchers suggest that women have been socialized to expect fewer intrinsic and extrinsic work rewards. Hence, the argument goes, women are more likely to be satisfied with lower-quality jobs, focusing instead perhaps on satisfying social relationships within the workplace (Phelan 1994).

However, we should not explain the job satisfaction of women with a *gender model* (differences due to prior socialization) while employing a *job model* (differences due to the nature of the job) to account for the satisfaction of men (Feldberg and Glenn 1979; de Vaus and McAllister 1991). In fact, it makes more theoretical sense to explain the satisfaction of both women and men with reference to the type of jobs they hold and their roles outside the workplace. While, on average, men might report high satisfaction with their relatively good jobs, women might be equally satisfied with less rewarding jobs, having modified their expectations because of the time spent in these same jobs. And as Chapter 4 discussed, men's and women's involvement in family roles differ greatly. This also needs to be taken into account when explaining the non-differences in job satisfaction between women and men.

The critical test would compare women and men doing similar work, as in a study of post office employees in Edmonton where men and women performed identical tasks (Northcott and Lowe 1987). The researchers found very few gender differences in job satisfaction or in work orientations after accounting for both job content and family roles. Thus, while gender differences in work orientations may exist, characteristics of the jobs women typically hold and family responsibilities, rather than prior socialization, are probably responsible.

Educational Attainment and Job Satisfaction

Educational attainment and job satisfaction might be linked in several different ways. Following human capital theory (see Chapter 3), we might hypothesize that higher education should lead to a better job and, in turn, more job satisfaction. A second, more complex hypothesis begins with the assumption that better-educated workers have higher expectations regarding their careers but recognizes that not all well-educated workers will have good jobs. Hence, well-educated workers in less-rewarding jobs would be expected to report low job satisfaction. As one commentator wrote several decades ago, "the placing of intelligent and highly qualified workers in dull and unchallenging jobs is a prescription for pathology—for the worker, the employer, the society" (O'Toole 1977: 60).

Job satisfaction studies completed in the 1970s and 1980s (Wright and Hamilton 1979; Martin and Shehan 1989) typically found that education had little effect on job satisfaction, perhaps because the two hypothesized effects cancelled each other out. Even when comparing well educated and less educated workers in the same blue-collar jobs, few differences in job satisfaction were observed. Perhaps the more educated workers anticipated future upward mobility, and so were willing to tolerate less rewarding work for a time. However, the more recent survey data highlighted in Figure 8.1 indicate that job satisfaction is somewhat higher among both the most- and least-educated Canadian workers. The explanation may be that the former are in better jobs because of their educational credentials while many of the latter are older (less educated) individuals who have slowly moved into better jobs over the course of their career. Thus, in explaining this U-shaped pattern, we find ourselves resorting to a job explanation of education differences in job satisfaction.

In previous chapters we have speculated that as education levels have been rising, the mismatch between workers' skills, credentials, and aspirations, on one hand, and their job content, on the other, may be rising. Although our single-point-in-time analysis (of 2000 survey data) cannot answer this question, we might hypothesize that levels of job dissatisfaction will slowly increase in the future as a result of well-educated young workers being unable to find jobs that meet their aspirations. Research has yet to compare the relationships among age, education, and job satisfaction today with the situation several decades ago. However, one recent study did show that workers who considered themselves to be underemployed in terms of their education and skill were much more likely to be dissatisfied with their jobs (Johnson and Johnson 1995). Given the extent to which youth, including the well educated, have been negatively affected by recent labour market changes, this is a trend that needs to be monitored.

Work Rewards, Work Orientations, and Job Satisfaction

Our review of the effects of age, gender, and education on job satisfaction indicates that work orientations are frequently part of the explanation. Nevertheless, research clearly demonstrates that "[j]ob conditions are more strongly related to job satisfaction than are the social characteristics of the workers or the predispositions they bring to the job" (Miller 1980). In fact, hundreds of studies have attempted to identify the specific job conditions that workers are most likely to find satisfying. Such studies have focused on pay, benefits, promotion opportunities, and other *extrinsic work rewards;* autonomy, challenge, social relationships in the workplace and a range of *intrinsic work rewards; work organization features* (for example, bureaucracy, health and safety concerns, and the presence of a union); and *job task design* characteristics, including the use of new technologies.

A popular theory developed several decades ago by Frederick Herzberg drew on all of these traditions, emphasizing both the extrinsic and intrinsic rewards of work. *Hygiene factors* like pay, supervisory style, and physical surroundings in the workplace could reduce job dissatisfaction, Herzberg argued. But only *motivators,* such as opportunities to develop one's skills and to make decisions about one's own work, could increase job satisfaction (Herzberg 1966, 1968). Herzberg also insisted that the presence of such motivators would lead, by way of increased job satisfaction, to greater productivity on the part of workers. We will return to that issue below.

Influenced by Herzberg's *two-factor theory,* most job satisfaction researchers now use multidimensional explanatory frameworks incorporating both intrinsic and extrinsic work rewards, as well as organizational and task characteristics. Although researchers categorize the specific features of work in somewhat different ways, there is considerable consensus at a broader level. Arne Kalleberg (1977), for example, identifies six major dimensions of work. The first, an intrinsic reward dimension, emphasizes interesting, challenging, and self-directed work that allows personal growth and development. Career opportunities form a second dimension, and financial rewards (pay, job security, and fringe benefits) a third. Relationships with co-workers, convenience (the comfort and ease of work), and resource adequacy (availability of information, tools, and materials necessary to do a job) complete the list.[34]

It is also clear from the research we have reviewed that work orientations or preferences must remain part of the job satisfaction equation. Indeed, Kalleberg argues that it is the specific match between work rewards (characteristics of the job) and work orientations that determines one's degree of job satisfaction. This would apply, he suggests, to both extrinsic and intrinsic dimensions of work. In his study, Kalleberg (1977) found that job rewards had positive effects on expressions of job satisfaction in the U.S. labour force, as predicted. But he also observed that, other things being equal, work preferences (orientations) had negative effects on satisfaction. In other words, the more one values some particular feature of work (the chance to make decisions, for example), the less likely it is that one's desires can be satisfied. However, job rewards had substantially greater effects on satisfaction than did work preferences. In addition, Kalleberg's analysis led him to conclude that intrinsic job rewards were more important determinants of job satisfaction than were extrinsic rewards.

Canadian Research on Intrinsic Job Rewards

What does Canadian research tell us about intrinsic and extrinsic work rewards and their fit or mismatch with the work orientations of workers? And have we seen any change over time in such patterns? Going back several decades, respondents in the 1973 national *Job Satisfaction Survey* were given a list of more than 30 specific job characteristics and asked to assess, first, how important each was to them and, second, how their own job rated on these characteristics. The analysts then compared the average "importance" and "evaluation" scores, and examined the gap between them. The largest discrepancies appeared in the areas of "opportunities for promotion" and "potential for challenge and growth" (Burstein et al. 1975: 31–34). These are not unusual findings since most workers seek intrinsic rewards from their work and wish to "get ahead" in their careers.

But has labour market restructuring, particularly downsizing and greater reliance on nonstandard workers, changed this pattern? Figure 8.2 presents selected findings from the CPRN 2000 national survey of employment relationships. For each of these five intrinsic and five extrinsic dimensions of work, sample members were asked to indicate how important it was to them personally (their own work orientation) and how much it was provided by their job (an evaluation of the specific job reward). Thus, these comparisons replicate the comparisons of "importance" and "evaluation" scores in the 1973 study. They are, in a sense, the ingredients for the contemporary patterns of job satisfaction and dissatisfaction that we have described above.

It is clear from this chart that there still are sizable gaps between what Canadian workers desire and what they get from their jobs, on both the intrinsic and extrinsic dimensions, with the largest gap (34 percentage points) for "good chances for career advancement." Thus, with respect to this specific finding, very little has changed since 1973 when "opportunities for promotion" was one of the two areas in which workers' desires far exceeded what their jobs provided.[35] But unlike the situation in 1973, the work orientation – work reward gap for all of the extrinsic dimensions considered in this analysis (pay, benefits, job security, balancing work and family) is larger than the gap for the five intrinsic dimensions (interesting work, feeling of accomplishment, freedom to decide how work will be done, chance to develop skills and abilities, receive recognition for work well done). Perhaps what we are seeing here reflects the growth in nonstandard employment and, more generally, the labour market restructuring and polarization that has occurred over the past decade or two.

That said, we still see that there are sizable gaps between workers' orientations and their job rewards on the five intrinsic dimensions of work featured in Figure 8.2. For example, 94 percent of Canadian workers report that having the freedom to decide how their job will be done is important to them, but only 76 percent feel that their job actually provides such freedom. Almost all (95%) value opportunities to develop their skills and abilities, but only 81 percent are in jobs that provide such opportunities. Similarly, 95 percent want an interesting job, but only 83 percent consider their current job to be interesting.

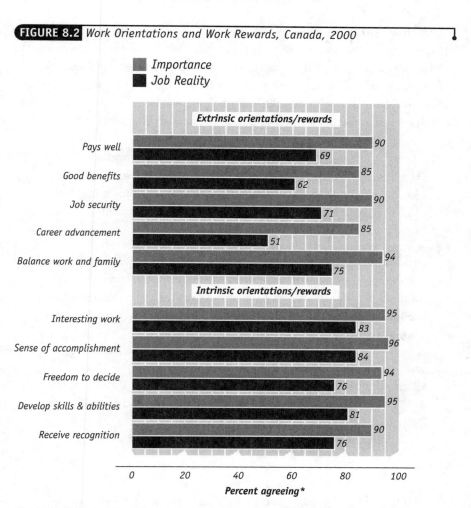

FIGURE 8.2 *Work Orientations and Work Rewards, Canada, 2000*

Importance
Job Reality

Extrinsic orientations/rewards

Pays well	90 / 69
Good benefits	85 / 62
Job security	90 / 71
Career advancement	85 / 51
Balance work and family	94 / 75

Intrinsic orientations/rewards

Interesting work	95 / 83
Sense of accomplishment	96 / 84
Freedom to decide	94 / 76
Develop skills & abilities	95 / 81
Receive recognition	90 / 76

Percent agreeing*

*For both work orientations ('how important is...?") and work rewards ('to what extent does your job provide...?"), survey respondents were asked to agree or disagree on a five-point scale. The percentage agreeing or agreeing strongly with each statement is presented in this chart. See www.jobquality.ca for more information on the discrepancy between work orientations and rewards.

Source: CPRN-Ekos 2000. *Changing Employment Relationships Survey.*

Researchers agree that, for most workers, jobs that provide considerable autonomy, complexity, and variety are more personally fulfilling. The opportunity to make decisions about how a job should be done, to develop and use a wide range of skills, and to do interesting work can also increase a worker's satisfaction with her or his job. In contrast, repetitive jobs with little variety often have the opposite effect. In the following quotations, compare the variety and challenge that are so satisfying for the male oil-field service company manager and the sense of accomplishment reported by the professional engineer (also male) with descriptions of repetitive, low-skill work by a female food-processing factory worker and a male assembly-line worker.[36]

> Every morning even now, I'm happy to come to work; I look forward to it. I think it's because this business is, well, you never know when you come in here in the morning what's going to be asked of you. It could be different every day; generally it is.

***

> I love it. I think I have one of the best jobs I know of ... I enjoy working on projects from start to finish as opposed to just having a small piece of them ... I have found over the years that I am very easily bored and in this field and this environment you don't get bored very often.

***

> Basically, I stand there all day and slash the necks of the chickens ... The chickens go in front of you on the line and you do every other chicken or whatever. And you stand there for eight hours on one spot and do it.

***

> Your brain gets slow. It doesn't function the way it should. You do the same thing day in and day out and your brain goes. I'm like a robot. I walk straight to my job and do what I have to do.

Fortunately, the jobs held by the majority of Canadians appear to be more challenging than those described in these last two quotations. The 2000 CPRN survey reveals, for example, that about three-quarters or more of Canadian workers report that their jobs are interesting, provide them with a sense of accomplishment, and offer some decision-making opportunities as well as chances to enhance skills and abilities (Figure 8.2). In addition, 77 percent of the respondents in this survey reported that their job required high skill levels, while a similar proportion (75%) agreed that "you get the training needed to do your job well" (results not shown in Figure 8.2).

Nevertheless, when asked to agree or disagree that "your job requires that you do the same tasks over and over," 59 percent of the 2000 survey respondents agreed or agreed strongly. These findings suggest that repetitious work (a lack of variety) is more common than non-challenging, low-skill work, or work with little autonomy. The 2000 survey also asked workers to respond with a yes or no to the question: "Considering your experience, education, and training, do you feel that you are overqualified for your job?" One in four workers (27%) said "yes." An earlier (1994) national survey of literacy skills also indicated that about 1 in 5 employed Canadian workers are underemployed with respect to their reading and writing skills Krahn (1997: 18). As we also have noted, there is strong evidence that underemployment may lead to job dissatisfaction (Johnson and Johnson 1995).

Consequences of Job Satisfaction and Dissatisfaction

"If the job's so bad, why don't you quit?" Many of us may have thought this about an unsatisfying job, but fewer have actually done so. There may be some features of the job—pay, hours, location, friendly workmates—that make it palatable, despite the absence of other work rewards. In addition, unless other jobs are available, most employees simply cannot afford to quit. Even during a period of relatively low unemployment in 2000, the CPRN national survey found 41 percent of Canadian workers agreeing that it would be difficult to find another job as good as their current job. Two-thirds (67%) agreed that it would be difficult to cope financially if they lost their job. Thus, job dissatisfaction will not necessarily translate into quitting behaviour, although there is some research evidence linking the two (McEvoy and Cascio 1985; Akerlof et al. 1988). But dissatisfied workers are more likely to call in sick or come in late (Clegg 1983).

Studies have also shown a relationship between job dissatisfaction and overt acts of employee deviance, such as theft of company property, or the use of drugs and alcohol on the job and away from work (Mars 1982; Martin and Roman 1996). Dissatisfaction with work is also correlated with the number of complaints and grievances filed in unionized work settings. As for nonunionized workers, surveys have shown that those dissatisfied with their work are more likely to view unions positively and are more likely to join a union, if given the chance.[37]

From an employer's perspective, however, the critical issue is whether increases in job satisfaction will boost productivity. If dissatisfaction leads to tardiness, absenteeism, deviance, or quitting, will improvements in the quality of working life lead to a happier and more productive workforce? Although one can find examples of research showing such a relationship, the safest answer to the question would be "don't count on it." Research has consistently shown that the relationship between satisfaction and productivity is very weak, or is only present in some work settings.[38]

There are several possible explanations for this. First, productivity is more often a function of technology and workers' skills than of their attitudes. Thus, even if high levels of satisfaction are evident, low skill levels, inadequate on-the-job training, or obsolete technology will limit opportunities for productivity increases. Second, work-group norms and expectations must be taken into consideration. Managers and consultants who have introduced job enrichment programs or high-performance work practices, and have perhaps even found higher levels of satisfaction as a consequence (Berg 1999), have frequently been disappointed when productivity increases did not follow. They failed to realize that workers might view an improved quality of working life as their just reward, or that informal work norms and long-standing patterns of behaviour are difficult to alter (Macarov 1982: 71).

Finally, it may be that productivity can be influenced by job satisfaction, but only under certain conditions. Our earlier discussion suggested that workers in low-level jobs might report job satisfaction because they were assessing their work with a limited set of alternatives in mind. Workers in higher-status jobs might, on the other hand, report satisfaction because of tangible work rewards. If so, perhaps productivity increases due to job satisfaction might only be expected in the latter group. In fact, a review of over 40 studies on this topic supports this hypothesis, demonstrating that the productivity–satisfaction link is strongest among professional, managerial, and supervisory workers (Petty et al. 1984).

WORK AND ALIENATION

William Faulkner once wrote that "You can't eat for eight hours a day nor drink for eight hours a day nor make love for eight hours a day—all you can do for eight hours is work. Which is the reason why man makes himself and everybody else so miserable and unhappy."[39] Faulkner didn't use the term *alienation*, but he might have since his cryptic observations about the misery of work capture some of the many meanings of the term as used by social philosophers and researchers.

Typically, the concept refers in some way to negative subjective reactions to work, but beyond that there is little consensus on its meaning. We might, for example, come across references to the causes and consequences of "job dissatisfaction and alienation," but seldom are the two concepts distinguished from each other. However, alienation is really a much broader philosophical concept. In fact, with reference to our earlier discussion of the meaning of work, we might conceive of alienation as the human condition resulting from an absence of fulfilling work.

Karl Marx and Alienating Work within Capitalism

The verb "alienate" refers to an act of separation, or to the transfer of something to a new owner. Marx used the term in the latter sense when he discussed the "alienating" effects of capitalist production relations on the working class. The noun "alienation" refers to the overall experience of work under these conditions.

Marx identified a number of sources of alienation under capitalism. Products did not belong to those who produced them. Instead, ownership of the product remained with those who owned the enterprise and who purchased the labour of workers. Decisions about what to produce and about the sale of the finished products were not made by the workers, and profits generated in the exchange remained with the owners of the enterprise. In fact, given an extensive division of labour, many of the workers involved might never see the finished product. Thus, workers were alienated from the product of their own work.

Marx also emphasized alienation from the activity of work. Transfer of control over the labour process from individual workers to capitalists or managers meant that individual workers lost the chance to make decisions about how the work should be done. In addition, extensive fragmentation of the work process had taken away most intrinsic work rewards. Alienation also involved the separation of individual workers from others around them. Obviously, bureaucratic hierarchies could have this effect. But more importantly, because capitalist employment relationships involve the exchange of labour for a wage, work was transformed from a creative and collective activity to an individualistic, monetary activity. Work itself had become a commodity. As a consequence, Marx argued, workers were alienated from themselves. Capitalist relations of production had reduced work from its role as a means of human self-fulfillment to being merely a market transaction.[40]

This structural perspective on alienation from work rests on several key assumptions. First, alienation occurs because workers have little or no control over the conditions of their work, and few chances to develop to their fullest potential as creative human beings. Second, the source of alienation can be traced to the organization of work under capitalism. Third, given that alienation is characteristic of capitalism, it exists even if workers themselves do not consciously recognize it.

Alienation, then, is a "condition of objective powerlessness" (Rinehart 2001: 11–21). Whether individual workers become aware of the cause of their discontent with work depends on a variety of factors. In the absence of a well-defined alternative to the current economic system, we would not expect most workers to be able to clearly articulate their alienation, or to act on it.[41] Apathy, or an attempt to forget about work as soon as one leaves it behind, are the common responses of many workers to a situation to which they see no viable alternative. But as we have seen in Chapter 7, discontent does exist, as demonstrated by the frequency of strikes, walkouts, and other behaviours showing frustration and unhappiness with the conditions of work.

The Social–Psychological Perspective on Alienation

The social–psychological perspective on alienation shares with the structural perspective an emphasis on the powerlessness of workers, and the conclusion that many jobs offer limited opportunities for personal growth and self-fulfillment. While the structural perspective emphasizes separation from the product and the activity of work, from co-workers and from oneself, the social–psychological approach attempts to measure feelings of powerlessness, meaninglessness, social isolation, self-estrangement, and normlessness (Seeman 1967, 1975). Thus, in a sense, the main focus of the social–psychological perspective is on the absence of intrinsic job rewards.

Social–psychological studies of alienation, moreover, are unlikely to lay all or much of the blame on capitalism itself. Instead, technologies that allow workers few opportunities for self-direction, bureaucratic work organizations, and modern mass society in general are identified as the sources of alienation. This perspective also differs from the structural approach in its emphasis on feelings of alienation—the subjective experience of alienating work conditions. Researchers within this approach have relied primarily on the self-reports of workers, in contrast with the Marxist focus on the organization and content of work.

Consequently, social–psychological accounts of alienation resemble job dissatisfaction, although their explanations of the sources of alienation have pointed more explicitly to the negative consequences of work fragmentation and powerlessness. The general job satisfaction literature examines a broader array of causal variables (work orientations, for example). But since some social–psychological studies of alienation actually define the phenomenon as an "extrinsic orientation to work" (Seeman 1975: 273), there is really more congruence between the two research traditions than first impressions would suggest. Hence, it is not surprising to find studies that examine alienation and job dissatisfaction simultaneously, or writers who use the terms interchangeably.

Robert Blauner on "Alienation and Freedom"

Almost four decades ago, Robert Blauner (1964) published *Alienation and Freedom*, a classic study of industrial differences in workers' responses to their jobs. Following the social–psychological tradition, he defined alienation in terms of powerlessness, meaninglessness, isolation (or social alienation), and self-estrangement. The centrality of powerlessness in Blauner's theory of alienation is clear from his use of the word *freedom* to refer to the ability to choose how one does one's work.

Blauner compared work in four different industries to test his theory that technology (and the attendant division of labour) is a major determinant of the degree of alienation experienced at work. He argued that the traditional printing industry, which at the time still operated largely in a craft-work mode, produced low levels of alienation because of the considerable autonomy of workers and the high levels of skill required. The textile manufacturing industry represented an intermediate step in the process of technological development, while the culmination occurred with the assembly lines of the automobile industry. Here, alienation was most acute because of low-skilled, repetitive tasks that deprived workers of control over their actions.

Blauner argued that new automated technologies reversed this trend. In work settings such as oil refineries, skill levels were higher, tasks were varied, and individuals could make a number of decisions about how they would do their work. Since this industry was providing us with a glimpse of the future of industrialized societies, he reasoned, the prospects for individual freedom were good. By predicting that alienation would decline as fewer workers were employed in mass production settings, Blauner was rejecting Marx's argument that work in a capitalist society was always alienating.

Alienation and Freedom has been both influential and controversial. Blauner was undoubtedly correct about the negative consequences of continued exposure to low-skill, routinized work. But critics have argued that a social–psychological definition does not address alienation in the broader way that Marx had defined it.[42] Furthermore, Duncan Gallie's (1978) comparative study of refinery workers in France and England has highlighted cross-cultural differences in workers' responses to technology, an important point Blauner overlooked. And as we have argued earlier, effects of technology are not predetermined. A position of *technological determinism* conveniently overlooks why different technologies are designed or chosen by those who control an enterprise, and how these technologies are built into the organizational structure of the workplace.

Richard Sennett on "The Corrosion of Character"

Writing in the middle of the 20th century, before the era of industrial restructuring, downsizing, and privatization began, and before the advent of widespread nonstandard employment, Robert Blauner was optimistic in his assessment of the future of work in western industrialized economies. Alienation would decline and freedom (to decide how work should be done) would increase. In contrast, Richard Sennett's recent book on "the corrosion of character" in the 21st-century economy is extremely pessimistic in its predictions.

While Sennett (1998) does not reference the social-psychological research literature on alienation, his analysis of the negative impact of contemporary work organizations and relationships on the minds and souls of American workers is firmly rooted in this tradition.

Sennett describes how today's labour market is characterized by the constant restructuring of work organizations, an emphasis on flexibility in production and the delivery of services, a greater reliance on nonstandard workers, and a glorification of risk-taking. Together, these new values and practices have combined to get rid of the order and routine that traditionally defined the lives of workers. Why is this a problem? Because, Sennett argues, order, routine, and stability lead to the formation of personal and occupational identities which give meaning to our lives. In a working world where constant change is glorified and the positive aspects of structure and routine are lost, individual identities are also lost or fail to take shape. Even the teamwork that is central to so many new management approaches is criticized by Sennett, since he sees it as merely a way of gaining compliance from workers, as "the group practice of demeaning superficiality" (1998: 99). He concludes that:

> The contradictions of time in the new capitalism have created a conflict between character and experience, the experience of disjointed time threatening the ability of people to form their characters into sustained narratives. (1998: 31).

Sennett recognizes that these fleeting personal identities and the resulting concerns about "who in society needs me?" (1998: 146) are shaped in a capitalist economy. But he does not blame the capitalist relations of production that separate workers from owners and that leave control of the labour process with the latter. Instead, the post-modern alienation that he describes is attributed to the forms of work organization and the much less stable divisions of labour that characterize the 21st century workplace. In this sense, Sennett's critique of the meaninglessness, social isolation, and normlessness of work today fits centrally within the social-psychological tradition of alienation research.

But where it fits is ultimately less important than whether he is correct in his analysis. The management theorists discussed in Chapter 5 see the changes taking place in today's workplace as largely positive, empowering workers and increasing their job satisfaction. Sennett is almost uniformly negative in his assessment of the alienating impact of contemporary work. These divergent perspectives on work experiences raise fundamental questions about whether, compared to earlier generations of workers, today's workers, individually and through their own organizations, are in a better or worse position to negotiate greater control over the labour process.

WORK AND STRESS

If we take a broader *work and well-being* approach to the subject of how workers experience and react to their jobs, both physical and psychological reactions to work become part of our subject matter. This approach also encourages us to consider how paid work might affect an individual's life in the family and the community. Workplace health and safety issues, discussed in Chapter 3, are also central to discussions of work and well-being, as are concerns about balancing work and family responsibilities (see Chapter 4). Here, we look more specifically at work and stress.

Defining Work-Related Stress

Defining *work-related stress* independent of job dissatisfaction is not easy. In fact, some researchers studying stress and its consequences rely on measures that might, in a different context, be considered indicators of job dissatisfaction. But there are important distinctions to be made between job dissatisfaction, anxiety and tension about work, job stress, and job burnout (Humphrey 1998: 4-9). It is possible to feel dissatisfied with work, perhaps even a little anxious about some aspects of a job, but without experiencing a great deal of stress. But work-related stress, with its physical and mental symptoms, can also accumulate to the point of burnout, where an individual is simply unable to cope in the job (Maslach and Leiter 1997). It is useful, then, to conceive of work-related stress as a many-sided problem—with job dissatisfaction as one of its components—that can lead to serious mental and physical health disorders.

It is also helpful to distinguish *stressors* (or *strains*) from an individual worker's reactions to them. Stressors are objective situations (for example, noisy work environments or competing job demands) or events (a dispute with a supervisor or news that some workers are about to be laid off) that have the potential to produce a negative subjective or physical response. Thus, work-related stress is an individually experienced negative reaction to a job or work environment (Kessler 1983). Obviously, the absence of stress does not imply the presence of job satisfaction. What distinguishes stress reactions are the wide range of ill health (physical and psychological) symptoms.

Causes and Consequences of Work-Related Stress

Research in many different settings has shown that physical reactions to stress can include fatigue, insomnia, muscular aches and pains, ulcers, high blood pressure, and even heart disease. Depression, anxiety, irritation, low self-esteem, and other mental health problems are among the documented psychological reactions to stressful work. The research literature has also shown that the effects of work-based stressors can be conditioned by individuals' psychological coping mechanisms and by the amount of social support they receive from family, friends, and co-workers.[43]

Constant worry over paying bills or losing one's job, concerns that have been increasing over the past decades, can be considered a form of work-related stress (Reynolds 1997). For example, a recent U.S. study of automobile workers revealed that the strongest predictor of symptoms of ill health was a chronic concern over job loss (Heaney et al. 1994). And, as Chapter 4 documented, equally stressful for some workers, especially women, are the pressures of looking after family responsibilities while trying to devote oneself to a job or career. As one of the young, university-educated women interviewed by Gillian Ranson (1998: 527) lamented:

> In this job, in this particular job, I don't think I could do justice to the child and I've made the decision that ... either after maternity leave or in the near future, I'm quitting, because it's not fair. I come home, I can't even talk to my husband because I'm so wound up, stressed out.

But most research in this area has concentrated on stressors in the work environment.[44] Continual exposure to health and safety hazards, sexual harassment, working in a physically uncomfortable setting, shift work, or long hours can all be stressors. Similarly, fast-paced work (especially when the pace is set by a machine) and inadequate resources to complete a task can generate stress. So too can the experience of constant organizational restructuring and/or the introduction of the latest management fad. In addition, working at tasks that underutilize one's skills and abilities, or that allow little latitude for decision making, are stressful for many workers. Finally, there is the stress that an unreasonable and overly demanding supervisor can create.

Statistics Canada's 1994/55 *National Population Health Survey* asked employed Canadians (age 15 to 64) about a number of sources of stress in their job. Forty-four percent of men and 37 percent of women indicated that their job had high physical demands. Seventeen percent of men and 31 percent of women reported high job strain, that is, "they were in hectic jobs, and had little freedom in controlling the pace of work or in deciding how to carry out their duties" (Statistics Canada 2000b: 22-4). Almost one in five (18% of men and 19% of women) stated that their jobs were insecure, while slightly fewer (16% of men and 15% of women) reported little support from their supervisors. CPRN's 2000 national survey provides a single umbrella question to help us gauge the extent of workplace stress. Sixty-one percent of the 2,500 sample members agreed that their job was very stressful, including 25 percent who strongly agreed. In short, a large number of working Canadians experience a significant amount of stress in their workplace.

The "Demand–Control" Model of Work-Related Stress

A useful perspective for understanding workplace stress is the *demand–control model*, which redefines stressors as *job demands* but also introduces the concept of worker control.[45] It distinguishes between active jobs where individual decision-making potential is high, and passive jobs where it is largely absent. If psychological demands on a worker are high, but she or he can do something about it, stress is less likely to result. If demands are high and control is low, stress and the health problems that can follow are far more often the outcome.

From this perspective, we can see why researchers have repeatedly found highly routinized, machine-paced work to be extremely stressful. Assembly-line jobs are often considered to be among the most stressful (Hamilton and Wright 1986: 266). Demand is constant, the physical work can be extremely taxing, and worker control is virtually absent. Solange de Santis describes her reaction to the assembly-line after several weeks of work in General Motors' Scarborough assembly plant:

> The line went down for a few minutes, and I sat on the stool attached to the job station, next to my table full of red and yellow lenses, ropes of black putty, boxes of screws and lightbulbs. Maybe it was because I had a few moments to think, maybe it was the sensory overload of the past few weeks, but for the first time an abrupt, raw hatred of the place rose in my craw, a loathing of the noise, the dirt. All the people are stupid, I thought. The work is meaningless and exhausting. There is no privacy. The line never stops. The last was a bit irrational, since I was thinking this during the instant that the line had stopped. (de Santis 1999: 85)

Earlier we suggested that instrumental work attitudes may be a coping mechanism—the paycheque becomes the only relevant work reward. Some assembly-line workers rely on alcohol or drugs to get through a shift (de Santis 1999: 111-14). Others adapt to assembly-line work by "tuning out" the boredom and waiting for the chance to get away from the job. Ben Hamper (1986: 88), better known as "Rivethead," describes how he was introduced to his new job on a truck-assembly line in Flint, Michigan:

> "Until you get it down, your hands will ache, your feet will throb and your back will feel like it's been steamrolled ... "

> "Are there any advantages to working down here?" I asked pitifully.

> The guy scratched at his beard. "Well, the exit to the time clocks and the parking lot is just down these stairs. Come lunchtime or quittin' time, you can usually get a good jump on the rest of the pack."

But psychological problems can also arise. Robert Linhart (1981: 57) describes an extreme reaction to the assembly line in a French automobile factory:

He was fixing parts of a dashboard into place with a screwdriver. Five screws to fix on each car. That Friday afternoon he must have been on his five hundredth screw of the day. All at once he began to yell and rushed at the fenders of the cars brandishing his screwdriver like a dagger. He lacerated a good ten or so car bodies before a troop of white and blue coats rushed up and overcame him, dragging him, panting and gesticulating, to the sick bay.

Highly routine, monotonous, mechanized, and closely supervised jobs are also found in the service industries. A study of Canada Post mail sorters and letter carriers in Edmonton revealed that the most stressful job in the organization involved "keying" postal codes using automated machinery. The relentless pace of the machinery, conflicting demands imposed by management, constant repetition, and lack of challenges and job autonomy were associated with diminished mental and physical health among coders. The use of pain relievers and tranquilizers was significantly higher among the coders using automated technology compared with those sorting mail by hand (Lowe and Northcott 1986).

With the rapid spread of computerized technologies, electronic surveillance has added a new source of stress. This practice might involve monitoring the telephone calls of workers who deal with the public by phone, recording output in settings where workers use computers to conduct their work, or even delivering warnings to those performing below certain levels. As e-mail and voice-mail systems have become more common, some employers have recognized their potential for maintaining control of workers. In 1993, for example, a study of large U.S. companies indicated that, in more than 30 percent of these firms, managers routinely read employees' e-mail or examined their personal computer files.[46]

Frederick Taylor would have applauded, but employees do not. A data entry clerk whose work group had been told that they had not met management productivity goals the previous week comments:

I feel so pressured, my stomach is in knots. I take tons of aspirin, my jaws are sore from clenching my teeth, I'm so tired I can't get up in the morning, and my arm hurts from entering, entering, entering. (Nussbaum and duRivage 1986: 18)

It is not difficult to see how such working conditions—high demands and virtually no worker control—can be stressful, and lead to physical and psychological ill health.

The "Person–Environment Fit" Model

A different theoretical model of work-related stress emphasizes the *person–environment fit.*[47] According to this model, stress results when there is a significant gap between an individual's needs and abilities and what the job offers, allows, or demands. To take a specific example, reports of "burnout" among social workers, teachers, and nurses are common. Individuals in these helping professions have work orientations (the desire to solve problems and help people) and useful skills (training in their profession) that are frequently thwarted by the need to deal with an excessive number of clients, limited resources, and administrative policies that make it difficult to be effective.[48]

We might also use this perspective to help us understand the stress many workers feel when they attempt to juggle their work and family roles. A paid job requires you to be present and involved; at the same time, family responsibilities demand time and attention. Because women continue to carry a large share of domestic and child-care responsibilities, they are much more likely to experience role conflict and stress, as this individual interviewed by Duffy and Pupo (1992: 134) reported:

> When I worked full-time, I felt very guilty about the children. If they were sick and I went to work, I felt guilty. If I stayed home with them, I felt guilty about work. Part-time work could offer the flexibility that full-time work cannot.

This woman chose part-time work to try to handle her problem, but gave up additional income and career options (which are limited in most part-time jobs). From a person–environment fit perspective, she was attempting to improve the fit between demands of her family and her job (or the financial need to work). But that fit could also have been improved if structural, rather than just individual, changes were implemented.

Thus, while the person–environment fit model of stress broadens our explanatory framework by bringing in work orientations, its individualistic focus advocates personal solutions. From the demand–control perspective, we are more inclined to seek solutions to the lack of worker control. In this case, if more men accepted an equal share of the responsibilities in their homes, if more employers offered flexible work schedules to their workers, and if afford-able, quality child care were more accessible, would the woman quoted above have been forced to make these choices? With respect to professional burnout, how could organizational structures and administrative policies be changed to allow social workers and nurses to be more effective? How can we use new technologies to reduce stress and increase job satisfaction, rather than merely to control workers?

CONCLUSION: THE "LONG ARM OF THE JOB"

Early in this chapter, we described how individuals are exposed to at least two competing work-value systems: the first suggests that monetary rewards are paramount; the second emphasizes how work can be personally self-fulfilling. This raises the possibility that, because of different socialization experiences, some workers would be primarily instrumentally oriented while others would be more motivated by the intrinsic rewards of a job. In short, it could be argued that work orientations or preferences are brought to the job, and will influence feelings of satisfaction or alienation.

But most research tends to support an alternative explanation, namely, that participation in low-skill or routinized work can produce instrumental work attitudes. For many workers, such attitudes may be a means of adapting to employment that has little but a paycheque to offer. Even so, studies of job satisfaction, alienation, and stress highlight the negative consequences of work that is repetitive and routine, offers few chances for individual decision making, and does not develop a person's skills and abilities. While it is impor-tant to recognize that work orientations affect how an individual feels about his or her job, the nature of the work itself is likely to have a stronger impact, both on an individual's feelings of satisfaction, alienation, and stress and on her or his work orientations.

We have suggested that work-related stress does not get left behind at the end of the workday. Chronic work pressures, as well as anxiety about poten-tial job or income loss, can undermine an individual's overall quality of life. At the same time, it is apparent that satisfaction with work translates into a broader sense of well-being. But are there any other more long-term, perhaps even permanent, psychological effects a job can have on an individual? The answer appears to be yes—continued exposure to some kinds of work can have long-lasting effects on nonwork behaviours and on one's personality.

In a study conducted over three decades ago, Martin Meissner argued that the "long arm of the job" has an impact on one's life away from work. He studied male British Columbia sawmill workers to test rival hypotheses about how the nature of work might affect after-work behaviours. The *compensatory leisure* hypothesis proposes that people will look for activities away from work that will compensate for what is absent in their jobs. Thus, workers who have little opportunity to develop their skills and abilities on the job might seek these opportunities away from work. The *spillover* hypothesis suggests that the effects of work will influence one's choice of after-work activities. Meissner concluded that there is a spillover effect. Workers who had little chance to make decisions about how their work should be done were considerably less likely to engage in free-time activities that required or allowed this kind of individual discretion. Similarly, those who had few opportunities for social interactions at work were more inclined toward solitary leisure-time activities (Meissner 1971: 260).

One could argue that the subjects in Meissner's study had chosen their jobs in order to satisfy their personal preferences. Such an emphasis on work orientations would explain, for example, that individuals with a preference for solitary activities would choose both their jobs and their leisure activities with this in mind. While plausible, this explanation is not convincing for several reasons. First, it suggests that individuals have a much greater range of job choices than is typically the case. Second, subsequent studies comparing these two hypotheses have agreed with Meissner (Staines 1980; Martin and Roman 1996). Third, there is research demonstrating even more conclusively that work with limited scope has a negative effect on personality.

Melvin Kohn and his associates have examined this relationship for many years using the concept of *occupational self-direction*. Kohn argues that work that is free from close supervision, that involves considerable complexity and independent judgement, and that is nonroutine will have a lasting positive effect on one's personality and psychological functioning. Specifically, individuals whose work allows self-direction are more likely to develop a personality that values such opportunities and a more self-confident, less fatalistic and less conformist approach to life. They also exhibit greater flexibility in dealing with ideas. Alternatively, jobs allowing little self-direction are more likely to lead to psychological distress, a finding we have already documented from stress research.

Kohn presents a convincing case, since he used longitudinal data in his studies. By comparing the jobs and personalities of workers at two points in time (up to ten years apart), he clearly demonstrated the personality changes in those who had and those who did not have the opportunity to work in jobs allowing self-direction. Hence, he has also been able to demonstrate that "both ideational flexibility and a self-directed orientation lead, in time, to more responsible jobs that allow greater latitude for occupational self-direction." [49] The overall conclusion of Kohn's studies and related research[50] is that because of the "long arm of the job," intrinsically rewarding work, particularly work that allows self-direction, can have important long-term consequences for the personalities and careers of those fortunate enough to participate in it.

NOTES

1. Bernstein (1997); also see Burstein et al. (1975: 10–11), Anthony (1977; Chapter 1) and Byrne (1990: Chapter 3).
2. Genesis (2: 17; 3: 19), *The Bible,* King James Version.
3. Weber (1958) emphasized the Calvinist belief in "predestination," a doctrine proposing that entry into heaven could not be influenced by good works on earth because it was already determined by God. According to Weber, hard work and economic success served to reduce anxiety about being among the "chosen." After all, the "chosen" must have been placed on earth to glorify God through their work and success.
4. See Kelvin and Jarrett (1985), Burman (1988, 1996), Warr (1987), Newman (1989), Feather (1990), Kirsh (1992), and Gallie and Russell (1998) on the social and psychological consequences of unemployment. Also see Sharpe (1999) and Sussman (2000) on contemporary Canadian patterns of unemployment.
5. The quotations in this section are from Burman (1988: 161, 113, 144, 86).
6. See Helen Russell (1999) for an interesting study of gender differences in the effects of unemployment on social relationships.
7. See Horvat (1983); Freeman (1993) and Nakanishi and Mikawa (1995) comment on a greater pursuit of leisure activities in Japan in the 1990s.
8. See *The Economist* (1996) for a critique of cultural explanations of economic growth, and the World Bank (1993) for a structural explanation of East Asian economic growth.

9. Jiang et al. (1995) suggest that family involvement in the work organization may be more important to Chinese than to American workers; Graham (1993, 1995) comments on problems experienced by Japanese firms setting up factories in North America. Also see Sivesind (1995) and Super and Šverko (1995) on cross-national differences in work values.

10. Kalleberg and Stark (1993: 182); Schooler (1996).

11. Kamata (1983); Gill (1985: 32); Thompson (1990).

12. Swift (1995: 221, 224); also see Schor (1991) on *The Overworked American*, a source for some of Swift's ideas.

13. Among other strategies, Rifkin (1995: 255–57) proposes tax deductions for voluntary work and a "social wage" for the unemployed who participate in voluntary work. But he does not recognize that such policies would still produce a very unequal income distribution. In a more recent book, Gorz (1999) proposes a guaranteed annual income and recommends cooperative economic organizations as solutions to the inequality problem.

14. On sharing work, see Best (1990), Human Resources Development Canada (1994), Yalnizyan et al. (1997), Hayden (1999), and Huberman and Lanoie (2000).

15. Peters (1995: 5, 69–71) presents data from public opinion polls spanning two decades, and from focus groups (group interviews) conducted in the mid-1990s.

16. The 1996 survey was conducted for the Royal Bank by Angus Reid (*Edmonton Journal*, 8 October 1996: F1). Wyatt Canada (1991: 11) completed the 1991 survey. See Reed (1997) for a recent Australian study of work orientations.

17. Unpublished findings from a survey conducted by Canadian Policy Research Networks Inc (www.cprn.org). See Lowe and Schellenberg (2001) for discussions of the same data analyzed in a slightly different manner.

18. Dex (1988); Lorence (1987); Loscocco (1990); Rowe and Snizek (1995: 226).

19. It is somewhat ironic that better-paid workers, who may be able to retire earlier, are also more likely to seek the same intrinsic rewards in their leisure and retirement activities that they obtained from their work (Stebbins 2000).

20. Barlow and Robertson (1994: 25–38); Osberg et al. (1995: 161–71).

21. National Center on Education and the Economy (1990: 24); Borman (1991: 33-34); Cappelli (1992: 6); Ainlay (1993: 24); Holzer (1996).

22. Côté and Allahar (1994); Meunier et al. (1998); Boyd and Norris (1999); Côté (2000); Schneider (2000).

23. Unpublished research findings; see Lowe and Schellenberg (2001) for discussion of the same data analyzed in a different fashion.

24. See Leinberger and Tucker (1991), Feldman et al. (1994), Nollen and Axel (1996), Booth (1997), and Sennett (1998) on reduced loyalty and the dilemmas of managing contingent workers.

25. Nixon's comment was quoted in *Time* (7 September 1987: 42).

26. Burstein et al. (1975: 12, 22, 60); also see Hamilton and Wright (1986: 288) and Furnham (1990: 196–208), who review a range of similar U.S. studies and draw the same conclusion.

27. Gallie et al. (1998: 303) draw the same conclusion about the U.K., namely, that the work ethic has not declined over the past several decades.

28. See Burman (1996: 42–45) on welfare state restructuring, Richards et al. (1995) for debates about "workfare" programs, and Swanson (2001) on stereotypes about the poor. Battle and Torjman (1999) and Riddell and St-Hilaire (2000) discuss more progressive employment policy options for dealing with unemployment and poverty.

29. See Economic Council of Canada (1992b), Statistics Canada (1997a), Laroche (1998), and Schecter and Pacquet (1999) on movement in and out of poverty in Canada; also see Newman (1989); Morris and Irwin (1992); Payne and Payne (1994); and Rank and Hirschl (1999).

30. Felt and Sinclair (1992); Wagner (1994); MacDonald (1994); Leonard (1998).

31. The survey results are reported in an Angus Reid Group–Royal Bank internal document titled *Workplace 2000: Part III* (1998: 10).

32. Maynard (1987: 115); *Edmonton Journal* (8 October 1996: F1); also see Burstein et al. (1975: 29) and Levitan and Johnson (1982: 76–79).

33. Kalleberg and Loscocco (1983) conclude that all of the explanations have some relevance; Hamilton and Wright (1986: 288) favour the "job effect," while Firebaugh and Harley (1995: 97) believe that "aging" and "life cycle" explanations fit the data best.

34. Ospina (1996) focuses on workers' perceptions about the justness of the opportunity structure in addition to work rewards and work orientations as determinants of job satisfaction.

35. See Jabes and Zussman (1988) and Zussman and Jabes (1989) for an insightful study of concerns about promotions and career opportunities in the Canadian public sector.

36. In order, the quotations are from House (1980: 335), Bailyn and Lynch (1983: 281), Armstrong and Armstrong (1983: 129), and Robertson and Wareham (1987: 29). For additional graphic "tales from the assembly line," see Hamper (1986) and de Santis (1999).

37. See Bender and Sloane (1998) on job dissatisfaction and filing grievances. Kochan (1979: 25) links dissatisfaction to willingness to join a union. Lowe and Northcott (1995), and Gordon and Denisi (1995) reverse the question by asking about the effects of union membership on job satisfaction.

38. Macarov (1982); Petty et al. (1984); Iaffaldano and Muchinsky (1985).

39. Faulkner is quoted by Studs Terkel (1971: xi).

40. See Archibald (1978: 35–43), Erikson (1990), Grabb (1997: 19–21), and Rinehart (2001: 11–21) for additional discussion of Marx's writings on alienation.

41. See Mann (1970) on the "social cohesion of liberal democracy," and Abercrombie et al. (1980) on the "dominant ideology."

42. Archibald (1978: 124–30); Hill (1981: 90–102). Hodson (1996) links Blauner's thesis to labour process debates about management control over workers.

43. McDonald and Doyle (1981); Baker (1985); Quick et al. (1987); Jex (1998).

44. See Lowe and Northcott (1986); Lowe (1989); Karasek and Theorell (1990); Roberts and Baugher (1995), Cartwright and Cooper (1997), Humphrey (1998), Wilkins and Beaudet (1998), Jex (1998), and Statistics Canada (2000b).

45. See Karasek (1979); Karasek and Theorell (1990); Sauter et al. (1989) on the "demand-control" explanation of workplace stress. For recent studies using this approach, see Soderfeldt et al. (1997), Carayon and Zijlstra (1999), and de Jonge et al. (2000).

46. The study, conducted by *Macworld* magazine, also revealed that 65 percent of the managers surveyed felt this practice was ethically acceptable (*Edmonton Journal*, 10 June 1993). Also see DeTienne (1993), Menzies (1996: 117-22), Frenkel et al. (1995), and Sewell (1998) on workplace electronic surveillance.

47. Kahn (1981); see Johnson (1989) for a comparison with the "demand–control" model.

48. Leiter (1991); see Wallace and Brinkerhoff (1991) and Maslach and Leiter (1997) on "burnout."

49. Kohn and Schooler (1983: 152); also see Kohn (1990); Miller et al. (1979); and Miller et al. (1985).

50. Krahn and Lowe (1997a) propose that underuse of literacy skills at work can lead to the loss of such skills. Schooler (1984) develops a more general theory of "psychological effects of complex environments" that has applicability beyond the workplace.

CONCLUSION

This discussion of work, industry, and Canadian society has ranged widely over many different topics. We have tried to review and synthesize key theoretical debates in the sociology of work and industry and, at the same time, document emerging industrial, technological, labour market, and workplace trends. Instead of attempting a detailed summary of all the issues we have covered, we conclude by highlighting some of the major themes in current debates about changing labour markets and workplaces. If there is one meta-theme linking the many subjects addressed in this book, it is this: a clear understanding of the factors affecting work and of the alternatives to existing workplace arrangements is an essential precondition for initiating and directing changes that could benefit more Canadians.

Debates about the emerging postindustrial society have been part of sociological discourse for several decades and will no doubt continue. But it is already clear that, like all major industrialized nations, Canada has become a service-based society. Natural resource, construction, and manufacturing industries will continue to play an important, if diminished, role in the economy. But it is the service sector, and the kinds of jobs it provides, that now dominates. Today, more than three out of four employed Canadians depend on the service sector for their livelihood. Some service industry jobs are highly skilled and well paying, yet a substantial number are relatively unskilled and less rewarding. Clearly one of the characteristics of the new postindustrial economy is the sharp distinction between "good jobs" and "bad jobs." In particular, while most working Canadians are still employed in permanent, full-time jobs that have a Monday-to-Friday daytime schedule, a growing portion of the labour force no longer fits this pattern, the definition of a "standard" job since World War II. Employment relationships and work arrangements have become much more varied and, in some key ways, less secure.

Equally important demographic changes have been quietly transforming the Canadian workforce. In particular, the population is slowly aging and the implications of this trend are only beginning to be understood. The baby boom generation is well into middle age. Having lived through the economic restructuring of the 1990s, many members of this large and privileged cohort have hit a career plateau and now eagerly anticipate retirement. Others love their work and can't imagine life without it. Still others may wish for retirement, but must keep working due to inadequate pensions. At the other end of the age distribution, in the 1980s and 1990s successive cohorts of younger workers experienced considerable difficulty finding good jobs, despite their increased investments in higher education.

But by the end of the 20th century, a strong economy, lower unemployment rates, and concerns about the imminent retirement of the baby boom cohort led some observers to predict labour shortages. However, this may be a short-sighted view, since labour market outcomes are an often unpredictable product of a complex mix of economics, demographics, and management decisions. Whether there will be a scarcity of workers, or of certain skills, in the next five years is an important but not yet answered question. Similarly, it is difficult to predict which cohort of workers, young, middle-aged, or old, will ultimately fare the best in today's rapidly changing economy.

These questions highlight the issue of growing social inequality in Canadian society, clearly the most disturbing trend we have observed. A significant level of structural unemployment remains with us, nonstandard jobs have clearly become more common, and the ranks of the working poor have slowly grown. After three decades of growth in the mid-20th century, family incomes stagnated in the 1980s and 1990s. It was only at the very end of the last century that Canadian families once again began to see real, albeit small, gains in income. The causes of the observed increase in social inequality are complex and intertwined, but involve transformation of the global economy, the desire for greater flexibility on the part of employers, the use of new technologies as labour replacements, shrinking employment in the goods-producing sector, polarization within the growing service sector, changing skill requirements in both sectors, and the continued popularity of downsizing. Together, these trends are creating a more segmented labour market in terms of income and benefits, job security, and skill requirements.

However, we are not convinced by the pessimistic futurists like Jeremy Rifkin (1995) who predict "the end of work" and a society in which the majority do not have employment. Recent labour market and economic trends simply do not support such dire predictions. Nor do we accept that the future labour market will be "dejobbed," that traditional paid jobs will be largely replaced by a fluid arrangement of postmodern contractual employment relationships (Bridges 1994). From our perspective, such predictions are more ideological justifications for the current heavy reliance on nonstandard workers than generalizations based on real trends. Nevertheless, there is evidence of growing polarization in the labour market, greater inequality in society as a whole, and increased anxiety among Canadians about their overall economic security (Lowe 2000). The key public policy question is whether we can do something about it.

Overlaid on the trend toward a more polarized labour market are inequities based on gender, age, race and ethnicity, disability, and region. With respect to the latter, some regions of the country remain underdeveloped, largely bypassed by the economic growth experienced by others. The lack of opportunities, outright discrimination, and other employment barriers faced by women, people with disabilities, racial and ethnic minorities, and Aboriginal Canadians are still very evident in Canadian society. When we look back at the long and difficult battles fought by organized labour to obtain the employment rights and standard of living we take for granted today, we are reminded that social inequities such as these are not easily eliminated. And as we look into the future, we recognize once again that some of the disturbing employment trends are age-differentiated. Throughout much of the 1990s, downsizing and work organization restructuring made it difficult for young people, especially those without university degrees, to find decent employment. Furthermore, corporate and government concerns about baby boom retirements have overshadowed the equally important, if not more important, problem of income security in retirement for the working poor and also for many members of the middle class.

Even so, there are a few signs of positive change. Over the past few decades, women have made some progress in their quest for labour market equality. While we acknowledge the flaws of current employment equity and pay equity policies, their very existence has nevertheless begun a slow process of institutional change. Although members of visible minorities continue to encounter labour market barriers, there is some evidence that discrimination against them is becoming less acceptable. Unfortunately, beyond the fact that their disadvantaged situation has been officially recognized in federal government employment equity initiatives, we can identify fewer positive employment trends for Aboriginal groups and people with disabilities. Recently, governments and employers have (once again) begun to concern themselves with "workforce diversity" issues, which could lead to improved opportunities for racial and ethnic minorities. But critics are quick to point out that relatively low unemployment rates and the resulting greater competition for skilled workers in some sectors of the economy lie behind this heightened concern. If so, will these concerns about increasing workforce diversity be maintained if the economy slows down?

Shifting topics, we draw attention to how the computer revolution has placed information technology at the centre of everyday life, at work and in the home. Most Canadians believe that these new digital technologies have had a positive impact on their work situation, and it is clear that new and challenging jobs have been created. There is also evidence of the new technologies being used to eliminate some jobs, deskill others, and increase management control over the labour process. But we need to remember that the effects of technology are not predetermined. Instead, the outcomes are a result of social choices made by real people within particular organizational contexts. Unfortunately, too often workers have not been involved as equal partners in the process of technological change, and the goals of such change have not included job creation and an improved quality of working life. Few would seriously advocate blocking the diffusion of new computer-based technology, given the potential it offers for economic prosperity and an improved quality of life. Rather, the public policy issue is how we can collectively manage technological change in a way that will benefit as many people as possible. We need to narrow the "digital divide" between individuals with computer skills and access to the new technology and those with neither.

Our examination of new management approaches within Canadian work organizations also identifies conflicting trends. On the one hand, we have documented how downsizing and an overreliance on nonstandard workers have frequently been a substitute for innovative approaches to increasing productivity. Similarly, despite their promise for humanizing work and empowering workers, the new management schemes have frequently been used to push workers harder with no compensation in terms of autonomy, skill enhancement, or improved incomes. Yet, on the other hand, some of the management literature advocates major workplace reforms that put people first, and there are positive examples of the implementation of such reforms.

Furthermore, there are important alternatives, including legislated industrial democracy and incentives to encourage worker ownership, that could lead to more worker autonomy, increased job security, and reduced social inequality. The challenge will be to convince employers of the benefits of real workplace reform and to assist workers in their struggle to obtain it.

The organized labour movement in Canada has reacted to the new technologies and new management schemes with some uncertainty. Some unions have strongly resisted change while others have been willing to accept it, so long as job and income security have been maintained. Others have insisted on being active partners in the change process, in return for their cooperation. Where equal-partner status has been obtained, and where real consultation has taken place, the outcomes have often been good. Recognizing that unions have been responsible for many of the gains made by working Canadians over the past century, it is extremely important, in our opinion, to maintain and strengthen the labour legislation that has allowed this to happen. Even in the new "knowledge economy," there are large numbers of low-wage, low-skilled workers who have virtually no bargaining power or employment security. At the same time, we need to find ways to support and protect more advantaged workers not likely to be covered by union contracts. For example, because of their education, status, and professional identities, the growing number of so-called 'knowledge workers' may be more likely to be represented by professional associations. How we address the needs of these and other currently vulnerable groups of workers will determine whether current labour market trends contribute to more or less social polarization.

Over the past decade, there has been a considerable amount of public policy debate about the social issues of unemployment, poverty, and growing inequality. But more often, the debate has had an economic tone, focusing on concerns about flexibility, productivity and competitiveness. Clearly, we have no quarrel with the desire to be competitive in the global economy, and recognize that greater labour market flexibility may be useful. But, as our comments throughout this book suggest, we are critical of single-factor solutions to the competitiveness problem that do not take job creation, the need for good jobs, and social equality into account.

Becoming more competitive could mean more than just leaner and meaner ways to increase corporate profits. From the perspective of individual workers, it could reflect the removal of barriers that prevent them from competing for good jobs and improving their standard of living. From the perspective of communities and regions in the country, it might indicate increased opportunities to benefit equally from economic growth. We are also unwilling to accept that flexibility has only one meaning, namely, that Canadian workers should be willing to accept whatever work opportunities they are offered by employers. As we have seen, flexibility can also describe labour market and workplace policies that provide workers with a wider array of options to improve their standard of living and quality of life. It might also refer to the willingness of corporations to consider job creation, local economic development, and other social goals as being on a par with profit making.

Training and education are being heavily promoted as a solution to the disadvantaged labour market position of some workers and, in the aggregate, as a way of improving Canada's economic position. Lifelong learning has become the centrepiece of both social and economic policy in Canada and throughout the Western industrialized nations. By obtaining additional education and training, some individuals can better compete for good jobs. Similarly, with a better stock of human capital, Canada can be more competitive. Investments in human capital may, perhaps, even lead to more job creation. But this is a long-term solution that, by itself, will not solve the longstanding problems of unemployment and underemployment. The more immediate challenge is to encourage employers to allow all workers to better utilize their full range of talents. Thus, we need to address how to create more skilled and autonomous jobs. These issues are not being addressed by most employers, or by the provincial and federal governments, which have been backing away from active labour market intervention.

. The issues we have been raising are ultimately about our societal goals. Is economic competitiveness at any social cost our objective? Or would Canadians prefer that the primary goal be a better quality of life, achieved through a reasonable standard of living, employment security, and good opportunities for personally rewarding work? If it is the latter—and we believe it should be—then a political response is also needed. As we have argued at various places in this book, a "let the market decide" approach (basically the position of most governments) is unlikely to assist us in reaching these social goals.

So what is the alternative? For a start, no single group—particularly employers—should have a monopoly on solutions. We believe that we have clearly documented the advantages of more collaborative union-management relationships, and this approach could be extended more widely to include governments, industry, and employee and community organizations. Multi-stakeholder forums are needed to address pressing issues such as income security, removing barriers to job-related training, flexible work designs, workplace equity and diversity, and sustainable economic development. In a sense, the ingredients of what used to be called industrial policy—economic growth, innovation, productivity—are now tightly intertwined with social policy concerns about equity, opportunity and human development.

Robert Reich, commenting on American society but with observations relevant to Canada as well, alerts us to the connection between economic globalization and polarization within national economies. In his view, left as things are, we will see further inequality between nations and within industrialized capitalist nations. In his words:

> The choice is ours to make. We are no more slaves to present trends than to vestiges of the past. We can, if we choose, assert that our mutual obligations as citizens extend beyond our economic usefulness to one another, and act accordingly (Reich 1991: 313).

We agree.

Abbott, Andrew 1988 *The System of Professions: An Essay on the Division of Expert Labor.* Chicago: University of Chicago Press.

Abella, Irving 1974 "Oshawa 1937." In Irving Abella, ed., *On Strike: Six Key Labour Struggles in Canada 1919–1949.* Toronto: James Lewis and Samuel.

Abercrombie, Nicholas, S. Hill, and B. S. Turner 1980 *The Dominant Ideology Thesis.* London: George Allen and Unwin.

Acker, Joan 1988 "Women and work in the social sciences." In Ann Helton Stromberg and Shirley Harkess, eds., *Women Working: Theories and Facts in Perspective.* 2nd ed. Mountain View, CA: Mayfield Publishing.

Adamchak, Donald J., Shuo Chen, and Jiangtao Li 1999 "Occupations, work units and work rewards in urban China." *International Sociology* 14(4): 423-41.

Adams, Roy J. 1995 "Canadian industrial relations in comparative perspective." In Morley Gunderson and Allen Ponak, eds., *Union–Management Relations in Canada.* 3rd ed. Don Mills, ON: Addison-Wesley Publishers.

———— **2000** "Canadian industrial relations at the dawn of the 21st century—prospects for reform." *Workplace Gazette: An Industrial Relations Quarterly* 3(4): 109-15.

Adams, Roy J., and Margaret Hallock 2001 "The anti-sweatshop movement and corporate codes of conduct." *Perspectives on Work* 5(1): 15-18.

Adams, Roy J., and Parbudyal Singh 1997 "Worker rights under NAFTA: experience with the North American Agreement on Labor Cooperation." In Rick Chaykowski, Paul-André Lapointe, Guylaine Vallée, and Anil Verma, eds., *Worker Representation in the Era of Trade and Deregulation. Selected Papers From the XXXIII Annual CIRA Conference. Brock University in St. Catharines, Ontario.*, Canadian Industrial Relations Association.

Adams, Tracy L. 1998 "Gender and women's employment in the male-dominated profession of dentistry: 1867-1917." *Canadian Review of Sociology and Anthropology* 35(1): 21-42.

Adams, Tracy L., and Kevin McQuillan 2000 "New jobs, new workers? Organizations restructuring and management hiring decisions." *Relations Industrielles/Industrial Relations* 55(3): 391-412.

Advisory Committee on Labour Management Relations in the Federal Public Service 2001 *Working Together in the Public Interest. Final Report.* Ottawa: Treasury Board of Canada (www.fryercommittee.com).

Aguayo, Rachael 1990 *Dr. Deming: The American Who Taught the Japanese About Quality.* New York: Simon and Schuster.

Aguren, Stefan, Christer Bredbacka, Reine Hansson, Kurt Ihregren, and K. G. Karlson 1985 *Volvo Kalmar Revisited: Ten Years of Experience.* Stockholm: Efficiency and Participation Development Council.

Ainley, Pat 1993 *Class and Skill: Changing Divisions of Knowledge and Labour.* London: Cassell Educational Limited.

Akerlof, G.A., A.K. Rose, and J.L. Yellen 1988 "Job switching and job satisfaction in the US. labor market." *Brookings Papers on Economic Activity* 2: 495-82.

Akyeampong, Ernest B. 1992 "Discouraged workers—where have they gone?" *Perspectives on Labour and Income* (Winter): 38–44.

———— **1993** "Flextime work arrangements." *Perspectives on Labour and Income* (Autumn): 17-30.

———— **1995** "Missing work." *Perspectives on Labour and Income* (Spring) 12–16.

———— 1997 "Work arrangements: 1995 Overview." *Perspectives on Labour and Income* (Spring): 48–52.

———— 1999a "Missing work in 1998—industry differences." *Perspectives on Labour and Income* 11(Autumn): 30-36.

———— 1999b "Saving for retirement: RRSPs and RPPs." *Perspectives on Labour and Income* (Summer): 18-22.

———— 2000 "Non-unionized but covered by collective bargaining." *Perspectives on Labour and Income* 12(Autumn): 33-8.

Akyeampong, Ernest B., and Jennifer Winters 1993 "International employment trends by industry – a note." *Perspectives on Labour and Income* (Summer): 33-37.

Alestalo, Matti, and Stein Kuhnle 1986–1987 "The Scandinavian route: economic, social, and political developments in Denmark, Finland, Norway, and Sweden." *International Journal of Sociology* 16: 3–38.

Alexander, Karl L., Doris R. Entwisle, and Carrie S. Horsey 1998 "From first grade forward: early foundations of high school dropout." *Sociology of Education* 70(2): 87-107.

Aligisakis, Maximos 1997 "Labour disputes in Western Europe: typology and tendencies." *International Labour Review* 136(1):73-94.

Althauser, Robert P. 1989 "Internal labor markets." *Annual Review of Sociology* 15: 143–61.

American Federation of Labour (AFL–CIO) 1995 *What's Wrong With Right-to-Work: A Tale of Two Nations.* rev. ed. Washington, DC: AFL–CIO.

Anderson, Kay J. 1991 *Vancouver's Chinatown: Racial Discourse in Canada, 1875–1980.* Montreal & Kingston: McGill–Queen's University Press.

Anderson, Robert D. 2000 "In for the long term: pension plans offered by employers." *Perspectives on Labour and Income* (Winter): 39-46.

Andres, Lesley 1993 "Life trajectories, action, and negotiating the transition from high school." In Paul Anisef and Paul Axelrod, eds., *Transitions: Schooling and Employment in Canada.* Toronto: Thompson Educational Publishing.

Andres, Lesley, Paul Anisef, Harvey Krahn, Dianne Looker, and Victor Thiessen 1999 "The persistence of social structure: cohort, class and gender effects on the occupational aspirations and expectations of Canadian youth." *Journal of Youth Studies* 2(3): 261-82.

Andres, Lesley, and Harvey Krahn 1999 "Youth pathways in articulated postsecondary systems: Enrolment and completion patterns of urban young women and men." *Canadian Journal of Higher Education* 29(1): 47-2.

Andres, Lesley, and E. Dianne Looker 2001 "Rurality and capital: educational expectations and attainments of rural, urban/rural and metropolitan youth." *Canadian Journal of Higher Education* 31(2): 1-46.

Angus, Charlie, and Brit Griffin 1996 *We Lived a Life and Then Some: The Life, Death, and Life of a Mining Town.* Toronto: Between the Lines.

Angus Reid Group 1996 "The public's agenda over 1996." *The Angus Reid Report* 11(6 Nov/Dec).

Angus Reid Interactive 1996 "Loyalty at work." (17 October): 1–3.

Anisef, Paul, and Paul Axelrod, eds. 1993 *Transitions: Schooling and Employment in Canada.* Toronto: Thompson Educational Publishing.

Anisef, Paul, Paul Axelrod, Etta Baichman-Anisef, Carl James, and Anton Turrittin 2000 *Opportunity and Uncertainty: Life Course Experiences of the Class of '73.* Toronto: University of Toronto Press.

Anthony, P. D. 1977 *The Ideology of Work.* London: Tavistock.

References

Antoniou, Andreas, and Robin Rowley 1986 "The ownership structure of the largest Canadian corporations, 1979." *Canadian Journal of Sociology* 11: 253–68.

Antos, Joseph R., Mark Chandler, and Wesley Mellow 1980 "Sex differences in union membership." *Industrial and Labor Relations Review* 33: 162–69.

Apostle, Richard, and Gene Barrett 1992 *Emptying Their Nets: Small Capital and Rural Industrialization in the Nova Scotia Fishing Industry.* Toronto: University of Toronto Press.

Apostle, Richard, D. Clairmont, and L. Osberg 1985 "Segmentation and wage determination." *Canadian Review of Sociology and Anthropology* 22: 30–56.

Appelbaum, Eileen, Thomas Bailey, Peter Berg, and Arne L. Kalleberg 2000 *Manufacturing Advantage: Why High-Performance Work Systems Pay Off.* Ithaca, NY: ILR.

Appelbaum, Eileen, and Rosemary Batt 1994 *The New American Workplace: Transforming Work Systems in the United States.* Ithaca, NY: ILR Press.

Arai, Bruce A. 1997 "The road not taken: the transition from unemployment to self-employment in Canada, 1961-1994." *Canadian Journal of Sociology* 22(3): 365-82.

——— **2000** "Self-employment as a response to the double day for women and men in Canada." *Canadian Review of Sociology and Anthropology* 37(2): 125-42.

Archibald, W. Peter 1978 *Social Psychology as Political Economy.* Toronto: McGraw-Hill Ryerson.

Argote, Linda 1999 *Organizational Learning: Creating, Retaining, and Transferring Knowledge.* Boston: Kluwer Academic.

Argyris, Chris 1999 "The next challenge for TQM—taking the offensive on defensive reasoning." *Journal for Quality and Participation* 22(6): 41-3.

Armstrong, Pat, and Hugh Armstrong 1983 *A Working Majority: What Women Must Do for Pay.* Ottawa: Canadian Advisory Council on the Status of Women.

——— **1990** *Theorizing Women's Work.* Toronto: Garamond Press.

——— **1994** *The Double Ghetto: Canadian Women and Their Segregated Work.* 3rd ed. Toronto: McClelland and Stewart.

Armstrong, Pat, Jacqueline Choiniere, and Elaine Day 1993 *Vital Signs: Nursing in Transition.* Toronto: Garamond Press.

Armstrong, Pat, Jacqueline Choiniere, Gina Feldberg, and Jerry White 1994 "Voices from the ward: a study of the impact of cutbacks." In Hugh Armstrong, Jacqueline Choiniere, Gina Feldberg, Jerry White, Pat Armstrong, eds., *Take Care: Warning Signals for Canada's Health System.* Toronto: Garamond Press.

Armstrong, Robin 1999 "Mapping the conditions of First Nations communities." *Canadian Social Trends* (Winter): 14-18.

Aronowitz, S. 1973 *False Promises: The Shaping of American Working Class Consciousness.* New York: McGraw-Hill.

Arsen, David D. 1996 "The NAFTA debate in retrospect: U.S. perspectives." In Karen Roberts and Mark I. Wilson, eds., *Policy Choices: Free Trade Among NAFTA Nations.* East Lansing: Michigan State University Press.

Arsen, David D., Mark I. Wilson, and Jonas Zoninsein 1996 "Trends in manufacturing employment in the NAFTA region: evidence of a giant sucking sound?" In Karen Roberts and Mark I. Wilson, eds., *Policy Choices: Free Trade Among NAFTA Nations,* East Lansing: Michigan State University Press.

Ashton, David 1986 *Unemployment Under Capitalism: The Sociology of British and American Labour Markets.* Brighton: Wheatsheaf Books.

Aston, T. H., and C. H. E. Philpin, eds. 1985 *The Brenner Debate: Agrarian Class*

Structure and Economic Development in Pre-Industrial Europe. Cambridge: Cambridge University Press.

Atkinson, J. 1984 *Flexibility, Uncertainty and Manpower Management*. Brighton: Institute of Manpower Studies Report No. 89.

———— 1985 "Flexibility: planning for an uncertain future." *Manpower Policy and Practice* 1 (Summer): 26–29.

Attewell, Paul 1987 "The deskilling controversy." *Work and Occupations* 14: 323–46.

Avery, Donald H. 1995 *Reluctant Host: Canada's Response to Immigrant Workers, 1896–1994*. Toronto: McClelland and Stewart.

Babcock, Robert H. 1974 *Gompers in Canada: A Study in American Continentalism Before the First World War*. Toronto: University of Toronto Press.

Bachmann, Kimberley 2000 *More Than Just Hard Hats: Creating Healthier Work Environments*. Ottawa: Conference Board of Canada.

Baer, Douglas E., Edward Grabb, and William A. Johnston 1991 "Class, crisis and political ideology in Canada: recent trends." *Canadian Review of Sociology and Anthropology* 24: 1–22.

Bailey, Thomas, and Annette D. Bernhard 1997 "In search of the high road in a low-wage industry." *Politics and Society* 25(2): 179-201.

Bailyn, Lotte, and John T. Lynch 1983 "Engineering as a life-long career: its meaning, its satisfactions, its difficulties." *Journal of Occupational Behaviour* 4: 263–83.

Bain, George S. 1978 *Union Growth and Public Policy in Canada*. Ottawa: Labour Canada.

Bain, George S., and H. A. Clegg 1974 "A strategy for industrial relations research in Britain." *British Journal of Industrial Relations* 12: 91–113.

Baines, Susan, and Jane Wheelock 1998 "Reinventing traditional solutions: job creation, gender and the micro-business household." *Work, Employment & Society* 12(4): 579-601.

Baker, D.B. 1985 "The study of stress at work." *Annual Review of Public Health* 6: 367–81.

Baldi, Stéphane, and Debra Branch McBrier 1997 "Do the determinants of promotion differ for blacks and whites? Evidence from the U.S. labor market." *Work and Occupations* 24(4): 478-97.

Balkin, David B., Gideon D. Markman, and Luis R. Gomez-Mejia 2000 "Is CEO pay in high-technology firms related to innovation?" *Academy of Management Journal* 43(6): 1118-29.

Bamber, Greg J., and Russell D. Lansbury 1998 "An introduction to international and comparative employment relations." In Greg J. Bamber and Russell D. Lansbury, eds., *International and Comparative Employment Relations*, 3rd ed. Thousand Oaks, CA: Sage Publications.

Bank of Montreal 1991 *Task Force on the Advancement of Women in the Bank*. Report to Employees.

———— 1993 *Advancing Workplace Equality*. Second Milestone Report.

Barbeau, Carole 2001 *Work-Related Child-Care Centres in Canada—2001*. Hull, QC: Human Resources Development Canada, Labour Program.

Barling, Julian, Clive Fullagar, and E. K. Kelloway 1992 *The Union and Its Members: A Psychological Approach*. New York: Oxford University Press.

Barlow, Maude, and Heather-Jane Robertson 1994 *Class Warfare: The Assault on Canada's Schools*. Toronto: Key Porter Books.

Barnard, Chester 1938 *The Functions of the Executive*. Cambridge, MA: Harvard University Press.

References

Barnet, Richard J., and John Cavanagh 1994 *Global Dreams: Imperial Corporations and the New World Order.* New York: Touchstone.

Barnett, William P., James N. Baron, and Toby E. Stuart 2000 "Avenues of attainment: occupational demography and organizational careers in the California civil service." *American Journal of Sociology* 106: 88-144.

Baron, James N., and Michael T. Hannan 2001 "Labor pains: change in organizational models and employee turnover in young, high-tech firms." *American Journal of Sociology* 4:960-1012.

Barro, Robert J. 2001 *Economic Growth in East Asia before and after the Financial Crisis.* Cambridge, MA: National Bureau of Economic Research.

Batstone, Eric, Ian Boraston, and Stephen Frenkel 1978 *The Social Organization of Strikes.* Oxford: Basil Blackwell.

Battle, Ken, and Sherri Torjman, eds. 1999 *Employment Policy Options.* Ottawa: Caledon Institute of Social Policy.

Baureiss, Gunter 1987 "Chinese immigration, Chinese stereotypes, and Chinese labour." *Canadian Ethnic Studies* 19: 15–34.

Beaud, Michel 1983 *A History of Capitalism 1500–1980.* New York: Monthly Review.

Beaujot, Roderic 1997 "Parental preferences for work and childcare." *Canadian Public Policy* 23(3):275-88.

Beaumont, P. B. 1995 *The Future of Employment Relations.* London: Sage.

Becker, Gary S. 1975 *Human Capital: A Theoretical and Empirical Analysis with Special Reference to Education.* 2nd ed. Chicago: University of Chicago Press.

Beckett, Elizabeth 1984 *Unions and Bank Workers: Will the Twain Ever Meet?* Ottawa: Labour Canada, Women's Bureau.

Bélanger, Jacques 2000 *The Influence of Employee Involvement on Productivity: A Review of Research.* Research Paper R-00-4E. Hull, QC: Applied Research Branch, Human Resources Development Canada.

Bélanger, Jacques, P. K. Edwards, and Larry Haiven, eds. 1994 *Workplace Industrial Relations and the Global Challenge.* Ithaca, New York: ILR Press.

Bell, Daniel 1973 *The Coming of Post-Industrial Society.* New York: Basic Books.

Bellin, Seymour S., and S. M. Miller 1990 "The split society." In Kai Erikson and Steven Peter Vallas, eds., *The Nature of Work: Sociological Perspectives.* New Haven: American Sociological Association and Yale University Press.

Bender, Keith A., and Peter J. Sloane 1998 "Job satisfaction, trade unions, and exit-voice revisited." *Industrial and Labor Relations Review* 51(2): 222-40.

Benders, Jos and Mark van Bijsterveld 2000 "Leaning on lean: the reception of a management fashion in Germany." *New Technology, Work, and Employment* 15(1):50-64.

Bendix, Reinhard 1974 *Work and Authority in Industry.* Berkeley: University of California Press.

Bennis, Warren 1999 "The end of leadership: exemplary leadership is impossible without full inclusion, initiatives, and cooperation of followers." *Organizational Dynamics* 28(1):71-80.

Bercuson, David J. 1974 *Confrontation at Winnipeg: Labour, Industrial Relations, and the General Strike.* Montreal and Kingston: McGill–Queen's University Press.

Berg, Maxine 1988 "Women's work, mechanization and the early phases of industrialization in England." In R. E. Pahl, ed., *On Work: Historical, Comparative and Theoretical Approaches.* Oxford: Basil Blackwell.

Berg, Peter 1999 "The effects of high performance work practices on job satisfaction in the United States steel industry."

Relations Industrielles/Industrial Relations 54(1): 111-34.

Berle, Adolf A., and Gardiner C. Means 1968 The Modern Corporation and Private Property. rev. ed. New York: Harcourt, Brace and World. [Originally published in 1932.]

Bernard, Richard B., and Michael R. Smith 1991 "Hiring, promotion, and pay in a corporate head office: an internal labour market in action?" Canadian Journal of Sociology 16: 353–74.

Bernhardt, Annette, Martina Morris, and Mark S. Handcock 1995 "Women's gains or men's losses? A closer look at the shrinking gender gap in earnings." American Journal of Sociology 101: 302–28.

Bernstein, Jared, and Lawrence Mishel 1997 "Has wage inequality stopped growing?" Monthly Labor Review (December): 3-16.

Bernstein, Paul 1997 American Work Values: Their Origin and Development. Albany, NY: State University of New York Press.

Best, Fred J. 1990 "Work sharing: an underused policy for combating unemployment?" In Kai Erikson and Steven Peter Vallas, eds., The Nature of Work: Sociological Perspectives. New Haven: American Sociological Association and Yale University Press.

Betcherman, Gordon 1993 "Research gaps facing training policy-makers." Canadian Public Policy 19: 18–28.

——— 1995 "Workplace transformation in Canada: policies and practices." Managing Human Resources in the 1990s and Beyond. In Bryan Downie and Mary L. Coates, eds., Managing Human Resources in the 1990s and Beyond. Kingston, ON: IRC Press, Queen's University.

——— 2000 "Structural unemployment: how important are labour market policies and institutions?" Canadian Public Policy (July Supplement): S131-40.

Betcherman, Gordon, and Norm Leckie 1995 "Age structure of employment in industries and occupations." Hull, QC: Human Resources Development Canada, Applied Research Branch, Research Paper (no. R-96–7E).

——— 1997 Youth Employment and Education Trends in the 1980s and 1990s. Ottawa: Canadian Policy Research Networks (CPRN) Working Paper no. W03.

Betcherman, Gordon, and Graham Lowe 1997 The Future of Work in Canada: A Synthesis Report. Ottawa: Canadian Policy Research Networks Inc.

Betcherman, Gordon, Kathryn McMullen, and Katie Davidman 1998 Training for the New Economy: A Synthesis Report. Ottawa: Canadian Policy Research Networks.

Betcherman, Gordon, Kathryn McMullen, Norm Leckie, and Christina Caron, eds. 1994 The Canadian Workplace in Transition. Kingston: IRC Press.

Betcherman, Gordon, and Rene Morissette 1994 Recent Youth Labour Market Experiences in Canada. Ottawa: Analytic Studies Branch, Statistics Canada.

Betcherman, Gordon, Keith Newton, and Joanne Godin, eds. 1990 Two Steps Forward: Human Resource Management in a High-Technology World. Ottawa: Economic Council of Canada.

Beynon, H. 1984 Working for Ford. 2nd ed. Harmondsworth, England: Penguin.

Bielby, Denise B., and William T. Bielby 1988 "She works hard for her money: household responsibilities and the allocation of work effort." American Journal of Sociology 93: 1031–59.

Billing, Yvonne D. 1994 "Gender and bureaucracies—a feminist critique of Ferguson's 'The feminist case against bureaucracy.'" Gender, Work and Organization 1: 179–93.

Birdi, Kamal, Peter Warr, and Andrew Oswald 1995 "Age differences in three components of employee well-being." *Applied Psychology: An International Review* 44: 345–373.

Birdsall, Nancy, and Carol Graham eds. 2000 *New Markets, New Opportunities? Economic and Social Mobility in a Changing World.* Washington, DC: Brookings Institution Press.

Black, Don, and John Myles 1986 "Dependent industrialization and the Canadian class structure: a comparative analysis of Canada, the United States and Sweden." *Canadian Review of Sociology and Anthropology* 23: 157–81.

Blackburn, Robert M., Jennifer Jarman, and Janet Siltanen 1993 "The analysis of occupational gender segregation over time and place: considerations of measurement and some new evidence." *Work, Employment & Society* 7: 335–62.

Blackburn, R.M., and Michael Mann 1979 *The Working Class in the Labour Market.* London: Macmillan.

Blau, Francine D., and Marianne A. Ferber 1986 *The Economics of Women, Men and Work.* Englewood Cliffs, NJ: Prentice-Hall.

Blau, Peter M. 1963 *The Dynamics of Bureaucracy.* 2nd ed. Chicago: University of Chicago Press.

Blau, Peter M., and Otis Dudley Duncan 1967 *The American Occupational Structure.* New York: John Wiley and Sons.

Blau, Peter M., and W. Richard Scott 1963 *Formal Organizations: A Comparative Approach.* London: Routledge and Kegan Paul.

Blaug, Mark 1985 "Where are we now in the economics of education?" *Economics of Education Review* 4: 17–28.

Blauner, Robert 1964 *Alienation and Freedom: The Factory Worker and His Industry.* Chicago: University of Chicago Press.

Bleasdale, Ruth 1981 "Class conflict on the canals of Upper Canada in the 1840s." *Labour/Le Travailleur* 7: 9–39.

Blishen, Bernard R., W. K. Carroll, and C. Moore 1987 "The 1981 socioeconomic index for occupations in Canada." *Canadian Review of Sociology and Anthropology* 24: 465–88.

Block, Fred 1990 *Postindustrial Possibilities: A Critique of Economic Discourse.* Berkeley, CA: University of California Press.

Block, Richard N., and Karen Roberts 2000 "A comparison of labour standards in the United States and Canada." *Relations Industrielles/Industrial Relations* 55(2): 273-306.

Bloom, Michael 1995 *Ethical Guidelines for Business–Education Partnerships.* Report 153-95. Ottawa: Conference Board of Canada.

Bluestone, Barry, and Bennett Harrison 1982 *The Deindustrialization of America.* New York: Basic Books.

———— 2000 *Growing Prosperity: The Battle for Growth with Equity in the Twenty-first Century.* Boston: Houghton.

Bognanno, Mario F., and Kathryn J. Ready, eds. 1993 *The North American Free Trade Agreement: Labor, Industry, and Government Perspectives.* Westport, CT: Praeger.

Boivin, Jean, and Esther Déom 1995 "Labour–management relations in Quebec. In Morley Gunderson and Allen Ponak, eds., *Union-Management Relations in Canada,* 3rd ed. Don Mills, ON: Addison-Wesley Publishers.

Bolman, Lee G., and Terrence E. Deal 1997 *Reframing Organizations: Artistry, Choice and Leadership.* 2nd ed. San Francisco: Jossey-Bass.

Boone, Louis E., David L. Kurtz, and C. Patrick Fleenor 1988 "The road to the top." *American Demographics* (March): 34–37.

Booth, Patricia 1997 *Contingent Work: Trends, Issues and Challenges for Employers.* Report 192–97. Ottawa: Conference Board of Canada.

Borman, Kathryn M. 1991 *The First "Real" Job: A Study of Young Workers.* Albany, NY: State University of New York Press.

Boulet, Jac-André, and Laval Lavallée 1984 *The Changing Economic Status of Women.* Ottawa: Supply and Services Canada (Economic Council of Canada).

Bourdieu, Pierre 1986 "The forms of capital." In J.C. Richardson, ed., *Handbook of Theory and Research for the Sociology of Education.* New York: Greenwood Press.

Bowden, Gary 1989 "Labour unions in the public mind: the Canadian case." *Canadian Review of Sociology and Anthropology* 26: 723–42.

Bowlby, Geoff 2000 "The school-to-work transition." *Perspectives on Labour and Income* (Spring): 43-48.

———— **2001** "The labour market: year-end review." *Perspectives on Labour and Income* (Spring): 9-19.

Boyd, Monica 1985 "Revising the stereotype: variations in female labour force interruptions." Paper presented at the annual meetings of the Canadian Sociology and Anthropology Association and the Canadian Population Society, Montreal.

Boyd, Monica, and Doug Norris 1999 "The crowded nest: young adults at home." *Canadian Social Trends* (Spring): 2-5.

Boyd, Monica, and Michael Vickers 2000 "100 years of immigration in Canada." *Canadian Social Trends* (Autumn): 2-12.

Boyer, Robert, and Daniel Drache, eds. 1996a *States Against Markets: The Limits of Globalization.* London: Routledge.

———— **1996b** "Introduction." In *States Against Markets: The Limits of Globalization.* London: Routledge.

Boyett, Joseph H., and Henry P. Conn 1991 *Workplace 2000: The Revolution Reshaping American Business.* New York: Dutton.

Bradbury, Bettina 1993 *Working Families: Age, Gender, and Daily Survival in Industrializing Montreal.* Toronto: McClelland and Stewart.

Bradley, Harriet 1989 *Men's Work, Women's Work: A Sociological History of the Sexual Division of Labour in Employment.* Cambridge: Polity Press.

Bradley, Keith, and Stephen Hill 1983 "After Japan: the quality circle transplant and productive efficiency." *British Journal of Industrial Relations* 21: 291–311.

Bradwin, Edmund 1972 *The Bunkhouse Man: A Study of Work and Pay in the Camps of Canada.* Toronto: University of Toronto Press. [Originally published in 1928.]

Braverman, Harry 1974 *Labor and Monopoly Capital: The Degradation of Work in the Twentieth Century.* New York: Monthly Review Press.

Breen, Richard, and David B. Rottman 1995 *Class Stratification: A Comparative Perspective.* London: Harvester Wheatsheaf.

Bridges, William 1994 *JobShift: How to Prosper in a Workplace without Jobs.* Don Mills, ON: Addison-Wesley.

Briskin, Linda, and Patricia McDermott 1993 *Women Challenging Unions: Feminism, Democracy, and Militancy.* Toronto: University of Toronto Press.

British Columbia Public Sector Employers' Council 1995 *Pay Equity Policy Framework.* (website: www.bcpsca.bc.ca)

Brohawn, Dawn K. ed. 1997 *Journey to an Ownership Culture: Insights from the ESOP Community.* Washington, DC: The ESOP Association and Scarecrow Press.

Brown, Amanda, and Jim Stanford 2000 *Flying Without a Net: The "Economic Freedom" of Working Canadians in 2000.* Ottawa: Canadian Centre for Policy Alternatives.

Brown, Leslie H. 1997 "Organizations for the 21st century? Co-operatives and 'new' forms of organization." *Canadian Journal of Sociology* 22: 65–93.

Brown, Lorne 1987 *When Freedom Was Lost: The Unemployed, The Agitator, and the State*. Montreal: Black Rose Books.

Bruno, Robert 1998 "Property rights or entitlements: how ESOPS influence what workers value about their unions." *Labor Studies Journal* 23(3): 55-83.

Brym, Robert 1996 "The third Rome and the end of history: notes on Russia's second communist revolution." *Canadian Review of Sociology and Anthropology* 33: 391–406.

Buckingham, Alan 1999 "Is there an underclass in Britain?" *British Journal of Sociology* 50(1): 49-5.

Burawoy, Michael 1979 *Manufacturing Consent: Changes in the Labor Process under Monopoly Capitalism*. Chicago: University of Chicago Press.

———— 1984 "Karl Marx and the satanic mills: factory politics under early capitalism in England, the United States, and Russia." *American Journal of Sociology* 90: 247–82.

Burchell, Brendan, and Jill Rubery 1990 "An empirical investigation into the segmentation of the labour supply." *Work, Employment & Society* 4: 551–75.

Burman, Patrick 1988 *Killing Time, Losing Ground: Experiences of Unemployment*. Toronto: Wall & Thompson.

———— 1996 *Poverty's Bonds: Power and Agency in the Social Relations of Welfare*. Toronto: Thompson Educational Publishing.

Burnham, J. 1941 *The Managerial Revolution*. Harmondsworth, England: Penguin.

Burns, T., and G. M. Stalker 1961 *The Management of Innovation*. London: Tavistock Publications.

Burrell, Gibson, and Gareth Morgan 1979 *Sociological Paradigms and Organizational Analysis: Elements of the Sociology of Corporate Life*. London: Heinemann.

Burris, Beverly H. 1998 "Computerization of the workplace." *Annual Review of Sociology* 24:141-57.

Burstein, M., N. Tienharra, P. Hewson, and B. Warrander 1975 *Canadian Work Values: Findings of a Work Ethic Survey and a Job Satisfaction Survey*. Ottawa: Information Canada.

Byrne, Edmund F. 1990 *Work, Inc.: A Philosophical Inquiry*. Philadelphia: Temple University Press.

Calás, Marta B., and Linda Smircich 1996 "From 'the woman's point of view': feminist approaches to organization studies." In Stewart R. Clegg, Cynthia Hardy, and Walter R. Nord, eds., *Handbook of Organization Studies*. London: Sage, 218–57.

Calliste, Agnes 1987 "Sleeping car porters in Canada: an ethnically submerged split labour market." *Canadian Ethnic Studies* 19: 1–20.

Cameron, David, and Janice Gross Stein 2000 "Globalization, culture and society: the state as place amidst shifting spaces," *Canadian Public Policy* 24 (2 Supplement): S15–34.

Canada 1969 *Canadian Industrial Relations: The Report of the Task Force on Labour Relations*. Ottawa: Queen's Printer.

———— 1984 *Report of the Commission on Equality in Employment* [The Abella Report]. Ottawa: Supply and Services.

———— 1985 *Employment Equity Act*. Chapter 23, 2nd Supplement, Revised Statutes of Canada.

———— 1992 *A Matter of Fairness. Report of the Social Committee on the Review of the Employment Equity Act*. Ottawa: House of Commons.

Canada, Department of Labour 1958 *Survey of Married Women Working for Pay in Eight Canadian Cities*. Ottawa: Queen's Printer.

Canadian Committee on Women in Engineering 1992 *More than Just Numbers: Report of the Canadian Committee on*

Women in Engineering. Fredericton: Faculty of Engineering, University of New Brunswick.

Canadian Conference of Catholic Bishops 1991 "The crisis of work." Canadian Conference of Catholic Bishops, Work and Solidarity Project.

Canadian Council on Social Development 2001. *The Progress of Canada's Children 2001.* Ottawa: Canadian Council on Social Development [http://www.ccsd.ca/pubs/2001/pcc2001/].

Canadian Labour Congress (CLC) 1997 *Women's Work: A Report.* Ottawa: Canadian Labour Congress.

Canadian Social Trends 1996 "Projections of visible minority groups, 1991 to 2016." *Canadian Social Trends* (Summer): 3.

——— **1997** "Canadian children in the 1990s: selected findings of the National Longitudinal Survey of Children and Youth." *Canadian Social Trends* 44 (Spring): 2–9.

Cant, Sarah, and Ursala Sharma 1995 "The reluctant profession–homeopathy and the search for legitimacy." *Work, Employment & Society* 9: 743–62.

Cao, Yang, and Victor G. Nee 2000 "Comment: controversies and evidence in the market transition debate." *American Journal of Sociology* 105(4):1175-89.

Cappelli, Peter 1992 "Is the 'skills gap' really about attitudes?" Philadelphia: National Center on the Educational Quality of the Workforce, University of Pennsylvania.

Caragata, Warren 1979 *Alberta Labour: A Heritage Untold.* Toronto: James Lorimer.

Carayon, Pascale, and Fred Zijlstra 1999 "Relationship between job control, work pressure and strain: studies in the USA and in the Netherlands." *Work and Stress* 13(1): 32-48.

Carey, Alex 1967 "The Hawthorne studies: a radical criticism." *American Sociological Review* 32: 403–16.

Carré, Françoise, Marianne A. Ferber, Lonnie Golden, and Stephen A. Herzenberg, eds. 2000 *Nonstandard Work: The Nature and Challenge of Changing Employment Relationships.* Champaign, IL: Industrial Relations Research Association.

Carroll, William K., John Fox, and Michael D. Ornstein 1982 "The network of directorate links among the largest Canadian firms." *Canadian Review of Sociology and Anthropology* 19: 44–69.

Carson, Paula P., Patricia A. Lanier, Kerry D. Carson, and Brandi N. Guidry 2000 "Clearing a path through the management fashion jungle: some preliminary trailblazing." *Academy of Management Journal* 43(6):1143-58.

Carter, Donald D. 1998 "Employment benefits for same sex couples: the expanding entitlement." *Canadian Public Policy* 14(1): 107–17.

Cartwright, Susan, and Cary L. Cooper 1997 *Managing Workplace Stress.* Thousand Oaks, CA: Sage.

Cascio, Wayne F. 1993 "Downsizing: what do we know? what have we learned?" *Academy of Management Executive* 7: 95–104.

——— **1996** *Issues of an Aging Workforce in a Changing Society: Cases and Comparisons.* Toronto: University of Toronto, Centre for Studies of Aging.

Castells, Manuel 1996 *The Information Age: Economy, Society and Culture. Vol. I: The Rise of the Network Society.* Oxford: Blackwell.

——— **1998** *The Information Age: Economy, Society and Culture. Vol. III: End of Millennium.* Oxford: Blackwell.

CAW–Canada Research Group on CAMI 1993 *The CAMI Report: Lean Production in a Unionized Auto Plant.* Willowdale, ON: Canadian Auto Workers Research Department.

Centre for Studies of Aging 1996. *Issues of an Aging Workforce in a Changing Society: Cases and Comparisons.* Toronto: University of Toronto, Centre for Studies of Aging.

Chaison, Gary N., and Joseph B. Rose 1990 "New directions and divergent paths: the North American labor movement in troubled times." *Proceedings of the Spring Meeting of the Industrial Relations Research Association.* Madison, WI: IRRA.

Chan, Tak W. 2000 "Revolving doors reexamined: occupational sex segregation over the life course." *American Sociological Review* 64(February):86-96.

Chandler, Jr., Alfred D. 1962 *Strategy and Structure: Chapters in the History of the American Industrial Enterprise.* Cambridge, MA: MIT Press.

———— **1977** *The Visible Hand: The Managerial Revolution in American Business.* Cambridge, MA: Harvard University Press.

Chang, Clara, and Constance Sorrentino 1991 "Union membership statistics in 12 countries." *Monthly Labor Review* (December): 46–53.

Chard, Jennifer, and Viviane Renaud 1999 "Visible minorities in Toronto, Vancouver, and Montreal." *Canadian Social Trends* (Autumn): 20-25.

Chawla, Raj K. 1992 "The changing profile of dual-earner families." *Perspectives on Labour and Income* (Summer): 22–29.

Chaykowski, Richard P., and George A. Slotsve 1999 "Unions, inequality, and the distribution of income in Canada: evidence from the 1994 Survey of Labour and Income Dynamics." *Workplace Gazette* 2(4):85-99.

Chelte, Anthony F., Peter Hess, Russell Fanelli, and William P. Ferris 1989 "Corporate culture as an impediment to employee involvement: when you can't get there from here." *Work and Occupations* 16: 153–64.

Chemers, Martin M., Stuart Oskamp, and Mark A. Costanzo, eds. 1995 *Diversity in Organizations: New Perspectives for a Changing Workplace.* Thousand Oaks, CA: Sage.

Cherns, A. 1976 "The principles of sociotechnical design." *Human Relations* 29: 783–92.

Child, John 1972 "Organizational structure, environment and performance: the role of strategic choice." *Sociology* 6: 2–22.

———— **1985** "Managerial strategies, new technology and the labour process." In David Knights, Hugh Willmott, and David Collison, eds., *Job Redesign: Critical Perspectives on the Labour Process.* Aldershot, England: Gower.

Chirot, Daniel 1986 *Social Change in the Modern Era.* San Diego: Harcourt Brace Jovanovich.

Church, Elizabeth 1996 "CEO pay packages not always 'justified.'" *The Globe and Mail* (25 September: B12).

———— **2001** "CEOs reap big bonuses as investors take losses." *The Globe and Mail* (14 June: A1).

Clairmont, Donald, R. Apostle, and R. Kreckel 1983 "The segmentation perspective as a middle-range conceptualization in sociology." *Canadian Journal of Sociology* 8: 245–71.

Clark, Andrew, Andrew Oswald, and Peter Warr 1996 "Is job satisfaction U-shaped in age?" *Journal of Occupational and Organizational Psychology* 69: 57–81.

Clark, R.D. 1982 "Worker participation in health and safety in Canada." *International Labour Review* 121: 199–206.

Clark, Warren 1999a "Search for success: finding work after graduation." *Canadian Social Trends* (Summer): 10-15.

———— **1999b** "Paying off student loans." *Perspectives on Labour and Income* (Spring): 28-33.

———— **2000** "100 years of education." *Canadian Social Trends* (Winter): 3-7.

Clarke, Jan 2000 "Skill as a complex gendered concept: a qualitative study of women, information work, and technology." *Knowledge and Society* 12: 209-228.

Clarke, Louise, and Larry Haiven 1999 "Workplace change and continuous bargaining: Saskatoon Chemicals then and now." *Relations Industrielles/Industrial Relations* 54(1):168-91.

Clarke, Thomas, and Stewart Clegg 1998 *Changing Paradigms: The Transformation of Management Knowledge for the 21st Century.* London: Harper Collins Business.

Clawson, Dan, and Mary A. Clawson 1999 "What has happened to the US labor movement?" *Annual Review of Sociology* 25:95-119.

Clegg, C.W. 1983 "Psychology of employee lateness, absence and turnover: a methodological critique and an empirical study." *Journal of Applied Psychology* 68: 88-101.

Clegg, Stewart R. 1990 *Modern Organizations: Organization Studies in the Postmodern World.* London: Sage.

Clegg, Stewart R., Cynthia Hardy, and Walter R. Nord, eds. 1996 *Handbook of Organization Studies.* Thousand Oaks, CA: Sage.

Clemenson, Heather A. 1992 "Are single industry towns diversifying? A look at fishing, mining and wood-based communities." *Perspectives on Labour and Income* (Spring): 31–43.

Clement, Wallace 1981 *Hardrock Mining: Industrial Relations and Technological Changes at INCO.* Toronto: McClelland and Stewart.

——— 1986 *The Struggle to Organize: Resistance in Canada's Fishery.* Toronto: McClelland and Stewart.

——— 1990 "Comparative class analysis: locating Canada in a North American and Nordic context." *Canadian Review of Sociology and Anthropology* 27: 462–86.

Clement, Wallace, and John Myles 1994 *Relations of Ruling: Class and Gender in Postindustrial Societies.* Montreal and Kingston: McGill–Queen's University Press.

Clinton, Angela 1997 "Flexible labor: restructuring the American labour force." *Monthly Labor Review* (August): 3-17.

Coates, Mary Lou, David Arrowsmith, and Melanie Courchene 1989 *The Canadian Industrial Relations Scene in Canada 1989: The Labour Movement and Trade Unionism Reference Tables.* Kingston: Industrial Relations Centre, Queen's University.

Cobb, Clifford, Ted Halstead, and Jonathan Rowe 1995 "If the GDP is up, why is America down?" *Atlantic Monthly* (October): 60–74.

Cockburn, Cynthia 1991 *In the Way of Women: Men's Resistance to Sex Equality in Organizations.* Ithaca, NY: ILR Press.

Cohen, Gary L. 1992 "Hard at work." *Perspectives on Labour and Income* (Spring): 8–14.

Cohen, Marjorie Griffen 1988 *Women's Work, Markets and Economic Development in Nineteenth Century Ontario.* Toronto: University of Toronto Press.

Cole, Robert E. 1979 *Work, Mobility, and Participation.* Berkeley CA: University of California Press.

Colling, Herb 1995 *Ninety-Nine Days: The Ford Strike in Windsor, 1945.* Toronto: NC Press.

Collins, James C., and Jerry I. Porras 1994 *Built to Last: Successful Habits of Visionary Companies.* New York: HarperCollins.

Collins, Randall 1990 "Market closure and the conflict theory of professions." In Michael Burrage and Rolf Torstendahl, eds., *Professions in Theory and History: Rethinking the Study of the Professions.* London: Sage.

Collinson, David L., David Knights, and Margaret Collinson 1990 *Managing to Discriminate.* London: Routledge.

Coltrane, Scott 1996 *Family Man: Fatherhood, Housework, and Gender Equity.* New York: Oxford University Press.

Comish, Shaun 1993 *The Westray Tragedy: A Miner's Story.* Halifax: Fernwood Publishing.

Commission for Labor Cooperation 1997 *North American Labor Markets: A Comparative Profile.* Dallas: Commission for Labor Cooperation.

—— **2000** *Standard and Advanced Practices in the North American Garment Industry.* Washington, DC: Secretariat of the Commission for Labor Cooperation.

Conference Board of Canada 1993 *Employability Skills Profile.* Ottawa: Conference Board of Canada.

—— **2000** *What To Do Before The Well Runs Dry: Managing Scarce Skills.* Ottawa: Conference Board of Canada.

Conley, James R. 1988 "More theory, less fact? social reproduction and class conflict in a sociological approach to working-class history." *Canadian Journal of Sociology* 13: 73–102.

Conrad, Peter 1987 "Wellness in the workplace: potentials and pitfalls of work-site health promotion." *Milbank Quarterly* 65: 255–75.

Conway, Hugh, and Jens Svenson 1998 "Occupational injury and illness rates, 1992-96: why they fell." *Monthly Labor Review* (November): 36-58.

Cooper, Robert, and Gibson Burrell 1988 "Modernism, postmodernism and organizational analysis: an introduction." *Organization Studies* 9: 91–112.

Co-operatives Secretariat 2000 *Worker Co-operative Success Stories.* Ottawa: Government of Canada, Co-operatives Secretariat.

Copp, Terry 1974 *The Anatomy of Poverty: The Condition of the Working Class in Montreal, 1897–1929.* Toronto: McClelland and Stewart.

Corak, Miles ed. 1998 *Labour Markets, Social Institutions, and the Future of Canada's Children.* Ottawa: Statistics Canada and Human Resources Development Canada.

Cornfield, Daniel B. 2001 "Shifts in Public Approval of Labor Unions in the United States, 1936-1999." *Guest Scholar Poll Review.* The Gallup Organization (www.gallup.com)

Cornforth, Chris 1995 "Patterns of cooperative management: beyond the degeneration thesis." *Economic and Industrial Democracy* 16(4): 487-523.

Coser, Lewis A. 1971 *Masters of Sociological Thought: Ideas in Historical and Social Context.* New York: Harcourt Brace Jovanovich.

Côté, James 2000 *Arrested Adulthood: The Changing Nature of Maturity and Identity.* New York: New York University Press.

Côté, James E., and Anton L. Allahar 1994 *Generation on Hold: Coming of Age in the Late Twentieth Century.* Toronto: Stoddart.

Coupland, Douglas 1993 *Generation X: Tales for an Accelerated Culture.* New York: St. Martin's Press.

Coverman, Shelley 1988 "Sociological explanations of the male–female wage gap: individual and structuralist theories." In Ann Helton Stromberg and Shirley Harkess, eds., *Women Working: Theories and Facts in Perspective.* 2nd ed. Mountain View, CA: Mayfield.

Craven, Paul 1980 *An Impartial Umpire: Industrial Relations and the Canadian State, 1900–1911.* Toronto: University of Toronto Press.

Creese, Gillian 1988–1989 "Exclusion or solidarity? Vancouver workers confront the oriental problem." *B.C. Studies* 80: 24–51.

—— **1999** *Contracting Masculinity: Gender, Class, and Race in a White-Collar Union, 1944-1994.* Don Mills, ON: Oxford University Press.

Creese, Gillian, Neil Guppy, and Martin Meissner 1991 *Ups and Downs on the Ladder of Success: Social Mobility in Canada.* Ottawa: Statistics Canada, General Social Survey Analysis Series 5 (Cat. No. 11-612E, No. 5).

Crocker, Diane, and Valery Kalemba 1999 "The incidence and impact of women's experiences of sexual harassment in Canadian workplaces." *Canadian Review of Sociology and Anthropology* 36(4):541-55.

Crompton, Susan 1991 "Who's looking after the kids? Child care arrangements for working mothers." *Perspectives on Labour and Income* (Summer): 68–75.

——— 1994 "Left behind: lone mothers in the labour market." *Perspectives on Labour and Income* (Summer): 23–28.

——— 1995 "Work and low income." *Perspectives on Labour and Income* (Summer): 12–14.

Crompton, Susan and Leslie Geran. 1995 "Women as main wage-earners." *Perspectives on Labour and Income* (Winter): 26–29.

Crompton, Susan, and Michael Vickers 2000 "One hundred years of labour force." *Canadian Social Trends* (Summer): 2-14.

Crouch, Colin 1982 *Trade Unions: The Logic of Collective Action.* Glasgow: Fontana.

Crozier, Michel 1964 *The Bureaucratic Phenomenon.* Chicago: University of Chicago Press.

Cunningham, J. B., and T. H. White, eds. 1984 *Quality of Working Life: Contemporary Cases.* Ottawa: Labour Canada.

Daft, Richard L. 1992 *Organization Theory and Design.* 4th ed. St. Paul, MN: West Publishing.

——— 1995 *Organization Theory & Design.* 5th ed. Minneapolis/St. Paul, MN: West Publishing Company.

Dai, S. Y., and M. V. George 1996 *Projections of Visible Minority Population Groups, Canada, Provinces and Regions, 1991–2016.* Cat. No. 91-541-XPE. Ottawa: Statistics Canada.

Dalton, Melville 1959 *Men Who Manage: Fusions of Feeling and Theory in Administration.* New York: John Wiley and Sons.

Dana, Leo-Paul 1992 "Why we must join NAFTA." *Policy Options* 13 (27): 6–8.

Danysk, Cecilia 1995 *Hired Hands: Labour and the Development of Prairie Agriculture, 1880 to 1930.* Don Mills, ON: Oxford University Press.

Das Gupta, Tania 1996 *Racism and Paid Work.* Toronto: Garamond Press.

Davies, Lorraine, and Patricia J. Carrier 1999 "The importance of power relations for the division of household labour." *Canadian Journal of Sociology* 24(1):35-51.

Davies, Scott, and Neil Guppy 1997 "Fields of study, college selectivity, and student inequalities in higher education." *Social Forces* 75(4): 1417-38.

——— 1998 "Race and Canadian education." In Vic Satzewich, ed., *Racism and Social Inequality in Canada: Concepts, Controversies and Strategies of Resistance.* Toronto: Thompson Educational Publishing.

Davies, Scott, Clayton Mosher, and Bill O'Grady 1996 "Educating women: gender inequalities among Canadian university graduates." *Canadian Review of Sociology and Anthropology* 33: 125–42.

Davis, Bob 2000 *Skills Mania: Snake Oil in our Schools?* Toronto: Between the Lines.

Davis, Kingsley, and Wilbert E. Moore 1945 "Some principles of stratification." *American Sociological Review* 10: 242–49.

Davis, Louis E., and Charles Sullivan 1980 "A labour–management contract and quality of working life." *Journal of Occupational Behaviour* 1: 29–41.

De Broucker, Patrice, and Laval Lavallée 1998a "Getting ahead in life: does your parents' education count?" *Canadian Social Trends* (Summer): 11-15.

———— 1998b "Intergenerational aspects of education and literacy skills acquisition." In Miles Corak, ed., *Labour Markets, Social Institutions, and the Future of Canada's Children.* Ottawa: Statistics Canada and Human Resources Development Canada.

De Jonge, Jan, Hans Bosma, Richard Peter, and Johannes Siegrist 2000 "Job strain, effort-reward imbalance and employee well-being: a large-scale cross-sectional study." *Social Science and Medicine* 50(9): 1317-27.

De Santis, Solange 1999 *Life on the Line: One Woman's Tale of Work, Sweat, and Survival.* New York: Doubleday.

De Silva, Arnold 1999 "Wage discrimination against natives." *Canadian Public Policy* 25(1): 65-83.

DeTienne, Kristen Bell 1993 "Big brother or friendly coach? Computer monitoring in the 21st century." *Futurist* 27 (September–October): 33–37.

de Vaus, David, and Ian McAllister 1991 "Gender and work orientation: values and satisfaction in Western Europe." *Work and Occupations* 18: 72–93.

de Witte, Marco, and Bram Steijn 2000 "Automation, job content, and underemployment." *Work, Employment & Society* 14(2): 245-64.

Dex, Shirley 1988 *Women's Attitudes Towards Work.* London: Macmillan.

Dhingra, Harbans L. 1983 "Patterns of ownership and control in Canadian industry: a study of large non-financial private corporations." *Canadian Journal of Sociology* 8: 21–44.

Dickinson, P., and G. Sciadas 1999 "Canadians connected." *Canadian Economic Observer* (February): 3.1 – 3.22.

Dickson, Tony, and Hugh V. McLachlan 1989 "In search of the spirit of capitalism: Weber's misinterpretation of Franklin." *Sociology* 23: 81–89.

DiGiacomo, Gordon 1999 "Aggression and violence in the workplace." *Workplace Gazette: An Industrial Relations Quarterly* 2(2):72-85.

Diprete, Thomas A. 1988 "The upgrading and downgrading of occupations: status redefinition vs. deskilling as alternative theories of change." *Social Forces* 66: 725–46.

Diprete, Thomas A., and Whitman T. Soule 1988 "Gender and promotion in segmented job ladder systems." *American Sociological Review* 53: 26–40.

Dohm, Arlene 2000 "Gauging the labour force effects of retiring baby boomers." *Monthly Labor Review* (July): 17-25.

Donaldson, Lex 1995 *In Defence of Organization Theory: A Reply to Critics.* Cambridge: Cambridge University Press.

———— 1996 *For Positivist Organization Theory.* London: Sage.

Doucouliagos, Chris 1995 "Worker participation and productivity in labor-managed and participatory capitalist firms: a meta-analysis." *Industrial and Labor Relations Review* 49(1): 58-77.

Downie, Bryan, and Mary L. Coates 1995 "Barriers, challenges, and future directions." In Bryan Downie and Mary L. Coates, eds., *Managing Human Resources in the 1990s and Beyond: Is the Workplace Being Transformed?* Kingston, Ontario: IRC Press.

Drache, Daniel 1994 "Lean production in Japanese auto transplants in Canada." *Canadian Business Economics* (Spring): 45–59.

———— 1995 "The decline of collective bargaining: is it irreversible?" *Proceedings of the XXXIst Conference.* Anthony Giles, Anthony E. Smith, and Kurt Wetzel, eds. Quebec: Canadian Industrial Relations Association.

Drache, Daniel, and Meric S. Gertler 1991 "The world economy and the nation-state: the new international order." In D.

Drache and M.S. Gertler, eds., *The New Era of Global Competition: State Policy and Market Power.* Montreal and Kingston: McGill–Queen's University Press.

Drolet, Marie 2001 *The Persistent Gap: New Evidence on the Canadian Gender Wage Gap.* Statistics Canada, Analytic Studies Branch, Research Paper Series, No. 157.

Drost, Helmar 1996 "Joblessness among Canada's Aboriginal peoples." In Brian MacLean and Lars Osberg, eds., *The Unemployment Crisis: All for Nought?* Montreal and Kingston: McGill–Queen's University Press.

Drucker, Peter F. 1993 *Post-Capitalist Society.* New York: HarperBusiness.

——— 1999 "Knowledge-worker productivity: the biggest challenge." *California Management Review* 41(2):79-94.

Dubin, Robert, J. E. Champoux, and L. W. Porter 1975 "Central life interests and organizational commitments of blue-collar workers." *Administrative Science Quarterly* 20: 411–21.

Dudley, Kathryn Marie 1994 *The End of the Line: Lost Jobs, New Lives in Postindustrial America.* Chicago: University of Chicago Press.

Duffy, Ann, and Norene Pupo 1992 *Part-Time Paradox: Connecting Gender, Work and Family.* Toronto: McClelland and Stewart.

Duncan, Greg J., Martha S. Hill, and Saul D. Hoffman 1988 "Welfare dependence within and across generations." *Science* (January): 467–71.

Duncan, Greg. J., W. Jean Yeung, Jeanne Brooks-Gunn, and Judith R. Smith 1998 "How much does childhood poverty affect the life chances of children?" *American Sociological Review* 63 (June): 406-23.

Dunlop, John T. 1971 *Industrial Relations Systems.* Carbondale, IL: Southern Illinois University Press. [Originally published in 1958.]

Durkheim, Émile 1960 *The Division of Labour in Society.* New York: Free Press. [Originally published in 1897.]

Duxbury, Linda, Lorraine Dyke, and Natalie Lam 2000 *Managing High Technology Employees.* Scarborough, ON: Carswell.

Duxbury, Linda, and Christopher Higgins 1998 *Work-Life Balance in Saskatchewan: Realities and Challenges.* Government of Saskatchewan (www.business.carleton.ca/sask.98).

Easterby-Smith, Mark, John Burgoyne, and Luis Araujo, eds. 2001 *Organizational Learning and the Learning Organization: Developments in Theory and Practice.* London: Sage.

Easterlin, Richard 1980 *Birth and Fortune: The Impact of Numbers on Personal Welfare.* New York: Basic Books.

Economic Council of Canada 1990 *Good Jobs, Bad Jobs: Employment in the Service Economy.* Ottawa: Supply and Services Canada.

——— 1991 *New Faces in the Crowd: Economic and Social Impacts of Immigration.* Ottawa: Supply and Services Canada.

——— 1992a *Pulling Together: Productivity, Innovation and Trade.* Ottawa: Supply and Services Canada.

——— 1992b *The New Face of Poverty: Income Security Needs of Canadian Families (Summary).* Ottawa: Supply and Services Canada.

Economist, The 1996 "Cultural explanations: the man in the Baghdad café." (9 November): 23–26.

Edin, Kathryn 1991 "Surveying the welfare system: how AFDC recipients make ends meet in Chicago." *Social Problems* 38: 462–74.

Edwards, Richard C. 1979 *Contested Terrain: The Transformation of the Workplace in the Twentieth Century.* New York: Basic Books.

References

Emery, F. E., and Einar Thorsrud 1969 *Form and Content in Industrial Democracy.* London: Tavistock Publications.

Employment and Immigration Canada 1990 *1990 Annual Report, Employment Equity Act.* Ottawa: Supply and Services Canada.

Enchin, Harvey 1992 "Canada loves quality, in theory." *The Globe and Mail* (15 May): B1–B2.

Engels, Friedrich 1971 *The Condition of the Working Class in England.* Oxford: Basil Blackwell. [Originally published in 1845.]

Erikson, Kai 1990 "On work and alienation." In Kai Erikson and Steven Peter Vallas, eds., *The Nature of Work: Sociological Perspectives.* New Haven: American Sociological Association and Yale University Press.

Erikson, Robert, et al., eds. 1986–1987 *International Journal of Sociology* 16. [Special issue on the Scandinavian model.]

Etzioni, Amitai 1975 *A Comparative Analysis of Complex Organizations.* 2nd. ed. New York: Free Press.

Evans, Peter, and James E. Rauch 1999 "Bureaucracy and growth: a cross-national analysis of the efforts of 'Weberian' state structures on economic growth." *American Sociological Review* 64: 748–65.

Ewan, Stuart 1976 *Captains of Consciousness: Advertising and the Social Roots of the Consumer Culture.* New York: McGraw-Hill.

Expert Panel on Skills 2000 *Stepping Up: Skills and Opportunities in the Knowledge Economy.* Ottawa: Advisory Council on Science and Technology. (Cat. No. C2-467/2000). (http://acst.ccst.gc.ca)

Farber, Henry S., and Daniel H. Saks 1980 "Why workers want unions: the role of relative wages and job characteristics." *Journal of Political Economy* 88: 349–69.

Fast, Janet E., and Judith A. Frederick 1996 "Working arrangements and time stress." *Canadian Social Trends* 43 (Winter): 14–19.

Fearfull, Anne 1992 "The introduction of information and office technologies: the great divide?" *Work, Employment & Society* 6 (3): 423–42.

Feather, Norman T. 1990 *The Psychological Impact of Unemployment.* New York: Springer-Verlag.

Federal, Provincial and Territorial Ministers Responsible for Social Services 2000 *In Unison 2000: Persons with Disabilities in Canada.* Ottawa: Human Resources Development Canada (Cat. no. SP-182-01-01E).

Feldberg, Roslyn, and Evelyn Nakano Glenn 1979 "Male and female: job versus gender models in the sociology of work." *Social Problems* 26: 524–38.

Feldman, Daniel C., Helen I. Doerpinghaus, and William H. Turnley 1994 "Managing temporary workers: a permanent HR challenge." *Organizational Dynamics* 23: 49–63.

Felstead, Alan, Harvey Krahn, and Marcus Powell 1999 "Young and old at risk: comparative trends in 'non-standard' patterns of employment in Canada and the United Kingdom." *International Journal of Manpower* 20(5): 277-96.

Felt, Lawrence, and Peter Sinclair 1992 "Everybody does it: unpaid work in a rural peripheral region." *Work, Employment & Society* 6: 43–64.

Ferber, Marianne A., and Jane Waldfogel 1998 "The long-term consequences of nontraditional employment." *Monthly Labor Review* (May): 3-12.

Ferland, Jacques 1989 "In search of the unbound Prometheia: a comparative view of women's activism in two Quebec industries, 1869–1908." *Labour/Le Travail* 24: 11–44.

Feuchtwang, Stephen 1982 "Occupational ghettos." *Economy and Society* 11: 251–91.

Figart, Deborah M., and June Lapidus 1996 "The impact of comparable worth on earnings inequality." *Work and Occupations* 23: 297–318.

Finnie, Ross 1999 "Patterns of inter-provincial migration, 1982-95." *Canadian Economic Observer* (December): 3.1- 3.12.

Finnie, Ross, and Gaétan Garneau 1996 "Student borrowing for postsecondary education." *Education Quarterly Review* 3(2): 10-34.

Firebaugh, Glenn, and Brian Harley 1995 "Trends in job satisfaction in the United States by race, gender, and type of occupation." *Research in Sociology of Work* 5: 87–104.

Fisher, E. G. 1982 "Strike activity and wildcat strikes in British Columbia: 1945–1975." *Relations industrielles/Industrial Relations* 37: 284–312.

Fisher, Susan R., and Margaret A. White 2000 "Downsizing in a learning organization: are there hidden costs?" *Academy of Management Review* 25(1):244-51.

Flanders, Allan 1970 *Management and Unions: The Theory and Reform of Industrial Relations.* London: Faber and Faber.

Foot, David K., and Jeanne C. Li 1986 "Youth employment in Canada: a misplaced priority?" *Canadian Public Policy* 12(3):499–506.

Foot, David K., with Daniel Stoffman 1998 *Boom, Bust & Echo 2000: Profiting from the Demographic Shift in the New Millennium.* Toronto: Macfarlane Walter & Ross.

Foot, David K., and Rosemary A. Venne 1990 "Population pyramids and promotional prospects." *Canadian Public Policy* 16: 387–98.

Forcese, Dennis 1997 *The Canadian Class Structure.* 4th ed. Toronto: McGraw-Hill Ryerson.

Forester, Tom 1989 *Computers in the Human Context: Information Technology, Productivity, and People.* Cambridge, MA: MIT Press.

Form, William 1983 "Sociological research on the American working class." *Sociological Quarterly* 24: 163–84.

——— 1987 "On the degradation of skills." *Annual Review of Sociology* 13: 29–47.

Forrest, Anne 2000 "Pay Equity: The State of the Debate." In Yonatan Reshef, Collete Bernier, Denis Harrison, and Terry H. Wager, eds., *Industrial Relations in a New Millennium. Selected Papers From the XXXVIIth Annual CIRA Conference. Edmonton, Alberta May 25-27, 2000.* Pp. 65–76. Canadian Industrial Relations Association.

Fortin, Pierre 1996 "The unbearable lightness of zero-inflation optimism." In Brian K. MacLean and Lars Osberg, eds., *The Unemployment Crisis: All for Nought?* Montreal and Kingston: McGill–Queen's University Press, 14–38.

Fox, Bonnie, and Pamela Sugiman 1999 "Flexible work, flexible workers: the restructuring of clerical work in a large telecommunications company." *Studies in Political Economy* 60 (Autumn): 59-84.

Fox, John, and Carole Suschnigg 1989 "A note on gender and the prestige of occupations." *Canadian Journal of Sociology* 14: 353–60.

Frager, Ruth A. 1992 *Sweatshop Strife: Class, Ethnicity, and Gender in the Jewish Labour Movement of Toronto 1900–1939.* Toronto: University of Toronto Press.

Frank, David 1986 "Contested terrain: workers' control in the Cape Breton coal mines in the 1920s." In Craig Heron and Robert Storey, eds., *On the Job: Confronting the Labour Process in Canada.* Montreal and Kingston: McGill–Queen's University Press.

Franke, Richard Herbert, and James D. Kaul 1978 "The Hawthorne experiments: first statistical interpretation." *American Sociological Review* 43: 623–43.

References

Frederick, Judith A. 1995 *As Time Goes By: Time Use of Canadians.* Ottawa: Statistics Canada. (Cat. no. 89–544E).

Frederick, Judith A., and Janet E. Fast 1999 "Eldercare in Canada: who does how much?" *Canadian Social Trends* 54(Autumn):26-30.

Freedman, Marcia 1976 *Labor Markets: Segments and Shelters.* Montclair, NJ: Allanheld, Osmun and Co.

Freeman, Alan 1993 "Japan gets a life." *The Globe and Mail* (13 March): D1.

Freeman, Bill 1982 *1005: Political Life in a Union Local.* Toronto: James Lorimer.

Freeman, Richard B. 1995 "The future for unions in decentralized collective bargaining systems: US and UK unionism in an era of crisis." *British Journal of Industrial Relations* 33: 519–36.

Freeman, R. B., and J. L. Medoff 1984 *What Do Unions Do?* New York: Basic Books.

Freeman, Richard B., and Joel Rogers 1999 *What Workers Want.* Ithaca, NY: Cornell University Press.

Freeman, Sarah J., and Kim S. Cameron 1993 "Organizational downsizing: a convergence and reorientation framework." *Organization Science* 4: 10–29.

Freidson, Eliot 1986 *Professional Powers: A Study of the Institutionalization of Formal Knowledge.* Chicago: University of Chicago Press.

Frenette, Marc 2001 "Overqualified? Recent graduates, employer needs." *Perspectives on Labour and Income* (Spring): 45-53.

Frenkel, Steve, Marek Korczynski, Leigh Donoghue, and Karen Shire 1995 "Reconstituting work: trends towards knowledge work and info-normative control." *Work, Employment & Society* 9: 773–96.

Friedman, Andrew L. 1977 *Industry and Labour: Class Struggle at Work and Monopoly Capitalism.* London: Macmillan.

Friedman, Thomas L. 2000. *The Lexus and the Olive Tree.* New York: Anchor Books.

Frost, Peter J., Larry F. Moore, Meryl Reis Louis, Craig C. Lundberg, and Joanne Martin, eds. 1991 *Reframing Organizational Culture.* Newbury Park, CA: Sage.

Fudge, Judy, and Patricia McDermott, eds. 1991 *Just Wages: A Feminist Assessment of Pay Equity.* Toronto: University of Toronto Press.

Fullerton, Howard N. Jr. 1997 "Labour force 2006: slowing down and changing composition." *Monthly Labor Review* (November): 23-38.

Furlong, Andy, Andy Biggart, and Fred Cartmel 1996 "Neighbourhoods, opportunity structures and occupational aspirations." *Sociology* 30: 551–65.

Furnham, Adrian 1990 *The Protestant Work Ethic: The Psychology of Work-Related Beliefs and Behaviours.* London: Routledge.

Galarneau, Diane, and Louise Earl 1999 "Women's earnings / men's earnings." *Perspectives on Labour and Income* (Winter): 20-26.

Gallie, Duncan 1978 *In Search of the New Working Class: Automation and Social Integration within the Capitalist Enterprise.* Cambridge: Cambridge University Press.

——— **1983** *Social Inequality and Class Radicalism in France and Britain.* Cambridge: Cambridge University Press.

——— **1991** "Patterns of skill change: upskilling, deskilling or the polarization of skills?" *Work, Employment & Society* 5: 319–51.

Gallie, Duncan, and Helen Russell 1998 "Unemployment and life satisfaction: a cross-cultural comparison." *Archives Européennes de Sociologie* 39(2): 248-80.

Gallie, Duncan, Michael White, Yuan Cheng, and Mark Tomlinson 1998 *Restructuring the Employment Relationship.* Oxford: Clarendon Press.

Gannagé, Charlene 1986 *Double Day, Double Bind: Women Garment Workers.* Toronto: Women's Press.

——— **1995** "Union women in the garment industry respond to new managerial strategies." *Canadian Journal of Sociology* 20 (4): 469–95.

Gardell, B. 1977 "Autonomy and participation at work." *Human Relations* 30: 515–33.

——— **1982** "Scandinavian research on stress in working life." *International Journal of Health Services* 12: 31–41

Gardell, B., and B. Gustavsen 1980 "Work environment research and social change: current developments in Scandinavia." *Journal of Occupational Behavior* 1: 3–17.

Garnsey, E., J. Rubery, and F. Wilkinson 1985 "Labour market structure and workforce divisions." In R. Deem and G. Salaman, eds., *Work, Culture and Society.* Milton Keynes and Philadelphia: Open University Press.

Garvin, David A. 1993 "Building a learning organization." *Harvard Business Review* (July/August) 78–91.

Gaskell, Jane 1991 "What counts as skill? Reflections on pay equity." In Judy Fudge and Patricia McDermott, eds., *Just Wages: A Feminist Assessment of Pay Equity.* Toronto: University of Toronto Press.

——— **1992** *Gender Matters from School to Work.* Milton Keynes, UK: Open University Press.

Gendell, Murray 1998 "Trends in retirement age in four countries, 1965-95. *Monthly Labor Review* (August): 20-30.

Gephart, Martha A., Victoria J. Marsick, Mark E. Van Buren, and Michelle S. Spiro 1996 "Learning organizations come alive." *Traning & Development* (December): 35–45.

Gera, Surendra, ed. 1991 *Canadian Unemployment: Lessons from the 80s and Challenges for the 90s.* Ottawa: Economic Council of Canada.

Gerber, Theodore P., and Michael Hout 1998 "More shock than therapy: market transition, employment, and income in Russia, 1991-1995." *American Journal of Sociology* 104(1):1-50.

Gerson, Kathleen 1993 *No Man's Land: Men's Changing Commitments to Family and Work.* New York: Basic Books.

Gherardi, Silvia 1999 "Learning as problem-driven or learning in the face of mystery?" *Organisation Studies* 20(1):101-23.

Gilbert, Sid, L. Barr, W. Clark, M. Blue, and D. Sunter 1993 *Leaving School: Results from a National Survey Comparing School Leavers and High School Graduates 18 to 20 Years of Age.* Ottawa: Minister of Supply and Services.

Gilbert, Sid, and Jeff Frank 1998 "Skill deficits among the young." *Canadian Social Trends* (Winter): 17-20.

Giles, Anthony 1996 "Globalization and industrial relations." In Anthony Giles, Anthony E. Smith, and Gilles Trudeau, eds., *The Globalization of the Economy and the Worker. Selected papers from the XXXIInd Annual Canadian Industrial Relations Association Conference,* Laval QC; CIRA.

——— **2000** "Industrial relations in the millennium: beyond employment?" *Labour/Le Travail* 46(Fall):37-67.

Giles, Anthony, and Hem C. Jain 1989 "The collective agreement." In John C. Anderson, Morley Gunderson, and Allen Ponak, eds., *Union–Management Relations in Canada.* 2nd ed. Don Mills: Addison-Wesley.

Gill, Colin 1985 *Work, Unemployment and the New Technology.* Cambridge: Polity Press.

Gillespie, Richard 1991 *Manufacturing Knowledge: A History of the Hawthorne*

Experiments. New York: Cambridge University Press.

Gindin, Sam 1989 "Breaking away: the formation of the Canadian Auto Workers." *Studies in Political Economy* 29: 63–89.

———— **1995** *The Canadian Auto Workers: The Birth and Transformation of a Union*. Toronto: James Lorimer.

Gingras, Yves, and Richard Roy 2000 "Is there a skills gap in Canada?" *Canadian Public Policy* (July Supplement): S159-74.

Gitter, Robert J., and Markus Scheuer 1997 "U.S. and German youths: unemployment and the transition from school to work." *Monthly Labor Review* (March): 16-20.

———— **1998** "Low unemployment in the Czech Republic: 'miracle' or 'mirage'?" *Monthly Labor Review* (August): 31-37.

Glass, Jennifer L. and Sarah B. Estes 1997 "The family responsive workplace." *Annual Review of Sociology* 23:289-313.

Godard, John 1994 *Industrial Relations: The Economy and Society*. Toronto: McGraw-Hill Ryerson.

———— **1997** "Managerial strategies, labour and employment relations and the state: the Canadian case and beyond." *British Journal of Industrial Relations* 35(3):399-426.

Goldfield, Michael 1987 *The Decline of Organized Labor in the United States*. Chicago: University of Chicago Press.

Goldthorpe, John H., D. Lockwood, F. Bechhofer, and J. Platt 1969 *The Affluent Worker in the Class Structure*. Cambridge: Cambridge University Press.

Gordon, Brett R. 1994 "Employee involvement in the enforcement of the occupational safety and health laws of Canada and the United States." *Comparative Labor Law Journal* 15: 527–60.

Gordon, David. M., R. Edwards, and M. Reich 1982 *Segmented Work, Divided Workers: The Historical Transformation of Labor in the United States*. New York: Cambridge University Press.

Gordon, Michael E., and Angelo S. Denisi 1995 "A re-examination of the relationship between union membership and job satisfaction." *Industrial and Labor Relations Review* 48: 222–36.

Gorham, Deborah 1994 "'No longer an invisible minority?': Women physicians and medical practice in late twentieth-century North America." In Dianne Dodd and Deborah Garham, eds., *Caring and Curing: Historical Perspectives on Women and Healing in Canada*. Ottawa: University of Ottawa Press, 183–211.

Gorz, Andre 1982 *Farewell to the Working Class: An Essay on Post-Industrial Socialism*. London: Pluto Press.

———— **1999** *Reclaiming Work: Beyond the Wage-Based Society*. Malden, MA: Polity Press.

Gouldner, Alvin W. 1954 *Patterns of Industrial Bureaucracy*. New York: Free Press.

———— **1955** *Wildcat Strike*. New York: Free Press.

Gower, David 1995 "Men retiring early: how are they doing?" *Perspectives on Labour and Income* 7: 30–34.

Grabb, Edward 1997 *Theories of Social Inequality: Classical and Contemporary Perspectives*. 3rd ed. Toronto: Harcourt Brace and Co.

Graham, Laurie 1993 "Inside a Japanese transplant: a critical perspective." *Work and Occupations* 20 (2): 147–73.

———— **1995** *On the Line at Subaru–Isuzu: The Japanese Model and the American Worker*. Ithaca, NY: ILR Press.

Grayson, Paul J. 1994 "Perceptions of workplace hazards." *Perspectives on Labour and Income* (Spring): 41–47.

Green, Francis, and David Ashton 1992 "Skill shortages and skill deficiency: a critique." *Work, Employment & Society* 6: 287–301.

Green, William C., and Ernest J. Yanarella, eds. 1995 *North American Auto Unions in Crisis: Lean Production as Contested Terrain.* Albany, NY: State University of New York Press.

Grenon, Lee 1996 "Are service jobs low-paying?" *Perspectives on Labour and Income* (Spring): 29–34.

——— 1997 "Northern earnings and income." *Perspectives on Labour and Income* (Spring): 28-32.

Grenon, Lee, and Barbara Chun 1997 "Non-permanent paid work." *Perspectives on Labour and Income* (Autumn): 21-31.

Grint, Keith 1991 *The Sociology of Work: An Introduction.* Cambridge: Polity Press.

Gunderson, Morley 1994 *Comparable Worth and Gender Discrimination: An International Perspective.* Geneva: International Labour Office.

——— 1998 "Harmonization of labour policies under trade liberalization." *Relations Industrielles Industrial Relations* 53(1):24-52.

Gunderson, Morley, and Douglas Hyatt 1995 "Union impact on compensation, productivity, and management of the organization." In Morley Gunderson and Allen Ponak, eds., *Union–Management Relations in Canada.* 3rd ed. Don Mills, ON: Addison-Wesley Publishers.

Gunderson, Morley, Douglas Hyatt, and Allen Ponak 1995 "Strikes and dispute resolution." In Morley Gunderson and Allen Ponak, eds., *Union–Management Relations in Canada.* 3rd ed. Don Mills, ON: Addison-Wesley Publishers.

——— 2001 "Strikes and disputes resolution." In Morley Gunderson, Allen Ponak, and Daphne G. Taras, eds., *Union—Management Relations in Canada.* 4th ed. Toronto: Addison Wesley Longman.

Gunderson, Morley, L. Muszynski, and J. Keck 1990 *Women and Labour Market Poverty.* Ottawa: Canadian Advisory Council on the Status of Women.

Gunderson, Morley, and W. Craig Riddell 2000 "The changing nature of work: implications for public policy." In W. Craig Riddell and France St-Hilaire, eds., *Adapting Public Policy to a Labour Market in Transition.* Montreal: Institute for Research on Public Policy, 1-37.

Gunderson, Morley, Jeffrey Sack, James McCartney, David Wakely, and Jonathan Eaton 1995 "Employee buy-outs in Canada." *British Journal of Industrial Relations* 33: 417–42.

Gunderson, Morley, Andrew Sharpe, and Steven Wald 2000 "Youth unemployment in Canada, 1976-1998." *Canadian Public Policy* (July Supplement): S85-S100.

Gustafsson, Bjorn, and Mats Johansson 1999 "In search of smoking guns: what makes income inequality vary over time in different countries?" *American Sociological Review* 64(August):585-605.

Guzda, Henry P. 1993 "Workplace partnerships in the United States and Europe." *Monthly Labor Review* (October): 67–72.

Haber, Samuel 1964 *Efficiency and Uplift: Scientific Management in the Progressive Era, 1890–1920.* Chicago: University of Chicago Press.

Hachen Jr., David S., 1988 "Gender differences in job mobility rates in the United States." *Social Science Research* 17: 93–116.

Hacker, Sally 1989 *Pleasure, Power and Technology: Some Tales of Gender, Engineering, and the Cooperative Workplace.* Boston: Unwin Hyman.

Hagan, John, and Fiona Kay 1995 *Gender in Practice: A Study of Lawyers' Lives.* New York: Oxford University Press.

Hage, J. T. 1999 "Organizational 'innovation' and organizational change." *Annual Review of Sociology* 25:597-622.

References

Haggerty, Kevin D., and Richard V. Ericson 2000 "The surveillant assemblage." *British Journal of Sociology* 51(4)605-22.

Hale, Thomas W., Howard V. Hayghe, and John M. McNell 1998 "Persons with disabilities: labor market activity, 1994." *Monthly Labor Review* (September): 3-12.

Hall, Karen 1999 "Hours polarization at the end of the 1990s." *Perspectives on Labour and Income* (Summer): 28-37.

Hall, Michael, Tamara Knighton, Paul Reed, Patrick Bussière, Don McRae, and Paddy Bowen 1998 *Caring Canadians, Involved Canadians: Highlights from the 1997 National Survey of Giving, Volunteering and Participating.* Ottawa: Statistics Canada (Cat. no. 71-542-XIE).

Hall, Michael, Larry McKeown, and Karen Roberts 2001 *Caring Canadians, Involved Canadians: Highlights from the 2000 National Survey of Giving, Volunteering and Participating.* Ottawa: Statistics Canada (Cat. no. 71-542-XPE).

Halpern, Norman 1984 "Sociotechnical systems design: the Shell Sarnia experience." In J. B. Cunningham and T. H. White, eds., *Quality of Working Life: Contemporary Cases.* Ottawa: Labour Canada.

Hamblin, Heather 1995 "Employees' perspectives on the dimension of labour flexibility: working at a distance." *Work, Employment & Society* 9(3): 473-98.

Hamilton, Gary G., and Nicole Woolsey Biggart 1988 "Market, culture, and authority: a comparative analysis of management and organization in the Far East." *American Journal of Sociology* 94: S52–S94.

Hamilton, Richard F., and James D. Wright 1986 *The State of the Masses.* New York: Aldine.

Hammer, Michael, and James Champy 1993 *Reengineering the Corporation: A Manifesto for Business Revolution.* New York: HarperBusiness.

Hamper, Ben 1986 *Rivethead: Tales From the Assembly Line.* New York: Warner Books.

Hampson, Ian 1999 "Lean production and the Toyota production system —or, the case of the forgotten production concepts." *Economic and Industrial Democracy* 20(3):369-91.

Harrington, Charles C., and Susan K. Boardman 1997 *Paths to Success: Beating the Odds in American Society.* Cambridge, MA: Harvard University Press.

Harris, Lloyd C., and Emmanuel Ogbonna 1999 "Developing a market oriented culture: a critical evaluation." *Journal of Management Studies* 36(2):177-96.

Harrison, Bennett 1997 *Lean and Mean: Why Large Corporations Will Continue to Dominate the Global Economy.* New York, NY: Guilford Press.

Hartmann, Heidi 1976 "Capitalism, patriarchy, and job segregation by sex." *Signs* 1: 137–69.

Hartnagel, Timothy F., and Harvey Krahn 1995 "Labour market problems and psychological well-being: a panel study of Canadian youth in transition from school to work." *British Journal of Education and Work* 8(3): 33-53.

Harvey, Andrew S., Katherine Marshall, and Judith A. Frederick 1991 *Where Does Time Go?* Ottawa: Statistics Canada, General Social Survey Analysis Series 4 (Cat. no. 11-612E, no. 4).

Hauser, Robert M., John Robert Warren, Min-Hsiung Huang, and Wendy C. Carter 2000 "Occupational status, education, and social mobility in the meritocracy." In Kenneth Arrow, Samuel Bowles, and Steven Durlauf, eds., *Meritocracy and Economic Inequality.* Princeton, NJ: Princeton University Press, 179-229.

Hayden, Anders 1999 *Sharing the Work: Sharing the Planet: Work Time, Consumption, and Ecology.* Toronto: Between the Lines.

Hayes, Robert H., and Ramchandran Jaikuma 1988 "Manufacturing's crisis: new technologies, obsolete organizations." *Harvard Business Review* (September/October): 77–85.

Health Canada and Statistics Canada 1999 *Statistical Report on the Health of Canadians.* Ottawa: Health Canada and Statistics Canada. (Cat. no. H39-467/1999E).

Heaney, Catherine, Barbara A. Israel, and James S. House 1994 "Chronic job insecurity among automobile workers: effects on job satisfaction and health." *Social Science and Medicine* 38: 1431–37.

Hearn, Jeff, Deborah L. Sheppard, Peta Tancred-Sheriff, and Gibson Burrell, eds. 1989 *The Sexuality of Organization.* London: Sage.

Heil, Gary, Warren Bennis, and Deborah C. Stephens 2000 *Douglas McGregor, Revisited: Managing the Human Side of the Enterprise.* New York: John Wiley & Sons.

Heinzl, John 1997 "Nike's hockey plans put Bauer on thin ice." *The Globe and Mail* (2 July 1997): B2.

Heisig, Ulrich, and Wolfgang Littek 1995 "Trust as a basis for work organization." In Wolfgang Littek and Tony Charles, eds., *The New Division of Labour: Emerging Forms of Work Organisation in International Perspective.* Berlin: Walter de Gruyter.

Heisz, Andrew, and Sylvain Coté 1998 "Job stability." *Perspectives on Labour and Income* (Winter): 24-29.

Helling, Jan 1985 *Innovations in Work Practices at Saab–Scania* (Saab–Scania Personnel Division). Paper delivered at the U.S.–Japan Automotive Industry Conference, Ann Arbor, MI., March 5–6.

Hendry, John 1999 "Cultural theory and contemporary management organization." *Human Relations* 52(5):557-77.

Henry, Frances, and Effie Ginzberg 1985 *Who Gets the Work? A Test of Racial Discrimination in Employment.* Toronto: The Urban Alliance on Race Relations and the Social Planning Council of Metropolitan Toronto.

Henson, Kevin D. 1996 *Just a Temp.* Philadelphia: Temple University Press.

Heron, Craig 1980 "The crisis of the craftsmen: Hamilton's metal workers in the early twentieth century." *Labour/Le Travailleur* 6: 7–48.

——— **1989** *The Canadian Labour Movement: A Short History.* Toronto: James Lorimer.

Heron, Craig, and Bryan Palmer 1977 "Through the prism of the strike: industrial conflict in southern Ontario, 1910–14." *Canadian Historical Review* 58: 423–58.

Heron, Craig, and Robert Storey, eds. 1986 *On the Job: Confronting the Labour Process in Canada.* Montreal and Kingston: McGill–Queen's University Press.

Herzberg, Frederick 1966 *Work and the Nature of Man.* New York: World.

——— **1968** "One more time: how do you motivate employees?" *Harvard Business Review* 46: 53–62.

Hessing, Melody 1991 "Talking shop(ping): office conversations and women's dual labour." *Canadian Journal of Sociology* 16: 23–50.

Hickson, David J. 1987 "Decision making at the top of organizations." *Annual Review of Sociology* 13: 165–92.

Hill, Stephen 1981 *Competition and Control at Work.* London: Heinemann.

——— **1988** "Technology and organizational culture: the human imperative in integrating new technology into organization design." *Technology in Society* 10: 233–53.

Hilton, Rodney, ed. 1976 *The Transition from Feudalism to Capitalism.* London: New Left Books.

Hinings, C. R., and Royston Greenwood 1988 *The Dynamics of Strategic Change.* Oxford: Basil Blackwell.

References

Hirschman, A.O. 1970 *Exit, Voice and Loyalty.* Cambridge, MA: Harvard University Press.

Hirst, Paul, and Grahame Thompson 1995 "Globalization and the future of the nation state." *Economy and Society* 24: 408–42.

Hitt, Michael A., Barbara W. Keats, Herbert F. Harback, and Robert D. Nixon 1994 "Rightsizing: building and maintaining strategic leadership and long-term competitiveness." *Organizational Dynamics* (Autumn): 18–32.

Hochschild, Arlie 1989 *The Second Shift: Working Parents and the Revolution at Home.* New York: Viking Penguin.

——— 1997 *The Time Bind: When Work Becomes Home and Home Becomes Work.* New York: Henry Holt and Company.

Hodson, Randy 1996 "Dignity in the workplace under participative management: alienation and freedom revisited." *American Sociological Review* 61: 719–38.

Hodson, Randy, and Robert L. Kaufman 1982 "Economic dualism: a critical review." *American Sociological Review* 47: 727–39.

Hofstede, Geert 1984 *Culture's Consequences: International Differences in Work-Related Values.* Beverly Hills, CA: Sage.

Hofstede, Geert, Bram Neuijen, Denise Daval Ohayv, and Geert Sanders 1990 "Measuring organizational cultures: a qualitative and quantitative study across twenty cases." *Administrative Science Quarterly* 35: 286–316.

Holzer, Boris 2000 "Miracles with a system: the economic rise of East Asia and the role of sociocultural patterns." *International Sociology* 15(3):455-78.

Holzer, Harry J. 1996 *What Employers Want: Job Prospects for Less-Educated Workers.* New York: Russell Sage Foundation.

Homans, George C. 1950 *The Human Group.* New York: Harcourt, Brace and World.

Horrell, Sara, J. Rubery, and B. Burchell 1990 "Gender and skills." *Work, Employment & Society* 4: 189–216.

Horvat, Andrew 1983 "Work comes before pleasure for Japanese." *The Edmonton Journal* (15 June): F6.

House, J. D. 1980 *The Last of the Free Enterprisers: The Oilmen of Calgary.* Toronto: Macmillan.

Hsiung, Ping-Chun 1996 *Living Rooms as Factories: Class, Gender, and the Satellite Factory System in Taiwan.* Philadelphia: Temple University Press.

Huberman, Michael, and Paul Lanoie 2000 "Changing attitudes toward work-sharing: evidence from Quebec." *Canadian Public Policy* 26(2): 141-55.

Hughes, Everett C. 1943 *French Canada in Transition.* Chicago: University of Chicago Press.

Hughes, Karen D. 1989 "Office automation: a review of the literature." *Relations Industrielles/Industrial Relations* 44: 654–79.

———. 1990 "Trading places: men and women in non-traditional occupations, 1971–86." *Perspectives on Labour and Income* (Summer): 58–68.

——— 1995 "Women in non-traditional occupations." *Perspectives on Labour and Income* (Autumn): 14–19.

——— 1996 "Transformed by technology? The changing nature of women's 'traditional' and 'non-traditional' white-collar work." *Work, Employment & Society* 10: 227–50.

——— 1999 *Gender and Self-Employment in Canada: Assessing Trends and Policy Implications.* CPRN Study No. W04. Ottawa: Canadian Policy Research Networks.

——— 2000 *Women and Corporate Directorships in Canada: Trends and Issues.* CPRN Discussion Paper No. CPRN-01. Ottawa, Ontario: Canadian Policy Research Networks.

Hughes, Karen D., and Graham S. Lowe 2000 "Surveying the 'post-industrial' landscape: information technologies and labour market polarization in Canada." *Canadian Review of Sociology and Anthropology* 37(1): 29-53.

Hughes, Karen D., Graham S. Lowe, and Allison L. McKinnon 1996 "Public attitudes towards budget cuts in Alberta: biting the bullet or feeling the pain?" *Canadian Public Policy* 22: 268–84.

Hum, Derek, and Wayne Simpson 1996 "Canadians with disabilities and the labour market." *Canadian Public Policy* 22: 285–97.

——— 1999a "Training and unemployment." In Ken Battle and Sherri Torjman, eds., *Employment Policy Options*. Ottawa: Caledon Institute of Social Policy.

——— 1999b "Wage opportunities for visible minorities in Canada." *Canadian Public Policy* 25(3): 379-94.

Human Resource Development Canada 1994 *Report of the Advisory Committee on Working Time and the Distribution of Work*. Ottawa: Supply and Services Canada.

——— 1997 *Adult Education and Training in Canada: Report of the 1994 Adult Education and Training Survey*. (Cat. No. 81-583).

——— 2000a *Statistical Analysis: Occupational Injuries and Fatalities Canada*. Hull, QC: HRDC.

——— 2000b *Occupational Injuries and their Cost in Canada 1993-1997*. Hull, QC: HRDC.

——— 2000c *Profile of Canadian Youth in the Labour Market. Second Annual Report to the Forum of Labour Market Ministers*. Hull, QC: HRDC.

Human Resources Development Canada, Workplace Information Directorate 2000 *Directory of Labour Organizations in Canada*. Hull, QC:HRDC.

Humphrey, James H. 1998 *Job Stress*. Boston: Allyn and Bacon.

Humphries, Jane 1977 "Class struggle and the persistence of the working class family." *Cambridge Journal of Economics* 1: 241–58.

Hunter, Alfred A. 1988 "Formal education and initial employment: unravelling the relationships between schooling and skills over time." *American Sociological Review* 53: 753–65.

Hunter, Alfred A., and Michael C. Manley 1986 "On the task content of work." *Canadian Review of Sociology and Anthropology* 23: 47–71.

Huxley, Christopher 1979 "The state, collective bargaining and the shape of strikes in Canada." *Canadian Journal of Sociology* 4: 223–39.

Hyman, Richard 1975 *Industrial Relations: A Marxist Introduction*. London: Macmillan.

——— 1978 *Strikes*. 2nd ed. Glasgow: Fontana.

——— 1987 "Strategy or structure? Capital, labour and control." *Work, Employment & Society* 1: 25–55.

Iacovetta, Franca, Michael Quinlan, and Ian Radforth 1996 "Immigration and labour: Australia and Canada compared." *Labour/Le Travail* (Fall): 90-115.

Iaffaldano, Michelle T., and Paul M. Muchinsky 1985 "Job satisfaction and job performance: a meta-analysis." *Psychological Bulletin* 97: 251–73.

Idle, Thomas R., and Arthur J. Cordell 1994 "Automating work." *Society* 36 (September–October): 65–71.

Ilg, Randy E. 1995 "The changing face of farm employment." *Monthly Labor Review* (April): 3–12.

Ingham, G. K. 1974 *Strikes and Industrial Conflict: Britain and Scandinavia*. London: Macmillan.

International Labour Office (ILO) 1995 *Yearbook of Labour Statistics*. Geneva: ILO.

———— 1997 *World Employment Report 1997-98: Industrial Relations, Democracy and Stability.* Geneva: ILO.

———— 1998 *World Employment Report 1998-99: Employability in the Global Economy: How Training Matters.* Geneva: ILO.

———— 1999 *Decent Work.* Geneva: ILO.

Jabes, Jak, and David Zussman 1988 "Motivation, rewards, and satisfaction in the Canadian federal public service." *Canadian Public Administration* 31: 204–25.

Jackson, Andrew, David Robinson, Bob Baldwin, and Cindy Wiggins 2000 *Falling Behind: The State of Working Canada, 2000.* Ottawa, ON: Canadian Centre for Policy Alternatives.

Jackson, Chris 1996 "Measuring and valuing household's unpaid work." *Canadian Social Trends* 42 (Autumn): 25–29.

Jacoby, Sanford M. 1985 *Employing Bureaucracy: Managers, Unions, and the Transformation of Work in American Industry, 1900–1945.* New York: Columbia University Press.

————. 1997 *Modern Manners: Welfare Capitalism Since the New Deal.* Princeton, NJ: Princeton University Press.

Jahoda, M. 1982 *Employment and Unemployment: A Social-Psychological Approach.* Cambridge: Cambridge University Press.

Jain, Hem C. 1990 "Worker participation in Canada: current developments and challenges." *Economic and Industrial Democracy* 11: 279–90.

Jain, Harish C. and Mohammed Al-Waqfi: 2000 "Racial discrimination in employment in Canada." In Yonatan Reshef et al., eds., *Industrial Relations in a New Millenium. Selected Papers from the XXXVIIth Annual CIRA Conference.* CIRA.

James, Carl E. 1990 *Making It: Black Youth, Racism and Career Aspirations in a Big City.* Oakville ON: Mosaic Press.

Jamieson, Stuart Marshall 1971 *Times of Trouble: Labour Unrest and Industrial Conflict in Canada, 1900–66.* Ottawa: Queen's Printer.

Jaynes, Gerald D. 2000 "Identity and economic performance." *Annals of the American Academy of Political and Social Science* 568 (March): 128-39.

Jenness, Diamond 1977 *Indians of Canada.* 7th ed. Toronto: University of Toronto Press.

Jenson, Jane 1989 "The talents of women, the skills of men: flexible specialization and women." In Stephen Wood, ed., *The Transformation of Work: Skill, Flexibility and the Labour Process.* London: Unwin Hyman.

Jenson, Jane, and Sherry Thompson 1999 *Comparative Family Policy: Six Provincial Stories.* CPRN Study No. F-08. Ottawa: Canadian Policy Research Networks.

Jermier, John M. 1998 "Introduction: critical perspectives on organizational control." *Administrative Science Quarterly* 43(2): 235-56.

Jex, Steve 1998 *Stress and Job Performance: Theory, Research, and Implications for Managerial Practice.* Thousand Oaks, CA: Sage.

Jiang, Shanhe, Richard H. Hall, Karyn L. Loscocco, and John Allen 1995 "Job satisfaction theories and job satisfaction: a China and U.S. comparison." *Research in the Sociology of Work* 5: 161–78.

Johnson, Carol 1996 "Does capitalism really need patriarchy? some old issues reconsidered." *Women's Studies International Forum* 19: 193–202.

Johnson, Gloria Jones, and Roy W. Johnson 1995 "Subjective underemployment and job satisfaction." *International Review of Modern Sociology* 25: 73–84.

Johnson, Holly 1994 "Work-related sexual harassment." *Perspectives on Labour and Income* (Winter): 9–12.

Johnson, Jeffrey V. 1989 "Control, collectivity and the psychosocial work environment." In S. L. Sauter, J. J. Hurrell Jr., and C. L. Cooper, eds., *Job Control and Worker Health.* New York: Wiley.

Johnston, William A., and Michael D. Ornstein 1985 "Social class and political ideology in Canada." *Canadian Review of Sociology and Anthropology* 22: 369–93.

Jones, Charles, Lorna Marsden, and Lorne Tepperman 1990 *Lives of Their Own: The Individualization of Women's Lives.* Don Mills, ON: Oxford University Press.

Jones, Frank E. 1996 *Understanding Organizations: A Sociological Perspective.* Toronto: Copp Clark Ltd.

—— **1999** "Seniors who volunteer." *Perspectives on Labour and Income* (Autumn): 9-17.

—— **2000** "Youth volunteering on the rise." *Perspectives on Labour and Income* (Spring): 36-42.

Jones, Oswald 2000 "Scientific management, culture and control: a first-hand account of Taylorism in practice." *Human Relations* 53(5):631-53.

Jones, Stephen R. G. 1990 "Worker interdependence and output: the Hawthorne Studies reevaluated." *American Sociological Review* 55: 176–90.

Jonsson, Berth 1980 "The Volvo experiences of new job design and new production technology." *Working Life in Sweden* 18 (September).

Kahn, R.L. 1981 *Work and Health.* New York: Wiley.

Kalleberg, Arne L. 1977 "Work values and job rewards: a theory of job satisfaction." *American Sociological Review* 42: 124–43.

—— **1988** "Comparative perspectives on work structures and inequality." *Annual Review of Sociology* 14: 203–25.

—— **2000** "Nonstandard employment relations: part-time, temporary and contract work." *Annual Review of Sociology* 26: 341-65.

Kalleberg, Arne, and Karyn A. Loscocco 1983 "Aging, values and rewards: explaining age differences in job satisfaction." *American Sociological Review* 48: 78–90.

Kalleberg, Arne, Barbara F. Reskin, and Ken Hudson 2000 "Bad jobs in America: standard and nonstandard employment relations and job quality in the United States." *American Sociological Review* 65: 256-78.

Kalleberg, Arne L., and David Stark 1993 "Career strategies in capitalism and socialism: work values and job rewards in United States and Hungary." *Social Forces* 72: 181–98.

Kalleberg, Arne L., and Mark E. Van Buren 1996 "Is bigger better? Explaining the relationship between organization size and job rewards." *American Sociological Review* 61: 47–66.

Kamata, Satoshi 1983 *Japan in the Passing Lane: An Insider's Account of Life in a Japanese Factory.* New York: Pantheon.

Kanter, Rosabeth M. 1977 *Men and Women of the Corporation.* New York: Basic Books.

—— **1989** *When Giants Learn to Dance: Mastering the Challenges of Strategy, Management, and Careers in the 1990s.* New York: Simon and Shuster.

—— **1995** *World Class: Thriving Locally in the Global Economy.* New York: Simon & Shuster.

Kaplan, William 1987 *Everything That Floats: Pat Sullivan, Hal Banks and the Seamen's Union of Canada.* Toronto: University of Toronto Press.

Kapsalis, Constantine 1998 "An international comparison of employee training." *Perspectives on Labour and Income* (Spring): 23-28.

Kapstein, Ethan B. 1996 "Workers and the world economy." *Foreign Affairs* 75: 16–37.

Karasek, Robert 1979 "Job demands, job decision latitude and mental health implications for job redesign." *Administrative Science Quarterly* 24: 285–308.

Karasek, Robert, and Töres Theorell 1990 *Healthy Work: Stress, Productivity, and the Reconstruction of Working Life.* New York: Basic Books.

Kazemipur, Abdolmohammad, and Shiva S. Halli 2001 "The changing colour of poverty in Canada." *Canadian Review of Sociology and Anthropology* 38(2): 217-38.

Kealey, Gregory S. 1980 *Toronto Workers Respond to Industrial Capitalism, 1867–1892.* Toronto: University of Toronto Press.

——— 1981a "Labour and working-class history in Canada: prospects in the 1980s." *Labour/Le Travail* 7: 67–94.

——— 1981b "The bonds of unity: The Knights of Labour in Ontario, 1880–1900." *Histoire sociale/Social History* 14: 369–411.

——— 1984 "1919: the Canadian labour revolt." *Labour/Le Travail* 13: 11–44.

——— 1986 "Work control, the labour process, and nineteenth-century Canadian printers." In Craig Heron and Robert Storey, eds., *On the Job: Confronting the Labour Process in Canada.* Montreal and Kingston: McGill–Queen's University Press.

——— 1995 *Workers and Canadian History.* Montreal and Kingston: McGill–Queen's University Press.

Keddie, V. 1980 "Class identification and party preference among manual workers." *Canadian Review of Sociology and Anthropology* 17: 24–36.

Keenoy, Tom 1985 *Invitation to Industrial Relations.* Oxford: Basil Blackwell.

Kelly, John E. 1982 *Scientific Management, Job Redesign and Work Performance.* London: Academic Press.

Kelly, Karen 1995 "Visible minorities: a diverse group." *Canadian Social Trends* (Summer): 2–8.

Kelly, Karen, Linda Howatson-Leo, and Warren Clark 1997 " 'I feel overqualified for my job…' " *Canadian Social Trends* (Winter): 11-16.

Kelvin, Peter, and Joanna E. Jarrett 1985 *Unemployment: Its Social–Psychological Effects.* Cambridge: Cambridge University Press.

Kerckhoff, Alan C., Richard D. Campbell, and Idee Winfield-Laird 1985 "Social mobility in Great Britain and the United States." *American Journal of Sociology* 91: 281–308.

Kerr, Clark, J. T. Dunlop, F. H. Harbison, and C.A. Myers 1973 *Industrialization and Industrial Man.* London: Penguin.

Kerr, Clark, and Abraham Siegel 1954 "The interindustry propensity to strike: an international comparison." In Arthur Kornhauser et al., eds., *Industrial Conflict.* New York: McGraw-Hill.

Kessler, Ronald C. 1983 "Methodological issues in the study of psychosocial stress." In Howard B. Kaplan, ed., *Psychosocial Stress: Trends in Theory and Research.* New York: Academic Press.

Kettler, David, James Struthers, and Christopher Huxley 1990 "Unionization and labour regimes in Canada and the United States." *Labour/Le Travail* 25: 161–87.

Kimmel, Jean, and Lisa M. Powell 1999 "Moonlighting trends and related policy issues in Canada and the United States." *Canadian Public Policy* 25(2): 207-31.

King, W. L. Mackenzie 1918 *Industry and Humanity: A Study in the Principles Underlying Industrial Reconstruction.* Toronto: Thomas Allen.

Kirsh, Sharon 1992 *Unemployment: Its Impact on Body and Soul.* Toronto: Canadian Mental Health Association.

Knight, Rolf 1978 *Indians at Work: An Informal History of Native Indian Labour in British Columbia 1858–1930.* Vancouver: New Star Books.

Knights, David, and Darren McCabe 2000 " 'Ain't misbehavin'? Opportunities for resistance under new forms of 'quality' management." *Sociology* 34(3): 421-36.

Knights, David, and Glenn Morgan 1990 "The concept of strategy in sociology: a note of dissent." *Sociology* 24: 475–83.

Knights, David, Hugh Willmott, and David Collison, eds. 1985 *Job Redesign: Critical Perspectives on the Labour Process.* Aldershot, England: Gower.

Kochan, Thomas A. 1979 "How American workers view labor unions." *Monthly Labor Review* 102 (April): 23–31.

Kochan, Thomas A., Harry C. Katz, and Robert B. McKersie 1986 *The Transformation of American Industrial Relations.* New York: Basic Books.

Kochan, Thomas, Russell Lansbury, and John Paul MacDuffie, eds. 1997 *After Lean Production: Evolving Practices in the World Auto Industry.* Ithaca, NY: ILR Press.

Kochan, Thomas A., and Paul Osterman 1994 *The Mutual Gains Enterprise: Forging a Winning Partnership Among Labor, Management, and Government.* Boston: Harvard Business School Press.

Kohn, Melvin L. 1990 "Unresolved issues in the relationship between work and personality." In Kai Erikson and Steven Peter Vallas, eds., *The Nature of Work: Sociological Perspectives.* New Haven: American Sociological Association and Yale University Press.

Kohn, Melvin L., and Carmi Schooler 1983 *Work and Personality: An Inquiry into the Impact of Social Stratification.* Norwood, NJ: Ablex.

Kompier, M., E. Degier, P. Smulders, and D. Draasisma 1994 "Regulations, policies and practices concerning work stress in five European countries." *Work and Stress* 8: 296–318.

Kopinak, Kathryn 1996 *Desert Capitalism: Maquiladoras in North America's Western Industrial Corridor.* Tucson: University of Arizona Press.

Krahn, Harvey 1992 *Quality of Work in the Service Sector.* Ottawa: Statistics Canada, General Social Survey Analysis Series 6 (Cat. no. 11 612E, No. 6).

——— 1995 "Non-standard work on the rise." *Perspectives on Labour and Income* (Winter): 35–42.

——— 1997 "On the permanence of human capital: use it or lose it." *Policy Options* 18(6): 17-21.

Krahn, Harvey, Tracey Derwing, Marlene Mulder, and Lori Wilkinson 2000 "Educated and underemployed: refugee integration into the Canadian labour market." *Journal of International Migration and Integration* 1 (Winter): 59-84.

Krahn, Harvey, and Trevor Harrison 1992 "Self-referenced relative deprivation and economic beliefs: the effects of the recession in Alberta." *Canadian Review of Sociology and Anthropology* 29: 191–209.

Krahn, Harvey, and Graham S. Lowe 1984 "Public attitudes towards unions: some Canadian evidence." *Journal of Labor Research* 5: 149–64.

——— 1997a *Literacy Utilization in Canadian Workplaces.* Ottawa: Human Resources Development Canada.

——— 1997b "School–work transitions and post-modern values: what's changing in Canada?" In Walter Heinz, ed., *From Education to Work: Cross-National Perspectives.* Cambridge: Cambridge University Press.

——— 1999 "Literacy in the workplace." *Perspectives on Labour and Income* (Summer): 38-44.

Krahn, Harvey, Norma Wolowyk, and Alison Yacyshyn 1998 *Metis Settlements General Council Census 1998. Report I: Enumeration Results and Settlement Profiles.* Edmonton: Population Research Laboratory, University of Alberta.

Krüger, Helga, and Bernd Baldus 1999 "Work, gender and the life course: social construction and individual experience." *Canadian Journal of Sociology* 24(3): 355-79.

Kruse, Douglas L. 1988 "Persons with disabilities: demographic, income, and health care characteristics, 1993." *Monthly Labor Review* (September): 13-22.

Kuhn, Thomas S. 1970 *The Structure of Scientific Revolutions.* 2nd ed. Chicago: University of Chicago Press.

Kumar, Krishnan 1995 *From Post-Industrial to Post-Modern Society: New Theories of the Contemporary World.* Oxford: Blackwell.

Kumar, Pradeep 1995 *Unions and Workplace Change in Canada.* Kingston, ON: IRC Press.

Kumar, Pradeep, and Lynn Acri 1991 "Women's issues and collective bargaining." In Donald Carter, ed., *Women and Industrial Relations, Proceedings of the 28th Conference of the Canadian Industrial Relations Association* (June 2–4): 581–95.

Kumar, Pradeep, David Arrowsmith, and Mary Lou Coates 1991 *Canadian Labour Relations: An Information Manual.* Kingston, ON: Industrial Relations Centre, Queen's University.

Kumar, Pradeep, and Mary Lou Coates 1991 *Industrial Relations in 1991: Trends and Emerging Issues.* Kingston: Industrial Relations Centre, Queen's University.

Kumar, Pradeep, and David Cowan 1989 *Gender Differences in Union Membership Status: The Role of Labour Market Segmentation.* Kingston: Industrial Relations Centre, Queen's University.

Kumar, Pradeep, Graham S. Lowe, and Grant Schellenberg 2001 "Workers' experience of job quality and the willingness to join a union." *Canadian Industrial Relations Association Annual Conference, May 27, 2001, Laval University, Quebec City* .

Kumar Pradeep, Gregor Murray, and Sylvain Schetagne 1998 "Adapting to change: union priorities in the 1990s." *Workplace Gazette* 1(3):84-98.

Kumazawa, Makoto, and Jun Yamada 1989 "Job skills under the lifelong nenko employment practice." In Stephen Wood, ed., *The Transformation of Work: Skill, Flexibility and the Labour Process.* London: Unwin Hyman.

Kunz, Jean Lock, Anne Milan, and Sylvain Schetagne 2000 Unequal Access: A Canadian Profile of Racial Differences in Education, Employment and Income. Canadian Race Relations Foundation.

Labour Canada 1986 *Women in the Labour Force, 1985–86 Edition.* Ottawa: Labour Canada, Women's Bureau.

———— **1990** *Women in the Labour Force 1990–91 Edition.* Ottawa: Women's Bureau, Labour Canada.

Labour Market Ministers 2000 *Profile of Canadian Youth in the Labour Market: Second Annual Report to the Forum of Labour Market Ministers.* Hull, QC: HRDC (Cat. no. RH61-1/2000E).

Lacroix, R. 1986 "Strike activity in Canada." In W. Craig Riddell, ed., *Canadian Labour Relations.* Toronto: University of Toronto Press.

Laliberte, Ron, and Vic Satzewich 1999 "Native migrant labour in the southern Alberta sugar-beet industry: coercion and paternalism in the recruitment of labour." *Canadian Review of Sociology and Anthropology* 36(1): 65-85.

Lam, Helen, and Yonatan Reshef 1999 "Are quality improvement and downsizing compatible? A human resources perspective." *Relations Industrielles/Industrial Relations* 54(4): 727-47.

Land, Hillary 1980 "The family wage." *Feminist Review* 6: 55–77.

Landes, David S. 1986 "What do bosses really do?" *Journal of Economic History* 46: 585–623.

Lane, Christel 1988 "Industrial change in Europe: the pursuit of flexible specialisation in Britain and West Germany." *Work, Employment & Society* 2: 141–68.

———— **1989** "From welfare capitalism to market capitalism: a comparative review of trends toward employment flexibility in the labour markets of three major European societies." *Sociology* 23: 583–610.

Langford, Tom 1996 "Effects of strike participation on the political consciousness of Canadian postal workers." *Relations Industrielles/Industrial Relations* 51 (3): 651–82.

Laroche, Mireille 1998 "In and out of low income." *Canadian Social Trends* (Autumn): 20-24.

Laroche, Mireille, Marcel Merette, and G.C. Ruggeri 1999 "On the concept and dimensions of human capital in a knowledge-based economy context." *Canadian Public Policy* 25(1): 87-100.

Lash, Scott 1984. *The Militant Worker: Class and Radicalism in France and America.* London: Heinemann.,
—— **1990** *Sociology of Postmodernism.* London: Routledge.

Laxer, Gordon 1989 *Open for Business: The Roots of Foreign Ownership in Canada.* Don Mills, ON: Oxford University Press.
—— **1995** "Social solidarity, democracy and global capitalism." *Canadian Review of Sociology and Anthropology* 32: 287–313.

Leach, Belinda 1998 "Industrial homework, economic restructuring and the meaning of work." *Labour/Le Travail* 41(Spring):97-115.

Leadbeater, David, and Peter Suschnigg 1997 "Training as the principal focus of adjustment policy: a critical view from northern Ontario." *Canadian Public Policy* 23: 2–19.

Leck, Joanne D., Sylvie St. Onge, and Isabelle Lalancette 1995 "Wage gap changes among organizations subject to the Employment Equity Act." *Canadian Public Policy* 21: 387–400.

Lehmann, Wolfgang 2000 "Is Germany's dual system still a model for Canadian youth apprenticeship initiatives?" *Canadian Public Policy* 26(2): 225-40.

Leicht, Kevin T., and Mary L. Fennell 1997 "The changing organizational context of professional work." *Annual Review of Sociology* 23: 215-31.

Leinberger, Paul, and Bruce Tucker 1991 *The New Individualists: The Generation after the Organization Man.* New York: HarperCollins.

Leiter, Michael P. 1991 "The dream denied: professional burnout and the constraints of human service organizations." *Canadian Psychology* 32: 547–55.

Lenski, Gerhard 1966 *Power and Privilege: A Theory of Social Stratification.* New York: McGraw-Hill.

Leonard, Madeleine 1998 "The long-term unemployed, informal economic activity, and the 'underclass' in Belfast: rejecting or reinstating the work ethic." *International Journal of Urban and Regional Research* 22(1): 42-59.

Lerner, Gerda 1986 *The Creation of Patriarchy.* New York: Oxford University Press.

Lettau, Michael K., and Thomas C. Buchmueller 1999 "Comparing benefit costs for full- and part-time workers." *Monthly Labor Review* (March): 30-35.

Levitan, Sar A., and Clifford M. Johnson 1982 *Second Thoughts on Work.* Kalamazoo, MI: W. E. Upjohn Institute for Employment Research.

Lewchuk, Wayne, A. Leslie Robb, and Vivienne Walters 1996 "The effectiveness of Bill 70 and joint health and safety committees in reducing injuries in the workplace: the case of Ontario." *Canadian Public Policy* 22: 225–43.

Lewicki, Roy J., Daniel J. McAllister, and Robert J. Bies 1998 "Trust and distrust: new relationships and realities." *Academy of Management Review* 23(3):438-58.

Lewis, Alan 1995 "The deskilling thesis revisited: Peter Armstrong's defence of Braverman." *Sociological Review* 43: 478–500.

References

Li, Peter 1982 "Chinese immigrants on the Canadian prairie, 1919–47." *Canadian Review of Sociology and Anthropology* 19: 527–40.

Lian, Jason Z., and David Ralph Matthews 1998 "Does the vertical mosaic still exist? Ethnicity and income in Canada, 1991." *Canadian Review of Sociology and Anthropology* 35(4): 461-81.

Liker, Jeffrey K., Carol J. Haddad, and Jennifer Karlin 1999 "Perspectives on technology and work organization." *Annual Review of Sociology* 25:575-96.

Lincoln, James R. 1990 "Japanese organization and organization theory." *Research in Organizational Behavior* 12: 255–94.

Lincoln, James R., and Arne L. Kalleberg 1985 "Work organization and workforce commitment: a study of plants and employees in the U.S. and Japan." *American Sociological Review* 50: 738–60.

———— **1990** *Culture, Control, and Commitment: A Study of Work Organization and Work Attitudes in the United States and Japan.* Cambridge: Cambridge University Press.

Lincoln, James R., and Kerry McBride 1987 "Japanese industrial organization in comparative perspective." *Annual Review of Sociology* 13: 289–312.

Lindenfeld, Fran, and Pamela Wynn 1997 "Success and failure of worker co-ops: the role of internal and external environmental factors." *Humanity and Society* 21(2): 148-61.

Lindsay, Colin 1999 "Seniors: a diverse group aging well." *Canadian Social Trends* (Spring): 24-26.

Linhart, Robert 1981 *The Assembly Line.* London: John Calder.

Lipset, Seymour Martin 1990a *Continental Divide: The Values and Institutions of the United States and Canada.* New York: Routledge.

———— **1990b** "Trade unionism in Canada and the United States: a reply to Bowden." *Canadian Review of Sociology and Anthropology* 27: 531–35.

Lipset, Seymour Martin, and Reinhard Bendix 1959 *Social Mobility in Industrial Society.* Berkeley, CA: University of California Press.

Lipset, Seymour M., and Noah M. Meltz 1997 "Canadian and American attitudes toward work and institutions." *Perspectives on Work* 1(3):14-19.

Lipset, Seymour Martin, Martin Trow, and James Coleman 1956 *Union Democracy: The Internal Politics of the International Typographical Union.* Garden City, NJ: Anchor Books.

Lipshitz, Raanan 2000 "Chic, mystique, and misconception: Argyris and Schon and the rhetoric of organizational learning." *Journal of Applied Behavioral Science* 36(4):456-73.

Lipsig-Mummé, Carla 1987 "Organizing women in the clothing trades: homework and the 1983 garment strike in Canada." *Studies in Political Economy* 22: 41–71.

Little, Bruce 1992 "Curing what ails the system." *The Globe and Mail* (18 January): A1, A6.

Little, Don 1997 "Financing universities: why are students paying more?" *Education Quarterly Review* 4(2): 10-26.

Littler, Craig R. 1982 *The Development of the Labour Process in Capitalist Societies.* London: Heinemann.

Littler, Craig R. and Graeme Salaman 1982 "Bravermania and beyond: recent theories of the labour process." *Sociology* 16: 251–69.

Livingstone David W. 1999 *The Education-Jobs Gap: Underemployment or Economic Democracy.* Toronto: Garamond Press.

Livingstone, D. W., and Meg Luxton 1996 "Gender consciousness at work: modification of the male breadwinner norm." In David W. Livingstone and J. M. Mangan, eds., *Recast Dreams: Class and Gender*

Consciousness in Steeltown. Toronto: Garamond Press, 100–29.

Livingstone, David W., and J. Marshall Mangan, eds. 1996 *Recast Dreams: Class and Class Consciousness in Steeltown.* Toronto: Garamond Press.

Lockwood, David 1966 "Sources of variation in working class images of society." *Sociological Review* 14: 249–67.

Logan, Ron, and Jo-Anne Belliveau 1995 "Working mothers." *Canadian Social Trends* 36 (Spring): 24–28.

Logue, John 1981 "Saab/Trollhattan: reforming work life on the shop floor." *Working Life in Sweden* 23 (June).

Logue, John, and Jacquelyn S. Yates 1999 "Worker ownership American style: pluralism, participation and performance." *Economic and Industrial Democracy* 20(2): 225-52.

Long, Richard J. 1984 "Introducing employee participation in ownership and decision making." In J. B. Cunningham and T. H. White, eds., *Quality of Working Life: Contemporary Cases.* Ottawa: Labour Canada.

——— **1989** "Patterns of workplace innovation in Canada." *Relations Industrielles/Industrial Relations* 44: 805–26.

Looker, Dianne 1993 "Interconnected transitions and their costs: gender and urban–rural differences in the transition from school to work." In Paul Anisef and Paul Axelrod, eds., *Transitions: Schooling and Employment in Canadian Society.* Toronto: Thompson Educational Publishers.

——— **1994** "Active capital: the impact of parents on youths' educational performance and plans." In Lorna Erwin and David MacLennan, eds. *Sociology of Education in Canada: Critical Perspectives on Theory, Research and Practice.* Toronto: Copp Clark Longman.

——— **1997** "In search of credentials: factors affecting young adults' participation

in postsecondary education." *Canadian Journal of Higher Education* 27(2/3): 1-36.

Looker, E. Dianne, and Peter Dwyer 1998 "Education and negotiated reality: complexities facing rural youth in the 1990s." *Journal of Youth Studies* 1(1): 5-22.

Looker, E. Dianne, and Victor Thiessen 1999 "Images of work: women's work, men's work, housework." *Canadian Journal of Sociology* 24(2): 225-54.

Lorence, Jon 1987 "A test of gender and job models of sex differences in job involvement." *Social Forces* 66: 121–42.

Lorence, Jon, and Jeylan T. Mortimer 1985 "Job involvement through the life course: a panel study of three age groups." *American Sociological Review* 50: 618–38.

Loscocco, Karyn A. 1990 "Reactions to blue-collar work: a comparison of women and men." *Work and Occupations* 17: 152–77.

Lowe, Graham S. 1981 "Causes of unionization in Canadian banks." *Relations Industrielles/Industrial Relations* 36: 865–92.

——— **1984** "The rise of modern management in Canada." In G. S. Lowe and H. J. Krahn, eds., *Working Canadians.* Toronto: Methuen.

——— **1987** *Women in the Administrative Revolution: The Feminization of Clerical Work.* Toronto: University of Toronto Press.

——— **1989** *Women, Paid/Unpaid Work, and Stress.* Ottawa: Canadian Advisory Council on the Status of Women.

——— **1997** "Computers in the workplace." *Perspectives on Labour and Income* (Summer): 29–36.

——— **1998** "The future of work: implications for unions." *Relations Industrielles/Industrial Relations* 53 (2): 235-57

——— **2000** *The Quality of Work: A People-Centred Agenda.* Don Mills, ON: Oxford University Press.

——— **2001** *Employer of Choice? Workplace Innovation in Government: A Synthesis*

References

Report. Ottawa, ON: Canadian Policy Research Networks.

Lowe, Graham S., and Harvey Krahn 1985 "Where wives work: the relative effects of situational and attitudinal factors." *Canadian Journal of Sociology* 10: 1–22.

———— **1989** "Recent trends in public support for unions in Canada." *Journal of Labor Research* 10: 391–410.

———— **1995** "Job-related education and training among young workers." *Canadian Public Policy* 21: 362–78.

———— **1999** "Reconceptualizing youth unemployment." In Julian Barling and E. Kevin Kelloway, eds., *Young Workers: Varieties of Experience.* Washington, D.C.: American Psychological Association.

———— **2000** "Work aspirations and attitudes in an era of labour market restructuring: a comparison of two Canadian youth cohorts." *Work, Employment & Society* 14(1): 1-22.

Lowe, Graham S., and Harvey Krahn, eds. 1993 *Work in Canada: Readings in the Sociology of Work and Industry.* Scarborough, ON: Nelson Canada.

Lowe, Graham S., Harvey Krahn, and Jeff Bowlby 1997 *1996 Alberta High School Graduate Survey: Report of Research Findings.* Edmonton, AB: Population Research Laboratory, University of Alberta.

Lowe, Graham S., and Herbert C. Northcott 1986 *Under Pressure: A Study of Job Stress.* Toronto: Garamond Press.

———— **1995** "Stressful working conditions and union dissatisfaction." *Relations Industrielles/Industrial Relations* 50: 420–42.

Lowe, Graham S., and Sandra Rastin 2000 "Organizing the next generation: influences on young workers' willingness to join unions in Canada." *British Journal of Industrial Relations* 38(2):203–222.

Lowe, Graham S., and Grant Schellenberg 2001 *What's a Good Job? The Importance of Employment Relationships.* CPRN Study W-05. Ottawa: Canadian Policy Research Networks.

Lucas, Rex A. 1971 *Minetown, Milltown, Railtown.* Toronto: University of Toronto Press.

Lum, Janet M. 1995 "The Federal Employment Equity Act: goals vs. implementation." *Canadian Public Administration* 38: 45–76.

Luxton, Meg 1980 *More Than a Labour of Love.* Toronto: Women's Press.

Luxton, Meg, and June Corman 1991 "Getting to work: the challenge of the Women Back Into Stelco Campaign." *Labour/Le Travail* 28: 149–85.

Mabey, Christopher, Graeme Salaman, and John Storey 1998 *Strategic Human Resource Management: A Reader.* London: The Open University/Sage.

Macarov, David 1982 *Worker Productivity: Myths and Reality.* Beverly Hills: Sage.

MacBride-King, Judith L. 1990 *Work and Family: Employment Challenge of the '90s.* Ottawa: Conference Board of Canada, Report.

MacBride-King, Judith L. and Kimberley Bachmann 1999 *Solutions for the Stressed-Out Worker.* Ottawa, ON: Conference Board of Canada.

Maccoby, Michael 1988 *Why Work: Motivating and Leading the New Generation.* New York: Simon and Schuster.

Macdonald, Keith, and George Ritzer 1988 "The sociology of the professions: dead or alive?" *Work and Occupations* 15: 251–72.

Macdonald, Martha 1991 "Post-Fordism and the flexibility debate." *Studies in Political Economy* 36: 177–201.

MacDonald, Robert 1994 "Fiddly jobs, undeclared working and the something for nothing society." *Work, Employment & Society* 8: 507–30.

MacKinnon, Malcolm H. 1981 "The industrial worker and the job: alienated or instrumentalized?" In K. L. P. Lundy and B. Warme, eds., *Work in the Canadian Context.* Toronto: Butterworths.

MacKinnon, Mark 1999 "Underground economy takes a big bite." *The Globe and Mail* (21 June): B1, B4.

Maclarkey, Robert L. 1997 "Information technology and the workplace: an empirical investigation of anti-technology theory." *International Review of Modern Sociology* 27(2): 33-44.

MacLean, Brian K., and Lars Osberg, eds. 1996 *The Unemployment Crisis: All for Nought?* Montreal and Kingston: McGill–Queen's University Press.

Macleod, Gus 1997 *From Mondragon to America: Experiments in Community Economic Development..* Sydney, NS: University College of Cape Breton Press.

Mahon, Rianne 1984 *The Politics of Industrial Restructuring: Canadian Textiles.* Toronto: University of Toronto Press.

——— **1987** "From Fordism to? New technology, labour markets and unions." *Economic and Industrial Democracy* 8: 5–60.

Mann, Michael 1970 "The social cohesion of liberal democracy." *American Sociological Review* 35: 423–39.

Manser, Marilyn E., and Garnett Picot 1999 "Self-employment in Canada and the United States." *Perspectives on Labour and Income* (Autumn): 37-44.

Marchak, M. Patricia 1981 *Ideological Perspectives on Canada.* 2nd ed. Toronto: McGraw-Hill Ryerson.

Marglin, Stephen A. 1976 "What do bosses do? the origins and functions of hierarchy in capitalist production." In Andre Gorz, ed., *The Division of Labour.* New York: Humanities Press.

Marquardt, Richard 1998 *Enter at Your Own Risk: Canadian Youth and the Labour Market.* Toronto: Between the Lines.

Mars, Gerald 1982 *Cheats at Work: An Anthropology of Workplace Crime.* London: Unwin Paperbacks.

Marsh, Catherine, R. McAuley, and S. Penlington 1990 "The road to recovery? Some evidence from vacancies in one labour market." *Work, Employment & Society* 4: 31–58.

Marshall, Katherine 1989 "Women in the professional occupations: progress in the 1980s." *Canadian Social Trends* (Spring): 13–16.

——— **1993** "Dual earners: who's responsible for housework?" *Canadian Social Trends* (Winter): 11–14.

——— **1996** "A job to die for." *Perspectives on Labour and Income* (Summer): 26–31.

——— **1997** "Job sharing." *Perspectives on Labour and Income* (Summer): 6–10.

——— **1998** "Stay-at-home dads." *Perspectives on Labour and Income* 10(Spring): 9-15.

——— **1999a** "Employment after childbirth." *Perspectives on Labour and Income* (Autumn): 18-25.

——— **1999b** "Seasonality in employment." *Perspectives on Labour and Income* (Spring): 16-22.

——— **2000** "Incomes of young retired women: the past 30 years." *Perspectives on Labour and Income* (Winter): 9-17.

——— **2001a** "Part-time by choice." *Perspectives on Labour and Income* (Spring): 20-27.

——— **2001b** "Working with computers." *Perspectives on Labour and Income* (Summer): 9-15.

Martin, Gary 2000 "Employment and unemployment in Mexico in the 1990s." *Monthly Labor Review* (November): 3-18.

Martin, Jack K., and Paul M. Roman 1996 "Job satisfaction, job reward characteristics, and employees' problem drinking behaviors." *Work and Occupations* 23: 4–25.

Martin, Jack K., and Constance L. Shehan 1989 "Education and job satisfaction: the influences of gender, wage-earning status, and job values." *Work and Occupations* 16: 184–99.

Martin, Joanne 2000 "Hidden gendered assumptions in mainstream organizational theory and research." *Journal of Management Inquiry* 9(2):207-16.

Martin, Joanne, Kathleen Knopoff, and Christine Beckman 1998 "An alternative to bureaucratic impersonality and emotional labor: bounded emotionality at The Body Shop." *Administrative Science Quarterly* 43(2):429-69.

Martinello, Felice 2000 "Mr. Harris, Mr. Rae and union activity in Ontario." *Canadian Public Policy* 26(1):17-33.

Maslach, Christina, and Michael P. Leiter 1997 *The Truth about Burnout: How Organizations Cause Personal Stress and What To Do About It.* San Francisco: Jossey-Bass.

Matthews, Roy A. 1985 *Structural Change and Industrial Policy: The Redeployment of Canadian Manufacturing, 1960–80.* Ottawa: Supply and Services Canada.

Maxim, Paul S., Jerry P. White, Paul C. Whitehead, and Daniel Beavon 2000 *An Analysis of Wage and Income Inequality: Dispersion and Polarization of Income among Aboriginal and Non Aboriginal Canadians.* London, ON.: Population Studies Centre, Discussion Paper no. 00-9.

Maynard, Rona 1987 "How do you like your job?" *Report on Business Magazine* (November): 112–22.

Mayo, Elton 1945 *The Social Problems of an Industrial Civilization.* Cambridge, MA: Harvard University Press.

McCabe, Darren 1999 "Total quality management: antiunion Trojan horse or management albatross." *Work, Employment & Society* 13(4): 665-91.

McCormack, A. Ross 1978 *Reformers, Rebels and Revolutionaries: The Western Canadian Radical Movement, 1899–1919.* Toronto: University of Toronto Press.

McCormick, Chris, ed. 1998 *The Westray Chronicles: A Case Study of an Occupational Disaster.* Halifax: Fernwood Publishing.

McDonald, Judith A. and Robert J. Thornton 1998 "Private-sector experience with pay equity in Ontario." *Canadian Public Policy* 24(2):185-208.

McDonald, N., and M. Doyle 1981 *The Stresses of Work.* Don Mills, ON: Nelson Canada.

McEvoy, G.M., and W.F. Cascio 1985 "Strategies for reducing employee turnover: a meta-analysis." *Journal of Applied Psychology* 70: 342-53.

McFarlane, Seth, Roderic Beaujot, and Tony Haddad 2000 "Time constraints and relative resources as determinants of the sexual division of domestic work." *Canadian Journal of Sociology* 25(1):61-82.

McGregor, Douglas 1960 *The Human Side of Enterprise.* New York: McGraw-Hill.

McIlwee, Judith S., and J. Gregg Robinson 1992 *Women in Engineering: Gender, Power, and Workplace Culture.* Albany, NY: State University of New York Press.

McKay, Shona 1991 "Willing and able." *Report on Business Magazine* (October): 58–63.

——— 1996 "You're (still) hired." *Report on Business Magazine* (December): 54–60.

McKinlay, Alan and Ken Starkey, eds. 1998 *Foucault, Management and Organization Theory: from Panopticon to Technologies of Self.* Thousand Oaks, CA: Sage.

McKinnon, Allison L., and Odynak, D. 1991 *Elder Care, Employees, and Employers: Some Canadian Evidence.* Discussion paper prepared for the Demographic Review Secretariat, Health and Welfare Canada. Edmonton: Population Research Laboratory, University of Alberta.

McLuhan, Marshall 1964 *Understanding Media: The Extensions of Man.* New York: McGraw-Hill.

McMullen, Kathryn 1996 *Skill and Employment Effects of Computer-Based Technology: The Results of the Working with Technology*

Survey III. Ottawa: Canadian Policy Research Networks Inc. Study no. W01.

Meissner, Martin 1971 "The long arm of the job: a study of work and leisure." *Industrial Relations* 10: 239–60.

Meissner, Martin, E. W. Humphreys, S. M. Meis, and W. J. Scheu 1975 "No exit for wives: sexual division of labour and the cumulation of household demands." *Canadian Review of Sociology and Anthropology* 12: 424–39.

Menzies, Heather 1996 *Whose Brave New World? The Information Highway and the New Economy.* Toronto: Between the Lines.

Merkle, Judith A. 1980 *Management and Ideology: The Legacy of the International Scientific Management Movement.* Berkeley, CA: University of California Press.

Merton, Robert K. 1952 "Bureaucratic structure and personality." In Robert K. Merton, A .P. Gray, B. Hockey, and H. C. Selvin, eds., *Reader in Bureaucracy.* New York: Free Press.

Meunier, Dominique, Paul Bernard, and Johanne Boisjoly 1998 "Eternal youth? Changes in the living arrangements of young people." In Miles Corak, ed., *Labour Markets, Social Institutions, and the Future of Canada's Children.* Ottawa: Statistics Canada.

Meyer, Stephen 1981 *The Five Dollar Day: Labor Management and Social Control in the Ford Motor Company, 1908–1921.* Albany, NY: State University of New York Press.

Michels, Robert 1959 *Political Parties: A Sociological Study of the Oligarchical Tendencies of Modern Democracy.* New York: Dover Publications. [Originally published in 1915.]

Micklethwait, John, and Adrian Wooldridge 1996 *The Witch Doctors: Making Sense of the Management Gurus.* New York: Times Books.

Middleton, Chris 1988 "The familiar fate of the *famulae:* gender divisions in the history of wage labour." In R. E. Pahl, ed., *On Work: Historical, Comparative and Theoretical Approaches.* Oxford: Basil Blackwell.

Miles, Raymond E. 1965 "Human relations or human resources." *Harvard Business Review* 43 (July-August): 148–63.

Milkman, Ruth 1991 *Japan's California Factories: Labor Relations and Economic Globalization.* Los Angeles: Institute of Industrial Relations, University of California at Los Angeles.

——— **1997** *Farewell to the Factory: Auto Workers in the Late Twentieth Century.* Berkeley, CA: University of California Press.

Milkman, Ruth, and Cydney Pullman 1991 "Technological change in an auto assembly plant: the impact on workers' tasks and skills." *Work and Occupations* 18: 123–47.

Miller, Danny 1990 *The Icarus Paradox: How Exceptional Companies Bring About Their Own Downfall.* New York: Harper/Business.

Miller, Joanne 1980 "Individual and occupational determinants of job satisfaction: a focus on gender differences." *Sociology of Work and Occupations* 7: 337–66.

Miller, Joanne, C. Schooler, M. L. Kohn, and K. A. Miller 1979 "Women and work: the psychological effects of occupational conditions." *American Journal of Sociology* 85: 66–94.

Miller, Karen A., Melvin L. Kohn, and Carmi Schooler 1985 "Educational self-determination and the cognitive functioning of students." *Social Forces* 63(4): 923-44.

Mills, C. Wright 1948 *The New Men of Power.* New York: Harcourt-Brace.

——— **1956** *White Collar: The American Middle Classes.* New York: Oxford University Press.

References

Mills, Terry L., Craig A. Boylstein, and Sandra Lorean 2001 " 'Doing' organizational culture in the Saturn corporation." *Organisation Studies* 22(1):117-.

Milner, Henry 1989 *Sweden: Social Democracy in Practice.* Oxford: Oxford University Press.

Mintzberg, Henry 1989 *Mintzberg on Management: Inside Our Strange World of Organizations.* New York: Free Press.

—— **1994** "The fall and rise of strategic planning." *Harvard Business Review* 72: 107–14.

—— **1998** "Covert leadership: notes on managing professionals." *Harvard Business Review* 76(6):140-147.

Mintzberg, Henry, Bruce Ahlstrand, and Joseph Lampel 1998 *Strategy Safari: A Guided Tour Through the Wilds of Strategic Management.* New York: The Free Press.

Mirus, Rolf, Roger J. Smith, and Vladimir Karoleff 1994 "Canadian underground economy revisited: update and critique." *Canadian Public Policy* 20: 235–52.

Mirchandani, Kiran 1999 "Legitimizing work: telework and the gendered reification of the work-nonwork dichotomy." *Canadian Review of Sociology and Anthropology* 36(1): 87-107.

Mishel, Lawrence, Jared Bernstein, and John Schmitt 1999 *The State of Working America 1998-99.* Ithaca, NY: Cornell University Press.

Mitchell, Alanna 1997 "The poor fare worst in schools." *The Globe and Mail* (18 April: A1).

Mitchell, Jared 1999 "The pink ceiling." *Report on Business Magazine* (June): 78-84.

Monette, Manon 1996 "Retirement in the 90s: going back to work." *Canadian Social Trends* 42 (Autumn): 12–14.

Morgan, Gareth 1997 *Images of Organization.* Thousand Oaks, CA: Sage Publications.

Morissette, René 1997 "Declining earnings of young men." *Canadian Social Trends* (Autumn): 8-12.

Morissette, René, and Marie Drolet 2001 "Pension coverage and retirement savings." *Perspectives on Labour and Income* (Summer): 39-46.

Morris, Lydia, and Sarah Irwin 1992 "Employment histories and the concept of the underclass." *Sociology* 26: 401–20.

Morton, Desmond 1989 "The history of the Canadian labour movement." In John C. Anderson, Morley Gunderson, and Allen Ponak, eds., *Union–Management Relations in Canada.* 2nd ed. Don Mills: Addison-Wesley.

Moulton, David 1974 "Ford Windsor 1945." In Irving Abella, ed., *On Strike: Six Key Labour Struggles in Canada 1919–1949.* Toronto: James Lewis and Samuel.

Murray Axmith and Associates 1997 *1997 Canadian Hiring and Dismissal Practices Survey.* Toronto: Murray Axmith and Associates.

Murray, Gregor 2001 "Unions: membership, structures, actions, and challenges." In Morley Gunderson, Allen Ponak, and Daphne G. Taras, eds. *Union –Management Relations in Canada* 4th ed. Toronto: Addison Wesley Longman.

Muszynski, Alicja 1996 *Cheap Wage Labour: Race and Gender in the Fisheries of British Columbia.* Montreal and Kingston: McGill-Queen's University Press.

Myles, John 1988 "The expanding middle: some Canadian evidence on the deskilling debate." *Canadian Review of Sociology and Anthropology* 25: 335–64.

—— **1996** "Public policy in a world of market failure." *Policy Options* (July–August): 14–19.

—— **2000** "Incomes of seniors." *Perspectives on Labour and Income* 12(4): 23–32.

Myles, John and Debra Street 1995 "Should the economic life course be redesigned? Old age security in a time of transition." *Canadian Journal on Aging* 14: 335–59.

Nadwodny, Richard 1996 "Canadians working at home." *Canadian Social Trends* (Spring): 16-20.

Naisbitt, John 1982 *Megatrends: Ten New Directions Transforming Our Lives.* New York: Warner.

Nakanishi, Nobuo, and Toshiki Mikawa 1995 "Work values and role salience in Japanese culture." In Donald E. Super and Branimir Sverko, eds., *Life Roles, Values, and Careers: International Findings of the Work Importance Study.* San Francisco: Jossey-Bass.

National Center on Education and the Economy (NCEE) 1990 *America's Choice: High Skills or Low Wages! Report of the Commission on the Skills of the American Workforce.* Rochester, NY: NCEE.

National Council of Welfare 2000 *Welfare Incomes 1999.* Ottawa: National Council of Welfare.

Neale, Deborah 1992 "Will Bob Rae deliver on his promise?" *Policy Options* (January–February): 25–28.

Nee, Victor, and Rebecca Matthews 1996 "Market transformation and societal transformation in reforming state socialism." *Annual Review of Sociology* 22: 401–35.

Neis, Barbara 1991 "Flexible specialization: what's that got to do with the price of fish?" *Studies in Political Economy* 36: 145–76.

Nelson, Daniel 1980 *Frederick W. Taylor and the Rise of Scientific Management.* Madison, WI: University of Wisconsin Press.

Nelson, Joel I. 1995 *Post-Industrial Capitalism: Exploring Economic Inequality in America.* Thousand Oaks, CA: Sage.

Nevitte, Neil 2000 "Value change and reorientations in citizen-state relations." *Canadian Public Policy* 24(2 Supplement):S73-94.

***New York Times, The* 1996** *The Downsizing of America: Millions of Americans are Losing Good Jobs. This Is Their Story.* New York: Times Books.

Newman, Katherine S. 1989 *Falling from Grace: The Experience of Downward Mobility in the American Middle Class.* New York: Vintage Books.

Nichols, Donald, and Chandra Subramaniam 2001 "Executive compensation: excessive or equitable?" *Journal of Business Ethics* .

Niezen, Ronald 1993 "Power and dignity: the social consequences of hydro-electric development for the James Bay Cree." *Canadian Review of Sociology and Anthropology* 30: 510–529.

Nightingale, Donald 1982 *Workplace Democracy: An Enquiry into Employee Participation in Canadian Work Organizations.* Toronto: University of Toronto Press.

Nilsson, Tommy 1996 "Lean production and white collar work: the case of Sweden." *Economic and Industrial Democracy* 17: 447–72.

Nishman, Robert F. 1995 *Worker Ownership and the Restructuring of Algoma Steel in the 1990s.* Kingston, ON: IRC Press.

Nissen, Bruce 1997 *Unions and Workplace Reorganization.* Detroit, MI: Wayne State University Press.

Noble, David 1985 "Social choice in machine design: the case of automatically controlled machine tools." In Donald Mackenzie and Judy Wajcman, eds., *The Social Shaping of Technology.* Milton Keynes: Open University Press.

——— **1995** *Progress without People: New Technology, Unemployment, and the Message of Resistance.* Toronto: Between the Lines.

Noble, Douglas D. 1994 "Let them eat skills." *The Review of Education / Pedagogy/ Cultural Studies* 16(1): 15-29.

Noël, Alain, and Keith Gardner 1990 "The Gainers strike: capitalist offensive, militancy, and the politics of industrial relations in Canada." *Studies in Political Economy* 31: 31–72.

Nolan, Peter, and P. K. Edwards 1984 "Homogenise, divide and rule: an essay on *Segmented Work, Divided Workers.*" *Cambridge Journal of Economics* 8: 197–215.

Nollen, Stanley, and Helen Axel 1996 *Managing Contingent Workers: How to Reap the Benefits and Reduce the Risks.* New York: American Management Association.

Northcott, Herbert C., and Graham S. Lowe 1987 "Job and gender influences in the subjective experience of work." *Canadian Review of Sociology and Anthropology* 24: 117–31.

Novek, Joel 1988 "Grain terminal automation: a case study in the control of control." *Labour/Le Travail* 22: 163–80.

——— **1989** "Peripheralizing core labour markets: the case of the Canadian meat packing industry." *Work, Employment & Society* 3: 157–77.

——— **1992** "The labour process and workplace injuries in the Canadian meat packing industry." *Canadian Review of Sociology and Anthropology* 29: 17–37.

Nussbaum, Karen, and Virginia duRivage 1986 "Computer monitoring: mismanagement by remote control." *Business and Society Review* 56 (Winter): 16–20.

Oakes, Leslie S., Barbara Townley, and David J. Cooper 1998 "Business planning as pedagogy: language and control in a changing institutional field." *Administrative Science Quarterly* 43: 257–92.

Oakeshott, Robert 1978 *The Case for Workers' Co-ops.* London: Routledge and Kegan Paul.

Oderkirk, Jillian 1996 "Computer literacy—a growing requirement." *Education Quarterly Review* (Autumn): 9–29.

Oderkirk, Jillian, Cynthia Silver, and Marc Prud'homme 1994 "Traditional-earner families." *Canadian Social Trends* 32 (Spring): 19–25.

O'Grady, John 2000 "Joint health and safety committees: finding a balance." In Terrance Sullivan, ed., *Injury and the New World of Work.* Vancouver and Toronto: UBC Press.

O'Hara, Bruce 1993 *Working Harder Isn't Working.* Vancouver: New Star Books.

Ollivier, Michèle 2000 " 'Too much money off other people's backs': status in late modern societies." *Canadian Journal of Sociology* 25(4): 441-70.

Olsen, Gregg 1991 "Labour mobilization and the strength of capital: the rise and stall of economic democracy in Sweden." *Studies in Political Economy* 34: 109–45.

——— **1999** "Half empty or half full? The Swedish welfare state in transition." *Canadian Review of Sociology and Anthropology* 36(2):241-67.

Olson, Mancur 1965 *The Logic of Collective Action.* Cambridge, MA: Harvard University Press.

O'Neill, Jeff 1991 "Changing occupational structure." *Canadian Social Trends* (Winter): 8–12.

Ontario Ministry of Education and Training 1996 *Excellence, Accessibility, Responsibility: Report of the Advisory Panel on Future Directions for Postsecondary Education.* Toronto: Minister of Education and Training.

O'Reilly III, Charles A., and Jeffrey Pfeffer 2000 *Hidden Value: How Great Companies Achieve Extraordinary Results With Ordinary People.* Boston: Harvard Business School Press.

Organisation for Economic Co-operation and Development 1989 *OECD Employment Outlook.* Paris: OECD.

——— **1991** Labour Force Statistics 1969

——— **1994** *Employment Outlook, July 1994.* Paris: OECD.

——— **1996** *Lifelong Learning for All.* Paris: OECD.

——— **1999** "New enterprise work practices and their labour market implications." In *OECD Employment Outlook* (June). Paris: OECD.

Organisation for Economic Co-operation and Development, Human Resources Development Canada, and Statistics Canada 1998 *Literacy Skills for the Knowledge Society: Further Results of the International Adult Literacy Survey.* Paris and Ottawa: OECD, HRDC and Statistics Canada (Cat. no. 89-556-XPE).

Organization Studies **1988** "Offence and defence: a symposium with Hinings, Clegg, Child, Aldrich, Karpik, and Donaldson." *Organization Studies* 9: 1–32.

Orme, Jr. W. A. 1996 *Understanding NAFTA: Mexico, Free Trade, and the New North America.* Austin: University of Texas Press.

Orr, Julian E. 1996 *Talking About Machines: An Ethnography of a Modern Job.* Ithaca, NY: ILR Press.

Osberg, Lars, and Pierre Fortin, eds. 1996 *Unnecessary Debt.* Toronto: Lorimer.

Osberg, Lars, and Zhengxi Lin 2000 "How much of Canada's unemployment is structural?" *Canadian Public Policy* (July Supplement): S141-S158.

Osberg, Lars, and Andrew Sharpe 1998 "An index of economic well-being for Canada." Ottawa: Centre for the Study of Living Standards [http://www.csls.ca]

Osberg, Lars, Fred Wein, and Jan Grude 1995 *Vanishing Jobs: Canada's Changing Workplace.* Toronto: Lorimer.

Ospina, Sonia 1996 *Illusions of Opportunity: Employee Expectations and Workplace Inequality.* Ithaca and London: Cornell University Press.

Osterman, Paul 1994 "How common is workplace transformation and who adopts it?" *Industrial and Labor Relations Review* 47: 173–88.

———— **1999** *Securing Prosperity: The American Labor Market: How It Has Changed and What to Do About It.* Princeton, NJ: Princeton University Press.

———— **2000** "Work reorganization in an era of restructuring: trends in diffusion and effects on employee welfare." *Industrial and Labor Relations Review* 53(2): 179-96.

Ostry, Sylvia 1968 *The Female Worker in Canada.* Ottawa: Queen's Printer.

O'Toole, James, ed. 1977 *Work, Learning and the American Future.* San Francisco: Jossey–Bass.

Ouchi, William 1981 *Theory Z: How American Business Can Meet the Japanese Challenge.* Reading, MA: Addison-Wesley.

Owram, Doug 1996 *Born at the Right Time: A History of the Baby Boom Generation.* Toronto: University of Toronto Press.

Pahl, R.E. 1984 *Divisions of Labour.* Oxford: Basil Blackwell.

Palmer, Bryan 1975 "Class, conception and conflict: the thrust for efficiency, managerial views of labor and the working class rebellion, 1902–22." *Radical Review of Political Economics* 7: 31–49.

———— **1979** *A Culture in Conflict: Skilled Workers and Industrial Capitalism in Hamilton, Ontario, 1860–1914.* Montreal and Kingston: McGill–Queen's University Press.

———— **1986** *The Character of Class Struggle: Essays in Canadian Working Class History, 1850–1985.* Toronto: McClelland and Stewart.

———— **1992** *Working Class Experience: Rethinking the History of Canadian Labour, 1800–1991.* 2nd ed. Toronto: McClelland and Stewart.

Palmer, Craig, and Peter Sinclair 1997 *When the Fish are Gone: Ecological Disaster and Fishers in Northwestern Newfoundland.* Halifax: Fernwood Publishing.

Panitch, Leo, and Donald Swartz 1993 *The Assault on Trade Union Freedoms: From Wage Controls to Social Contract.* Toronto: Garamond.

Paris, Hélène 1989 *The Corporate Response to Workers with Family Responsibilities.* Ottawa: Conference Board of Canada, Report 43–89.

References

Parr, Joy 1990 *The Gender of Breadwinners: Women, Men and Change in Two Industrial Towns 1880–1950*. Toronto: University of Toronto Press.

Patterson, E. Palmer II 1972 *The Canadian Indian: A History Since 1500*. Don Mills, ON: Collier–Macmillan.

Pauls, Syd 1996 "Racism and Native schooling: a historical perspective." In Ibrahim Alladin, ed., *Racism in Canadian Schools*. Toronto: Harcourt Brace Canada.

Pauly, Edward, H. Kopp, and J. Haimson 1995 *Homegrown Lessons: Innovative Programs Linking School and Work*. San Francisco, CA: Jossey–Bass.

Payette, Suzanne 2000 "What's new in workplace innovations?" *Workplace Gazette* 3(1):110-119.

Payne, Joan, and Clive Payne 1994 "Recession, restructuring and the fate of the unemployed: evidence in the underclass debate." *Sociology* 28: 1–19.

Pendleton, Andrew, John McDonald, Andrew Robinson, and Nicholas Wilson 1996 "Employee participation and corporate governance in employee-owned firms." *Work, Employment & Society* 10: 205–26.

Penn, Roger 1982 "The contested terrain : a critique of R.C. Edwards' theory of working class fractions and politics." In Graham Day, ed., *Diversity and Decomposition in the Labour Market*. Aldershot, England: Gower.

Penn, Roger, and Hilda Scattergood 1985 "Deskilling or enskilling? an empirical investigation of recent theories of the labour process." *British Journal of Sociology* 36: 611–30.

Pentland, H. Claire 1979 "The Canadian industrial relations system: some formative factors." *Labour/Le Travail* 4: 9–23.

——— **1981** *Labour and Capital in Canada, 1650–1860*. Toronto: James Lorimer.

Perlman, Mark, ed. 1958 *Labor Union Theories in America: Background and Development*. Evanston, IL: Row, Peterson.

Perlman, Selig 1928 *A Theory of the Labor Movement*. New York: Macmillan.

Perrow, Charles 1986 *Complex Organizations: A Critical Essay*. 3rd ed. New York: Random House.

Peters, Suzanne 1995 *Exploring Canadian Values: Foundations for Well-Being*. Ottawa: Canadian Policy Research Networks Study Inc.

Peters, Tom 1987 *Thriving on Chaos: Handbook for a Management Revolution*. New York: Alfred A. Knopf.

——— **1990** "Get innovative or get dead, Part I." *California Management Review* 33, 1: 9–26.

——— **1991** "Get innovative or get dead, Part II." *California Management Review* 33, 2: 9–23.

Peters, Thomas J., and Robert H. Waterman Jr. 1982 *In Search of Excellence*. New York: Warner.

Peterson, Trond, Ishak Saporta, and Marc-David L. Seidel 2000 "Offering a job: meritocracy and social networks." *American Journal of Sociology* 106: 763-816.

Pettigrew, Andrew M. 1979 "On studying organizational culture." *Administrative Science Quarterly* 24: 570–81.

Petty, M. M., G. McGee, and J. Cavender 1984 "A meta-analysis of the relationship between individual job satisfaction and individual performance." *Academy of Management Review* 9: 712–21.

Pfeffer, Jeffrey 1994 *Competitive Advantage through People: Unleashing the Power of the Workforce*. Boston: Harvard University Press.

——— **1997** *New Directions in Organization Theory: Problems and Prospects*. New York: Oxford University Press.

Phelan, Jo 1994 "The paradox of the contented female worker: an assessment of alternative explanations." *Social Psychology Quarterly* 57: 95–107.

Phillips, Paul, and Erin Phillips 1993 *Women & Work: Inequality in the Canadian Labour Market.* Toronto: James Lorimer & Company.

Picard, André 1994 "Who Gets UI?" *Perspectives on Labour and Income* (Summer): 29–35.

Picot, Garnett 1987 "The changing industrial mix of employment, 1951–1985." *Canadian Social Trends* (Spring): 8–11.

——— 1998 "What is happening to earnings inequality and youth wages in the 1990s?" *Canadian Economic Observer* (September): 3.1- 3.18.

Pineo, Peter C. 1984 "Revisions of the Pineo-Porter-McRoberts socioeconomic classification of occupations for the 1981 census." Hamilton: McMaster University, Program for Quantitative Studies in Economics and Population, Research Paper No. 125.

Pineo, Peter C., and John Porter 1967 "Occupational prestige in Canada." *Canadian Review of Sociology and Anthropology* 4: 24–40.

Pinfield, Lawrence T., and John S. Atkinson 1988 "The flexible firm." *Canadian Business Review* (Winter): 17–19.

Piore, Michael J., and Charles F. Sabel 1984 *The Second Industrial Divide: Possibilities for Prosperity.* New York: Basic Books.

Piva, Michael J. 1979 *The Condition of the Working Class in Toronto, 1900–1921.* Ottawa: University of Ottawa Press.

Podolny, Joel M., and Karen L. Page 1998 "Network forms of organization." *Annual Review of Sociology* 24:57-64.

Poggio, Barbara 2000 "Between bytes and bricks: gender cultures in work contexts." *Economic and Industrial Democracy* 21(3):381-402.

Polanyi, Karl 1957 *The Great Transformation.* Boston: Beacon Press.

Pold, Henry 2001 "Trends in part-time work." *Perspectives on Labour and Income* (Summer): 36-38.

Pold, Henry, and Fred Wong 1990 "The price of labour." *Perspectives on Labour and Income* (Autumn): 42–49.

Policy Options 1996 *Special Issue on Unemployment.* (July–August).

Pollert, Anna 1988 "The flexible firm: fixation or fact?" *Work, Employment & Society* 2: 281–316.

Pollitt, Christopher 1995 "Management techniques for the public service: pulpit and practice." In B. G. Peters and D. J. Savoie, eds., *Governance in a Changing Environment.* Montreal and Kingston: McGill-Queen's University Press.

Ponak, Allen, and Larry F. Moore 1981 "Canadian bank unionism: perspectives and issues." *Relations Industrielles/Industrial Relations* 36: 3–30.

Ponak, Allen and Daphne Taras 1995 *Right-to-Work.* Submission to Alberta Economic Development Authority Joint Review Committee

Poole, Michael 1981 *Theories of Trade Unionism.* London: Routledge and Kegan Paul.

Popper, Micha, and Raanan Lipshitz 2000 "Organizational learning: mechanisms, culture, and feasibility." *Management Learning* 31(2):181-96.

Porter, John, Marion Porter, and Bernard R. Blishen 1982 *Stations and Callings: Making It through the School System.* Toronto: Methuen.

Powell, Gary N. 1993 *Women & Men in Management.* 2nd ed. Newbury Park, CA: Sage.

Pringle, Rosemary 1989 "Bureaucracy, rationality and sexuality: the case of secretaries." In Jeff Hearn, Deborah L. Sheppard, Peta Tancred-Sheriff, and Gibson

References

Burrell, eds., *The Sexuality of Organization*. London: Sage.

Pugh, D. S., D. J. Hickson, and C. R. Hinings 1985 *Writers on Organizations*. Beverly Hills, CA: Sage.

Pupo, Norene 1997 "Always working, never done: the expansion of the double day." In Ann Duffy, Daniel Glenday, and Norene Pupo, eds., *Good Jobs, Bad Jobs, No Jobs: The Transformation of Work in the 21st Century*. Toronto: Harcourt-Brace Canada.

Purcell, Kate 1979 "Militancy and acquiescence amongst women workers." In Sandra Burman, ed., *Fit Work for Women*. London: Croom Helm.

——— **1988** "Gender and the experience of employment." In Duncan Gallie, ed., *Employment in Britain*. Oxford: Basil Blackwell.

Purcell, Patrick J. 2000 "Older workers: retirement and retirement trends." *Monthly Labor Review* (October): 19-30.

Quaid, Maeve 1993 *Job Evaluation: The Myth of Equitable Assessment*. Toronto: University of Toronto Press.

Quarter, Jack 1992 *Canada's Social Economy: Co-operatives, Non-Profits, and Other Community Enterprises*. Toronto: Lorimer.

Quick, J. D., R. S. Horn, and J. C. Quick 1987 "Health consequences of stress." *Journal of Organizational Behavior Management* 8: 19–36.

Randle, Keith 1996 "The white-coated worker: professional autonomy in a period of change." *Work, Employment & Society* 10: 737–53.

Rank, Mark, and Thomas A. Hirschl 1999 "The likelihood of poverty across the American adult life span." *Social Work* 44(3): 201-16.

Rankin, Tom 1990 *New Forms of Work Organization: The Challenge for North American Unions*. Toronto: University of Toronto Press.

Ranson, Gillian 1998 "Education, work and family decision-making: finding the 'right time' to have a baby." *Canadian Review of Sociology and Anthropology* 35(4): 517-33.

Ranson, Stewart, Bob Hinings, and Royston Greenwood 1980 "The structure of organizational structures." *Administrative Science Quarterly* 25: 1–17.

Rashid, Abdul 1994 "High income families." *Perspectives on Labour and Income* (Winter): 46–57.

——— **1999** "Family income: 25 years of stability and change." *Perspectives on Labour and Income* (Spring): 9-15.

Ray, Carol Axtell 1986 "Corporate culture: the last frontier of control?" *Journal of Management Studies* 23: 287–97.

Reagan, Barbara B., and Martha Blaxall 1976 "Occupational segregation in international women's year." In M. Blaxall and B. B. Reagan, eds., *Women and the Workplace*. Chicago: University of Chicago Press.

Redman, Tom, Adrian Wilkinson, and Ed Snape 1997 "Stuck in the middle? Managers in building societies." *Work, Employment & Society* 11: 101–14.

Reed, Ken 1997 "Orientations to work: the cultural conditioning of motivation." *Australian and New Zealand Journal of Sociology* 33 (3): 364-86.

Reed, Mike 1989 *The Sociology of Management*. London: Harvester Wheatsheaf.

Reed, Paul B., and L. Kevin Selbee 2001 "Canada's civic core: on the disproportionality of charitable giving, volunteering and civic participation." *ISUMA: Canadian Journal of Policy Research* (Summer): 28-33.

Reich, Robert B. 1991 *The Work of Nations: Preparing Ourselves for 21st-Century Capitalism*. New York: Alfred A. Knopf.

Reichheld, Frederick F. 1996 *The Loyalty Effect: The Hidden Force Behind Growth,*

Profits, and Lasting Value. Boston: Harvard Business School Press.

Reid, Donald G., and Roger C. Mannell 1994 "The globalization of the economy and potential new roles for work and leisure." *Society and Leisure* 17: 251–66.

Reid, Frank 1982 "Wage-and-price controls in Canada." In John Anderson and Morley Gunderson, eds., *Union–Management Relations in Canada.* Don Mills ON: Addison-Wesley.

Reimer, Neil 1979 "Oil, Chemical and Atomic Workers International Union and the quality of working life: a union perspective." *Quality of Working Life: The Canadian Scene* (Winter): 5–7.

Reiter, Ester 1991 *Making Fast Food: From the Frying Pan into the Fryer.* Montreal and Kingston: McGill–Queen's University Press.

Reitz, Jeffrey G. 1988 "Less racial discrimination in Canada, or simply less racial conflict?: Implications of comparisons with Britain." *Canadian Public Policy* 14: 424–41.

Reshef, Yonatan 1990 "Union decline: a view from Canada." *Journal of Labor Research* 9: 25–39.

Reskin, Barbara 2000 "Getting it right: sex and race inequality in work organizations." *Annual Review of Sociology* 26:707-9.

Reskin, Barbara F., and Debra B. McBrier 2000 "Why not ascription? Organizations' employment of male and female managers." *American Sociological Review* 65:210-233.

Reskin, Barbara, and Irene Padavic 1994 *Women and Men at Work.* Thousand Oaks, CA: Pine Forge Press.

Reynolds, John R. 1997 "The effects of industrial employment conditions on job-related distress." *Journal of Health and Social Behavior* 38(2): 105-16.

Richards, John, Aidan Vining, David M. Brown, Michael Krashinsky, William J. Milne, Ernie S. Lightman, and Shirley

Hoy 1995 *Helping the Poor: A Qualified Case for "Workfare."* Ottawa: C. D. Howe Institute.

Richardson, Charley 1996 "Computers don't kill jobs, people do: technology and power in the workplace." *Annals of the American Academy of Political and Social Science* (March): 167–79.

Riddell, W. Craig 1985 "Work and pay: the Canadian labour market: an overview." In W. Craig Riddell, ed., *Work and Pay: The Canadian Labour Market.* Toronto: University of Toronto Press.

——— 1986 "Canadian labour relations: an overview." In W. Craig Riddell, ed., *Canadian Labour Relations.* Toronto: University of Toronto Press.

Riddell, W. Craig, and France St-Hilaire, eds. 2000 *Adapting Public Policy to a Labour Market in Transition.* Montreal: Institute for Research on Public Policy.

Riddell, W. Craig, and Andrew Sharpe 1998 "The Canada-US unemployment rate gap: an introduction and overview." *Canadian Public Policy* (February Supplement): S1-S37.

Riddell, W. Craig, and Arthur Sweetman 2000 "Human capital formation in a period of rapid change." In W. Craig Riddell and France St-Hilaire, eds., *Adapting Public Policy to a Labour Market in Transition.* Montreal: Institute for Research on Public Policy, 85-141.

Rifkin, Jeremy 1995 *The End of Work: The Decline of the Global Labor Force and the Dawn of the Post-Market Era.* New York: Putnam.

Rinehart, James 1978 "Contradictions of work-related attitudes and behaviour: an interpretation." *Canadian Review of Sociology and Anthropology* 15: 1–15.

——— 1984 "Appropriating workers' knowledge: quality control circles at a General Motors plant." *Studies in Political Economy* 14: 75–97.

—— 1986 "Improving the quality of working life through job redesign: work humanization or work rationalization?" *Canadian Review of Sociology and Anthropology* 23: 507–30.

—— 2001 *The Tyranny of Work: Alienation and the Labour Process.* 4th ed. Toronto: Harcourt Canada.

Rinehart, James, Christopher Huxley, and David Robertson 1997 *Just Another Car Factory: Lean Production and its Discontents.* Ithaca, NY: ILR Press.

Rioux, Marcia H. 1985 "Labelled disabled and wanting to work." In *Research Studies of the Commission on Equality in Employment* (Abella Commission). Ottawa: Supply and Services Canada.

Roberts, J. Timmons, and John E. Baugher 1995 "Hazardous workplaces and job strain: evidence from an eleven nation study." *International Journal of Contemporary Sociology* 32: 235–249.

Roberts, Karen, Doug Hyatt, and Peter Dorman 1996 "The effect of free trade on contingent work in Michigan." In Karen Roberts and Mark I. Wilson, eds., *Policy Choices: Free Trade Among NAFTA Nations,* East Lansing, MI: Michigan State University Press.

Roberts, Wayne 1990 *Cracking the Canadian Formula: The Making of the Energy and Chemical Workers Union.* Toronto: Between the Lines.

Robertson, David, and Jeff Wareham 1987 *Technological Change in the Auto Industry.* Willowdale, ON: Canadian Auto Workers (CAW).

—— 1989 *Changing Technology & Work: Northern Telecom.* Willowdale, ON: Canadian Auto Workers (CAW).

Robin, Martin 1968 *Radical Politics and Canadian Labour: 1880–1930.* Kingston: Queen's University, Industrial Relations Centre.

Robinson, Ian 1994 "NAFTA, social unionism, and labour movement power in Canada and the United States." *Relations Industrielles/Industrial Relations* 49 (4): 657–93.

Robson, Karen, and Jean E. Wallace 2001 "Gendered inequalities in earnings: a study of Canadian lawyers." *Canadian Review of Sociology and Anthropology* 38(1):75-95.

Rodrigues, Suzana B., and David J. Hickson 1995 "Success in decision making: different organizations, differing reasons for success." *Journal of Management Studies* 32(5):655-78.

Roethlisberger, F. J., and W. J. Dickson 1939 *Management and the Worker.* Cambridge, MA: Harvard University Press.

Rollings-Magnusson, Sandra 2000 "Canada's most wanted: pioneer women on the western prairies." *Canadian Review of Sociology and Anthropology* 37(2): 223-38.

Rollings-Magnusson, Sandra, Harvey Krahn, and Graham S. Lowe 1999 *Does a Decade Make a Difference? Education and Work among 1985 and 1996 University Graduates.* Edmonton: Population Research Laboratory, University of Alberta.

Rónas-Tas, Ákos. 1994 "The first shall be last? Entrepreneurship and Communist cadres in the transition from socialism." *American Journal of Sociology* 100: 40–69.

Rones, Philip L., Randy E. Ilg, and Jennifer M. Gardner 1997 "Trends in hours of work since the mid-1970s." *Monthly Labor Review* (April): 3-14.

Rose, Joseph 2001 "From softball to hardball: the transition in labour-management relations in the Ontario public service." In Gene Swimmer, ed., *Public-Sector Labour Relations in an Era of Restraint and Restructuring,* Toronto, ON: Oxford University Press.

Rose, Joseph B., and Gary N. Chaison 2001 "Unionism in Canada and the United States in the 21st century: the prospects for revival." *Relations Industrielles/Industrial Relations* 56(1):34-62.

Rosenberg, Samuel, ed. 1989 *The State and the Labor Market.* New York: Plenum.

Rosenthal, Patrice, Stephen Hill, and Riccardo Peccei 1997 "Checking out service: evaluating excellence, HRM and TQM in retailing." *Work, Employment and Society* 11(3): 481-503.

Ross, Becki: L. 2000 "Bumping and grinding on the line: making nudity pay." *Labour/Le Travail* 46 (Fall): 221–50.

Ross, Peter, Greg J. Bamber, and Gillian Whitehouse 1998 "Employment, economics and industrial relations: comparative statistics." In Greg J. Bamber and Russell D. Lansbury, eds., *International and Comparative Employment Relations.* 3rd ed. Thousand Oaks, CA: Sage Publications.

Rossides, Daniel W. 1998 *Professions and Disciplines: Functional and Conflict Perspectives.* Upper Saddle River, NJ: Prentice Hall.

Rothschild, Joyce, and Raymond Russell 1986 "Alternatives to bureaucracy: democratic participation in the economy." *Annual Review of Sociology* 12: 307–28.

Rowe, Reba, and William E. Snizek 1995 "Gender differences in work values: perpetuating the myth." *Work and Occupations* 22: 215–29.

Rowlinson, Michael, and Stephen Procter 1999 "Organizational culture and business history." *Organisation Studies* 20(3):369-96.

Roy, Arun S., and Ging Wong 2000 "Direct job creation programs: evaluation lessons on cost-effectiveness." *Canadian Public Policy* 26(2): 157-69.

Roy, Donald 1952 "Quota restriction and goldbricking in a machine shop." *American Journal of Sociology* 57: 427–42.

——— 1959–60 " 'Bananatime': job satisfaction and informal interaction." *Human Organization* 18: 158–68.

Rubenson, Kjell, and Hans G. Schuetze 2000 "Lifelong learning for the knowledge society: demand, supply, and policy dilemmas." In Kjell Rubenson and Hans G. Schuetze, eds., *Transition to the Knowledge Society: Policies and Strategies for Individual Participation and Learning.* Vancouver, BC: University of British Columbia, Institute for European Studies.

Rubery, Jill 1988 "Employers and the labour market." In Duncan Gallie, ed., *Employment in Britain.* Oxford: Basil Blackwell.

Rubery, Jill, and Colette Fagan 1995 "Gender segregation in societal context." *Work, Employment & Society* 9: 213–40.

Russell, Bob 1990 *Back to Work? Labour, State, and Industrial Relations in Canada.* Scarborough, ON: Nelson.

——— 1995 "The subtle labour process and the great skill debate: evidence from a potash mine-mill operation." *Canadian Journal of Sociology* 20: 359–385.

——— 1997 "Rival paradigms at work: work reorganization and labour force impacts in a staple industry." *Canadian Review of Sociology and Anthropology* 34: 25–52.

——— 1999 *More with Less: Work Reorganization in the Canadian Mining Industry.* Toronto: University of Toronto Press.

Russell, Helen 1999 "Friends in low places: gender, unemployment and sociability." *Work, Employment & Society* 13(2): 205-24.

Ryerson, Stanley B. 1968 *Unequal Union: Confederation and the Roots of Conflict in the Canadas, 1815–1873.* Toronto: Progress Books.

Ryscavage, Paul 1995 "A surge in growing income inequality?" *Monthly Labor Review* (August): 5l–61.

Sandberg, Ake 1994 "'Volvoism's at the end of the road?" *Studies in Political Economy* 45: 170–82.

References

Sangster, Joan 1978 "The 1907 Bell telephone strike: organizing women workers." *Labour/Le Travail* 3: 109–30.

Sass, Robert 1986 "Workplace health and safety: report from Canada." *International Journal of Health Services* 16: 565–82.

——— **1995** "A conversation about the work environment." *International Journal of Health Services* 25: 117–128.

——— **1996** "A message to the labor movement: stop and think!" *International Journal of Health Services* 26: 595–609.

Satzewich, Vic, ed. 1998 *Racism and Social Inequality in Canada: Concepts, Controversies, and Strategies of Resistance.* Toronto: Thompson Educational Publishing.

Satzewich, Vic, and Peter S. Li 1987 "Immigrant labour in Canada: the cost and benefit of ethnic origin in the job market." *Canadian Journal of Sociology* 12: 229–41.

Saul, John R. 1995 *The Unconscious Civilization.* Toronto: Anansi.

Sauter, Steven L., J. J. Hurrell Jr., and C. L. Cooper 1989 *Job Control and Worker Health.* New York: Wiley.

Sawhill, Isabel V. 2000 "Opportunity in the United States: myth or reality?" In Nancy Birdsell and Carol Graham, eds., *New Markets, New Opportunities? Economic and Social Mobility in a Changing World.* Washington, DC: Brookings Institution Press.

Schecter, Stephen, and Bernard Pacquet 1999 "Contested approaches in the study of poverty: the Canadian case and the argument for inclusion." *Current Sociology* 47(3): 43-64.

Schein, Edgar H. 1992 *Organizational Culture and Leadership* 2nd ed. San Francisco: Jossey–Bass.

Schellenberg, Grant, and David P. Ross 1997 *Left Poor by the Market: A Look at Family Poverty and Earnings.* Ottawa: Canadian Council on Social Development.

Schneider, Judy 2000 "The increasing financial dependency of young people on their parents." *Journal of Youth Studies* 3(1): 5-20.

Schooler, Carmi 1984 "Psychological effects of complex environments during the life span: a review and theory." *Intelligence* 8: 259–81.

——— **1996** "Cultural and social-structural explanations of cross-national psychological differences." *Annual Review of Sociology* 22: 323–49.

Schor, Juliet 1991 *The Overworked American: The Unexpected Decline of Leisure.* New York: Basic Books.

Schwartz, Barry 1999 "Capitalism, the market, the 'underclass,' and the future." *Society* 37(1); 33-42.

Scott, John 1988 "Ownership and employer control." In Duncan Gallie, ed., *Employment in Britain.* Oxford: Basil Blackwell.

Seager, Allen 1985 "Socialists and workers: the Western Canadian coal miners, 1900–21." *Labour/Le Travail* 16: 25–39.

Secretariat of the Commission for Labor Cooperation 1996 *North American Labor Markets: A Comparative Profile 1984–1995. Preliminary Findings.* Dallas: Commission for Labor Cooperation.

Sedivy-Glasgow, Marie 1992 "Nursing in Canada." *Canadian Social Trends* (Spring): 27–29.

Seeman, Melvin 1967 "On the personal consequences of alienation in work." *American Sociological Review* 32: 273–85.

——— **1975** "Alienation studies." *Annual Review of Sociology* 1: 91–125.

Semler, Ricardo 1993 "Workers' paradise?" *Report on Business Magazine* (December): 39–48.

Senge, Peter M. 1990 *The Fifth Discipline: The Art and Practice of the Learning Organization.* New York: Doubleday.

Senge, Peter, Art Kleiner, Charlotte Roberts, Richard B. Ross, and Bryan J. Smith 1994 *The Fifth Discipline Fieldbook: Strategies and Tools for Building a Learning Organization.* New York: Currency Doubleday.

Sennett, Richard 1998 *The Corrosion of Character: The Personal Consequences of Work in the New Capitalism.* New York: W.W. Norton.

Sennett, Richard, and Jonathon Cobb 1972 *The Hidden Injuries of Class.* New York: Knopf.

Sev'er, Aysan 1999 *Special Issue: Sexual Harassment. Canadian Review of Sociology and Anthropology* 36(4).

Sewell, Graham 1998 "The discipline of teams: the control of team-based industrial work through electronic and peer surveillance." *Administrative Science Quarterly* 43: 397-428.

Shadd, Adrienne L. 1987 "Dual labour markets in core and periphery regions of Canada: the position of Black males in Ontario and Nova Scotia." *Canadian Ethnic Studies* 19: 91–109.

Shain, Alan 1995 "Employment of people with disabilities." *Canadian Social Trends* (Autumn): 8–13.

Shapiro, Daniel M., and Morton Stelcner 1997 "Language and earnings in Quebec: trends over twenty years, 1970-1990." *Canadian Public Policy* 23(2): 115-40.

Sharpe, Andrew 1999 "The nature and causes of unemployment in Canada." In Ken Battle and Sherri Torjman, eds., *Employment Policy Options.* Ottawa: Caledon Institute of Social Policy.

Sharpe, Dennis B., and Gerald White 1993 *Educational Pathways and Experiences of Newfoundland Youth.* St. John's: Centre for Educational Research and Development, Memorial University.

Sherman, Barrie, and Phil Judkins 1995 *Licensed to Work.* London: Cassel.

Shieh, G. S. 1992 *"Boss" Island: The Subcontracting Network and Micro-Entrepreneurship in Taiwan's Development.* New York: Peter Lang.

Shields, Margot 2000 "Long working hours and health." *Perspectives on Labour and Income* (Spring): 49-56.

Shorter, Edward, and Charles Tilly 1974 *Strikes in France, 1830–1968.* Cambridge, MA: Cambridge University Press.

Silcoff, Sean 2001 "Corporate bigwigs took home whopping 43-per-cent pay raise." *Edmonton Journal* (23 May): F8.

Siltanen, Janet 1994 *Locating Gender: Occupational Segregation, Wages and Domestic Responsibilities.* London: UCL Press.

Sinclair, Peter R., and Lawrence F. Felt 1992 "Separate worlds: gender and domestic labour in an isolated fishing region." *Canadian Review of Sociology and Anthropology* 29: 55–71.

Sitkin, Sim B., Denise M. Rousseau, Ronald S. Burt, and Colin Camerer 1998 "Special topic forum on trust in and between organizations." *Academy of Management Review* 23(3):387-92.

Siu-Kai, Lau, and Kuan Hsin-Chi 1988 *The Ethos of the Hong Kong Chinese.* Hong Kong: Chinese University Press.

Sivesind, Karl Henrik 1995 "The indispensable role of culture: explaining different understandings of work through a comparison of German and Norwegian factories." *Comparative Social Research* 15: 35–101.

Skrypnek, Berna J., and Janet E. Fast 1996 "Work and family policy in Canada." *Journal of Family Issues* 17: 793–812.

Sloan, Richard P. 1987 "Workplace health promotion: a commentary on the evolution of a paradigm." *Health Education Quarterly* 14: 181–94.

Smith, Adam 1976 *The Wealth of Nations.* Chicago: University of Chicago Press. [Originally published in 1776.]

References

Smith, Gerry 2000 *Work Rage: Identify the Problems, Implement the Solutions.* Toronto, ON: Harper Collins.

Smith, Michael R. 1978 "The effects of strikes on workers: a critical analysis." *Canadian Journal of Sociology* 3: 457–72.

Smith, Michael 1999a "Insecurity in the labour market: the case of Canada since the Second World War." *Canadian Journal of Sociology* 24(2): 193-224.

———— **1999b** "The production of flexible attitudes in the Canadian pulp and paper industry." *Relations Industrielles/Industrial Relations* 54(3): 581-608.

———— **2001** "Technological change, the demand for skills, and the adequacy of their supply." *Canadian Public Policy* 27(1): 1-22.

Smith, Michael R., Anthony C. Masi, Axel van den Berg, and Joseph Smucker 1995 "External flexibility in Sweden and Canada: a three industry comparison." *Work, Employment & Society* 9: 689–718.

———— **1997** "Insecurity, labour relations, and flexibility in two process industries: a Canada/Sweden comparison." *Canadian Journal of Sociology* 22: 31–63.

Smith, Vicki 1994 "Braverman's legacy: the labour process tradition at 20." *Work and Occupations* 21: 403–21.

———— **1997** "New forms of work organization." *Annual Review of Sociology* 23:315-39.

Smucker, Joseph 1980 *Industrialization in Canada.* Scarborough, ON: Prentice-Hall.

Smucker, Joseph, Axel van den Berg, Michael R. Smith, and Anthony C. Masi 1998 "Labour deployment in plants in Canada and Sweden: a three-industry comparison." *Relations Industrielles/Industrial Relations* 53(3): 430-56.

Social Research and Demonstration Corporation 1996 *When Work Pays Better Than Welfare: A Summary of the Self-Sufficiency Project's Implementation, Focus Group, and Initial 18-Month Impact Reports.* Vancouver: Social Research and Demonstration Corporation.

Soderfeldt, Bjorn, Marie Soderfeldt, Kelvyn Jones, and Patricia O'Camp 1997 "Does organization matter? A multilevel analysis of the demand-control model applied to human services." *Social Science and Medicine* 44(4): 527-34.

Sonnenfeld, Jeffrey A. 1985 "Shedding light on the Hawthorne Studies." *Journal of Occupational Behaviour* 6: 111–30.

Sorrentino, Constance 1995 "International unemployment indicators, 1983–93." *Monthly Labor Review* (August): 31–50.

Sosteric, Mike 1996 "Subjectivity and the labour process: a case study in the restaurant industry." *Work, Employment & Society* 10: 297–318.

Spain, Daphne, and Suzanne M. Bianchi 1996 *Balancing Act: Motherhood, Marriage, and Employment among American Women.* New York: Russell Sage Foundation.

Spenner, Kenneth I. 1983 "Deciphering Prometheus: temporal change in the skill level of work." *American Sociological Review* 48: 824–37.

———— **1990** "Skill: meanings, methods, and measures." *Work and Occupations* 14: 399–421.

Spilerman, Seymour 2000 "Wealth and stratification processes." *Annual Review of Sociology* 26: 497-524.

Staber, Udo 1993 "Worker cooperatives and the business cycle: are cooperatives the answer to unemployment?" *The American Journal of Economics and Sociology* 52: 129–43.

Stabler, Jack C., and Eric C. Howe 1990 "Native participation in northern development: the impending crisis in the NWT." *Canadian Public Policy* 16: 262–83.

Staines, Graham L. 1980 "Spillover versus compensation: a review of the literature on the relationship between work and non-work." *Human Relations* 33: 111–29.

Stark, David 1988 "Rethinking internal labour markets: new insights from a comparative perspective." In R.E. Pahl, ed., *On Work: Historical, Comparative and Theoretical Perspectives.* Oxford: Basil Blackwell.

Statistics Canada 1992 *CALURA Part II Labour Unions 1989.* (Cat. No. 71–202).

—— **1994** *Schooling, Work and Related Activities, Income, Expenses and Mobility: 1991 Aboriginal Peoples Survey.* Ottawa: Statistics Canada. (Cat. no. 89–534–XPB)

—— **1995a** "Moving with the times: introducing change to the LFS" *The Labour Force* (December): C–2–C–19.

—— **1995b** *1994 General Social Survey (Cycle 9) Microdata File.* Ottawa: Statistics Canada.

—— **1996a** *Education in Canada, 1995.* (Cat. no. 81–229).

—— **1996b** *Income Distribution by Size in Canada 1995.* (Cat. no. 13–207).

—— **1997** *Income After Tax, Distributions by Size in Canada, 1995.* (Cat. no. 13–210–XPB). Ottawa: Statistics Canada.

—— **1998a** "Older workers." *Labour Force Update* (Spring). (Cat. no. 71-005-XPB).

—— **1998b** "Canada—US labour market comparison." *Labour Force Update* (Autumn). (Cat. no. 71-005-XPB).

—— **1999** *Earnings of Men and Women 1997.* (Cat. no. 13-217-XIB).

—— **2000a** *Income in Canada 1998.* (Cat. no. 75-202-RPE).

—— **2000b** "Stress and well-being." *Health Reports* (Winter): 21-32.

—— **2000c** "Unionization: an update." *Perspectives on Labour and Income* 12(3):39-59.

—— **2000d** *Women In Canada 2000: A Gender-Based Statistical Report.* Ottawa, ON: Statistics Canada, Cat. no. 89-503-XPE.

—— **2001** *Historical Labour Force Review 2000.* Ottawa, ON: Statistics Canada, Cat. no. 71F004XCB.

Statistics Canada and Human Resources Development Canada 1996 *Reading the Future: A Portrait of Literacy in Canada.* (Cat. no. 89–551).

—— **1998** *The Evolving Workplace: Findings from the Pilot Workplace and Employee Survey.* Ottawa: Statistics Canada and HRDC (Cat. no. 71-583-XPE).

—— **2001** *A Report on Adult Education and Training in Canada: Learning a Living.* Ottawa, ON: Statistics Canada and Human Resource Development Canada (Statistics Canada Cat. no. 81-586-XPE).

Staw, Barry M., and Lisa D. Epstein 2000 "What bandwagons bring: effects of popular management techniques of corporate performance, reputation, and CEO pay." *Administrative Science Quarterly* 45(3):523-56.

Stebbins, Robert A. 2000 "The extraprofessional life: leisure, retirement, and unemployment." *Current Sociology* 48(1): 1-27.

Steinberg, Ronnie J. 1990 "Social construction of skill: gender, power, and comparable worth." *Work and Occupations* 17: 449–82.

Stern, David, N. Finkelstein, J. R. Rose III, J. Latting, and C. Dornsife 1995 *School to Work: Research on Programs in the United States.* Washington: Falmer.

Stern, Robert N. 1976 "Intermetropolitan pattern of strike frequency." *Industrial and Labor Relations Review* 29: 218–35.

Stewart, A., and R. M. Blackburn 1975 "The stability of structured inequality." *Sociological Review* 23: 481–508.

Stewart, Paul, and Phillip Garahan 1995 "Employee responses to new management techniques in the auto industry." *Work, Employment & Society* 9: 517–36.

References

Stinson, John F. Jr. 1997 "New data on multiple jobholding available from the CPS." *Monthly Labor Review* (March): 3-8.

Stone, Leroy 1994 *Dimensions of Job–Family Tension*. Ottawa: Statistics Canada.

Storey, Robert 1983 "Unionization versus corporate welfare: the Dofasco way." *Labour/Le Travaill* 12: 7–42.

———— **1991** "Studying work in Canada." *Canadian Journal of Sociology* 16: 241–64.

Storey, Robert, and Wayne Lewchuk 2000 "From dust to DUST to dust: asbestos and the struggle for worker health and safety at Bendix Automotive." *Labour/Le Travail* 45 (Spring): 103-40.

Strong-Boag, Veronica 1988 *The New Day Recalled: Lives of Girls and Women in English Canada, 1919–1939*. Markham, ON: Penguin Books.

Strong-Boag, Veronica, and A. Fellman, eds. 1997 *Rethinking Canada: The Promise of Women's History*. 3rd ed. Don Mills, ON: Oxford University Press.

Sturdy, Andrew, David Knights, and Hugh Willmott, eds. 1992 *Contemporary Studies in the Labour Process*. London: Routledge.

Sufrin, Eileen 1982 *The Eaton Drive: The Campaign to Organize Canada's Largest Department Store, 1948 to 1952*. Toronto: Fitzhenry and Whiteside.

Sugiman, Pamela 1992 "That wall's comin' down: gendered strategies of worker resistance in the UAW Canadian region (1963–1970)." *Canadian Journal of Sociology* 17: 24–27.

Sullivan, Terrance, ed. 2000 *Injury and the New World of Work*. Vancouver and Toronto: UBC Press.

Sunter, Deborah 1997 "Youths and the labour market." *Canadian Economic Observer* (May): 3.1–3.7.

———— **2001** "Demography and the labour market." *Perspectives on Labour and Income* (Spring): 28-39.

Sunter, Deborah, and Geoff Bowlby 1998 "Labour force participation in the 1990s." *Perspectives on Labour and Income* (Autumn): 15-21.

Sunter, Deborah, and Rene Morissette 1994 "The hours people work." *Perspectives on Labour and Income* (Autumn): 8–13.

Super, Donald E., and Branimir Šverko, eds. 1995 *Life Roles, Values, and Careers: International Findings of the Work Importance Study*. San Francisco: Jossey-Bass.

Suplee, Curt 1997 "Robot revolution." *National Geographic* (July): 76–93.

Sussman, Deborah 1998 "Moonlighting: a growing way of life." *Perspectives on Labour and Income* (Summer): 24-31.

———— **2000** "Unemployment kaleidoscope." *Perspectives on Labour and Income* (Autumn): 9- 15.

Swanson, Jean 2001 *Poor-Bashing: The Politics of Exclusion*. Toronto: Between the Lines.

Swift, Jamie 1995 *Wheel of Fortune: Work and Life in the Age of Falling Expectations*. Toronto: Between the Lines.

Swimmer, Gene, ed. 2001 *Public-Sector Labour Relations in an Era of Restraint and Restructuring*. Toronto, ON: Oxford University Press.

Szelényi, Iván, and Eric Kostello 1996 "The market transition debated: toward asynthesis?" *American Journal of Sociology* 10: 1082–96.

Tancred, Peta 1995 "Women's work: a challenge to the sociology of work." *Gender, Work and Organization* 2: 11–20.

Tanner, Julian 1984 "Skill levels of manual workers and beliefs about work, management, and industry: a comparison of craft and non-craft workers in Edmonton." *Canadian Journal of Sociology* 9: 303–18.

Tanner, Julian, and Rhonda Cockerill 1986 "In search of working-class ideology: a test of two perspectives." *Sociological Quarterly* 27: 389–402.

Tanner, Julian, Harvey Krahn, and Timothy F. Hartnagel 1995 *Fractured Transitions from School to Work: Revisiting the Dropout Problem.* Don Mills, ON: Oxford University Press.

Tanner, Julian, Rhonda Cockerill, Jan Barnsley, and A. P. Williams 1999 "Flight paths and revolving doors: a case study of gender desegregation in pharmacy." *Work, Employment & Society* 13(2):275-93.

Tanner, Julian, Scott Davies, and Bill O'Grady 1992 "Immanence changes everything: a critical comment on the labour process and class consciousness." *Sociology* 26: 439–53.

Tapscott, Don 1996 *The Digital Economy: Promise and Peril in the Age of Networked Intelligence.* San Francisco, CA: McGraw-Hill.

Taras, Daphne G. 1997 "Why nonunion representation is legal in Canada." *Relations Industrielles/Industrial Relations* 52(4):763-83.

Taras, Daphne G., Allen Ponak, and Morley Gunderson 2001 "Introduction to Canadian industrial relations." In Morley Gunderson, Allen Ponak, and Daphne G. Taras, eds. *Union–Management Relations in Canada.* 4th ed. Toronto: Addison Wesley Longman.

Taylor, Frederick W. 1919 *Shop Management.* New York: Harper.

Taylor, Jeff 1995 "Labour in the Klein revolution." In Trevor Harrison and Gordon Laxer, eds., *The Trojan Horse: Alberta and the Future of Canada.* Montreal: Black Rose Books.

Teeple, Gary 1972 "Land, labour and capital in pre-Confederation Canada." In Gary Teeple, ed., *Capitalism and the National Question in Canada.* Toronto: University of Toronto Press.

Terkel, Studs 1971 *Working.* New York: Pantheon.

Thomas, Alan Berkeley 1988 "Does leadership make a difference to organizational performance?" *Administrative Science Quarterly* 33: 388–400.

Thomas, Graham, and Sally Wyatt 2000 "Access is not the only problem: using and controlling the Internet." In Sally Wyatt, Flis Henwood, Nod Miller, and Peter Senker, eds., *Technology and In/Equality.* London: Routledge.

Thompson, Elizabeth 1990 "Worked to the bone." *Perception* 14: 45–47.

Thompson, Paul, and Chris Smith 2000/1 "Follow the redbrick road." *International Studies of Management & Organization* 30(4): 40-67.

Thorsrud, Einar 1975 "Collaborative action research to enhance the quality of working life." In L. E. Davis and A. B. Cherns, eds., *The Quality of Working Life.* Vol. 1. New York: Free Press.

Tilly, Charles 1979 *From Mobilization to Revolution.* Reading, MA: Addison-Wesley.

Tindale, Joseph A. 1991 *Older Workers in an Aging Workforce.* Ottawa: National Advisory Council on Aging.

Tobin, James 1996 "Business cycles and economic growth: current controversies about theory and policy." In Lars Osberg and Pierre Fortin, eds., *Unnecessary Debts.* Toronto: Lorimer.

Toffler, Alvin 1980 *The Third Wave.* New York: Bantam.

Trentini, Giancarol, and Giovanni Battista Muzio 1995 "Values in a cross-cultural perspective: a further analysis." In Donald E. Super and Branimir Šverko, eds., *Life Roles, Values, and Careers: International Findings of the Work Importance Study.* San Francisco: Jossey-Bass.

Trice, Harrison M., and Janice M. Beyer 1993 *The Cultures of Work Organizations.* Englewood Cliffs, NJ: Prentice-Hall.

References

Trist, E. L., and K. W. Bamforth 1951 "Some social and psychological consequences of the longwall method of coal-getting." *Human Relations* 4: 3–38.

Tucker, Eric 1992 "Worker participation in health and safety regulation: lessons from Sweden." *Studies in Political Economy* 37: 95–127.

Turk, James L., ed. 2000 *The Corporate Campus: Commercialization and the Dangers to Canada's Colleges and Universities.* Toronto: Lorimer.

Tushman, Michael L., and Philip Anderson, eds. 1996 *Managing Strategic Innovation and Change.* New York: Oxford University Press.

Ulrich, Dave 1998 "Intellectual capital=competence × commitment." *Sloan Management Review* 39(2):15-26.

United Auto Workers. 1985 "Can capital and labour cooperate?" In Daniel Drache and Duncan Cameron, eds., *The Other Macdonald Report.* Toronto: James Lorimer.

Useem, Michael, and Jerome Karabel 1986 "Pathways to top corporate management." *American Sociological Review* 51: 184–200.

Vallas, Steven Peter 1990 "The concept of skill." *Work and Occupations* 14: 379–98.

Van den Berg, Axel, and Joseph Smucker, eds. 1997 *The Sociology of Labour Markets: Efficiency, Equity, Security.* Scarborough, ON: Prentice-Hall.

Van Houten, Donald R. 1990 "The political economy and technical control of work humanization in Sweden during the 1970s and 1980s." *Work and Occupations* 14: 483–513.

Van Kirk, Sylvia 1980 *Many Tender Ties: Women in Fur-Trade Society, 1670–1870.* Winnipeg: Watson and Dwyer.

Vaughan, Diane 1999 "The dark side of organizations: mistake, misconduct, and disaster." *Annual Review of Sociology* 25:271-305.

Veltmeyer, Henry 1983 "The development of capitalism and the capitalist world system." In J. Paul Grayson, ed., *Introduction to Sociology: An Alternative Approach.* Toronto: Gage.

Vosko, Leah F. 1998 "Regulating precariousness? The temporary employment relationship under the NAFTA and the EC treaty." *Relations Industrielles/Industrial Relations* 53(1):123-53.

——— **2000** *Temporary Work: The Gendered Rise of a Precarious Employment Relationship.* Toronto: University of Toronto Press.

Wagner, David 1994 "Beyond the pathologizing of nonwork: alternative activities in a street community." *Social Work* 39: 718–27.

Wajcman, Judy 1991 "Patriarchy, technology, and conceptions of skill." *Work and Occupations* 18: 29–45.

Walby, Sylvia 1989 "Flexibility and the changing sexual division of labour." In Stephen Wood, ed., *The Transformation of Work?* London: Unwin Hyman.

——— **1990** *Theorizing Patriarchy.* Oxford: Basil Blackwell.

Waldram, James B. 1987 "Native employment and hydroelectric development in northern Manitoba." *Journal of Canadian Studies* 22: 62–76.

Waldrop, Judith 1992 "Less work, more play, same pay." *American Demographics* (August): 13.

Walker, C. R., and R. H. Guest 1952 *Man on the Assembly Line.* Cambridge, MA: Harvard University Press.

Wallace, Jean E. 1995a "Corporatist control and organizational commitment among professionals: the case of lawyers working in law firms." *Social Forces* 73: 811–39.

——— **1995b** "Organizational and professional commitment in professional and nonprofessional organizations." *Administrative Science Quarterly* 40: 228–55.

Wallace, Jean E., and Merlin B. Brinkerhoff 1991 "The measurement of burnout revisited." *Journal of Social Service Research* 14: 85–111.

Wallace, Jo-Ann 1995 " 'Fit and qualified': the equity debate at the University of Alberta." In Stephen Richer and Lorna Weir, eds., *Beyond Political Correctness: Toward the Inclusive University,* Toronto: University of Toronto Press.

Walmsley, Ann 1992 "Trading places." *Report on Business Magazine* (March): 17–27.

Walsh, Janet 1997 "Employment systems in transition? a comparative analysis of Britain and Australia." *Work, Employment & Society* 11: 1–25.

Walsh, Mark 1999 "Working past age 65." *Perspectives on Labour and Income* (Summer): 16-20.

Walters, Vivienne 1985 "The politics of occupational health and safety: interviews with workers' health and safety representatives and company doctors." *Canadian Review of Sociology and Anthropology* 22: 57–79.

Walters, Vivienne, and Ted Haines 1988 "Workers' use and knowledge of the internal responsibility system: limits to participation in occupational health and safety." *Canadian Public Policy* 14: 411–23.

Wanner, Richard A. 1993 "Patterns and trends in occupational mobility." In James Curtis, Edward Grabb, and Neil Guppy, eds., *Social Inequality in Canada: Patterns, Problems, Policies.* 2nd ed. Scarborough: Prentice-Hall.

——— 1999 "Expansion and ascription: trends in educational opportunity in Canada, 1920-1944." *Canadian Review of Sociology and Anthropology* 36(3): 409-42.

——— 2000 "A matter of degree(s): twentieth-century trends in occupational status returns to educational credentials in Canada." *Canadian Review of Sociology and Anthropology* 37(3): 313-43.

Wanner, Richard A., and Bernadette C. Hayes 1996 "Intergenerational occupational mobility among men in Canada and Australia." *Canadian Journal of Sociology* 21: 43–76.

Warhurst, Christopher 1998 "Recognizing the possible: the organization and control of a socialist labor process." *Administrative Science Quarterly* 43(2): 470-97.

Warr, Peter 1987 *Work, Unemployment, and Mental Health.* Oxford: Clarendon Press.

Watkins, Mel 1977 "From underdevelopment to development." In Mel Watkins, ed., *Dene Nation: The Colony Within.* Toronto: University of Toronto Press.

——— 1991 "A staples theory of economic growth." In Gordon Laxer, ed., *Perspectives on Canadian Economic Development.* Toronto: Oxford University Press.

Webb, Janette 1996 "Vocabularies of motive and the 'new' management." *Work, Employment & Society* 10: 251–71.

Webb, Sidney, and Beatrice Webb 1894/1911. *The History of Trade Unionism.* London: Longmans, Green.

Weber, Max 1946 "Bureaucracy." In H. H. Gerth and C. Wright Mills, eds., *From Max Weber.* New York: Oxford University Press.

——— 1958 *The Protestant Ethic and the Spirit of Capitalism.* New York: Scribner.

——— 1964 *The Theory of Social and Economic Organization.* New York: Free Press.

Weiner, Nan, and Morley Gunderson 1990 *Pay Equity: Issues, Options and Experiences.* Toronto: Butterworths.

Weiss, Donald D. 1976 "Marx versus Smith on the division of labour." *Monthly Review* 28: 104–118.

Weitzel, William, and Ellen Jonsson 1989 "Decline in organizations: a literature integration and extension." *Administrative Science Quarterly* 34: 91–109.

Wells, Donald M. 1986 *Soft Sell: Quality of Working Life Programs and the Productivity*

References

Race. Ottawa: Canadian Centre for Policy Alternatives.

———— 1997 "When push comes to shove: competitiveness, job security and labour-management cooperation in Canada." *Economic and Industrial Democracy* 18(2):167-200.

Welsh, Sandy, and Annette Nierobisz 1997 "How prevalent is sexual harassment: a research note on measuring Sexual harassment in Canada." *Canadian Journal of Sociology* 22(4):505-22.

Westergaard, John 1995 *Who Gets What? The Hardening of Class Inequality in the Late Twentieth Century*. Cambridge: Polity Press.

Westmoreland-Traoré, Juanita 1999 "Employment equity in Canada: legal and social objectives." In Colette Bernier, Reynald Bourque, Renaud Paquet, and Terry H. Wagar, eds., *New Forms of Employment and Labour Force Diversification. Selected Papers From the XXXVIth Annual CIRA Conference*. Quebec, QC: Canadian Industrial Relations Association.

Wetzel, Kurt, Daniel G. Gallagher, and Donna E. Soloshy 1991 "Union commitment: is there a gender gap?" *Relations Industrielles/Industrial Relations* 46: 564–83.

White, Jerry P. 1990 *Hospital Strike: Women, Unions, and Public Sector Conflict*. Toronto: Thompson Educational Publishing.

White, Julie 1990 *Male and Female: Women and the Canadian Union of Postal Workers*. Toronto: Thompson Educational Publishing.

White, Lynn, Jr. 1962 *Medieval Technology and Social Change*. Oxford: Oxford University Press.

Whitehead, T. N. 1936 *Leadership in a Free Society*. Cambridge, MA: Harvard University Press.

Whitfield, K, and M Poole 1997 "Organizing employment for high performance:

theories, evidence and policy." *Organisation Studies* 18(5):745-64 .

Whitley, Richard 1992 *Business Systems in East Asia: Firms, Markets and Societies*. London: Sage.

Whittaker, D. H. 1990 "The end of Japanese-style employment?" *Work, Employment & Society* 4: 321–47.

Whyte, William Foote, and Kathleen King Whyte 1988 *Making Mondragon: The Growth and Dynamics of the Worker Cooperative Complex*. Ithaca, NY: ILR Press.

Wilensky, Jeanne L., and Harold L. Wilensky 1951 "Personnel counseling: the Hawthorne case." *American Journal of Sociology* 57: 265–80.

Wilgosh, Lorraine R., and Deborah Skaret 1987 "Employer attitudes toward hiring individuals with disabilities: a review of the recent literature." *Canadian Journal of Rehabilitation* 1: 89–98.

Wilkins, Kathryn, and Marie P. Beaudet 1998 "Work stress and health." *Health Reports* (Winter): 47-62.

Wilson, John 2000 "Volunteering." *Annual Review of Sociology* (26): 215-40.

Wilson, William J. 1997 *When Work Disappears: The World of the New Urban Poor*. New York: Alfred A. Knopf.

Winson, Anthony. 1996 "In search of the part-time capitalist farmer: labour use and farm structure in central Canada." *Canadian Review of Sociology and Anthropology* 33: 89–110.

Wolfson, Michael C., and Brian B. Murphy 1998 "New views on inequality trends in Canada and the United States." *Monthly Labor Review* (April): 3-23.

Womack, James P., Daniel T. Jones, and Daniel Roos 1990 *The Machine That Changed the World*. New York: Harper Perennial.

Women in Capital Markets 2001 *Women in Canadian Investment Dealers: Growing the Pipeline*. Toronto: Women in Capital

Markets [http://www.wcm.ca/news-front/news].

Wood, Stephen 1987 "The deskilling debate, new technology and work organization." *Acta Sociologica* 30: 3–24.

——— 1989a "The Japanese management model." *Work and Occupations* 16: 446–60.

——— 1989b *The Transformation of Work? Skill, Flexibility and the Labour Process.* London: Unwin Hyman.

——— 1989c "New wave management?" *Work, Employment & Society* 3: 379–402.

Woodward, Joan 1980 *Industrial Organization: Theory and Practice.* 2nd ed. Oxford: Oxford University Press.

Workplace Gazette 2000 "Union membership in Canada—2000." *Labour Gazette* 3(3):68-75.

World Bank 1993 *The East Asian Miracle: Economic Growth and Public Policy.* New York: Oxford University Press.

——— 2001 *Rethinking the East Asian Miracle.* New York: Oxford University Press and the World Bank.

World Commission on Environment and Development 1987 *Our Common Future.* Oxford: Oxford University Press.

Wotherspoon, Terry 1995 "Transforming Canada's education system: the impact on educational inequalities, opportunities, and benefits." In B. Singh Bolaria, ed., *Social Issues and Contradictions in Canadian Society.* 2nd ed. Toronto: Harcourt Brace Jovanovich.

Wrege, Charles D., and Richard M. Hodgetts 2000 "Frederick W. Taylor's 1899 pig iron observations: examining fact, fiction, and lessons for the new millennium." *Academy of Management Journal* 43(6):1283-91.

Wright, Erik Olin 1997 *Class Counts: Comparative Studies in Class Analysis.* Cambridge: Cambridge University Press.

Wright, Eric Olin, C. Costello, D. Hachen, and J. Sprague 1982 "The American class structure." *American Sociological Review* 47: 709–26.

Wright, James D., and Richard F. Hamilton 1979 "Education and job attitudes among blue-collar workers." *Sociology of Work and Occupations* 6: 59–83.

Wright, Susan 1993 "Blaming the victim, blaming society, or blaming the discipline: fixing responsibility for homelessness." *Sociological Quarterly* 34: 1–16.

Wyatt Canada 1991 *The New National Benchmark on Worker Attitudes.* Vancouver: The Wyatt Company.

Wylie, William N. T. 1983 "Poverty, distress, and disease: labour and the construction of the Rideau Canal, 1826–1832." *Labour/Le Travail* 11: 7–30

Yakabuski, Konrad 2001 "The extended family." *Report on Business Magazine* (July): 55-56.

Yalnizyan, Armine, T. Ran Ide, and Arthur J. Cordell 1994 *Shifting Time: Social Policy and the Future of Work.* Toronto: Between the Lines Press.

Yammarino, Frances J., Fred Dansereau, and Christina J. Kennedy 2001 "A multiple-level multidimensional approach to leadership: viewing leadership through an elephant's eye." *Organizational Dynamics* 29(3):149-63.

Yanow, Dvora 2000 "Seeing organizational learning: a 'cultural' view." *Organization* 7(2):247-68.

Yates, Charlotte 1990 "The internal dynamics of union power: explaining Canadian autoworkers' militancy in the 1980s." *Studies in Political Economy* 31: 73–105.

——— 1998 "Unity and diversity: challenges to an expanding Canadian autoworkers' union." *Canadian Review of Sociology and Anthropology* 35(1):93-118.

References

Yoder, Janice D. 1991 "Rethinking tokenism: looking beyond numbers." *Gender & Society* 5: 178–92.

Yun, Hing Ai 1995 "Automation and new work patterns: cases from Singapore's electronics industry." *Work, Employment & Society* 9: 309–27.

Zbaracki, Mark J. 1998 "The rhetoric and reality of total quality management." *Administrative Science Quarterly* 43:602-636.

Zeitlin, Irving M. 1968 *Ideology and the Development of Sociological Theory.* Englewood Cliffs, NJ: Prentice-Hall.

Zeitlin, M. 1974 "Corporate ownership and control." *American Journal of Sociology* 79: 1073–1119.

Zetka, James R. Jr., 1992 "Work organization and wildcat strikes in the U.S. automobile industry, 1946–1963." *American Sociological Review* 57: 214–26.

Zeytinoglu, Isik U., and Jacinta K. Muteshi 2000 "Gender, race and class dimensions of nonstandard work." *Industrial Relations* 55(1):133-65.

Zhao, John, Doug Drew, and T. Scott Murray 2000 "Knowledge workers on the move." *Perspectives on Labour and Income* (Summer): 32-46.

Zhou, Xueguang 2000 "Economic transformation and income inequality in urban China: evidence from panel data." *American Journal of Sociology* 105(4):1135-74.

Zuboff, Shoshana 1988 *In the Age of the Smart Machine: The Future of Work and Power.* New York: Basic Books.

Zussman, David, and Jak Jabes 1989 *The Vertical Solitude: Managing in the Public Sector.* Halifax: Institute for Research on Public Policy.

Index

McNab, Donald, 10
Means of production, 17
Mechanistic organization, 220
Medoff, James, 345
Megatrends (Naisbitt), 26
Meissner, Martin, 171, 453
Mercantile period, 3
Meritocracy, 126
Merton, Robert, 216
Michels, Robert, 342
Microelectronic production technology, 267
Milkman, Ruth, 265
Miller, Danny, 219
Milliken & Company, 248
Mills, C. Wright, 20
Minimum wages, 105
Minorities, 45
Mintzberg, Henry, 222, 226, 245
Mobility chains, 133
Mode of production, 17
Modern Times, 229
Mondragon co-ops, 329
Monopoly capitalism, 130
Monopoly face of unionism, 345
Morgan, Gareth, 215
Morgan, Glenn, 223
Motivators, 434
Mulroney, Brian, 34
Multinational corporations, 30
Multiskilling/multitasking, 291
Myles, John, 117, 150, 187, 291, 292

NAFTA, 29, 31–33, 323
Naisbitt, John, 26, 298
National Action Committee on the Status of Women, 169
National day of protest, 384
National Occupational Classification (NOC), 61, 62, 63, 64
National War Labour Order (P.C. 1003), 351

Native Canadians
disadvantaged labour market position, 140–142
discrimination, 137, 138
historical role, 160–161
hunting/gathering societies, 54
unemployment, 76
unions, 344
Natural rate of unemployment, 80
Nenko, 263, 266
Neo-Fordist, 308
New Democratic Party, 395
New economy, 27
New human resource management, 374
New management literature, 244–252
New middle class, 117
New social contract, 246
Newly industrializing countries (NICs), 12
Nightingale, Donald, 317, 328
Nike, 28
Nine-Hour Movement, 346, 383
Nixon, Richard, 426
No-fault compensation systems, 311
NOC, 61, 62, 63, 64
Nonpaid work, 54–56
Nonstandard jobs, 268
Nonstandard work, 32
Nonstandard work arrangements
part-time work, 88–91
part-year work, 92
temporary employment, 91, 92
varieties, 86–88
youth, 88–89
Normative control, 240
Nortel, 28, 104, 278
North American Free Trade Agreement (NAFTA), 29, 31–33, 323
Nova Corporation, 251
Novek, Joel, 288, 313
Numerical flexibility, 269